Web Server Administration

Steve Silva
DeVry University, Phoenix

Australia • Canada • Mexico • Singapore • Spain • United Kingdom • United States

Web Server Administration

by Steve Silva

Senior Vice President, Publisher:
Kristen Duerr

Executive Editor:
Jennifer Locke

Senior Product Manager:
Barrie Tysko

Developmental Editor:
Lisa Ruffolo

Production Editor:
Brooke Booth

Associate Product Manager:
Janet Aras

Editorial Assistant:
Amanda Piantedosi

Cover Designer:
Joseph Lee
Black Fish Design

Manufacturing Coordinator:
Laura Burns

Compositor:
GEX Publishing Services

Printed in Canada

1 2 3 4 5 6 7 8 9 WC 08 07 06 05 04

For more information, contact Course Technology, 25 Thomson Place, Boston, Massachusetts, 02210.

Or find us on the World Wide Web at: www.course.com

ISBN 0-619-06439-0

BRIEF

Contents

TABLE OF

Contents

Preface

Web servers have rapidly evolved from being useful additions to an organization's network to being essential parts of its information structure. Web servers have dramatically improved their ability to convey information through the use of databases and programming languages, which allow a Web site to customize and rapidly change its content in response to user actions and other events. Web servers can now make organizations of any size more productive, responsive, and dynamic. To realize this potential, Web server administrators need to know how to install, configure, manage, and troubleshoot their Web servers.

Web Server Administration discusses the basic structure of a Web server and examines topics that are important to organizations connected to the Internet, such as providing Web access, maintaining performance, ensuring security, and integrating e-mail, file transfer, and media services. The book begins with a thorough explanation of the Internet and a review of networking building blocks. It also defines the tasks of a Web server administrator, which focus on making sure that Internet services are available to network users. To offer these services, Web server administrators usually need to evaluate and select a Web server and related components, such as servers, routers, and firewall products. Another critical task involves setting up Internet Protocol (IP) addressing in preparation for integrating the Web server into the Internet using a DNS server.

After explaining how to install a Web server and configure Transmission Control Protocol/Internet Protocol (TCP/IP), this book discusses other topics involved with Web server administration, including daily Web server management, customizing a Web server, and monitoring its performance. It also describes how to extend the power of a Web server by establishing a programming environment and providing a variety of Web services, such as e-mail. While discussing every aspect of Web server administration in the context of security, this book also devotes a chapter to securing the Web server environment.

Special Features

To provide concrete examples, this book establishes a fictional sample business named TechnoWidgets, Inc., and guides you through the steps of setting up its Web site using the URL *www.technowidgets.com*. You will perform typical Web server administration tasks for TechnoWidgets, such as selecting hardware and software, configuring an IP addressing scheme for the company, and creating e-mail accounts for its employees.

Both Linux and Microsoft Windows are common operating systems for developing a Web presence. *Web Server Administration* presents all topics in the context of both Linux and

Windows, including separate, step-by-step instructions for performing Web server administration tasks using Red Hat Linux, Windows 2000 Server, and Windows Server 2003. Each chapter balances the coverage of topics, instructions, and exercises between Linux and Windows. Because the topics discuss using both Windows and Linux to manage a Web server, you can use either operating system and apply all of the topics in this book.

Although Windows Server 2003 is an improvement over Windows 2000 Server, it will take time for Windows 2003 to replace Windows 2000. To overcome this practical limitation, this book can be used with Windows 2000 or Windows 2003. Although many procedures are similar, this book indicates where steps differ to avoid confusion. This book therefore provides an excellent way to master the transition from one operating system or version to another.

The Intended Audience

Web Server Administration was developed to help the student with a basic background in networking to understand how to set up and maintain an Internet presence. Although this book reviews many networking and operating system topics, you should have completed course work that includes the basics of operating systems and networking. This knowledge is especially useful in troubleshooting, understanding how to install and run an application, and navigating the folder structure of a Web server.

The Approach

This book combines the concepts of Web server administration with plenty of opportunities for hands-on practice to apply the concepts. Each chapter introduces a networking or Web server topic, discusses it in the context of Windows and Linux, and then provides steps for each operating system. Chapter by chapter you build a Web environment that becomes increasingly more sophisticated. However, beyond the basics of installing an operating system (covered in Chapter 3), setting up DNS (Chapter 4), and intalling a Web server (Chapter 6), the topics discussed in other chapters are independent of each other.

Each chapter concludes with a summary to help you understand the major points and review questions to test your knowledge. Chapters also include Hands-on Projects and Case Projects. The Hands-on Projects build on the step-by-step procedures in the chapter and include variations to enhance independent learning. While the Hands-on Projects offer details needed to complete the project, the Case Projects require you to apply the solution on your own. The Case Projects introduce a problem many Web server administrators face, and then ask you to use the skills you developed in the course to solve the problem.

Overview of This Book

The concepts, step-by-step procedures, Hands-on Projects, and Case Projects in this book will help you achieve the following objectives:

- Understand the basics of server and Web server administration
- Evaluate server and network components
- Install Red Hat Linux 8, Windows 2000, and Windows 2003
- Learn about the domain name service (DNS) and identify the components of DNS
- Install and configure DNS in Windows and Linux
- Learn the basics of managing a server
- Install the Internet Information Services (IIS) and Apache Web servers
- Configure new Web sites and virtual directories in IIS and Apache
- Program dynamic Web sites with databases
- Install and administer the Exchange 2000 e-mail server in Windows and sendmail in Linux
- Install and configure FTP in Windows and Linux
- Install and configure remote access in Windows and Linux
- Use a variety of techniques to secure a Web environment
- Learn how to monitor a Web environment

In **Chapter 1**, you learn about the basics of server and Web server administration, including the common tasks and services of administrators. To prepare for installing a Web server, you also compare Web server platforms. **Chapter 2** explains how to prepare to install the server by identifying the server categories and evaluating server and network components. You also learn about setting up IP addressing, and planning for fault tolerance and system backup. In **Chapter 3**, you learn how to install Windows 2000, Windows 2003, and Red Hat Linux 8. You configure TCP/IP in each of the operating systems, and learn the basic Linux commands that you use throughout the rest of the book.

Chapter 4 discusses name resolution, which allows you to use names such as *www.technowidgets.com* instead of an actual IP address such as 0.192.155.3. You install and configure the domain name service (DNS) server in Windows and Linux, and examine WINS, which provides a way to resolve IP addresses in a Windows LAN. In **Chapter 5**, you learn how to manage a server, primarily from the perspective of a Web server administrator. Besides examining networking models, you review how users are authenticated and how to share resources on a network. You also explore how to manage file system permissions, users, and groups.

In **Chapter 6**, you install and configure the Internet Information Services (IIS) and Apache Web servers. You learn the various ways to host multiple Web sites and you configure virtual directories. In **Chapter 7**, you install and test a programming environment for the Web server. You evaluate the need for programming languages and database management systems (DBMSs) in an effort to create dynamic Web sites, and then install the SQL Server DBMS in Windows and MySQL in Linux. You also create programs that interact with the DBMSs.

Chapter 8 discusses e-mail services, including their environment and protocols. You install e-mail servers in Windows (Exchange 2000) and Linux (sendmail). You also configure e-mail clients. In **Chapter 9**, you learn how to extend the Web environment by installing and configuring FTP, news servers, remote access, and streaming media servers. **Chapter 10** explains how to secure the Web environment. You first identify the threats and vulnerabilities of a Web environment, and then learn how to secure data transmission, the operating system, and the server applications. You also authenticate Web users to help prevent unwanted users from accessing your Web server, learn how to use a firewall to filter TCP/IP packets, and how to use intrusion detection software. In **Chapter 11**, you monitor and analyze the Web environment, including the operating system, the Web server, and other Web applications. You also examine the analysis tools that are used to better understand Web traffic.

Each chapter in *Web Server Administration* includes the following elements to enhance the learning experience:

- **Chapter Objectives:** Each chapter in this book begins with a list of the important concepts to master within the chapter. This list provides you with a quick reference to the contents of the chapter, as well as a useful study aid.
- **Step-By-Step Methodology:** As new concepts are presented in each chapter, step-by-step instructions allow you to actively apply the concepts you are learning.
- **Tips:** Chapters contain Tips designed to provide you with practical advice and proven strategies related to the concept being discussed. Tips also provide suggestions for resolving problems you might encounter while proceeding through the chapters.
- **Chapter Summaries:** Each chapter's text is followed by a summary of chapter concepts. These summaries provide a helpful way to recap and revisit the ideas covered in each chapter.
- **Review Questions:** End-of-chapter assessment begins with a set of approximately 20 review questions that reinforce the main ideas introduced in each chapter. These questions ensure that you have mastered the concepts and understand the information you have learned.
- **Hands-on Projects:** Along with conceptual explanations and tutorials, each chapter provides Hands-on Projects related to each major topic aimed at providing you with practical experience. Some of these involve enhancing or extending the exercises in the chapter tutorials, and some involve creating new applications. Many Hands-on Projects provide detailed step-by-step instructions, whereas others encourage independent thinking and learning by encouraging you to apply the material presented in the current and previous chapters with less guidance. As a result, the Hands-on Projects provide you with practice implementing various aspects of the Web environment.

- **Case Projects:** Four cases are presented at the end of each chapter. Each case involves a fictional sample business, and is designed to help you apply what you have learned in the chapter to real-world situations. You work with the same sample businesses in each chapter, so you can build on what you have learned and applied from one chapter to the next. The Case Projects give you the opportunity to independently synthesize and evaluate information, examine potential solutions, and implement them, much as you would in an actual business situation.

In addition to these book-based features, Web Server Administration includes a CD with a Microsoft Windows Server 2003 Enterprise Edition 180-day Evaluation copy, located at the back of this book. Please note that 180 days after installation, this trial software will expire and no longer function. Also in this book (in envelopes bound in the text) are three CDs with a copy of the Publisher's Edition of Red Hat® Linux® from Red Hat, Inc. More information about this software can be found in the "Read This Before You Begin" section that follows this Preface.

Certified Internet Webmaster Program (CIW)

This textbook covers many of the objectives of the CIW Server Administrator exam, one of the certification exams offered by CIW. CIW offers certification for the knowledge economy; their exams are designed to help people enter the IT industry as well as assist experienced professionals in building on existing IT skills. For those interested in using this book to help prepare for this exam, this book offers a mapping grid online that lists each CIW exam objective and identifies where that objective is addressed in the book. This exam objective mapping grid is available for download at *www.course.com*, via the "Student Downloads" link, on the Web page for this book. For more information about CIW certification, visit their Web site at *www.ciwcertified.com.*

Teaching Tools

The following supplemental materials are available when this book is used in a classroom setting. All of the teaching tools available with this book are provided to the instructor on a single CD-ROM.

Electronic Instructor's Manual The Instructor's Manual that accompanies this textbook includes additional instructional material to assist in class preparation, including suggestions for lecture topics, sample syllabi, and ideas for small projects for students to be assigned either in class or as homework.

ExamView ExamView® is the ultimate tool for your objective-based testing needs. It is a powerful objective-based test generator that enables you to create paper, LAN, or Web-based tests from testbanks designed specifically for your Course Technology text. Use the ultra-efficient QuickTest Wizard to create tests in less than five minutes by taking advantage of Course Technology's question banks, or customize your own exams from scratch.

PowerPoint Presentations This book comes with Microsoft PowerPoint slides for each chapter. These are included as a teaching aid for classroom presentation, to make available to students on the network for chapter review, or to be printed for classroom distribution. Instructors can add their own slides for additional topics they introduce to the class.

Data Files Data files, containing all of the data necessary for steps within the chapters and the Hands-on Projects, are provided through the Course Technology Web site at *www.course.com*, and are also available on the Instructor's Resources CD-ROM.

Solution Files Solutions to the end-of-chapter review questions are provided on the Instructor's Resources CD-ROM and can also be found on the Course Technology Web site at *www.course.com*. The solutions are password protected.

ACKNOWLEDGMENTS

First, I would like to acknowledge the hard-working students at DeVry University who have given me the incentive to write this book, and my wife, who painstakingly read every chapter and offered suggestions. Special thanks to my editor Lisa Ruffolo, who is not only a great editor, but very technically savvy too. I would also like to thank Barrie Tysko from Course Technology for making the process of writing this book as pleasurable as possible.

The reviewers were very forthcoming and helpful in every chapter. They include: Anthony Austin, Seneca College; Albert DiCanzio, Webster University; Daniel Gompert, Central Community College; Malcolm JW Gibson, DeVry Institute of Technology-Georgia/Decatur Campus; Kenneth Kleiner, Fayetteville Technical Community College; Jim Martinez, GoCertify.com; Robert McCloud, Sacred Heart University; Margaret Moony, Peralta Community College District; and Cindi A. Nadelman, New England College.

Steve Silva

Read This Before You Begin

To the User

Data Files

In Chapters 4 and 7, you use data files, which your instructor will provide for you. You also can obtain the files electronically from the Course Technology Web site by connecting to *www.course.com*, and then searching for this book title.

In the book, you are asked to copy files from the floppy disk drive in both Linux and Windows. While you are usually reminded that your drive letter (and path) may be different, keep in mind that you might be copying data files from a drive other than the floppy disk drive.

Using Your Own Computer

To use your own computer to complete the chapters, Hands-on Projects, and Case Projects in this book, you will need the following:

- **550 MHz Pentium III or faster computer is strongly recommended.** This computer should have at least 256 MB of RAM, at least a 6 GB blank hard drive, and a floppy disk drive. The faster the computer, the faster it starts, which is a significant advantage when using this book. By the later chapters, your computer will contain a lot of software, and can take a few minutes to start.
- **Microsoft Windows Server 2003 or Windows 2000 Server.** You can use either version of the Windows operating system—the instructions for using either are very similar. Any differences are noted in the steps and descriptions. *Note*: Chapter 3 explains how to install Windows and Linux on a single hard drive. In addition, a 180-day trial version of Windows Server 2003 is included at the back of this book. System requirements, uninstall instructions, and other important information regarding the evaluation copy of this software are located on the last page of this book.
- **Red Hat Linux 8.** This book includes a copy of the Publisher's Edition of Red Hat® Linux® from Red Hat, Inc., which you may use in accordance with the license agreement. Official Red Hat® Linux®, which you may purchase from Red Hat, includes the complete Red Hat® Linux® distribution, Red Hat's documentation, and may include technical support for Red Hat® Linux®. You also may purchase technical support from Red Hat. You may purchase Red Hat® Linux® and technical support from Red Hat through the company's Web site (*www.redhat.com*) or its toll-free number 1-888-REDHAT1. There is a sticker on the top of the envelope containing the

Red Hat® Linux® CD-ROMs (this sticker may also be on the inside back cover of the text). By ripping this seal, you agree to the terms listed above.

- **Data files.** You will not be able to complete the projects in Chapters 4 and 7 using your own computer(s) unless you have the data files. You can get the data files from your instructor, or you can obtain the data files electronically from the Course Technology Web site by connecting to *www.course.com* and then searching for this book title.
- **Additional software**. Some of the steps and projects refer to SQL Server 2000 and Exchange 2000, which are not included with the book. If you do not have access to SQL Server 2000 to work with database files, a Microsoft Access database file is included. If you do not have access to Exchange 2000, you can install the basic e-mail server that comes with Windows Server 2003. You also need .NET Framework, which is available for download on the Microsoft Web site.

The book is organized so the concepts are applied in Windows 2000, Windows Server 2003, and Red Hat 8, so even if you only use one of the operating systems, you will still be applying all the concepts. Your instructor may have you use just a single operating system.

As you work through the chapters, you can use all of the default names and IP addresses that are given in the book. For example, you can name the computer web1, use the domain of technowidgets.com, and use an IP address of 192.168.0.100. However, in a computer lab, the default names and IP addresses might conflict with other computer names and IP addresses. Consult with your instructor or technical support staff to make sure each computer has a unique name and IP address.

Although you complete most of the steps and projects with a single computer, some of them suggest or require more than one computer. However, the other computers are used for testing so you can still perform the main part of the project on a single computer. For example, in Hands-on Project 4-4, you acquire the IP addresses of two other DNS servers in your student lab. However, the project uses two sample IP addresses that you can use to complete the project. In Hands-on Project 4-8, you configure a DNS client for multiple servers. You can still complete the project, though you configure it to use your own server. Hands-on Project 10-8 shows you how to set up a proxy server. As the project explains, you only need the other computers for testing.

You should also have access to a computer connected to the Internet so you can download some small freeware programs, which fit on a floppy disk.

Visit Our World Wide Web Site

Additional materials designed especially for you might be available for your course on the World Wide Web. Go to *www.course.com*. Periodically search this site for more details.

TO THE INSTRUCTOR

The steps, Hands-on Projects, and Case Projects in this book were written and tested using Windows Server 2003, Windows 2000 Server, and Red Hat Linux 8 along with the default browser included with each operating system. All the other applications, such as the MySQL DBMS and the sendmail e-mail server, are included on the Red Hat Linux 8 CDs. However, .NET Framework, SQL Server 2000, and Exchange 2000 are not included. .NET Framework is available for download from the Microsoft Web site.

If the computers in your lab are not networked, you can follow the guidelines as described in "Using Your Own Computer." Because the Web server is part of a client/server technology, some projects use two, and occasionally three computers. However, these projects are designed to show how Web servers work in a client/server environment. With few changes, most of these projects can work on a single computer.

If the computers in your lab are networked, students must use unique computer names, IP addresses, and domains. If the computers are also used to connect to the Internet, the students should use domain names that are not real to reduce DNS resolution problems. You could also require that students use alternate top-level domain names. For example, instead of using .com, students could use .cxm.

Because the book discusses the same Web server concepts in each operating system, you can use any supported operating system to cover virtually all the concepts. Some projects suggest using a browser in one operating system to connect to a Web server in another operating system. These projects work even if you only use one operating system.

Course Technology Data Files

You are granted a license to copy the data files to any computer or computer network used by individuals who have purchased this book.

CHAPTER

1

THE BASICS OF SERVER AND WEB SERVER ADMINISTRATION

In this chapter, you will:

- Review the Internet and the World Wide Web
- Learn about server administration
- Learn about Web server administration
- Explore the common tasks and services performed by administrators
- Examine networking building blocks
- Compare Web server platforms

This chapter introduces the basics of server administration and Web server administration for anyone interested in being a Web server administrator. Whereas a server administrator focuses on the computing needs inside the business, a Web server administrator focuses on making sure that a variety of services are available on the Internet. To offer these services, you may need to evaluate and select options from among a variety of hardware, such as servers, routers, and firewall products. You also need to choose a Web server platform, such as Windows or Linux. The Windows platform offers more than one operating system, while more than one company produces the Linux operating system. After you choose the server and operating system, you should select server software products, such as software needed to run and maintain the Web server and to offer other services, such as File Transfer Protocol (FTP), e-mail, database, programming languages, and security software. After you select and install the Web server software, you must maintain the server daily by monitoring its performance and usage, installing software updates and security patches, and generally making sure that the Web server environment continues to meet the needs of the organization.

When you administer a Web server, you need to understand the Web server environment, which includes the network on which the Web server runs. In this chapter, you will review the basic components of a network and learn how the Web server fits into both the local area network (LAN), and the wide area network (WAN). A LAN is a group of computers along with the devices and media that connect them, which are all under the direct control of the administrator. The WAN is primarily a public, shared network that connects regions and countries. For example, the Internet is a WAN.

REVIEWING THE INTERNET AND THE WORLD WIDE WEB

The Internet is a worldwide network of networks. The term "World Wide Web" (or "Web" for short) refers to the part of the Internet used by the HTTP protocol. Web browsers and Web servers use the HTTP protocol to communicate with one another. When you use a Web browser, you are using the Web. For example, in a browser, you could type *www.technowidgets.com* to visit the Web site of TechnoWidgets, Inc. When you do so, you use the Web to access information provided by TechnoWidgets, Inc. When you send an e-mail message to *info@technowidgets.com*, your message may go to an e-mail server that TechnoWidgets, Inc., runs. Although you use the same connection between you and the server at TechnoWidgets, Inc., to send the message, in this case you use the Internet, not the Web. The Web is not separate from the Internet, but rather represents a way to identify a type of communication on the Internet that relies on HTTP. Web administrators often manage applications that use the Internet, but not the Web.

The Internet is not centrally controlled. Instead, it depends on the cooperation of many entities to make sure that the thousands of networks that make up the Internet function correctly. In some countries, market competition determines how the Internet is configured. In other countries, the national telecommunications monopoly controls the Internet. The Internet shares part of the WAN that is also used by the international telecommunications network, but is distinguished by its use of TCP/IP.

Although the Internet had its origins in the 1960s, major changes began in 1995 when a new backbone was created along with four **network access points (NAPs)**. A **backbone** is a high-speed network that connects to other networks—no users connect to a backbone. The NAPs provide the major Internet connection points and are designed to serve the public. Over time, more NAPs have been created. Just as important, much Internet traffic is now handled without going directly through NAPs because of **peering agreements**, which are agreements between network owners and Internet service providers (ISPs) to exchange traffic. Historically, peering agreements did not involve payment, but today large ISPs often charge smaller ISPs for peering.

Peering arrangements are relevant to any business considering connecting to the Internet using a particular ISP. If the ISP is small, it may have unfavorable peering arrangements that may slow traffic between your business and the rest of the Internet. If you are considering a small, local ISP, you need to find out about its peering arrangement with its upstream ISP and about the performance of its network.

The Web comprises the network of Web servers on the Internet. The Internet is a very large WAN. However, a WAN serves purposes other than supplying the network for the Internet. Namely, it carries voice data for the telephone system and can be used to connect the main office of a business to a branch office.

UNDERSTANDING SERVER ADMINISTRATION

Server administrators focus on their LAN, provide access to the software and services their users need, and make sure that the users' environment is reliable and consistent. Although users must have enough network access to perform their work, server administrators must also control that access to minimize the harm that users can do to the network, either intentionally or unintentionally. Often, the server administrator's job extends to the whole network, as all components must work together.

Working with Users

Users are central to server administration because the purpose of the server—and of the LAN in general—is to make users productive. A LAN can serve hundreds or even thousands of users who need to perform their work as efficiently as possible, and the server administrator makes sure they can access the resources they need, whether those resources are on or controlled by the server. For example, many users need access to a single program on the server or to printers managed by the server.

Users like consistency. If they have to move from one computer to another, they usually want the desktop interface to be as familiar as possible. **Roaming profiles** provide this familiarity. A profile is stored on the user's hard disk and contains information such as the user's preferred desktop settings, Windows Explorer folder options, files stored in My Documents, and Internet Explorer Favorites. A roaming profile resides on the server and allows a user to access his or her profile from other computers on the LAN. If the LAN supports users who work from many computers, the server administrator can make sure that these users have roaming profiles. When the user logs on, the profile is transferred to his or her current hard disk. Because the profile includes all the files in My Documents, it can become very large and slow the logon step.

Establishing Access Control

Controlling access to the network is the principal job of server administrators. They need to give users just enough access to do their jobs, but not more. Access control prevents users from harming the system, and it lets everyone use the system efficiently. To ease administration, server administrators organize users into logical groups based on their common needs. For example, one group may consist of the users in accounting and another group may include everyone in marketing. The users in accounting need access to the accounting software and the printers in the accounting department, but they do not need the forecasting software that the marketing personnel use. Accounting users should not be able to modify marketing forecasts or access the printers in the marketing department, because it is inconvenient for the accounting group and ties up the printers for the marketing group, frustrating both groups of users.

Users often need to share documents on the server. Server administrators can control access to these documents by assigning permission to users, thereby allowing some users to add documents, others to modify documents, and others to only read documents.

Understanding the Server Environment

All but the smallest network includes more than one server, meaning that the server administrator needs to manage many servers. To simplify this task, networks can group servers. Windows, for example, provides a number of ways to do so. In Windows NT, servers and the associated user computers are grouped into domains. Users log on to a domain, which can be completely separate from or related to other domains. In Windows 2000 and 2003, domains can be part of a larger group called a forest. Server groups, domains, and forests increase the complexity of a network, which complicates server administration because the server administrator must then manage thousands of users.

In addition to setting up servers, the server administrator must understand and often maintain the other devices that surround the server. For example, switches or hubs connect the computers to the network, and routers divide the network into manageable parts. These devices can be connected by wires, fiber-optic cables, or even wireless connections.

UNDERSTANDING WEB SERVER ADMINISTRATION

Whereas server administrators focus on LANs, Web server administrators focus on the Internet. The primary purpose of a Web server is to provide information to anyone who requests it on the Internet. As Web server administrator, this means you allow users outside of your organization to access your server when they visit the Web site that your organization hosts. Because this situation can be like opening your doors to allow anyone access to your computers, security and control become even more important with a Web server than when the computers that access your servers are on a LAN. Unlike server administrators, who have complete control over their environment, Web server administrators need cooperation from people outside the organization, such as the support personnel from an ISP, to solve problems with the Internet connection.

You need many technical skills to administer a Web server. You may need to control access to Web pages, create virtual Web sites on a single server, and make sure that the programming environment and e-mail services are functioning correctly. You must also set up and provide other services. For example, you might provide FTP services to allow users to transfer files from one computer to another across the Internet. You must also work with the domain name service (DNS), which translates host names such as *www.microsoft.com* into Internet Protocol (IP) addresses so that the server can find the appropriate computer when exchanging data across the Internet. You should also understand the roles played by firewalls and proxy servers, which protect the organization's computers from unauthorized users who try to access them via the Internet. These many Web server management tasks are often divided among a number of administrators.

Understanding the Web Environment

The connection that a network maintains to the Internet complicates your job as Web server administrator. Although you may control the Web server and related servers, you can't control the Internet. The best that you can do is to control the access that Internet users have to your servers. You do so by working with the Web environment, which contains all the server software that typically is accessed from outside the organization.

For Web administration, you install and maintain many types of software, such as databases and programming languages that create and update Web pages. You typically install each type of software on separate computers for two reasons. First, if you store your Web pages on the same computer containing the database that supplies data to the Web pages, along with e-mail, FTP, and firewall software, requests for using this software might slow the throughput to an unacceptable point. Second, if one software component malfunctions, it can't affect the other components. The steps and Hands-on Projects in this book simplify the lab environment by instructing you to store all components on a single computer, but you should not follow this practice outside of the lab.

Unlike server administrators, who primarily work with users, Web server administrators work with developers and other administrators, not users. Web developers need to access one or more programming languages and databases to create Web pages, then need to access your Web site to update the pages. Developers might also need to use test sites that remain separate from the production Web server. Web server administrators work with other administrators as well, including the database administrator who controls access to the databases that the Web developers use. The e-mail administrator makes sure that everyone can send and receive mail. Depending on the size of the organization, this administrator may not install and configure the software, but merely maintain the users. As Web server administrator, you need to support these development and administration activities. In particular, you need to determine how developers can access their Web pages securely. If any software develops a problem, you might be involved in troubleshooting to solve the problem.

Selecting Programs and Databases

Although Web server administrators do not necessarily need to know how to program, you do need to know how to install languages so that programmers can use them. Most Web sites display Web pages dynamically. For example, a Web page might display advertisements or products based on user preferences. A Web page is considered to be dynamic when it refers to stored data and then displays information based on that data. To display dynamic Web pages, a Web developer uses a programming language to access information in a database and then displays that information on a Web page. For example, suppose you visit an online bookstore and search for books on Linux. At the Web server, a program takes your search request and examines a database for books on Linux. It then displays a list of all the books that the bookstore has on Linux.

Web developers use a variety of programming languages. Perl was one of the first programming languages used to create dynamic Web pages. Web-based programming languages have evolved significantly since Perl was introduced in the mid-1990s, however. Although Perl was originally designed to process text, it remains popular today.

Microsoft has relied on **Active Server Pages (ASP)**, which uses a scripted environment that usually relies on VBScript, a subset of Visual Basic, for programming logic. Because it is scripted and not compiled, ASP does not offer the features or speed of a compiled language. Microsoft has addressed these concerns and more with ASP.NET, which compiles programs and supports more languages than ASP, including Visual Basic .NET, C# .NET (similar to C++), J# .NET (similar to Java), and COBOL .NET. ASP.NET increases its flexibility by using Web services and **Extensible Markup Language (XML)**. A **Web service** consists of one or more programming modules that reside on the Web server and can be accessed from a client computer. XML allows developers to create text files containing tags that define information. Developers can create their own tags within strict syntax guidelines, which allow them to send data in text form to be interpreted by otherwise incompatible systems. Web services and XML work together so that data, as opposed to simple Web pages, can be sent to a computer for processing. Of course, sending data with a Web page leaves the data vulnerable to hackers, and the Web server administrator must work to keep the data secure.

Programs solve specific problems. For example, an accounting program performs calculations to solve accounting problems, and a server program is software that runs on a server to solve data transfer problems. (A server program is not identical to the operating system.) A Web server refers to both the program that runs on the server and the physical server computer.

A **service** is a program that runs in the background. In the UNIX/Linux environment, a service is called a **daemon**. Web servers and e-mail servers are considered services because they are always running in the background. Because a Web service has come to mean a programming technique used on the Web, the Web server is not called a Web service.

Because of their overlapping meaning, you can use the terms "e-mail software," "e-mail application," "e-mail service," and "e-mail program" interchangeably, though these terms actually have slightly different meanings.

Besides the Microsoft .NET languages, one of the most popular programming languages is Java, which is an object-oriented, standards-based language with industry-wide support. Web server environments often include Java because developers can use it to create dynamic Web pages. To write Java programs, developers can use Java Server Pages (JSP), which has a scripting language and a structure similar to Active Server Pages. One difference is that a JSP page is compiled into a servlet, which is then run on a server. A **servlet** is a program written in Java and designed to produce Web pages. A skilled programmer can write servlet programs to optimize code and precisely control the behavior of a Web page.

One of the easiest Web development languages to use is PHP, which was originally designed to allow relatively unsophisticated users to create home pages on a Web site. PHP originally meant Personal Home Page, but as its popularity grew and it evolved into a complete programming language, it came to stand for PHP Hypertext Preprocessor. PHP has a structure similar to that of ASP and JSP, and a syntax similar to that of Perl and Java.

Macromedia ColdFusion is another popular Web development language that was introduced before ASP. Although ColdFusion is more extensive than the other languages previously mentioned, it offers many features that make producing sophisticated Web pages relatively easy. The ColdFusion syntax is also similar to that of ASP and JSP, so programmers who know those languages can learn ColdFusion quickly.

All Web development programming languages are limited unless they can connect to a database to extract and save data. A **database management system (DBMS)** lets you store and access data on a computer. Relational databases contain data in table form and share a common language called **Structured Query Language (SQL)** that you can use to manipulate the data in the database. Many Web sites employ databases to perform tasks such as storing customer information, producing reports, and displaying product information. Database management systems range from simple to complex in terms of features and capabilities, and from free to expensive in terms of price.

At the low end of DBMS capabilities is Microsoft Access. It is an appropriate choice for Web sites that do not have sophisticated needs, such as a site that looks up employee e-mail names and phone numbers.

Microsoft SQL Server 2000 is a more complex DBMS than Access, though it is also easy to use. Combining SQL Server 2000 and ASP.NET provides a capable system because ASP.NET has code specifically optimized for SQL Server 2000. For example, you can use ASP.NET to extract data from a database, produce a report in HTML, and then send the report to another user. Although many organizations hire a database administrator (DBA) to manage their databases, SQL Server 2000 is often installed without a DBA. In these cases, the Web server administrator must install SQL Server 2000 and provide security measures while the developers create the databases and tables.

Oracle9*i* is another sophisticated DBMS that can be installed on a variety of server platforms, including Windows, UNIX, and Linux. Oracle9*i* products are built on a core database, and they work with a family of related products such as application servers, e-commerce servers, and e-mail servers. When you install Oracle9*i*, it also installs an Apache Web server and associated modules configured to work with the database. Soon after installing the database, developers can test sample JSP pages and servlets to see how they connect to Oracle9*i*. A knowledgeable DBA should maintain Oracle9*i*.

While Access, SQL Server 2000, and Oracle9*i* range in price from moderate to expensive, MySQL is a capable DBMS that is freely available. In a test with Oracle9*i* on a quad-processor server, MySQL could handle almost as many simultaneous users as Oracle9*i*.

Where Oracle9*i* is suitable for large organizations with extensive and specific requirements, MySQL should be considered for other environments. The Web server administrator can install MySQL and provide some support; Web developers can then provide the rest of the support.

Managing E-mail Servers

E-mail servers are common in many businesses. By design, they are open because users need to send e-mail to anyone and receive e-mail from anyone. The e-mail server generally sends and accepts messages without imposing any security, which can lead to abuse of the e-mail service. For example, most people are annoyed with the volume of spam they receive. Viruses and worms sent through e-mail continue to create problems. All of this unwanted traffic can cause problems for the Web server administrator. In smaller organizations, the Web administrator may also act as the e-mail administrator. Even in larger organizations, the two administrators need to work closely together. In some organizations, the Web administrator provides technical support while someone else performs maintenance tasks such as adding and deleting users to the system.

Microsoft strives to make products that are easy to install and configure, yet are powerful and flexible enough to grow in a complex environment. Microsoft Exchange 2000, for example, is designed to manage e-mail services. In some environments, the Web administrator can readily install and easily maintain Exchange 2000, which lets users exchange e-mail, coordinate meetings on a group calendar, manage contacts and tasks, and be involved with discussion groups. You can also use Exchange 2000 with other products such as Exchange 2000 Conferencing Server, which manages data, voice, and video conferencing.

Besides the Microsoft servers, one of the most popular e-mail server products is sendmail, an open-source software package that is available in both free and commercial versions. Sendmail does not provide a full range of e-mail services, however—it only sends and receives mail, and does not route the e-mail it receives to users. If you are a Web server administrator supporting sendmail, you must install another product such as imapd to let users access their e-mail. (You will install sendmail and imapd in Chapter 8.)

Working with Other Web Applications

In addition to programming languages, databases, and e-mail services, your Web server might support other applications that you need to manage, including firewall, FTP, and DNS services, depending on the size of your organization. Some organizations choose to have an ISP provide some of these applications, such as DNS, while large organizations often hire specialists to take charge of these applications.

Firewall is a general term for specialized software designed to control access to your Web environment. A firewall helps to control access to your Web environment as well as access from your internal network to the Internet. As Web server administrator, you need detailed information on what type of access the other Web applications need, such as e-mail and

Web server software. The firewall makes sure that only the applications you specify can be accessed. Good firewall products help to prevent attacks on the Web environment by malicious hackers, and they can monitor access to and from your Web environment. This means that you can track how internal users use the Web, which is particularly helpful if internal users are not using the Web for business purposes and slow your connection to the Internet.

FTP is a service that allows users to download files from and upload files to a server; the Web server administrator controls who can download and who can upload files. Many users employ FTP to download software programs, updates, data files, and software patches from Web sites. FTP can operate in two standard modes: anonymous and protected. The anonymous mode does not require a password and lets anyone access files. Protected mode requires a user to enter a user name and password to access files. Because the user name and password are sent as clear (unencrypted) text, hackers can easily find out the user name and password to download sensitive information or upload damaging files that could harm the FTP server. For this reason, it is difficult to make FTP secure.

A **DNS** server translates host names such as *www.technowidgets.com* into an IP address such as 38.246.165.12. DNS can also translate an IP address into a host name. An IP address is the way each computer is identified on a network. (IP addresses are covered in detail in Chapter 2.) The DNS server typically controls the hosts in a single domain. For example, the DNS server in an organization with the domain name technowidgets.com would control hosts such as *www.technowidgets.com*, *mail.technowidgets.com*, and *ftp.technowidgets.com*. A DNS server receives an IP address and responds with a host name; security programs and e-mail programs can take advantage of this feature to determine which host is sending the message. An ISP can readily maintain the DNS server because its information rarely changes.

Managing the Internet Connection

Naturally, the Web administrator needs to maintain a connection with the Internet. When a LAN experiences a problem, the LAN administrator is responsible for checking the wiring and connections. The Web administrator, on the other hand, works with many other administrators or organizations to connect a Web environment to the Internet and then to maintain that connection.

As a Web server administrator, your responsibility ends at your connection to the Internet. From that point, you need to contact your ISP to obtain additional support. Your ISP may have to contact your local phone company to confirm that your connection from your building is working. The local phone company, in turn, might have to work with a long-distance telephone carrier to complete a connection or to solve a problem. In the WAN environment, many organizations are responsible for maintaining connectivity.

You may also need to contact your ISP to change your service. For example, you might want a faster Internet connection or multiple connections for redundancy. However, not all ISPs can offer all services. For example, an ISP that specializes in low-speed connections might not provide high-speed connections.

Now that you've examined the differences between server administrators and Web server administrators, you can explore their similarities.

Exploring Administrators' Common Tasks and Services

While server administrators and Web server administrators work in different environments and perform different tasks, they share many types of tasks. In smaller organizations, the server administrator and the Web server administrator might be the same person. Although both administrators maintain security, for example, each takes a different approach to that task—both are interested in security, but security on a LAN can be different from security in a Web server environment.

Installing and Configuring Systems

The Web administrator needs to determine the hardware and software requirements of the environment. This includes not only the servers, but also everything that connects to the servers, such as switches that connect servers and other computers together, and routers that connect the server network with the internal LAN or Internet. Administrators install the operating system and applications on the servers.

For the Web server administrator, installing the operating system is a simple task because the Web server is more isolated than a typical server on a LAN. The more challenging task for the Web server administrator is to determine which other applications the organization needs and then to install them.

Both Web and server administrators need to maintain a correct configuration. Server administrators focus on configuring users and their environment. Web server administrators seek to maintain a correct configuration on a variety of applications. Unfortunately, knowing how to configure one application, such as e-mail, does not necessarily help to configure another application, such as DNS.

Maintaining Security

Everyone is concerned about security. However, an organization should be concerned about more than simply preventing a hacker from attacking its system. Disgruntled and inept employees can do damage, too. As a consequence, administrators need to consider both physical security and software security.

Physical security involves protecting your server environment from others. For example, you should stop outsiders from engaging in malicious behavior and prevent internal users from surfing the Internet and potentially downloading viruses. Some users with technical skills might want to change the server and create difficult-to-resolve problems. External users might try to detect the traffic between your Web server and the Internet.

Just as Web server administrators use firewalls to restrict access to the Web server, so should server administrators restrict access to the server environment. To do so, they can use a Demilitarized Zone (DMZ), a configuration where the servers are isolated from both outside attacks and inside attacks.

Monitoring the System

Systems can be monitored to track performance, troubleshoot problems, and record usage, for example. Server performance reflects the server's ability to perform its duties, such as transmitting Web pages or e-mail messages to users, with minimal delay. Although Web and server administrators have different criteria for adequate performance, their objective is the same. Users should find performance acceptable, while the cost for the performance must make business sense. For the server administrator, traffic typically travels at 100 Mbps in a LAN. For the Web administrator, traffic is often limited to speeds of 1.544 Mbps or less. Both administrators want to keep their users happy. Users accessing Web pages, for example, will not accept significant delays while waiting for the pages to appear in their browsers. What is considered "significant" can vary depending on the environment. If the user constantly accesses a Web-based application that is critical to job performance, he or she may require very quick response times. If the user is ordering seat belts for a classic car, response time is less important.

As an administrator, you may use many methods to monitor your system for troubleshooting purposes. The operating system, whether Windows or Linux, monitors itself and communicates information to you using software tools and log files. Windows uses the Event Viewer to organize log files. Linux also maintains log files and can notify you about them through e-mail. Figure 1-1 shows an example of the Windows Event Viewer. To find out more about each message, you could double-click it.

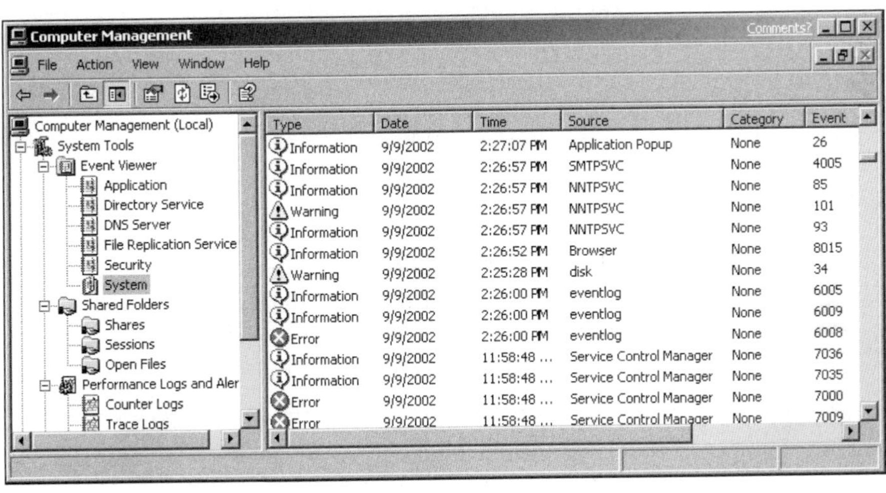

Figure 1-1 Windows Event Viewer

Both Apache and Microsoft Internet Information Server (IIS) Web servers have extensive logging capabilities, as you will see in Chapter 11. Figure 1-2 shows an example of an Apache log file that you can track to see who is accessing what part of your site and how often.

```
10.2.5.3 - - [25/Sep/2002:10:16:52 -0400] "GET / HTTP/1.1" 304 - "-" "Mozilla/4.0"
10.2.5.3 - - [25/Sep/2002:10:16:52 -0400] "GET /icons/apache_pb.gif HTTP/1.1" 304 -
"http://10.11.22.33/" "Mozilla/4.0"
10.2.5.3 - - [25/Sep/2002:10:16:52 -0400] "GET /poweredby.png HTTP/1.1" 304 -
"http://10.11.22.33/" "Mozilla/4.0"
10.2.5.3 - - [25/Sep/2002:10:28:16 -0400] "GET /test.htm HTTP/1.1" 200 31 "-"
"Mozilla/4.0"
10.11.22.33 - - [16/Sep/2002:09:06:43 -0400] "GET / HTTP/1.1" 200 2890 "-" "Mozilla/4.0"
10.11.22.33 - - [16/Sep/2002:09:06:43 -0400] "GET /poweredby.png HTTP/1.1" 200 1154
"http://localhost:55555" "Mozilla/4.0"
10.11.22.33 - - [16/Sep/2002:09:06:43 -0400] "GET /icons/apache_pb.gif HTTP/1.1" 200 2326
"http://localhost:55555" "Mozilla/4.0"
```

Figure 1-2 Apache log file

Because system monitoring takes resources, you must balance the desire to understand certain aspects of your system against the resources required by that effort. Extensive system monitoring may decrease performance to an unacceptable level and quickly fill your hard disk with log files.

Windows and Linux also provide software tools that monitor a system by gathering data about system usage or helping to troubleshoot a performance problem. For example, you can use the Windows System Monitor to create a graph that tracks processor usage over time, thereby enabling you to identify programs or resources that consume excessive processing power.

Maintenance and Backup

After you install and configure a computer system, you need to maintain it. For example, you should periodically upgrade your operating system and applications. You might also need to eliminate security holes by installing software patches and enhancements. While these changes usually improve a system, they can occasionally introduce new problems. For example, a patch designed to solve one problem might cause another. An upgrade that has produced no problems in other environments might unexpectedly cause serious problems in your environment. In general, you should plan for the worst and test changes thoroughly in isolation as much as possible before making them on the overall system. For example, schedule maintenance tasks during a slow time on the system, such as late at night, to avoid interrupting services. Because it can be difficult to determine which patches you need, you should monitor the Web sites of the manufacturers of your software to see what they suggest. User groups and e-mail notification can also prove useful.

In addition to performing software maintenance, server administrators typically create and maintain system backups. Backup software stores data from your server on another device such as a tape. You can use the tapes to restore data if someone accidentally overwrites Web pages or realizes that they need files deleted earlier. All the tasks related to backing up data and restoring it can be complex. For example, normally you cannot back up open files, although open files can be the most important ones on your server. Microsoft SQL Server and most other SQL servers keep their data files open so they can't be backed up. Thus, when you buy your backup software, you should either make sure that it can back up open files, such as those associated with SQL Server and Microsoft Exchange Server, or require the database administrator and mail server administrator to do their own backups.

System problems can be so severe that the only solution is to completely reinstall all the software and its associated data. As you set up a new server, you should always test your ability to reinstall software and data, including your operating system, DBMS, mail server, Web server, and other applications. Enter data in all the applications, and then install your backup software and do a complete backup. Format your drive to simulate a catastrophic failure, and then verify that you can restore the system from your backup. Take these steps to confirm that you can recover from a disaster:

1. Install the operating system.
2. Install applications such as the DBMS, e-mail, and others your organization uses, including backup software.
3. Create sample transactions and other data for all the applications.
4. Back up the complete system.
5. Format the hard disk and reinstall the operating system.
6. Reinstall the backup software.
7. Restore the system.
8. Test applications to make sure that the data was restored correctly.

Examining Network Building Blocks

Many parts of the network need to work together in harmony. Administrators must understand how these parts fit together so they can determine how to create an efficient and balanced network. For example, you should not buy an extremely fast server when your connection to the Internet is very slow. Administrators must also prevent malicious hackers from penetrating or disrupting the Web environment. Because hackers exploit the basics of the TCP/IP model to do damage, you must understand these basics so you can protect your system.

This chapter provides an overview of networking and telecommunications. Chapter 2 focuses on the addressing part of the networking model. When you learn about securing the Web server in Chapter 10, you will examine other parts of the model to see how you can protect the server against attacks such as a SYN flood, Ping of Death, smurf attack, fragmentation bomb, and spoofing.

As a Web server administrator, you need to look at the network as a logical model to understand how computers communicate, and as a physical structure to understand how network components work together. In the following section, you first examine the logical model, and then learn about the components of a LAN and a WAN.

Understanding the OSI Model and the TCP/IP Model

You use the **Open Source Interconnection (OSI)** model and **Transmission Control Protocol/Internet Protocol (TCP/IP)** model to understand network communication. The OSI model defines the building blocks that divide data communications into discrete parts. TCP/IP comprises a suite of protocols that are used in data communication. A **protocol** is a set of communication rules. For example, when you mail a letter, you follow a protocol to correctly address the envelope. In data communications, protocols define the details of how each task is performed.

The objective of the OSI and TCP/IP models is to show the division of tasks needed to communicate on a network. For example, suppose the sales manager at TechnoWidgets, Inc., in Phoenix, Arizona, decides to send a sample of a new widget to an important customer in San Francisco, California. To send the widget from one place to another, many specialists are involved, as shown in Figure 1-3. The sales manager gives the widget to an assistant, who packages it and calls the transportation company that will carry the package to the customer. The person who picks up the package doesn't know where the customer lives, but takes it to a central sorting center. The people at the central sorting center don't care about the street address, but send the package to the San Francisco sorting center. The people at the San Francisco sorting center deliver it to the customer's business. There, an assistant takes the device out of the package to allow the customer to admire the new widget. When the sales manager calls to find out whether the customer likes the widget, he or she does not need to know all the steps taken to convey the device from one place to another—only that the customer has received it. The sales manager and the customer communicate at the same level, yet the sales manager needs to understand only how to transfer the package to the assistant. This process is very similar to the way in which the networking models function. Each level communicates with its corresponding level at the other end without needing to understand what happens outside that level except to communicate to level(s) adjacent to it.

Examining the OSI Model

The OSI model was designed in the 1970s and implemented in the 1980s to show how networking protocols should function. It consists of seven layers, which separate the complex task of communication into manageable parts. By dividing the tasks into layers, a protocol needs to be concerned only with specific tasks and the way in which it communicates with the layer below and above it. The highest layer describes the link between the computer system and TCP/IP, and the lowest level describes the data as it is either leaving or entering the computer. See Table 1-1.

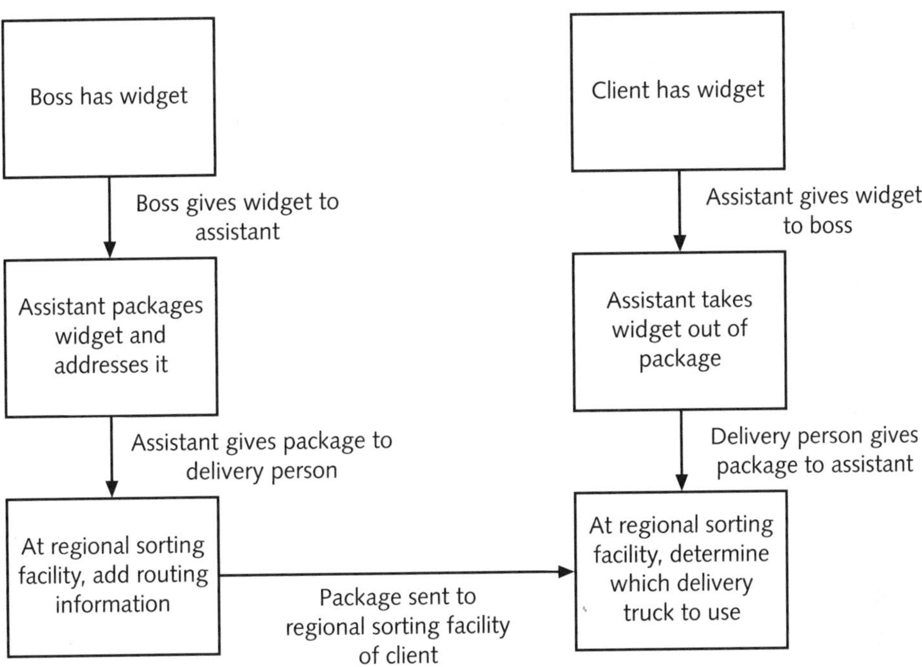

Figure 1-3 Sending a package divides tasks

Table 1-1 OSI model

Layer	Name	Description
7	Application	Responsible for low-level application access to the network. An example of an application that works at this level would be FTP, which transfers files from one computer to another.
6	Presentation	Can convert data into a format that is understandable to the Application layer. Encryption and decryption occur at this layer.
5	Session	Can open communication with another computer, maintain it for a specified period, and then shut down the communication.
4	Transport	Responsible for transporting the data from one computer to another. Protocols at this level include TCP (used for communications between the browser and the Web server) and UDP (used for communication with a DNS server).

Table 1-1 OSI model (continued)

Layer	Name	Description
3	Network	Primarily responsible for addressing between two computers. It is also responsible for fragmentation and reassembly of packets if the devices through which the packets flow have different capabilities. The IP protocol is at this layer. Another protocol, ICMP, provides error messages.
2	Data Link	Responsible for the interface between the packets coming down through the upper layers and the physical layer. It puts the interface in a data frame that is designed for a specific medium and then sends it on to the Physical layer.
1	Physical	Responsible for transferring the data to the network medium. Ethernet is a common transfer method.

The OSI model is part of the networking vocabulary. For example, a switch is a device that takes data from one computer and sends it to another computer to which it is directly connected. This situation is analogous to sending a package in Phoenix to another place in Phoenix. Such communication takes place at Layer 2 of the OSI model. Other switches are Layer 3 switches, which means that they can work at the Network layer. This situation is analogous to moving the package from Phoenix to San Francisco. By stating that a product is a Layer 3 switch, you should understand that the term refers to Layer 3 of the OSI model and recognize what that entails.

Examining the TCP/IP Model

As opposed to the theoretical OSI model, the TCP/IP model is a real-world model based on how TCP/IP actually works. The TCP/IP model doesn't correspond exactly with the more common OSI model, as Table 1-2 shows. Actually, TCP not only performs the tasks at the Transport level of the OSI model, but also handles some of the tasks at the Session level of the OSI model. The first three layers constitute the TCP/IP protocol suite.

Table 1-2 TCP/IP model

Layer	Common components	OSI reference layer
Application	HTTP, SMTP, POP3, FTP, DNS	Application Presentation Session
Transport	TCP, UDP	Transport
Network	IP, ICMP	Network
Physical	Ethernet, FDDI	Data Link Physical

Because the OSI model is a general-purpose model, you can use it to better understand other protocols such as IPX/SPX, NetBEUI, and Appletalk. These protocols have been used in LANs for many years but are not common today.

Most of the protocols will be explained in depth in the following chapters. For now, understand that the protocols provide the rules to make sure that all TCP/IP systems can interoperate. They need to interoperate both the application level and the lower-level data communication layers. The following list briefly describes the main protocols:

- *Hypertext Transfer Protocol (HTTP)*—Web servers implement this protocol, which allows you to request a Web page or send a completed form to a Web server for processing. Examples include IIS and Apache.
- *Simple Mail Transfer Protocol (SMTP)*—E-mail servers implement this protocol, which allows you to send mail to another e-mail server. Examples include Microsoft Exchange and Sendmail.
- *Post Office Protocol Version 3 (POP3)*—E-mail servers implement this protocol, which allows users to retrieve mail from an e-mail server. Examples include Microsoft Exchange and Sendmail.
- *File Transfer Protocol (FTP)*—FTP servers implement this protocol, which is used to transfer files to and from a server. Both Windows and Linux have FTP servers that are included with the operating system.
- *Domain Name Service (DNS)*—DNS servers implement this protocol to translate names into IP addresses and IP addresses into names. For example, when you type *www.technowidgets.com* into a browser, a DNS server must first translate that name into an IP address before the request can be sent to the Web server. Berkeley Internet Name Domain (BIND) is the most popular program used to implement DNS. Microsoft also has a DNS server.
- *Transmission Control Protocol (TCP)*—This protocol creates a reliable connection between two computers. TCP is used as a primary means of communication by HTTP, SMTP, POP3, and FTP.
- *User Datagram Protocol (UDP)*—This protocol does not establish a connection between two computers as TCP does, but simply sends a message. This ability makes it a good protocol for sending short, discrete messages, such as requesting the IP address for *www.microsoft.com* from a DNS server. UDP relies on the application that implements it to make sure that the message gets to its destination.
- *Internet Protocol (IP)*—This protocol provides an addressing scheme so that it can determine whether the data packet should be sent to a computer that is physically connected on the same network or to another computer that can route it to the destination computer. It can also provide fragmentation and reassembly of data. (See Chapter 2 for more information about IP and addressing.)
- *Internet Control Message Protocol (ICMP)*—This protocol provides error messages. When you use the ping utility and it returns an error, it is from ICMP.

Now that you have learned about the networking building blocks, you need to see how the components in a network come together to transfer the data from one computer to another.

Identifying Network Components

To design an appropriate Web environment for the needs of your organization, you must first understand the common network components. The overall design needs to be balanced so that a bottleneck will not cause problems with the rest of the network. In a Web server environment, data must travel between your Web server and the user's computer. This section discusses the common components you need to consider when designing a Web network environment. After considering the specifics of the network configuration, you must evaluate the performance of the network and determine its capacity. You also need to determine how to measure network performance.

Identifying Common LAN Components

Recall that a LAN is a network that spans a relatively small geographic area, such as an office, a single floor in a building, an entire building, or even multiple buildings in an office park or campus. The most common network technology in use today is **Ethernet**, which connects multiple devices, such as PCs and printers, on a LAN. With Ethernet, these devices can send information across the cables that connect them, thereby passing information from one device to another. Figure 1-4 diagrams a simple LAN.

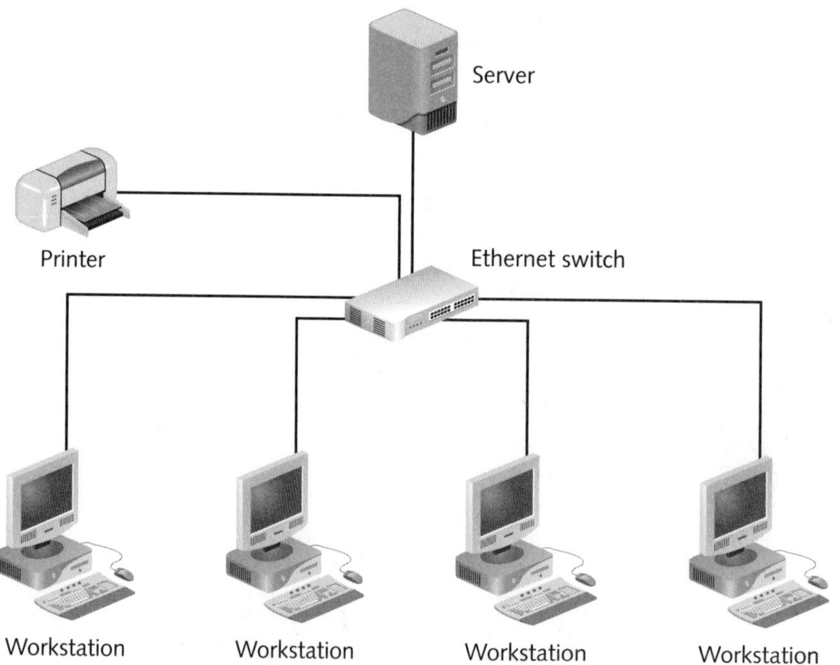

Figure 1-4 Simple network diagram

Note the Ethernet switch shown in Figure 1-4. A **switch** is a central device that allows PCs to communicate with one another. A data cable connects the NIC of each computer to the switch. Ethernet switches work at several speeds. Standard Ethernet communicates at 10 Mbps, but other Ethernet speeds include 100 Mbps and 1 Gbps. Switches operating at a speed of 100 Mbps are the most common today.

Whatever configuration your network uses, the server should have a higher connection speed than the workstations that are accessing it, because the server is a central resource. For example, suppose you have a network of 100 workstations and one server, all connected at 10 Mbps. If all 100 of those workstations wanted to access the server at the same time, they would overload the connection to the server. Even if the server had enough processing power to supply the data, its connection speed would allow it to send data only at 10 Mbps to the network, so the data would take longer to travel to each workstation. Although that number of workstations could technically overload a server even if it had a 100 Mbps connection, normally traffic is not so sustained that a 100 Mbps connection could not manage it. For this reason, it is common practice to connect servers at 100 Mbps, 1 Gbps, or even higher rates.

Your connection speed to the Internet is even more critical. The typical connection speed of 1.544 Mbps is merely a fraction of the speed possible with standard Ethernet. You want to make sure that your users and your Web server exchange data in an acceptable amount of time, but minimize the cost of your Internet connection by purchasing only what you need in terms of the speed of your connection.

Connecting Your LAN to the Internet

A WAN is a telecommunications network operating over an area that can span a few miles or reach another country. Whereas you control the cabling in a LAN, the WAN is typically a shared, public network. You connect your LAN to a WAN that is connected to your ISP, and your ISP provides the connection to the Internet. In essence, a WAN is a network that begins where the connection at your building ends. Although your focus in using the WAN is to connect to the Internet, you could also use the WAN to connect your main office in Chicago to your branch office in Walnut Creek.

A common method of connecting to a WAN from a business is through a T1 line, which is a digital connection that is used only for data and voice transmission. Alternatively, you could use other types of T-Carrier WAN connections, as listed in Table 1-3. You will learn about other WAN connection options shortly, but for now note these T-Carriers are the most common building blocks for WANs. Many other connection types exist as well, including ISDN, DSL, and cable modems.

When deciding which connection to use, you must consider your organization's overall needs for speed and cost. For instance, a small company with a small Web server could use a 64 Kbps fractional T1, but a larger company with a much busier Web server might require multiple T1s. In these cases, you can keep increasing the capacity to the point of matching companies such as Microsoft, which use multiple T3s.

Table 1-3 Common T-Carrier connections

Connection type	Speed	Description
Fractional T1	64 Kbps increments up to T1	Used when you do not need a full T1 connection. A T1 connection is divided into 24 channels, and one channel is 64 Kbps.
T1	1.544 Mbps	T1 is the most common digital leased-line service. Each channel in a T1 circuit can carry voice or data transmissions, and you can combine multiple T1s to provide additional speed.
T3	44.736 Mbps	T3 is equivalent to 28 T1 circuits. Its speed is often rounded and referred to as 45 Mbps. Like fractional T1s, fractional T3s allow customers to lease less than the full T3 rate.

The appropriate connection speed for your Web server is difficult to gauge accurately. Ask the following questions to determine the speed you need:

- How much data will a typical user request?
- How many users will access your Web server simultaneously?
- How many pages will the typical user view?
- What is the typical user's tolerance for delay?
- Will the access be spread throughout the day or will it be focused on a few hours in a day?
- How long will it take for the estimated number of users to double? A month? A year?
- What is the average size of your Web page?
- How will the average size of your Web page increase over the next year as you incorporate more graphics? (This factor could easily increase the average size of your Web pages by five or ten times.)
- If your Web server shares its connection with users in your organization who need a connection to the Internet, how will their needs change over time?

Selecting a connection type and determining the optimal connection speed are more of an art than a science for a company connecting its Web server to the Internet for the first time. The main thing to consider is the need for future growth. The T-Carrier connections offer the most growth potential.

Connecting Your Network to a WAN Using a T-Carrier Line

You use a few standard components when you connect your network to a WAN using any T-Carrier line, whether fractional T1, full T1, or T3. Even though T1 and Ethernet networks are digital, they send data in very different ways. You need certain components to translate the digital format of the data arriving via a T1 line to the digital format that is acceptable to your LAN. In an organization where users share the connection to the Internet, your Web server will share the network with users. Although Figure 1-5 shows one way to connect these devices, technology has advanced to the point that you can connect a T1 line directly into a WAN interface card in a computer.

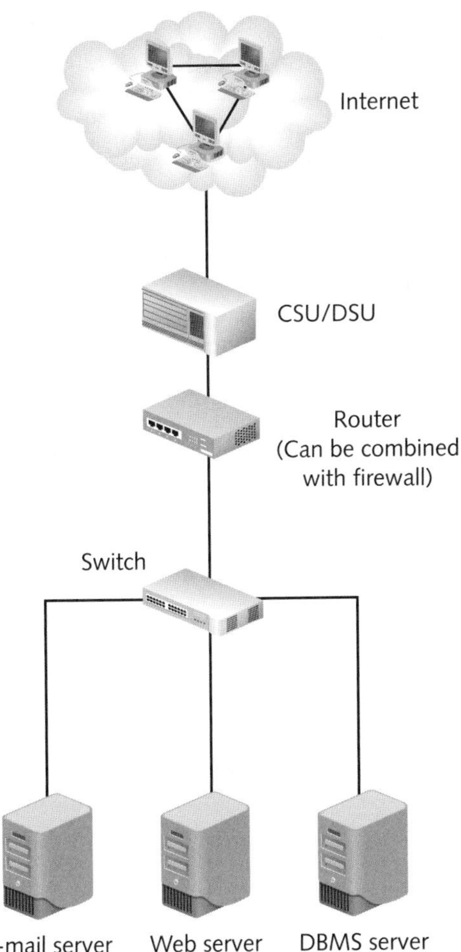

Figure 1-5 Network diagram showing T1 WAN components

The following list describes the typical components in a connection to a T-Carrier WAN line:

- *Channel Service Unit/Data Service Unit (CSU/DSU)*—This unit really includes two devices in one. The CSU portion is on the WAN side and serves two purposes: It transmits and receives the digital signal, and it provides an electrical buffer from either side of the device. The DSU translates between the digital signal on the T1 side and the serial connection on the LAN side.
- *Multiplexor*—This optional component provides a mechanism to load multiple voice and data channels into a single digital line. This strategy could be used in a case where you want to split your T1 line into two parts and then carry data across one part and phone traffic across the other part. A multiplexor is not required.
- *Router*—Although routers can serve a variety of functions, the router used to connect a T1 line to a WAN is specialized. A serial connection provides communication with the CSU/DSU or multiplexor. That connection routes to one or more Ethernet ports. The Ethernet port, in turn, provides the connection to your LAN. More details about routing are in the "IP Addressing" section of Chapter 2.

It is easiest to think of the CSU/DSU as being a kind of digital modem. Just as a modem provides an interface between the telephone line and your computer, so the CSU/DSU provides the same interface for your LAN. Likewise, a modem provides a serial connection to your computer just as a CSU/DSU device provides a serial connection to your LAN.

Using an Integrated Services Digital Network Connection

An integrated services digital network (ISDN) connection offers a digital service capable of carrying voice, video, or data communications. Although it was defined in 1984, ISDN connections became popular only in the 1990s as compatibility problems eased. ISDN remains popular in applications where users need a private connection to a company network to telecommute but speeds higher than those offered by a typical modem. ISDN is also used as a backup when the main line malfunctions. It is a dial-up service: You must dial a number to reach the system that accepts the ISDN connection and connect to the local telephone service, just as you do with a standard telephone call with a modem. However, because ISDN is a completely digital service, it can provide higher capacity across the phone system's wires. ISDN lines connect to the LAN via a **terminal adapter (TA)**, sometimes referred to as an ISDN modem.

ISDN offers two service types:

- *Basic Rate Interface (BRI)*—This service provides three channels of data transfer. Two channels carry up to 64 Kbps of data and are referred to as "B" or "bearer" channels. The third channel carries data at a speed of 16 Kbps and is referred to as a "D" or "delta" channel. In a typical BRI connection, the two B channels transmit the data and the D channel manages the link.
- *Primary Rate Interface (PRI)*—This type of service provides a significantly higher amount of bandwidth and divides the equivalent of a T1 line into 24 channels. PRI uses 23 B channels, each capable of carrying data at 64 Kbps, and one 64 Kbps D channel to manage the link.

The BRI provides data transfers at a speed of 128 Kbps, which may be appropriate for a user to connect to a private company network, but probably is not adequate for a typical Web server. The PRI channels use a T1 line, so their capacity is 1.544 Mbps, which is appropriate for a small to medium-size company.

Using a Digital Subscriber Line

As with ISDN, a **digital subscriber line (DSL)** allows you to transfer data at high speeds over conventional telephone lines. Many types of DSL connections are available, and they are characterized by their download and upload speeds. Download speed measures how fast you can transfer data from a server such as a Web page or a file, while upload speed indicates how fast you can send data to the server such as a Web page request or an e-mail message with attachments. Typically, download speeds are more important than upload speeds for users. The most common include the following:

- *ADSL (Asymmetric DSL)*—DSL recognizes that typical home users are more interested in fast downloads than fast uploads, so ADSL has a faster download speed than upload speed. The speeds vary depending on the service that you request. ADSL supports rates ranging from 1.544 Mbps to 6.1 Mbps for downloads and from 16 Kbps to 640 Kbps for uploads.
- *IDSL (ISDN DSL)*—IDSL has only one speed, 128 Kbps. It is typically used by those who live out of range of the other DSL options.
- *RADSL (Rate Adaptive Digital Subscriber Line)*—RADSL is a variation of ADSL. When the modem starts, it tests the line to adjust its operating speed to the fastest speed that the line can support. RADSL supports rates ranging from 640 Kbps to 2.2 Mbps for downloads and from 272 Kbps to 1.088 Mbps for uploads.

- *SDSL (Single Digital Subscriber Line)*—Although the word "single" means that it just needs a single line as opposed to earlier DSL standards that required more lines, the main significance of SDSL is that the upload and download speeds are the same. SDSL operates at rates up to 1.544 Mbps.

You can use the information in the preceding list to determine which types of DSL are appropriate for a home user and which are appropriate for a business user with a Web server. A Web server receives very small packets of data requesting Web pages. The Web server responds to each request by transmitting a relatively large Web page. The Web server needs more upload speed than download speed, so SDSL is appropriate. On the other hand, ADSL provides the opposite of what a typical business with a Web server needs, because it provides faster download speed than upload speed. ADSL is therefore more appropriate for a home user, though it can be appropriate for a business in some cases. For example, a business with many users needs fast downloads because their requests for Web pages are small compared to the size of the Web pages returned. Perhaps the users have a Web server that just has basic information about their company, but the Web server is never expected to have many simultaneous users. ADSL would be appropriate for this type of business. SDSL is the best solution where the emphasis in the business is the Web server and allowing users to access the Web server at relatively high speeds.

Note that not all ISPs offer services that reach speeds of up to 1.544 Mbps. Your ISP should allow you to start with a slow speed and grow to the maximum speed.

Download is often referred to as "downstream," and upload is often referred to as "upstream." The Web site *www.dslreports.com* is a good resource for information about DSL service and its providers.

One limitation of all varieties of DSL is **signal degradation**, although this concept is not unique to DSL. (ISDN is also particularly susceptible to signal degradation.) Signal degradation involves the loss of signal strength as the signal moves farther from the source. To use DSL, you must be located within a certain distance of a telephone switch to avoid signal degradation. The distances vary, but with some versions of DSL a client must be located within 3,000 meters of a switch. Some DSL variants allow distances of up to 8,000 meters. Generally, the DSL provider will conduct a line test to determine whether a business or home telephone line can handle a DSL connection. Telecommunication technology has advanced to the point that most business and home users can get DSL. Figure 1-6 shows a typical way to connect to the Internet using DSL.

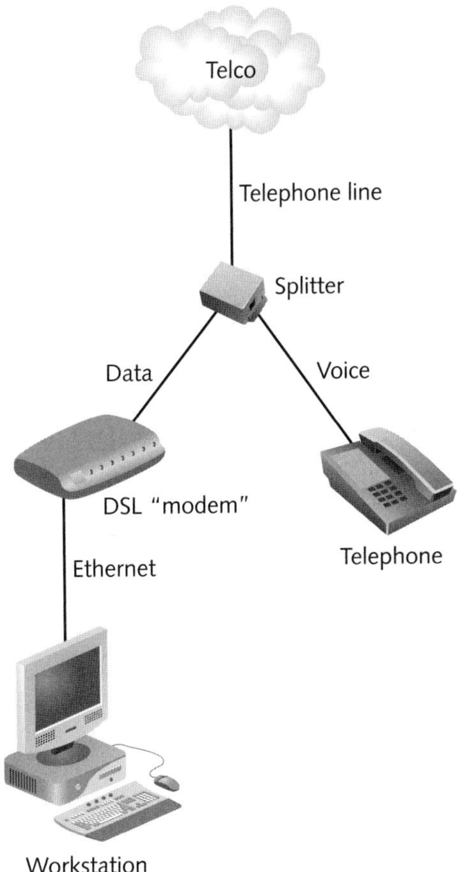

Figure 1-6 DSL connection

Using Cable Modems

Although cable modems are designed for the home user market, they are used in business as well. Like DSL, cable modems allow a wide range of communication speeds and often have different upstream and downstream speeds. Unlike DSL, cable modems do not use standard phone lines, but transmit a signal along the same line as your cable TV. See Figure 1-7.

Cable modems typically share access, which means that everyone receiving cable service from the same provider in the same area or neighborhood competes for the amount of capacity available. (Standard Ethernet operates in the same way.) This shared access won't be a problem if your service provider expands its service as it adds new users. Unlike with T-Carrier, ISDN, and DSL connections, however, the performance of cable modem connections can degrade significantly over time. You should therefore make sure to work out a quality-of-service agreement with your cable provider that guarantees a certain level of performance. Many cable providers offer a dedicated cable connection of up to 1.544 Mbps that costs less than many ISPs offering T1 service using standard T-Carriers.

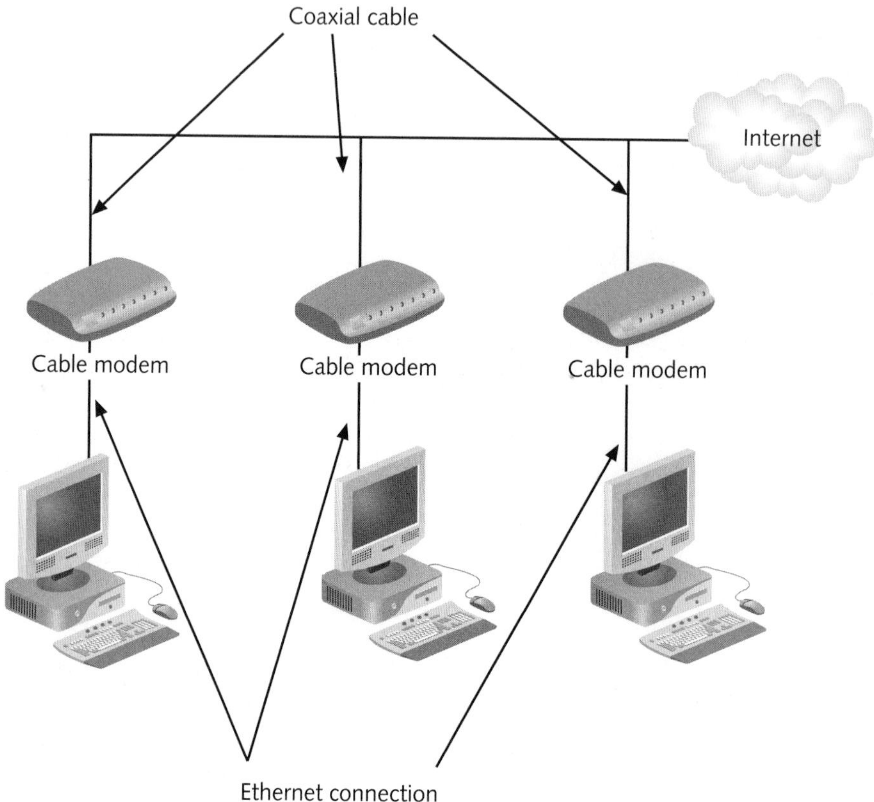

Figure 1-7 Cable modems share a connection to Internet

Much of the previous discussion focused on the speed of connections using a variety of technologies. Because this consideration is so important, you need a deeper understanding of how speed applies to connecting a Web server to the Internet.

Understanding Bandwidth and Throughput

Although **bandwidth** technically means the width of a band of frequencies, it is expressed in bits per second (bps)—that is, the theoretical maximum amount of bits that can be sent in a second. The speed estimates in the previous section were calculated in terms of their bandwidth. Another factor that affects the actual speed is **throughput**, which is the amount of data you can move from one place to another in a given time period. A pipe carrying water is a common analogy for bandwidth and throughput. In this case, the bandwidth is the total capacity of the pipe; the throughput is the amount of water flowing through the pipe in a certain amount of time. Both bandwidth and throughput are typically measured in units of bits per second: kilobits, megabits, or gigabits, as appropriate. Mbps and Gbps are typically used when specifying the speeds of the network.

Be sure to distinguish between measurements in bits (e.g., Mbps) and those in bytes (e.g., MBps). Measures relating to speed are usually expressed in bits per second when describing data transfer speeds for networks, whereas data transfer rates within a computer such as hard drive transfers are often expressed in bytes per second. There are eight bits in one byte, so 1 MBps is eight times faster than 1 Mbps.

Throughput as a percentage of bandwidth is a useful measure of how much data you can expect to transfer between your Web server and the user. This "bandwidth utilization" rate tells you how much of the bandwidth you are actually using. Keeping track of your utilization patterns allows you to plan for future growth. For instance, the bandwidth of a typical Internet connection is 1.544 Mbps. If you have an average throughput of 768 Kbps (meaning that 768 Kbps of a potential 1.544 Mbps of data is passing through the network), then your network has a utilization of approximately 50 percent. This bandwidth utilization rate is desirable because it shows that you are not overloading your connection. It is important to keep track of the utilization rate during times that your users are most often connecting to your server. For instance, it is misleading to analyze throughput over a 24-hour period if most of your traffic occurs in a 4-hour time span during the day. If your bandwidth utilization typically remains under 80 percent, your users should be able to display pages without too much of a delay. If the demand for Web pages exceeds these levels, your users will have to wait longer to see each page.

Your ISP can often provide you with software to monitor your throughput so that you can determine when your network experiences the heaviest traffic. You also need to realize that you can never reach 100 percent utilization. A difficult task when trying to select the ISP that will provide your Internet connection is finding out what the average throughput will be. Just because all the companies you are considering offer a 1.544 Mbps connection, it does not mean that your maximum throughput will be the same in all cases. Some ISPs sell so many T1 lines that their connections to the Internet cannot adequately support them all.

The puzzle of identifying LAN components and connecting the LAN to the WAN has many pieces. The most complex piece is learning about the WAN connection. Because the ISP industry is highly competitive, pricing and services change rapidly. What is the most popular and cost-effective solution one year may not be as popular the next year. Although the T-Carrier approach offers virtually unlimited expandability, most businesses will probably never need to expand beyond 1.544 Mbps. At 1.544 Mbps, you can select between T1, SDSL, and a dedicated cable modem. Which option you choose depends on the combination of services that is available in your area.

For many organizations, setting up a Web environment on their own premises is not appropriate. These businesses may choose instead to have another business host their Web sites.

Understanding Web Hosting Solutions

Web hosting offers an alternative to setting up your own Web server environment. There are many types of Web hosting services to fit every budget.

Web hosting can be a viable solution if you do not currently have the in-house expertise necessary to install, configure, and maintain your own Web environment.

Having another company host your Web site offers some significant advantages. When you let another company host your Web site, you do only the Web site development. The Web hosting company can even help you register your domain name and supply e-mail for you. You do not have to worry about bandwidth, because the Web hosting company should have enough bandwidth for your Web site. The Web hosting company is also responsible for keeping you connected to the Internet and typically has technical support personnel available 24 hours a day to ensure connectivity. It can offer many services that you can add as you grow. The following list includes some common types of Web hosting services:

- *Standard hosting*—Your site resides on the same computer with many other sites. This option is the cheapest solution, but your response times may vary depending on the popularity of the other sites. You will probably use FTP to upload and download pages. Standard hosting is similar to having a Web site like the one that is typically available when you sign up for a home connection.
- *Dedicated server*—You have a server that only you use. There are a variety of sizes from which to choose, so you get only the type of computer that you need.
- *Co-location*—Your own server is physically located at the company that does your Web hosting. The firm is responsible for maintaining the connection to the WAN, and you are responsible for configuring the software on the server. Co-location makes it easier to take the final step of moving the Web server to your own environment because the hosting company supplies only the connection.

Although Web hosting seems like an easy and straightforward solution, consider the problems it can present. Always remember that you are putting a system with significant importance to your organization in the hands of someone else. What happens if the Web hosting company suddenly goes out of business? Also, if you want to create dynamic pages, what programming language do you use? Not all Web hosting companies offer the same languages, and some languages might cost more than others. What kind of DBMS can you use? Will Microsoft Access be sufficient? Will you need Microsoft SQL Server? Will you require a server just for your own use, or can you share it with one or more organizations? How will you get your data and Web pages to and from the server? How much traffic can you expect on your Web site? The more traffic you get, the more you will have to pay. Be sure to find answers to these types of questions before contracting with a Web hosting company.

A Web hosting company can also provide the following services:

- Help in registering your domain name—it probably has access to the two DNS servers required when you register the domain name
- E-mail setup for you and other members of your organization
- Templates to facilitate Web site development
- E-commerce services, including shopping carts and credit card processing

Web hosting solutions are an important option to consider for an organization that seeks to create a Web presence. They can be a cost-effective method to get started on the Web.

COMPARING WEB SERVER PLATFORMS

One of your major decisions as a Web server administrator is to select a computing platform for your Web server, a decision that usually involves choosing between Microsoft Windows and a UNIX-related operating system. Each platform has its strengths and weaknesses. In addition, you need to select which version of the platform you want to run. Within Windows, you have to consider the Windows NT, Windows 2000, and Windows 2003 operating systems. Each operating system also offers different editions, such as Windows Server 2003 Web Edition and Windows Server 2003 Standard Edition. Likewise, UNIX and Linux are provided in different versions and distributions. Some computer manufacturers offer their own versions, such as Sun Solaris and IBM AIX. Linux comes in several different varieties, such as Red Hat and Mandrake.

With Linux, both the server and the client workstation can use the same operating system. The Windows environment is different. Microsoft client operating systems include Windows NT Workstation, Windows 2000 Professional, and Windows XP. You cannot run Microsoft Exchange on any of the client operating systems. Instead, you must purchase the corresponding server product to run Microsoft Exchange and any of Microsoft's server products. Some client products also offer reduced versions of software that is available in the server products. For example, the client operating system might include a Web server, but it will be less capable than the Web server offered on the server operating systems.

Microsoft Windows Platforms: NT, 2000, and 2003

All Windows platforms can fulfill the basic requirements of a Web server and all related tasks. Windows NT Server was released before Microsoft recognized the importance of the Internet. Windows 2000 Server offers much better integration between the operating system and Web-based applications. Windows 2003 completely integrates and extends the Web-based application model. It represents a major shift toward putting the Internet and all the related software at the center of the operating system.

Windows NT Server

Windows NT, a product of the early 1990s, remains a reliable platform for a Web server. It was designed without considering Web servers, but Microsoft has since improved successive versions to accomodate Web servers. Although Windows NT was originally less reliable than its successors, service packs and improved drivers have enhanced its reliability over time.

The Web server from Microsoft is called Internet Information Server (IIS), and it was first released in the mid-1990s to provide Web pages, FTP, and Gopher, a technology to organize information that predates the Web server. Microsoft later added the ability to program using Active Server Pages. CGI scripts were available, but they proved less popular than they were on UNIX/Linux systems. Throughout the 1990s and into the new millennium, Microsoft has continued to improve IIS and its support for languages and security. Under Windows NT, IIS progressed to version 4.0.

Windows 2000 Server

Although Windows 2000 has been replaced by Windows 2003, it remains a capable operating system that works with many hardware devices and software packages. The Windows 2000 Server family has three members: Windows 2000 Server, Windows 2000 Advanced Server, and Windows 2000 Datacenter. Windows 2000 Server is the basic model, and Windows 2000 Advanced Server is the more advanced version. The major advantages of Windows 2000 Advanced Server are that it doubles RAM support from 4 GB to 8 GB, doubles the maximum number of processors from 4 to 8, and supports **clustering**, which enables you to group several servers to act as one server. Windows 2000 Datacenter offers up to 64 GB of RAM and up to 32 processors.

One significant difference between Windows NT and Windows 2000 is the addition of Active Directory Services (ADS) in Windows 2000. You can use ADS to support a much larger network with many more aspects to configure. See Figure 1-8. Whereas Windows NT allows you to manage relatively small networks, ADS provides a single point of management for Windows resources in very large network environments. This capability simplifies the management process and allows for a much higher level of scalability than is possible with Windows NT. Although Windows 2000 uses domains, many more network resources beside users and groups can be tracked. Even within the concept of the user, much more information about the user can be stored. Domains can be broken down into organizational units (OUs).

Naming and keeping track of computers are more complicated tasks in a larger network. To ease these tasks, Windows 2000 introduced **Dynamic Domain Name Service (DDNS)**, which offers an Internet-oriented method of tracking computers. Similar to how a browser finds the location of a Web server, DDNS allows individual computers in a network to find other computers and resources. DDNS also changed computer naming to fit the Internet model. Instead of calling your computer PC1, for example, it can be called PC1.technowidgets.com.

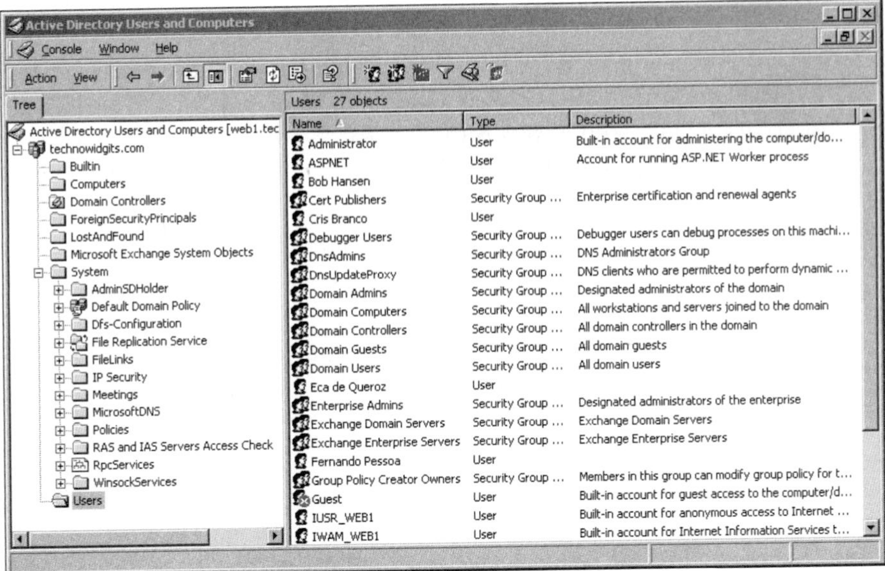

Figure 1-8 ADS computers and users

Windows 2000 comes with IIS 5.0, which is a more reliable Web server than IIS 4.0 under Windows NT. With IIS 5.0, you can restart Web services without rebooting the computer, and you can run applications isolated from the Web server program. The isolation means that if the application fails, it won't cause the Web server to shut down. You can also create custom error messages and track more detailed information when managing the server, such as the amount of time used by processes. For example, instead of displaying the standard HTTP 404 error, "This page cannot be found," you can display a more helpful page that may include a link to a site map. IIS 5.0 also provides significantly improved remote administration and browser-based administration.

Under IIS 5.0, Active Server Pages has been improved. Although HTML pages are still simply sent to the user who requests them, ASP pages are processed by another program; this strategy increases the time it takes to get the page to the user. This delay is acceptable because normally the processing generates HTML code. However, in some cases, you might send an ASP file that does not need to be processed. This so-called scriptless ASP processing bypasses the service that processes ASP pages.

The life of Windows 2000 has been extended by the ability to install .NET Framework, which changes the programming capabilities of the Web server. The .NET Framework is explained in the next section.

Windows Server 2003

Windows Server 2003 represents a significant departure in the area of the Web server environment. It builds on Windows 2000, providing many improvements to implementing and maintaining a Windows 2000 network design. The Windows Server 2003 family has four members. The following list highlights their features that are most important for the Web server environment:

- *Web Edition*—Full use of .NET Framework, IIS 6.0, Network Load Balancing, maximum RAM of 2 GB, and up to 2 processors.
- *Standard Edition*—Same as Web Edition, except that it has Windows Media Services, Internet Connection Firewall, Terminal Server, Internet Authentication Service, Internet Connection Sharing, and up to 4 GB of RAM.
- *Enterprise Edition*—Same as Standard Edition, except that it supports the 64-bit Intel Itanium-based computers, up to 8 processors, up to 64 GB of RAM for Itanium-based computers, and 32 GB for others.
- *Datacenter Edition*—Same as Enterprise Edition, except that it supports up to 64 processors, up to 512 GB for Itanium-based computers, and 64 GB for others. However, it does not have Windows Media Services, Internet Connection Firewall, or Internet Connection Sharing.

New to the Windows Server 2003 family is product activation. To use the product beyond a specified number of days, it must be activated with a special code from Microsoft. This requirement ensures that each server product purchased will be used on only a single computer.

The .NET Framework is central to the .NET Web environment. This improved programming model allows sophisticated programs to be developed for use on the Web. One important aspect of .NET Framework is its use of XML, which basically turns data into text that can easily be transmitted from computer to computer. Instead of allowing users to connect to Web servers to view pages, computers can contact other computers to transfer purchase orders or a variety of other information. Because XML and its associated technologies have industry support, servers with different operating systems can communicate readily. The underlying programming language is more powerful than the older ASP.

Other Microsoft Server Products

Server products besides a DBMS can run on a Microsoft server, and perform specialized tasks that may be useful in some organizations. Many are appropriate in a Web environment.

- *Application Center*—Allows you to manage a cluster of servers as if it is one server. This ability can be important when your Web site is spread across multiple servers in a cluster. Application Center is also compatible with other server products such as Biztalk Server.
- *Biztalk Server*—Connects to your business partners over the Internet using XML. XML is data in text form, which allows computers to easily send data to one another. Biztalk helps you model your business processes so you can

describe exactly what needs to be sent and received. To make this task easier, Microsoft offers hundreds of adapters, which are processes that are already configured for such popular systems as SAP. They allow you to integrate your custom applications with other products.

- *Commerce Server*—Builds an effective e-commerce site in a short amount of time by using the built-in templates for shopping carts and products. Targeted marketing is simplified by being able to store customer profile information. The model used is a pipeline: At various points in the pipeline, the programmer can customize the code to the needs of the business.
- *Content Management Server*—Creates large and complex Web sites. The people throughout your organization may be responsible for managing their own set of pages, and the Content Management Server is designed to organize this process. It helps in delivering personalized content to customers, employees, and other users. It organizes development, staging, and live Web servers and the flow between them. Sample templates and Web sites can help speed your development.
- *Internet Security and Acceleration Server*—Combines a firewall product with a Web cache. The firewall allows you to set policies regarding what type of traffic you will allow into and out of your Web environment, which helps to prevent someone from doing harm to your system. A Web cache takes Web pages that are requested frequently and stores them locally. When a user requests the same page again, the request does not have to go to the Internet, but can be retrieved locally.
- *Operations Manager*—Helps decrease support costs for a server environment. It comes with a preset series of alerts and rules to get you started. It can even help you manage an environment with non-Microsoft products, such as Oracle DBMS and UNIX-based servers.
- *Mobile Information Server*—Gives you the capability to organize and send data to a variety of mobile devices. It can deliver secure wireless communications to members of your organization. This server contains Outlook Mobile Access, which allows you to track e-mails, tasks, and calendars on mobile devices.
- *SharePoint Portal Server*—Allows you to set up a site that can be highly personalized. A good example is *my.yahoo.com*, where you can choose the kind of news you want to read, the color scheme of your pages, and many other options. This server product helps you to set up such a site.

UNIX/Linux

UNIX was introduced in 1969 and continues to evolve today. Many variations of the UNIX operating system have been introduced, and these multiuser operating systems are employed as network operating systems by most non-PC networks today. Although UNIX was the first open operating system, meaning that anyone could make their own version of it, the UNIX name remained an AT&T trademark for many years. It was eventually purchased by such networking companies as Novell and Santa Cruz Operations, and is now owned by The Open Group.

UNIX consists of a kernel, a file system, and a shell. The **kernel** is a central high-security portion of the operating system that contains its core elements. By isolating the kernel from other applications so that computer processes or users cannot modify the core code and interrupt services, UNIX provides a stable platform. The **file system** provides the input and output mechanisms for the operating system. The **shell** provides the user interface to UNIX. Because UNIX uses more than 600 commands, graphical user interfaces (GUIs) were developed to simplify its operations. Even so, most UNIX administrators still perform a significant amount of their work at the command line. Popular UNIX versions include Sun Solaris, Hewlett-Packard HP-UX, IBM AIX, and the increasingly popular Linux.

Although Windows is a tightly integrated system, UNIX versions are different in that you have more flexibility in combining the components that you need. When you start a basic version of UNIX, all you see is a command prompt. There is no GUI as in Windows. However, you can add a variety of GUIs. For example, **KDE (K Desktop Environment)** is available on systems such as Linux, Sun Solaris, and FreeBSD.

As mentioned earlier, several companies and organizations have developed separate versions of UNIX since its introduction. By the 1980s, two strands of UNIX development, AT&T and Berkeley, continued in parallel. The Berkeley strand was adopted by Sun Microsystems, which used the Berkeley code as the basis for SunOS. IBM and Hewlett-Packard chose the AT&T version. By the late 1980s, several groups of companies had formed associations with the goal of producing a single UNIX standard. This effort failed, although the AT&T and Sun alliance produced UNIX **System V**, which remains in use today. Solaris is the most popular example of a System V system. Another standard developed around the **Berkeley Systems Distribution (BSD)**. Examples of the BSD implementation include FreeBSD and SunOS.

OpenBSD has a reputation for security, mainly because its developers made security a priority during the development process. Although Sun intended Solaris to replace SunOS, both remain in use today because customer demand keeps SunOS alive.

Linux was developed separately from these other versions of UNIX. Because of this separate history, technically it is not a true UNIX version; instead, it is an operating system that was written to appear and act like UNIX. However, most people approach Linux as a version of UNIX. Linus Torvalds began his work on Linux in 1991, basing it on Minix, which was included in a textbook on operating systems. Minix was very close to UNIX but its purpose was to serve as a teaching tool. Because the source code is freely available, Linux has been successfully enhanced and supported by a number of organizations, including Red Hat, Mandrake, SuSe, and Caldera. Although it is often more convenient to purchase Linux on a CD, you can also download it for free.

For a more complete listing of organizations that distribute their versions of Linux, see *www.linux.org/dist/index.html*.

While each distribution of Linux has different strengths and weaknesses, all of them share several elements. Each Linux distribution is built on the same Linux core code and distributed under the **GNU General Public License**, which states that while companies can charge a fee for their customized versions of the core Linux code, they need to make the source code available. As a consequence, you can typically obtain the Linux distribution for a low price, often for free. Companies that distribute the Linux code raise revenues by selling support for their software products. Linux's popularity has also been helped by ongoing announcements of support from large companies such as IBM and Oracle. Even Sun, which has its own version of UNIX called Solaris, offers a SUN server based on Linux.

Linux has been gaining popularity for a number of other reasons other than its low cost. For one, it is very stable and is easier to make secure than a Windows server. Stability is important because you rely on your server to keep functioning correctly. You do not want it to stop running, nor do you want parts of the system to malfunction. Security is highly desirable because you want to prevent intruders from harming your system. Historically, Microsoft Windows has focused on functionality rather than security. Although Windows is known for its extensive features, it has also been plagued by numerous security holes.

Linux also runs on many hardware platforms, including those from Intel, AMD, and Sparc. Processors from Intel and AMD are used in computers that run Windows; Sparc processors are used in computers from Sun. This wide support increases the system's flexibility. In the case of Intel processors, Linux runs well on a processor with far less computing power than a corresponding Windows server requires.

Linux can be used as both a workstation and a server. When used as a workstation, the major difference is that you add a GUI and its associated applications. As mentioned previously, KDE is popular as a GUI, as is GNOME (pronounced *guh-nome*).

So far, Linux has not penetrated the corporate market to any significant extent. This is partly due to the less sophisticated programs available for this system. However, the applications available are constantly improving and increasing in number.

Support from Oracle and IBM has given Linux the potential to become a platform for capable database servers.

Linux server and workstation versions are really the same, except that the server installation includes server applications such as Apache Web server. For more information on the Linux versions, see Chapter 3.

Chapter Summary

3/27/04

- Server administration involves managing local users and their access to network resources. The focus of the server administrator is within the organization.
- Web server administration involves managing the many applications that make up the Web environment. It can encompass managing not only the Web server, but also an e-mail server, FTP server, and others.
- Both server administrators and Web server administrators have to install, configure, and maintain their servers. They have to make sure that if data is lost on their servers, they can retrieve it. Security is always important, even though they may use different techniques to ensure security.
- Many pieces make up a network, and they must all work together. A Web server administrator must understand both the physical aspects of the network and the underlying logical aspects. Without this knowledge, problems that require a simple solution could seem baffling.
- There are many Web server platforms from which to choose. All have their strengths and weaknesses, and all are constantly evolving. As a Web server administrator, you should understand as much as possible about all the platforms.
- The Internet is a network of networks that is not controlled by a single organization. The cooperation of many entities, both governmental and private, ensures that it continues to function. Although it is amazing that the Internet works so well, it can also prove frustrating to a Web administrator who cannot find exactly who is to blame when an e-mail message does not reach its destination.

Review Questions

1. A(n) ___LAN___ is a network that connects computers and printers in a building.
2. The bandwidth of a T1 line is ________________.
   a. 45 Mbps
   b. 1.544 Mbps
   c. 10 Mbps
   d. 1 Gbps
3. Which of the following is *not* a component that connects a T1 line to a LAN?
   a. CSU/DSU
   b. switch
   c. multiplexor
   d. router

4. An ISDN Basic Rate Interface (BRI) line is composed of 23 D channels and 1 B channel. True or False?
5. ________________DSL and ________________DSL support different downstream and upstream speeds.
6. Which of the following is the measure of how much data is actually transmitted through a line in a given amount of time?
   a. bandwidth
   b. throughput
   c. speed
   d. utilization
7. Which of the following is a measure of the total capacity that a data line can carry?
   a. bandwidth
   b. throughput
   c. speed
   d. utilization
8. The name of the most common programming language on Microsoft Web servers is ________________.
9. Which of the following DBMS products is available for free?
   a. Access
   b. MySQL
   c. SQL Server
   d. Oracle9*i*
10. Which of the following is *not* a Linux distribution?
    a. Red Hat
    b. Susie
    c. Caldera
    d. Mandrake
11. Windows Server 2003 is available in four editions. They are ________________, ________________, ________________, and ________________.
12. Although cable modems are appropriate for home use, they cannot be used for business. True or False?
13. Windows ________________ Server 2003 has all the capabilities that you would need on a Web server and can run on computers that use the Intel Itanium processor.

14. An agreement that ISPs make to exchange data is called ________________.
    a. viewing
    b. peeking
    c. peering
    d. seeing
15. Which two devices are usually combined to form a single device?
    a. CSU
    b. router
    c. DSU
    d. multiplexor
16. When you send an e-mail message to someone, you are using the ________________.
    a. Web
    b. Internet
    c. e-mail network
    d. none of the above
17. An example of a GUI environment for Linux is ________________.
    a. Windows
    b. NAP
    c. KDE
    d. BSD
18. Which of the following has the fastest speed?
    a. SDSL
    b. T3
    c. T10
    d. ISDN
19. Which version of Linux is considered the most secure?
    a. Red Hat
    b. Mandrake
    c. SuSe
    d. OpenBSD
20. A drawback of Linux is that it takes more computing power than a Windows server. True or False?

21. Why is FTP not secure for uploading files?
    a. The protocol is flawed.
    b. The user name and password are sent to the server as clear text.
    c. You cannot use user names and passwords.
    d. FTP is extremely secure.
22. A firewall is a device that controls access to a network. True or False?

HANDS-ON PROJECTS

Project 1-1

Visit the Linux Web site at *www.linux.org* and find the list of Linux distributions. How many distributions are currently available? Choose three and describe in one to two pages how they differentiate themselves from the other versions. Also explain which of the three you would choose for a Web server and why.

Project 1-2

Put together a shopping list and search the Web for the components that you would need to connect a T1 line to your LAN. Write one to two pages describing which components are on your list. Which brands, models, and prices for these hardware devices did you find on the Web?

Project 1-3

Go to the DSL site at *www.dslreports.com*. Research the different types of DSL products available in your area. Write one to two pages describing the types of DSL lines available and their price range.

Project 1-4

Search the Microsoft Web site for information on the company's server products that could be used in a Web environment besides Windows Server 2003 Web Edition, Standard Edition, Enterprise Edition, and Datacenter Edition. List the primary uses of at least two of the products.

Project 1-5

This project involves using a command called tracert (pronounced *trace route*). Its primary purpose is to display the names of the routers between your computer and another computer. A router connects one network with another. In this chapter, you learned the basics of how the Internet fits together. This project shows you the actual path your data takes. Your objective is to compare the paths that your data takes from a school computer to two destinations. What are the similarities in the results? What are the differences in the results? If possible, try the same commands from home or from some other location. Once again, compare the results with each other and with the results you got from school.

Each time your data is transferred from one router to another, the step is called a hop. Which result took the most hops? Can you decipher where *www.linux.org* is located just by looking at the result of the tracert?

To answer these above questions, go to the command prompt by clicking **Start**, pointing to **Programs**, pointing to **Accessories**, and clicking **Command Prompt**, and then type the following two tracert commands:

```
tracert www.yahoo.com
tracert www.linux.org
```

Project 1-6

Interview the server administrator or Web server administrator at your school. What operating system does the Web server at your school use? How fast is the connection at school? What other software related to the Web environment does your school have? For example, does it have e-mail, programming languages, or a DBMS?

Case Project

In the Case Projects throughout this book, you will set up and work with a simple Web server. In each Case Project, you will examine and practice various aspects of the Web server environment. For example, in one chapter you will install and test the programming environment. In another chapter, you will focus on e-mail or firewalls. When you reach the end of the book, you will have set up the major software components of a Web environment. The Case Projects can be done in Linux, Windows, or both.

Case Project 1-1

You work for CWA, an accounting firm with five departments in one building and a total of 600 employees. The firm runs a Windows 2000 LAN, with a UNIX e-mail server. CWA leases space on a Internet service provider's computer to host a simple Web site that lists the services CWA provides. CWA wants to upgrade its Web site to accept and process online financial forms and to calculate investment information for its clients. The company has asked you to research the kinds of hardware and software it needs to move its Web site from its ISP to its place of business. Using this chapter and information you find on the Internet, write two to three pages that identify CWA's hardware and software needs. Be sure to include computer specifications, network devices, connection types, and operating systems.

CHAPTER

2

PREPARING FOR SERVER INSTALLATION

In this chapter, you will:

- Identify server categories
- Evaluate server components
- Plan for system disasters and reduce their effects
- Evaluate network components
- Set up IP addressing

In Chapter 1, you learned about network components, with an emphasis on the Web server and related server products. In this chapter, you will focus on server hardware and learn that how you use the server influences which components you select. Because a server malfunction affects more people than a single workstation malfunction does, you need to minimize server problems, typically through duplication of hardware. You will learn which server hardware enables you to optimize performance, and which hardware components allow you to communicate with the other servers in your Web environment and the Internet. Finally, you will learn about configuring IP addressing for the servers.

IDENTIFYING SERVER CATEGORIES

Before examining the detailed components of a server, you need to know the general categories of servers and understand how each type is used. For example, if you want to configure an entertainment center, you need to know whether it will be used mostly for watching television or for listening to music. You also need to know whether the entertainment center is intended for a large room or a small apartment. The answers to both questions will help you determine what kind of speakers to buy.

Similarly, determining the primary use of the server helps to determine the types of components you need. For example, a file server requires high-speed disk drives, whereas application servers require high-speed processors. Determining the necessary types of components can be difficult in a Web server environment because you must consider the need for a Web server, database management servers, and e-mail servers, as well as the server requirements of programming languages and other systems.

Understanding File Servers

As its name suggests, a file server sends and receives files. For file servers, a fast disk subsystem is more important than the processor type. Nevertheless, you should make sure that the file server's processor is powerful enough to run applications efficiently.

The classic LAN typically used a file server. Novell, a manufacturer of LAN operating systems, dominated the market for many years with its NetWare product, which used disk systems very efficiently. However, adding applications to a NetWare server was not as easy as adding applications to UNIX- or Windows-based servers.

In the Web environment, you can use a Web server that primarily contains static HTML files as a file server. Because the Web server simply sends files from its hard disk to the network, the processor does not have to do much work. Figure 2-1 illustrates this process. However, many Web sites mix static HTML files and dynamic files that require processing by a programming language. To offset the processing burden of a programming language, large Web sites use application servers that specialize in creating dynamic pages.

You can also use an FTP server in the Web environment to transfer files, usually from the server to users. For example, when you download applications, service packs, and other large files, you are probably transferring them from an FTP server.

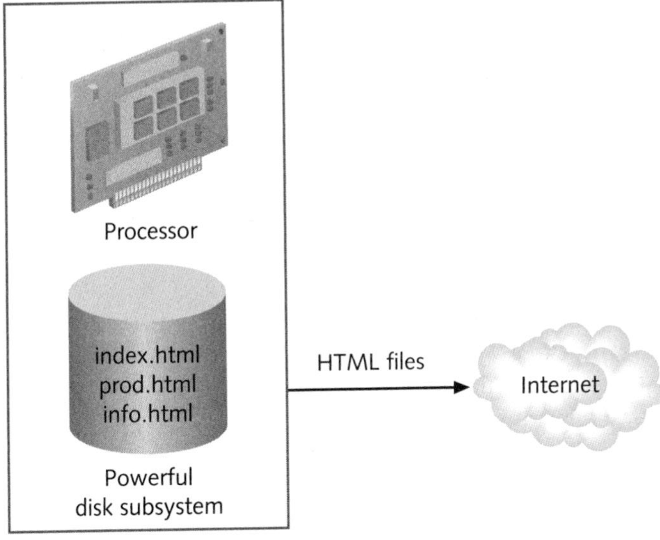

Figure 2-1 File server

Understanding Application Servers

The tasks performed by an application server are more complex than those carried out by a file server. An application server runs server applications that wait in the background, ready to process requests, rather than user applications such as Microsoft Word. Typically, a server application processes requests from many users at the same time. For example, a server that contains a database management system (DBMS) is an application server. Although the disk subsystem is important, a DBMS requires extensive processing power because it often processes complex requests from many users. Figure 2-2 shows a Web server working as an application server along with a DBMS.

An e-mail server is another example of an application server. While some e-mail servers simply transfer files that contain e-mail messages, many also process data by verifying that a user is valid and by testing connections with other e-mail servers to send and receive files. Microsoft's e-mail server, Exchange, is considered a groupware server that performs services such as collaboration, task management, and meeting management, making it an application server.

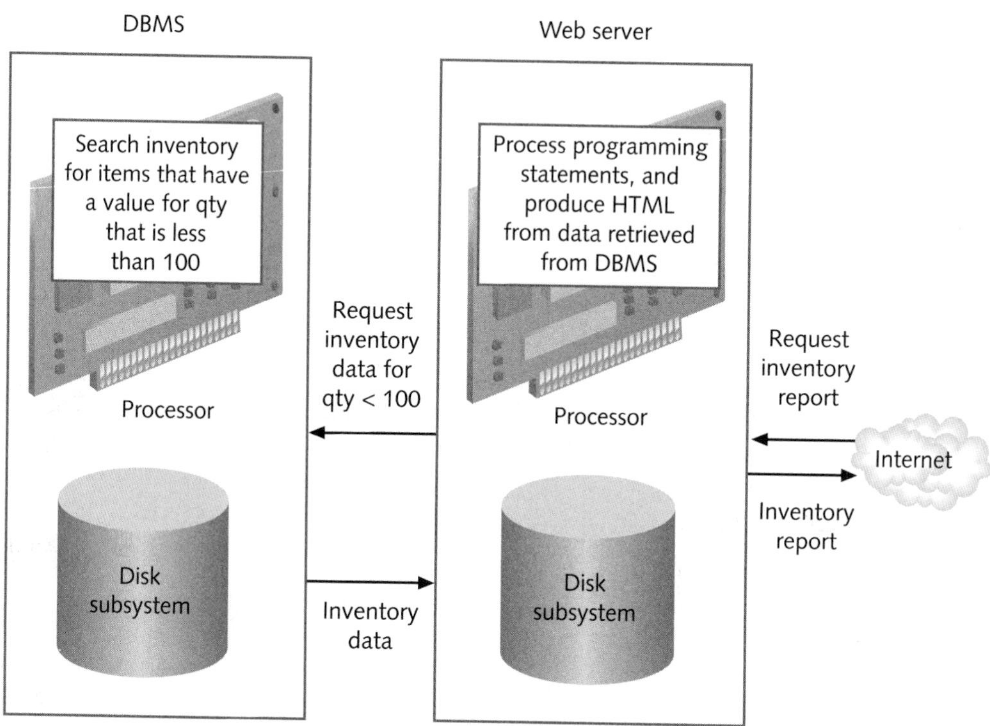

Figure 2-2 Application servers

A Web server that sends static HTML files to the network requires no logical operations or file processing. However, when the Web server adds support for programming languages such as Active Server Pages (ASP) or JavaServer Pages (JSP) technology, the HTML pages work like applications. For example, ASP might process a text file to search a database and produce a report on certain products. These operations could require extensive processing power.

When considering which servers to select, you need to determine how they will be used, which applications will run on them, and how the applications will be used. To help select the appropriate mix of features, also consider whether these applications are more disk intensive or processor intensive.

Evaluating Server Components

As you learned in the previous section, the purpose of the server determines which components you need. Just as you need to balance the parts of a Web server system, so you also need to balance components within the server computer. For example, if you choose a fast disk subsystem for a server and a slow processor for a DBMS, you have made the following mistakes:

- The processor is a **bottleneck**, or a component of the server that generally slows the system, keeping parts of the system from working optimally. Creating a bottleneck can be a costly waste of resources.
- You have wasted money on a disk subsystem that could be put to better use elsewhere.
- The bottleneck may not be obvious, so you may end up spending more on a faster Internet connection or other network component to try to increase throughput.

Study your needs and try to identify the potential bottlenecks in your environment. Ideally, all the components in a server should work together to optimize performance.

Evaluating Processors

The processor is the main focus of most server purchases because it makes everything else work. When the processor is the bottleneck, the solution often involves an expensive upgrade to a new server, although some servers do allow you to add processors. Additional processors can be used by some server applications, such as a DBMS, to process complex requests more rapidly.

Examining the Intel Family of Processors

Most Microsoft Windows computers use Intel processors. The most common type of Intel processor is based on the 386 chip, which includes the Pentium processors. In these 32-bit processors, data is processed 32 bits at a time.

When you install Linux software on a new server with an Intel processor, the name of the file typically ends in i386. The i386 designation means that the program is designed to run on any member of the Intel family that is currently available in servers, except for the Itanium processor.

The Itanium, the latest generation of processors, is a 64-bit processor that requires special versions of operating systems. Figure 2-3 shows that 64-bit processors accept twice as much data as 32-bit processors. Even so, most of today's servers still use Pentium processors.

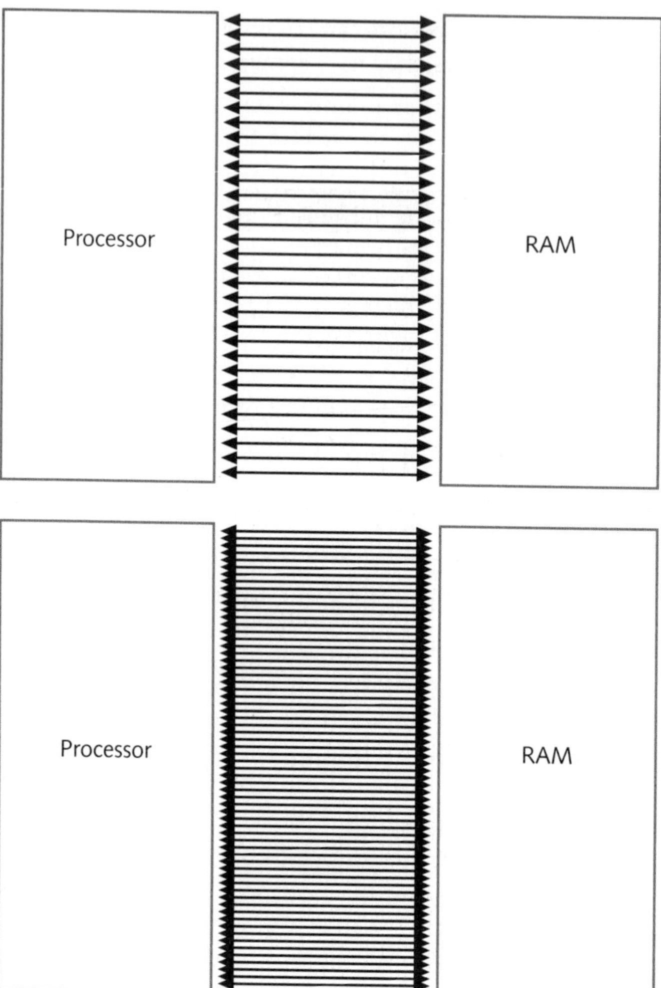

Figure 2-3 32-bit and 64-bit processors

When a processor doubles in speed, it effectively becomes more than twice as fast, because the amount of work it can do is not solely based on speed. As processors get faster, they increase the number of instructions they can process. Comparing the same speeds across different versions of a processor can be like trying to determine the amounts of freight that an economy car and a diesel truck can carry by looking at how fast they go.

The current generation of the 386 family has three principal members: the Celeron is designed for low-end desktop computers; the Pentium 4, the fastest member of the family, is designed for more capable workstations; and the Pentium III Xeon is the workhorse designed for servers. Multiprocessor servers use the Xeon, which can easily handle up to eight processors; more Xeon processors can be added by manufacturers. Although all of these processors are used in servers, they have some important differences, as shown in Table 2-1.

Table 2-1 Processor differences

Processor	Relative speed	RAM	L2 cache	Bus speed
Pentium 4	Fastest	Dual Channel RDRAM; PC 133 SDRAM; DDR 200/266 SDRAM	512 KB	More than 400 MHz
Pentium III Xeon	Not as fast as Pentium 4; some versions not as fast as Celeron	Dual Channel DDR; SDRAM	Up to 2 MB	Up to 400 MHz
Celeron	Usually the versions are about half the speed of a Pentium 4	SDRAM	128 KB or 256 KB	Up to 100 MHZ

RAM allows the processor to quickly process information without accessing the hard disk. Generally speaking, increasing RAM is the least expensive way to increase server performance. When choosing from the many types of RAM available, consider the trade-off between price and performance. Dual Channel RDRAM is the fastest option on Intel processors. RDRAM runs at 800 MHz, PC2100 DDR runs at 266 MHz, and SDRAM runs at 100 MHz or 133 MHz. The effectiveness of the RAM speed depends on the processor, the bus speed, and the L2 cache.

The L2 cache is extremely high-speed RAM. When the processor needs to process data, it first looks in this cache. If it finds the data in the cache, throughput is enhanced. Thus, the more cache you have, the more work the processor can handle at any time. In Table 2-1, note that the major difference among processors appears in the L2 cache column.

Bus speed measures the rate at which signals are sent between devices such as the hard drive, network interface card, and memory. The path that the data travels between devices is called the **bus**.

Among processors that are compatible with the Intel family members but are manufactured by other companies, the AMD processor is the most popular. This capable chip is most closely related to the Pentium 4. The AMD processor can be a viable, low-cost alternative to the more expensive chips from Intel. For example, an AMD-based server from a second-tier manufacturer can often provide the required processing power at a significantly reduced price.

Examining the UltraSPARC Family of Processors

Sun produces an operating system, Solaris, and associated hardware based on the UltraSPARC family of processors. These 64-bit processors have an architecture that is different from that of the Intel processors. Summarized briefly, Intel uses a **Complex**

Instruction Set Computer (CISC) architecture that emphasizes the number of different instructions that the processor can handle. UltraSPARC uses a **Reduced Instruction Set Computer (RISC)** architecture, where the focus is on efficiently processing a few types of instructions.

Table 2-2 compares important characteristics of different members of the UltraSPARC family. You cannot directly compare UltraSPARC processors and Intel processors based on these characteristics because their architecture is different and they typically work in computers that use different operating systems. Windows systems commonly use Intel processors, whereas Sun systems typically use UltraSPARC processors to run the Solaris operating system. Sun also offers Linux as an operating system option on some of its low-end servers.

Table 2-2 UltraSPARC characteristics

Processor	Relative speed	Maximum L2 cache	Maximum number of processors	Bus speed
UltraSPARC III Cu	Fastest	8 MB	More than 1,000	150 MHz
UltraSPARC II	About 50% of III Cu	8 MB	64	66 MHz
UltraSPARC IIi	About 50% of III Cu	2 MB	4	66 MHz
UltraSPARC IIe	About 50% of III Cu	256 KB	4	66 MHz

Using Multiple Processors

One way to prevent the processor from becoming a bottleneck is to use more than one processor and spread the work among the various processors. Some applications, such as BEA WebLogic, can assign several servers to a single processor. Figure 2-4 shows a Web server configuration using more than one processor.

Other applications, such as a DBMS, are designed to work together across processors, as shown in Figure 2-5. Other applications cannot benefit from multiple processors at all. A server's ability to use multiple processors depends on the combined capabilities of the processor, the motherboard, the operating system, and the design of the application. With Intel processors, the Pentium Xeon is used in servers with multiple processors. Although motherboards for two processors are commonly available at computer stores, motherboards with four processors are typically available only as part of a server package. The Windows Server 2003 Datacenter Edition allows for up to 64 processors, but the hardware manufacturer of the server must provide support for all these processors as an integral part of the server.

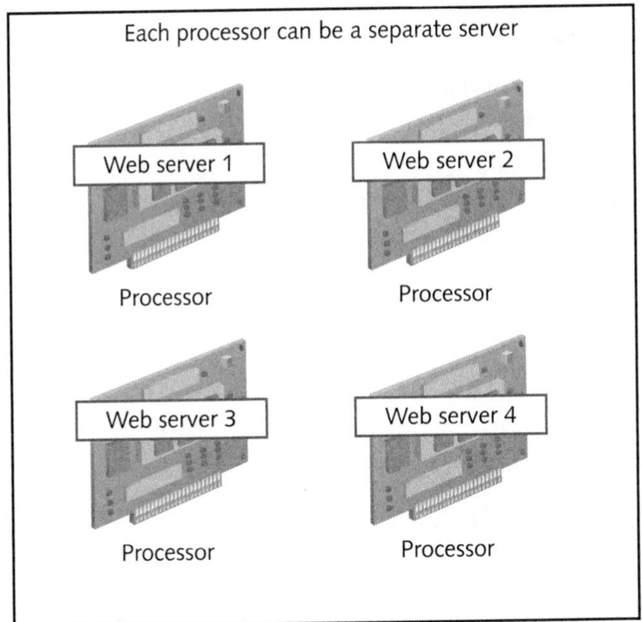

Figure 2-4 Multiprocessor configuration

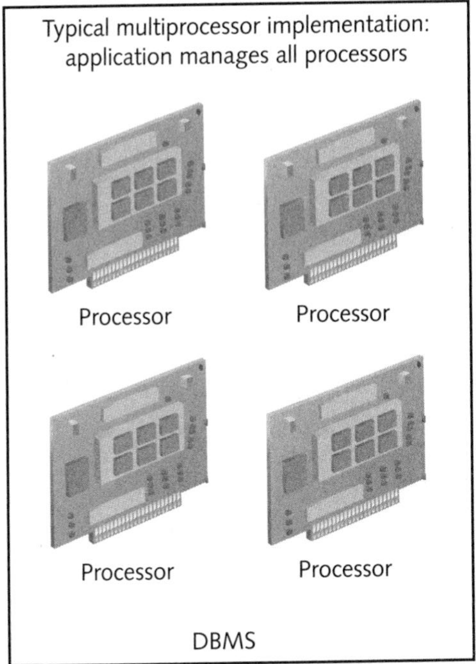

Figure 2-5 DBMS multiprocessor configuration

The most common form of multiple-processor support used in servers is **symmetric multiprocessing (SMP)**. SMP allows a server to divide processes and assign them to available processors. The system can then handle more requests. Dual SMP systems are a popular server platform, and some systems support more than two processors. In such a case, the processors share RAM and the system bus. SMP can be contrasted with asymmetric multiprocessing, in which each processor is a specialist assigned to handle one particular task.

SMP is not the only way to implement systems with multiple processors. In clustering, multiple computers work together as a single computer. Clustering is discussed later in this chapter in the section on fault tolerance.

Selecting a Hard Drive Interface

Besides the processor, the disk subsystem is the most important server component. It includes two parts:

- The hard drive interface, which connects drives to the motherboard
- The hard drive itself

Steps for putting together a reliable disk subsystem are discussed in the section on fault tolerance; see "Planning for System Disasters and Reducing Their Effects" later in this chapter.

The hard drive is another component that can significantly affect overall system performance. When choosing a hard drive interface, balance the desired performance with your budget. **Integrated Drive Electronics (IDE)**, the least expensive alternative, is the most commonly used interface for workstations. For servers that need higher performance and scalability, the interface of choice is **Small Computer System Interface (SCSI)**.

Using Integrated Drive Electronics

As its name suggests, an IDE drive has its controlling electronics directly attached to, or integrated with, the hard drive. By contrast, the attachment to the system bus goes through a relatively simple controller. The IDE design contributed to the explosive development of larger hard drives by allowing drive manufacturers to design larger drives and simultaneously improve data access mechanisms without having to worry about potential incompatibilities with the systems containing the drives.

However, IDE drives do have some limitations. A server can support only two IDE drives at a time, which is a limitation for two reasons:

- *Expandability*—Server administrators want to be able to increase capacity by adding drives.
- *Overall speed*—Because disk drives are relatively slow compared to bus speeds, you can reduce the bottleneck by dividing access across many drives. This

limitation is overcome to some extent with Enhanced Integrated Drive Electronics (EIDE) drives that support a maximum of four devices—two on a primary interface and two on a secondary interface. See Figure 2-6. Otherwise, EIDE is simply an extension of the original IDE standard.

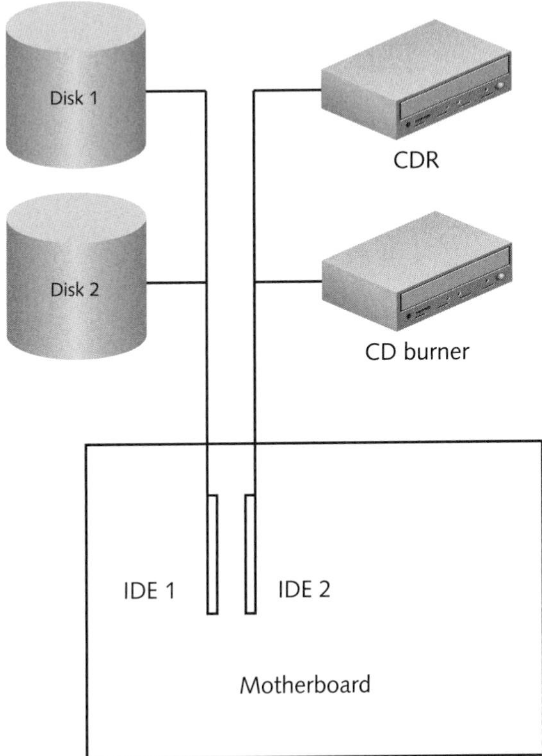

Figure 2-6 EIDE connections

Another limitation of IDE drives is that they require direct action from the processor when data is read or written. This strategy presents a significant drawback for a server, as it consumes computing time that could otherwise be used for other processes. While most modern computer workstations come with built-in support for EIDE, and work well in that capacity, SCSI is the interface of choice for most servers.

Using the Small Computer System Interface

SCSI, pronounced "skuzzy," is a parallel interface that allows multiple devices to communicate with the local system at the same time. Unlike the EIDE interface, which supports only hard drives and CDs, the SCSI interface can support several additional devices, including tape drives and scanners.

SCSI allows you to daisy-chain up to seven devices using one SCSI adapter, and up to 15 devices using two adapters. An adapter is hardware that modifies the capabilities of a computer. SCSI adapters can be embedded in the motherboard when it is manufactured or a SCSI adapter can be added to an existing motherboard by purchasing the adapter and plugging it in to a **PCI slot**. A PCI slot is a connector on the motherboard that can accept a variety of hardware adapters. Figure 2-7 shows an example of a SCSI configuration. The devices that are chained together can also communicate independently of the processor. This strategy can increase the overall performance of the system because the processor can use its clock cycles to carry out other tasks. SCSI systems are more costly than IDE drives, and their increased capabilities make them more complex to install and troubleshoot. Nevertheless, SCSI's higher expandability and increased performance make up for any drawbacks.

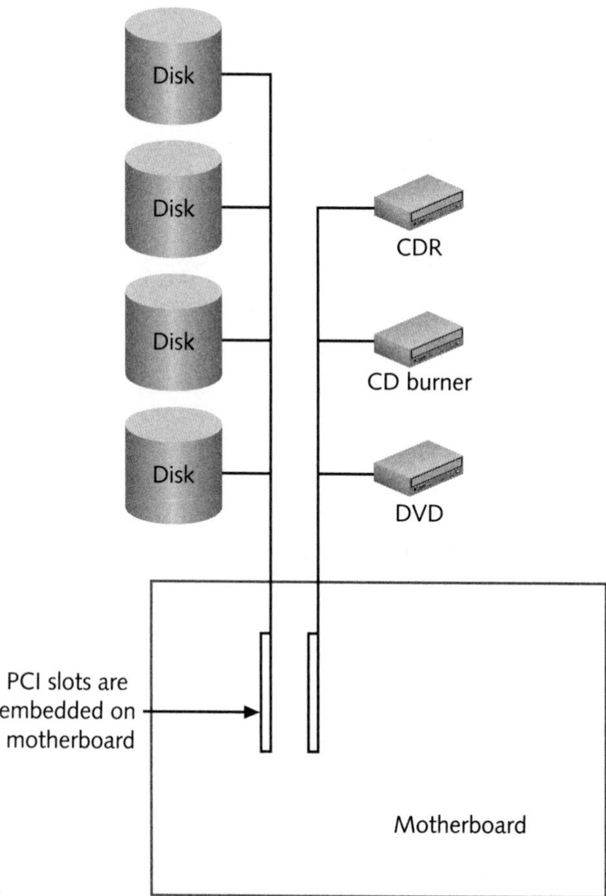

Figure 2-7 SCSI with multiple adapters

Selecting compatible hard drives, tape drives, and other hardware devices for a SCSI system can be difficult because a number of SCSI standards exist. Some servers are configured with multiple types of SCSI, which makes installing the operating system more challenging. Each SCSI interface requires software drivers to function correctly, and the drivers must be installed in the correct order. Also, a server may have a very fast SCSI for the disk drives but a slow one for the CD. To make sure that the devices match and will work together, you should understand the following SCSI standards:

- *SCSI-2*—SCSI-2 uses an 8-bit bus and supports data rates of 4 MBps. Also known generically as Fast SCSI, it incorporates the following distinct standards:

  Wide SCSI uses a wider cable (168 cable lines to 68 pins) to support 16-bit data transfers.

  Fast SCSI uses an 8-bit bus, but doubles the clock rate to support data transfer rates of 10 MBps.

  Fast Wide SCSI uses a 16-bit bus and supports data transfer rates of 20 MBps.

- *SCSI-3*—SCSI-3 is actually a family of technologies, not one specific standard. **Ultra Wide SCSI** often referred to as SCSI-3, uses a 16-bit bus and supports data transfer rates of 40 MBps.

  Ultra SCSI uses an 8-bit bus and supports data transfer rates of 20 MBps.

  Ultra2 SCSI uses an 8-bit bus and supports data transfer rates of 40 MBps.

  Wide Ultra2 SCSI uses a 16-bit bus and supports data transfer rates of 80 MBps.

  Ultra3 (Ultra160) SCSI is a fairly new standard that supports data transfer rates up to 160 MBps. It is the most common interface used in servers.

When choosing an interface for a modern server, you should select an interface from at least the SCSI-3 family. As with all other server components, it may be tempting to buy a less expensive card, but purchasing a SCSI interface card from a reputable vendor is worth the additional expense. You can find more information about SCSI at *www.adaptec.com;* Adaptec is the principal manufacturer of SCSI adapters. Some top server manufacturers embed Adaptec SCSI adapters in their server motherboards. These manufacturers, such as Compaq and Dell, call the SCSI adapters Ultra3. Adaptec calls the same adapter the Ultra160.

Selecting a Hard Drive

No matter how fast the hard drive interface can pass along information, the actual speed of the transmission will be limited by the specifications of the drive itself. When evaluating hard drive performance, consider the following factors:

- *Vendor*—You should select products from a reliable vendor. Investigate the **mean time between failure (MTBF)**, which is the average time interval that elapses before a hardware component fails and requires service. Also find out what kind of support the vendor provides.

- *Capacity*—You can choose from a wide range of capacities, typically starting at about 9 GB for SCSI and increasing significantly for IDE.
- *Data transfer rate*—This rate can be represented by two speeds—hard drive to buffer and buffer to adapter.
- *Buffer size*—The buffer consists of RAM storage between the adapter and the hard drive. Buffer size is measured in megabytes.
- *Average seek time*—This measure indicates the time it takes, in milliseconds, to get to a position on the drive.
- *Rotational speed*—This measures how fast the disk drive spins. Typical rotational speeds are 7,200 RPM, 10,000 RPM, and 15,000 RPM.

When configuring a server sold by a major vendor such as Dell, Compaq, or Hewlett-Packard, the most important factors to consider are the type of SCSI adapter, the capacity, and the rotational speed. All of the vendors use Ultra3 adapters. To obtain more information about a specific drive, visit the Web site for the drive manufacturer. Compare servers from different vendors before you make a decision.

A key measure of hard drive performance is the **access time**, or the amount of time it takes the drive to retrieve a single piece of data. The access time, which is measured in milliseconds, includes the seek time, or time needed for the drive's read/write head to find a particular cylinder on the disk. The seek time is typically higher for a larger disk because it has more space to search. Another factor that affects access time is the spindle rotation speed of the drive, also referred to as the **drive speed**. A higher rotation speed lowers the access time. Typical IDE drive speeds are 5,400 RPM and 7,200 RPM; SCSI drives can operate at 7,200 RPM, 10,000 RPM, 15,000 RPM, and higher.

You can configure multiple drives in a system in many ways. With IDE, you can use two drives to increase your storage capacity. SCSI adapters can have many more drives to expand the system's storage capacity. This approach can also improve the system's overall speed if you divide the drives to isolate the operating system on one drive and the applications on the rest of the drives. Isolating system components is a relatively inexpensive solution, but each drive introduces another potential point of system failure. That is, if one drive fails, the whole system fails. To circumvent this problem, you can use a **redundant array of inexpensive/independent disks (RAID)**, a common drive configuration on servers. RAID allows multiple drives to operate together as a single drive, and it uses a SCSI interface. If one drive malfunctions, the system continues to work. This stability is part of the important concept of fault tolerance, which is discussed later in this chapter.

Selecting a Network Interface Card

The network interface card (NIC) is another server component that can affect overall performance. The NIC provides the pathway for data to enter and leave the server. Table 2-3 provides an overview of common NIC types and speeds along with their usage. Note that the 100 Mbps card is the most popular NIC. The "Use" column in Table 2-3 refers to current common usage. History has shown that the higher-speed connections currently used for servers will eventually migrate to workstations. Figure 2-8 compares two Intel NIC configurations.

Table 2-3 Common network interface cards

NIC type	Speed	Media	Use
Standard Ethernet	10 Mbps	Twisted pair (sometimes fiber)	Workstations
Fast Ethernet	100 Mbps	Twisted pair (sometimes fiber)	Workstations and small to medium-sized servers (most popular)
Gigabit Ethernet	1,000,000 Mbps	Fiber (sometimes twisted pair)	High-end servers
10-Gigabit Ethernet	10,000,000 Mbps	Fiber	Backbone connections
ATM	25 Mbps–622+ Mbps	Fiber	Workstations and servers (rare)

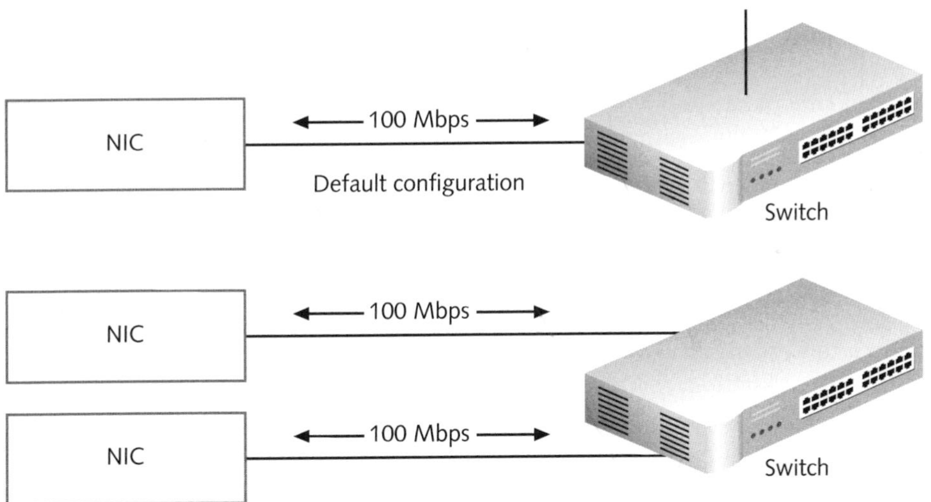

Figure 2-8 NIC configurations

Because a T1 connection offers a data transfer rate of only 1.544 Mbps, a standard Ethernet connection at 10 Mbps appears to be more than adequate. However, the Intel Pro 100 offers an excellent option even if you do not need the extra speed. You can connect two NICs to a switch and configure the NICs so that if one fails, the other will continue to supply data. This approach provides an inexpensive kind of insurance against NIC failure. In a server environment, redundancy is used to prevent a single point of failure.

NICs are the least expensive components in a server environment, so it is usually best to choose NICs from major vendors such as Intel and 3COM. As you have seen with the Intel Pro 100, NICs have features that can enhance both performance and reliability.

Purchasing and Supporting a Server

It is much easier to make a mistake in the purchase of a server than a workstation. Most users never exceed the capabilities of their workstations; when they do need higher performance, they can upgrade to a new processor without affecting the rest of the system. Support is also more important for a server than a workstation because of the larger number of people affected. Make sure that the server is extremely reliable and that support is available when you need it. The following section on fault tolerance stresses the need to ensure that the server can continue to function even if a component fails.

When selecting the server on which your organization will depend, work with a well-known vendor. You can choose a local company with a long track record of producing high-quality servers or a national vendor such as Dell, Sun, Compaq, or Hewlett-Packard. These companies sell servers with prices ranging from less than $1,000 to more than $1,000,000, with widely varying levels of reliability and support.

One important reason for purchasing a complete server from a vendor is to ensure that the components will work together. Typical workstations do not have SCSI adapters, so getting them to work within a network can be challenging. Selecting high-performance motherboards and making sure that everything is compatible with your operating system can be difficult. Some components, such as redundant power supplies, can be difficult to find on your own. You must also know which components do not work together. On a workstation, for example, any NIC will function properly, but for years, 3COM NICs would not work in a Dell server.

Having access to reliable support is another reason to purchase a server from a major vendor. When your server stops running, you might not know whether the problem is limited to the power supply or the motherboard, and you probably do not have the diagnostic equipment to find out. An experienced support staff can help you troubleshoot and solve the problem, saving you hours of work.

Vendors provide various levels of support based on your needs and budget. They often offer 24-hour response time, although 24 hours can be a long time when people depend on e-mail to do their jobs. Also, this response time does not necessarily mean that the problem will be fixed in 24 hours. The vendor may need to order a motherboard or other device, and it could take a few days to get your server working again.

A major vendor should also know what works and what doesn't, and it might know how to troubleshoot server behavior you haven't experienced before. For example, a server at DeVry University in Phoenix, Arizona, developed an apparent software problem. When the IP configuration was changed, the setting changed when the server was rebooted. The baffled administrators assumed that software was causing the problem and reinstalled the operating system, but the problem with the IP configuration persisted. When contacted, the vendor traced the problem to the motherboard. Once a new motherboard was installed, the problems were solved.

Planning for System Disasters and Reducing Their Effects

Disaster planning can help you avoid problems with hardware, software, and even business procedures. Planning for system disasters is like buying insurance—you might not like paying for it, but you are glad to have it when you need it. Also, just as it may be economically infeasible to insure your company against every conceivable problem, it may not make good business sense to make sure that systems will never fail. Always balance the cost of disaster planning against the benefit to the organization and others. For example, a disaster plan for computer systems in a nuclear power plant is more critical than one for a small retail business.

Servers can be critical to a business. For example, on an e-commerce site, a server failure could cost a business thousands of dollars for each minute of lost revenue. Virtually anything you can do to keep servers running represents time and money well spent, but spending money on **fault tolerance** must provide a distinct business benefit. Fault tolerance is the ability of a system to keep running even when a component fails.

Not every server needs to be 99.999 percent reliable (the coveted "five nines"), which would mean about five minutes of downtime per year. This level of reliability can be expensive to achieve, and only critical servers need such high reliability. For example, DNS servers have built-in fault tolerance. (Recall that a DNS server converts host names to IP addresses for your domain.) You might have a local DNS server and your ISP might have another DNS server. If your DNS server malfunctions, the DNS server at your ISP can take over and resolve names. This fact means that your local DNS server is not a critical server. Indeed, some companies use recycled workstations running Linux as a DNS server. They keep all the DNS scripts on a floppy disk and set up an old workstation to use as a DNS server when necessary.

In creating a reliable system, you need to justify the cost involved. Top-level managers usually make the initial decisions to address the cost of business downtime, though they often do not realize its full impact. You can help them in this effort by doing a disaster assessment.

Disaster Assessment and Recovery

To understand how disasters would affect your system and business, start by identifying which disasters could strike your server and pinpointing how long they could last. Determine which disasters could result from computer malfunction, simple human error, or the actions of disgruntled employees. For example, important documents can be accidentally deleted, accounts receivable can be closed at the wrong time in an accounting program, or data can be accidentally deleted from a database.

Focus on the disasters you can prevent. For example, a server that uses a single disk drive might take advantage of RAID technology to prevent problems in case the drive fails. Lost data from an accounting program could be restored by a tape backup, by the program itself (which might offer an option to restore the data), or by a database administrator (who might restore the data from detailed logs kept by the DBMS).

Think creatively about disasters that can cause monetary loss and ways to prevent them. If a disaster does occur, have a recovery plan that minimizes the cost to the organization. Be sure to maintain adequate documentation of your systems. Because you are responsible for the Web server environment, you could be the first person blamed for its failure. Document the hardware, software, and configuration decisions made by you and your managers.

Preventing Hardware Disasters

The hardware problems on which Web server administrators focus are those involving the server. Because these computers are complex, you need high-quality technical support for them. However, servers aren't the only devices that can fail—all the components in a Web server environment must work together. For example, a working server won't help you if the router that connects it to the Web fails.

For this reason, you need a plan of action to address hardware failures in a Web environment. If a component fails and you have support for it, for example, you need to know the support phone number and the location of the support contract. The support person may in turn need the contract number and the serial number of the failed component. Make sure that these numbers are written down and that more than one person knows about them, because components can fail when you are on vacation.

If you do not have support on a device, a disaster recovery plan is even more important. If the router fails and you need to purchase a new one, you might need preapproval to buy it. Management needs to know in advance the cost of the component, the cost of support for the component, its role in the Web environment, and the importance of expediting an order in case the component fails.

Preventing Software Disasters

Software disasters are more complex than hardware disasters because so many types of software exist. No administrator can be expected to understand the intricacies of every application in a company. However, the administrator is often the person responsible for knowing who to call to get a problem solved. When the problem involves a computer, you are likely to be the first person whom users call for help. Software companies often have support lines that you can recommend as a resource. For a complex DBMS, your company may not need or be able to afford a full-time database administrator, so it might contract with a local firm to fix problems.

As with hardware components, you need to document every software component and devise a plan for dealing with problems. The plan could be as simple as providing a list of phone numbers for internal software experts. In other cases, you might need to call the software support number. As with hardware, a software application may offer only 30 days of free support. If a software maintenance contract is needed, you need to make management aware of the annual or per-incident cost. If you need to pay a per-incident cost in an emergency, make sure you can have the payment expedited so you can get support. Typically, your company should have a general budget for emergency support.

Web server administrators occasionally encounter software that does not work properly from the day it is installed. It may not work correctly, it may stop unexpectedly, or it may lose data. Also, it may not have features that were promised. If the software is important to the company, however, it is your job to make it work successfully.

In such situations, be sure to document your problems with the software and the actions you take to solve them. Document your conversations with support personnel, any patches you apply to the software, and any other procedures you perform to fix the problems. Beware of relying too much on workarounds. For example, a support technician may tell you that when the application stops, you can simply go to the Web server and restart the service that controls the application. This workaround may suffice when you are available, but it won't help on a weekend, when no one is near the Web server.

Maintain a good working relationship with support personnel; you may need a favor some day.

Solving Electrical Problems

The old saying that "the memory of a computer is only as long as its power cord" highlights the importance of a constant electrical supply. Even if the original server room was expertly planned and the electrical needs of each component were carefully researched, with dedicated circuits provided for all components that required them, electrical problems can arise later. For example, servers might be added and other components might be upgraded without the addition of any new circuits. If components are not attached to an **uninterruptible power supply (UPS)**, an overloaded circuit could cause a component to restart itself. If you overload the UPS, the battery within it will become too drained to keep components running. Make sure you have an adequate supply of electricity and enough UPSs for your server room, and make sure each UPS has enough capacity.

In a large, complex environment you need an expert to tell you how many circuits and UPSs you need. Nevertheless, you can typically make a reasonably good estimate yourself. Start by calculating **watts**, a unit of power. Wattage is equal to volts multiplied by amperes (amps); each circuit is usually 15 or 20 amps and 110 to 120 volts, so the number of watts for a 15-amp circuit is about 1,725 (115 × 15).

Your next challenge is to find out from building maintenance which wall sockets are part of which circuit. In some cases, you could have a dedicated 20-amp circuit for a single device; often, however, a number of wall sockets will be part of the same circuit. Offices adjoining the server room might also share a circuit. Once you map the sockets to the circuits and find out how many amps are on the circuit, you need to know which components will use that circuit. The components' power supplies usually indicate the number of watts they use. Typically, a power supply on a server may be 300 watts, but the environment might include three power supplies. Total the wattage and find out how many circuits will be needed.

A 300-watt power supply is not like a 300-watt bulb. The power supply does not consume a constant 300 watts, but only the power that it actually needs at a given time. However, make sure that your electrical supply can give you maximum power so that you have room to expand. Remember to gather information on future needs so your server room has enough circuits. Also, keep in mind that some devices, such as large Cisco switches, need significantly more watts when they start up than when they are running. Make sure that your supply of electricity can handle this kind of fluctuating demand.

In a server room, you should always place a UPS between the wall socket and the devices. A UPS is rated in watts, so you can calculate how much power you need. Also, consider how long the server should run on the battery when the electricity goes out. In most cases, you want just enough electricity to shut down the servers properly. Software/hardware combinations from the UPS manufacturer can handle this task automatically, so if an electrical outage occurs when no one is near the server room, the servers will shut down without any human intervention. When servers are shut down properly, data in RAM that could be critical to the operating system and applications is stored on the disk where it belongs. For example, files that are open are closed properly. If systems lose power and cannot shut down correctly, data can be lost and hard disks can suffer serious problems.

Although disaster assessment and recovery are complex tasks, Web server administrators are not solely responsible for preventing and recovering from disasters. In larger organizations, for example, the help desk is charged with resolving many application software problems. The IT director should have an adequate budget to make sure that any monetary issues related to support get resolved quickly.

Allowing for System Redundancy

After acknowledging that hardware occasionally fails, you need to assess which components are most prone to failure and then determine how to avoid failure, how much it costs to avoid it, and whether the cost justifies the benefits to the organization. This section will help you determine which components are most likely to fail and learn how you can avoid failure through redundancy.

Power supplies on larger devices such as servers and switches are not only critical components, but also relatively inexpensive. Often, servers have two or three power supplies; switches may have two such supplies. If some of your servers have only one power supply, you should purchase spares.

Achieving Disk Redundancy Through RAID

A RAID system can prevent data loss when a single drive malfunctions. The six original RAID levels were designed by a research group at the University of California in Berkeley, but a number of RAID levels have been added since then. Each level represents a different way to make multiple disk drives act as a single drive. Although RAID 0 is not fault tolerant, the other levels are.

The RAID levels are described in the following list:

- *RAID 0*—In this technique, called disk striping, data is split into small pieces and spread over a number of drives. Disk striping in RAID 0 is the fastest of all the RAID levels because it does not have to store the data necessary to allow a single disk to fail.
- *RAID 1*—Data is duplicated across two drives, which can make writing data slower. This method, called mirroring, is ideal for IDE drives because you can have only two high-speed drives. If you are using SCSI, you can have two SCSI adapters; each goes to a drive, so even if one of the adapters fails, the system will keep running. This technique is called disk duplexing. Figure 2-9 compares these approaches.
- *RAID 2*—This technique uses special error-correcting codes for drives that do not have built-in error detection. SCSI drives come with error correction, so this RAID level is not important for them.
- *RAID 3*—This technique stripes data across the disk drives at the byte level. Information needed to rebuild data is stored on one drive. RAID 3 is not commonly used.
- *RAID 4*—This technique is similar to RAID 3, in that information needed to rebuild the data is stored on one drive. Reads are as fast as with RAID 0, but writes are slow because extra information must be stored for rebuilding purposes. RAID 4 is not commonly used.
- *RAID 5*—This technique is by far the most common disk redundancy method found in servers. RAID 5 distributes data across the drives and stores the redundancy, or parity, information needed to rebuild the drives; thus, if

any drive fails, it can be replaced with no loss of data. Figure 2-10 shows an example of a RAID 5 implementation. Although all Windows versions from NT to 2003 can implement RAID 5 in software, it requires too much extra memory and processing power to be generally feasible. It is much less of a burden on the operating system to have RAID 5 implemented in hardware via special SCSI RAID controllers. All major server vendors configure their servers in this manner.

- *RAID 10*—Instead of using an array of single drives, RAID 10 is an array of RAID 1 mirrored drives. It is much more expensive than the other RAID levels because you have twice as many drives. Nevertheless, RAID 10 is better than RAID 5 because it eliminates the immediate need to replace a drive; each disk in the array is mirrored. Also, it is more fault tolerant than RAID 5; if two disks in a RAID 5 array fail before one is replaced and the array is rebuilt, then you will lose your data. With RAID 10, two pairs of disks would have to stop functioning before you had to replace any drives.

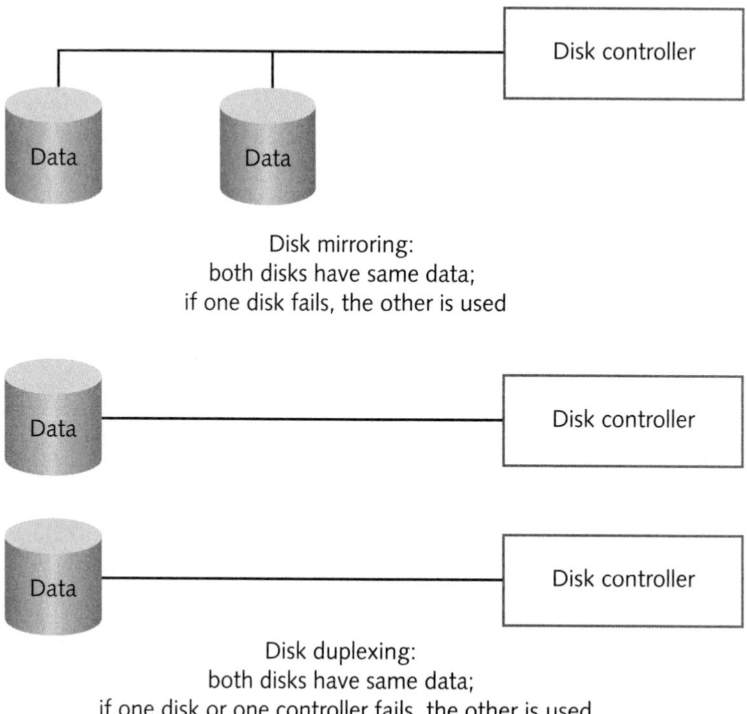

Figure 2-9 RAID 1 disk mirroring and duplexing

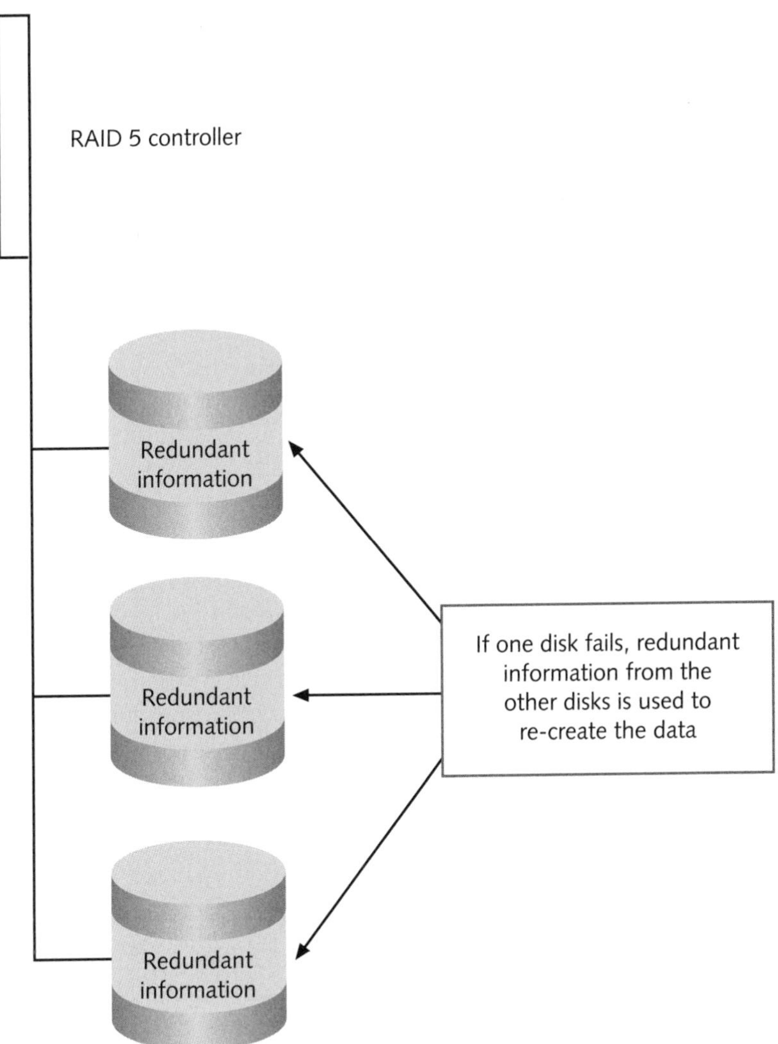
RAID 5 controller
Redundant information
Redundant information
Redundant information
If one disk fails, redundant information from the other disks is used to re-create the data

Figure 2-10 RAID 5

Disk mirroring and disk duplexing (RAID 1) are very common in the low-priced segment of the server market. Setting up disk mirroring in a Windows server with IDE drives is very easy. If your computer has two 20 GB drives, you can install a Windows server on one of the drives and make it a dynamic disk (as opposed to a basic disk). In the Disk Management utility, you can mark the other disk and create a mirror. If one of the disks fails, you can then use the Disk Management utility to break the mirror, which makes the disks independent again. At that point, you can simply replace the broken drive and re-create the mirror.

Outside of the low-end market, RAID 5 is the most popular method of disk redundancy. In mirroring, you can have only two drives; in RAID 5, however, you can have dozens of drives. The equivalent of one drive is used for redundancy, and you need a minimum of three drives. For example, if a RAID 5 array includes three 20 GB drives, the storage capacity would be 40 GB. With ten 20 GB drives, you would have 180 GB of storage. If you have n number of drives, with n being at least 3, and y is the capacity of each drive, the available storage capacity is $(n - 1) \times y$. If one of the drives then malfunctions, the other drives have the data from the malfunctioning drive, so the only difference is a slight slowdown because data must be re-created from the other drives. Once you put a new drive back into the system, it is automatically rebuilt.

Some RAID 5 installations allow for a hot swap, meaning that you can replace the drive while the server continues running. You can even have multiple RAID 5 systems in a single computer, or a mix of RAID 5 and other RAID technologies. For example, a Microsoft Exchange benchmark test uses a server with four 18.35 GB disks for the operating system, sixteen 18.37 GB disks for log files, and forty-eight 18.35 GB disks for information storage files.

All major server vendors support hardware-based RAID 5 systems. Most RAID 5 technology is implemented in hardware through a special utility in the RAID 5 controller; upgrading from a simple SCSI adapter to a RAID 5 controller is relatively inexpensive. In the utility, you set up the size of the C: drive partition and other partitions as required. When you install Windows or Linux, the operating system does not know or care that you have RAID 5; it appears to the operating system as just another disk drive. Although Windows server products allow you to set up RAID 5 in software, you should avoid using software-based RAID 5 because of the processing and memory burden it imposes on the operating system.

Achieving High Availability with Multiple Servers

Clustering is a technology in which many computers act as one. You can also use a simpler technique called load balancing to distribute the work among many computers.

Clustering has three major purposes:

- *Computing power*—You may need so much computing power that no single computer can handle the demand. A cluster of relatively inexpensive computers can offer more computing power than one large supercomputer. For example, a company called Accelerated Servers has put together clusters of up to 60,000 connections. Clustering software from NASA Goddard's Beowulf project is freely available but rather complex to install; the Beowulf products are available primarily for Linux servers. A variety of vendors, including PSSC Labs and Accelerated Servers, have implemented Beowulf in their products. These types of servers are often used in the scientific community to handle advanced mathematics applications.

- *Fault tolerance*—At the other end of the spectrum from computing power is fault tolerance. Pure fault tolerance is very difficult to achieve, because clusters are very complex and include many components. For example, a PCI slot can fail, as can a single processor on a multiprocessor server or a component in the switch that connects them together. The cluster that comes closest to true fault tolerance is produced by Compaq's NonStop Himalaya servers. In this cluster, each server is extremely fault tolerant—if any component fails, the cluster will keep running. According to Compaq, 95 percent of all security transactions and 80 percent of all ATM transactions go through NonStop Himalaya servers.
- *High availability*—Between the two extremes lies what IBM, Microsoft, and others call high availability through clustering. This approach provides redundancy and failover for fault tolerance, but its definition is not quite as strict as that of pure fault tolerance. (Failover is the ability to have a server fail and yet have the other servers continue to function.)

IBM's approach to clustering is more complex than Microsoft's approach. IBM uses computers it calls nodes to serve different purposes. Most servers are used as compute nodes, which is where the real work occurs. For each group of 32 to 64 compute nodes, a head node controls the compute nodes. Each system requires a management node, and external disk subsystems may require other nodes.

An IBM cluster must have three functional networks:

- One network facilitates interprocess communication. It allows the processors to work together.
- A second network supports the disk subsystem. In a cluster, the computers share a single disk subsystem. The first two networks typically rely on specialized high-speed networks.
- The third network provides system management, which is usually implemented via 10/100 Mbps Ethernet. IBM uses Red Hat Linux for the operating system.

IBM's solution to clustering is hardware-based; it makes all the computers in a cluster truly act as one.

In contrast, Microsoft's approach to clustering is to distribute the computing load (load balancing) among distinct servers. This approach to high availability must be able to accommodate any computer that uses Microsoft Windows server products. The Microsoft solution uses a software product that ties together multiple servers into a single system, and it focuses on Web server availability.

Before Windows Application Center 2000 became available, the simplest form of load balancing was a **DNS round-robin**. In a DNS round-robin, one host is associated with 10 IP addresses that correspond to 10 Web servers, instead of one host being associated with one IP address. As requests for Web pages arrive, they are sent to the next IP address on the list. To add new Web servers, you simply add IP addresses to the list. Although this round-robin approach provided basic functionality, it required too much maintenance and software development was too complex. For example, you had to make sure that each server was exactly the same, and that all Web links accessed by users existed on all servers. Also, it was difficult to keep track of user information as users explored a site, a common scenario in a shopping-cart application in e-commerce.

Microsoft has solved these problems with the Microsoft Application Center. Figure 2-11 shows an example of a Microsoft cluster created with this approach. You can synchronize applications and data on all the servers, and you can load-balance based on IP addresses and the needs of certain software components. You can readily add and remove servers from the cluster, and you can add an application and have it distributed to all servers in the cluster. Because all servers in the cluster are configured in the same way, if one server fails, the other servers can perform its work.

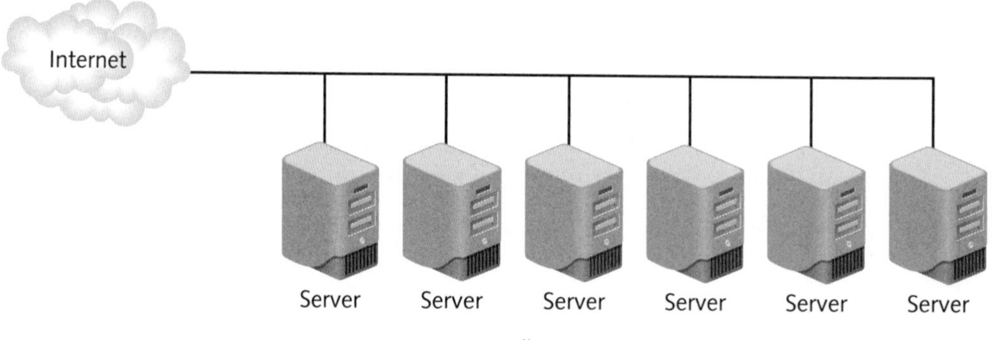

Figure 2-11 Microsoft cluster

No system can achieve fault tolerance without having a good backup system in place. Imagine a cluster of 20 servers in which each server uses RAID 5 technology. If an administrator accidentally overwrote a major part of the Web site with old pages, many valuable Web pages would be destroyed. The only solution at that point would be to restore the pages from tape backups.

Setting Up Backup Systems

As you know, a backup of your data files protects against user error, and it can prove invaluable if a data error goes unnoticed for days. Not only should you keep data backups, but you should also maintain a number of backups made over a period of time so that data can be restored from a specific date.

When setting up a backup system, consider the following issues:

- *Your backup procedures*—How many backup procedures do you need? How often do you need to make the backups?
- *The backup technologies you can use*—How many tape drives do you need in a multiserver environment? How do you make sure everything is backed up, including specialized applications such as DBMS and e-mail servers?

Backup Procedures

The number of tape backups you make and the frequency of backups depend on the needs of the organization. Typically, you will need daily backups for the previous week and weekly backups for the previous month. Many organizations also may have special backup needs based on certain occurrences. For example, a company may need a backup immediately before month-end closings in the accounting system and another backup immediately after the month-end closing. You may want to back up the system before installing any new software, in case the software causes serious system problems that you cannot solve by simply uninstalling it.

Once you have decided on your schedule of backups, you have to decide on the backup method. Each type entails certain trade-offs:

- *Full backup*—All backup schedules begin with a full backup of everything on the drive. The advantage is that all the data is in one place; if data must be restored, you need to access only one storage location. The disadvantage is that a full backup takes more time than other techniques.
- *Differential backup*—This method backs up all files that are new or changed since the last full backup. The advantage is that if data must be restored, it can be found in only two possible places: on the tape with the full backup or on the tape with the differential backup. The disadvantage is that you keep backing up the same old information since the full backup, because you back up new data every day.
- *Incremental backup*—This method backs up only the data that has changed since the last incremental backup. The advantage is that data is backed up only once, which doesn't take as many system resources as the previous two methods. The disadvantage is that to restore data, you might have to search through the full backup or any one of the incremental backups. Most backup software deals with this problem by quickly going through all the backups for you. Often, the full backup and the incremental backups are found on the same tape.

Figure 2-12 compares the incremental and differential backup approaches.

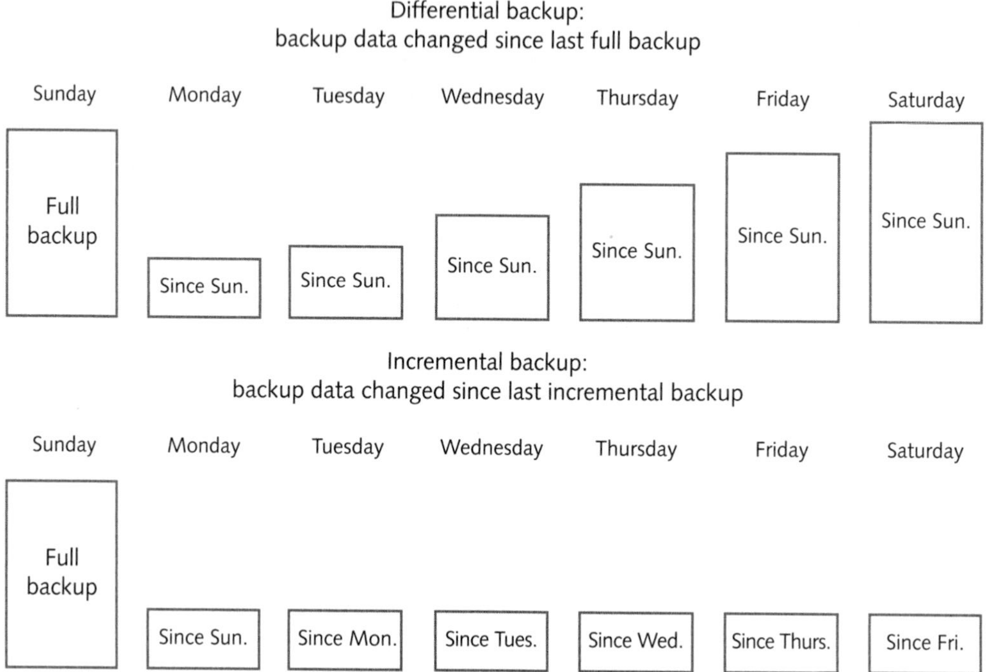

Figure 2-12 Tape backup approaches

You can use a combination of these backup types if desired. For example, on Sunday you might make a full backup. On Monday, suppose you add a new file called filea.doc and change a file called fileb.doc, so you need only a differential backup of filea.doc and fileb.doc. On Tuesday, you add filec.doc and change filed.doc, so your differential backup will include filea.doc, fileb.doc, filec.doc, and filed.doc. Now assume that you start over on Sunday and use incremental backups. On Monday, you add filea.doc and change fileb.doc; if you do an incremental backup, only filea.doc and fileb.doc will be backed up. On Tuesday, you add filec.doc and change filed.doc, so your incremental backup will include only filec.doc and filed.doc.

Often, full backups are scheduled to take place once per week during a slow time, such as 1 A.M. on Sunday. During the week, incremental or differential backups might be done at 1:00 every morning. Place the weekly full backups on a new tape and be sure to store the old tape off site, in case the computer room becomes damaged by fire or fire sprinklers. Some companies use a fire-proof safe for tape storage.

Choosing Backup Technologies

You can back up data in more than one way and should consider whether you need more than the basic procedures. For example, these procedures may prove inadequate for a server environment containing eight servers. Likewise, your system might include multiple LAN servers, multiple specialized Web servers, a database server, a print server, and an e-mail server.

You should consider three issues when performing backups:

- **Backing up the operating system**. In a Windows server, the Registry is always open, and open files are not backed up by default. You need to make sure that your backup software explicitly backs up the Registry.
- **Backing up special application files**. DBMSs keep files open, as do Microsoft Exchange and other applications. These critical files will not be backed up unless your backup software has special modules for each of these applications. These software modules usually cost extra money and are available only for popular software. Also, you may have a custom application that keeps files open. Open files are not included in a backup, even though some of them could be important files used by your applications. For a solution to this problem, contact the company that supplied the custom application. The only way to close the application files may be to manually stop the application before you make a backup. Some applications, such as Oracle DBMSs, require part of the backup procedures to take place through utilities that are part of the software before the files will be backed up.
- **Backing up simple data files such as text files, spreadsheet files, or executable files**. These files are easy to back up, assuming that the user does not have them open. Make sure you can back up every file in case the disk subsystem is completely destroyed, thereby ensuring that you can rebuild the system after a disaster. This is not a trivial task. Verify that your software can restore the system by practicing on every new server you get and documenting the procedures.

Although it is best to have a tape drive on every server, budget constraints may not allow it. Good digital tape drives can cost thousands of dollars. To add to the complexity, configuring one tape drive to back up multiple servers makes it more difficult to back up the Windows Registry, DBMSs, Microsoft Exchange, and other special applications. Typically, you need to buy software modules from the manufacturer of your backup software and install them on the servers without tape drives. If you implement such a system, note that when you back up data on another server on the network, you place a severe burden on the network. Some backup systems can easily clog a 100 Mbps network. To prevent this problem, backups should always be done when no one is using the network. In addition, put an extra NIC in each server and implement a second network just for backups.

Evaluating Network Components

There is more to a Web server environment than a few servers. The servers need to be connected together and the connections need to communicate with the Internet. This section examines these components and explains how to put together a complete system.

Switches and Hubs

You use switches and hubs to connect computers. A twisted-pair wire usually connects the NIC in the computer to the hub or switch. A switch is a device that controls the routing and operation of data signals. Standard switches communicate at Layer 2 of the OSI model. However, as explained in Chapter 1, Layer 3 switches can also act as routers.

Hubs are shared devices found at Layer 1 of the OSI model; computers share the connections in the hub much like old-fashioned telephone party lines. With a party line, you picked up the phone to find out whether anyone else was using it. If no one was on the line, then you could talk. Imagine that so many conversations took place on the party line that you spent more time checking the line than actually talking. In the computer world, this situation is called **contention**. The more traffic, the slower it travels. Using a hub between a workstation and a server is fine with light data traffic, but switches are a much more common solution to heavier traffic management.

A switch is analogous to a modern telephone system. You dial a specific number and then communicate, even though others may be using the same telephone system at the time. A switch simulates a direct connection between two computers. Although these devices should be really called switching hubs, they are commonly called switches. Because servers handle a lot of traffic, this section focuses on switches; hubs are not an option when connecting servers.

Not all switches are the same. Some cost $100, while others cost 10 times as much. As with most components, you need to balance your needs with your budget. For example, assume that you have a 12-port switch. (A port is where you connect the network cable.) When only two computers are connected to a 12-port switch, traffic flows without interruption. As traffic increases, however, you need to consider the following characteristics:

- *Packets per second*—The number of packets that can go from one port to another port. More expensive switches promise **wire speed**, which is the same speed two computers could achieve if they were physically connected.
- *Data switching backplane*—The total speed the switch can handle. It should be measured in gigabits per second.
- *Connection types*—Can you use full-duplex NICs that allow 100 Mbps data transfers in both directions at once? As you add more switch capacity, can the switches function as if they were one switch?

Once you have a switch to connect the servers in a network, you must connect the server network to your ISP's network. Your ISP then connects your system to the Internet.

Routers

Routers connect one network to another network and can serve many purposes, including connecting an internal network to an external network. Chapter 1 discussed connecting your network to the Internet. Recall that the digital signal coming from the Internet differs from the digital signal in your network. The router not only moves packets from one network to another, but can also transform the packet into another type. For example, when a router links to your internal network and your CSU/DSU, its Ethernet port connects to your internal network and its serial port connects to your CSU/DSU.

Not all routers are separate devices, and any server can become a router. All you need are two or more NICs. The connection into one NIC comes from one network, and the other connection goes to the second network. As you will see in Chapter 10, a firewall computer can take packets from the Internet on one NIC and then send them to an internal network with a special network address that cannot be detected from the Internet on the other NIC. A firewall computer can also act as a router.

Maintaining Internet Connections

There are many pieces to the puzzle of identifying LAN components and connecting them to the WAN, as you discovered in Chapter 1. The most complex piece involves learning about the WAN connection. Due to the competitive nature of the ISP industry, both pricing and services change rapidly. As a consequence, the most popular and cost-effective solution one year may not be the best solution the next year. Although the T-Carrier approach offers virtually unlimited expandability, most businesses will probably never need to expand beyond a capacity of 1.544 Mbps. At this level, you can select between T1, SDSL, and a dedicated cable modem. Your choice will depend on the combination of services that are available in your area, the cost of the service, the reputation of the ISP, and the expandability you need.

Organizations that are just getting started in Internet connectivity should consider the Web hosting solutions outlined in Chapter 1. They involve much less risk and you do not need on-site technical expertise.

Setting Up IP Addressing

As you learned in Chapter 1, IP is one of the protocols in the TCP/IP protocol suite. Its purpose is to provide addressing, which is how information gets from one computer to another on the Internet. Every Web server has a unique address that is valid on the Internet. However, workstations on an organization's LAN often use private IP addresses that are not accessible on the Internet, but rather have meaning only on the company network.

Understanding the Addressing Structure

The addressing structure determines how addresses are created and how you can determine the difference between the network portion of the address and the **host** (or individual computer) portion. This structure is like a world where every house has a Zip code that identifies both the local post office and the house. A computer's "Zip code" also supplies information about the country from which it came; large countries with many houses get certain types of codes, whereas countries with few houses get special codes that can handle fewer residences. IP addresses are organized in much the same way.

IP addresses are divided into four numbers separated by periods, such as 192.168.0.100. Each number, with certain restrictions, can range from 0 to 255. An IP address has two parts: a host portion and a network portion. All computers that are directly connected to each other form a network with regard to IP addressing. In such a case, the network portion of the IP address must be the same for all computers, and the host portion of each machine's address must be different to distinguish one computer from the rest of the computers on the same network.

Subnet Mask

The subnet mask tells you what part of the IP address represents a network number and what part of the address represents the number for the host.

IP addresses are classified into three principal classes, as shown in Table 2-4. The addresses are grouped according to how many hosts each class can accommodate. A class A address can have over 16 million hosts, whereas a class C address can have only 254 hosts. Figure 2-13 gives an example that shows the differences among the classes with regard to network and host portions of the address.

Table 2-4 Common TCP/IP classes

Class	First number	Subnet mask	Number of networks	Number of hosts
Class A	1–127	255.0.0.0	126	> 16,000,000
Class B	128–191	255.255.0.0	> 16,000	> 65,000
Class C	192–223	255.255.255.0	> 2,000,000	254

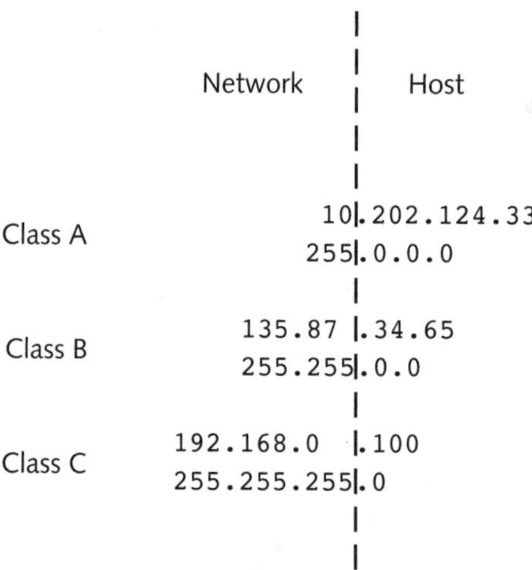

Figure 2-13 Subnet mask used to separate network from host

Determining the network portion and the host portion is critical for the following reason: when your computer needs to send a packet based on an IP address, it must determine whether the packet should stay on the local network or be sent through the gateway to another network. To do so, your computer compares the IP address of the destination to the subnet mask. If the network portions of both your computer's address and the destination address match, the packet stays on the local network. If the network portions are different, the packet is sent to the gateway (router) address. When you set up an IP address in your computer, the third value—usually called the gateway—is the IP address of the computer that will take the packet out of the local network so that it can ultimately be routed to the correct network.

Private Networks

Private networks are special network addresses reserved exclusively for use on networks that do not communicate across the Internet. These networks offer two advantages. First, you don't have to worry about packets from the private network getting to the Internet, because Internet routers cannot route packets that use these addresses. Second, hackers cannot easily access computers in your local network that use such IP addresses.

The private addresses have the following designations:

- 10.0.0.0–10.255.255.254 (a single class A network address)
- 172.16.0.0–172.31.0.0 (16 class B network addresses)
- 192.168.0.0–192.168.255.254 (256 class C network addresses)

Your objective, whether for your Web server or for users in your organization, is to achieve interaction with the Internet. Private network addresses become very powerful in this effort when they are combined with **network address translation (NAT)**.

Network Address Translation

NAT allows an IP address from one network to be translated into another address on an internal network. You need to use NAT if your ISP gave you only one address for your organization instead of 254 addresses for your servers and users. Some routers and firewalls allow you to take single (or multiple) IP addresses that are destined for your network from the Internet and translate them into your local set of addresses. This approach allows you to have a single IP address of 38.246.165.10, for example, which is then translated to the address of your Web server at 192.168.0.100. Although this technique does a good job of isolating your Web server, NAT can do even more. It can take a single IP address that is valid on the Internet and translate it into a pool of local addresses. For example, 38.246.165.10 may be translated into a pool of addresses ranging from 192.168.3.1 to 192.168.3.254. Now as many as 254 users can share a single Internet connection. Figure 2-14 shows an example of this type of network. Proxy servers can keep track of which packet belongs to which internal user. (Proxy servers will be discussed in detail in Chapter 10.)

This technique has been very useful in allowing a dwindling pool of valid Internet IP addresses to serve an ever-increasing number of Internet users. Also, by ensuring that your internal IP address pool is a private network address, you make it more difficult for a hacker to penetrate your system.

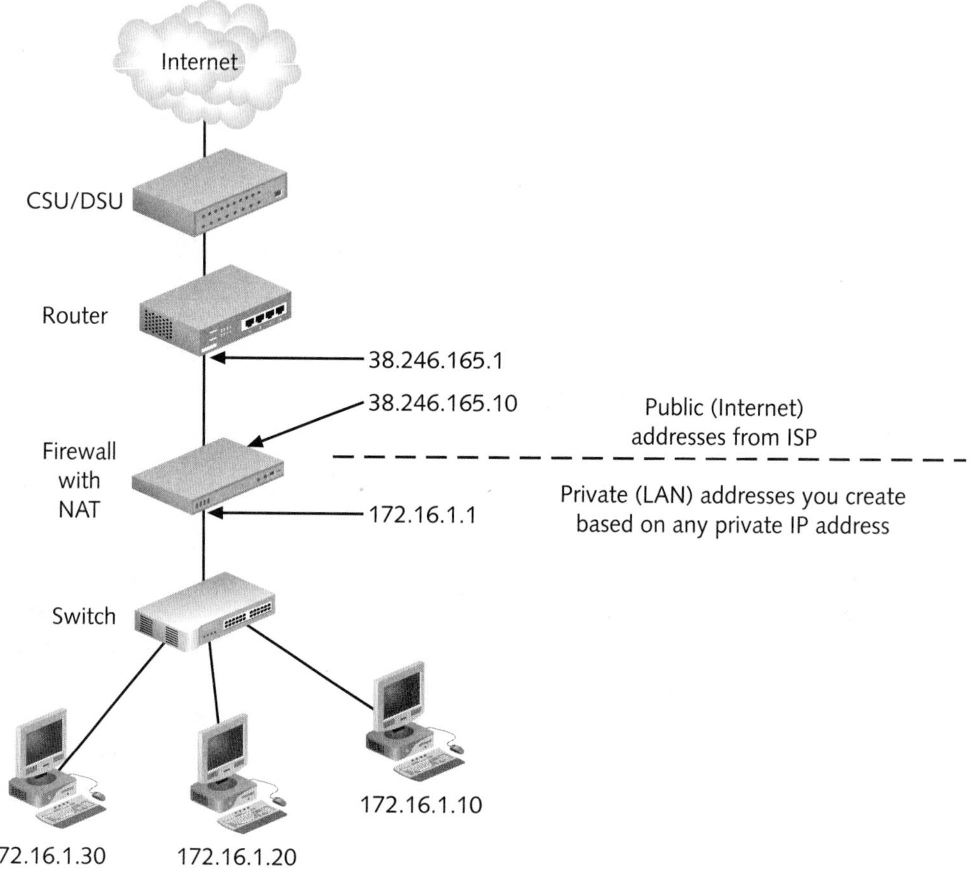

Figure 2-14 Network diagram

NAT is very flexible. For example, you could receive three IP addresses from your ISP: one destined for your Web server, one destined for your e-mail server, and one destined for your FTP server. All three will be translated to different internal IP addresses to help protect your servers.

An important aspect of NAT is that it allows multiple internal users to use a single IP address on the Internet. This type of single-address NAT is called port address translation (PAT). When a browser connects to a Web site, it typically links to port 80 on the Web server. However, for the Web server to send the Web page back to the browser, it needs to access a specific port on the browser. This port information is sent to the Web server when the user initially requests the Web page. Then a device that uses PAT, such as a router, associates each internal user with a different port. When a Web page comes back to the assigned port on the router, the port is translated into the user's port and the Web page is sent to the user. See Figure 2-15.

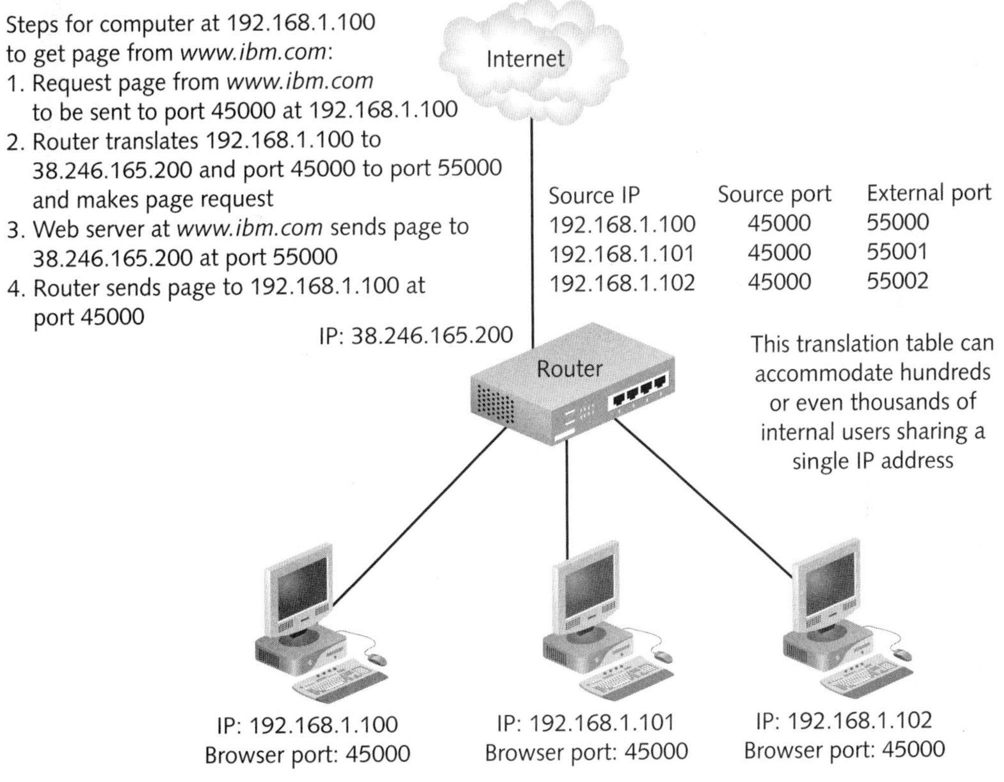
Steps for computer at 192.168.1.100
to get page from www.ibm.com:
1. Request page from www.ibm.com
to be sent to port 45000 at 192.168.1.100
2. Router translates 192.168.1.100 to
38.246.165.200 and port 45000 to port 55000
and makes page request
3. Web server at www.ibm.com sends page to
38.246.165.200 at port 55000
4. Router sends page to 192.168.1.100 at
port 45000
Internet
IP: 38.246.165.200
Router
Source IP
Source port
External port
192.168.1.100
45000
55000
192.168.1.101
45000
55001
192.168.1.102
45000
55002
This translation table can
accommodate hundreds
or even thousands of
internal users sharing a
single IP address
IP: 192.168.1.100
Browser port: 45000
IP: 192.168.1.101
Browser port: 45000
IP: 192.168.1.102
Browser port: 45000

Figure 2-15 Using port address translation

CHAPTER SUMMARY

- The two basic types of servers are the file server and the application server. Often, it is not easy to distinguish between them. For example, a Web server could be considered a file server or an application server, depending on how you use it. How you categorize a server affects the capabilities of the server components you choose.
- Many components make up a server, but all of them work together to produce the appropriate throughput. If one of the components is not sufficient for the task, a bottleneck occurs and the server as a whole is affected. Various families of processors are available from Intel, Sun, and other companies. Not all servers use Windows operating systems; some use Solaris or Linux instead.
- Computer components can fail and data can be lost. You must anticipate as many problems as possible and then determine how to avoid them, or at least lessen their

repercussions. You can prevent many problems by providing fault tolerance or at least high availability of components in the Web environment.

- RAID technology is an excellent method of preventing a single disk failure from causing a loss of data. You need a minimum of three hard disks to implement RAID 5. The storage equivalent of one disk is used to provide redundancy.
- Clustering can achieve fault tolerance by configuring multiple servers to act as one. There are two basic types of clustering. In one approach, the cluster appears as a single computer. In the other approach, multiple servers work together.
- Be careful when you back up data to make sure that you include all of it; by default, open files are not copied in a backup. Many important applications, such as e-mail and DBMSs, keep files open and so have special backup needs.
- A complete Web server environment includes switches and hubs to connect the computers, routers to connect the networks, and Internet connections.
- Correct IP addressing is essential to network communication. IP addresses include both a network portion and a host portion and are classified into three categories based on the numbers of networks and hosts they can support. Network address translation (NAT) can translate a single IP address into multiple addresses that exist in the internal network.

Review Questions

1. In a file server, which component is most important?
   a. processor
   b. NIC
   c. disk subsystem
   d. bus
2. In an application server, which component is most important?
   a. processor
   b. NIC
   c. disk subsystem
   d. bus
3. A Web server can be used as ______________.
   a. a file server only
   b. an application server only
   c. a combination of file server and application server, depending on how it is used
   d. neither a file server nor an application server

4. A DBMS server is used as ______________.
   a. a file server only
   b. an application server only
   c. a combination of file server and application server, depending on how it is used
   d. neither a file server nor an application server
5. ______________ is a term that refers to any cause of performance degradation in a system.
6. Which one of the following processors is not compatible with the others? That is, in which is the underlying architecture significantly different?
   a. Intel
   b. UltraSPARC
   c. AMD
   d. All of the above are compatible.
7. The Itanium processor is manufactured by ______________.
   a. IBM
   b. AMD
   c. Intel
   d. Sun
8. The Itanium is a ______________-bit processor.
   a. 16
   b. 32
   c. 64
   d. 128
9. When a processor doubles in speed, it often becomes more than twice as fast as its predecessor. True or False?
10. The UltraSPARC is manufactured by ______________.
    a. IBM
    b. AMD
    c. Intel
    d. Sun
11. The UltraSPARC architecture is ______________.
    a. CISC
    b. DISC
    c. RISC
    d. MISC

12. The Windows Server 2003 Datacenter Edition allows up to how many processors?
    a. 16
    b. 32
    c. 64
    d. 128
13. Which disk interface allows for the most drives?
    a. IDE
    b. PCI
    c. ISA
    d. SCSI
14. Which interface is popular for RAID 5?
    a. IDE
    b. PCI
    c. ISA
    d. SCSI
15. RAID 1 is also known as ________________.
    a. redundant copying
    b. mirroring
    c. duplicating
16. The device that allows servers to continue running when the electricity stops is a(n) ________________.
17. A 20-amp circuit can handle about ________________ watts.
18. It is better to use the Microsoft RAID 5 technology that is part of the operating system than to use the hardware-based RAID 5 technology. True or False?
19. The simplest form of load balancing is ________________.
20. Which backup method backs up all files that are new or changed since the last full backup?
    a. full
    b. differential
    c. secondary
    d. incremental
21. ________________ connect one network to another network.

HANDS-ON PROJECTS

Project 2-1

Create a table with one column titled "Most Economical" and a second column titled "The Best." In each row of the table, list a component such as processor, disk, RAM, or NIC. Given a configuration for Windows 2000, fill in the cells in the table. Write a paragraph describing the trade-offs required between choosing the most economical and the best.

Project 2-2

You are configuring backup procedures in a Web server environment where the Web server is used constantly. You want an approach that minimizes the amount of time it takes to back up the Web server. What approach would you take and why? Write one to two pages explaining and defending your decision.

Project 2-3

Your supervisor has heard that there is more than one way to implement a fault-tolerant disk subsystem. He wants to know what the methods are and under which circumstances each should be used. Write one to two pages identifying ways that you can create a fault-tolerant disk subsystem and recommend when each strategy should be used.

Project 2-4

The information in Tables 2-1 and 2-2 is constantly changing. Use the Internet to research Intel and UltraSPARC processors, including information on their relative speed, RAM, L2 cache, and bus speed. Write one to two pages detailing the changes that have occurred since this book was published. Mention the sources of your information.

CASE PROJECTS

Case Project 2-1

A local real estate agency has asked you for help in setting up a presence on the Internet. The agency has started to create a budget and needs to determine how much the server hardware will cost. Its plan is to start with a fairly small Web site, but in the near future the agency wants to have listings of all local homes for sale, including pictures and virtual tours. The agency averages about 1,000 listings at a time. Unfortunately, the agency can't give you many details on how many simultaneous users the site will have; the site's reliability is the most important consideration at the moment.

Because the agency hasn't yet decided on which operating system and applications to use, you'll need to provide some choices. Put together a two- to three-page proposal listing two hardware configurations—one that would run a Windows 2003 system and one that would run a Red Hat Linux system. Your objective is to find servers that come preconfigured with the operating systems. The servers need to have tape backups. The agency is on a tight budget so it wants as cheap a solution as possible but with on-site support.

Case Project 2-2

The real estate agency is happy with your proposal (see Case Project 2-1), but needs some time to make a decision. In the meantime, your boss has suggested that you prepare for any decision that the agency makes. This means that you need to develop some documentation.

Prepare a diagram like the one in Figure 2-15 that shows the real estate agency's network. It has six machines in the office and a router with a fractional T1 connection to the Internet. Assume that the router's IP address is 24.16.5.200 and that the port on the Internet side of the firewall is 24.16.5.201. For the computers on the private side of the network, you get to choose the addresses; base them on the class C private address 192.168.0.0.

Case Project 2-3

The real estate agency (see Case Project 2-1) has also been selected to support regional home listings. As a result, its new Web site will require a Web server environment that is not only many times larger, but also able to grow rapidly without requiring a new, bigger server. How would you build this environment? Write two to three pages to justify your conclusions.

Case Project 2-4

Identify appropriate servers for an organization that requires an FTP server, a DBMS server, and a Web server that is in between a file server and an application server. Basically, the company has a lot of static HTML files but also supports Active Server Pages files. You have a budget of $15,000 for each server. Go to Web sites for major vendors such as Dell, Compaq, Hewlett-Packard, Sun, and IBM. Describe in detail at least two servers in each category from at least two vendors; show the range of possibilities for each server, including information on processors and disk capacity. Write two to three pages explaining and defending your choices.

CHAPTER

3

INSTALLING THE SERVER

In this chapter, you will:

- Prepare the server for system installation
- Understand the installation process
- Install Windows 2000 Server, Windows Server 2003, and Red Hat Linux 8
- Examine basic Linux commands
- Configure TCP/IP

Whether you are installing a Windows server or a Linux server, you typically perform the same tasks when preparing for installation. First, you determine how to organize the disk into partitions. Then, you examine the licensing requirements, which vary from one operating system to another. Although you can download Linux for free, licensed versions from Red Hat and others come with support and extra software. For the Microsoft operating systems, licenses are based on client access. You must also make sure that the NIC, video adapter, and disk subsystem on the server are compatible with the operating system that you install. After you complete these preparation tasks, you are ready to install an operating system on your server.

This chapter includes instructions for installing Microsoft Windows 2000 Server, Windows Server 2003, and Red Hat Linux 8. With few exceptions, you will install the default components for each server. If you are new to Linux, you can take an introductory tour of the KDE windowing environment and learn the basic commands of the shell interface. Finally, you will learn how to configure TCP/IP properties, which is necessary for communicating with other computers.

PREPARING THE SERVER FOR SYSTEM INSTALLATION

Before you install the operating system on your server, you need to perform a variety of tasks to prepare for the installation. If you are installing multiple operating systems on a single disk, your preparation steps are more complicated than when you are installing one operating system per computer.

Although you will probably install the operating system using a CD, this chapter covers other methods as well, including installing from a bootable CD, installing from a floppy disk with a nonbootable CD, and performing a network installation. Whichever installation method you use, make sure all of your hardware components are compatible with the operating system before you start installing the operating system. You should also document your findings for future reference.

Single-Boot and Multi-Boot Systems

Single-boot systems have one operating system, whereas **multi-boot systems** have more than one operating system on a single disk. Virtually all servers used in production environments are single-boot systems. (Production environments are those where servers work in a business or organization other than a computer lab, which runs the server only for educational purposes.) Multi-boot systems are often used in development or training. It is easier to set up a multi-boot system with operating systems from a single manufacturer such as Microsoft, because the software is designed to coexist with different versions. However, even if you use only Microsoft operating systems on a single hard disk, you must still install current service packs after you install Windows. **Service packs** are operating system improvements and corrections issued by Microsoft after the company releases an operating system. You can download Windows service packs from the Microsoft Web site at *http://www.microsoft.com/downloads*. Red Hat Linux calls its improvements and corrections errata and divides them into three categories: security alerts, bug fixes, and enhancements. The errata are available at *http://www.redhat.com/apps/support/errata*.

If you want to install two operating systems on one hard disk, you need to plan the installations carefully. Most operating systems are designed to control the **master boot record** (**MBR**), a sector on the hard disk that contains a **boot loader** program intended to start the boot process. When you turn on a multi-boot computer, a menu appears, listing the operating systems available on the computer; you then select which one you want to use. When Microsoft operating systems use the MBR, the menu of operating systems lists only the Microsoft software. You cannot easily add a Linux menu item to the Microsoft boot menu. Therefore, if you install Windows first and Linux second, you must rely on a Linux boot method to allow both operating systems to coexist on the same hard disk. Linux can recognize a Windows installation even though Windows cannot recognize the Linux installation.

Red Hat Linux can boot your computer in a number of ways. Like Windows, Linux uses a boot loader at startup. Older versions of Linux used LILO, which is an excellent boot loader. However, LILO typically needs to be reconfigured when it is combined on the same hard disk with a Windows operating system. To boot your computer with Red Hat Linux, you use a boot loader called GRUB. When GRUB is installed in the MBR and you boot the system, a menu appears with two entries: Linux and DOS. You select DOS to open a menu that lists Microsoft operating systems, such as Windows 2000 Server. In rare cases, GRUB may not work on a system. In this situation, you can use a boot floppy disk. When you install Linux, the Setup program asks for a floppy disk to configure as a boot floppy disk. Save that floppy disk in a safe place in case you cannot boot your system from the hard disk.

Installation Methods

You can install operating systems using one of several methods. For Windows servers, you can use a bootable CD, a floppy disk with a nonbootable CD, or a network installation. For Linux, depending on the distribution, you can use a bootable CD, a floppy disk with a nonbootable CD, or FTP, which allows you to transfer the operating system files from a server on the Internet.

The most common—and fastest—method for installing a server operating system is to use a bootable CD. Although the option to boot from a CD should be available on all newer PCs, sometimes the BIOS is set up so that the boot order starts with the hard disk instead of the CD. Because different BIOSs are available, check with your network supervisor to confirm that your computer is configured so that the CD drive is the first device in the booting sequence.

If you are using a computer that cannot boot from a CD, such as an older PC or one with a nonstandard SCSI configuration, you can start installing a server operating system with a boot floppy disk. For Linux, if you do not have a bootable CD and need to start the installation process from a floppy disk, format a floppy disk and then insert the Linux CD 1 in the CD drive of any Windows PC. From a command prompt, type the information shown in Figure 3-1. The figure assumes that the CD is the D: drive.

To create a boot floppy disk in Windows 2000, use the command **d:\bootdisk\makeboot.exe** where D: is the CD drive. Windows 2003 does not support boot floppy disks.

Both Linux and Windows allow you to install them from a network. To install Linux, you first connect to the network, then transfer the files using FTP or HTTP. You can create a network boot disk to connect to the network before you install an operating system. For a network boot disk, follow the same steps as shown in Figure 3-1, with one exception: instead of using boot.img as the filename, use bootnet.img. See Figure 3-2.

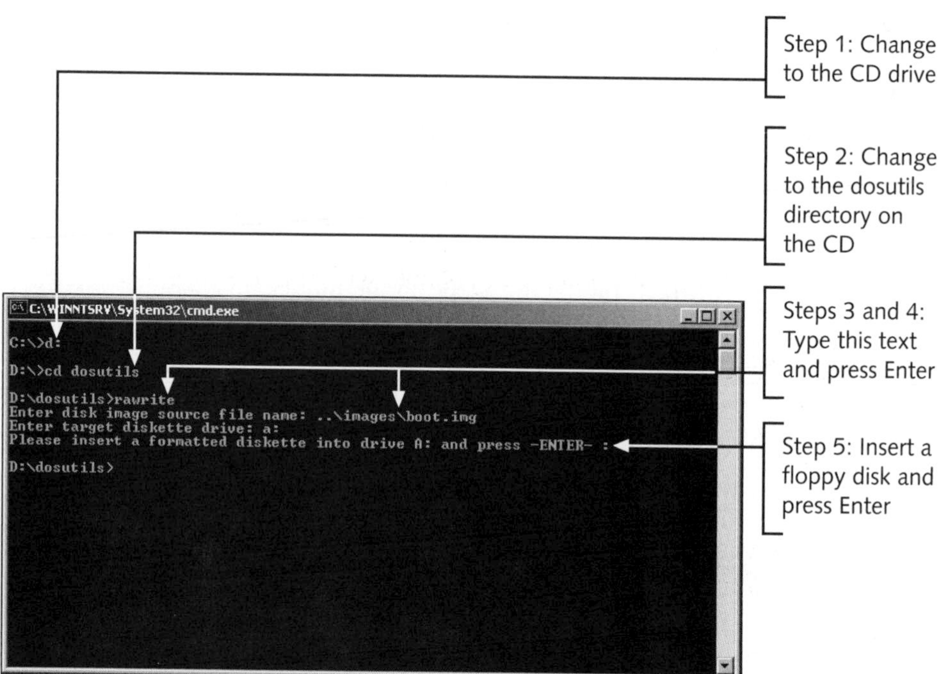

Figure 3-1 Creating a Linux install floppy disk

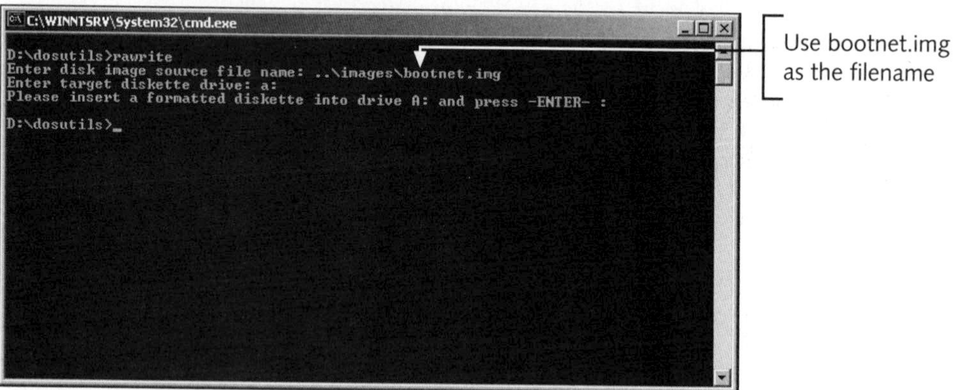

Figure 3-2 Creating a network boot disk

To install any Microsoft Windows server product over a network to a hard disk without an operating system, you must first create an MS-DOS boot disk that contains drivers you can use to connect to the network. This task poses a challenge in two ways. First, you can create a DOS boot disk only if you can access a computer running a Windows operating system. Second, you need to access DOS drivers for your NIC. Some NICs do not provide DOS drivers, and others are difficult to find. Also, because operating systems are so large, installing over a network is very slow, especially for multiple installations.

Checking Hardware Compatibility

If you are using computer hardware that is designed for a server, you should not have any problems when you install a server operating system. However, if you are installing the operating system in a lab environment, as you will in this chapter, the video adapter, NIC, or hard disk might not be compatible with the new software.

If you are using an IDE drive, then you should not have a compatibility problem with the hard disk. However, SCSI and RAID controllers can pose problems. Although the manufacturers usually include drivers for these types of controllers, you often have to make sure that they are the latest version. Always check the manufacturer's Web site for the latest drivers. You may need different drivers for the different controllers, and they must be loaded in the correct order. For example, there may be a SCSI RAID controller for the hard drives, and another SCSI controller for the CD-ROM. Reliable server vendors often provide Setup programs that automate driver installation. For this reason, it is usually wise to purchase a server from a top vendor. For example, Dell now provides special startup CDs that guide you through an installation and make sure that all the drivers are installed correctly.

In the past, video adapters have posed some problems for Linux installations. Older versions of Linux sometimes requested the name of the manufacturer of the chip set on your video adapter, which is not a commonly known piece of information. Today's Linux distributions, particularly Red Hat, include virtually all the current video drivers.

NIC compatibility is not a problem if you use NICs from a major vendor, such as Intel or 3COM. If you use discounted NICs, however, they might not be compatible with Windows or Linux. In that case, you would have to make sure that the NICs include appropriate drivers for the operating system you are installing.

Windows 2003 provides the best support for existing hardware. Since the release of Windows 2000, Microsoft has provided **signed drivers**, which means that the drivers are certified to work as described.

However, dozens of companies manufacture hardware components. Although the video adapter, NIC, and hard disk are the components that are most often incompatible with server operating systems, you could experience problems with a component as basic as a motherboard. Upgrading a computer can also result in hardware problems. For example, you might have an excellent, high-quality server running the Windows NT server software, but the specialized RAID controller on the server might not be compatible with Windows 2000 or Windows 2003. If you are upgrading an old server, make sure you have a detailed list of components. Many video adapters, RAID controllers, and SCSI adapters are compatible with Windows NT but not with Windows 2000 or

Windows 2003. To a lesser extent, an older Windows 2000 server might have devices that are not compatible with Windows 2003.

To check whether a device is compatible with a particular Windows operating system, visit *www.microsoft.com/hwdq/hcl*. At the Microsoft site, you can select a device to see whether it is compatible with a particular version of Windows, ranging from Windows 98 to Windows 2003. If you want to check whether a device is compatible with Linux 8, start at *hardware.redhat.com/hcl*.

Preparing System Documentation

System documentation should be detailed enough so that even an inexperienced network administrator could reinstall and configure the server. This documentation should include information about the operating system and all applications, including the Web server or e-mail server.

System documentation is an ongoing process, not something you create only once. Begin by listing the basic hardware characteristics of your system to document how it is configured when you purchased your server. Next, list the configuration information for the operating system—primarily the partition information and the drivers that may be needed beyond the ones that come with the operating system, such as SCSI drivers. Then, describe the partitions in the next section of the documentation by identifying the number of partitions, the size of the partitions, and the rationale for the configuration. Also describe the procedures for the steps in the installation where you do not accept the defaults. Next, describe the software you have added and deleted, along with any patches that have been applied; this section can change over time. In a prominent place on the document, include all support information, such as the support Web site, phone number, contract number, support type, and expiration date of the support agreement. Some support contracts allow you to call 24 hours a day, seven days a week. Others are available only during business hours.

Keep the system documentation in a notebook with all associated CDs. In addition, store the system documentation with any software documentation for backup software and other applications on the server. If you build the system yourself, document every component you purchase, including the following components and related information:

- *Server*—Include the manufacturer and complete model number.
- *Processor*—List the type, speed, and number of processors.
- *RAM*—Indicate the amount of installed RAM.
- *Drive interface*—If the drive is a SCSI or RAID, list the manufacturer, model, and drivers needed.
- *Hard disk*—Include the manufacturer and complete model number.
- *NIC*—Include the manufacturer and complete model number.

- *Partition information*—List the number of partitions and the size of each; for Windows, also list the size of each drive.
- *Operating system version installed*—Indicate the version of the operating system, which is especially important for Linux as there are many distributions and the versions change more often than in Windows.
- *Latest software patches*—List the patches you installed and when you installed them.
- *Support information for hardware and software*—Include any Web site addresses and phone numbers. If you have a contract, include the contract number, type of support, and date of its expiration.

Understanding the Installation Process

During the installation process, the Setup program will ask about your system and its configuration. You should know the answers to these questions *before* you start the installation. Because many of these questions are common to all operating systems, understanding these similarities will help you to install any operating system.

Partitioning the Hard Disk

You need to understand how you will **partition** the hard disk. A partition is a logical division of the hard disk. Because you might be installing three operating systems, you must create a number of partitions. Although the concept of partitioning is the same across all operating systems, Windows and Linux use partitions in different ways.

Windows Partitioning

On a Windows computer, you can create a **primary partition**, which is a drive or part of a drive where the system starts its boot process, and an **extended partition**, where more drives can be added as needed. Usually, the operating system boots from the C: drive. When configuring a server, you should isolate the system software from other software and data files on this drive by keeping the files in separate partitions; doing so improves security and system performance. If hackers access a partition through your Web site, they can likely access data, which is stored on the Web partition that doesn't contain the operating system. They may find it difficult to move from that drive to the one with the operating system, where they could cause more damage. If you install system, software, and data files on the same drive, and then hackers or users store so many files on the system that they fill the drive, the operating system will stop functioning. If you store programs and data on a separate partition and fill up that partition, however, only the programs are affected; the operating system keeps running so that you can clean up the disk.

On a Windows production server, it is a good idea to make the C: drive partition at least 2 GB. Typically, the rest of the drive is given to the next drive letter available. On most systems, the D: drive is the CD-ROM drive, so the E: drive would be the disk partition. Allow plenty of space for the E: drive because you will often add temporary files, log files, and other files over time.

If you install Windows on a new hard disk that is not a preconfigured RAID 5 drive, the Setup program will ask you to first create a partition into which it will install Windows. If you are setting up a multi-boot computer, you could store all of the operating systems in the same partition. In this chapter, however, you will install the first Windows operating system on the C: drive; if you install a second Windows operating system, it will be on the next drive letter available.

Linux Partitioning

The concept of dividing the hard disk into more than one partition in Linux is the same as it is for Windows. You should also keep the Linux operating system separate from applications. However, unlike Windows, Linux does not assign drive letters to disks or partitions. Instead, the drive begins at the root, which is designated with a forward slash (/). Two partitions are required for Linux—the root partition and the swap partition. Linux uses the swap partition to swap instructions and data in and out of RAM when a program requires more space than is available in RAM. Note that the swap partition requires a special file format called swap.

Red Hat Linux can create a number of default partitions for you. Table 3-1 identifies these default partitions and indicates the amount of space Linux allocates for each partition on a 6.4 GB drive and an 80 GB drive.

Table 3-1 Linux default partitions

Name	Description	6.4 GB drive	80 GB drive
/ (root)	The root partition is the top of the directory structure. It does not contain many files when you first install Linux. If you create directories at the root, it will use up this space.	510 MB	510 MB
swap	Linux stores **virtual memory** in the swap partition. The processor uses virtual memory when it does not have enough RAM. A rule of thumb is that the swap partition should be at least the size of your physical memory. By default, Red Hat makes the swap partition double the size of your physical memory. Unlike the other partitions, swap is not part of the directory structure, which means that you cannot explicitly store files on this partition. Rather, the operating system uses it behind the scenes.	1,020 MB	1,020 MB

Table 3-1 Linux default partitions (continued)

Name	Description	6.4 GB drive	80 GB drive
/boot	Linux stores the basic files for starting your system in the boot partition. These files include the operating system kernel, along with the few support files needed to boot the system. This is the smallest partition, usually 47 MB in size.	102 MB	102 MB
/usr	Linux stores the files and programs that are shared among all users in the usr partition. Because this partition can contain the most files, it should be the largest. By default, it takes up about 70 percent of the disk after Linux allocates space for the other partitions.	2,761 MB	54,627 MB
/home	Users create their directories in the home partition. Depending on how many users are on the system, this partition can be quite large. By default, it takes up about 30 percent of the disk after Linux allocates space for the other partitions. On a Web server, however, the home partition can be smaller because users should not store files in the home directory, unless the user is an ISP with user Web sites associated with the home directories.	1,012 MB	19,979 MB
/var	The var partition contains your Web site, FTP site, log files, and e-mail spool files. Log files and e-mail files can take up a lot of room on a server, so you should increase this partition to at least a few gigabytes. You can take some space away from either /home or /usr to do so.	753 MB	753 MB

Notice that the only partitions that differ depending on the size of the hard disk are the /usr partition and the /home partition. Red Hat assumes that you want to use the additional space for applications (/usr) and user home directories (/home). For a Web server installation, however, you need more space in the var partition and less space in the home and user directories. As you go through the installation, text boxes will offer you the default partition sizes. You can easily change the sizes to whatever is appropriate for your environment.

Managing Multiple Operating Systems

For production servers where you install one operating system on a hard disk, create partitions as suggested in the previous sections. When you install more than one operating system on the same hard disk, however, you should start with an unpartitioned hard disk and then add partitions for each operating system. Create one partition for each

Windows operating system, and allow Linux to create its default partitions. Table 3-2 lists suggested partition sizes for each operating system.

Table 3-2 Suggested partition sizes

Operating system	Partition size
Windows 2000	6,000 MB
Windows 2003	6,000 MB
Linux partitions	Remaining space on drive, but at least 3 GB

Making Space for Multiple Operating Systems

To partition a hard disk, you can use low-level commands such as fdisk for DOS and some versions of Windows, and fips for Linux. However, it is much easier to partition the hard disk as you install each operating system. The Setup program for each operating system will allow you to delete partitions and create partitions of any size.

Booting Multiple Operating Systems

You must install the Windows operating systems first and then Linux. You already have learned that because Windows does not recognize Linux, it is the responsibility of Linux to recognize Windows. In Linux, you can use a specially configured floppy disk to avoid the Windows boot menu or take advantage of Red Hat's GRUB boot menu to select between Linux and Windows.

When you install a new Windows operating system, it detects the previous installation and adds the new installation to the boot menu automatically. After you add Windows 2003, the menu includes choices for Windows 2003 and any other Windows operating systems that you installed, as shown in Figure 3-3.

```
Please select the operating system to start:
     Windows Server 2003, Enterprise
     Microsoft Windows 2000 Server


Use the up and down arrow keys to move the highlight to your choice.
Press ENTER to choose.
```

Figure 3-3 Windows boot menu

The information in this section applies to installing operating systems in a lab environment. If you are installing a single operating system on a computer in a production environment, you do not need to perform the installation steps in this section to boot multiple operating systems.

Naming Computers

The primary purpose of naming a computer in either Windows or Linux is to distinguish it from other computers on your LAN. You can name a computer as you install it. Recognize also that you can share that name and its aliases with the rest of the network, even the Internet.

You must give your Windows computer a name that is unique throughout your network. To make it easy to recognize and remember, keep the name simple and descriptive, such as web1 or web2. The name you assign is used on the LAN for communication; it is not related to how the computer is recognized on the Internet. For example, you might name the computer web1, but to the Internet it may be *www.technowidgets.com*. To an e-mail user, it may be technowidgets.com as in *info@technowidgets.com*.

In Linux, computer names are usually referred to as host names. You can create a network with Linux computers that share the same host name with no problems, because in Linux you communicate with other computers by IP address. Of course, it is helpful in general to have unique names associated with each IP address, so it is still a good idea to have unique names that are also descriptive. (The method used to associate names and IP addresses is a separate issue discussed later.)

Licensing the Software

A software license describes how you can use the software. Software licenses differ among the operating systems. Microsoft assumes that the users of Windows 2000 have purchased a legal copy. In contrast, Windows 2003 users must verify that they are compliant with licensing by activating the software once it is installed. To activate Windows 2003, you must contact Microsoft either by the Internet or phone. Licensing is not a concern for Linux, because copies of the operating system are free, although packaging, support, and special additions may cost extra.

When you purchase a Windows server operating system, it probably comes with a few client licenses. Simply purchasing a server and client operating systems does not mean that you can legally connect computers together in a LAN. Each computer that connects to a LAN must have a **client access license** (**CAL**). Two types of licenses for Windows servers exist: per server and per seat. You use a **per server license** when you have a single server and not all client computers need to connect to it at the same time. You use **per seat licenses** in network environments with multiple servers. Per seat licensing means that each client computer has its own license and can connect to as many servers as you have. Because most networked environments have multiple servers, per seat licensing is the most common type. Connecting to a Web-based application, whether it is on a LAN or WAN, does not require a CAL, but it may require another type of license such as a per processor license. Typically, however, all computers in a LAN have a CAL.

Linux takes a different licensing approach. Linux is produced under the **GNU general public license**. GNU, pronounced "guh-NEW," is a recursive acronym for "GNU's Not UNIX." According to the GNU general public license, "the GNU general public license is intended to guarantee your freedom to share and change free software—to make sure the software is free for all its users." Some companies, including Red Hat, bundle Linux with extra software for specific purposes and charge more for that. For many environments, the personal version of Red Hat Linux is satisfactory for basic Web connectivity and networking. The personal version is used in all the examples in this book. You can also obtain Red Hat Professional, which has more installation options and better support. For mission-critical systems, you can license Red Hat Linux Advanced Server.

Identifying Devices

The most significant improvement in the installation procedures in servers over the past few years has been the increased ability of the operating system to correctly identify devices. When installing Windows NT and early versions of Linux, it was difficult to have the operating system perform this task. PCI slots introduced the possibility of using Plug and Play devices, which means that the operating system automatically configures a device such as a NIC as it is being installed. Windows 2000, Windows 2003, and Linux support Plug and Play devices. Windows 2000 and Windows 2003 recognize a wide variety of devices, but recall that you need to verify that your devices are included on the appropriate Hardware Compatibility List. Problems can arise when you try to use old specialized devices, such as RAID controllers designed for Windows NT, in a Windows 2003 server.

Until a few years ago, Linux had a reputation as being difficult to install because it often supported only older NICs and video adapters. Also, when it did support a video adapter, you had to know the details of the chip set and other information. At that time, because Linux was not yet popular and was primarily managed by volunteers, it did not support as many devices as Windows. Although it is still a good idea to check whether a device is compatible with Linux by visiting *hardware.redhat.com/support/hcl*, Linux will probably work on today's typical PC. Special-purpose servers, such as high-capacity, high-performance Web servers that support multiple processors or RAID controllers, might not be supported by Linux. In this case, be sure to purchase both the server and the operating system from a top vendor. Doing so increases the probability that they will work together.

Selecting a File System

A file system determines the way in which files are organized on a computer disk; in Windows, the file system also determines the characteristics of a file. With Windows 2000, Windows 2003, and Linux, you can choose from more than one type of file system. In the Windows operating systems, you use either the File Allocation Table (FAT) or New

Technology file system (NTFS). With Linux, ext3 is the current choice, although you can use others, such as ext2.

The **FAT** file system for Windows is based on the original DOS operating system from 1981. For server installations, FAT is obsolete because it does not provide adequate file system security. In the past, one advantage of using the FAT file system was that if the server did not boot correctly, you could boot from a DOS disk in the floppy disk drive, access a FAT volume on the hard disk, and correct the problem by copying or editing files. Today, a number of utilities allow you to boot from the floppy disk drive, so you no longer need to use the FAT file system to enjoy this advantage.

The **NTFS** was first introduced with Windows NT. It offers better performance with large hard disks than does FAT, better error correction, and, most important, built-in file system security. The security in NTFS controls file access for all users. In a Web server, everyone who receives a Web page is associated with a user name. The user associated with the Web server can access only those files that are part of the Web site, not the whole hard disk. This restriction greatly improves security.

In Red Hat Linux, all file systems have the same security capabilities. The latest file system from Red Hat is **ext3**. According to Red Hat, this file system offers many improvements, especially in terms of access speed.

Verifying Installation Requirements

The final preparation step before installing an operating system on your server is to verify both the minimum and the recommended installation requirements. The software manufacturer typically sets the minimum requirements needed to allow the software to function. However, most Web server administrators require more than the minimum hardware resources to handle Web traffic efficiently.

For Windows 2000 and Windows 2003, the minimum processor required is a Pentium running at 133 MHz with 128 MB of RAM. For Windows 2000, you need about 1 GB of space for the operating system; Windows 2003 requires about 1.5 GB. For adequate performance, the processor should be at least four times faster and you should have double the amount of RAM. Fortunately, even an entry-level server is many times faster than the minimum required, which is appropriate for most Web servers. From 1996 to 1998, DeVry University in Phoenix had a Web server running Windows NT that it also used as an e-mail server. For part of this time, Microsoft SQL Server, DBMS, was used by Active Server Pages, which is a programming environment for the Web server. The server ran on a 166 MHz Pentium III server with 64 MB of RAM.

Linux is less stringent in its minimum requirements. In fact, a special-purpose version of Linux can be embedded on a chip with very little RAM. However, for a Web server, even a computer with a Pentium III processor would be appropriate for most environments.

Because Web pages do not take up much space, the size of the disk needed for a typical Web server is not much larger than the requirements for the operating system itself. Much of the space is needed for other software that you may put on the Web server, such as e-mail software or a DBMS. For example, to install the Oracle9*i* DBMS, which includes the Apache Web server, you need nearly 3 GB of space.

In a student lab environment, to install all of the software and operating systems, the minimum requirements are a 15 GB drive and a Pentium computer with 128 MB of RAM. If you plan to install one Windows operating system, such as Windows 2000 or Windows 2003, plus Linux, you need a 10 GB drive.

INSTALLING MICROSOFT WINDOWS 2000 SERVER

In a production environment, you will often install the operating system on the C: partition and put all other software, such as the Web server, e-mail, and DBMSs, on the E: partition. Recall that you install the operating system on a separate partition to make sure that it can continue to run even if the applications partition runs low on disk space. For most environments, a C: partition with 2 to 3 GB is sufficient.

A student lab requires a different configuration than does a production environment. For ease of configuration, you will install all the software on a single drive in this chapter. You will also need to create a computer name and IP address that are unique on your network. If the network includes more than one computer, ask your instructor for the computer name and IP address.

Throughout the text, the name of the computer is web1 and the IP address is 192.168.0.100, with a subnet mask of 255.255.255.0.

In the following steps, you will install Windows 2000 Server with the default components, including the Web server. You will configure the Web server and other related components in later chapters.

Before you start the installation, write down the 25-character product key from the program CD. You will need it to complete the installation.

To begin installing Windows 2000 Server and create a partition:

1. Turn on the computer and insert the Windows 2000 Server CD in the CD drive. If a message appears instructing you to press any key to boot from the CD, press a key. The Setup program inspects your computer's hardware configuration and then loads files for the installation. When the Welcome to Setup window opens, press **Enter** to begin the installation.

   If any other messages appear during this step, consult with your instructor or technical support staff for assistance.

2. In the Licensing Agreement window, press **F8** to accept the licensing agreement. The Disk Partitions window opens, shown in Figure 3-4.

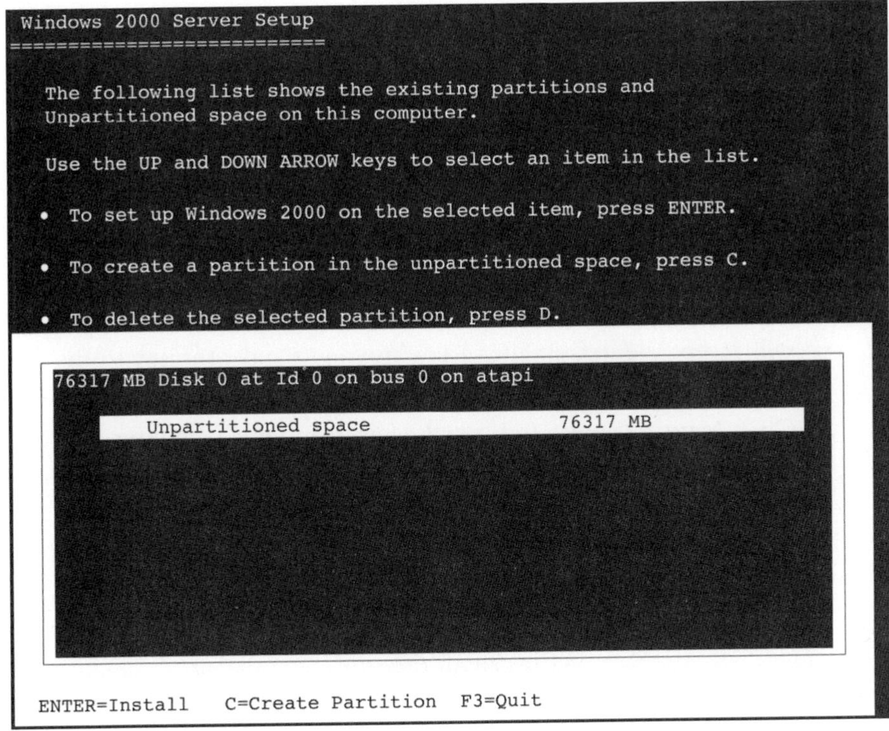

Figure 3-4 Disk Partitions window

You use this window to create a disk partition. In a production environment, you might create a partition of 2 to 3 GB; in a student lab, create a partition of at least 6 GB for Windows 2000 Server. The partition size is given in megabytes, so for a 3 GB partition, you would enter 3,000, and for a 6 GB partition, you would enter 6,000.

3. Press **C** to create a partition. The "C" stands for Create, not the drive letter. A text box appears with the maximum size for the partition. Change the size to one that is appropriate for your environment, typically 3,000 for a production environment or 6,000 for a student environment. Press **Enter** to create the disk partition.
4. The next window states: "The following list shows the existing partitions and the unpartitioned space on this computer." This is where you select the partition on which you will install the operating system. There should be a single new partition that begins "C: New (Unformatted)." Select the partition you just created and press **Enter** to install the operating system.
5. In the Disk Formatting window, accept the default selection of "Format the partition using the NTFS file system" by pressing **Enter**. Recall that NTFS is an appropriate file system for Web servers because of its security features.

The Setup program formats the partition, examines the disk, copies the installation files to the hard disk, and reboots the computer.

The screens in the first part of the installation were text-based because Windows was not installed on the hard disk yet. In the second part of the installation, a minimal version of Windows is installed to support and test the configuration options.

To continue installing Windows 2000 Server and specify settings:

1. After the computer reboots, a welcome window appears. Wait until the Detect and Install Devices dialog box appears. Pay close attention to the dialog boxes and answer the questions as they appear. If you do not, Windows will accept the default after a few moments and continue to the next screen. This choice will cause problems when you do not want to accept the default.

   Click **Next** to detect and install devices on your computer. The Setup program automatically detects your NIC and video adapter. This step could take a few minutes.

2. In the Regional Settings dialog box, you can change the user locale and keyboard settings from the standard U.S. selections, if necessary. For example, changing the locale can alter the date format and allow you to type foreign characters. Click **Next** to accept the default U.S. settings.

3. In the Personalize Your Software dialog box, type your name and the name of your organization, and then click **Next**.

4. In the Your Product Key dialog box, type your 25-character product key, and then click **Next**.

5. In the Licensing Modes dialog box, you select the type of licensing agreement you are using, either Per Seat or Per Server. If you are working in a student lab environment, accept the default licensing mode of Per Server with five licenses by clicking **Next**.

   You would use the Per Seat option button in an environment with multiple servers that user workstations need to access, where each workstation has its own CAL.

6. In the Computer Name and Administrator Password dialog box, change the default computer name to **web1** or a name provided by your instructor. Recall that names must be unique on the network. For the password, type **password** in both text boxes, and then click **Next**.

In a production environment, you should use a more secure password than "password." More secure passwords have at least eight characters and include both uppercase and lowercase letters, digits, and special characters such as # or %.

7. The Windows 2000 Components dialog box opens, listing the operating system components you can install on the server. See Figure 3-5. Internet Information Services (IIS), which is the Web server, is installed by default. However, some components within IIS, such as the FTP server, are not installed by default. You will install FTP and other software associated with the Web environment in later chapters. Accept the default selections by clicking **Next**.

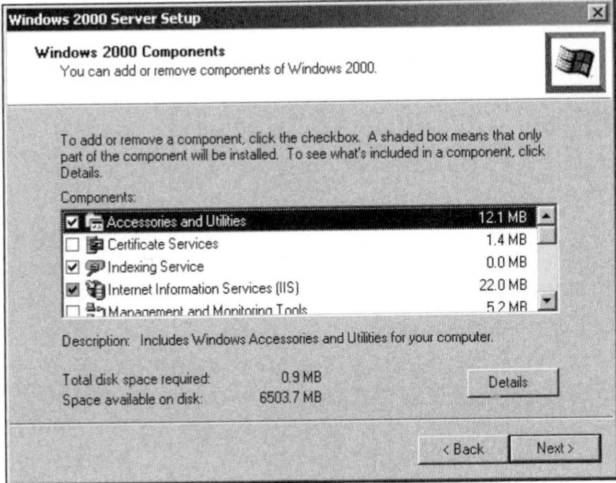

Figure 3-5 Windows 2000 Components dialog box

In a production environment, you may want to install a variety of services as you install the operating system. If you selected Internet Information Services (IIS) and clicked Details, you would be able to add the FTP server or the NNTP service. At the same time, you could unselect the SMTP service, which allows e-mail to be sent from a Web page. Within the Networking Services component, you could choose to install DNS.

8. The Date and Time Settings dialog box opens, listing the time zone, date, and time for your system. If these settings are not correct, use the list boxes to change them, and then click **Next**.

9. As Setup installs the networking components, the Network Settings dialog box appears. After it installs the components, it prompts you to choose between typical settings and custom settings. Click the **Custom settings** option button, and then click **Next**. You select the Custom settings option so that you can later enter an IP address. You have to pay close attention to this dialog box because if you do not choose options appropriately, the installation program will accept the default—typical settings—and continue with the installation.

10. The Networking Components dialog box displays the networking components that you can customize. Click **Internet Protocol (TCP/IP)**, and then click the **Properties** button.
11. The Internet Protocol (TCP/IP) Properties dialog box opens. To enter an IP address, click the **Use the following IP address** option button.
12. In the IP address text box, type your IP address, such as **192.168.0.100**. In the Subnet mask dialog box, type your subnet mask, such as **255.255.255.0**. If your network uses a default gateway, type the IP address of your router in the Default gateway text box. (In a student lab, you probably do not have a default gateway.)

    In the Preferred DNS server text box, type the IP address of your DNS server. In the student lab, you will be installing a DNS server on this computer, so enter the same IP address as you used for this computer—**192.168.0.100**. In a production environment, your ISP usually gives this IP address to you. See Figure 3-6. Click **OK** to save the changes and return to the Networking Components dialog box. Click **Next** to continue.

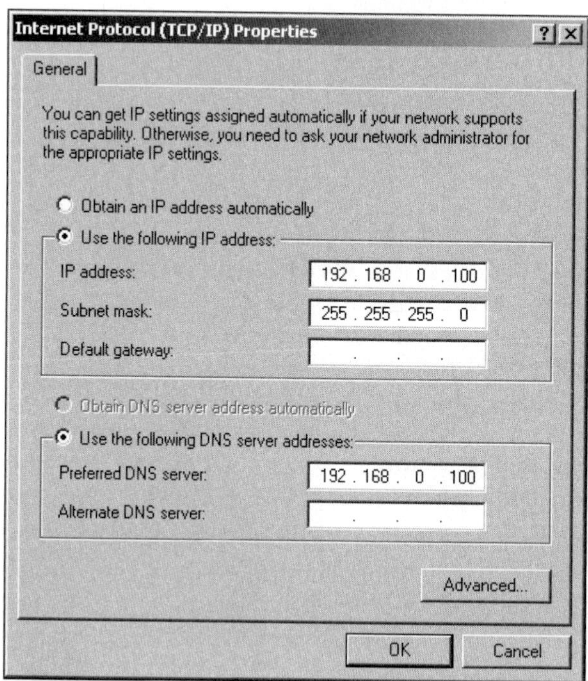

Figure 3-6 Windows 2000 Internet Protocol (TCP/IP) Properties dialog box

13. The Workgroup or Computer Domain dialog box opens. If this computer is part of a domain, you could click the option button to make it part of a domain and enter the name of the domain. In a student lab, you accept the default of no domain with a workgroup name of WORKGROUP by clicking **Next**.
14. The Installing Components and Performing Final Tasks dialog boxes appear in succession to inform you about the tasks that Setup is performing during the install process. This might take a few minutes. When the installation is complete, click **Finish** and then remove the CD. The computer restarts automatically.

Now you can test the installation to make sure that it works correctly by logging on and then shutting down the computer.

To test the installation:

1. After your computer restarts, the logon window appears. Log on using the password you created earlier, **password**, and then click **OK**.
2. In the Windows 2000 Configure Your Server dialog box, you can choose to configure the server now or later. Click the **I will configure this server later** option button, and then click **Next**.
3. To prevent this dialog box from appearing every time you start the computer, click the **Show this screen at startup** check box to remove the check mark. Then close the Windows 2000 Configure Your Server dialog box.
4. Click **Start** on the taskbar, click **Shutdown**, and then click **OK** to shut down the server.

INSTALLING MICROSOFT WINDOWS SERVER 2003

The Windows 2003 Web Server is Microsoft's entry-level server, which is useful for companies that need only basic Web services. If you need to add more advanced features such as Internet Authentication Service, Internet Connection Sharing, Windows Media Services, and Internet Connection Firewall, you must use Microsoft 2003 Standard Server. In the following procedure, you will install 2003 Standard Server; it includes an option called Active Directory that you will need if you plan to install Microsoft Exchange. Active Directory is not available with 2003 Web Server.

The 2003 servers provide excellent Internet features because they were designed to work in a complex Internet environment and offer dramatically improved security. Their programming environment, including Web Services, ASP.NET, and other components of the .NET Framework, is built into the operating system.

To install Windows 2003:

1. Turn on your computer and insert the Windows 2003 Standard Server CD. When prompted, press any key to boot from the CD.
2. The installation program displays "Windows Setup" as it loads files. When the Windows 2003 Standard Server Setup screen appears, press **Enter** to begin the Setup program.
3. In the next window, press **F8** to accept the licensing agreement.
4. In the next window, create a partition of 6 GB for the operating system. Select **Unpartitioned space** in the menu, and then press **C** to create the partition. Refer back to Figure 3-4, which shows the same dialog box. (Note that the Windows 2003 dialog box uses a different title.) A text box appears with the maximum size for the partition. Change the size to **6000**, and then press **Enter**.
5. Select the partition you just created, which is labeled as [New (Raw)]. Press **Enter** to set up Windows in the partition.
6. To format the disk, click **Format the partition using the NTFS file system (Quick)**.

When the Setup program successfully completes the first part of the installation, it reboots the computer. Do not press a key to have the computer boot from the CD, as you did in a previous procedure. Instead, let the computer continue when it reboots so that it will not start the Setup program again. After the computer reboots, a screen appears with the following option buttons:

- Collecting information
- Dynamic Update
- Preparing installation
- Installing Windows
- Finalizing Installation

The Setup program displays the option buttons as it completes the tasks, and it displays the approximate time remaining until the installation is finished. As with Windows 2000 Server, you need the 25-character product key from the program CD to complete the installation.

To finish the Windows 2003 installation:

1. After the computer restarts and the Setup program finishes installing devices, the Regional and Language Options dialog box opens. Unless you have changes to make, click **Next** to accept the default regional and language options.
2. The Personalize Your Software dialog box opens. To personalize your system, enter your name and organization, and then click **Next**.
3. The Your Product Key dialog box opens. Enter the 25-letter product key from the program CD. In a production environment, you must also register your software—the software will stop functioning in 14 days unless you register it. Click **Next** to continue.
4. The Licensing Modes dialog box opens. Select the licensing mode. In a student lab environment, accept the default of Per server by clicking **Next**. You would use the Per Seat option button in an environment with multiple servers that user workstations need to access, where each workstation has its own CAL.
5. In the Computer Name and Administration Password dialog box, change the default computer name to **web1** if you are on an isolated network. In a student environment, a good way to make the computer name unique is to use WEB as the first part of the name, followed by the last octet of your IP address. For the administrator password, enter **password** in both text boxes. If a message appears, click **Yes** to use this password. In a production environment, you would enter a more secure password. Click **Next** to continue.
6. The Date and Time Settings dialog box opens. Modify the date, time, and time zone settings if necessary, and then click **Next**.
7. In the Network Settings dialog box, click the **Custom settings** option button so that you can define your own network settings. If you accept the default of Typical Settings, the server would use DHCP to automatically receive an IP address from a DHCP server. This choice is not appropriate for a Web server. Click **Next**.
8. In the Networking Components dialog box, click **Internet Protocol (TCP/IP)**, and then click the **Properties** button.
9. Click the **Use the following IP address** option button, and then enter your IP address. You can use **192.168.0.100** as the IP address and **255.255.255.0** as the subnet mask, unless the instructor tells you otherwise. For DNS, enter **192.168.0.100**. See Figure 3-7. When you finish, click **OK** to return to the Networking Components dialog box, and then click **Next**.

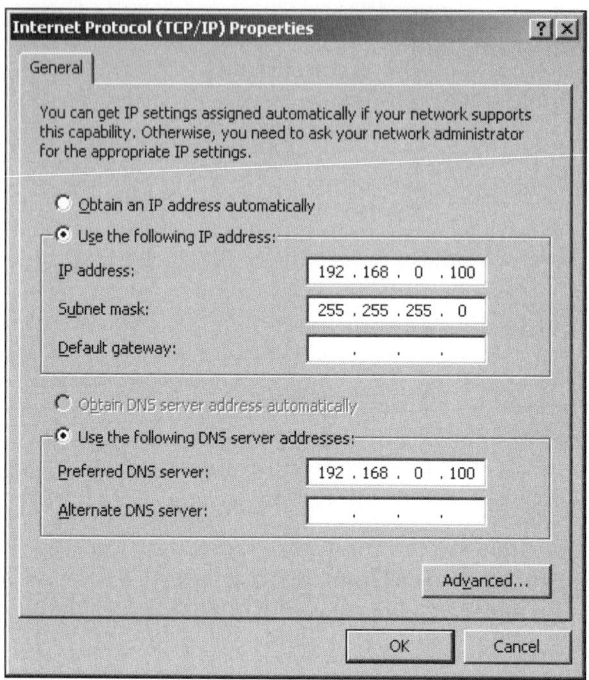

Figure 3-7 Windows 2003 Internet Protocol (TCP/IP) Properties dialog box

10. In the Workgroup or Computer Domain dialog box, accept the default selection of **No, this computer is not on a network or is on a network without a domain** and the default workgroup name, **WORKGROUP**, by clicking **Next**. In a production environment where this computer is part of a domain, you could enter that information after clicking the **Yes, make this a member of the following domain** option button. The installation finishes after a few minutes, and Setup then restarts the computer.

11. When the computer restarts, press **Ctrl+Alt+Del** and enter your administrator password, which is **password**. The Manage Your Server dialog box opens. See Figure 3-8. You have access to wizards that help set up server roles such as Web application, DNS server, and others. You will learn about these roles in subsequent chapters. To prevent this dialog box from opening the next time you log on, select the **Don't display this page at logon** check box. Close the window.

12. Click **Start**, and then click **Shut Down**. The Shut Down Windows dialog box opens. Make sure that "Shut down" appears in the list box. Enter a comment in the text box, if necessary, and then click **OK**.

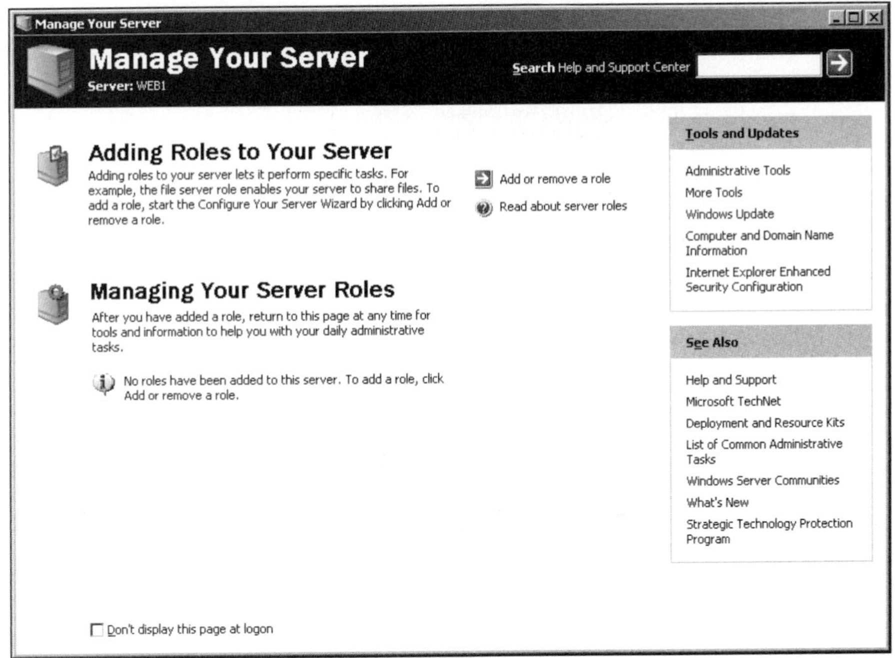

Figure 3-8 Manage Your Server window

INSTALLING RED HAT LINUX 8

Installing Red Hat Linux 8 is easier than installing earlier versions of Linux. The current version recognizes most devices automatically and offers a wide range of optional software components you can install. You will install some of the software you will need in later chapters, such as the Apache Web server and FTP.

To begin installing Red Hat Linux 8:

1. Make sure that you have the first two Linux installation CDs. Turn on the computer and insert Linux Red Hat CD 1.
2. A screen appears and describes the various boot modes. Press **Enter** to accept the default graphic installation. Note that each screen includes online help in the left panel.
3. The Welcome window opens. Click **Next**.
4. The Language Selection window opens. Click **Next** to accept English as the default language.
5. The Keyboard window opens. Click **Next** to accept the default U.S. English keyboard configuration.

6. The Mouse Configuration window opens. If you know what type of mouse you have, select it from the list in the Mouse Configuration window and then click **Next**. Otherwise, accept the default selection. The Installation Type window opens, shown in Figure 3-9.

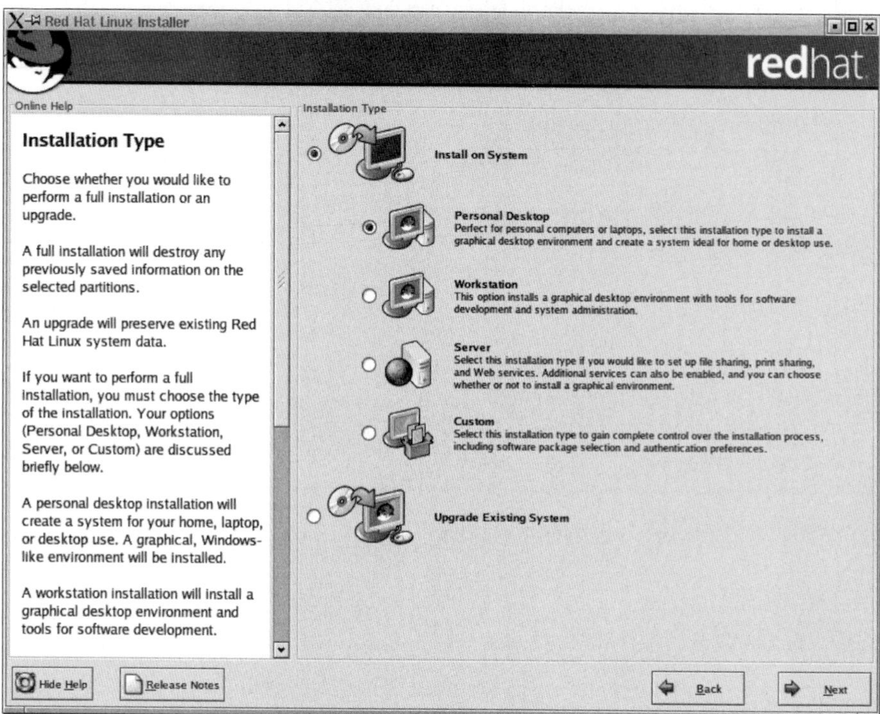

Figure 3-9 Installation Type window

7. Click **Server** in the Installation Type window, and then click **Next**. The installation type you select determines which components are installed and which packages you can select later in the installation.

8. The Disk Partitioning Setup window opens. Leave the default to automatically partition the drive, and then click **Next**.

9. The Automatic Partitioning window opens. See Figure 3-10. If you installed any of the Windows operating systems, *do not* accept the default of Remove all partitions on this system. If you do, the Windows installation(s) will be removed. However, this option would be appropriate for a production Web server with a single operating system. The "Remove all Linux Partitions on this system" option button is appropriate if you are reinstalling Linux. If this is the first time you are installing Linux in a student lab environment, select the **Keep all partitions and use existing free space** option button, and then click **Next**.

The Warning During Automatic Partitioning dialog box opens, suggesting that you create a boot disk. Click **OK** to continue.

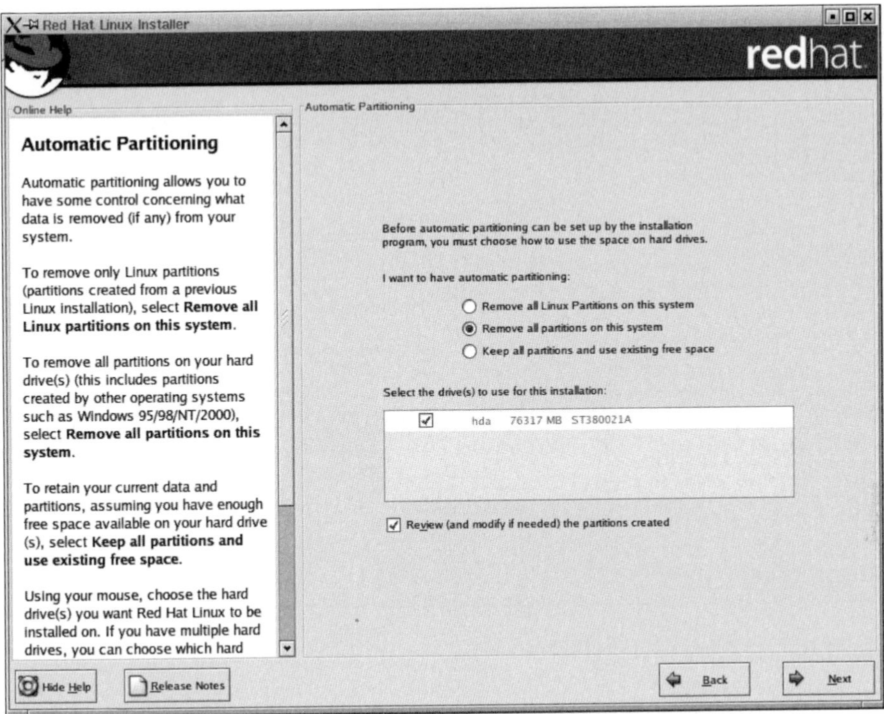

Figure 3-10 Automatic Partitioning window

10. The Partitioning window opens. See Figure 3-11. In a production environment, you would probably want to use space from the /home partition by highlighting /home and clicking Edit. You could then add space to the /usr partition for software such as DBMSs. Normally, however, you can just accept the default disk setup of five partitions and click **Next**.

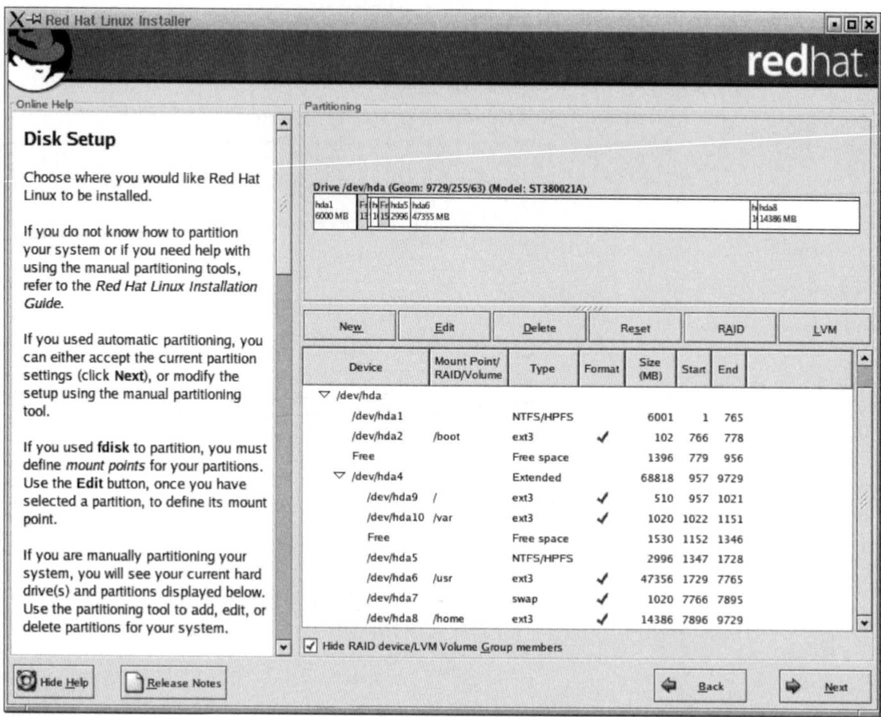

Figure 3-11 Disk Setup window

11. The Boot Loader Configuration window automatically detects the Windows installation, if you have one, and lists it under the DOS label. See Figure 3-12. The selected Red Hat Linux check box indicates that it will be the default operating system when you reboot. Accept the defaults, and then click **Next**.

Now you are ready to select the network configuration settings and a Red Hat Linux windowing environment.

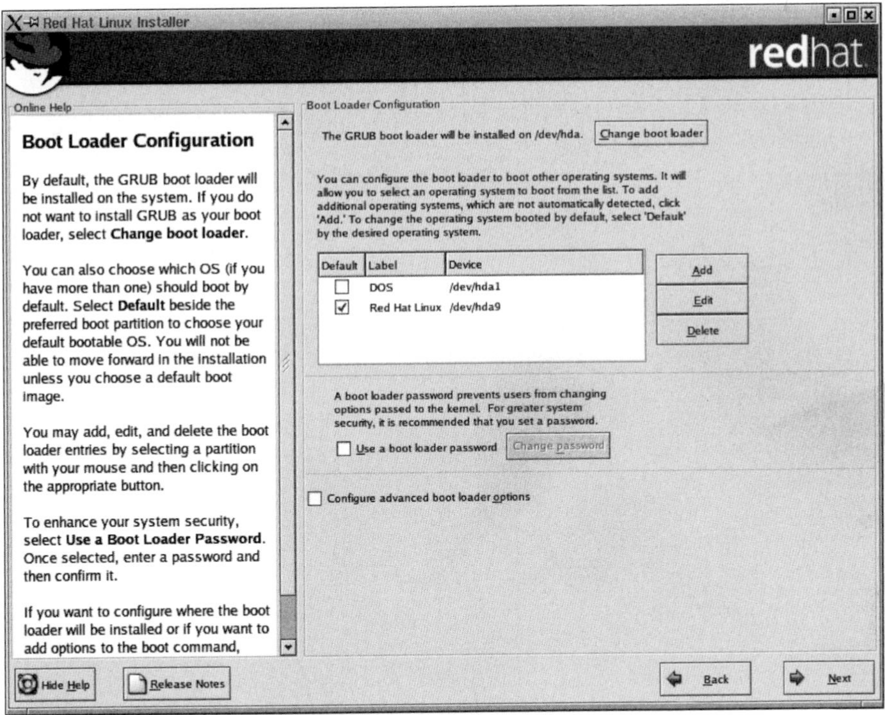

Figure 3-12 Boot Loader Configuration window

To select network configuration settings and a Red Hat Linux windowing environment:

1. In the Network Configuration window, the top section is entitled Network Devices. See Figure 3-13. This section shows the NIC that the Setup program detected. Click the **Edit** button to change the IP configuration.
2. The Edit Interface eth0 dialog opens. See Figure 3-14. Click the **Configure using DHCP** check box to remove the check mark. When you do, the text boxes for the IP Address and Netmask become enabled. Enter your IP address and netmask in these text boxes. The examples use **192.168.0.100** as the IP address, and **255.255.255.0** as the netmask. Click **OK** to return to the Network Configuration window.

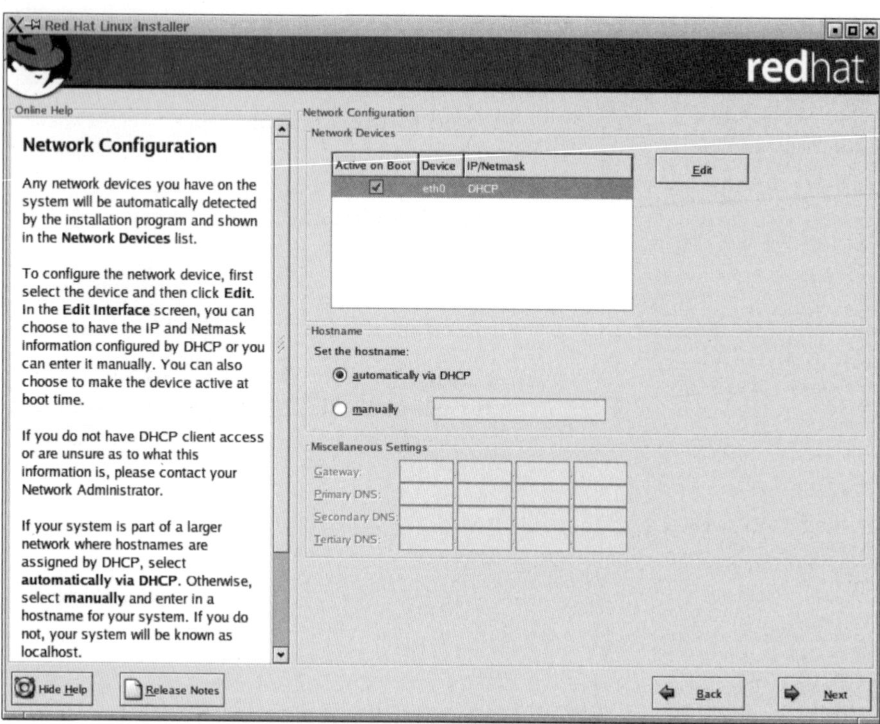

Figure 3-13 Network Configuration window

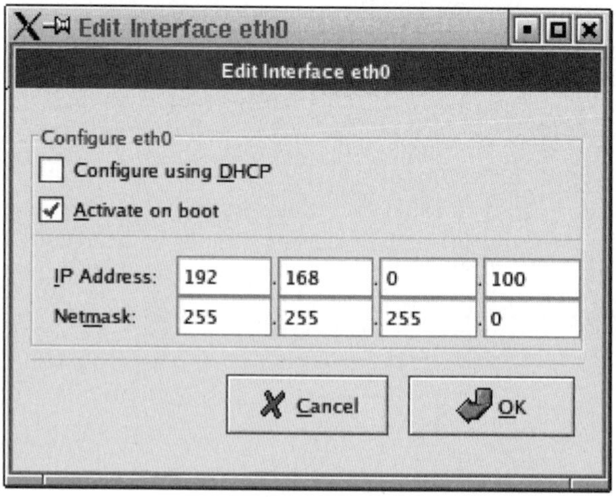

Figure 3-14 Edit Interface eth0 dialog box

3. Enter a host name such as **web1**, which corresponds to the computer name you used for Windows. If appropriate for your environment, you can enter the gateway address, which is the address of your router. For a Web server, the router would be connected to the Internet. You should also enter the primary DNS address, which you would get from your ISP unless you are installing DNS yourself. You will install DNS in the next chapter so for the primary DNS, enter the same IP address that you used in Step 2, and then click **Next**.
4. The Error With Data dialog box opens if you did not specify a gateway address, which you do not need in a student environment. Click **Continue**.
5. You will set up network security later, so click **No firewall** in the Firewall Configuration window, and then click **Next**. In a production environment, you could select the medium security level and allow selected services such as FTP.
6. Click **Next** in the Additional Language Support window, unless you have specific language requirements.
7. The Time Zone Selection window opens. Use the list boxes if you want to make changes to the time zones, and then click **Next**.
8. In the Account Configuration window, enter **password** as the root password, and then confirm it by typing **password** again in the second field for the student environment. (You will add users in Chapter 5.) In a production environment, you would enter a more secure password as described under the section on Windows 2000. Click **Next**.
9. The Package Group Selection window opens. See Figure 3-15. Under Desktops, you can select either GNOME or KDE. Because KDE is more common in most Linux distributions, click the **KDE Desktop Environment** check box.

   Production environments often have each computer specialize in a single server software package. In a computer lab, make sure that the following are checked under servers: **Web Server**, **Windows File Server**, **DNS Name Server**, **FTP Server**, and **News Server**. You will configure these servers and manually install other servers later. Click the **Text-based Internet** and **Printing Support** check boxes to remove the check marks, because they are not typically used in a Web environment. Click **Next** when you finish.
10. Click **Next** in the About to Install window to start the installation.

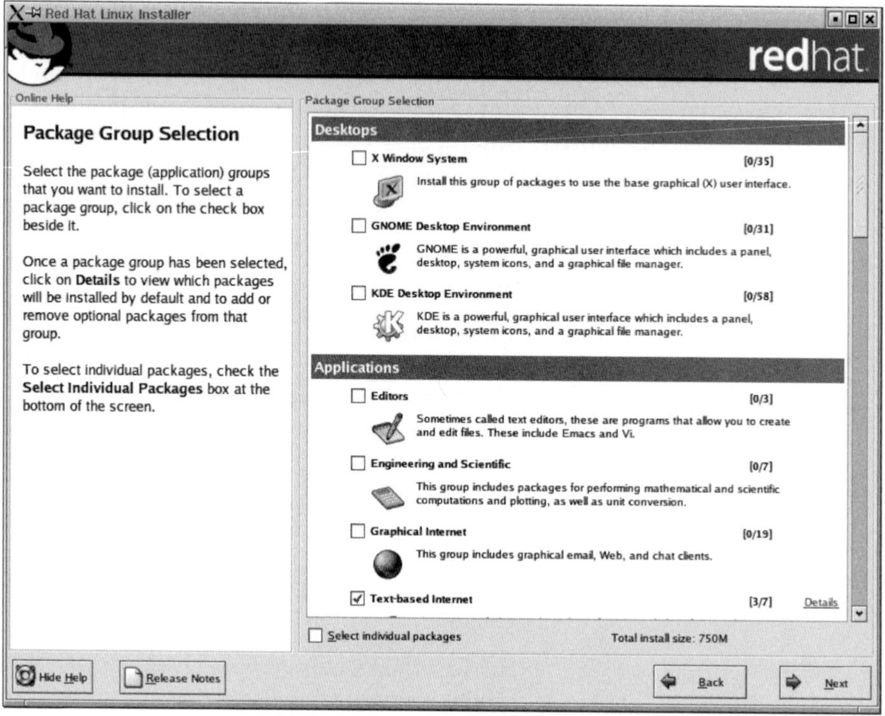

Figure 3-15 Package Group Selection window

The Setup program formats the Linux partitions and then installs the operating system while the Installing Packages window is active. Have Red Hat Linux CD 2 available.

To finish installing Red Hat Linux 8:

1. When the computer ejects CD 1, insert CD 2 and then click **OK**.
2. After the packages are installed, the Boot Disk Creation window opens. Because you may need a boot disk to start Linux, accept the default of **Yes, I would like to create a boot disk** by clicking **Next**. The Insert a floppy disk dialog box opens. Insert a floppy disk and click **Make boot disk**.
3. Your video adapter should be highlighted in the Graphical Interface (X) Configuration window. Click **Next**. If you do not have a supported video adapter, select **Unsupported VGA compatible** before clicking **Next**.
4. The Monitor Configuration window opens. If your monitor is highlighted, click **Next**. Otherwise, select the configuration closest to your monitor in the Generic section.

5. The Customize Graphical Configuration window opens. You can change the color depth and screen resolution, if necessary. Click **Next** to continue.
6. The Congratulations window opens. Remove the floppy disk and click **Exit**. The computer reboots.

To start Linux for the first time:

1. After your computer restarts, the GRUB window opens. If you installed Windows, that option appears under the selection for DOS. Accept the default of **Red Hat Linux** by pressing **Enter**.
2. Because this is the first time you have started Linux, the Red Hat Setup Agent is started to guide you through some basic configuration steps. Click **Forward**.
3. The Date and Time Configuration window opens. Make any necessary changes, and then click **Forward**.
4. If Setup detected a sound card, you can click **Play test sound** to test it. Click **Forward** to continue.
5. The Red Hat Update Agent window opens. If the product was purchased and you are connected to the Internet, you can register the product. In a student environment, you click the **No, I do not want to register my system** option button. Click **Forward** to continue.
6. The Install Additional Software window opens. This window allows you to install the Red Hat Linux Documentation CD, the Red Hat Installation CDs, and any additional CDs. Because you have already installed the software you need for now, click **Forward**.
7. Click **Forward** in the Finished Setup! window.
8. The login window prompts you for a user name. Type **root**, and then press **Enter**. Enter your password, such as **password**, and then press **Enter**. If a message appears regarding a missing sound driver, click **OK**.
9. Click the **Red Hat** icon in the lower-left corner of the desktop, and then click **Logout**.
10. The End session for root dialog box opens. Click **Logout**.
11. You are prompted again for your user name. On the bottom of the screen, click **System**.
12. A dialog box opens, giving you the default option of shutting down the computer. You can also click the **Reboot the computer** option button. Once you have selected the appropriate option, click **OK**. When the Are you sure you want to shut down the machine? dialog box opens, click **Yes** to continue.

An Introduction to Linux Commands

If this occasion marks your first exposure to Linux, you need to know enough commands to perform basic functions such as editing files and finding directories. When you use Linux as a Web server, you edit only a few files. In Linux, the two common windowing environments are GNOME and KDE; both environments are similar to Windows and easy to use.

Figure 3-16 shows the typical desktop for Linux using KDE. Because you might work in a different windowing environment in Linux or none at all, the following examples use the command-line interface, also called the shell interface. To open the shell interface in KDE, you click the Red Hat icon in the panel at the bottom of the screen, point to System Tools, and click Terminal.

Figure 3-16 KDE desktop

If you have used the command-line interface in any Windows product, you will find the shell interface very similar. However, some notable differences exist:

- Linux has no drive letters; in Windows, different partitions have different drive letters, such as C: and D:.

- In Linux, the root of the disk is /. Even though you may create different partitions for /home and /usr, all of them still start at /.
- In Linux, you use the forward slash (/) instead of the backward slash (\) that you use in Windows.

The Linux file system is organized in a hierarchy that is similar to the Windows file hiearchy. Shell commands typically require a reference to the file system, so it is a good idea to understand how you refer to files and directories. For example, suppose you need to edit, move, or copy a file called products.html, which is found in /var/www/research. The exact location of this file is called the **path**. The complete path to the previous file, including the file itself, is /var/www/research/products.html.

You can use this path with any command that requires a reference to the file. The "/" at the beginning of the path means to start at the root of the drive. If you do not have a "/" at the beginning, the path begins at the current position in the directory structure. For example, if you are working in the /var/www directory and you want to reference the products.html file, you would type research/products.html.

You can also use two dots in your command (..) to move up one directory in the structure. For example, if you were working in the /var/www/html directory and you wanted to reference the products.html file, you could type ../research/products.html.

Before you can use a floppy disk, you must perform a special step: You must **mount** the drive. Mounting the drive makes the system recognize the floppy disk in the drive. For example, if you insert a floppy disk in the drive and then type mount /mnt/floppy, the path to the floppy disk becomes /mnt/floppy.

Armed with this introduction to paths, you are ready to learn some useful commands:

- *ls*—List the contents of a directory. You can type `ls -a` to list hidden files and `ls -l` to see all the characteristics of a file, including the file permissions. You can use the asterisk (*) wildcard character to represent one or more characters. For example, to display all.conf files, you would type `ls *.conf`. You can also combine options, as in `ls -a -l*.conf`. If you have mounted a floppy disk, you can type `ls /mnt/floppy` to see the disk contents.
- *cd*—Change the directory. If you need to perform a number of operations in a single directory, such as editing multiple files, it might be easier to move to that directory and then start the editor. For example, to reach the www directory, which is below /var, you would type `cd /var/www`. To move to the html directory, which is below /var/www, you could type `cd /var/www/html` or `cd html`.

- *mkdir*—Make (create) a directory. For example, you may need to create a directory in your Web site for HTML files. To create a directory called secure in the /var/www/html directory, you could type **`mkdir /var/www/html/secure`**. If you were already in the /var/www/html directory, you could simply type **`mkdir secure`** to create the directory.
- *rmdir*—Remove a directory. If you created a directory called secure with the previous command and then decided to remove it, you could type **`rmdir secure`**, assuming that you were already in /var/www/html.
- *mv*—Move and/or rename a file. To move a file called ftpaccess from /etc to /var/ftp, you could type **`mv /etc/ftpaccess /var/ftp/ftpaccess`**. If you were in the /var/www/html directory and just finished editing a file called info.tml, you could rename it by typing **`mv info.tml info.html`**.
- *cp*—Copy a file. This command is like the **`mv`** command, except that it does not delete the original copy. For example, to copy a file called ftpaccess from /etc to /var/ftp, you could type **`cp /etc/ftpaccess /var/ftp/ftpaccess`**. The **`cp`** command is useful when you want to make a backup file before you start editing a configuration file. Assuming that you were in the /etc directory, you could make a backup copy of ftpaccess before editing it by typing **`cp ftpaccess ftpaccess.backup`**. To copy /etc/ftpaccess to the floppy disk, you would type **`cp /etc/ftpaccess /mnt/floppy/ftpaccess`**.
- *locate*—Find a file if you forget where it is located. For example, to find a file called httpd.conf, you would type **`locate httpd.conf`**.
- *kedit*—Edit a file. This command is unique to the KDE windowing environment and assumes that KDE has been installed. It allows you to edit an existing file or create a file to edit. To edit /etc/ftpaccess, for example, you would type **`kedit /etc/ftpaccess`**. If the ftpaccess file did not exist, this command would create it.

Many other shell commands exist, but the preceding list covers the most important ones. Other commands with special purposes, such as monitoring programs that are running, are covered in a later chapter.

All Web administrators need to know the commands described in this section, but students without a background in command-line interfaces can perform the same tasks more easily in the KDE windowing environment using a program called **Konqueror**. You can open this program by double-clicking the Home icon on the KDE desktop. The screen that appears is similar to Figure 3-17.

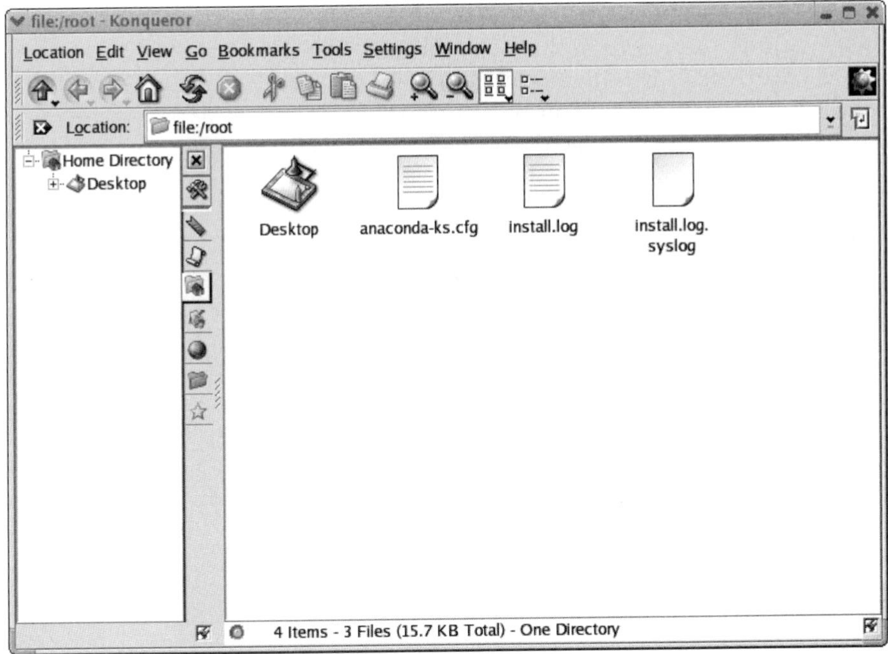

Figure 3-17 Home directory

Notice that the location is identified as file:/root. You can use the panel on the left to move to a new directory.

To move to the etc directory in Linux using the KDE desktop:

1. Start the Linux server, and log on with your user name and password. Double-click the **Home** icon on the desktop. The Konqueror window shown in Figure 3-17 opens.
2. Click the **Root Directory** tab icon in the vertical tab bar (the second tab from the bottom), and then click the **etc** folder in the left panel. The right panel displays a list of the directories and files within etc. Directories are indicated by folder icons, and text files are indicated by page icons, as shown in Figure 3-18.

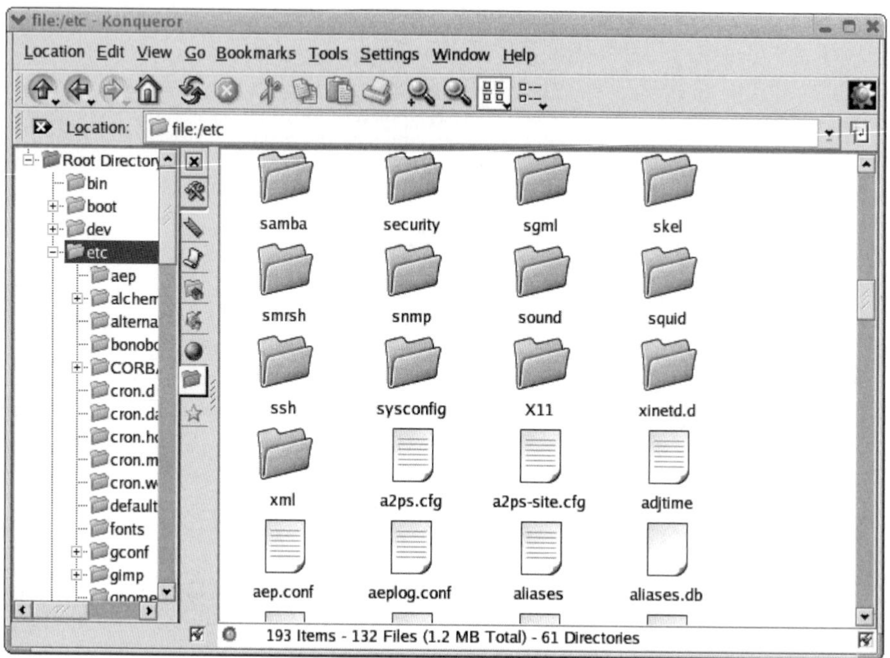

Figure 3-18 Contents of etc directory

Directory and text file manipulation are similar in Windows and Linux. You should practice working with directories and files in Linux, but you should not delete or rename any existing directory or file unless your instructor requests it.

To create directories and files in Linux:

1. In the Konqueror window, click the **Home Directory** tab in the vertical tab bar, and then click **Home Directory** in the left panel. Right-click a blank part of the right panel, point to **Create New**, and then click **Directory**.
2. Type the name of the new directory, and then press **Enter**.
3. Find the name of the directory in the list and double-click it. You are now in your new directory.
4. Create a file called **test.txt** by right-clicking the right panel, pointing to **Create New**, and clicking **Text File**.
5. Type the filename, and then press **Enter**.
6. To edit the file, right-click it, point to **Open With**, and then click **Text Editor**. The icons in the text editor should be familiar to anyone who has used Windows Notepad, as you can see in Figure 3-19.

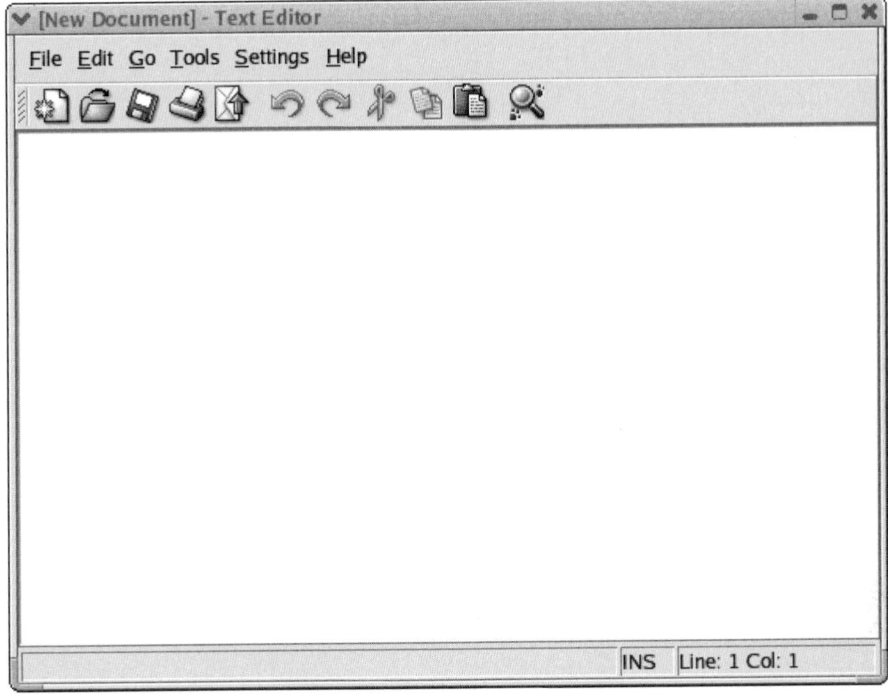

Figure 3-19 Kedit text editor

7. Type some sample text, and then click the floppy disk icon to save the file.
8. To close the file, click **File** on the menu bar, and then click **Quit**.

When you return to the file listing, it includes another file with the same name as the one you created, except that it ends with a tilde (~). This file is a backup of the original file.

If you have a floppy disk in the drive and the drive is mounted, you can view its contents by clicking the Root Directory tab and using the left panel to find /mnt/floppy. As in Windows, you can drag a file from the right panel to any directory in the left panel, including /mnt/floppy, to copy the file.

CONFIGURING TCP/IP IN WINDOWS AND LINUX

Understanding TCP/IP configuration is important, because you might need to change it if you type your IP address incorrectly, if another computer on the network has the same IP address, or if you move the computer to a different network. You might also need to add or change DNS information. Before you make any changes, you should determine your TCP/IP configuration.

Determining the TCP/IP Configuration

You can see the basic TCP/IP configuration from the command prompt in both Windows and Linux.

To see the basic TCP/IP configuration in Windows:

1. Click **Start**, point to **Programs** (**All Programs** in Windows 2003), point to **Accessories**, and then click **Command Prompt**.
2. At the command prompt, type **ipconfig** and then press **Enter**. Figure 3-20 shows a Command Prompt window similar to the one that you see.

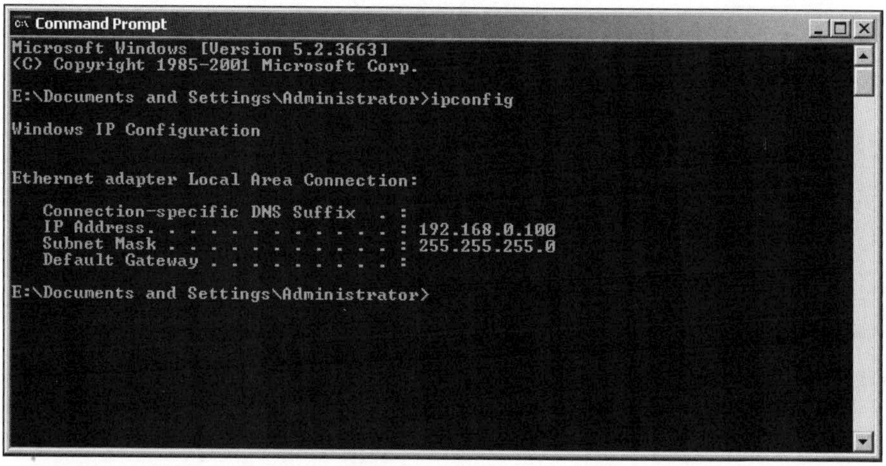

```
Command Prompt
Microsoft Windows [Version 5.2.3663]
(C) Copyright 1985-2001 Microsoft Corp.

E:\Documents and Settings\Administrator>ipconfig

Windows IP Configuration


Ethernet adapter Local Area Connection:

    Connection-specific DNS Suffix  . :
    IP Address. . . . . . . . . . . . : 192.168.0.100
    Subnet Mask . . . . . . . . . . . : 255.255.255.0
    Default Gateway . . . . . . . . . :

E:\Documents and Settings\Administrator>
```

Figure 3-20 Basic Windows TCP/IP configuration using ipconfig

Figure 3-20 shows the TCP/IP information based on the installation example in this chapter. If a network is connected to the Internet, a value appears for the default gateway, which is the IP address of a computer with a connection to another network. For a typical Web server, the default gateway would be the IP address of your router connected to the CSU/DSU.

To see the basic TCP/IP configuration in Linux, type the command `ifconfig` in the shell interface. The window that appears looks like Figure 3-21.

The Linux response is more detailed, but you can still determine the IP address and the subnet mask. The name *eth0* refers to the NIC in your computer. If your computer had second NIC, it would be named *eth1*. The name *lo* refers to the loopback address; if TCP/IP is installed, the loopback IP address of 127.0.0.1 is available, even if the NIC is not configured. If you need to make changes to the TCP/IP configuration, use the GUI in Windows and KDE in Linux.

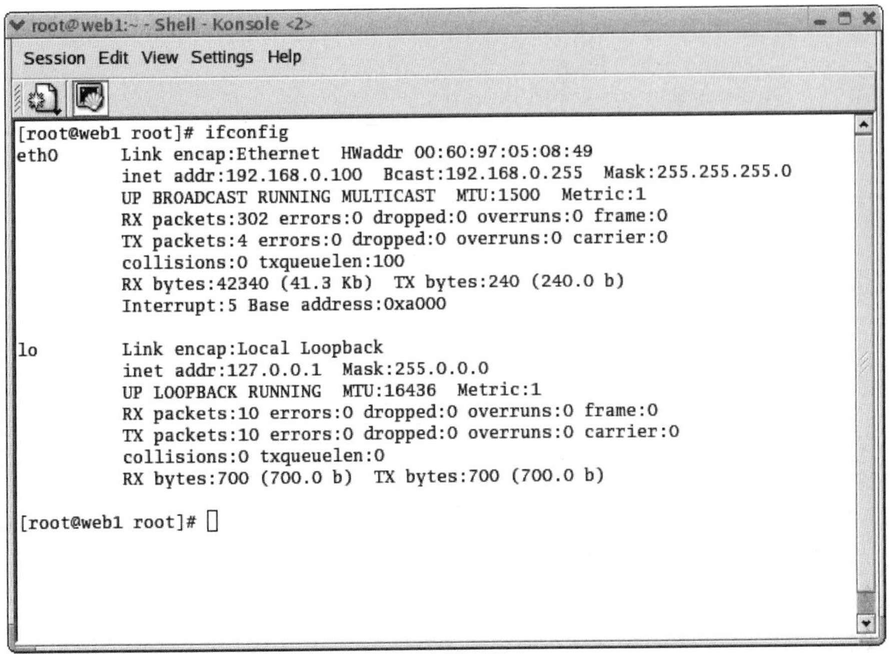

Figure 3-21 Basic Linux TCP/IP configuration using ifconfig

Configuring the IP Address in TCP/IP

This section focuses on setting up the IP address in TCP/IP.

To change the TCP/IP configuration in Windows 2000 or Windows 2003:

1. *In Windows 2003*: Click **Start**, point to **Control Panel**, point to **Network Connections**, and then click **Local Area Connection**.

   In Windows 2000: Click **Start**, point to **Settings**, point to **Network and Dial-up Connections**, and then click **Local Area Connection**.

2. In the Local Area Connection Status dialog box, click the **Properties** button.
3. In the next dialog box, select **Internet Protocol (TCP/IP)**, and then click the **Properties** button.
4. If necessary, change the IP address and the subnet mask.
5. To exit, click **OK** twice, and then click **Close** twice.

In Linux, you perform the following steps to change the IP address and subnet mask.

To change the TCP/IP configuration in Linux:

1. Click the **Red Hat** icon in the lower-left corner of the desktop, point to **System Settings**, and then click **Network**.
2. The Network Configuration dialog box opens, as shown in Figure 3-22.

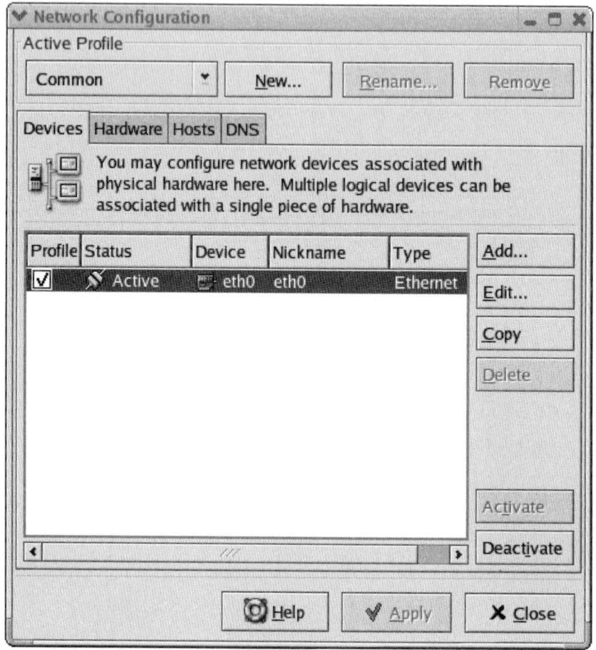

Figure 3-22 Network Configuration dialog box

3. Click the **Edit** button to change the properties of the NIC. The Ethernet Device dialog box opens. See Figure 3-23.
4. Now you are ready to change the IP configuration. Click **OK** to exit the Ethernet Device dialog box.
5. Click **Apply**, and then click **Close** in the Network Configuration dialog box.

Now that you have confirmed that your IP configuration is correct, you need to test it.

Testing the TCP/IP Configuration

You can test whether the TCP/IP protocol has been installed correctly by pinging the **loopback** IP address, which is 127.0.0.1. This IP address tests basic TCP/IP connectivity. In Windows, pinging will stop after four attempts; in Linux, it stops when you press Ctrl+C. At a command line, you type `ping` followed by an IP address or host name. In both Windows and Linux, you can use the name *localhost* in place of 127.0.0.1. Once you have made sure that TCP/IP has been installed correctly, you can ping the actual IP address that you configured: `ping 192.168.0.100`.

Figure 3-23 Ethernet Device dialog box

If you were connected to a router, the next step would be to ping its IP address. If the router was connected to the Internet, then you would ping an IP address on the Internet. Finally, assuming that you had DNS installed, you could ping *www.redhat.com* and see the replies from that site. In some cases, a site such as *www.microsoft.com* will not respond to ping requests, even though you can use the URL *www.microsoft.com* in a browser. Pinging is a commonly used technique when you are configuring a firewall.

Chapter Summary

- Windows and Linux installations share many common tasks, such as disk partitioning. It is a good idea to keep the operating system and the application programs on separate partitions.
- The same computer can have multiple operating systems. You can group the Windows operating systems in a single boot menu and then use a boot floppy disk to boot to Linux.
- Naming computers is similar in both Windows and Linux. It is a good idea to keep the names simple and descriptive. Although Linux allows two computers to have the same name, it is nevertheless a good practice to use unique names.

- Windows and Linux are licensed in different ways, and different versions of Windows vary in their licensing procedures. In Windows products before Windows 2003, Microsoft trusted the customer to fulfill the licensing requirements. In Windows 2003, the product must be activated by Microsoft after installation to avoid piracy constraints. Linux is based on the GNU general public license, so the product is free.
- Microsoft and Red Hat Linux products have improved in their ability to recognize NICs and video adapters. In Windows NT, the recognition process is manual; in Windows 2000 and Windows 2003, the process is automatic.
- Installing Microsoft operating systems has become easier with each new product. Windows NT required some detailed information, including the exact path to the network drivers for your NIC. With Windows 2003, the selections focus on overall configuration information, such as internationalization data, date, time, and time zone. Red Hat Linux has also streamlined its installation process, supplementing it with online help.
- In Linux, you use basic commands such as `ls` to list the contents of a directory, `mkdir` to create a directory, `rmdir` to remove a directory, `mv` to move or rename a file, `cp` to copy a file, `cd` to change directories, and `locate` to find files.
- When you install an operating system, TCP/IP is one configuration you typically do not need to change. However, you do need to correct mistakes, and you must add TCP/IP entries, such as for DNS servers.

Review Questions

1. Multi-boot systems offer multiple options for booting a single operating system. True or False?
2. The ________________ is used by the hard disk to start the boot process.
   a. GRUB
   b. MBR
   c. LILO
   d. CDR
3. Which of the following are boot loaders?
   a. GRUB
   b. MBR
   c. LILO
   d. CDR

4. MBR stands for _______________.
   a. multi-booter
   b. master break record
   c. master boot record
   d. multiple boot recorder
5. Which of the following is *not* a Windows installation method?
   a. FTP installation
   b. network installation
   c. bootable CD installation
   d. floppy disk with nonbootable CD
6. What is an NFS drive?
   a. a Windows partition with security
   b. a high-speed CD-ROM
   c. a network drive to which Linux can connect
   d. a Linux drive with security
7. Which of the following operating systems use signed drivers?
   a. Windows NT
   b. Windows 2000
   c. Windows 2003
   d. Linux
8. The URL for the Microsoft Hardware Compatibility List is _______________.
9. Which of the following items does not need documenting?
   a. processor type
   b. PCI version
   c. amount of RAM
   d. drive interface
10. A(n) _______________ is a logical division of the hard disk.
    a. drive letter
    b. root
    c. MBR
    d. partition

11. The boot partition contains ________________.
    a. the specific files needed to boot Windows
    b. the Windows operating system files
    c. the MBR
    d. none of the above
12. In Linux, which partition is not needed?
    a. swap
    b. /
    c. /usr
13. Which Linux partition would contain HTML files?
    a. /usr
    b. /web
    c. /var
    d. /boot
14. If you let Linux automatically partition the hard disk, which partition does not increase as the size of the hard disk increases?
    a. /var
    b. /usr
    c. /home
    d. /web
15. In Windows, a(n) ________________ contains improvements and corrections to an operating system after it has been installed.
    a. service pack
    b. service update
    c. patch
    d. update pack
16. In a Windows network with multiple servers, the per server method of licensing is typically the best. True or False?
17. Red Hat Linux is licensed under the ________________.
    a. Red Hat proprietary license
    b. Linux standard licensing
    c. GNU general public license
    d. any of the above, depending on the version

18. For Windows, which file system gives you the most security?
    a. FAT
    b. NTFS
    c. NFS
    d. HiSec
19. Which of the following has the least demanding hardware requirements?
    a. Windows 2000
    b. Windows 2003
    c. Linux
20. What is the Linux command to move to a new directory?
    a. `mv`
    b. `cd`
    c. `md`
    d. `cv`

Hands-on Projects

To complete most of the Hands-on Projects in this book, you need to install Linux and then install either Windows 2000 or Windows 2003. If you decide to install Windows or Linux, but not both, you can still complete some Hands-on Projects in each chapter.

Project 3-1

Check with your instructor to find another IP address that you can use for your Web server. You will return to your Windows 2000 or Windows 2003 server installation and change the IP address. The following steps assume an IP address of 10.1.2.3, a subnet mask of 255.0.0.0, and a default gateway of 10.1.1.1.

To change the IP address in Windows 2000 or Windows 2003:

1. *In Windows 2003*: Click **Start**, point to **Control Panel**, point to **Network Connections**, and then click **Local Area Connection**.

   In Windows 2000: Click **Start**, point to **Settings**, point to **Network and Dial-up Connections**, and click **Local Area Connection**.
2. The Local Area Connection Status dialog box opens. Click the **Properties** button. The Local Area Connection Properties dialog box opens. See Figure 3-24 for the version for Windows 2003. The dialog box for Windows 2000 is very similar.

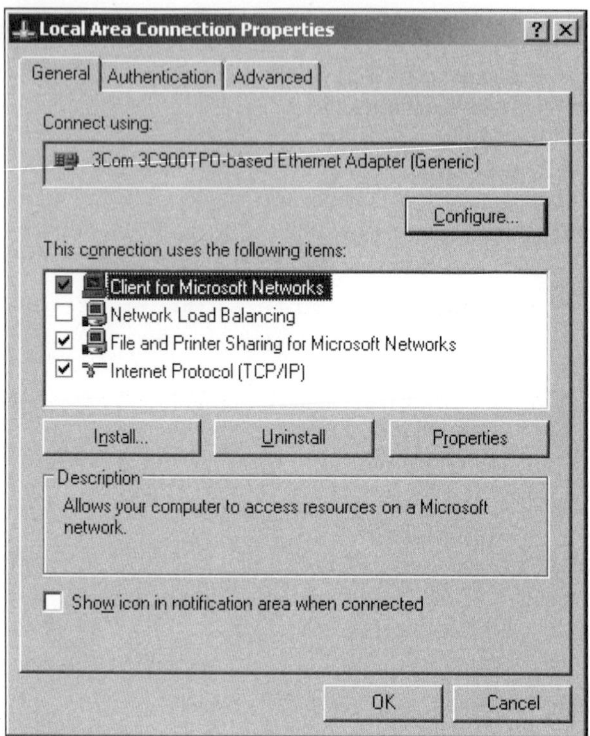

Figure 3-24 Local Area Connection Properties dialog box

3. Click **Internet Protocol (TCP/IP)** (just the text, not the check box next to it). The text in the Description box changes to describe TCP/IP.
4. Click **Properties**. The Internet Protocol (TCP/IP) Properties dialog box opens.
5. Enter an IP address of **10.1.2.3**. The IP address uniquely defines this computer.
6. Enter a subnet mask of **255.0.0.0**. The subnet mask defines which part of the address refers to the network and which part of the address refers to the specific computer (host). The 255 in the first octet defines the first octet in the IP address as the network portion of the address, which is 10. The other octets define the host portion of the address, which is 1.2.3.
7. Enter a default gateway of **10.1.1.1**. The computer uses this IP address to send packets if the destination IP address is outside the local network.
8. Click **OK** to return to the Local Area Connection Properties dialog box.
9. Click **OK** to return to the Local Area Connection Status window.
10. Close the window.

Project 3-2

In this project you test the configuration change that you made in Project 3-1. You use the ping utility to make sure that the IP address responds.

To use the ping utility to test the IP address:

1. *In Windows 2000*: Click **Start**, point to **Programs**, point to **Accessories**, and then click **Command Prompt**.

   In Windows 2003: Click **Start**, and then click **Command Prompt**.

2. Type **ping 10.1.2.3** and press **Enter**. If you do not receive an error message, the IP address is correct.

Project 3-3

In Windows, you might need to change the computer name, especially if you accept the default during installation.

To change the computer name from web1 to web1a in Windows 2003:

1. Click **Start**, point to **Control Panel**, and then click **System**.
2. The System Properties dialog box opens. See Figure 3-25. This dialog box shows the basic system configuration, including registration information and the type of computer on which it is running.

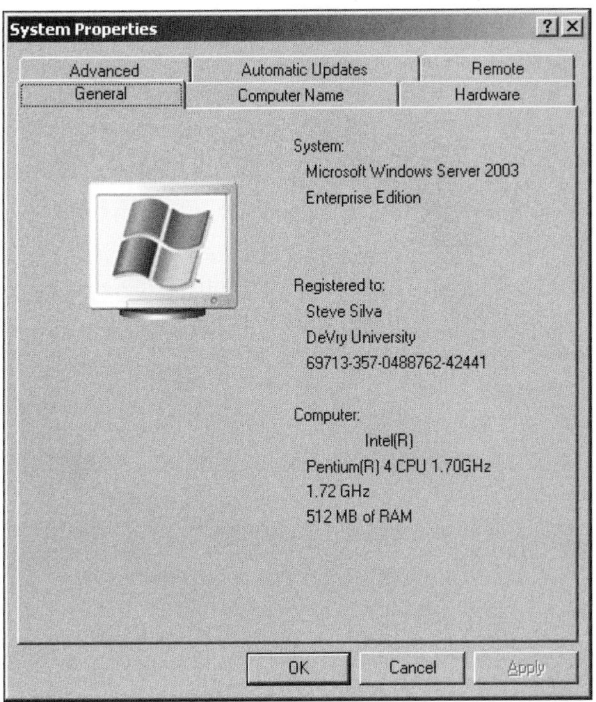

Figure 3-25 Windows 2003 System Properties dialog box

3. Click the **Computer Name** tab. See Figure 3-26. Now you can enter a description for the server.

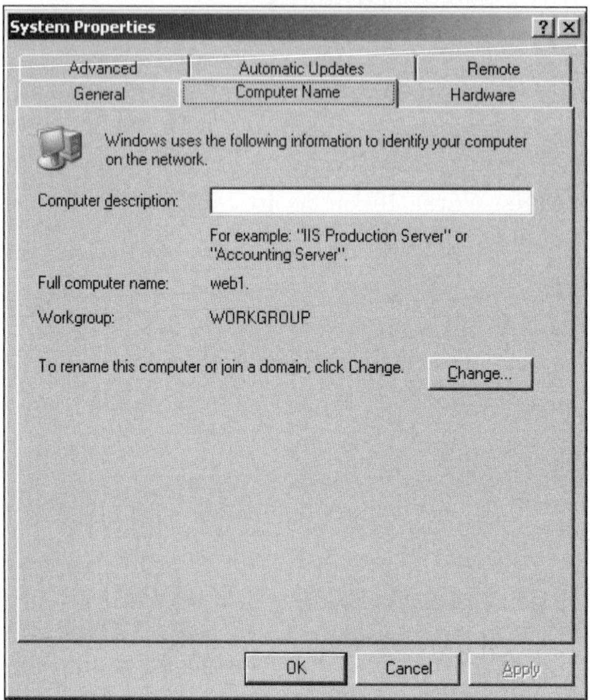

Figure 3-26 Computer Name tab

4. Click **Change**. The Computer Name Changes dialog box opens. See Figure 3-27.
5. Enter **web1a** for the computer name.
6. Click **OK** to accept the change. The Computer Name Changes message box opens, explaining that you must restart this computer for the changes to take effect.
7. Click **OK** to acknowledge the message and return to the System Properties dialog box.
8. Click **OK** to exit the System Properties dialog box. The System Settings Change message box opens.
9. Click **Yes** to restart the computer.

Now repeat the steps and change the computer back to its original name, such as web1.

Computer Name Changes

You can change the name and the membership of this computer. Changes may affect access to network resources.

Computer name:

web1

Full computer name:

web1.

More...

Member of

Domain:

Workgroup:

WORKGROUP

OK Cancel

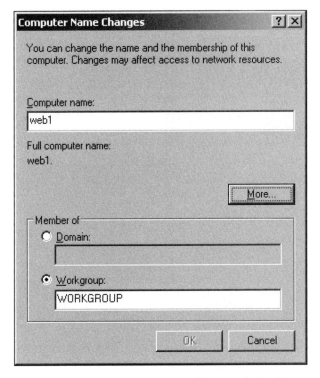

Figure 3-27 Computer Name Changes dialog box

Project 3-4

Although changing the computer name in Windows 2000 is similar to changing it in Windows 2003, there are some differences, which you examine in this project.

To change the computer name in Windows 2000:

1. Click **Start**, point to **Settings**, and then click **Control Panel**.
2. Double-click **System**. The System Properties dialog box opens. See Figure 3-28. You see the basic system configuration, including registration information and the type of computer on which it is running.
3. Click the **Network Identification** tab. The computer name and workgroup are displayed. See Figure 3-29.

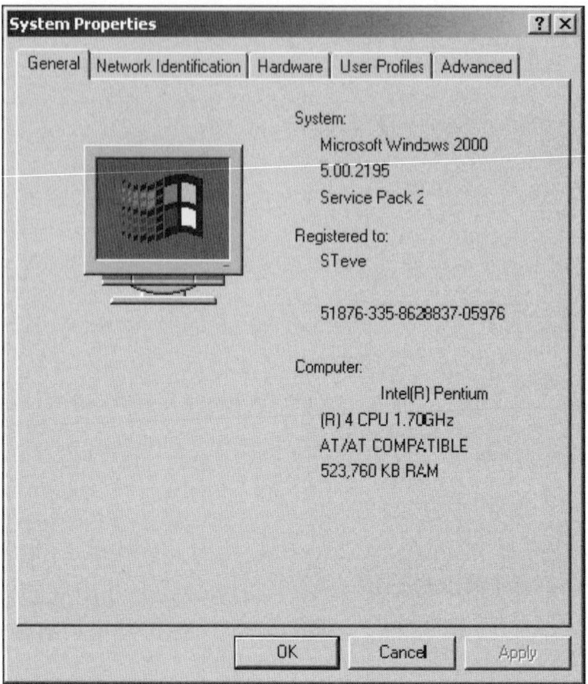

Figure 3-28 Windows 2000 System Properties dialog box

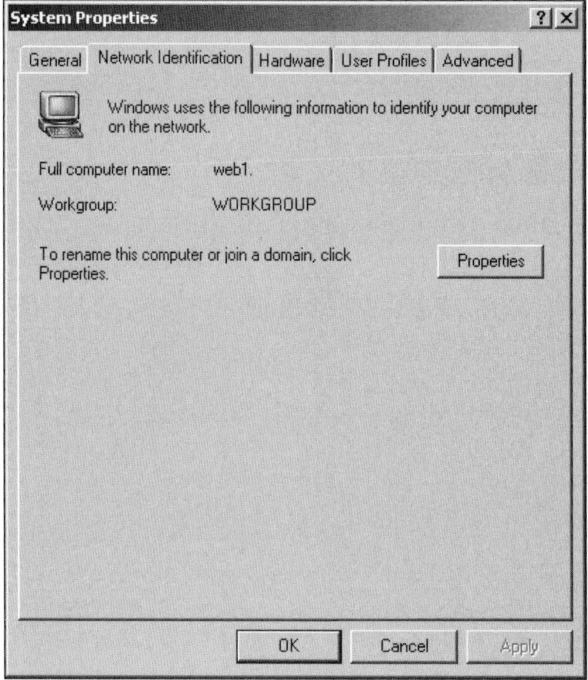

Figure 3-29 Network Identification tab

4. Click **Properties**. The Identification Changes dialog box opens. See Figure 3-30. Change the computer name to web1a.

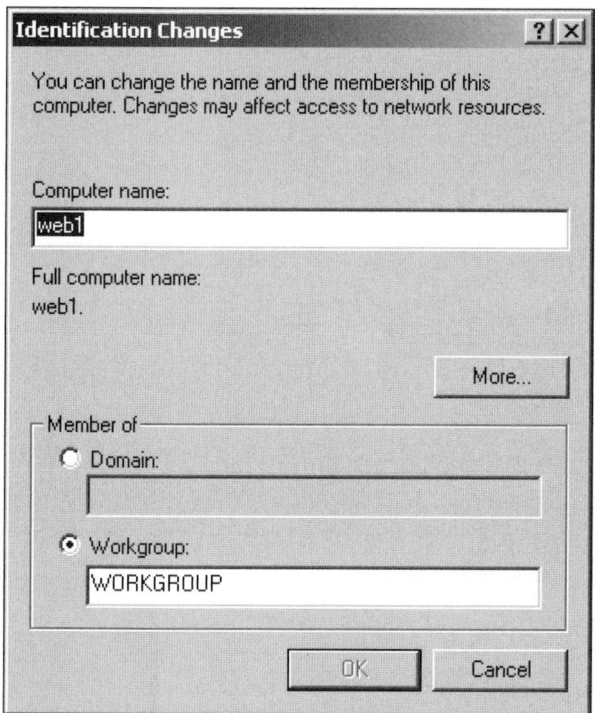

Figure 3-30 Identification Changes dialog box

5. Click **OK**. The Network Identification message box opens, reminding you to reboot the computer for the changes to take effect.
6. Click **OK** to acknowledge the reminder. You return to the System Properties dialog box.
7. Click **OK**. The System Settings Change message box appears, asking whether you want to restart the computer.
8. Click **Yes** to restart the computer.

Now repeat the steps and change the computer back to its original name, such as web1.

Project 3-5

The Windows installation wizard installed the Windows components for a typical server. Sometimes, however, you need to check which components you have installed. In this project you will discover which components are installed and add a component.

To display Windows components:

1. *In Windows 2003*: Click **Start**, point to **Control Panel**, and then click **Add or Remove Programs**.

   In Windows 2000: Click **Start**, point to **Settings**, and then click **Control Panel**. The Control Panel window opens. Double-click **Add or Remove Programs**.
2. The Add or Remove Programs window opens. The right panel of this window is for programs you have installed, so it is blank. Click **Add/Remove Windows Components**. The Windows Components Wizard opens. See Figure 3-31. Notice that the Accessories and Utilities component is highlighted. The list will be slightly different for Windows 2000.

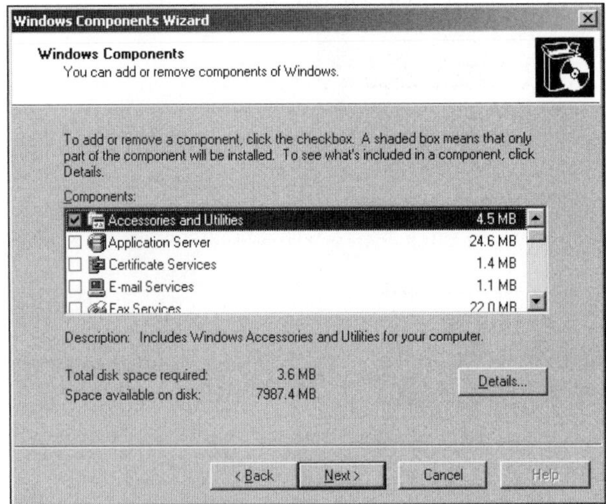

Figure 3-31 Windows Components Wizard

3. Click **Details** to find out the names of the subcomponents of Accessories and Utilities. The Accessories and Utilities dialog box opens. See Figure 3-32. The Accessories and Communications subcomponents have subcomponents of their own.
4. Click **OK** to close the window and return to the Windows Components Wizard dialog box. You can scroll down the window to find the Windows components that have been installed.
5. Click **Cancel** to exit the Windows Component Wizard dialog box.
6. Close the Add or Remove Programs window.
7. Close the Control Panel window, if necessary.

Project 3-6

When you install a Windows server, the screen resolution is often set to the maximum allowable by the hardware. This level may not be comfortable for you, so it is a good idea to know how to change the resolution.

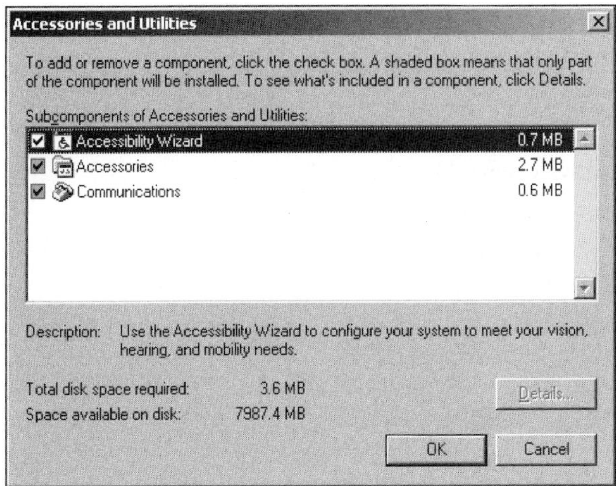

Figure 3-32 Accessories and Utilities dialog box

To change the screen resolution:

1. Right-click the desktop, and then click **Properties**. The Display Properties dialog box opens.
2. Click the **Settings** tab. You can change the screen resolution and the color quality.
3. Adjust the slider bar for screen resolution (screen area in Windows 2000) to lessen the resolution.
4. Click **OK**. The Monitor Settings dialog box opens, stating that you have 15 seconds to accept the changes.
5. Click **OK** to accept the changes.
6. Repeat Steps 1 through 5 to reset the screen resolution.

Project 3-7

You will use the Linux terminal program to get to the shell and the text editor called kedit often as you go through the rest of the chapters. It is much easier to copy shortcuts to these programs to the KDE panel, which is also known as the kicker. This bar is found along the bottom of the desktop. Another useful button to put on the KDE panel is one used to find files. To copy this button to the panel, you will drag and drop it.

To add the terminal program to the panel:

1. Right-click the panel (the bar at the bottom of the desktop), point to **Add**, point to **Button**, point to **System Tools**, and then click **Terminal**. Note the terminal icon on the panel.

To add the kedit icon to the panel:

1. Right-click the panel, point to **Add**, point to **Button**, point to **Extras**, point to **Accessories**, and then click **Text Editor**.

To add the locate icon to the panel:

1. Double-click the **Start Here** icon on the desktop. The Konqueror window opens in the Start Here directory. See Figure 3-33.

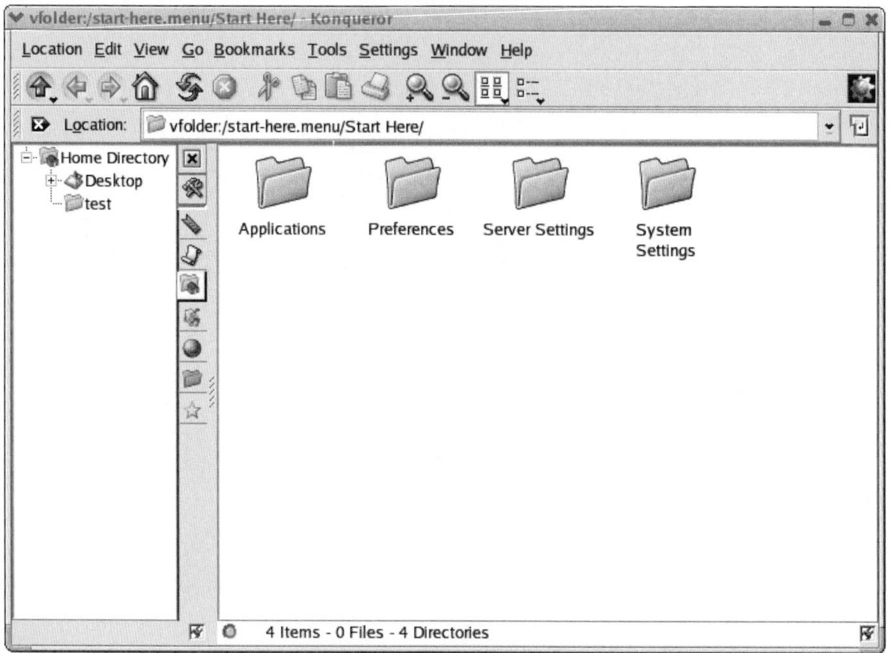

Figure 3-33 Start Here directory window

2. Double-click **Applications**. Konqueror displays the contents of the Application directory in the right panel. Note the icon labeled Find Files. See Figure 3-34.
3. Drag the **Find Files** icon to the panel.

To find the rc.local file:

1. Click the **Find Files** icon on the panel.
2. In the Named text box, type **rc.local**, which contains a list of programs to run when Linux is started.
3. Click **Find**. Nothing was found because it started looking in your home directory of /root.
4. Click the **Look in** list arrow and then click **file:/**, which represents the root of the server.
5. Click **Find**. You will notice what appears to be two copies of rc.local. Right-click each copy of rc.local, and then click **Properties**. What is the difference between the properties?

3

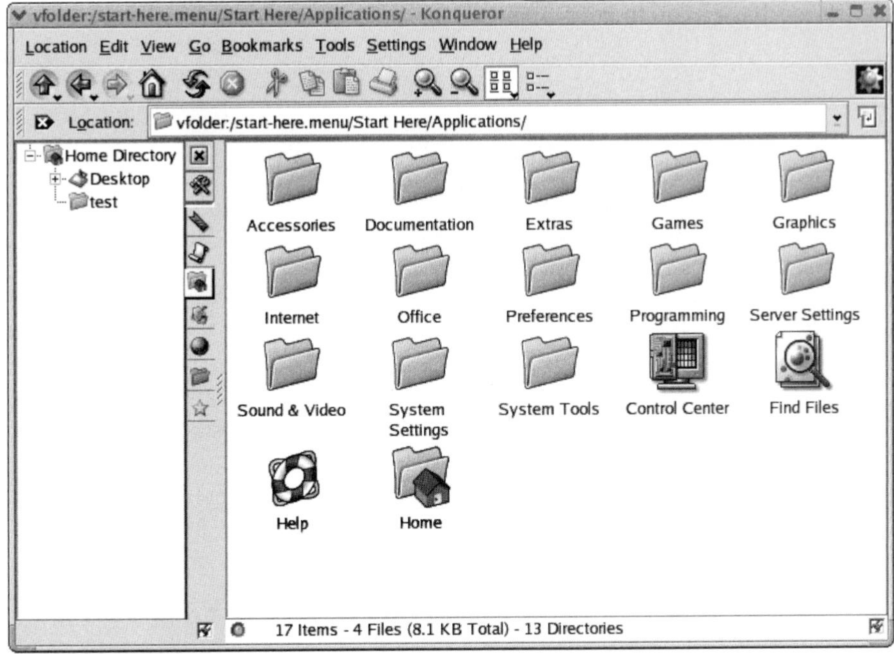

Figure 3-34 Konqueror window with Application icons

Project 3-8

Linux uses text files for configuration. It is a good idea to keep backup copies of these files. Because you use the shell so much, you need to know how to copy files between a floppy disk and your hard drive using the cp command-line copy utility.

To copy files to a floppy disk:

1. Click the **terminal icon** on the panel to open a shell.
2. Put a floppy disk in the drive.
3. Type **mount /mnt/floppy** to mount the floppy disk so that Linux will recognize it. (Be sure to press the spacebar after typing "mount".) Now the directory called floppy corresponds to the floppy disk. Notice that when you type the commands in steps 4 and 5, the light on the floppy disk does not become illuminated because the files are actually being stored in memory. It is only in Step 6 that the files are actually put on the floppy disk. If you took out the floppy disk before Step 6, there would be no files on it.
4. Type **cp /etc/named.conf /mnt/floppy** and press **Enter** to copy named.conf to the floppy disk. This file will be used in the next chapter.
5. Type **cp /etc/httpd/conf/httpd.conf /mnt/floppy** and press **Enter** to copy httpd.conf to the floppy disk. You will use this file to configure the Web server.

6. Type **umount /mnt/floppy** and press **Enter** to unmount the floppy disk. (Be sure to press the spacebar after typing "umount".) Linux will take whichever files in memory are destined for the floppy disk and write them to the disk.

Project 3-9

Because you are probably more accustomed to working with a GUI, it is also useful to know how to use KDE to copy files.

Use KDE to copy /etc/rc.d/rc.local to a floppy disk:

1. Put a floppy disk in the drive.
2. Double-click the **floppy icon** on the desktop. For a brief moment, a window opens, stating that it is mounting the floppy drive. The file:/mnt/floppy - Konqueror window opens. See Figure 3-35. The default starting point is your home directory, as you can see in the left panel.
3. Click the **Root Directory** tab on the vertical tab bar, which is the second tab from the bottom. Now you see the list of directories in the left panel.
4. In the left panel, expand the etc directory by clicking the **+** next to it.
5. In the left panel, click **rc.d** to display the contents of the directory. You now see the file named rc.local in the right panel; you want to copy this file. However, before you copy it, you have to be able to drop it on the /mnt/floppy directory in the left panel.
6. In the left panel, scroll down until you see the mnt directory. Click the **+** next to mnt. The window should be similar to Figure 3-36.
7. Drag **rc.local** from the right panel to the floppy directory in the left panel. A small dialog box opens asking whether you want to copy, move, or link the file.
8. Click **Copy Here** to copy the file to the floppy disk.
9. Close the window.

Project 3-10

In this project, you change the IP address of your Linux installation. Check with your instructor to find another IP address that you can use in this project. The following steps assume an IP address of 10.1.2.3, a subnet mask of 255.0.0.0, and a default gateway of 10.1.1.1.

To change the IP address in Linux:

1. Click the **Red Hat** icon, point to **System Settings**, and then click **Network**. By default, the Network Configuration dialog box opens to the Devices tab, which you use to change the IP address.
2. Click **Edit** to change the properties of the NIC. The Ethernet Device dialog box opens.

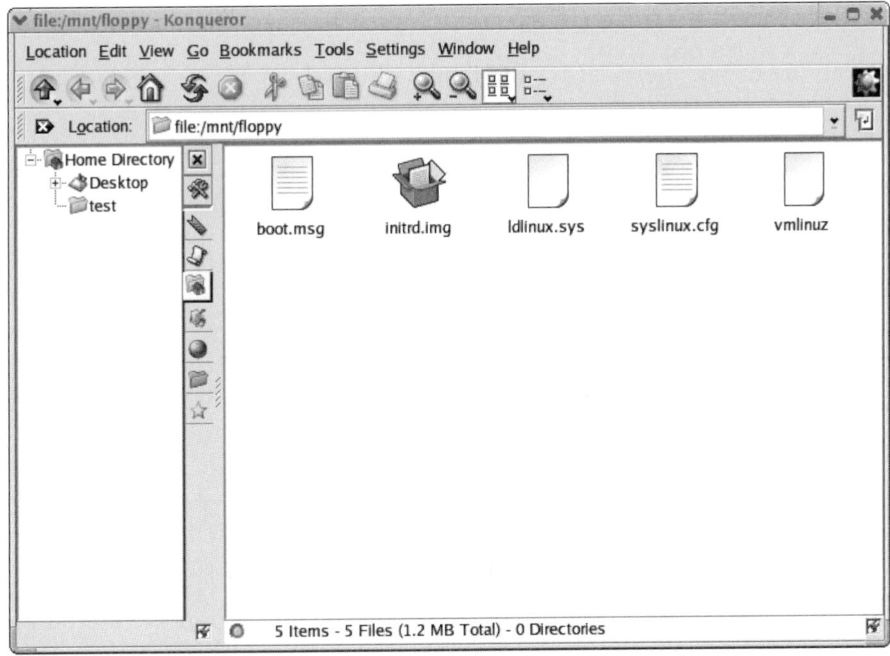

Figure 3-35 file:/mnt/floppy - Konqueror window

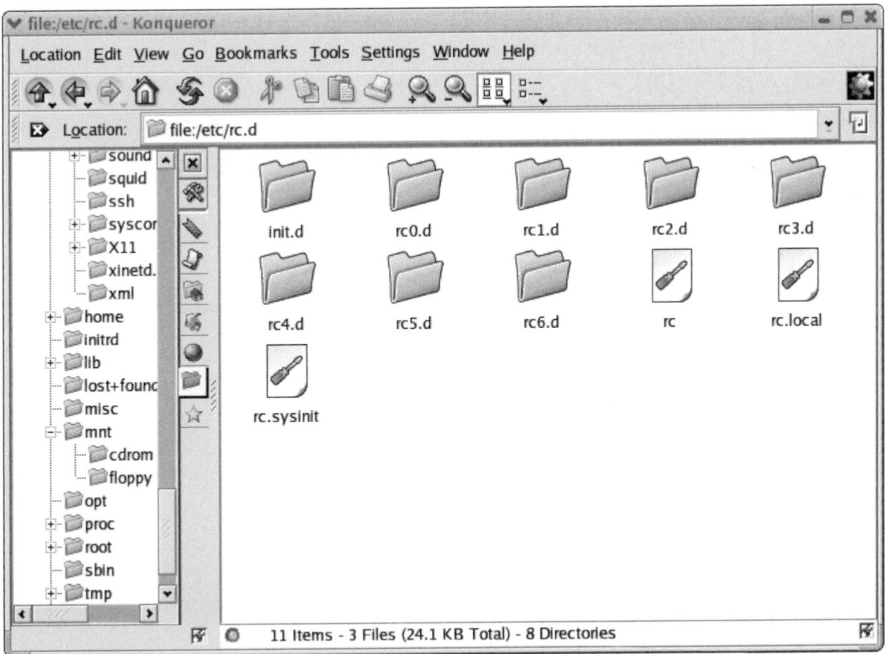

Figure 3-36 Window with files ready to copy

3. Enter **10.1.2.3** for the address.
4. Enter **255.0.0.0** for the subnet mask.
5. Enter **10.1.1.1** for the default gateway address.
6. Click **OK** to exit the Ethernet Device dialog box.
7. Click **Apply**, and then click **Close** on the Network Configuration dialog box.

Project 3-11

Locate and install the latest service pack for Windows. Some Windows 2000 software in future chapters will not function without a service pack.

Check whether there are any bug fixes for Red Hat Linux and, if so, install them.

CASE PROJECTS

Case Project 3-1

Your boss at TechnoWidgets, Inc., does not want to use Linux; she used it once before, when only the shell interface was available. Create a table of the shell interface commands and the corresponding way of achieving the same result in Konqueror. Your boss also referred to a shell command called `chown`; find out what it means and whether Konqueror can perform the same function.

Case Project 3-2

Your company is considering implementing a new Linux Web server. Until now, all of your servers have been Windows-based. Your boss is unfamiliar with Linux and has asked you to provide some information—specifically, data on how Linux compares with Windows with respect to support. Write a memo that compares the support needs of a Windows 2000 or Windows 2003 system versus a Linux system. Your boss wants a balanced comparison that draws on multiple sources. Include the cost of contacting Microsoft and Red Hat with a support question.

Case Project 3-3

Based on your memo, your boss is considering integrating Linux into the company. She has provided you with a test machine with which to become familiar with Linux. You want your initial configuration of the test machine to work as long as possible, and you've heard that proper partitioning can ease long-term growth on a system. Research some of the possible UNIX/Linux partitioning schemes and provide a document that can be used to configure the drive partitions on your new server. Provide an explanation of the partition setup you want to use.

CHAPTER

4

NAME RESOLUTION

In this chapter, you will:

- Understand the domain name service (DNS)
- Identify the components of DNS
- Configure zone files
- Install and configure DNS in Linux
- Understand name resolution in Windows
- Install and configure DNS in Windows 2000 and 2003
- Troubleshoot DNS
- Use WINS to resolve computer names in Windows

To allow users to access a Web site, Web server administrators need to know how to resolve names. In general, name resolution involves taking a common name of a network resource—a Web server, for instance—and converting it into a corresponding IP address. This scheme is convenient for computer users, because they remember names more easily than complex numbers. The Web server administrator is usually the person who makes sure that all servers connected to the Internet have appropriate names and reference valid IP addresses so that users can access them.

You can use the domain name service (DNS) and Windows Internet naming service (WINS) for name resolution. The primary purpose of DNS is to resolve an Internet name such as *www.redhat.com* to its corresponding IP address. A Microsoft Windows 2000 or Windows 2003 network uses DNS to resolve computer names on a local area network (LAN). Networks that still use Windows 9x and Windows NT Workstation require WINS to translate computer names to IP addresses. In the computer lab, you need to set up DNS servers for the operating systems you installed in Chapter 3 so you can simulate connecting to the servers using names such as *www.technowidgets.com* instead of IP addresses. Although browsers do not require that you use DNS names, e-mail servers do, as explained in Chapter 8. That is, you can type http://192.168.0.100 in a browser, but you cannot use ajones@192.168.0.100 in an e-mail client.

UNDERSTANDING THE DOMAIN NAME SERVICE (DNS)

You use DNS every time you surf the Internet, although you might not be aware of it. If you type *www.redhat.com* in your browser, for example, the DNS server translates that text into 66.187.232.56 because your request for the page must be sent to that IP address. In the following sections, you will learn about DNS components and their operation. First, examine the structure of the system.

DNS works like a telephone directory service. That is, just as a phone book correlates a person's name and phone number, DNS resolves common names for network resources to corresponding IP addresses. This process of converting a name to a numeric IP address, called **address resolution**, is convenient for Internet users—it is much easier to remember *www.linux.org* than 198.182.196.56. Address resolution also makes it easy for an administrator to move a server from one IP address to another. Without a naming service, the administrator would need to inform everyone using the server that the address had changed. With DNS, the administrator simply changes a record in a DNS configuration file and does not need to inform users.

While the best-known function of DNS is an Internet-wide service that converts host names into their corresponding IP addresses in browsers, DNS serves other important Internet functions. For example, it finds the IP addresses of e-mail servers for e-mail client software.

DNS is needed for more than the Internet. In a LAN, for example, computers must communicate with each other; therefore, the network requires a central directory of all its computers and their associated IP addresses. Windows 2000, Windows XP, and Windows 2003 Server support Dynamic DNS (DDNS), which updates DNS automatically when the IP address of a workstation changes or a new workstation is added to the network. In contrast, earlier Windows operating systems must use WINS for name resolution, as described later in this chapter.

Examining the Structure of the Internet Domains

DNS is organized into a hierarchical structure that defines domains. Likewise, the file system on your computer is arranged in a hierarchy. For example, the C: drive may have a folder called Program Files; within that folder could be a folder called Microsoft Office; and so on. Thus, each folder may contain one or more files. Linux uses a similar hierarchical structure. Just as you create folders to organize files, DNS arranges host names in a hierarchy to make them easier to manage and find. With tens of millions of hosts to organize, it faces a challenging task. The DNS hierarchical naming system consists of three levels:

- *Root level*—This level is the top of the hierarchy. The root is expressed by a period ("dot"). In common use, the trailing period is removed from domain names, but when you configure DNS services you must include it.

- *Top-level domain (TLD)*—This level identifies the most general portion of the domain name. It is the last part of the domain name—for example, com, edu, or org.
- *Second-level domain (SLD)*—This level identifies an entity within a top-level domain. The second-level domain name includes the top-level domain. Second-level domains can also be divided into further domain levels, called **subdomains**, as in the URL *www.arda.jones.name*. In this case, jones.name is the second-level domain controlled by the .name TLD, and arda.jones.name represents the subdomain that a person can register.

Identifying Top-Level Domains

Recall that a top-level domain identifies the most general part of the domain name, which is the highest category used to distinguish domain names. Table 4-1 lists some of the top-level Internet domains. The first seven listed are the original domains that were available on the Internet. The Internet Corporation for Assigned Names and Numbers (ICANN) approved the last seven in November 2000, so they are just coming into common use.

Table 4-1 Top-level Internet domains

Top-level domain	Description
com	Commercial organizations
edu	Educational institutions
gov	Government institutions
mil	Military
net	Network support centers (ISPs)
org	Other organizations (originally nonprofit)
in-addr.arpa	Used for reverse lookups; that is, given an IP address, it finds the name
biz	Businesses
info	Open to anyone
name	Personal registrations
pro	Licensed professionals, such as lawyers, doctors, and accountants
aero	Anything related to air transport
museum	Museums
coop	Cooperative businesses, such as credit unions

Originally, the .net TLD was intended for networking organizations and the .org TLD was geared toward nonprofit organizations. In recent years, these definitions have expanded and no longer meet these requirements. Some new TLDs, such as .pro, .aero, .museum, and .coop, have specific requirements.

Table 4-2 shows a partial list of the codes used to categorize top-level domains by country. (For a complete list, see *www.iana.org/cctld/cctld-whois.htm*.)

Table 4-2 Top-level domain country codes

Country code	Country
br	Brazil
ca	Canada
ch	Switzerland
de	Germany
ie	Ireland
mx	Mexico
pt	Portugal
uk	United Kingdom
us	United States

Identifying Second-Level Domains

Second-level domains include businesses and institutions that register their domain names with top-level domains through their respective registrars. They include registered names such as *iso.ch* and *amazon.com*. They can also be subcategories of top-level domains. For example, the United States domain (us) is categorized into second-level domains for each state, such as *ca.us* for California. Companies and academic institutions in the United Kingdom and most other countries are also categorized using second-level domains such as *co.uk* and *ac.uk*. Thus, in the United Kingdom, companies and academic institutions can register names under their respective second-level domain.

A subdomain is a further division of a second-level domain. In other words, a company that registers a domain can divide it into subdomains. For example, a subdomain of *technowidgets.com* may be *support.technowidgets.com*, and a host computer of this subdomain may be identified as *www.support.technowidgets.com*. However, on the Internet, subdomains created by owners of domain names are not common. An organization might create subdomains when it has autonomous divisions that run their own Web servers and e-mail, yet want to be recognized as part of the domain. For example, the people at TechnoWidgets, Inc., could create a host called *www.support* within *technowidgets.com* to use as a subdomain for TechnoWidgets, Inc. Figure 4-1 shows a sample DNS namespace structure.

While many second-level domains, such as the ones under .com, need to be registered through a designated Internet authority such as *www.register.com*, you can create as many subdomains as you like within your own domain. The subdomain information is then propagated through the DNS system.

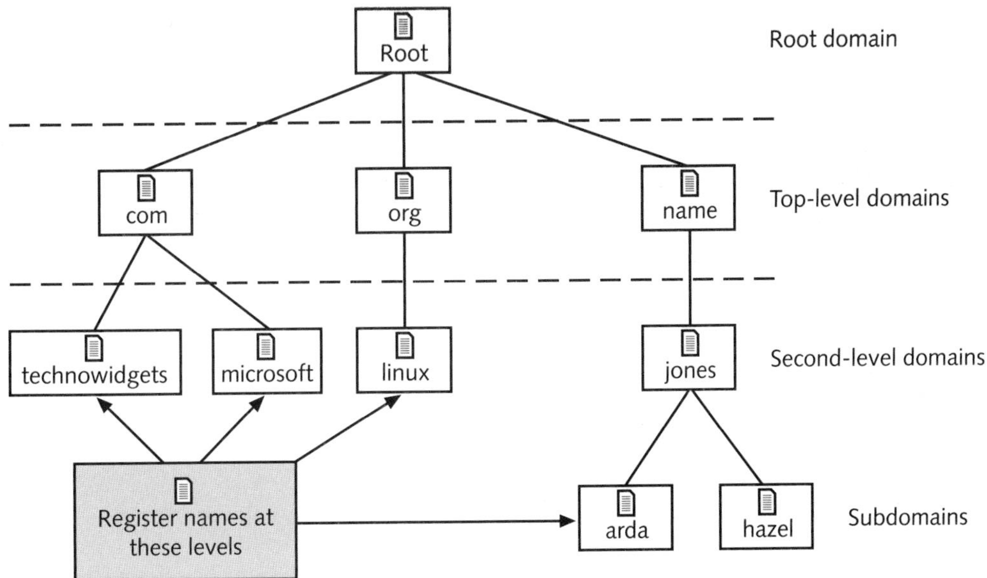

Figure 4-1 Structure of the DNS namespace

Understanding Host Names

The first portion of a URL is typically a host name. For example, in *www.technowidgets.com*, the www represents the Web server. Likewise, an FTP server could be called *ftp.technowidgets.com*. Although the Web server and the FTP server could reside on different computers, they could also be on the same computer with different IP addresses or even on the same computer with the same IP address, depending on how the DNS administrator configured the system.

Do not confuse the host name in DNS with the computer name that you used when you installed the operating system. Typically, the name you used when installing the operating system (web1) is not a name commonly associated with the Internet.

When you access a host by using its DNS name, note that information moves from specific to general as you read from left to right. For example, to access a domain of *technowidgets.com* in a browser, you would enter *www.technowidgets.com*. The name "www" is most specific, because it refers to a particular host acting as a Web server. The name "technowidgets" refers to an entire domain, and "com" means it is one of many commercial entities. Figure 4-2 shows the components of *www.technowidgets.com*.

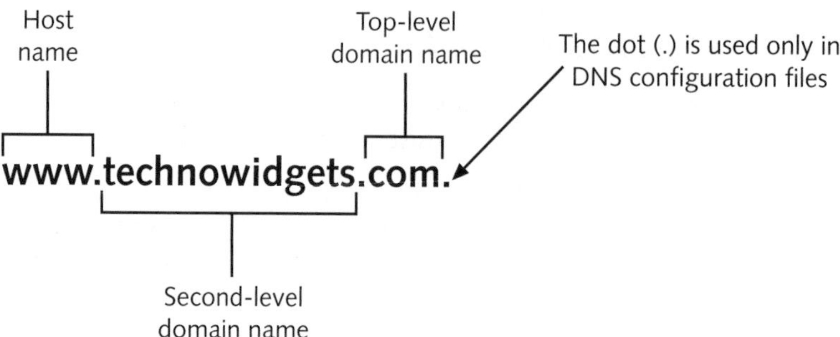

Figure 4-2 Components of a URL

Figure 4-3 shows what happens when a user types *www.technowidgets.com* into a Web browser. DNS is a distributed database of IP addresses; the root servers know only the addresses for all of the top-level domain servers. Each TLD server (such as for com) knows only the addresses for the second-level domain servers, such as the one for *technowidgets.com*. Finally, the DNS server for *technowidgets.com* returns the IP address for www. Every domain name such as *technowidgets.com* must have associated DNS servers. If you worked at TechnoWidgets, it could be your job to configure the *technowidgets.com* DNS server.

1. User types www.technowidgets.com in browser
2. Browser queries DNS server to get IP address
3. DNS server queries root server to find IP address of COM server
4. DNS server queries COM server to find IP address of technowidgets.com server
5. DNS queries technowidgets.com server to find IP address of www
6. IP address for www.technowidgets.com is sent back to browser

Step 3
Root DNS server
Step 2
Step 4
Step 6
COM DNS server
DNS caching
or forwarding
server
Step 1
www.technowidgets.com
typed in browser
Step 5
DNS primary or
secondary server for
technowidgets.com

Figure 4-3 Finding the IP address for *www.technowidgets.com*

IDENTIFYING THE COMPONENTS OF DNS

Now that you have explored the structure of the domain system, you are ready to explore the parts of the DNS system. It consists of two key components:

- *Name server*—Also known as a DNS server, the name server is an application that supports name-to-address and address-to-name translation. You will learn about the various types of name servers later in this chapter. When you configure DNS files, the term "name server" will be used within the files.
- *Name resolver*—Commonly called a DNS client, a name resolver is technically the client software component that uses the services of one or more name servers. Each client must know how to contact at least one name server so that the name resolver software can exchange query packets with the DNS server. When the client software needs to send a DNS query to look up an IP address for a given name, the resolver sends the query to the name server. The address of the name server is part of the TCP/IP configuration. Windows clients use the term "DNS server address" to describe this information, while Linux clients use the term "nameserver address." Notice that nameserver is a single word when used in a Linux configuration.

DNS follows the standard client/server model—the client makes a request and the server fulfills it. DNS servers can fill several different roles, depending on the needs of an organization. No matter which role the server undertakes, however, the client must specify the IP address of the DNS server.

Two categories of DNS servers exist. The first category includes primary and secondary DNS servers, which are necessary for the Internet to function. These servers contain the host names for an individual domain on the Internet. The second category of DNS servers includes caching and forwarding servers, which search the Internet for the host names.

A special type of server called the **root server** identifies all top-level domains on the Internet. If a client requests information about a host in another domain, a caching or forwarding DNS server can communicate the request to the root server. The InterNIC determines which systems are root servers. You can obtain the list of Internet servers at *ftp.rs.internic.net/domain/named.cache*.

Understanding DNS Servers That Define the Internet

Primary and secondary servers define the hosts for a particular domain such as *technowidgets.com*. The primary server defines the domain and contains the host names and associated IP addresses for each host. The secondary server retrieves the domain data from the primary server at regular intervals.

Working with Primary Servers

The **primary server** stores files for a domain. Configuration files refer to the primary server as a master server because a primary server is the authority for the current domain, meaning that it controls host names and updates to the secondary server. The primary server maintains the DNS databases for its DNS **zone**, the set of records contained within a domain. For example, if the domain name for your company is *technowidgets.com*, then you need to create a forward lookup zone for the *technowidgets.com* domain on the primary server. In the zone files, you create records that have the host names and corresponding IP addresses for all hosts in the zone. If your organization decided to create subdomains, they would be maintained in separate zones.

Working with Secondary Servers

A **secondary server** receives its authority and database from the primary server. It provides fault tolerance, load distribution, and remote name resolution for the primary DNS server. When the secondary server first starts, it requests from the primary server all the data for a zone. The secondary server then periodically checks with the primary name server to determine whether it needs to update its data. Configuration files refer to the secondary server as a slave server. Each primary server can have multiple secondary servers.

Even when you configure your own primary server, your ISP will probably maintain your secondary server because the ISP has a more reliable connection to the Internet.

Understanding DNS Servers That Resolve Names

Primary and secondary servers rely on other servers to search the data they store. The caching and forwarding servers search primary and secondary servers. When you install a DNS server, it is a caching server by default, so no extra configuration is needed. You can configure a caching server to use a forwarding server for resolving names instead of using the root servers on the Internet. In addition, you can combine the caching server that is configured by default with a primary server, secondary server, or forwarding server. However, caching and forwarding DNS servers can be used in organizations that do not have domain names. Remember, they are used only to resolve names.

Working with Caching Servers

A **caching server** is not authoritative for any zone. Instead, it handles queries by asking other servers for information. All servers cache the information they receive until the time specified in the Time to Live (TTL) field expires. That is, a caching server stores name resolution information until the data expires. Caching servers can be used in organizations in which many users connect to the Internet and access many common sites. Using a local caching server can significantly reduce response time for URL resolution. If you install a DNS server in Linux, it remains only a caching server until you modify it to become a primary or secondary server.

4

Working with Forwarding Servers

Forwarding servers, or forwarders, process requests that DNS servers cannot resolve locally. A forwarding server is not a separate type of server, but rather a caching server used in a particular way. A forwarding server accesses the Internet, as shown in Figure 4-4. To make a DNS server become a forwarding server, you add a record to reference the DNS server on the Internet that will resolve names. You then add records in the caching servers that reference the forwarding server.

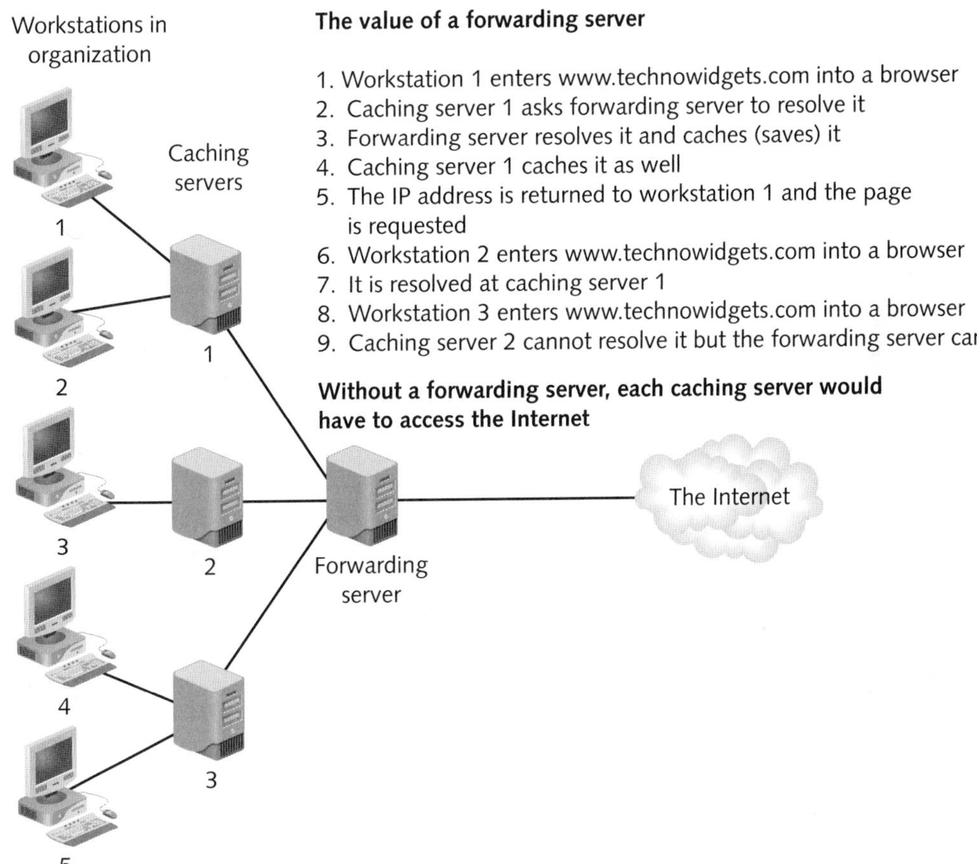
Workstations in organization
Caching servers
The value of a forwarding server
1. Workstation 1 enters www.technowidgets.com into a browser
2. Caching server 1 asks forwarding server to resolve it
3. Forwarding server resolves it and caches (saves) it
4. Caching server 1 caches it as well
5. The IP address is returned to workstation 1 and the page is requested
6. Workstation 2 enters www.technowidgets.com into a browser
7. It is resolved at caching server 1
8. Workstation 3 enters www.technowidgets.com into a browser
9. Caching server 2 cannot resolve it but the forwarding server can
Without a forwarding server, each caching server would have to access the Internet
1
2
3
4
5
1
2
3
Forwarding server
The Internet

Figure 4-4 Caching servers using a forwarding server

Forwarding servers work in combination with caching servers. They are useful in organizations that have many caching servers but want to reduce traffic on their connection to the Internet. If all the caching servers cached names and IP addresses independently, then information would be duplicated because each caching server would access the Internet to resolve names. A forwarding server acts as the single point of contact for the Internet, so it caches often-used names requested by the other servers. For example, if the users of five caching servers wanted to access *www.redhat.com*, then each caching server would have to contact the Internet to resolve the address. If the caching servers used a forwarding server, then the forwarding server would get the IP address for *www.redhat.com* and cache it. When the other caching servers needed the IP address for *www.redhat.com*, they could get it from the cache at the forwarder.

The primary and secondary servers are accessed by users throughout the Internet to determine the IP addresses of your hosts, such as *www.technowidgets.com*. The caching and forwarding servers are accessed by users in your organization to determine the IP addresses of hosts on the Internet.

CONFIGURING ZONE FILES

Recall that a zone file contains records that specify the host names and corresponding IP addresses for all hosts in the zone. Once you configure the zone, you can use the information in these files for name resolution, regardless of whether you use DNS in Linux or Windows.

Often, your ISP configures the zone files; in some cases, the ISP may have a Web interface to make it easy for you to change these files. If your organization operates its own primary DNS server, then you will configure the zone files directly. When you register a domain name, you must provide the addresses of a primary DNS server and a secondary DNS server. Smaller organizations often use only the DNS servers at their ISP. This is an easy but inflexible approach; for example, you would need to contact your ISP every time you changed your domain. If you determine that you want more control over changes to your domain, you can set up a primary DNS server in your organization and have your ISP maintain the secondary server. Controlling your own DNS server also makes it easier to move to a new ISP because you control all the records that you need to change.

A primary server is the authoritative server for managing information on IP addresses and associated host names in your domain. All other systems on your network should be configured so that the DNS server entry in the TCP/IP configuration has the IP address of your DNS server. You can also enter an IP address for a second DNS server, which will be used if the first server cannot be contacted or cannot resolve the name. Typically, this entry applies to the DNS server at your ISP.

Understanding Zone Files and DNS Records

A zone file helps define a branch of the DNS namespace under the administrative control of a primary DNS name server. A **namespace** is a common grouping of related names—for example, hosts within a LAN. Although many IT professionals use the terms "domain" and "zone" interchangeably, they are not identical. A zone refers to a specific file that resides on a server. For instance, a company that registers the domain name *technowidgets.com* gains administrative control of the domain *technowidgets.com*. To exert control over that domain, the company must create zones. When you create a DNS server, you generally populate it with two types of zones:

- *Forward lookup*—These zones contain entries that map names to IP addresses.
- *Reverse lookup*—These zones contain entries that map IP addresses to names.

4

Every domain zone file consists of DNS records. A DNS record is an entry in a DNS database on a primary server that provides additional routing and resolution information. You can configure many different types of records, but only a few are essential for full address resolution routing. Common DNS records are listed in Table 4-3.

Do not confuse forward and reverse zone files with primary or secondary servers. A primary or secondary server usually *contains* a forward or reverse zone. Zone files make it possible to populate a DNS server, either primary or secondary, with individual host information.

Table 4-3 Common DNS records

DNS record	Function
Address (A)	The most commonly used record; associates a host to an IP address. For example, you can establish an association between an IP address and a Web server by creating an address record.
Canonical name (CNAME)	Creates an alias for a specified host. As an example, suppose the name of a WWW server is *server1.company.com*. (Web servers are commonly named WWW.) A CNAME record creates an alias for the *server1.company.com* host.
Internet (IN)	Identifies Internet records; precedes most DNS record entries.
Mail Exchanger (MX)	Identifies a server used for processing and delivering e-mail for the domain.
Name server (NS)	Identifies DNS servers for the DNS domain. It can also refer to a DNS server that will resolve names for clients, making the DNS server act as a forwarding server.
Pointer (PTR)	Performs reverse DNS lookups. The PTR record allows DNS to resolve an IP address to a host name.
Start of Authority (SOA)	Identifies the DNS server with the most current information for the DNS domain. Because several secondary DNS servers may exist, this record identifies the primary server for the specified DNS domain. Although RFC 1035, the document that defines DNS, specifies SOA as the "start of the zone of authority," many authors define SOA as the "statement of authority."

Configuring the Forward Lookup Zone

The forward lookup zone maps host names to IP addresses. Although Windows uses a GUI and Linux uses text files, both must supply the same information so that any other DNS server can read the forward lookup zone. Figure 4-5 shows a sample forward lookup zone file for *technowidgets.com*. For the purposes of this example, IP addresses that are invalid on the Internet are used. Spacing is not important in the files. However, each name, such as @, web1, or www, must appear in the first column of the line.

```
$TTL  86400
@      IN     SOA   web1.technowidgets.com. admn.technowidgets.com. (
                                         2002072100 ; Serial
                                         28800      ; Refresh
                                         14400      ; Retry
                                         3600000    ; Expire
                                         86400 )    ; Minimum
              IN       NS       web1
              IN       A        192.168.0.100
              IN       MX   10  mail.technowidgets.com.

web1          IN    A      192.168.0.100
www           IN    CNAME web1
www.support IN    CNAME web1
research      IN    A      192.168.0.150
              IN    MX 10 mail
mail          IN    A      192.168.0.200
```

Figure 4-5 Forward lookup zone for *technowidgets.com*

Each statement except for the first line contains `IN`, which stands for the Internet class; historically, there were other classes but the Internet class is the only one used today. The `$TTL 86400` tells caching software how long to cache the resource records such as www. The time is measured in seconds.

Starting with the first character on the next line, the `@` signifies the name of the zone, which is *technowidgets.com*. This line defines the **Start Of Authority** (**SOA**) record; it states that the primary DNS server resides on *web1.technowidgets.com*. The e-mail address of the contact person for this domain is *admn@technowidgets.com*.

Make sure that you replace the @ in the e-mail name with a period when you type the e-mail address for the domain's contact name.

The next five items define the relationship between the primary server and the secondary server. Other than the first item, the numbers are represented in seconds.

- The **serial number** can be any valid 32-bit number. When you change the DNS configuration, changing the serial number informs the secondary server that it should update its database. The standard format for the serial number is YYYYMMDDnn, where YYYYMMDD is the date of the configuration change and nn represents a sequential number allowing up to 100 changes per day.
- The **refresh** interval tells the secondary server how often to check for updates from the primary server.
- The **retry** interval describes how often the secondary server should try to contact the primary server if it fails to make contact after the refresh interval.
- The secondary server also needs to know how long to keep trying to contact the primary server before giving up and stopping all requests for name resolution. This information is provided by the value for **expire**.
- The last item, **minimum**, refers to the length of time that a negative response to a query should remain cached.

Although older versions of DNS software could describe time only in seconds, current versions can use m, h, and d to describe minutes, hours, and days, respectively. For example, you could translate the previous SOA record into the following record:

```
2002072100 ; Serial
8h         ; Refresh
4h         ; Retry
1000h      ; Expire
1d )       ; Minimum
```

The SOA record is followed by the line `IN NS web1`. Because nothing precedes `IN` in the line, it takes the value of the previous `IN` statement, which was the `@`, meaning *technowidgets.com*. The `NS` stands for name server, which is shorthand for DNS server, and `web1` is the name of the host that has the DNS server. In other words, the line means that web1 has the DNS server for *technowidgets.com*. Notice that `web1` does not end in a period, yet *web1.technowidgets.com.* does. When a name ends in a period, it is called a **fully qualified domain name (FQDN)**, which is the complete name of the host. When no period appears at the end, the host name is given relative to the zone name. In this case, using web1 is the same as using *web1.technowidgets.com.* for the name. Again, notice the period after "com."; if the first line does not end with a period, the server appends the zone name. In this case, the server would interpret the host name as *web1.technowidgets.com.technowidgets.com*. The most common error in configuring DNS servers is forgetting the period at the end of the FQDN.

The next line, `IN A 192.168.0.100`, means that the name *technowidgets.com* resolves to the IP address 192.168.0.100. To refer mail for *technowidgets.com* to a mail server, you need a mail exchange record of `IN MX 10 mail.technowidgets.com`. Because the system could include multiple mail servers, the value of 10 helps determine which mail server is the primary one. If there were multiple MX records, they would have different numeric values. The one with the lowest value would be the first e-mail server contacted; if it did not respond, the next e-mail server in numeric order would be contacted.

Instead of the FQDN of *mail.technowidgets.com.*, you could have used "mail" without a period at the end. The FQDN you decide to use depends on personal preference.

So far, the record refers to web1 twice without describing the IP address of the host. It is finally described in the line `web1 IN A 192.168.0.100`, which tells you that web1 is located at 192.168.0.100. However, because it is not standard practice to have a URL of *web1.technowidgets.com*, you must create a **canonical name**, also known as an alias, which states that www is equivalent to web1. This alias is shown in the next line, `www IN CNAME web1`, which means that *www.technowidgets.com* is the same as *web1.technowidgets.com*.

The next line includes a host for research at 192.168.0.150. Because the line following `research` does not have a name to the left of `IN`, it takes the value of the previous line, which is "research." That is, mail sent to *research.technowidgets.com* should go to the same mail server. Finally, the last line describes the IP address of the mail server.

The previous example incorporates all the elements of a typical forward lookup zone file. You use many of the same elements to configure the reverse lookup zone file, so the next section covers only the unique parts of this file.

Configuring the Reverse Lookup Zone

Along with converting domain names into IP addresses, the DNS system can do the reverse: it can convert IP addresses into names. For example, suppose that an e-mail system receives an e-mail from bgates@microsoft.com. The IP address of the sender is 38.246.165.21. The e-mail system may want to know whether 38.246.165.21 is actually associated with *microsoft.com*. A reverse lookup can tell the system the domain of the IP address. A reverse lookup is also useful when using DNS-based troubleshooting utilities such as nslookup and dig.

Although a forward lookup zone is required when setting up DNS, a reverse lookup zone is not required.

DNS converts IP addresses to names by associating a domain name with a network address and placing the domain name in the top-level in-addr.arpa domain. To implement reverse lookups, you create reverse zone files and populate them with PTR records in the proper format.

For example, suppose that your company has the class C network address 192.168.0.0. The associated in-addr.arpa zone name is 0.168.192.in-addr.arpa. You create this name by reversing the order of the bytes in the network address and adding in-addr.arpa at the end. By placing this information in a PTR record, you create the proper reverse DNS entry for the host. Figure 4-6 shows an example.


```
$TTL  86400
@     IN     SOA    web1.technowidgets.com. admn.technowidgets.com. (
                                       2002072100 ; Serial
                                       28800      ; Refresh
                                       14400      ; Retry
                                       3600000    ; Expire
                                       86400 )    ; Minimum
            IN        NS       web1

100         IN       PTR     web1.technowidgets.com.
150         IN       PTR     research.technowidgets.com.
200         IN       PTR     mail.technowidgets.com.
```

Figure 4-6 Reverse lookup zone

Conventionally, the bytes in IP addresses move from general to more specific networks as you proceed from left to right. However, URLs are opposite—the most specific is on the left. For example, in the URL *www.technowidgets.com*, "www" represents the specific host. With the corresponding IP address, 192.168.0.100, the host portion of the address is 100, and is on the right. To have the most specific portion on the left, you must reverse the address. You already know that the @ represents the name of the zone, which is 0.168.192.in-addr.arpa. You also know that a name without a period at the end means that the zone name is appended to it. Thus the text `100 IN PTR web1.technowidgets.com.` is the same as `100.0.168.192.in-addr.arpa. IN PTR web1.technowidgets.com.` These addresses now match; web1 is on the left in both cases. Matching is necessary because the search is similar; just as searches always start at the top-level domain of com for forward lookups, so searches start at in-addr.arpa for reverse lookups.

Now that you have learned about the forward and reverse lookup zones in a DNS server, you are ready to learn how to set them up in Linux and Windows.

INSTALLING AND CONFIGURING DNS IN LINUX

The software used for DNS in Linux and other non-Windows servers is called **BIND** (Berkeley Internet Name Domain). Even organizations that have only Windows servers for the Web environment typically use BIND on a UNIX/Linux computer for their Internet DNS.

At the time of this book's publication, Red Hat Linux shipped with version 9 of BIND; a newer version might now be available on the Red Hat Web site. One advantage of using the Linux distribution from Red Hat is that it employs the rpm method of installing software, which not only installs software but also maintains a record of files used for the application. The record can later help you update or delete an application without affecting other applications.

You probably installed the DNS name server when you installed Linux in the previous chapter. If you did not, use Hands-on Project 4-1 to install the DNS server software directly from the CD. This procedure could prove helpful if you need to upgrade the software in the future.

When you installed Linux, it added a number of files and directories to your system. Table 4-4 describes the most important files.

Table 4-4 Common DNS configuration files and directories in Linux

File	Description
/etc/rc.d/init.d/named	The name server daemon is the file that starts DNS.
/etc/named.conf	This file describes the location of your zone files.
/var/named	This directory contains your zone files.

Configuring DNS in Linux

After you configure the forward and reverse lookup zone files for the DNS server in Linux, you store the files in the correct location and make sure that DNS knows about the files. Refer to the sample zone files in Figures 4-5 and 4-6 to better understand how to complete the following tasks. The specific steps are covered in Hands-on Project 4-2.

To configure DNS in Linux:

1. Use a consistent standard to name the zone files.

   Begin the name of the forward lookup zone file with "named" followed by a dot and then the name of the zone. Because the name of the forward lookup zone is *technowidgets.com*, you would name the file "named.technowidgets.com". For the reverse zone, start the filename with "named" followed by a dot and then add the network address of the zone with the octets reversed; the name of the reverse lookup zone file in Figure 4-6 would then be "named.0.168.192".

2. Store these files in the /var/named directory.
3. Tell DNS about the zone files.

   Modify the file in /etc called **named.conf**, which is shown in Figure 4-7.

   This file starts as a caching DNS server, because it is not acting as a primary DNS server for a domain yet. Once you add the zone information (explained later), the server will be a primary DNS server.


```
// generated by named-bootconf.pl


options {
        directory "/var/named";
        /*
         * If there is a firewall between you and nameservers you want
         * to talk to, you might need to uncomment the query-source
         * directive below. Previous versions of BIND always asked
         * questions using port 53, but BIND 8.1 uses an unprivileged
         * port by default.
         */
        // query-source address * port 53;
};


//
// a caching-only nameserver config
//
controls {
        inet 127.0.0.1 allow { localhost; } keys { rndckey; };
};
zone "." IN {
        type hint;
        file "named.ca";
};


zone "localhost" IN {
        type master;
        file "localhost.zone";
        allow-update { none; };
};


zone "0.0.127.in-addr.arpa" IN {
        type master;
        file "named.local";
        allow-update { none; };
};


include "/etc/rndc.key";
```

Figure 4-7 Contents of named.conf

In Figure 4-7, the entry for the "localhost" zone provides a model for adding your forward and reverse lookup zones to named.conf.

- *zone "localhost" IN* {—The name of the zone is in quotation marks. Be sure to type the name of your zone correctly, because the @ uses this name in the zone file. Recall from Figures 4-5 and 4-6 that the @ represents the zone name.
- *type master;*—The configuration file uses this term to denote a primary server. The term for a secondary server is slave.
- *file "localhost.zone";*—This is the name of the zone file. At the beginning of Figure 4-7 is `directory "/var/named";`, which is the name of the directory that must contain the zone files.
- *allow-update { none; };*—No secondary server needs this information. When a secondary server requests an update of the zone files, this file will be skipped. Because you want your zone files to be updated, do not add this line to the forward and reverse zone entries in named.conf.

Given this information, add the forward and reverse zones for Technowidgets, Inc., so named.conf resembles Figure 4-8.

Starting DNS in Linux

Once you have added the forward and reverse zone entries to named.conf, you can start DNS in Linux by typing the following command:

```
/etc/rc.d/init.d/named start
```

If you find a mistake in a zone file and want to restart the server, type the following command:

```
/etc/rc.d/init.d/named restart
```

To stop the DNS server, type the following command:

```
/etc/rc.d/init.d/named stop
```

Because it is easy to overlook starting DNS, set it to start every time you start the server.

To have DNS start automatically in Linux:

1. Type the following command to open the rc.local file and then press **Enter**:

   kedit /etc/rc.d/rc.local

   The rc.local file runs the files contained in it when Linux starts.
2. Add the following line to the file:

   /etc/rc.d/init.d/named start
3. Save the file and then exit.

```
// generated by named-bootconf.pl

options {
      directory "/var/named";
      /*
       * If there is a firewall between you and nameservers you want
       * to talk to, you might need to uncomment the query-source
       * directive below. Previous versions of BIND always asked
       * questions using port 53, but BIND 8.1 uses an unprivileged
       * port by default.
       */
      // query-source address * port 53;
};

//
// a caching-only nameserver config
//
controls {
      inet 127.0.0.1 allow { localhost; } keys { rndckey; };
};
zone "." IN {
      type hint;
      file "named.ca";
};

zone "localhost" IN {
      type master;
      file "localhost.zone";
      allow-update { none; };
};

zone "0.0.127.in-addr.arpa" IN {
      type master;
      file "named.local";
      allow-update { none; };
};
zone "technowidgets.com" IN {
      type master;
      file "named.technowidgets.com";
};

zone "0.168.192.in-addr.arpa" IN {
      type master;
      file "named.0.168.192";
};

include "/etc/rndc.key";
```

Figure 4-8 named.conf with zone information for TechnoWidgets, Inc.

To review the steps for setting up DNS in Linux, suppose that your company developed an idea for a domain called *ProductsWithPizazz.com*. First, you would register the domain name. To add the domain to your existing DNS server, you would do the following:

- Add a forward lookup entry in named.conf.
- Add the associated zone file in /var/named.
- Modify the reverse lookup zone.

For example, you could add the following code to named.conf:

```
zone "ProductsWithPizazz.com" IN {
      type master;
      file "named.productswithpizazz.com";
};
```

Configuring a Caching Server

After you install the DNS server in Linux, you can set it up as a caching server by adding a reverse lookup zone for your host address.

When you configure the client software to resolve names through a caching server, it refers to the following section of the configuration in named.conf (refer back to Figure 4-7):

```
zone "." IN {
      type hint;
      file "named.ca";
};
```

This code refers the client to the root zone. The file named.ca contains the names and IP addresses of the root servers, which can be accessed to resolve names. The resolved names are then cached locally.

Configuring a Caching Server to Use a Forwarding Server

To configure a caching server to use a forwarding server, open the file named.conf in the caching server, and then add the IP address of the forwarding server to the options. If your organization has more than one forwarding server, you can add the servers' IP addresses in the same line, separated by semicolons. In named.conf, the only option specified at first is the directory of the zone files. For example, the following code is from named.conf, minus the comments:

```
options {
      directory "/var/named";
};
```

To refer name resolution to a forwarding server, add the forwarders option. If the IP address of the forwarding server is 192.168.0.250, change the options code as follows:

```
options {
      directory "/var/named";
      forwarders {192.168.0.250;};
};
```

Remember to add a semicolon after the IP address and again after the closing bracket (}). Although you have only one forwarder, the option is still called "forwarders."

4

Configuring Client DNS in Linux

After configuring the DNS server, you need to configure the client portion of DNS. Recall that when the client software needs to resolve a name, it looks in the TCP/IP configuration for a DNS server. In the case of Linux, the server is called a nameserver.

Assuming that your Linux computer has an IP address of 192.168.0.100, you need to tell the client software that the address belongs to your DNS server.

To configure client-side DNS in Linux:

1. In a terminal window, type **kedit /etc/resolv.conf** and then press **Enter**.
2. The file might already reference the nameserver. If it does not, add the following line to the end of the file, assuming that the IP address of your DNS server is 192.168.0.100: **nameserver 192.168.0.100**
3. Because this computer is part of a domain, you should add the name of the domain. For example, if the name is technowidgets.com, type **domain technowidgets.com** on a new line in the file.
4. Save the file by clicking the floppy disk icon on the kedit toolbar at the top of the window.
5. Close the window to exit the file. Now the Linux computer will resolve names.

Even though you are configuring this computer to use just one DNS server, you could add two more nameserver lines. It is a good idea to reference multiple DNS servers in case one cannot be contacted.

Now that the DNS server is running and the client configuration is using the DNS server for name resolution, you need to perform the same procedures in Windows.

Understanding Name Resolution in Windows

Name resolution can mean more than just DNS. Although basic DNS is perfect for the Internet, name resolution also needs to take place within LANs. This chapter focuses on the Web server environment, but it is important to compare the DNS of the Internet with other methods of name resolution. For example, DNS assumes that each computer will have a **static** IP address—an address that is allocated to a computer once and doesn't change. In a LAN environment, by contrast, it is common for computers to have **dynamic** IP addresses, which can change over time.

The dynamic IP address is assigned through **Dynamic Host Configuration Protocol (DHCP)**. DHCP holds a pool of addresses that are given to a computer for a specific amount of time. Typically, a computer continues to renew the IP address indefinitely, but it can change at any time. As you can imagine, if the IP address of a computer changed often, the zone file described earlier in this chapter would not be very useful. Someone would have to constantly update the zone file as computers changed addresses.

Because such a solution obviously is not feasible, Microsoft developed Dynamic DNS (DDNS). In this system, computers and their associated IP addresses are automatically added, changed, and deleted from the DDNS as computers are turned on and shut down. Both Windows 2000 and Windows 2003 allow you to use DDNS for the LAN and simple DNS for connections to the Internet. The other possibility is to have a single DDNS configuration for both internal LAN use and the Internet. Before LANs could use DDNS, Microsoft had to incorporate a hierarchical namespace into this service, similar to the Internet, as you will learn in the next chapter.

Microsoft operating systems before Windows 2000 cannot use DDNS, so they need an older technology to support name resolution. Servers used with Windows NT Workstation, Windows 95, and Windows 98 get this support from **WINS (Windows Internet name service)**. In the case of WINS, the term "Internet" simply means name resolution between networks; this term was created before Microsoft became involved with the Internet as we know it. Just as the IP address of the DNS server is part of the TCP/IP configuration in Windows, so there is a place to enter the address for the WINS server. Although Windows 2000, Windows XP, and Windows 2003 support a hierarchical naming scheme similar to that of the Internet, the older systems understood a computer name only within a **domain**. A domain in Windows is simply a logical grouping of computers. The only way older computers can be recognized on a LAN is to ensure they are registered in a WINS database.

DNS is not required with Windows NT, but it is required in Windows 2000 and Windows 2003 if you want to take advantage of **Active Directory Service (ADS)**. ADS keeps track of all users throughout the network and all resources they can use, such as printers and files. It works from a single point of administration, which eases maintenance. You will set up ADS in the next chapter, then use it to install a Microsoft Exchange server in Chapter 8.

Although DNS is required for ADS, you do not have to use Microsoft DNS. When you install ADS, you could use the IP address of a Linux server that has DNS.

Installing and Configuring DNS in Windows 2000 and 2003

In Chapter 3, the Windows Setup program allowed you to install DNS when you installed Windows 2000. However, you did not install DNS, so you can do so now. Windows 2003 does not allow you to install components with the operating system.

4

To install DNS in Windows :

1. Insert the Windows installation CD. When the installation window opens, click **Exit**.
2. From the Control Panel, click **Add or Remove Programs** (double-click **Add/Remove Programs** in Windows 2000).
3. Click **Add/Remove Windows Components** in the left panel. The Windows Components Wizard opens.
4. Scroll down to click and select **Networking Services**, and then click the **Details** button.
5. Select the **Domain Name System (DNS)** check box and click **OK**.
6. Click **Next** to install the DNS server.
7. Click **Finish**, and then close the window.

After installing DNS, you need to configure it. Configuring DNS is the same in both Windows 2000 and Windows 2003. Figure 4-9 shows the DNS configuration window in Windows 2003, but you would see a similar window in Windows 2000.

To begin configuring DNS in Windows:

1. Open the DNS configuration window.

   In Windows 2003: Click **Start**, point to **Administrative Tools**, and then click **DNS**.

   In Windows 2000: Click **Start**, point to **Programs**, point to **Administrative Tools**, and then click **DNS**.

2. Click the **+** icon next to the name of the server to open the window shown in Figure 4-9. You see two standard folders: one for Forward Lookup Zones and one for Reverse Lookup Zones. You will not use the Event Viewer system folder.

Your objective is to set up the DNS for *technowidgets.com*. You will skip the wizard, which is more focused on LAN-based use of DDNS; your focus is the Internet. The first procedure sets up a file for the *technowidgets.com* zone.

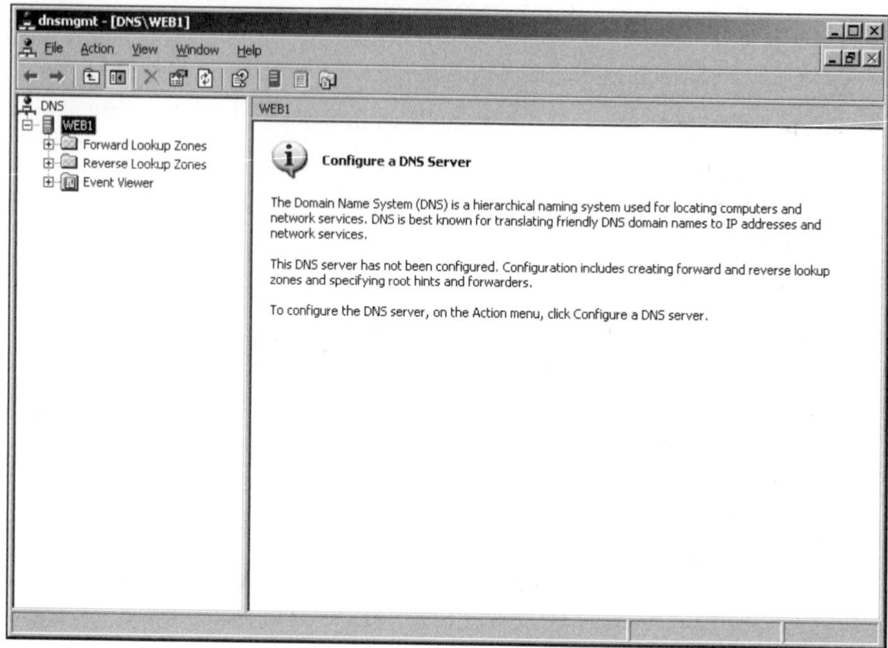

Figure 4-9 DNS configuration window

To set up a forward lookup zone file in DNS in Windows:

1. In the left pane of the DNS configuration window, click **Forward Lookup Zones**, right-click **Forward Lookup Zones**, and then click **New Zone** on the shortcut menu.
2. The New Zone Wizard starts to guide you through the process of creating a zone. Click **Next**.
3. In the Zone Type window, accept the default zone type of Primary zone, and then click **Next**.
4. The Zone Name dialog box appears. For the zone name, type **technowidgets.com**, and then click **Next**.
5. The Zone File dialog box appears. You use this dialog box to define the name of the file in which to store the zone information. Accept the default filename of technowidgets.com.dns, and then click **Next**.
6. *Windows 2003 only:* The Dynamic Update dialog box opens. You are creating a DNS for the Internet only, so you do not want other computers automatically adding records to your DNS. Accept the default option of **Do not allow dynamic updates** by clicking **Next**.
7. Click **Finish** to create the forward lookup zone file. This is just a blank file. In subsequent steps, you will fill it with zone information for *technowidgets.com*.

Although you do not have to set up the reverse lookup zone yet, it is easier to do it now. Later, when you add a new host record, it can automatically add the PTR record in the reverse lookup zone, if the zone already exists.

To set up a reverse lookup zone file in DNS in Windows:

1. In the left pane of the DNS configuration window, click **Reverse Lookup Zones**, right-click **Reverse Lookup Zones**, and then click **New Zone** on the shortcut menu.
2. The New Zone Wizard starts and the welcome screen appears. Click **Next**.
3. In the Zone Type dialog box, accept the Primary zone (Standard primary in Windows 2000) as the default. Click **Next**.
4. The Reverse Lookup Zone Name dialog box appears. It asks for the network ID or the name of the zone. You need to enter the network portion of the IP address; for example, if your IP address was 192.168.0.0, you would type **192.168.0**. Notice that "0.168.192.in-addr.arpa" appears in the dimmed box; this is exactly what you created under Linux.
5. Click **Next**. In the Zone File dialog box, accept the default filename of 0.168.192.in-addr.arpa.dns by clicking **Next**.
6. *Windows 2003 only:* The Dynamic Update dialog box opens. Accept the default option of **Do not allow dynamic updates**. You want to specify hosts yourself, and you do not want workstations on the LAN adding their host names to the DNS. Click **Next**.
7. Click **Finish** to exit the New Zone Wizard and create the reverse lookup zone file.

Notice that the window shown in Figure 4-9 has now changed. In the left pane of the DNS configuration window, you see a folder for *technowidgets.com*, which indicates you have created the zone file. (Expand the Lookup Zones folder, if necessary.) Now you need to configure it. You want this zone file to contain the same information as the one you created in Linux. Instead of editing a text file, you will use dialog boxes in Windows to add and modify information.

The first task in configuring DNS is to add the host records. In the Linux configuration, you added the Mail Exchanger (MX) record, but the Windows GUI does not let you refer to a host name that does not exist yet. The following code shows a list of host names and related information from the Linux configuration:

```
web1       IN  A      192.168.0.100
www        IN  CNAME  web1
research   IN  A      192.168.0.150
mail       IN  A      192.168.0.200
```

To add hosts to the DNS configuration in Windows:

1. In the left pane of the DNS configuration window, click **technowidgets.com**, and then right-click **technowidgets.com**. The window that appears is similar to Figure 4-10.

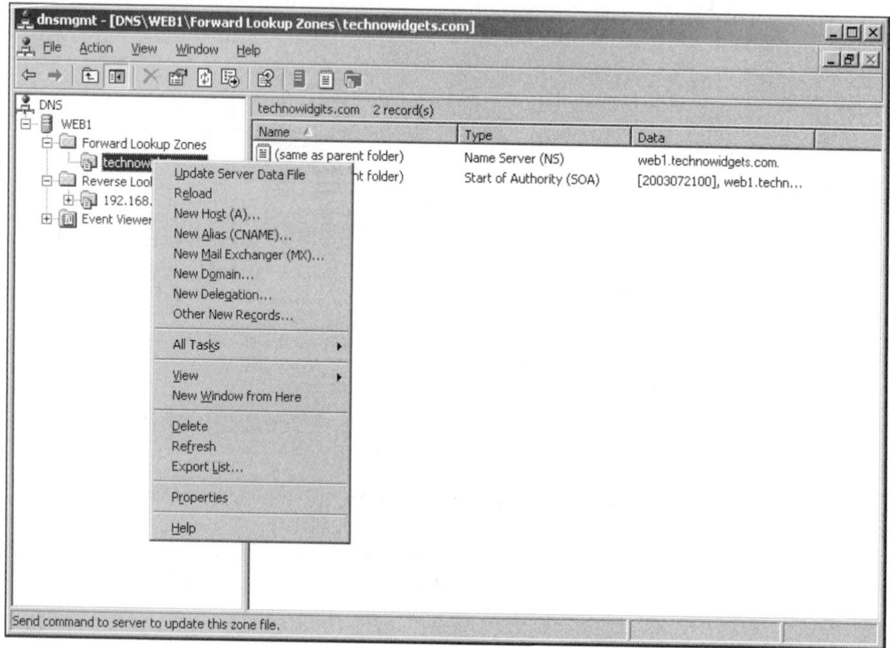

Figure 4-10 Shortcut menu for *technowidgets.com*

2. Click **New Host (A)**. The New Host dialog box appears.
3. In the Name text box, type **web1**.
4. In the IP address text box, type **192.168.0.100**.
5. Make sure that the check box next to **Create associated pointer (PTR) record** is selected. This option will save you time in creating a reverse lookup zone. Click **Add Host** and then click **OK**. Step 5 completes the steps for adding a host record.
6. Repeat Steps 3 through 5 to add **research** at **192.168.0.150** and **mail** at **192.168.0.200**. Remember to click **Add Host** and then **OK** after entering each name and IP address.
7. Click **Done** to exit the New Host dialog box.

8. To add the canonical name www, which is an alias for web1, right-click **technowidgets.com** and then click **New Alias (CNAME)** or **New Alias** in Windows 2000. The New Resource Record dialog box appears.
9. In the Alias name text box, type **www**.
10. In the Fully qualified domain name text box, type **web1.technowidgets.com**.
11. Click **OK** to finish adding the new alias.

In Chapter 8 you will install a mail server, so you need to add an MX record.

To add an MX record in Windows:

1. In the left pane of the DNS configuration window, right-click **technowidgets.com**.
2. Click **New Mail Exchanger (MX)**.
3. The New Resource Record dialog box states that the default mail exchanger is for the domain, so you do not enter anything in the Host or child domain text box. In the Fully qualified domain name (FQDN) of mail server text box, type **mail.technowidgets.com**.
4. Click **OK** to finish adding the new MX record.

Your next task is to configure the Start of Authority (SOA) and name server sections of the zone file. Recall from Figure 4-5 that you have the following Start of Authority:

```
@      IN     SOA   web1.technowidgets.com. admn.technowidgets.com. (
                                      2002072100 ; Serial
                                      28800      ; Refresh
                                      14400      ; Retry
                                      3600000    ; Expire
                                      86400 )    ; Minimum
```

To configure the Start of Authority and name server of a zone in Windows:

1. In the left pane, make sure that the **Forward Lookup Zones** folder is open so you can see the name of the zone. Right-click **technowidgets.com**, and then click **Properties**. You see the information you entered when you created the zone.
2. Click the **Start of Authority (SOA)** tab.
3. Make the Windows DNS the same as the one in Linux by changing the following settings. Windows DNS configuration is forgiving. If you forget to add a dot after "com," it will add it for you in the configuration file.

- Change the serial number to **2003072100**.
- Change the primary server to **web1.technowidgets.com**.
- Change the responsible person to **admn.technowidgets.com**. The dialog box should look like Figure 4-11.

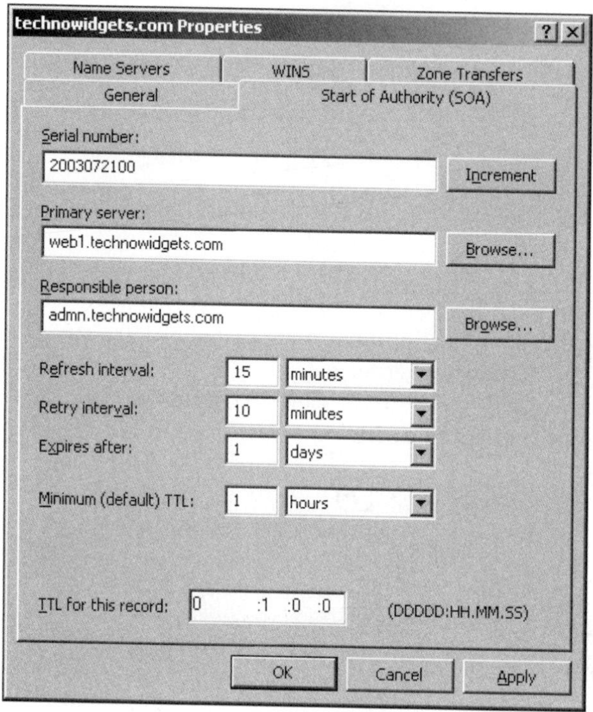

Figure 4-11 Start of Authority (SOA) tab

4. To configure the name servers, click the **Name Servers** tab. Click **Edit**, and then click **Browse**. In the Records box, expand WEB1 until you see the host record for web1. Highlight **web1**, and then click **OK** to return to the Name Servers tab. This is like adding an NS record to DNS. The dialog box should look like Figure 4-12.
5. Click **OK** to return to the main DNS screen.

You have now duplicated the steps necessary to create the same DNS configuration that you had in Linux, except for the extra alias and MX record. When you click the forward lookup zone of *technowidgets.com*, you should see the window shown in Figure 4-13.

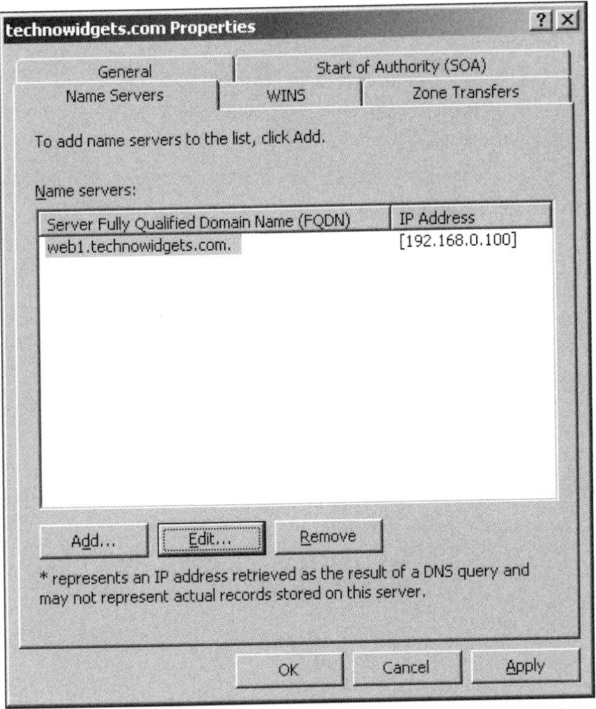

Figure 4-12 Name Servers tab of the DNS properties dialog box

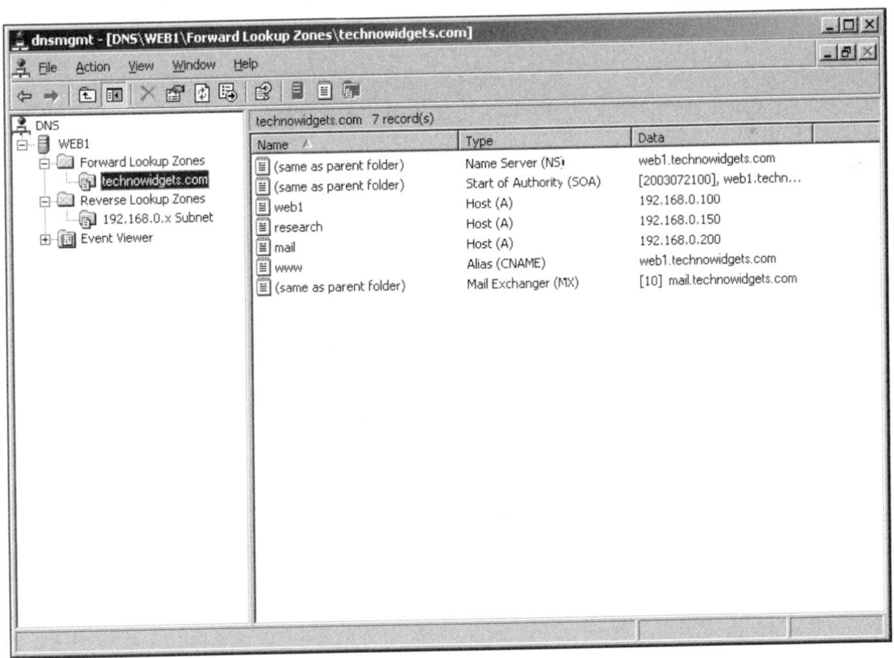

Figure 4-13 Finished DNS configuration for *technowidgets.com*

Configuring Client-Side DNS in Windows

Just as with Linux, you need to configure Windows computers to use the DNS server you just created to resolve names. Because DNS works the same way on any computer, you can have a Linux client computer using a DNS server on a Windows computer, and vice versa. The steps for configuring DNS on the client side are the same for Windows 2000 and Windows 2003. You can skip this procedure if you added a DNS server when you installed Windows.

To add client-side DNS in Windows:

1. Open the Local Area Connection window.

   In Windows 2003: Click **Start**, point to **Control Panel**, point to **Network Connections**, and then click **Local Area Connection**.

   In Windows 2000: Click **Start**, point to **Settings**, and then click **Network and Dial-up Connections**. In the Network and Dial-up Connections window, click **Local Area Connection**.

2. The Local Area Connection Status dialog box opens. Click **Properties**.
3. In the Local Area Connection Properties dialog box, click **Internet Protocol (TCP/IP)**, and then click **Properties**.
4. In the Internet Protocol (TCP/IP) Properties dialog box, click **Advanced**.
5. In the Advanced TCP/IP Settings dialog box, click the **DNS** tab, as shown in Figure 4-14.
6. To add a DNS address, click **Add**.
7. The TCP/IP DNS Server dialog box appears. Type **192.168.0.100**, and then click **Add**.
8. Although the DNS configuration is complete, note the references to DNS suffixes. They simply mean that if you enter a suffix of *technowidgets.com*, you can just use the host names of "www" and "mail" instead of the full names of *www.technowidgets.com* and *mail.technowidgets.com*. Click **OK**.
9. Close the remaining windows.

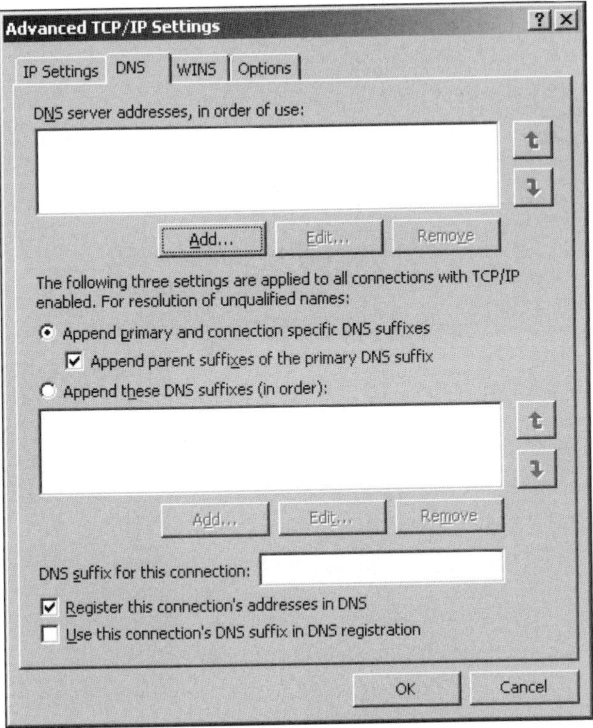

Figure 4-14 TCP/IP configuration window for DNS

You have set up both the DNS server and the TCP/IP property in the client software to have your server resolve names. Windows offered you more guidance than the same process in Linux, but it was still easy to forget to add the period at the end of an FQDN.

TROUBLESHOOTING DNS

There is more than one way to make sure that DNS is working, and many of these techniques are similar in Windows and Linux. The most common technique is to use the **ping** utility, which you learned about in Chapter 3. Another helpful utility is **nslookup**, which is available on both Linux and Windows. The nslookup utility can give you more information about a host name because it actually reads DNS information; for example, it can tell you that *www.technowidgets.com* is a canonical name for *web1.technowidgets.com*. In Linux, an even better utility for getting DNS information is **dig**. The dig utility can extract more DNS information, such as the SOA record, from the DNS.

Using ping to Test Connectivity

In Chapter 3, you used ping with an IP address to test connectivity. You can also use this utility to determine whether the DNS server can translate a host name into an IP address. It is not important that the addresses for mail and research do not exist yet; you just want to make sure that the names are resolved. In Figure 4-15, you can see the result of typing "ping mail.technowidgets.com". The second line of the `ping` statement shows you that the name was translated to 192.168.0.200, so you know that DNS is working. Even though it was translated correctly by DNS, there is no IP address of 192.168.0.200, so the reply timed out.

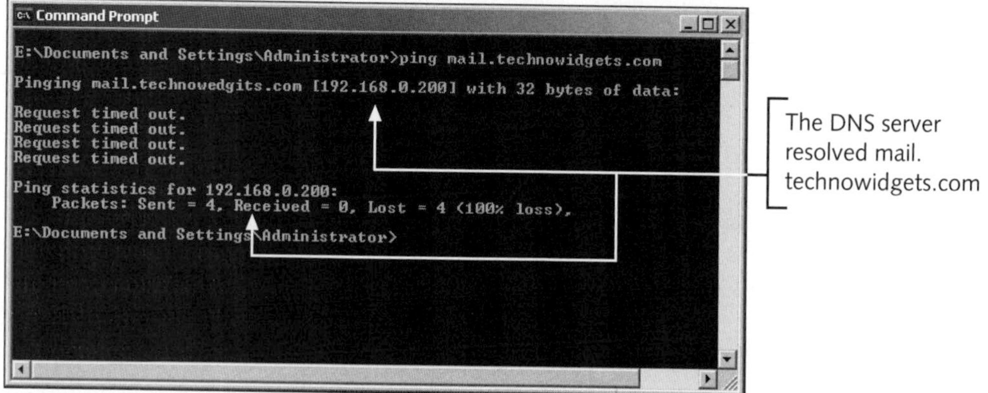

Figure 4-15 Pinging to test connectivity

Using nslookup to Check DNS

Another utility specifically designed to test DNS functionality is **nslookup**. The first two letters in the name of the utility's name stand for "name server," indicating that nslookup is designed to look up information in a name (DNS) server. The utility works in two modes: command-line mode and interactive mode.

In command-line mode, you type the command plus an address or name; nslookup responds with the answer and comes back to the command prompt. For an example, look at the top of Figure 4-16. When the user entered the command "nslookup www.technowidgets.com", nslookup responded that the actual host name is *web1.technowidgets.com* at 192.168.0.100 and noted that *www.technowidgets.com* is an alias. The utility works the same way in both Windows and Linux, but in Linux it displays a message stating that the command is **deprecated**. A deprecated command is considered obsolete and may be dropped from future versions of the software.

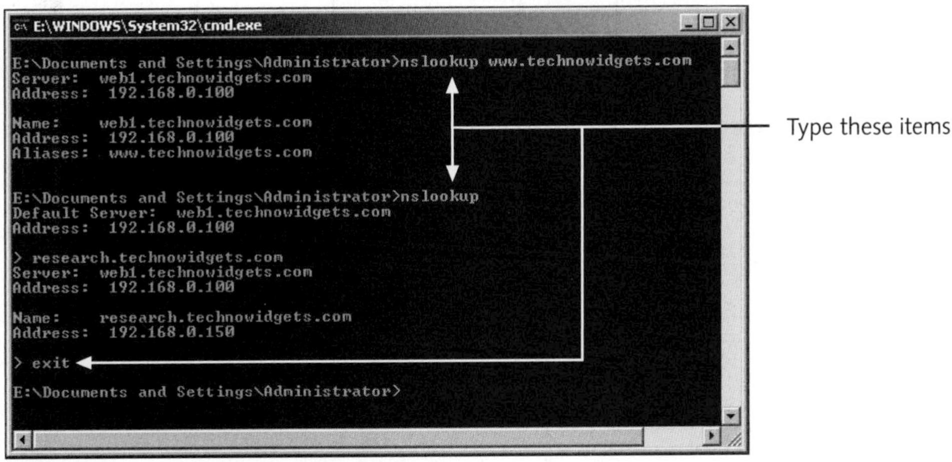

Figure 4-16 Example of nslookup

You can use nslookup in interactive mode when you want to look up more than one piece of information. Interactive mode means that you type commands from within the nslookup program. As shown in Figure 4-16, you simply type `nslookup` and press Enter to get into interactive mode. You are then ready to request information for the local DNS server. If you type `research.technowidgets.com`, nslookup responds with the IP address that corresponds to *research.technowidgets.com*. If you type an IP address that exists in DNS, nslookup responds with the host name. For example, if you type `192.168.0.200`, nslookup responds with *mail.technowidgets.com*. To exit interactive mode, type exit.

Using dig to Find DNS Information in Linux

The **dig (domain information groper)** utility can find more information about DNS records than nslookup does. It is not included in Windows, but it is available with Linux. As with nslookup, you can use dig in either command-line mode or interactive mode.

By default, dig looks at the local DNS server. You need to specify two items in your command. The first item is the name or IP address, such as *www.technowidgets.com* or 192.168.0.200. The second item describes the information you want, such as "a" for IP address, "ns" for information on the name server itself, "mx" for the mail exchanger for the domain, or "soa" for the SOA record for the domain. Table 4-5 lists some sample commands using dig.

Table 4-5 Sample commands using dig

Command	Description
`dig technowidgets.com soa`	Display the soa record for the *technowidgets.com* domain. Display the host name that corresponds to the domain name and its IP address.
`dig www.technowidgets.com a`	Display the IP address for *www.technowidgets.com*. If it is a canonical name (alias), display the actual host name.
`dig technowidgets.com ns`	Display the name of the DNS server (name server) and its IP address.

The actual output of the **`dig`** command includes more than a corresponding command using nslookup. The lines preceded by semicolons (;) are comments inserted by the **`dig`** command. The other lines, which are the actual output you are seeking, appear in the Answer section. Figure 4-17 shows an example of the **`dig technowidgets.com ns`** command. The name server is *web1.technowidgets.com* and the IP address for *web1.technowidgets.com* is 192.168.0.100.

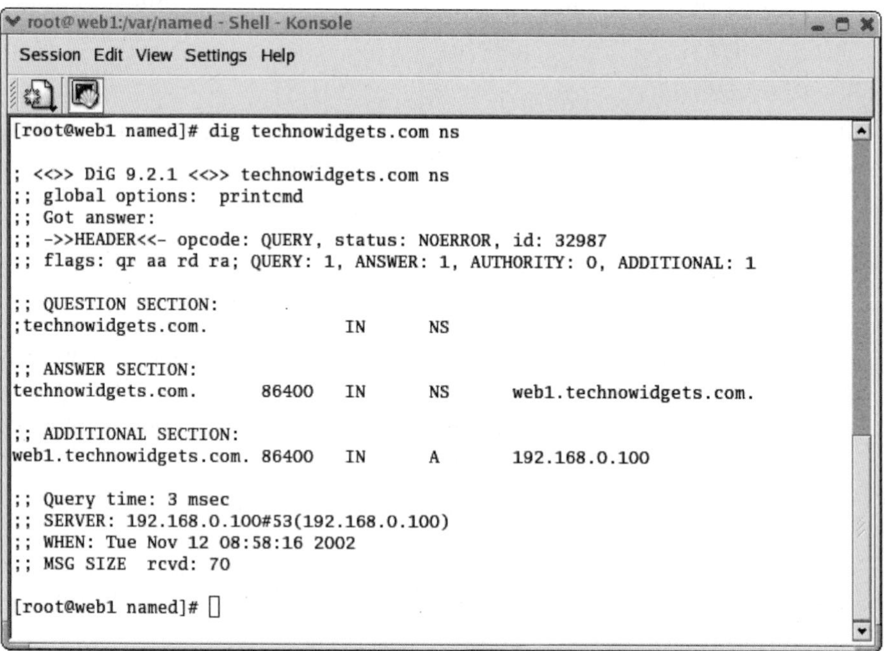

Figure 4-17 Example of a `dig` command

Other Troubleshooting Techniques for DNS

If ping, nslookup, and dig do not give you the correct results, you need to track down the errors and fix them yourself. In Linux, for example, you have to make sure that you started the DNS server by typing the following command:

```
/etc/rc.d/init.d/named start
```


If it still does not work, make sure you set the DNS client configuration to the address of the DNS server. In Linux, this information is in /etc/resolv.conf; in Windows, check the steps in the "Configuring Client-Side DNS in Windows" section earlier in this chapter. Another common problem is mistakenly entered combinations of IP addresses. If you used different IP addresses, make sure that you entered them consistently throughout the configurations.

In Linux, the `/etc/rc.d/init.d/named start` Command Fails

You probably have a syntax error in one or more of the following files: named.conf, named.technowidgets.com, or named.192.168.0. Check the files for errors.

In Linux, DNS Starts, But the `ping` and `nslookup` Commands Do Not Work

The filenames in named.conf probably do not match the actual files in /var/named. For example, the named.conf file contains the following line:

```
file "named.technowidgets.com";
```

Do you have a file with that name in var/named? To check, type the following command:

```
ls /var/named/named.technowidgets.com
```

I Receive a Response from Some Hosts, But Not All

You probably have a typographical error in one of your host names. The most common error is an FQDN without a period at the end of the name. Conversely, if you just have a host name, make sure no period appears at the end.

Using WINS to Resolve Computer Names in Windows

WINS is another method for resolving names besides DNS. It is used by Windows NT Workstation, Windows 95, and Windows 98 to resolve computer names in a LAN, although these clients still use DNS to resolve host names for the Internet. WINS and DNS serve different purposes in these older systems.

Understanding Computer Names

Technically, computer names for Windows computers are called **NetBIOS** names. A NetBIOS name is based on the NetBIOS interface, which was developed in the 1980s to link software with network services and thereby allow computers to communicate with one another. Each NetBIOS name was broadcast to every computer physically connected to other computers on the network, and the names could not be routed to other networks. This scheme prevented computers on one network from accessing resources on another network. WINS was created to act as a centralized database of computer names and their associated IP addresses. For example, if you wanted to access a printer on a computer named corp1, the printer software on your computer could look up the IP address for the corp1 computer in WINS so it could communicate with the printer.

Installing WINS

Installing WINS is as easy as installing DNS. Both are components of networking services. The following procedures explain how to install WINS on Windows 2000 and Windows 2003.

To install WINS on Windows 2000 or Windows 2003:

1. Insert the Windows CD in the drive. When the installation begins, click **Exit**.
2. In the Control Panel, double-click **Add or Remove Programs**.
3. Click **Add/Remove Windows Components**.
4. Scroll down and click the words **Networking Services**, but not the check box next to it.
5. Click **Details** to display the available networking services.
6. Click the **Windows Internet Name Service (WINS)** check box.
7. Click **OK** to return to the Windows Components Wizard.
8. Click **Next**, and then click **Finish** to complete the installation of WINS. Close the window.

Configuring WINS

From the client perspective, setting up WINS is as easy as setting up DNS. You enter the IP address for the WINS server, and the WINS database is updated automatically every time you turn on the computer.

To configure a WINS client for a Windows NT Workstation or server:

1. Right-click the **Network Neighborhood** icon on the desktop.
2. Click **Properties**. The Network dialog box opens.
3. Click the **Protocols** tab.

4. Click **TCP/IP Protocol**.
5. Click **Properties**.
6. Click the **WINS Address** tab.
7. Enter the IP address of the WINS server in the Primary WINS Server text box.
8. Click **OK**, and then click **Close** to finish configuring the WINS client.

The most common error in setting up WINS is forgetting to configure it on the server. You might think that installing WINS on the server would automatically change the server's TCP/IP settings to include the server name in the WINS database, but it does not. You have to configure WINS on the server just as you did on the workstation.

Administering WINS

Typically, WINS does not require much administration. Because it is a dynamic database, it should add and delete names automatically. However, sometimes problems arise. For example, a record might be stuck in the database and have to be deleted. Figure 4-18 shows an example of a WINS database with just the server on the network.

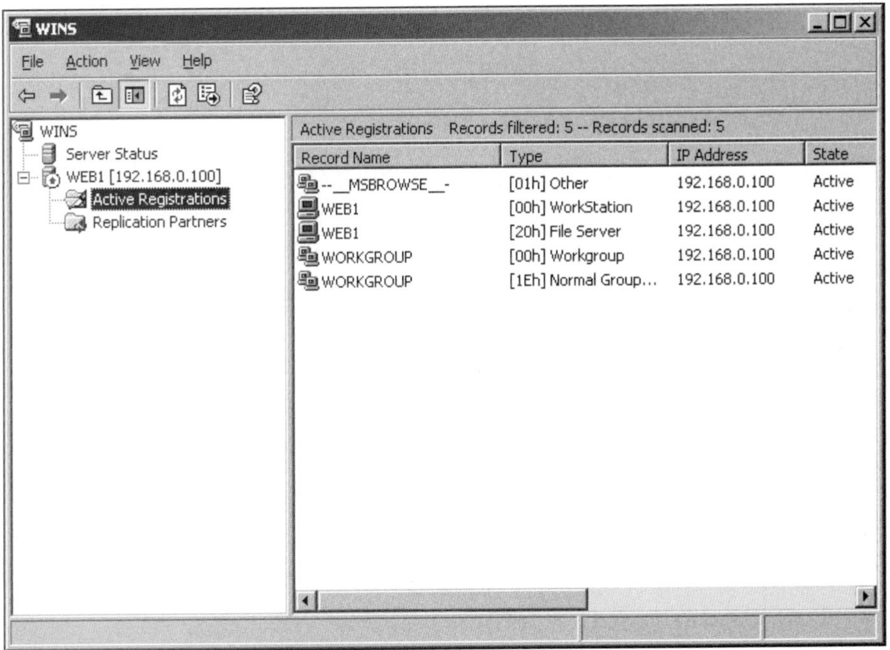

Figure 4-18 WINS database

Note that a single computer can have a number of entries. Not only are NetBIOS names associated with the computer, but they are also associated with the group and the login name. Even the server name web1 has two entries, which Windows uses to differentiate between a computer used as a workstation and a computer used as a server.

Chapter Summary

- DNS is an application that translates names to IP addresses and IP addresses to names. These names exist in a hierarchical structure. At the top of the structure is the root-level domain, which is where searches begin. The next level is the top-level domain, which has names such as .com, .org, .uk, and .name that are controlled by ICANN. Second-level domain names include *microsoft.com* and *redhat.com*. Often these domain names can be registered. Thus, if one is not already being used, you can pay a fee and use it yourself.
- Servers come in many forms. Root servers know the location of the DNS servers that take care of the top-level domains. Servers in the top-level domains know the location of the servers in the second level, which are typically DNS servers controlled by an organization. At the level of these DNS servers are primary servers, secondary servers, caching servers, and forwarding servers. The primary server defines the hosts for a domain. The secondary server provides backup for the primary server. The caching server caches IP addresses of hosts requested by users. The forwarding server passes requests to another DNS server when it cannot answer the request itself.
- To configure DNS, you must configure a forward lookup zone and a reverse lookup zone. The forward lookup zone translates host names to IP addresses. The reverse lookup zone translates IP addresses to host names.
- To configure DNS files in Linux, you modify three text files. The /etc/named.conf file contains the names of the zones and the names of the zone files. The other two files are the zone files for forward and reverse lookups.
- You configure DNS files in Windows using a GUI. Windows provides more guidance during DNS configuration than Linux does, but the concepts underlying both processes are exactly the same.

- Troubleshooting DNS problems involves using utilities such as ping, nslookup, and dig. Ping tests basic connectivity. Nslookup can provide more detail about specific DNS records. Dig offers detailed information about the DNS configuration. If you find a problem, work through it step by step. The most common error is an FQDN that does not end with a period.
- Although DNS is used on the Internet and DDNS is used for some Windows operating systems such as Windows 2000, Windows XP, and Windows 2003, older Microsoft operating systems need WINS to resolve names in a LAN.

Review Questions

1. Name resolution means ______________.
   a. translating names to IP addresses
   b. translating IP addresses to names
   c. both a and b
   d. neither a nor b
2. DNS can be used for name resolution on the Internet and LANs. True or False?
3. The IP address 10.1.2.3 could be associated with ______________.
   a. *www.mycompany.com*
   b. *mycompany.com*
   c. com
   d. both a and b
4. At the top of the DNS hierarchy are the top-level domain names. True or False?
5. Linux.org is an example of a(n) ______________.
   a. root server
   b. TLD
   c. SLD
   d. XLD
6. Which of the following TLDs was added in 2000?
   a. org
   b. in-addr.arpa
   c. pt
   d. info

7. In which of the following TLDs can the general public register names?
   a. pro
   b. org
   c. aero
   d. coop
8. Second-level domains can be further subdivided into ________________.
   a. subdomains
   b. third-level domains
   c. host-level domains
   d. other-level domains
9. When you register a domain, how many DNS servers are required?
   a. 0
   b. 1
   c. 2
   d. 3
10. Which of the following is not a type of DNS server?
    a. primary
    b. secondary
    c. forwarding
    d. reversing
11. Which server type would be configured by the administrator to contain host names?
    a. primary
    b. secondary
    c. forwarding
    d. reversing
12. By having a local ________________ server, response time for URL resolution can be reduced significantly.
13. Which type of zone maps names to IP addresses?
    a. forward
    b. reverse
    c. primary
    d. secondary

14. Which type of record is used in a reverse lookup zone file?
    a. CNAME
    b. A
    c. MX
    d. PTR

15. What does the @ mean?
    a. the name of the server
    b. the name of the zone
    c. "at this time"
    d. nothing; it is just a placeholder
16. In the line "@ IN SOA web1.xyz.com. admn.xyz.com. (", admn refers to ________________.
    a. an e-mail name
    b. a host name
    c. an alternative name of the DNS server
    d. the secondary server
17. In an SOA record, the number for the refresh interval of 28800 is in ________________.
    a. milliseconds
    b. seconds
    c. minutes
    d. hours
18. In Linux, the name of the file that contains the names of the zone files is ________________.
    a. zone.conf
    b. conf.zone
    c. named.conf
    d. dns.conf
19. Which of the following would be correct for configuring a DNS client in Linux?
    a. nameserver 10.1.1.1
    b. name server 10.1.1.1
    c. dnsserver 10.1.1.1
    d. dns server 10.1.1.1

20. Which of the following utilities is not installed with Windows?
    a. ping
    b. nslookup
    c. dig
    d. All of the above are installed.

Hands-on Projects

In the following projects, you will work with DNS. DNS should be installed and running before you perform the Hands-on Projects, except for Project 4-1, which guides you through installing DNS on a Linux computer.

Projects 4-1 through 4-4 and Project 4-9 assume that you are logged on to Linux as the root and that you are starting at a shell prompt in a terminal window. To open the terminal window, click the red hat icon, point to System tools, then click Terminal.

Project 4-1

Complete this project *only* if you did not install DNS when you installed Linux in Chapter 3. Although you can use the Konqueror file system manager to double-click the package to install, you should learn how to install it from a shell prompt because that procedure is the same on all Linux distributions that support rpm files.

To install DNS on your Red Hat system:

1. Open a terminal window.
2. Insert your Red Hat installation CD1 in the drive.
3. Make the CD available by mounting it. Type **mount /mnt/cdrom**, and press **Enter**. Be sure to press the spacebar after typing "mount."
4. Install the BIND software by entering the following command:

   rpm –ivh /mnt/cdrom/RedHat/RPMS/bind-9*.
5. Be sure to type a space after "rpm". Install the bind utilities by entering the following command:

   rpm –ivh /mnt/cdrom/RedHat/RPMS/bind-util*

   Be sure to type a space after "rpm".

Your system is ready to be configured.

Project 4-2

The purpose of this project is to create a DNS server in Linux. The first step is to create a domain name and host addresses. Use the IP addresses shown in parentheses only if your computer is not part of a network. If it is part of a network, your instructor will have to assign IP addresses.

To create a domain name and host addresses:

1. Choose your own domain name and enter it below. You can be creative because no organization is telling you what TLDs you can use.

   Domain name: ______________

2. Use the domain name and the IP address of your computer to create entries for the IP address of the domain and web1.

   IP address of your domain: ______________ (192.168.0.100)

   The host, web1, will have the same address as the domain. The hosts mail and www will have the same addresses as web1. Earlier in the chapter, mail had a different IP address because typically a mail server is not on the same computer. However, for the projects in Chapter 8, you will install the e-mail server on the same computer.

3. Ask your instructor for the IP addresses for intranet and research and write them in the following spaces.

   IP address of intranet: ______________ (192.168.0.150)

   IP address of research: ______________ (192.168.0.200)

To copy DNS configuration files to Linux directories:

1. Open a terminal window and insert the floppy disk with the DNS files from the Chapter 4 folder of your data disk.

   You will use the configuration files for *technowidgets.com* as a guide.

2. To make the floppy disk available for copying, type the following command:

   mount /mnt/floppy

3. To copy the named.conf file to the /etc directory, type the following command:

   cp /mnt/floppy/Chapter4/named.conf /etc/named.conf

4. Note the spaces after "cp" and "named.conf". In the following command, replace x.com with your domain name. To copy named.technowidgets.com to /var/named and rename it named.x.com, type the following command:

   cp /mnt/floppy/Chapter4/named.technowidgets.com /var/named/named.x.com

   Make sure that the filename in /var/named matches the filename you configure in named.conf for your domain name.

5. In the following command, change the second occurrence of 0.168.192 with the reversed network portion of your IP address. To copy named.0.168.192 to /var/named, type the following command:

   cp /mnt/floppy/Chapter4/named.0.168.192 /var/named/named.0.168.192

6. Open the rc.local file in the rc.d directory, add the command that starts the DNS server to the rc.local file (**/etc/rc.d/init.d/named start**) on a new line at the end of the file.

Now you can modify the existing files or type them in from the beginning.

To create a DNS server in Linux for your domain:

1. At the shell prompt, type **kedit /etc/named.conf**.

   A file opens, similar to the one shown earlier in Figure 4-8. Your objective is to add references for a forward lookup zone and a reverse lookup zone. Replace *technowidgets.com* with your domain. Be careful to create a reverse lookup zone name that is the reverse of the network portion of your IP address. It should be placed just before the last line:

```
zone "technowidgets.com" IN {
    type master;
    file "named.technowidgets.com";
};

zone "0.168.192.in-addr.arpa" IN {
    type master;
    file "named.0.168.192";
};
```

2. Create a forward lookup zone file. The name of your file is the reference you just created in named.conf. For *technowidgets.com*, it was called named.technowidgets.com. Type **kedit /var/named** followed by the name of your file. Press **Enter**. Create a file that looks like the following code. Again, remember to replace the domain name and IP addresses with your own.

```
$TTL 86400
@    IN    SOA    web1.technowidgets.com. admn.technowidgets.com. (
                        2002072100 ; Serial
                        28800      ; Refresh
                        14400      ; Retry
                        3600000    ; Expire
                        86400 )    ; Minimum
```

```
IN      NS      web1
            IN      A       192.168.0.100
            IN      MX  10  mail.technowidgets.com.

web1        IN  A       192.168.0.100
www         IN  CNAME       web1
mail        IN  CNAME       web1
intranet    IN  A       192.168.0.150
research    IN  A       192.168.0.200
```

3. Click the floppy disk icon to save the file and close the window.
4. Create a reverse lookup zone file. The name of your file is the reference you just created in named.conf. For the network 192.168.0.0, it was named.0.168.192. Type **kedit /var/named/**, followed by the name of your file, and press **Enter**. Create a file that looks like the following code. Again, remember to replace the domain name and IP addresses with your own.

```
$TTL 86400
@     IN     SOA    web1.technowidgets.com. admn.technowidgets.com. (
                          2002072100 ; Serial
                          28800      ; Refresh
                          14400      ; Retry
                          3600000    ; Expire
                          86400 )    ; Minimum
            IN      NS      web1

100   IN   PTR     web1.technowidgets.com.
150        IN      PTR     intranet.technowidgets.com.
200        IN      PTR     research.technowidgets.com.
```

5. Click the floppy disk icon and close the window.

Check the two zone files and make sure that each FQDN, such as *research.technowidgets.com.*, ends with a period. Missing periods are by far the most common reason that the DNS server does not work.

6. Start the DNS server by typing the following command:

/etc/rc.d/init.d/named start

You cannot test the server until you configure the DNS client in Project 4-4.

Project 4-3

Add a second domain to an existing DNS server. Create only the forward lookup zone. Notice how similar this project is to Project 4-2. You can use this technique to add as many domains as you want.

To add a new domain to an existing DNS server.

1. In a terminal window, type **kedit /etc/named.conf** and then press **Enter**.
2. Type the following code starting on the next-to-last line of the file:

```
zone "dnstest.com" IN {
    type master;
    file "named.dnstest.com";
};
```

3. Click **File** on the menu bar, and then click **Save** to save the file.
4. Click **File** on the menu bar, and then click **New** to create a configuration file for dnstest.com.
5. Type the following information. Although the information is almost the same as that in Project 4-2, you enter the data in a different but equivalent format:

```
$TTL  86400
@      IN     SOA   web1 admn.dnstest.com. (
                        2002072100 ; Serial
                        28800      ; Refresh
                        14400      ; Retry
                        3600000    ; Expire
                        86400 )    ; Minimum
dnstest.com. IN    NS      web1
dnstest.com. IN    A       192.168.0.100
dnstest.com. IN    MX    10  mail

web1.dnstest.com.      IN    A       192.168.0.100
www.dnstest.com.       IN    CNAME       web1
mail.dnstest.com.      IN    A       192.168.0.200
```

6. Click **File** on the menu bar, and then click **Save As**. The Save File As dialog box opens.
7. In the Location text box, type **/var/named/named.dnstest.com** and then click **OK**. This saves the file as named.dnstest.com in the /var/named directory—the file name designated in Step 2.

8. Close the kedit window.
9. Type **/etc/rc.d/init.d/named restart**, which will restart the DNS server so you can test the new domain after completing Project 4-4.

Project 4-4

Configure a DNS client in Linux to recognize multiple DNS servers. Get IP addresses from two other student DNS servers on the network. The steps assume that other DNS servers are located at 192.168.0.110 and 192.168.0.120. Configuring references for multiple servers is common practice—in case one DNS server is not available, you can then use the next DNS server in the list.

To configure multiple DNS servers in Linux:

1. In a terminal window, type **kedit /etc/resolv.conf** and then press **Enter**.
2. The first line of the file should have the reference to the DNS server on your computer. For example, if your IP address was 192.168.0.100, you would enter **nameserver 192.168.0.100** and press **Enter**.
3. Type the following lines, remembering to substitute the IP addresses given with the IP addresses of the other student DNS servers:

   nameserver 192.168.0.110

   nameserver 192.168.0.120
4. Type the following line but replace the domain name with your own:

   domain technowidgets.com
5. Click **File** on the menu bar, and then click **Save**.
6. You should be able to ping your Web server now. If your domain name was *technowidgets.com*, you would type **ping www.technowidgets.com**. If you completed Project 4-3, you could ping the hosts you created.
7. Get the host names of the other student Web servers and use the ping utility to make sure that the servers are resolving the names.

Project 4-5

Install the DNS server. This project is required for Windows 2003 because you are not given the option of installing DNS during the OS installation. With Windows 2000, you could have installed the DNS server as you installed the operating system.

To install the DNS server in Windows 2003:

1. Insert the Windows installation CD. When the installation window opens, close it.
2. From the Control Panel, click **Add or Remove Programs**.
3. Click **Add/Remove Windows Components** in the left panel. The Windows Components Wizard opens.

4. Scroll down and click **Networking Services**, and then click **Details**.
5. Select the **Domain Name System (DNS)** check box, and then click **OK**.
6. Click **Next** to install the DNS server.

Project 4-6

Create a DNS server in Windows 2003 based on your own domain name. First, gather the information as you did in the first three steps in Project 4-2 for your own domain name and IP addresses. Remember to replace *technowidgets.com* with your domain name and the sample IP addresses with your addresses. To allow the other IP addresses for intranet and research to work, you should add these IP addresses to your computer. You will use them in subsequent chapters.

To add IP addresses in Windows 2003:

1. From the Windows 2003 Control Panel, point to **Network Connections**, and then click **Local Area Connection**.
2. The Local Area Connection Status window opens. Click **Properties**. The Local Area Connection Properties window opens. Click **Internet Protocol (TCP/IP)**.
3. Click **Properties**. The Internet Protocol (TCP/IP) Properties window opens.
4. Click **Advanced**. The Advanced TCP/IP Settings dialog box opens.
5. Under IP address, click **Add**. The TCP/IP Address dialog box opens.
6. Type the IP address and subnet mask for the intranet host. Click **Add**.
7. Add the IP address for the research host.
8. Click **OK** twice and close the windows.

To add a new zone using the wizard:

1. In Administrative Tools, click **DNS**. The dnsmgmt window opens. See Figure 4-9.
2. Right-click **WEB1** (the name of your computer) in the left pane, and then click **Configure a DNS Server**. The Configure a DNS Server Wizard opens. See Figure 4-19. The first time you open this window, you may find the selections disabled. If so, click the name of the computer.
3. Click **Next**. The Select Configuration Action dialog box opens. Click the **Create forward and reverse lookup zones** option button to create a DNS server similar to the one described for Linux. See Figure 4-20.

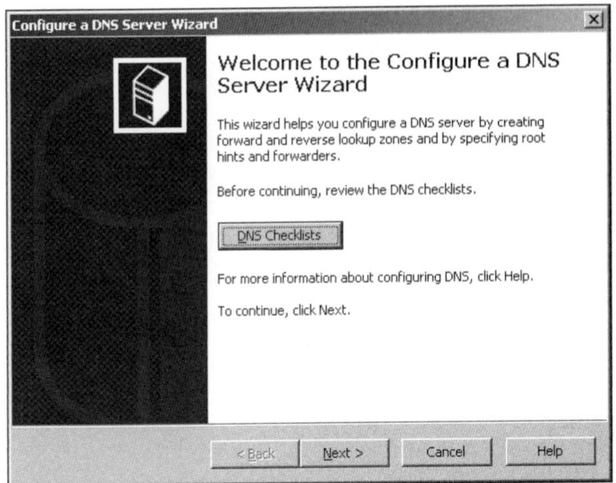

Figure 4-19 Configure a DNS Server Wizard

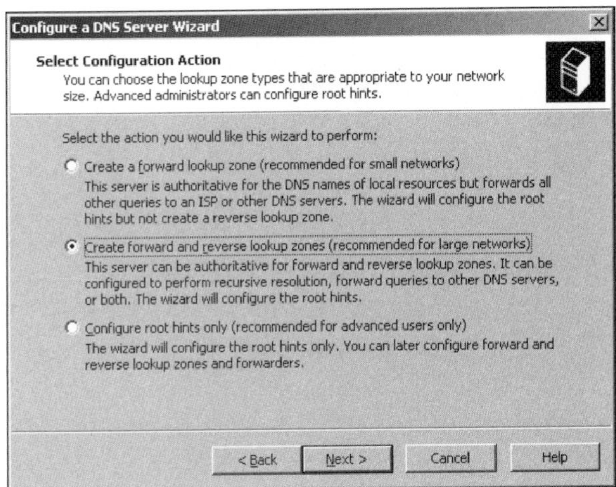

Figure 4-20 Select Configuration Action dialog box

4. Click **Next**. The Forward Lookup Zone dialog box opens. Keep the default of creating a forward lookup zone now. Click **Next**.
5. The Zone Type dialog box opens. See Figure 4-21. Keep the default of Primary zone. Note that you could also create a secondary zone, which gets its information from another server, or a stub zone, which just creates basic information.

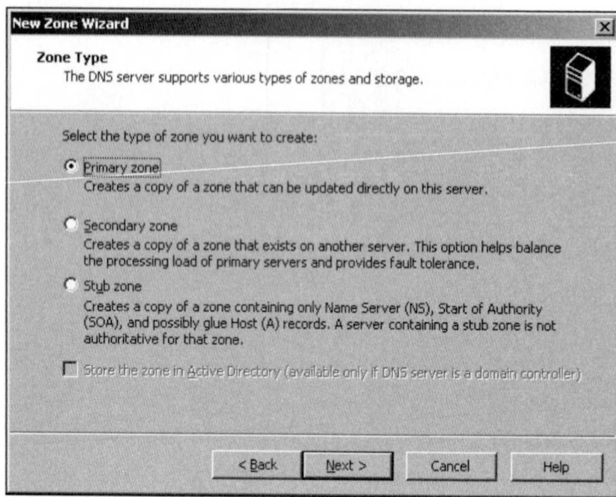

Figure 4-21 Zone Type dialog box

6. Click **Next**.
7. The Zone Name dialog box opens. See Figure 4-22. Enter your own domain name for the zone, such as **technowidgets.com**.

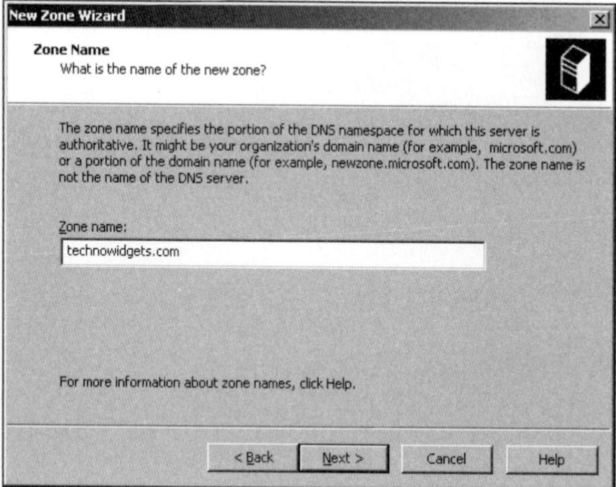

Figure 4-22 Zone Name dialog box

8. Click **Next**. The Zone File dialog box opens. See Figure 4-23. Accept the default filename based on your domain name.

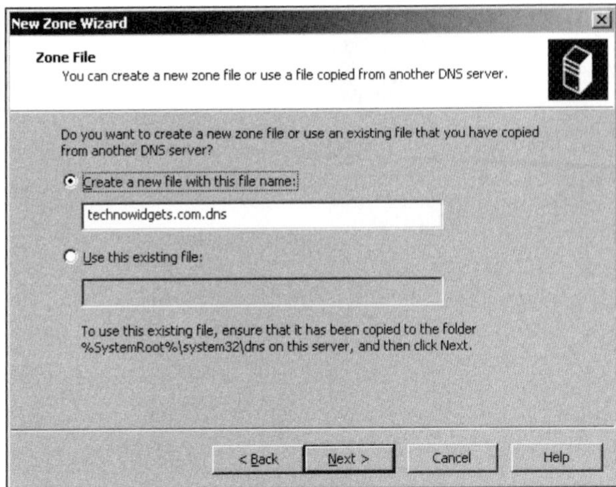

Figure 4-23 Zone File dialog box

9. Click **Next.** The Dynamic Update dialog box opens. See Figure 4-24. The two choices determine whether you will accept dynamic DNS update from your network. Keep the default option button of Do not allow dynamic updates.

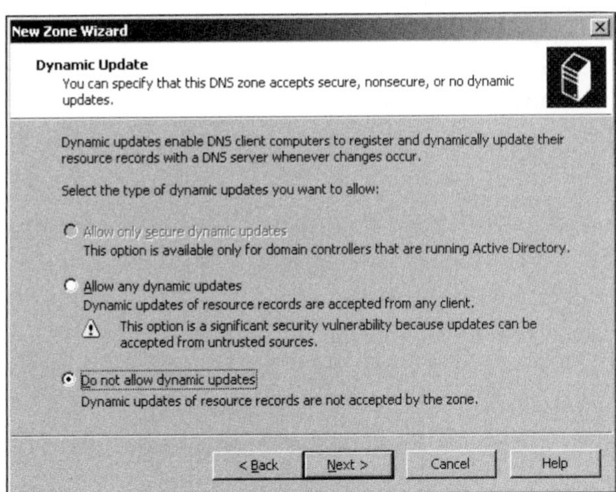

Figure 4-24 Dynamic Update dialog box

10. Click **Next.** The Reverse Lookup Zone dialog box opens. See Figure 4-25. Note that it states that "Reverse lookup zones are usually necessary only if programs require this information." You are creating a reverse lookup zone in case programs do require one.

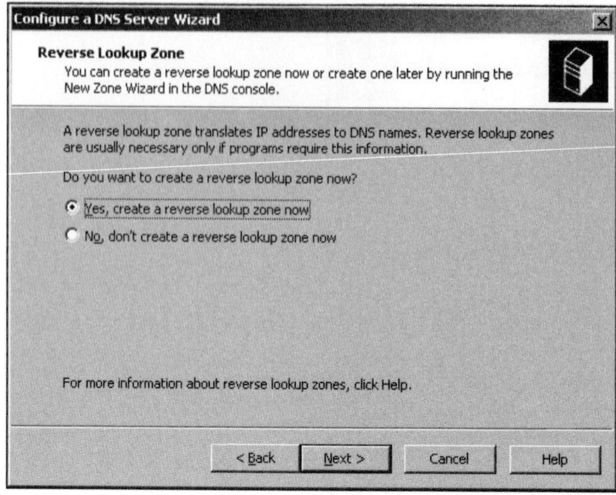

Figure 4-25 Reverse Lookup Zone dialog box

11. Accept the default of "Yes, create a reverse lookup zone now". Click **Next**. The Zone Type dialog box opens. It is the same as Figure 4-21 but now refers to the reverse lookup zone. Keep the default of Primary zone.
12. Click **Next**. The Reverse Lookup Zone Name dialog box opens. Enter the network portion of your IP address. For a class C address, you would enter the first three octets, such as 192.168.0. As you enter the address, the appropriate filename is created in the other text box.
13. Click **Next**. The Zone File dialog box opens. Leave the default filename for your reverse lookup zone file.
14. Click **Next**. The Dynamic Update dialog box opens. It looks like Figure 4-24 except that it is for the reverse lookup zone. Keep the default option button of Do not allow dynamic updates.
15. Click **Next**. The Forwarders dialog box opens. Typically, the IP address of the forwarder belongs to your ISP. For this project, click **No, it should not forward queries**.
16. Click **Next**. The Searching for Root Hints message box might open, followed by the Completing the Configure a DNS Server Wizard dialog box opens. See Figure 4-26. Note that settings are summarized.
17. Click **Finish** to exit the wizard. You may receive a message that the wizard could not find root hints. That will not create a problem for these projects. Click **OK**.

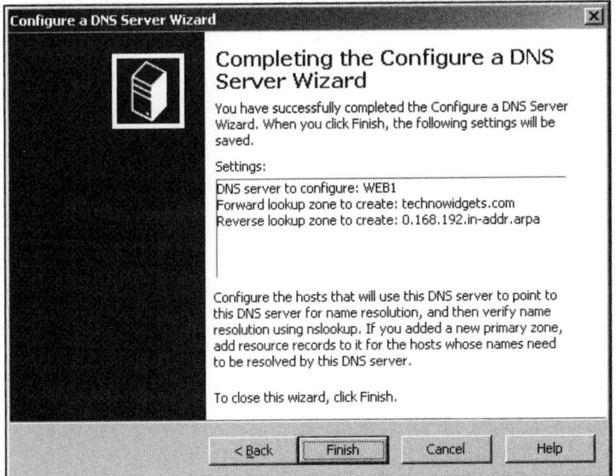

Figure 4-26 Completing the Configure a DNS Server Wizard

Now you have created the correct file structure. The next procedure is to fill the files with information about the hosts in your Web environment such as www, intranet, research, and mail.

To set up hosts for your domain:

1. In the dnsmgmt window, expand the left pane until you see the name of your domain name under Forward Lookup Zones.
2. Right-click the name of your domain and then click **New Host (A)**. In the Name text box, type the name of your computer. In the IP address text box, type the IP address of your server. Select **Create associated pointer (PTR) record**, if necessary.
3. Click **Add Host**. The DNS message box opens stating that the record was added. Click **OK**.
4. You return to the New Host dialog box so you can add more hosts. Add the hosts **research** and **intranet** with different IP addresses. When you are finished adding the extra hosts, click **Done**.
5. Next, you need to add a host for www. Because www is on the same computer and you have already created a host name for the computer in Step 2, you will create an alias for the name of the computer called www. Right-click the name of your domain, and then click **New Alias**. The New Resource Record dialog box opens.
6. In the Alias Name text box type, **www**. For the Fully qualified name for target host, type the name of the computer followed by a dot, followed by the name of your domain. For example, if the computer name is web1 and the domain name is technowidgets.com, type **web1.technowidgets.com**. However, do not add a dot at the end. Click **OK**.

7. Create an alias for the mail host as you did for www in the previous step, using **mail** as the alias name. In this case, the mail server is at the same IP address as the Web server. The "To add hosts to the DNS configuration in Windows" steps earlier in the chapter show how to create a mail server at a different IP address.
8. Although you have a host called mail, you have not set it up as a mail exchanger so that e-mail server names can be resolved. Right-click your domain name, and then click **New Mail Exchanger**.
9. Because you want to send mail to a host that corresponds to your domain name, you need to leave the Host or domain text box blank. In the Mail server text box, type the fully qualified host name for the mail server. For technowidgets.com, it would be mail.technowidgets.com. Leave the priority at **10**. Click **OK**.

To test your DNS server, complete Project 4-8.

Project 4-7

Create a DNS server in Windows 2000 based on your own domain name. First, gather the information as you did in the first three steps in Project 4-2 for your own domain name and IP addresses. Remember to replace technowidgets.com with your domain name and the sample IP addresses with your addresses. To allow the other IP addresses for intranet and research to work, you should add these IP addresses to your computer. You will use them in subsequent chapters.

To add IP addresses in Windows 2000:

1. In Windows 2000, right-click **My Network Places**, and then click **Properties**. The Network and Dial-up Connections window opens. Double-click **Local Area Connection**.
2. The Local Area Connection Status window opens. Click **Properties**. The Local Area Connection Properties window opens. Highlight **Internet Protocol (TCP/IP)**.
3. Click **Properties**. The Internet Protocol (TCP/IP) Properties window opens.
4. Click **Advanced**. The Advanced TCP/IP Settings dialog box opens.
5. Under IP address, click **Add**. The TCP/IP Address dialog box opens.
6. Type the IP address and subnet mask for the intranet host. Click **Add**.
7. Click **Add** again and add the IP address for the research host. Click **Add** and close the window.
8. Click **OK** twice and then close the windows.

To configure a DNS server in Windows 2000 with the wizard:

1. From the Control Panel, open the Administrative Tools window. Double-click **DNS** to open the DNS window.
2. Right-click the name of your computer, and then click **Configure the server**. The Configure DNS Server Wizard opens.

3. Click **Next**. The Root Server dialog box opens. This is the first DNS server so you should keep the default.
4. Click **Next**. The Forward Lookup Zone dialog box opens. You want to create a forward lookup zone so you will keep the default.
5. Click **Next**. The Zone Type dialog box opens. You want to create a primary server so you will keep the default of Standard primary.
6. Click **Next**. The Zone Name dialog box opens. Type the name of your domain name (for example, technowidgets.com).
7. Click **Next**. The Zone File dialog box opens. It suggests a name based on your zone (domain) name. Keep the default name.
8. Click **Next**. The Reverse Lookup Zone dialog box opens. Accept the default of Yes, create a reverse lookup zone.
9. Click **Next**. The Zone Type dialog box opens. It is the same dialog box previously displayed, except that this time it is for the reverse lookup zone. As in Step 5, keep the default of Standard primary.
10. Click **Next**. The Reverse Lookup Zone dialog box opens. Remember that you have to enter the network portion of your IP address. For example, the network 192.168.0.0 is entered as 192.168.0.
11. Click **Next**. The Zone File dialog box opens. Accept the default filename.
12. Click **Next**. The Completing the Configure DNS Server Wizard dialog box opens with a summary of your actions.
13. Click **Finish** to exit the wizard.

Now you have created the correct file structure. The next step is to fill the files with information about the hosts in your Web environment such as www, research, and mail.

To set up hosts for your domain:

1. In the DNS window, expand the **Forward Lookup Zones** folder in the left pane. Your domain name appears in the window.
2. Right-click the name of your domain, and then click **New Host**. In the Name text box, type the name of your computer. In the IP address text box, type the IP address of your server. Select **Create associated pointer (PTR) record**.
3. Click **Add Host**. The DNS message box opens stating that the record was added. Click **OK**.
4. You return to the New Host dialog box so you can add more hosts. Add the hosts **research** and **intranet** with different IP addresses. When you are finished adding the extra hosts, click **Done**.
5. Next, you can add a host for www. Because www is on the same computer and you have already created a host name for the computer in Step 2, you will create an alias for the name of the computer called www. Right-click the name of your domain, and then click **New Alias**. The New Resource Record dialog box opens.

6. In the Alias Name text box, type **www**. For the Fully qualified name for target host, type the name of the computer followed by a dot, and then type the name of your domain. For example, if the computer name is web1 and the domain name is technowidgets.com, type **web1.technowidgets.com** (with no dot at the end). Click **OK**.
7. Create an alias for the **mail** host as you did for www.
8. Although you have a host called mail, you have not set it up as a mail exchanger so e-mail server names can be resolved. Right-click your domain name, and then click **New Mail Exchanger**.
9. Because you want to send mail to a host that corresponds to your domain name, you need to leave the Host or domain text box blank. In the Mail server text box, type the fully qualified host name for the mail server. For technowidgets.com, it would be mail.technowidgets.com. Leave the priority at **10**. Click **OK**.

Project 4-8

Configure a DNS client in Windows to recognize multiple DNS servers. Get IP addresses from two other student DNS servers on the network. The steps assume that other DNS servers are located at 192.168.0.110 and 192.168.0.120. Configuring references for multiple servers is common practice—in case one DNS server is not available, you can then use the next DNS server in the list.

To add DNS servers to Windows:

1. In Windows 2003 from the Control Panel, point to **Network Connections**, and then click **Local Area Connection**. In Windows 2000, right-click **My Network Places**, and then click **Properties**. The Network Connections window opens. Double-click **Local Area Connection**.
2. The Local Area Connection Status window opens. Click **Properties**. The Local Area Connection Properties window opens. Highlight **Internet Protocol (TCP/IP)**.
3. Click **Properties**. The Internet Protocol (TCP/IP) Properties window opens. For the **Preferred DNS server**, enter the IP address of your computer. For the **Alternate DNS server**, enter the address of a second student's computer that has a DNS server. You need to add a text box for the third address you want to add.
4. Click **Advanced**. The Advanced TCP/IP Settings dialog box opens. Click the **DNS** tab.
5. Click **Add** to add another DNS server. The TCP/IP DNS Server dialog box opens.
6. Enter the DNS server address of another student's computer.
7. Click **Add** to add the IP address to the list of DNS servers and return to the Advanced TCP/IP Settings dialog box. Notice the third address.
8. Click **OK** to return to the Internet Protocol (TCP/IP) Properties dialog box.

9. Click **OK** to return to the Local Area Connection Properties dialog box.
10. Click **OK** to return to the Local Area Connection Status window.
11. Click **Close** to return to the Network Connections window.
12. Close the Network Connections window.
13. Using the host names of the other student Web servers, use the ping utility to make sure that the servers are resolving the names.

Project 4-9

Set up a forwarding server to see the effects of a caching server. You need to work with another student on this project. Before you start, make sure that /etc/resolv.conf has only one entry for nameserver, and that the IP address is for your server.

To set up a caching server to use a forwarding server:

1. Get the IP address of the Linux server of another student who is running DNS.
2. In a terminal window, type **kedit /etc/named.conf** and then press **Enter**. Immediately after the line "directory "/var/named"" add the following line. It assumes that the IP address of the other DNS server is 192.168.0.10:
   forwarders {192.168.0.10; };
3. Click **File** on the menu bar, and then click **Save** to save the file.
4. Close the kedit window.
5. Restart your DNS server at a shell prompt by typing the following command and then pressing **Enter**:

   /etc/rc.d/init.d/named restart
6. To test the functionality of the forwarding server, ask the other student for a host on the student's DNS server. For example, if it is *www.ecopolice.org*, you would type the following command in a terminal window and then press **Enter**:

   ping www.ecopolice.org

   Because your DNS server cannot resolve *www.ecopolice.org*, the server will forward it to the other student's DNS server for resolution.
7. Have the other student stop the DNS server by typing the following command and then pressing **Enter**:

   /etc/rc.d/init.d/named stop
8. From your computer, ping the host on the other student's computer as you did in Step 6. The command still works, even though the other student's DNS server is stopped, because you have a caching server. The name resolution was cached on your DNS server, so it does not have to go to the forwarder to resolve the name.

CASE PROJECTS

Case Project 4-1

You are starting a company on a tight budget. You can get a DSL line to your office with a static IP address, but the ISP does not offer any DNS services. At this point you do not want to set up your own DNS, so you want to find out if any companies offer such a service. Somebody told you about UltraDNS. What exactly does this firm offer? Find at least two other companies that will provide DNS servers for you.

Case Project 4-2

Think of a domain name for your new business. Where can you register the name? How much does it cost? What information do you have to provide before you can register a domain name?

Case Project 4-3

Congratulations—you just passed the bar exam. You now want to register a domain name in the .pro TLD, which is reserved for professionals. What are the rules for registering domain names in the .pro domain? Can your friend, who is a professional wrestler, register a domain, too?

Case Project 4-4

Find at least four Web sites that have information on BIND, the DNS software you used with Linux. What is the current version of BIND? Which site is most helpful for someone who wants to configure DNS?

Case Project 4-5

Write a two- to five-page paper on the issue of security and DNS. What are some of the problems? What are some of the solutions?

CHAPTER

5

MANAGING A SERVER

In this chapter, you will:

- Understand the Web server administrator's view of server management
- Examine networking models
- Learn how users are authenticated
- Manage users and groups
- Manage file system permissions
- Share resources in a network
- Enforce network policies

Because Web server administration is a part of network administration, you should understand the basics of server administration in a LAN environment and network issues in a typical organization. To help you plan the structure and functioning of a network, you use networking models that guide you in determining how users and computers work together.

Managing a server primarily involves controlling access to resources such as files and printers. You can control two areas: users' access to the server, and what users can do once they access the server. You can control these areas for users originating from the Internet as well as users on the LAN. One way to manage user access is through user authentication, which makes sure that only valid users gain access to the server. Although both Linux and Windows share the same objective of controlling access, they implement security features differently. The Windows operating systems are rich in LAN management capabilities, whereas Linux focuses on the advantages of a multiuser server. Although this chapter mainly focuses on the LAN user, most of the concepts discussed here apply to controlling Web access, too.

UNDERSTANDING THE WEB ADMINISTRATOR'S VIEW OF SERVER MANAGEMENT

When you learned about servers in Chapter 2, the focus was on the hardware—the computer and its capabilities. In this chapter, the focus is on the server software that allows you to manage server resources. When sharing files on a Windows network, this kind of software is an integral part of the operating system. When providing a Web page, the Web server software is a separate product that works with the operating system. The server computer can run more than one server software product. As a consequence, you can use the same computer as a Web server and as your e-mail server and FTP server.

Before you as the Web administrator can allow access to the Web server, e-mail server, and other Web applications, access controls need to be in place. In many organizations, the Web server is not isolated from the LAN. Users on the LAN might be responsible for updating Web pages for their departments. You might therefore need to handle a variety of LAN administrator tasks such as sharing folders that reside on your Web site and setting permissions to control access to the folders.

The principles involved in controlling access from a LAN and from the Internet are similar. You need to make sure that the users who gain access to your server are valid. The LAN operating system, in fact, is designed to ensure that users are valid. It is your job to match the users with the resources they need. When controlling access from the Internet, you have other options, however. Applications such as e-mail typically are based on user accounts that are part of the operating system. Other applications, such as ones requiring membership to a Web site, often rely on a database of user names and passwords that might also contain other information about the user. If your Web site depends on a database of user information, user names cannot be used to penetrate the operating system, although storing user names and passwords in a database is not as secure as storing them in the operating system. You need to explore the capabilities of the LAN environment to decide which approach is best in your case.

Although there are more UNIX/Linux Web servers than Microsoft Windows Web servers, virtually all LAN workstations are Windows-based. The dominance of Windows in LANs means that Microsoft alone can determine how computers communicate in the LAN environment. As you will learn, the way computers communicate with a Windows server in a LAN environment is very different from the way they communicate with an Internet-based server such as a Web server. In contrast, all computers communicate with a Linux server in a similar way, whether they are part of a LAN or connected only by the Internet. Because of the Microsoft-based LAN environment, managing a Windows server requires more planning and knowledge than managing a Linux server. You must know the basics of being a LAN administrator because your Web server environment might be integrated into the LAN.

Examining Networking Models

Because a server is part of a network, you should understand how a server fits into the network before you can consider such issues as users, resources, and control. In this section, you examine two approaches to networking models. The first is the Microsoft LAN approach to networking. The second is the client/server approach to networking, which is the basic model used for Web and e-mail servers. Whereas Microsoft does employ the client/server model for some network tasks, Linux primarily uses this model for all functions.

5

Microsoft LAN Networking Models

You configure a Microsoft Windows LAN using one of two networking models: the workgroup or the domain. The model determines how users are organized. The workgroup networking model, also known as the peer-to-peer model, considers each computer as an independent entity. Any access to resources on a computer depends on local user accounts. The domain model, on the other hand, centralizes users and the control of resources. Note that Microsoft's definition of a domain in a LAN is not related to an Internet domain.

Workgroup Networking Model

The workgroup networking model treats each computer in the network as an equal, or peer. This model does not use a centralized server. Instead, each computer acts as both a server and a client. When you allow other users to access resources on your computer, your computer is acting as a server. When you access resources on another computer, your computer is acting as a client. Because each user's computer acts as a server, each user must therefore be an administrator.

This decentralized approach has several disadvantages. First, most users are not interested in learning about administration. Second, because each computer must have a complete list of user names and passwords of other users wanting to access resources on the computer, security is compromised. It is also difficult to keep track of changing passwords. When a user changes his or her password, the password must be changed on the other computers that the user accesses. Because of these limitations, the workgroup networking model is best suited to small networks consisting of up to ten computers for which security is not a major concern.

Figure 5-1 shows an example of a workgroup and its limitations. The user Mary Noia (mnoia) can access the printer attached to Bob Cabral's (bcabral) computer only if bcabral does certain things. First, bcabral has to add mnoia's user name and password to the list of users. Second, bcabral must share the printer. Third, bcabral must specifically allow mnoia to use the shared printer.

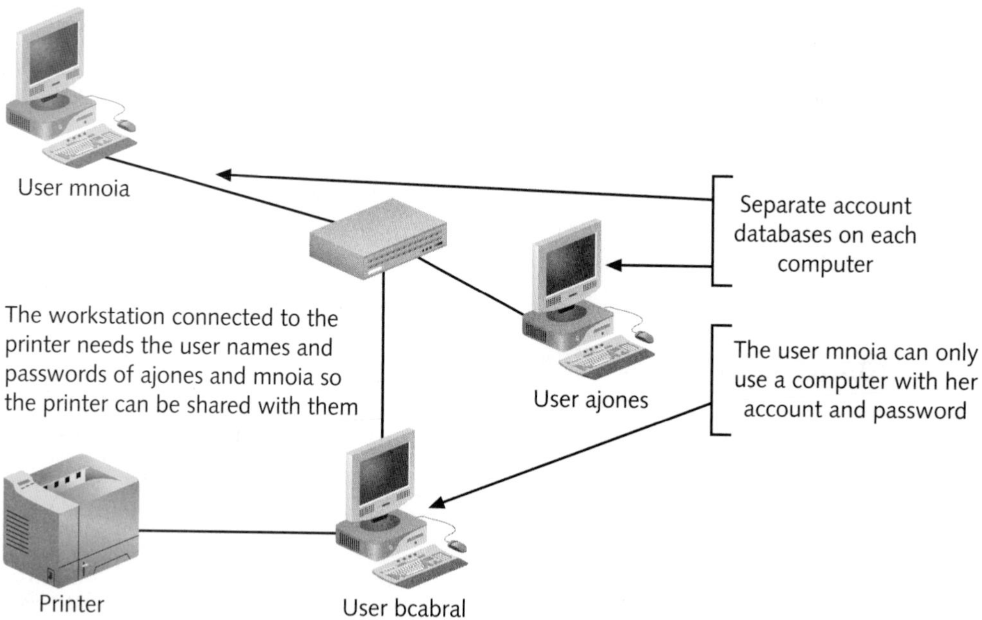
User mnoia
Separate account databases on each computer
The workstation connected to the printer needs the user names and passwords of ajones and mnoia so the printer can be shared with them
The user mnoia can only use a computer with her account and password
User ajones
Printer
User bcabral

Figure 5-1 Workgroup networking model

Domain Networking Model

The domain networking model uses one or more servers to centralize control. Instead of each computer and user being independent, they are all part of a domain. This centralization allows an administrator to use a single point of control. With a single logon, the user can be given access to any resource in the domain, as shown in Figure 5-2. Because the user name and password are stored only once, changing the password does not have the same negative effects that it would have in a workgroup network. In a workgroup network, if you changed your password on your computer, you could not access resources on other computers until your user name on the other computers was changed. Microsoft suggests that you use the domain networking model for networks with more than ten computers, which makes it the dominant networking model for LANs.

Client/Server Networking Model

In the client/server networking model, the client represents a program such as a browser that accesses resources. The server is a program such as a Web server that provides resources. The client and the server communicate using a protocol. You already know that TCP/IP is a protocol suite, and that one of the protocols in this suite is HTTP. Browsers and Web servers use HTTP to communicate.

Networking in Linux uses the client/server model. Each computer has its own database of users and passwords. If you want to use a resource on another computer, you must supply a user name and password on that computer.

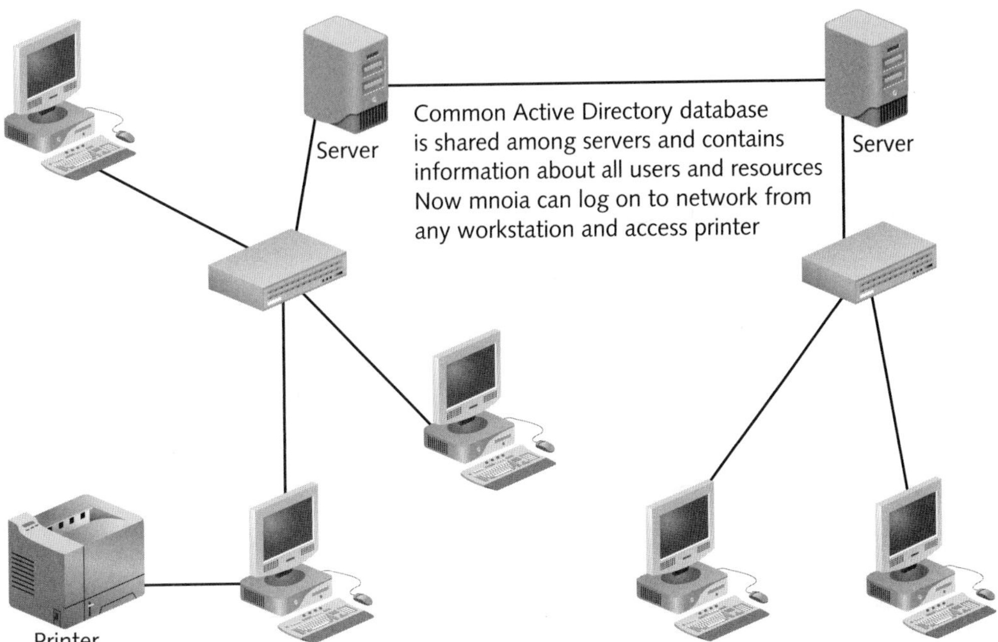
Server
Common Active Directory database
is shared among servers and contains
information about all users and resources
Now mnoia can log on to network from
any workstation and access printer
Server
Printer

Figure 5-2 Domain network

You can designate one computer to act as a server and store hundreds or even thousands of user accounts on it. On the client computer, you can use a program such as Telnet to log on to the server. Using this configuration, everyone can share the applications and resources on that centralized computer. A big difference between the client/server approach and Microsoft's domain model is that Linux typically lets you access only a single computer at a time. In Microsoft, your identity can be carried throughout the network to allow you to access any resources. Furthermore, when you use Telnet, for example, to connect to a server, processing occurs on the server, not the client. With Windows, processing usually occurs at the client, not the server.

Even when you use a Web browser to connect to a Web page on another computer, you first have to log on to that computer. Typically, the Web server provides a guest account that it uses automatically when someone wants to access a Web page. A guest account is a very restricted user account that can access only resources related to the Web site. A Web server requires an account to be associated with anyone who accesses the computer.

Access to a server is controlled by a program that runs in the background, called a **service** in Windows and a **daemon** (pronounced "demon" or "daymon") in Linux. Multiple services can run simultaneously, such as a Web server and an e-mail server. Client programs are designed to access the service. For example, a Web browser connects to a Web server, an e-mail client connects to an e-mail server, and a Telnet client connects to a Telnet server, even if both reside on the same computer.

To allow all these server services to run on a single computer, the server uses port numbers to distinguish them. You can imagine ships sailing to specific ports in a certain city, where each port has a specific purpose and can handle only certain types of cargo. Likewise, a packet of data from a Web browser goes to a specific port on the Web server, while a packet of data from an e-mail client goes to a different port. For example, the default port for a Web server is 80, the port used to send e-mail is 25, and the port used for DNS is 53. Each server application listens at a port, waiting for packets of data destined for it. The server sends data back to a client in a similar manner, with client programs using ports to accept data from various servers. A detailed understanding of these concepts is critical in designing a secure environment for your Web server, e-mail server, and other related applications. You will learn these details in Chapter 10 on securing the Web environment.

AUTHENTICATING USERS

Authentication is the process of determining a user's true identity. That is, when you log on to a network or supply user information to a Web site, authentication is how the system verifies whether you are who you say you are. Authentication involves two processes. First, you need a mechanism such as user names and passwords to identify users. Second, you need to know how secure the process is to get the identification information to the server. A complex password may not ensure security if it is sent to the server in such a way that it is easy to intercept.

Identifying Authentication Methods

Networks can employ three methods to authenticate users. These methods can be used alone or in combination with other security-related methods. You can prove your identity by using the following methods:

- What you know
- What you have
- Who you are

The following sections examine these authentication methods in more detail.

What You Know

This method is the most common form of authentication, and it typically uses passwords. That is, when you log on to a computer network, you are prompted to type a password that you have chosen or that a network administrator has given to you. The password is *what you know*. The computer bases its authentication on this password by checking it against a list. If the password you typed matches a password on the list, you are allowed access to the system. If it does not, you are locked out.

If you give your password to someone else, the computer grants this other person access because the authentication scheme is based on knowing the password. In this case, the security measure has not failed—the other person gained access by a legitimate authentication method.

What You Have

This method requires that you use a physical item, such as a key, for authentication. An example would be an entry card that you insert into a card reader to gain access to a room or building. Anyone who runs the card through the reader is granted access to the building. In this case, the authentication is based on *what you have*.

Of course, if someone takes the card from you, he or she can enter the building even though the card was originally given to you. Therefore, to create a more sophisticated authentication system for entering the building, an administrator may require not only a card, but also a password. Taking both a card and a password from someone is more difficult. ATM cards, which use personal identification numbers (PINs), are based on this combination of what you have and what you know.

Smart card logon became available with Windows 2000. The smart card contains information that provides the most secure logon procedure—namely, encrypted codes that uniquely identify the user. Putting this information on a card is much more secure than putting the information on a computer, because a computer is more readily accessible.

Who You Are

Biometrics is the science of connecting authentication schemes to unique physical attributes. Examples of this method include using fingerprints, visual and photographic identification, and voice recognition. Each method attempts to validate an individual's claim concerning his or her identity by verifying a specific physical characteristic. These *who you are* methods of authentication are becoming increasingly common as the hardware verification tools become less expensive and the recognition tools are built into operating systems.

Each of the three authentication methods is used in systems today, either individually or in combination with the others. How they are implemented varies from system to system.

Implementing an Authentication System

If a network has older computers such as those running Windows NT, Windows 95, and Windows 98, a server must use the **NTLM (NT LanManager)** protocol for authentication. It is not as secure as **Kerberos**, which is the default authentication protocol in Windows 2000, Microsoft Windows Server 2003, and Windows XP. Both NTLM and Kerberos are designed specifically for authenticating users who have accounts in the operating system. Windows has another mechanism, called **certificates**, for authenticating users over the Internet. Certificates guarantee the identity of an organization or user. Certificates will be fully discussed in Chapter 10.

Using the NTLM Protocol

The NTLM protocol was first used with Windows NT. Service Pack 4 included version 2 of the protocol, which added a better security mechanism. Unfortunately, you can now use many programs to crack these passwords. If users create passwords based on common words, they can be found in a short time. Even complex passwords can be cracked given enough time.

NTLM is used when anyone on a Windows NT workstation logs on to any Windows server, even Windows 2003. This is one important reason to upgrade your workstations to Windows 2000 or XP. NTLM is also used when a Windows 2000 user logs on locally to a computer instead of a domain and then uses a network resource. The user name and the password used to log on locally are sent to the server with the resource, such as a shared folder. This technique to gain access to network resources should be discouraged because it is not as secure as Kerberos.

Using Kerberos

Kerberos is an authentication system developed at the Massachusetts Institute of Technology (MIT). It is designed to enable two parties to exchange private information across an otherwise open network. Kerberos works by having an authentication server assign a unique key, called a ticket, to each user who logs on to the network. The ticket is then embedded in messages to identify the sender of the message and is used to grant access to other resources. Many implementations of Kerberos are available, including a free implementation available from MIT at *web.mit.edu/kerberos/www*. This site also provides more detailed information about Kerberos.

Managing Users and Groups

Users need accounts to access resources on a server. Even when the resource is a Web page, the Web server has a default user account that it uses on your behalf. This default account has restricted access, but at least allows you to view the Web page. In a LAN environment, access to resources such as printers and files are controlled based on user accounts. If a number of user accounts have common resource needs, the administrator can organize them into groups. For example, suppose everyone in the accounting department needs access to the accounting software and the printers in the accounting department. All of these users could be organized into a single group. The users are members of the group, and the administrator gives the group access to the resources. As resource needs change, the administrator simply modifies the group's access instead of setting new access limits for each member of the group. This section discusses adding users and groups; the next section focuses on giving the users and groups access to resources (that is, managing file system permissions).

Identifying Special Accounts

Applications that operate as a service need to use accounts to perform work tasks. For example, assume that you have a DBMS such as MySQL on Linux or SQL Server on Windows. Even though your personal user account does not have the access necessary to modify the physical DBMS files that exist on the computer, when you use the DBMS, the DBMS has the ability to modify its own files. The DBMS is associated with an account.

Windows has a special **system account**. The system account represents the operating system and has many of the same privileges as the administrator. This powerful account is a favorite target of hackers. If the hacker's program becomes associated with a system account or the hacker can manipulate a program associated with a system account, the hacker has almost complete access to the computer. When you install SQL Server, for example, you have the choice of using the system account or a user account that is created especially for operating under it. Normally, you would use the system account. However, you should use a special user account if you have multiple computers with SQL Server and they merge data.

Services such as the Web server use special, highly restricted accounts. When you install the IIS Web server in Windows, for example, a guest user account is created to permit anonymous logon to the Web server. Basically, this user has only permission to read Web pages.

Be careful about deleting user accounts that you do not recognize. They could be special accounts that are used by applications such as the Web server or DBMS. By default, these special accounts are not displayed.

Linux implements daemons in a different way. Although Linux does not have a system account, it does have the root account, which is similar. The root account has full access to everything in Linux. Even though programs could run as if they were root, the standard in Linux is that each daemon is associated with an individual account that restricts the daemon to specific directories and files. For instance, when you use the Red Hat User Manager for the first time after installing Linux, you will find more than 30 users already defined. (Your actual number may vary depending on the applications that you chose when you installed Linux.) Figure 5-3 shows some of these users. Typically, these user accounts are restricted so that they cannot be used to log on to a system.

Understanding Users and Groups in Windows

You need to create user accounts for individuals, and in some cases for applications, that need access to your resources. Windows has two types of user accounts: **local accounts** and **domain accounts**. When you create a local account on a computer, it exists only on that computer and can be used to control access to resources on only that computer. When you create a domain account, it is recognized throughout the whole domain. Recall that a **domain** is a logical grouping of computers that administrators use to organize common resource needs. A domain user can access resources on any computer in the domain.

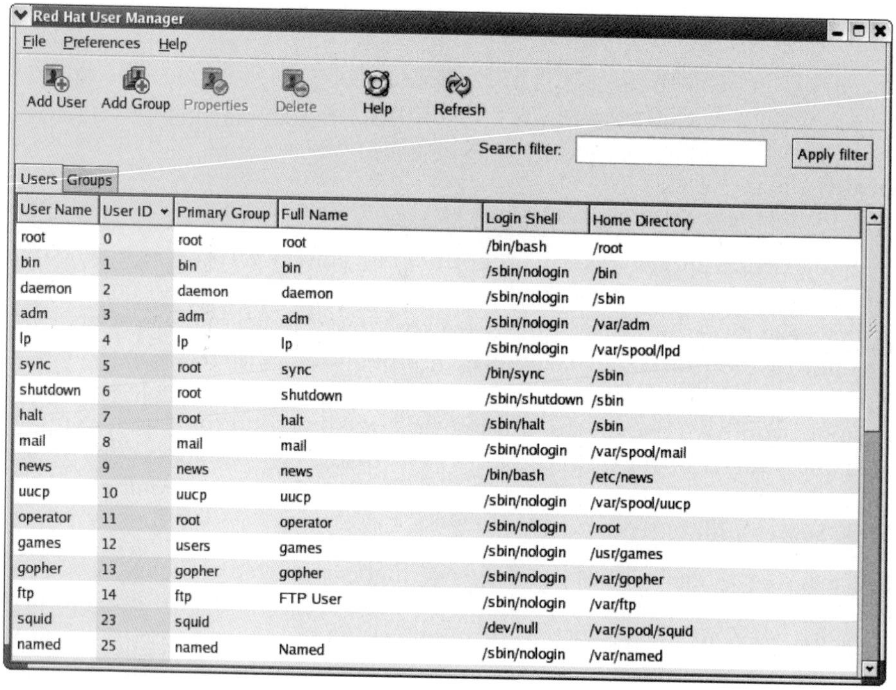

Red Hat User Manager

File Preferences Help

Add User Add Group Properties Delete Help Refresh

Search filter: Apply filter

Users Groups

User Name	User ID	Primary Group	Full Name	Login Shell	Home Directory
root	0	root	root	/bin/bash	/root
bin	1	bin	bin	/sbin/nologin	/bin
daemon	2	daemon	daemon	/sbin/nologin	/sbin
adm	3	adm	adm	/sbin/nologin	/var/adm
lp	4	lp	lp	/sbin/nologin	/var/spool/lpd
sync	5	root	sync	/bin/sync	/sbin
shutdown	6	root	shutdown	/sbin/shutdown	/sbin
halt	7	root	halt	/sbin/halt	/sbin
mail	8	mail	mail	/sbin/nologin	/var/spool/mail
news	9	news	news	/bin/bash	/etc/news
uucp	10	uucp	uucp	/sbin/nologin	/var/spool/uucp
operator	11	root	operator	/sbin/nologin	/root
games	12	users	games	/sbin/nologin	/usr/games
gopher	13	gopher	gopher	/sbin/nologin	/var/gopher
ftp	14	ftp	FTP User	/sbin/nologin	/var/ftp
squid	23	squid		/dev/null	/var/spool/squid
named	25	named	Named	/sbin/nologin	/var/named

Figure 5-3 Default user accounts in Linux

Understanding Local User Accounts

Web servers typically have local user accounts. When you view a Web page or use FTP to upload or download files, you are doing so while logged on as a local user. You would add a local user if you wanted to give individuals the ability to use FTP to upload files to their Web directory. Although some user accounts are necessary, you should add only the ones that are absolutely essential to a server that is connected to the Internet. After all, the more users you have, the more opportunities hackers have to gain access to your system.

The user name is the account name that users need to log on to the computer. When you set up your user accounts, establish a consistent naming convention. For example, you could use the first letter of the user's first name plus the last name. A user named Cristina Salinas would then have the user name CSalinas. Although the steps to add a user appear later in this section, Figure 5-4 shows the principal dialog box involved.

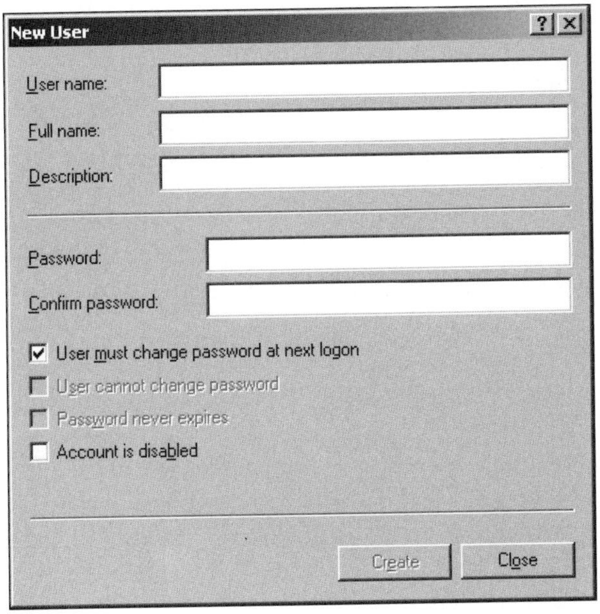

Figure 5-4 New User dialog box in Windows 2003

In the New User dialog box, the Full name and Description text boxes are optional, but are useful to help you remember the details of the account. The password can be up to 128 characters, and you can use all the symbols on a keyboard. Make sure that passwords are difficult to discover because hackers (and even coworkers) can easily obtain programs that can find passwords. The more complex the password, the more difficult it is to discover. Here are some rules to follow when creating passwords:

- Include at least eight characters.
- Use a mix of uppercase and lowercase letters and numerals.
- Use non-alphanumeric symbols.
- Do not use a recognizable word as part of the password.

To create a complex password that is easy to remember, start by thinking of an easily remembered sentence such as, "I really want to go to San Diego." Replace any occurrence of "I" with a 1. Replace a "to" with 2. Alternate uppercase and lowercase letters. Add one or more symbols. Now you have: 1Rw2G2sD:). This password would be extremely difficult to crack.

The four check boxes in the New User dialog box let you control account properties. By default, Windows selects the "User must change the password at next logon" check box. This option forces the user to change the password the next time he or she logs on to one that the administrator does not know. If you uncheck "User must change password at next logon," two check boxes become available. One is "User cannot change password." Select this check box for a common account that is used by more than one person. An administrator is then responsible for changing the password and notifying the users. Select the "Password never expires" check box if you are creating a user that is associated with a service. In this case, you want the service to run without having to change a password every 42 days, which is otherwise the default. Select the "Account is disabled" check box if you want to suspend the use of the account but do not want to delete it. For example, if a user were taking a six-month family leave, you could disable her account.

In the following steps, you add a user called ajones with a password of pass in Windows 2000 or Windows 2003.

To add a user account:

1. From the Control Panel, open the Administrative Tools window, and then open **Computer Management**.
2. In the left pane of the Computer Management window, click the **plus sign** (+) next to Local Users and Groups.
3. Click the **Users** folder. The current users for this computer appear in the right pane of the Computer Management window.
4. To add a user, click **Action** on the menu bar, and then click **New User**. The New User dialog box opens. (Refer back to Figure 5-4.)
5. In the User name text box, type **ajones**.
6. For the Full name, type **Arda Jones**. For the description, type **Director of Accounting**.
7. In the Password text box, type **pass**.
8. Type the same password (**pass**) in the Confirm Password text box. Because you entered a password that is not secure, make sure the "User must change password at next logon" check box is selected.
9. Click the **Create** button. Windows creates a new user account for the user named ajones.
10. Close all open windows.

Understanding Domain Accounts and Active Directory Services

Although Web servers often use only local accounts, there are typically other servers in the Web environment that have more complex requirements. For example, you can set up an e-mail server with Microsoft Exchange 2000. Microsoft Exchange 2000 requires the capabilities of the **Active Directory (AD)** service. AD allows users to use only a single logon for the whole network. All resources throughout the network are then available to them, including those outside their own domains. AD organizes the domains in your network so you can administer them as a whole. It requires DNS, which you set up in Chapter 4.

AD is designed for large networks. Any server that has AD is called a domain controller. Domain controllers share information about the network. If one domain controller cannot be contacted, the other domain controllers can take over its duties.

Windows has two modes for AD servers. **Mixed mode** allows Windows NT domain controllers to communicate with Windows 2000 and Windows 2003 domain controllers. **Native mode** allows only Windows 2000 and Windows 2003 domain controllers to communicate. The main advantage of native mode is its more efficient use of server resources, because this mode does not have to support two different ways of keeping track of users and computers. Another advantage of using native mode is that you have an additional group type, Universal, which is described in the following section. When AD is installed, the default is mixed mode. If you change it to native mode, you cannot go back to mixed mode.

Computers and other resources in AD follow the same naming format as the naming scheme that the Internet uses. That is why AD requires DNS. A major planning decision is whether the internal naming scheme, or **namespace**, should match the external namespace. If both are the same, your logon name (internal namespace) would be the same as your e-mail name (external namespace). For example, if your domain is *technowidgets.com*, your user with the account ajones could use *ajones@technowidgets.com* for both a logon name and an e-mail name. If you keep the namespaces separate, configuration would be more flexible because for the external namespace, you need to focus on only those computers that will be accessed from the Internet. You could then use a DNS like the one you created in Chapter 4, and it could reside either within your organization or at your ISP.

Once AD is installed, you add users with a special administrative tool called Active Directory Users and Computers. The process is similar to the one you used to add a new user in the previous steps, except that there are two possibilities for logon names. For Windows 2000 and Windows 2003, the logon name looks like an e-mail address, such as *ajones@technowidgets.com*, although you can still enter the user name alone, such as ajones.

Installing the Active Directory Service in Windows

To configure Microsoft Exchange in Chapter 8, you need to install the Active Directory service. Doing so significantly changes the setup of your operating system, so this step is not like adding DNS or another Windows component. To install AD on a Windows computer, you run the dcpromo.exe program from a command prompt. If you decide later that you do not want AD, you can uninstall it by running dcpromo.exe again.

To install the Active Directory service for *technowidgets.com* using Windows:

1. Click **Start**, click **Run**, type **dcpromo.exe**, and then press **Enter** to start the Active Directory Installation Wizard.
2. In the Welcome to the Active Directory Installation Wizard dialog box, click **Next**.

3. *Windows 2003 only:* The Operating System Compatibility dialog box opens, explaining that Windows 95 and Windows NT 4.0 SP3 and earlier cannot log on to a Windows 2003 domain. Click **Next**.

   The Domain Controller Type dialog box opens, allowing you to specify the type of domain controller you want to set up. See Figure 5-5. If there was an existing domain, you could add this computer to it. For this procedure, you want to create a new domain controller.

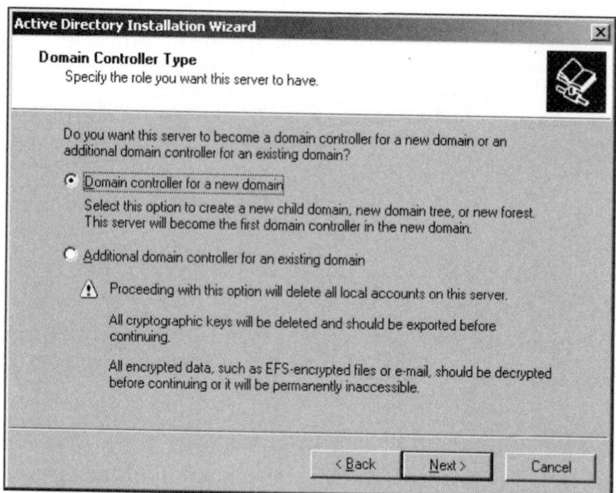

Figure 5-5 Domain Controller Type dialog box

4. Accept the default of **Domain controller for a new domain** by clicking **Next**.

5. Now you have to determine how the new domain fits into your network. Windows 2003 uses one dialog box to gather this information and Windows 2000 uses two dialog boxes.

   In Windows 2003: In the Create New Domain dialog box, you need to specify how the new domain will fit into your network. See Figure 5-6. This domain could be a child domain within an existing domain, a domain in a new forest, or a domain tree in an existing forest. In this chapter, assume that it is the first domain controller in the organization, so accept the default of Domain in a new forest by clicking **Next**. Note that if you were creating an independent domain within an existing network, you would most likely create a domain tree in an existing forest.

   In Windows 2000: In the Create Tree or Child Domain dialog box, accept the default of **Create a new domain tree** by clicking **Next**. Accept the default of Create a new forest of domain trees by clicking **Next**.

The other option permits you to create a domain within a domain, which is called a child domain. In the Create or Join Forest dialog box, you determine whether the new domain is the first domain in the organization, which is the default, or you decide to place it in an existing forest.

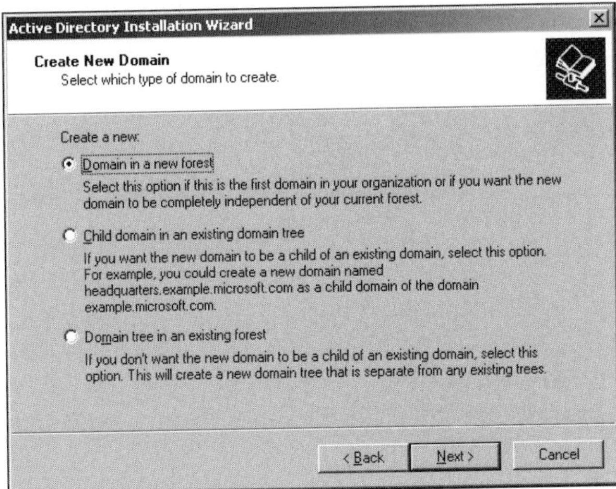

Figure 5-6 Create New Domain dialog box

6. In the New Domain Name dialog box, type the fully qualified domain name that the DNS uses. In the text box, type the name of your domain, such as **technowidgets.com**. See Figure 5-7. Click **Next**.

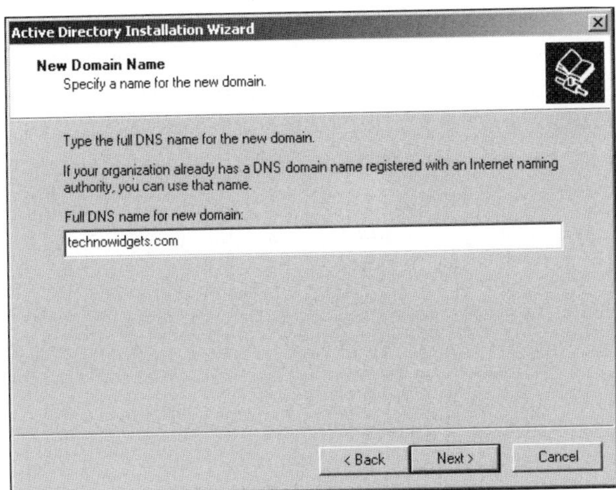

Figure 5-7 New Domain Name dialog box

7. In the NetBIOS Domain Name dialog box, the first 15 characters of the domain name up to the dot appear in the Domain NetBIOS name text box. In the case of *technowidgets.com*, TECHNOWIDGETS appears as the default. The NetBIOS domain name is used in Windows operating systems created before Windows 2000. See Figure 5-8. Click **Next**.

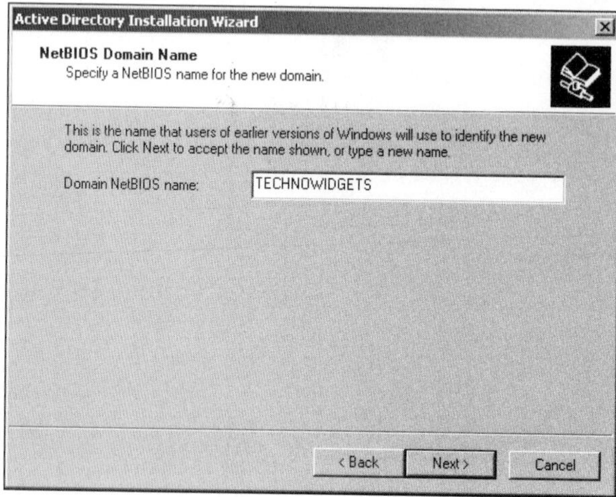

Figure 5-8 NetBIOS Domain Name dialog box

8. In the Database and Log Folders dialog box (called the Database and Log Locations dialog box in Windows 2000), accept the default locations for storing the Active Directory database and log. See Figure 5-9. The default is to store them in the WINDOWS folder in Windows 2003, and the WINNT folder in Windows 2000. Your drive may differ from the one shown in the figure. Click **Next**.

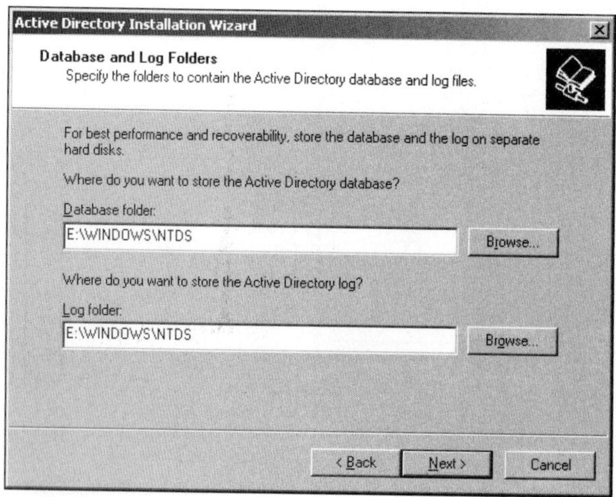

Figure 5-9 Default locations in the Database and Log Folders dialog box

9. In the Shared System Volume dialog box, accept the default location for the shared system volume. As with the Database and Log folders, the default location is the SYSVOL folder in the Windows folder in Windows 2003 and the WINNT folder in Windows 2000. Windows uses the information in this folder to send to other domain controllers. Click **Next**.

10. *In Windows 2003:* The DNS Registration Diagnostics dialog box opens if you installed DNS as described in Chapter 4. See Figure 5-10. In Chapter 4, you installed a DNS that would be used only for the Internet. Now that you are creating a domain controller, you need to allow dynamic updates. Click the **Install and configure the DNS server on this computer, and set this computer to use this DNS server as its preferred DNS server** option button. This will use your existing configuration files and add only dynamic updates. Click **Next**.

    In Windows 2000: The Configure DNS dialog box opens, stating that DNS is not available, which means that dynamic updates are not available. Accept the default of **Yes, install and configure DNS on this computer (recommended)** to keep your existing configuration files by clicking **Next**.

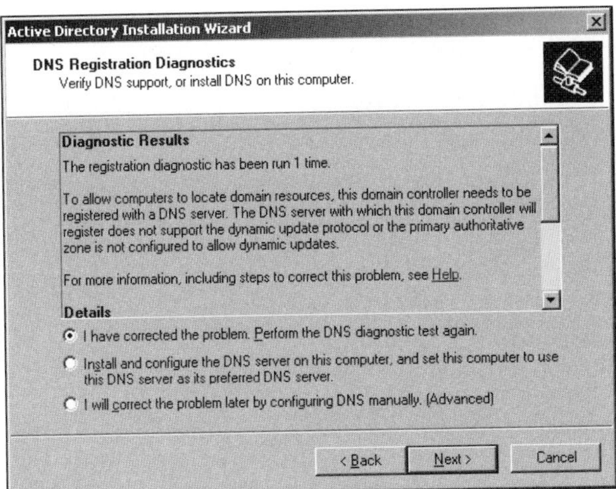

Figure 5-10 DNS Registration Diagnostics dialog box

11. In the Permissions dialog box, click the **Permissions compatible only with Windows 2000 or Windows Server 2003 operating systems** option button. In Windows 2000, this is the **Permissions compatible only with Windows 2000 servers** option button. Selecting this option indicates that you do not have any Windows NT domain controllers on this network. Click **Next**.

12. In the Directory Services Restore Mode Administrator Password dialog box, type **password** in the Password and Confirm Password text boxes, and then click **Next**. This password would be used to enter the restore mode of AD, which should be restricted to only those administrators who know how to use this advanced mode (which is why a separate password is required for this mode). On a production server, you would use a more complex password.
13. The Summary dialog box lists the choices that you have made. Review them and then click **Next**.

    Windows installs and configures AD. A window notifies you of the steps that are occurring, which can take a few minutes. After Windows creates and configures the databases necessary for AD, the Completing the Active Directory Installation dialog box opens. Click **Finish** to exit the wizard.
14. *Windows 2000 only:* You might receive a message stating that your zone already exists. If this happens, click **OK**. DNS will still be configured correctly.
15. A message box appears, asking whether to restart the server. Click the **Restart Now** button. It will take longer than normal to restart as Windows finishes the configuration.

Configuring Groups in Windows

You use groups to organize common needs among users. Typically, these needs are related to accessing resources such as printers and files. For example, only certain people may require access to a high-speed color printer. You would put the user accounts of those people needing to use this printer into a group, and then you would give the group access to the color printer. You could use the same technique to restrict the actions of a specific group of users while using a Web site.

If you do not install AD, Windows has only one local group, which you use for your local users. With AD, you can assign users to two types of groups. One type is called a security group; you use the groups in this category to assign permissions to users and thereby control access. You use the other type, called a distribution group, for combining users for other purposes, such as e-mailing groups of users. This chapter discusses only the security groups and assumes that AD is running in native mode.

Three types of security groups exist. **Domain local groups** have members from the same domain. You can use such groups to assign permissions to resources in the same domain. **Global groups** have members from the same domain, but you can use them to assign permissions to resources in any domain. **Universal groups** can have members from any domain, and you can use them to assign permissions to resources in any domain. What a group can have as members varies by group. Besides user accounts, members of domain local groups can include local groups from the same domain, global groups, and universal groups. Global groups can have other global groups as members, and universal groups can have other universal groups and global groups as members.

When you create a user account, the account becomes a member of a group called **Users** if the network has no domain, and a member of the **Domain Users** group if it does have a domain. Both of these groups are built-in groups. That is, when you install Windows, they are created automatically to help with managing users.

Windows has a number of other built-in groups. The most commonly used are Domain Admins and Administrators, for administrators; Account Operators, who can administer user accounts; and Server Operators, who can shut down the server, back up data, and restore data.

5

Understanding Linux User and Group Accounts

Setting up user accounts in Linux is simpler than the equivalent process in Windows. Like Windows local users, Linux users have permissions only on the computer where the user account is created. Linux offers two ways to create users. You can use the command-line utility useradd, which is found in all Linux distributions. Alternatively, you can use a GUI tool. Remember that you can use either the GNOME or the KDE windowing environment, and that a number of Linux distributions are available, so the GUI tools vary. Historically, the most popular GUI tool was linuxconf. Red Hat has deprecated linuxconf in favor of the company's own tool, called the Red Hat User Manager. This chapter uses the Red Hat tool, but the others work in a similar fashion.

When you add a user in Linux, you specify the properties of the user account. Table 5-1 lists these properties.

Table 5-1 Properties of user accounts in Linux

Item	Description
User name	Logon name of the user
Full name	The full name of the user or any comment
Password	The password must be at least six characters
Home directory	The default is /home/*username*
Group	The default is to create a group with the same name as the user
Login shell	The default is /bin/bash, which determines the characteristic of the shell environment

In the following steps, you will set up a new user account in Linux for a user named Mary Noia. You will use mnoia as her user name and Azore$ as her password.

To add a user with the Linux Red Hat GUI:

1. Click the **Red Hat** icon on the Panel, point to **System Settings**, and click **Users and Groups**. See Figure 5-11.

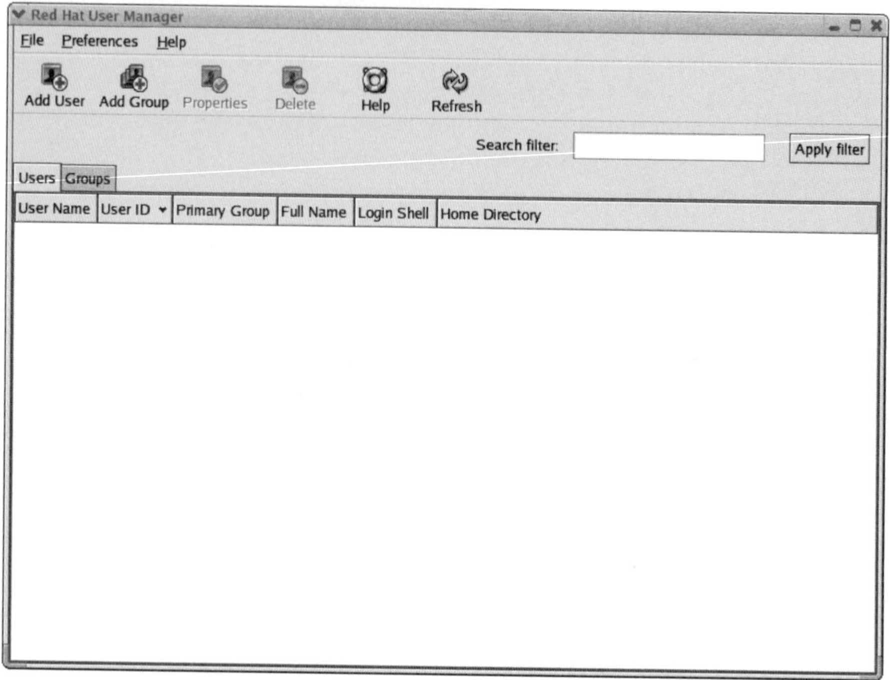

Figure 5-11 Red Hat User Manager

2. In the Red Hat User Manager window, click **Add User**. The Create New User dialog box opens, as shown in Figure 5-12.
3. In the User Name text box, type **mnoia** for the user name and then press **Tab**. The Home Directory text box shows /home/mnoia, which is the default location for user directories.
4. Press the **Tab** key to move the insertion point to the Full Name text box. Type **Mary Noia**, and then press the **Tab** key to move to the Password text box.
5. Type **Azore$** in both the Password and the Confirm Password text boxes.
6. Click **OK** to create the user. You return to the Red Hat User Manager window, where you can now see an entry for mnoia.

The window now displays a single entry for mnoia. To view all the system users, click Preferences on the menu bar, and then click Filter system users and groups.

Now that you know how to add a user with the GUI tool, you should also know how to add a user using the command-line version because it is available on all Linux distributions. To add the user ajones with a password, you must complete two steps. You use useradd to add the user and then use passwd to create a password. You cannot use the ajones account until you create a password.

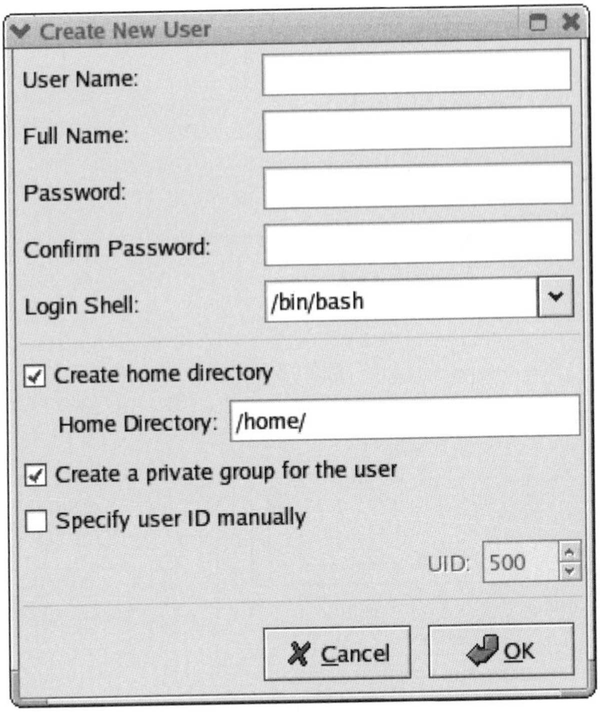

Figure 5-12 Create New User dialog box

To add a user using useradd and passwd in Linux:

1. From a shell prompt, type **useradd ajones** and then press **Enter**. This creates the user and the user's home directory, which is /home/ajones.
2. Type **passwd ajones** and then press **Enter** to start the utility to change the password for ajones.
3. Type **NorthDakota** as the password, press **Enter**, and then type the password again to confirm it. Now ajones can log on to the server.
4. To display the user you just added, click the **Red Hat** icon, point to **System Settings**, and then click **Users and Groups**.
5. Close the Red Hat User Manager window.

When you create a user, Linux enters information in three files. The first file is /etc/passwd, shown in Figure 5-13, which is a text file that contains user names and information related to user names. You can edit this file directly to change the full name of the user or other attributes. However, this file does not contain passwords. Instead, Red Hat Linux stores the encrypted passwords in the second file, /etc/shadow. The information is kept separated so that only the person who logs on as root (the **superuser**) and the authentication application can read /etc/shadow. Some distributions of Linux leave the encrypted passwords in /etc/passwd, which can be more easily cracked by hackers. By default, a group is created with the same name as the user account and then stored in /etc/group.

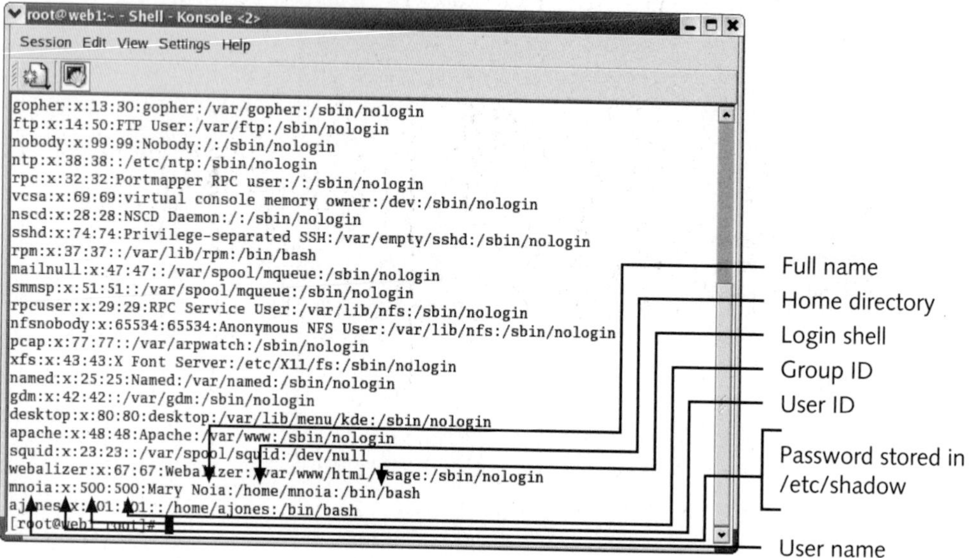

Figure 5-13 The /etc/passwd file

Figure 5-13 shows a partial listing of users in /etc/passwd. Items in the /etc/passwd file are separated by a colon (:). The "x" in the second position represents the password, which is actually stored in /etc/shadow. The next-to-last line is for Mary Noia, who was the first user added. The number 500 appears in two places. The first 500 represents the **user ID** (**uid**). The second 500 represents the **group ID** (**gid**). By convention, uids less than 100 are reserved for special system users and programs. Red Hat starts numbering users at 500 instead of 100. The root user has a uid of zero and a gid of zero—the defining factor for the root account is the zeros for uid and gid. You could change the account name from root to whatever you want, however. In Chapter 10, you will use these uid and gid number ranges to secure your Web server.

Managing File System Permissions

Permissions allow you to control access to the resources on a computer. A resource may be a Web page, a document, a program, or a printer. You give permissions to users and groups. File system permissions exist in Windows only if you format a hard disk using NTFS.

Managing File System Permissions in Windows

File system permissions in Windows offer more detailed control than their counterparts in Linux. Windows 2000 has 13 individual file system permissions organized into six standard permissions; only one is geared toward folders. Windows 2003 adds a new standard file permission called Special Permissions, plus a new individual file system permission called Full Control. This section focuses on the standard permissions, which are listed in Table 5-2. All the permissions are the same for folders and files except the List Folder Contents permission, which is for folders only. When a permission is set at a folder level, the permission applies, by default, to the files in the folder and is inherited by all subfolders.

Table 5-2 Windows permissions

Permission	Description
Full Control	Full Control includes all other permissions, such as Modify and Read, and allows you to take ownership of the file or folder and change the attributes of a file.
Modify	To modify a file, you need to be able to read it and write it. Because the modification could be to delete the contents, this permission lets you delete a file. When you have this permission, you have Read, Write, Read & Execute, and List Folder Contents permissions.
Read	With this permission, you can read files but cannot execute them. For example, you can view a text file or your local program can read a configuration file. You must have at least Read permissions in all folders above the folder containing the file. For example, if you have permission to read a file called test.cfg in C:\config\app, but you do not have Read permission in config and app, you cannot read test.cfg.
Write	When set on a file, this permission allows you to write to files. When set on a folder, you can write to the folder, meaning that you can create and delete files in the folder.
Read & Execute	In addition to the Read permission, this permission allows you to run programs. It also includes the List Folder Contents permission.
List Folder Contents	This permission allows you to view the contents of a folder. It can only be set at the folder level. It allows you to see the files and folders inside the folder.
Special Permissions (Windows 2003 only)	This is not a specific permission. Under the list of permissions for users, when this permission is checked, it means that this user has one or more of the 14 individual permissions set. These individual permissions are combined to form the other permissions in this table, which are appropriate in the vast majority of circumstances.

If a user is a member of multiple groups that have certain permissions on a folder or file, the permissions are typically added together. For example, if the Users group has Read permission and the Managers group has Write permission, and you are a member of both groups, then you have both Read and Write permissions. When a particular permission is denied, that denial takes priority over when it is allowed. For example, if you were a member of Users and Managers, and also a member of a group that was denied the Read permission, you would have only the Write permission.

Configuring File System Permissions in Windows

Assume that you just created a folder called config, a subfolder called app, and a file in app called test.txt. In Windows 2003, the default settings for users are Read & Execute. But what if you wanted to allow users to write to the file? You have to configure the properties of the file and click the check box next to the Write permission in the Allow column. Figure 5-14 shows the default settings for the test.txt file.

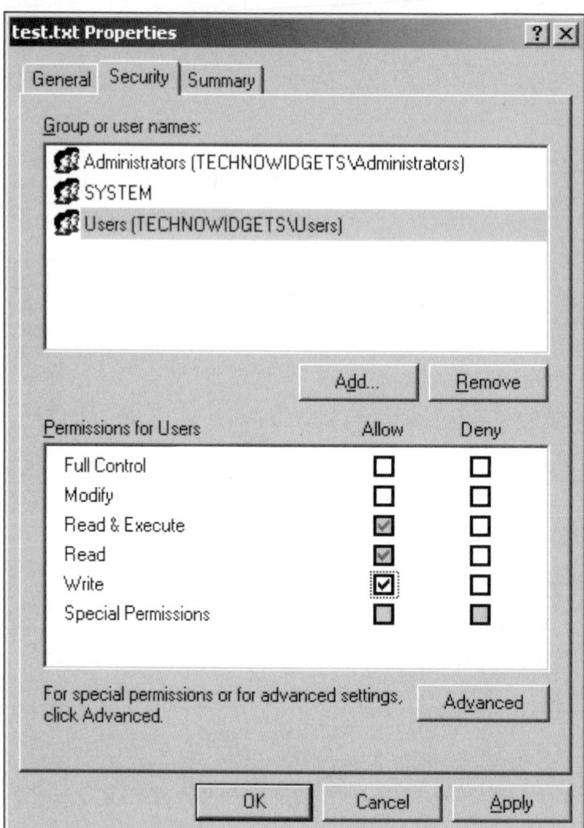

Figure 5-14 Setting Write permissions on a file

In the dialog box shown in Figure 5-14, the Read & Execute (and the related Read) permission is gray, meaning that it inherited its permissions from the permissions listed above it. The Special Permissions check box is grayed because the special permissions are actually set on another screen, shown by the Advanced button. In the following steps, you will set the Write permission on the test.txt file.

To create a sample file called test.txt in Windows 2003 or 2000:

1. Right-click **Start**, and then click **Explore**.
2. In the left pane, click the drive that corresponds to the root of the Windows installation. Typically, it is labeled **Local Disk (C:)** if you just installed one version of Windows. The contents are displayed in the right pane.
3. Click **File** on the menu bar, point to **New**, and then click **Folder**. A text box and a folder icon opens.
4. Type **config**, which is the name of the folder, and then press **Enter**.
5. Double-click **config** to display the contents in the right pane.
6. Click **File** on the menu bar, point to **New**, and then click **Text Document**. A text box and a text icon opens.
7. Type **test.txt**, and then press **Enter**.

To set a file permission in Windows 2003:

1. In Windows Explorer, right-click **test.txt**, and then click **Properties** on the shortcut menu. The test.txt Properties dialog box opens.
2. Click the **Security** tab. You use this property sheet to assign permissions to the test.txt file.
3. In the Group or user names window, click **Users** to allow changes for user accounts in the Users group.
4. Click the **Write** check box in the allow column to allow the users who have accounts in the Users group to have Write permission on the test.txt file.
5. Click **OK** to close the dialog box.

It is more difficult to do the same thing in Windows 2000, because when you installed it, the default permission gave full control to Everyone, a special group that includes anyone logged on to the computer. The Users group, by default, includes all Users, although users can be deleted from the Users group. In the following steps, you will give the Users group the Write permission along with the default Read & Execute permissions and allow only the Administrators group to have the Full Control permission.

To add the Write permission to Users and the Full Control permission to Administrators using Windows 2000:

1. Make sure that you have created a file called test.txt.
2. In Windows Explorer, right-click **test.txt**, and then click **Properties** on the shortcut menu. The test.txt Properties dialog box opens.

3. Click the **Security** tab. You use this property sheet to assign permissions to the test.txt file. See Figure 5-15.

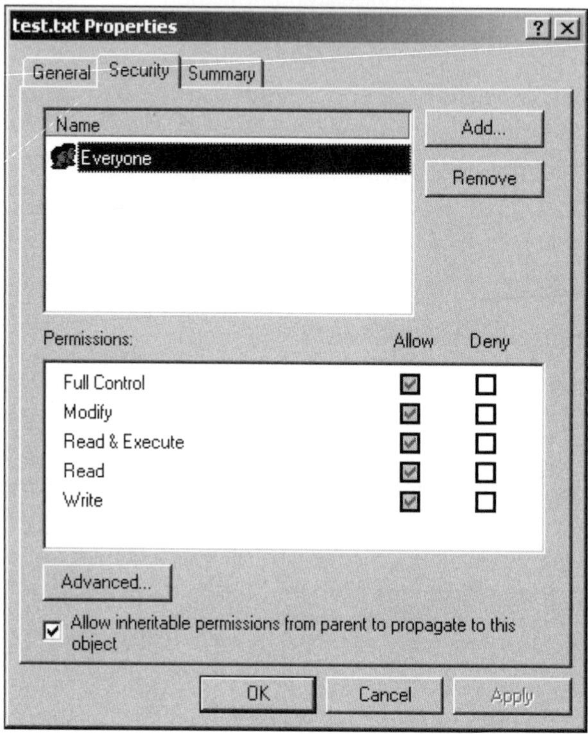

Figure 5-15 Default settings in the Security tab of the test.txt Properties dialog box in Windows 2000

4. Click the **Add** button to select the Administrators group and define the permissions for administrators with regard to this file.
5. In the Select Users, Computers, or Groups dialog box, click **Administrators**, and then click **Add**. Notice that the Administrators group appears in the lower dialog box. See Figure 5-16.
6. Click **OK** to set permissions for Administrators. The test.txt Properties dialog box now shows that the Administrators group has only Read & Execute permission, which is the default.
7. Click the **Full Control** check box in the Allow column, which also selects the other check boxes in the Allow column.
8. Click **Add** to start the process of setting permissions for the Users group.

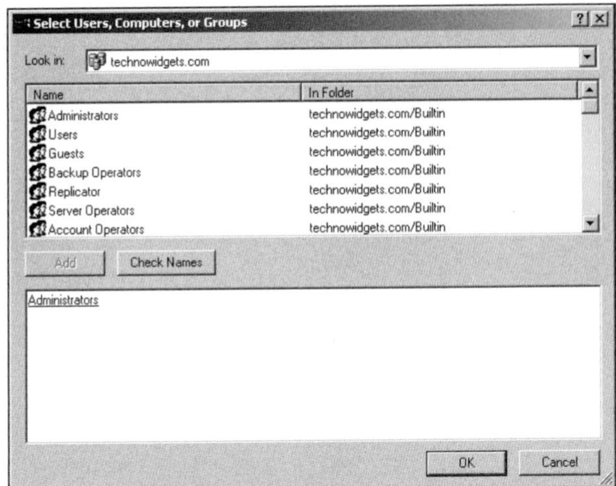

Figure 5-16 Select Users, Computers, or Groups dialog box

9. In the Select Users, Computers, or Groups dialog box, click **Users** and then click **Add**. Now the Users group appears in the lower dialog box instead of the Administrators group that you saw in Figure 5-16.
10. Click **OK** to set permissions for Users.
11. In the test.txt Properties dialog box, click the **Write** check box in the Allow column.
12. Next, you should remove the group Everyone because you want to control users through the Users group instead of the Everyone group. The Users group can be controlled by adding and deleting users, but you have no control over the Everyone group. Any nonguest user logged on is automatically part of the Everyone group. Click **Everyone** to see the permissions set for this group. The check boxes in the Allow column are grayed, meaning that these permissions are inherited. To remove Everyone, click the **Allow inheritable permissions from parent to propagate to this object** check box to uncheck it.
13. In the security warning dialog box, click **Remove** to remove the inherited permissions for the Everyone group and keep Administrators and Users in their current folder.
14. Click **Users** to review the permissions you set. See Figure 5-17.
15. Click **OK** to save the changes.

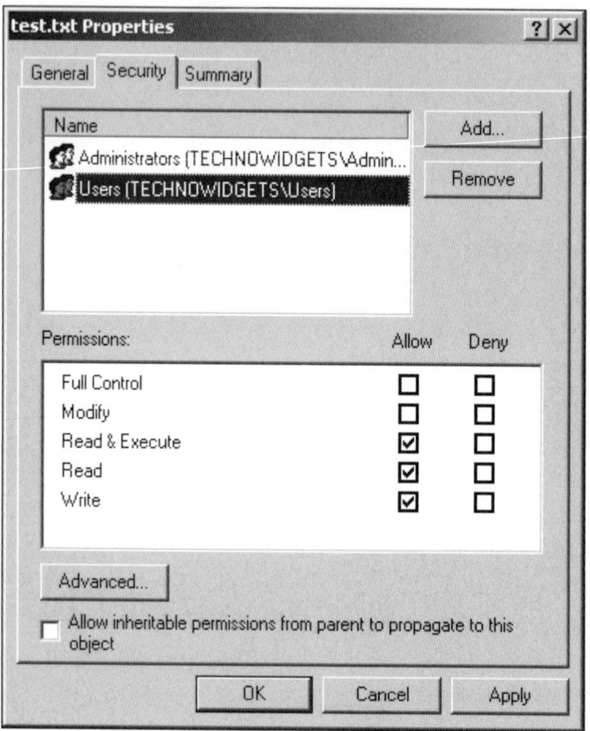

Figure 5-17 Setting Write permission for members of the Users group

Managing File System Permissions in Linux

To better understand file system permissions in Linux, you have to understand the file system itself. Linux does not have a file system equivalent to the Windows FAT file system, which does not have any security. (All Linux file systems have security.) In Linux, a directory is nothing more than a file that contains other files. This structure helps in determining what the permissions allow you to do. Linux directories correspond to folders in Windows.

Linux has three permissions that you can apply to directories and files: read, write, and execute. Table 5-3 describes these permissions.

Table 5-3 File and directory permissions in Linux

Permission type	When used with files	When used with directories
Read	Read a file or copy a file	List the contents of a directory
Write	Write to the file, including deleting the file	Create files
Execute	Execute programs and shell scripts, which are text files containing Linux commands	Modify the file permissions

The read, write, and execute permissions can be applied to three categories of users. First, they can be set for the owner of the file. When a file is created, ownership is given to the user who created it. Second, the permissions can be set for a group that is assigned to the directory or file. Third, you can set permissions for accounts that are not members of the group. This approach is different from Windows. In Windows, the file or folder remains separate from the permissions assigned to it. Thus, in Windows, you could have dozens of groups and users with differing permissions assigned to a single file. In contrast, in Linux, the permissions are part of the file. Groups exist only in the context of the file. As a consequence, there can be only one group assigned to a file and only one user assigned to the file. In Windows, zero or more users and groups can be assigned permissions in a file. In Linux, the three categories are the only assigned permissions, and they are assigned to every file.

Because three sets of permissions are assigned to every directory and file, the designers of Linux had to come up with an efficient method of designating permissions. Their approach was to have three bits represent each set of permissions. The first bit corresponds to the read permission and has a value of 4. The second bit corresponds to the write permission and has a value of 2. The third bit corresponds to the execute permission and has a value of 1. The permission can either be described as a single digit ranging from 0 to 7 or a combination of r, w, and x. Table 5-4 lists the various combinations of permissions, which are always represented as rwx, meaning read, write, and execute permissions, respectively. The dash (-) indicates that no permissions are set for that item. For example, r-x means that the write permission is not given, only the read and execute. For a directory, the execute permission allows you to use the directory name when accessing files in it. The numeric equivalent can be used to change permissions.

Table 5-4 Linux permissions

Permissions r = 4, w = 2, x = 1	Numeric equivalent
---	0
--x	1
-w-	2
-wx	3
r--	4
r-x	5
Rw-	6
rwx	7

The primary utility for changing permissions is chmod. The format of the chmod utility is `chmod nnn name`, where `nnn` represents the three digits for each of the three permissions and `name` represents the name of the directory or file. Each digit corresponds to one of the numeric values in Table 5-4. The first digit represents the permission for the owner. The second digit is for the group, and the third digit is for everyone else. Table 5-5 shows several examples of using the chmod utility.

Table 5-5 Using chmod to set permissions

Command	Permissions		
	Owner	Group	Other
`chmod 755 myfile`	rwx	r-x	r-x
`chmod 540 myfile`	r-x	r--	---
`chmod 744 myfile`	rwx	r--	r--

Linux provides another way to use chmod. Instead of setting all the permissions at once, you can change existing permissions. To do so, use the following syntax: **`chmod x +|-p filename`**. The **`x`** represents which set of permissions is being changed. The values can be `u` for user, `g` for group, `o` for others, `s` for user and group, and `a` for all sets of permissions. The `a` is the default. The + or the – designates whether the permission will be added or deleted. The `p` represents the permissions. Instead of digits, you use a combination of r, w, and x. Table 5-6 lists some examples.

Table 5-6 Use of the `chmod` command

Command	Description
`chmod g+rx myfile`	For members of the group for myfile, add the read and execute permissions.
`chmod o-wx+r myfile`	For anyone outside of the group for myfile, delete the write and execute permissions and add the read permission.
`chmod +rwx myfile`	Change all the permissions for myfile to rwx. Because there was no designator, the a, for all sets, is assumed.

To display the permissions for a file or directory, you use the `-l` modifier of the `ls` command that is used to list the contents of a directory. The `-l` contains the letter "l," not the digit one. It stands for long listing. For example, the command `ls -l` may produce the following output:

```
drwxr-xr-x 2 ajones   ajones   1024  Oct 17 11:38  apps
-rw-r—r— 1 ajones   ajones   349  Dec  3 10:44  myfile
-rwxrwxrwx 1 root     root     3245  Oct 18 12:12  mfile
```

The first line states that it is a directory because the character in the first position is a `d`. The permissions for the owner are rwx, the permissions for the group are r-x, and the permissions for others are r-x. The owner is ajones. The group is also ajones. The size of the file is 1,024 bytes. The file was last modified on October 17 at 11:38 A.M. The name of the directory is apps.

Figure 5-18 shows how to create file permissions to allow others to edit a file. Then you change the permissions to allow others to create files in a directory. In Figure 5-18, the text after the "#" prompt is what you type.

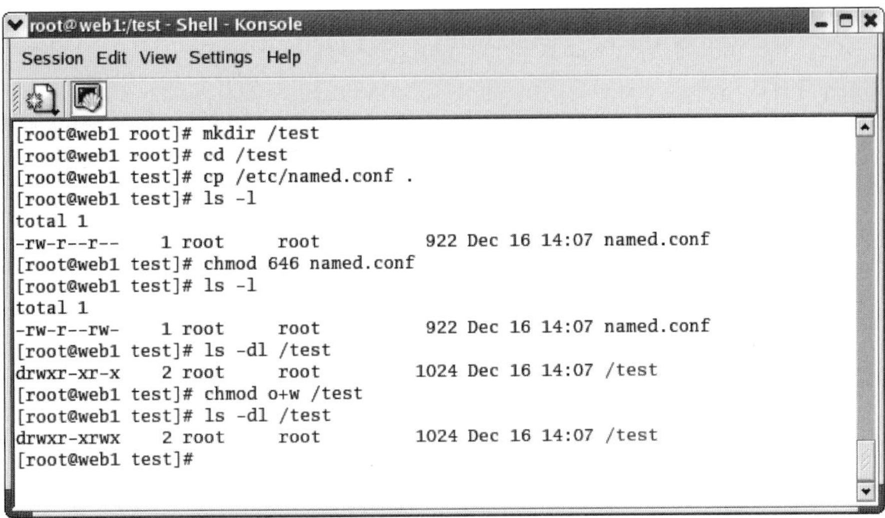

Figure 5-18 Exploring file permissions in Linux

To explore file permissions in Linux:

1. In a terminal window, create the /test directory by typing **mkdir /test** and pressing **Enter**.
2. Change to the /test directory by typing **cd /test** and pressing **Enter**.
3. Type **cp /etc/named.conf .** and press **Enter** to copy the named.conf file from /etc to your current directory (the /test directory). Be sure to include the ending dot, which indicates the current directory. You will change the permissions of the named.conf file.
4. Type **ls -l** and press **Enter**. A file listing appears, similar to the one shown earlier in Figure 5-18. The permissions allow the owner (root) with read and write permissions.
5. To allow others write permission, type **chmod 646 named.conf** and press **Enter**.
6. Type **ls -l** and press **Enter** to see the changes to the named.conf file. Now you could log on as any user and edit the file. However, when you save the file after editing it, Linux would warn you that it could not make a backup of the file. Although you can change the file, you need write permissions in the /test directory to make a backup of the file. By default, the permissions for the /test directory are rwsr-xr-x.
7. To allow others to create files in the directory using the alternate form of chmod, type **chmod o+w /test** and press **Enter**.

SHARING RESOURCES IN A WINDOWS NETWORK

Sometimes a user needs files on other computers. If you have the needed files, you can share the folder with the rest of the Windows network. When you create a shared folder, you need to set permissions on it. Although you will learn how to share folders in this section, note that the steps for sharing a printer are similar. You need to determine who can access the shared folder and what they can do. For example, you may just want the user to read files from your folder but not store new files there. You have already learned about file system permissions. Shares have their own permissions, though they are not as complex as those for files. Linux has only three permissions, which are listed in Table 5-7.

Table 5-7 Share permissions

Permission	Description
Full Control	Allow files to be added, deleted, changed, and read
Change	Allow existing files to be written to
Read	Can only read files

When you compare the permissions on a shared folder to the file system (NTFS) permissions that were described earlier, note that the most restrictive permissions always take priority. For example, if the shared folder has given a user Full Control, but the underlying NTFS permissions are Read & Execute, the effective permissions are Read & Execute. If the shared folder permission is Read and the NTFS permission is Full Control, the effective permission is Read. It can be confusing to keep track of the differences between shared folder permissions and NTFS permissions. Microsoft suggests that you set shared folder permissions at Full Control and then implement the restrictive permissions using NTFS permissions.

To create a shared folder named config using Windows 2000 or Windows 2003:

1. In a previous section, you created a folder called config that you will modify. In Windows Explorer, right-click the folder **config**, and then click **Sharing and Security** (on Windows 2000, **Sharing**) on the shortcut menu. The config Properties dialog box opens to the Sharing tab.
2. To share the config folder with other users, click the **Share this folder** option button.
3. The name of the shared folder appears in the Share name text box. By default, the name of the share is the same as the folder name. See Figure 5-19.

   Click the **Permissions** button to open the permissions for the config folder, which indicates that, by default, everyone gets Read permission for Windows 2003 but Full Control for Windows 2000. Click **OK** to return to the config Properties dialog box.
4. Click **OK**. The icon for the config folder changes, indicating that it is shared.

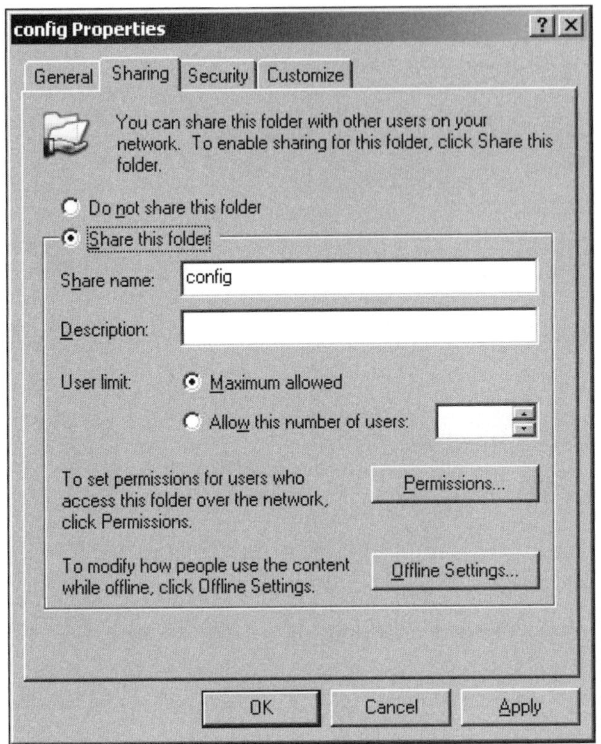

Figure 5-19 config Properties dialog box showing the shared folder

If you want to access a folder that is stored on another computer, that folder must first be set up as a shared folder. Then the shared folder on the other computer can become a virtual drive on your computer. A **virtual drive** is a drive that does not physically exist on your computer. For example, when you install Windows, it creates a partition to which it assigns the identifier C:. Your CD-ROM drive may be drive D. Both C: and D: are physical drives. In contrast, a virtual drive assigns a drive letter to a shared folder on another computer. Microsoft uses the term **map a drive**, meaning that the folder corresponds (maps) to a drive letter. Actually, you can even map a drive using a shared folder on the same computer for practice.

To map a drive to a shared folder in Windows:

1. In Windows Explorer, click **Tools** on the menu bar, and then click **Map Network Drive**.
2. The Map Network Drive dialog box appears. In the Folder text box, assuming that the name of the server with the share is web1, type: **\\web1\config**. See Figure 5-20. Your drive letter may be different.

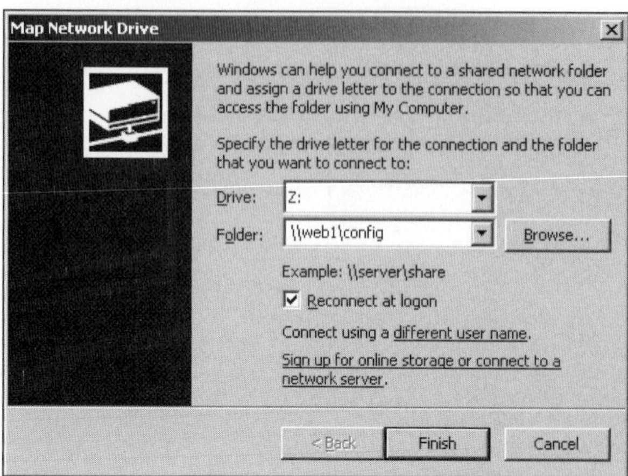

Figure 5-20 Map Network Drive dialog box

3. Click **Finish** to create the mapping. You can now access the config folder from your computer. It appears on the left panel of Windows Explorer.

   Note that the icon for the config mapped drive now represents a network connection.

Enforcing Network Policies

You may want to exert even more control over users who have an account on your network. You can set network policies in both Windows and Linux, although Windows has significantly more policies. Both Windows and Linux, however, have policies concerning passwords. For example, you can set policies such as the number of days before the user's password must be changed.

Enforcing Network Policies in Linux

In Linux, network policies are part of the entries in the /etc/shadow file. As you learned earlier, the /etc/shadow file contains the encrypted password for each user. It also contains network policies. The items are separated by a colon (:) and appear in a specific order.

The following is an example from /etc/shadow:

```
mnoia:$3498jhhd8:11816:20:40:10:15:12379:-1
```

Table 5-8 explains each of the fields in the record.

Table 5-8 Fields in the /etc/shadow record

Field	Description
`mnoia`	User account name
`$3498jhhd8`	Encrypted password
`11816`	Starting at January 1, 1970, the number of days since the password was changed
`20`	The number of days before a change is allowed
`40`	The number of days before a change is required
`10`	The number of days of warning before a change is required
`15`	The number of days before the account becomes inactive after the password has expired
`12379`	The number of days since January 1, 1970, that the account is set to expire
`-1`	Reserved field

Although you can manually change the file, doing so is prone to error. The Red Hat User Manager—the GUI that you used when you added a user account—is a better choice. To change the user information, select a user account and then click Properties. The expiration of the user account appears under the Account Info tab. Figure 5-21 shows the information under the Password Info tab with the Enable password expiration check box selected.

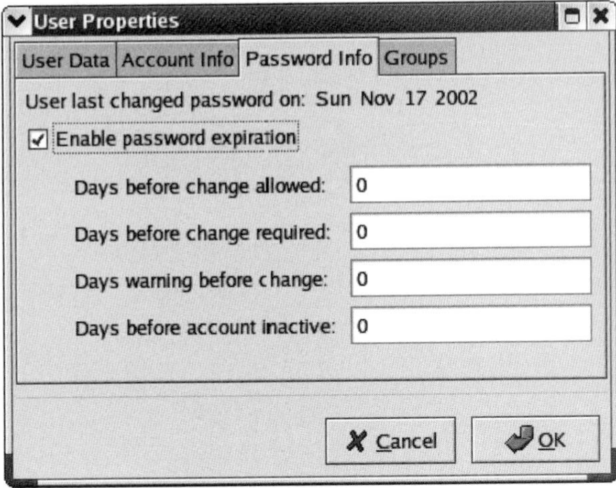

Figure 5-21 Password Info tab of User Properties dialog box for mnoia

Enforcing Network Policies in Windows

The number of network polices in Windows changed drastically from Windows NT to Windows 2000 and Windows 2003. Windows NT has a fraction of the policies available in Windows 2000 and Windows 2003. Windows 2000 and Windows 2003 call network policies **group policies**. You can set up a hierarchy of group policies, with one group policy overriding the policies in another group. Group policies exist only under Active Directory. Windows 2000 and Windows 2003 have similar policies.

To display the default domain group policy in Windows 2000 and Windows 2003:

1. *In Windows 2003:* In the Control Panel, point to Administrative Tools, and then click **Active Directory Users and Computers**.

   In Windows 2000: In the Control Panel, double-click the Administrative Tools icon, and then click **Active Directory Users and Computers**.

2. Right-click the name of your domain, such as **technowidgets.com**, and then click **Properties** on the shortcut menu.
3. In the technowidgets.com Properties dialog box, click the **Group Policy** tab. The default Domain Policy is selected.
4. Click **Edit** to open the Group Policy window.
5. In the left pane of the Group Policy window, under Computer Configuration, expand **Windows Settings**, expand **Security Settings**, expand **Local Policies**, and then click **User Rights Assignment**. The user rights you can assign appear in the right pane. See Figure 5-22.

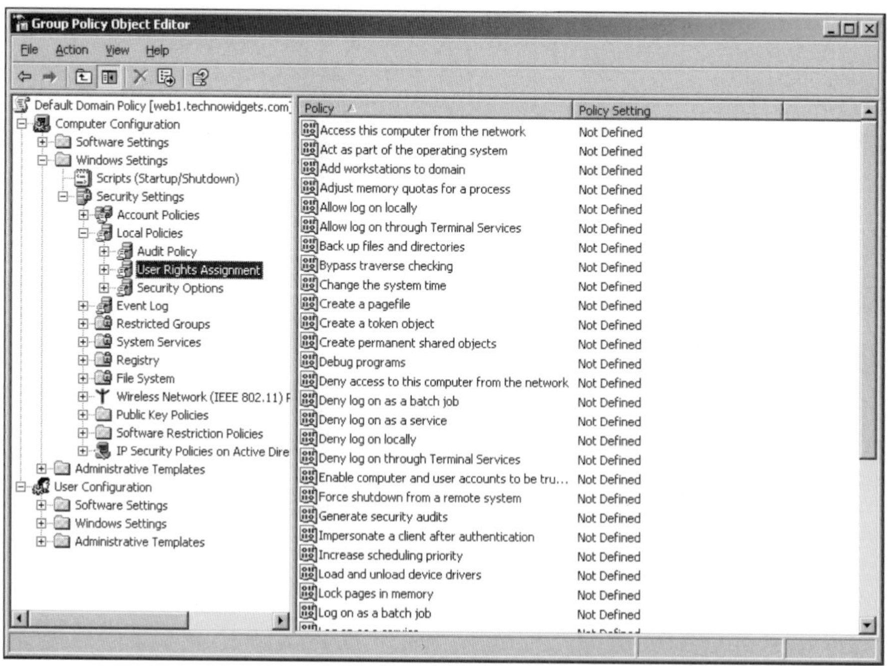

Figure 5-22 Group Policy window in Windows 2003

As you can see in Figure 5-22, the left pane of the Group Policy window also displays categories. Windows has two major groups of policies: computer configuration policies and user configuration policies. Each category has three subcategories: software settings, windows settings, and administrative templates. You can explore this area to find hundreds of settings. The default settings allow you to configure what the settings will be when you add a new computer or user to the network. This is very different from Linux, in which settings are specified after the user is created.

The right pane displays the policies related to User Rights Assignment, which you selected in Step 5. In the left pane, under the Policy Setting column, you can define which users or groups apply to this setting.

Chapter Summary

- The Web Administrator's view of server management focuses on controlling access to resources but from a different perspective. Typically, the Web server has a guest user account that allows people to contact the Web server without having a user account and password. However, the Web server can also be connected to the LAN, so LAN techniques for controlling access are important as well.
- Networking models are split between the methods typically used in a LAN and the client/server networking model. The Microsoft LAN models are divided between the workgroup networking model, in which each computer stores user accounts for that computer, and the domain networking model, in which user accounts are stored in a central location. The workgroup networking model is designed for groups of 10 or fewer computers. The domain model is designed for larger groups. The client/server networking model uses programs running on the server and client programs that access them. Examples include a Web server and Telnet, the technique that people use to log on to a Linux server.
- Authenticating users is based on a combination of three things: (1) what you know, such as a user name and password; (2) what you have, such as a smart card; and (3) who you are, or biometrics. Kerberos is the most secure method introduced to date in the Microsoft environment to authenticate. Under some circumstances, however, NTLM is still used. NTLM is used with Windows NT, for example, but hackers have many tools available to crack passwords with this system.
- At the core of the security system are the user accounts and the groups created to organize users. You should put users into global groups, assign global groups to local groups, and then assign permissions to local groups. Microsoft servers can operate in two modes. First, they can be standalone servers that just have local user accounts; this is the typical mode for Web servers. Second, they can be domain controllers. In Windows 2000 and Windows 2003, this means adding the Active Directory service. AD is a comprehensive repository of information related to users, computers, and other resources on a network.

- File system permissions in Windows are more detailed than those in Linux. Windows 2000 has 13 primary permissions and Windows 2003 has 14. By default, permissions are inherited, meaning that when you set permissions in a folder, the same permissions will be applied in subfolders and files. You can assign many groups and users permissions to a single folder or file in Windows. Linux has three permissions: read, write, and execute. The file system assigns permissions in each directory and file for the owner of the file, the group associated with the file, and all others.
- You can share folders and printers in a Windows network. The permissions available on a shared folder are Full Control, Modify, and Read. These permissions are used in conjunction with the underlying NTFS permissions. Once a resource is shared, you can map a drive to it, thereby creating a virtual drive that is associated with the folder.

REVIEW QUESTIONS

1. The LAN networking model that involves a centralized user accounts database is ______________.
   a. workgroup
   b. domain
   c. client/server
   d. both b and c
2. The LAN networking model that involves user accounts on each computer is ______________.
   a. workgroup
   b. domain
   c. client/server
   d. both b and c
3. Which LAN networking model is also known as peer-to-peer?
   a. workgroup
   b. domain
   c. client/server
   d. AD
4. Which networking model is related to the way Web servers work?
   a. workgroup
   b. domain
   c. client/server
   d. AD

5. The default authentication method in Windows 2000 and Windows 2003 is ________________.
6. Which of the following Windows operating systems first used the NTLM protocol?
   a. Windows 2003
   b. Windows 2000
   c. Windows NT
   d. Windows 98
7. The ________________ is a special account in Windows that represents the operating system.
8. One of the first things you should do when you install Windows or Linux is to delete all the user accounts that you do not recognize so as to increase security. True or False?
9. Linux has an account that corresponds to the Windows system account that is typically used when installing programs that use daemons. True or False?
10. A domain is ________________.
    a. a group of up to 10 computers
    b. a group of up to 10 users
    c. a logical grouping of computers, users, and resources
    d. another word for permissions
11. By default, passwords in Windows expire in ________________ days.
12. AD stands for ________________ ________________.
13. Mixed mode and native mode are related to ________________.
    a. PDC
    b. AD
    c. BDC
    d. NTLM
14. Once you convert from mixed mode to native mode, you cannot go back to mixed mode. True or False?
15. Once you install Active Directory, you cannot uninstall it. True or False?
16. In Linux, which file typically has passwords?
    a. /etc/shadow
    b. /etc/passwd
    c. /etc/userpasswords
    d. passwords are not in a file

5

17. In Windows, the Modify permission does not include which of the following permissions?
    a. Read
    b. Write
    c. Read & Execute
    d. List Folder Contents
18. The shell command to change a password in Linux is ________________.
19. The shell command to add a user in Linux is ________________.
20. Network policies in Windows 2003 are called ________________.

HANDS-ON PROJECTS

Project 5-1

The following project assumes that Active Directory has already been installed on your computer. In this project, you add a user in Windows by creating your own user name and password.

To add a user in AD:

1. In Administrative Tools, open the **Active Directory Users and Computers** window.
2. Right-click **Users**, point to **New**, and then click **User**. The New Object - User dialog box opens.
3. Enter the first and last name of the user. Notice how the system fills in the full name for you.
4. In the first User logon name text box, enter the first letter of the first name, followed by the last name. The system fills in the logon name for pre-Windows 2000 computers.
5. Click **Next**. Enter the password in both text boxes. Leave the default check boxes.
6. Click **Next**. The dialog box displays a summary of what you entered. Click **Finish** to create the user.

To determine the properties of an AD user and change one in Windows:

1. Double-click the user you created in the previous set of steps to display the properties for that user. Click the **Account** tab to configure the user account options.
2. Scroll the Account options and then click **Smart card is required for interactive logon**. Click **OK**.
3. Log out of the administrator account and log on as the user you just modified. Can you log on? What message do you receive?

Project 5-2

Although Active Directory is common in LANs because it offers more control over users, you do not usually make the Web server an Active Directory domain controller on a LAN because doing so requires extra processing. In this project, you uninstall Active Directory. You only need to reinstall AD if you want to install the Microsoft Exchange 2000 e-mail server in Chapter 8. After you uninstall AD, you will add a local user account in Windows 2000 or Windows 2003 and modify its properties.

To uninstall Active Directory in Windows:

1. Open a Command Prompt window, type **dcpromo.exe**, and then press **Enter**. The Welcome to the Active Directory Installation Wizard opens.
2. Click **Next**. A message box opens stating that "This domain controller is a Global Catalog server. Global Catalogs are used to process user logons. You should make sure other Global Catalogs are accessible to users of this domain before removing Active Directory from this computer." Because you are not using a real domain, you do not need to accommodate other domain controllers. Click **OK**.
3. The Remove Active Directory dialog box opens. A warning states that if this is the last domain controller in your domain, you will lose your user accounts. Click the **This server is the last domain controller in the domain** check box and then click **Next**.
4. *In Windows 2003:* The Application Directory Partitions dialog box opens. Click **Next** to delete the application directory partition. In the Confirm Deletion dialog box, select the **Delete all application directory partitions on this domain controller** check box, and then click **Next**. The Administrator Password dialog box opens. You must observe complexity rules for the password that you enter in this dialog box so you cannot type "password." Type **Lisboa&** and then click **Next**.

   In Windows 2000: The Network Credentials dialog box opens, requesting the user name and password of the Enterprise Administrator. Note that in a large network this could be different from the administrator in a single domain. In the User name text box, type **Administrator** and in the Password text box, type **password**. Click **Next**.

   The Administrator Password dialog box opens. In effect, you are being demoted from an Enterprise Administrator of the domain to an administrator for this single server. In the Password text box, type **password**, and type **password** again in the Confirm Password text box. Click **Next**.
5. The Summary dialog box opens, stating that you are going to remove Active Directory. Click **Next**.
6. A message box opens and describes the progress of configuration, which can take several minutes. The Completing the Active Directory Installation Wizard opens. Click **Finish**.
7. A dialog box opens explaining that you must restart Windows, click **Restart Now** to have the changes you made take effect.

In Windows 2003, you must create a secure password. To make it easier to remember your password, you can change the administrator password back to "password."

To change the administrator password:

1. After you log on as administrator, press Ctrl+Alt+Del. The Windows Security dialog box opens.
2. Click the **Change Password** button. The Change Password dialog box opens.
3. Type your old password in the Old Password text box. If you are using Windows 2003, your old password is **Lisboa&**. In the New Password and Confirm New Password text boxes, type **password**. Click **OK**.
4. The Change Password message states that your password has been changed. Click **OK**.
5. The Windows Security dialog box opens. Click the **Cancel** button.

To add a user and determine the capabilities of a user:

1. Create a user called **lcamoes** with a full name of **Luis de Camoes** and a description of **Writer** with a password of **pass**.
2. Log on as lcamoes and change the password.
3. Try to add a user. (Recall that you add a user in the Administrative Tools window, which you can open from the Control Panel.) Were you successful?
4. Try to add a group. Were you successful?
5. Try to change the description of lcamoes from Writer to **Poet**. Were you successful?
6. In the left pane of the Computer Management window under System Tools, Event Viewer has four categories of events. Double-click each category. Which ones can you see? Which ones are blocked from viewing?
7. Log off as lcamoes.

As an administrator, you can modify the properties of the users. In the following steps, you will modify lcamoes so he can become a member of the built-in group called Power Users. Being a member of the Power Users group increases a user's permissions on the system. In this project, you explore some of these new capabilities.

To modify the properties of lcamoes and test them:

1. Log on as an administrator.
2. Open the Properties dialog box for lcamoes.
3. Click the **Member Of** tab.
4. Click **Add** to start adding lcamoes to a group. The Select Groups dialog box opens.
5. *In Windows 2003:* Type **Power Users** in the Enter the object names to select text box.

   In Windows 2000: Select **Power Users** and then click **Add**.

   Click **OK** to return to the lcamoes Properties dialog box. Power Users is now listed on the Member Of tab.

6. Click **OK** to close the lcamoes Properties dialog box.
7. Log off as administrator and log on as lcamoes.
8. Repeat Steps 3-7 in "To add a user and determine the capabilities of a user." What has changed now that lcamoes is a Power User?

Project 5-3

Create a group called tech in Windows and add the user you created in Project 5-2 to the group. Give this group full control over the \inetpub directory.

To create a group called tech:

1. In Administrative Tools, open **Computer Management**.
2. Click the **plus sign** (+) next to Local Users and Groups.
3. Click **Groups**.
4. To add a group, click **Action** on the menu bar and then click **New Group**.
5. For the group name, type **tech**.
6. Click **Create** to create the group.
7. Click **Close** to close the New Group dialog box.

You now have a group called tech that appears in the right pane of the Computer Management window. Now you want to add a user.

To add a user to a group in Windows 2000:

1. Double-click **tech** in the right pane of the Computer Management window.
2. Click **Add** to add a user. The Select Users or Groups dialog box opens.
3. In the top text box, scroll down to the user that you created and select it.
4. Click **Add** to add the user to the bottom text box.
5. Click **OK** in the Select Users or Groups dialog box, which adds the user to the Members area of the properties for the tech group.
6. Click **OK** to accept the changes to the tech group.

To add a user to a group in Windows 2003:

1. Double-click **tech** in the right pane of the Computer Management window.
2. Click **Add** to add a user.
3. When you are asked for the user name, suppose that you are not sure of the name you used. Click **Advanced** in the Select Users dialog box to search for the user.
4. Click **Find Now** in the Select Users dialog box. All the users and groups are listed.
5. Click the user you created, and then click **OK** in the Advanced option of the Select Users dialog box to add the user to the object names text box.
6. Click **OK** in the Select Users dialog box, which adds the user to the Members area of the properties for the tech group.
7. Click **OK** to accept the changes to the tech group.

To give the tech group Full Control in the \inetpub folder:

1. In Windows Explorer, display the **\inetpub** folder.
2. Right-click **inetpub**, and then click **Sharing and Security (Sharing** in Windows 2000).
3. Click the **Security** tab.
4. *In Windows 2003:* Click **Add** to add a group to the directory. The Select Users or Groups dialog box opens. In the text box, type **tech**.

   In Windows 2000: In the top text box, select the **tech** group and then click **Add**.
5. Click **OK** to add the tech group to the list of groups for \inetpub. Notice that the tech group is highlighted. What are the default permissions?
6. Click the **Full Control** check box.
7. Click **OK** to close the inetpub Properties dialog box.

Project 5-4

In Windows, create a folder called apps in the root of your drive and allow the user you created in Project 5-1 or 5-3 to have the Read permission, and administrators to have the Full Control permission. You can work in either Windows 2000 or Windows 2003 but, as you learned from the text, the steps are different.

To create the folder apps in Windows:

1. Right-click **Start**, and then click **Explore**.
2. Click the drive letter that is the default for your operating system. Because there could be more than one operating system, the drive letter may not be C. In the Windows Explorer window, it will be the drive with a dash (-) next to it.
3. Now the right pane shows the folders in the root of the drive. Right-click in the right pane, point to **New**, and then click **Folder**.
4. Type **apps**, and then press **Enter** to create the apps folder.

To share the apps folder with Read & Execute permissions in Windows:

1. Share the folder as **apps**.
2. Click **Permissions**. What are the default share permissions?
3. Select the **Security** tab. What are the default folder permissions for Users? Notice that the share permissions and the file permissions are different.

To test the share from another computer in Windows:

1. From another computer, open Windows Explorer.
2. Click **Tools** on the menu bar, and then click **Map Network Drive**. The Map Network Drive dialog box opens. Leave the drive letter as the default.
3. Click the link to **Connect using a different user name**.

4. Type the user name and password of the user that you created earlier, and then click **OK**.
5. The easiest way to map a drive to a folder is to use the IP address. For example, if the IP address is 192.168.0.100, you would type **\\192.168.0.100\apps**.
6. Click **Finish**. A window opens with the contents of the apps folder. It should be empty. Drag a file to the apps window. Did it succeed?

Project 5-5

The Red Hat Linux User and Groups utility makes it easier to manage users than do the command-line utilities. Once you add a user, it is beneficial to understand the capabilities of the new user.

To add a user and determine the capabilities of a user in Linux:

1. Use the Red Hat User and Groups utility to create a user called **lcamoes** with a full name of **Luis de Camoes** and a password of **password**. What is the name of the login shell? Where is the home directory?
2. Log on as lcamoes and change the password.
3. Try to add a user. Were you successful?
4. Change your password to **password1** by using the command **passwd**. Were you successful?
5. Find your current directory by typing **pwd** at a command prompt. What is it?
6. Create a directory in your current directory. Type **mkdir test**, and then press **Enter**. Were you successful?
7. Create a directory in the usr directory. Type **mkdir /usr/test**, and then press **Enter**. Were you successful?
8. Create a directory in the tmp directory. Type **mkdir /tmp/test**, and then press **Enter**. Were you successful?
9. Display a long listing of the root directory. Type **ls -l**, and then press **Enter**. What is the difference between the permissions for /usr and the permissions for /tmp?
10. Log out as lcamoes.

Project 5-6

Once you create a user, you need to understand which file permissions the user has and how to modify them.

To check permissions and set permissions for lcamoes in Linux:

1. Log on as root.
2. Create a directory in the home directory of lcamoes. In a terminal window, type **mkdir /home/lcamoes/test2**, and then press **Enter**. Were you successful?

3. Look at the permissions for /home/lcamoes. What do they tell you about who can create directories and files in the directory? The root user is not constrained by permissions.
4. Create a directory called **/usr/lcamoesapp**.
5. Display a long listing of the /usr directory. What are the permissions for /usr/lcamoes? What does the rest of the entry display for this directory?
6. Change the owner of the directory to lcamoes. Type **chown lcamoes /usr/lcamoesapp**, and then press **Enter**. (Be sure to insert a space after "lcamoes".)
7. Display a long listing of the /usr directory. What is different about the entry for /usr/lcamoesapp? Can lcamoes create directories and files in this directory now?
8. Change the permissions for /usr/lcamoesapp so others cannot read or execute files in this directory.
9. Create a file and store it in **/usr/lcamoesapp**.
10. Create a user called **cbranco**.
11. Log on as cbranco and try to edit the file you created in /usr/lcamoesapp. What error message do you receive?

Project 5-7

Although the text described sharing folders in Windows networks, you can share directories in Linux using NFS (Network File System). Once you select the directory to share, any computer with NFS client software can access the information. NFS allows you to set up security in a variety of ways, including determining who has access, what the permissions are once the user accesses the directory (read/write), and what IP addresses are allowed.

On the client side, you use the `mount` command to associate a local directory with the remote shared directory. This technique is similar to mounting a CD.

To share the /var directory in Linux:

1. Click the **Red Hat** icon, point to **Server Settings**, and then click **NFS Server**. The NFS Server Configuration dialog box opens. See Figure 5-23.
2. Click **Add** to add a shared directory. The Add NFS Share dialog box opens. See Figure 5-24. Besides filling in the text box with the name of the directory, you can specify which hosts can access it. The hosts can be specific computers or network address ranges.
3. In the Directory text box, type **/var** to share the /var directory. You can leave the permission at Read-only but, as the option button states, you could change it to Read/Write to give you the ability to change the contents.

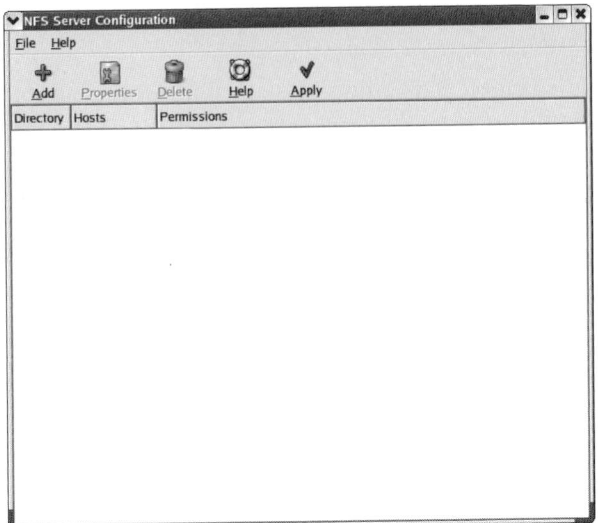

Figure 5-23 NFS Server Configuration dialog box

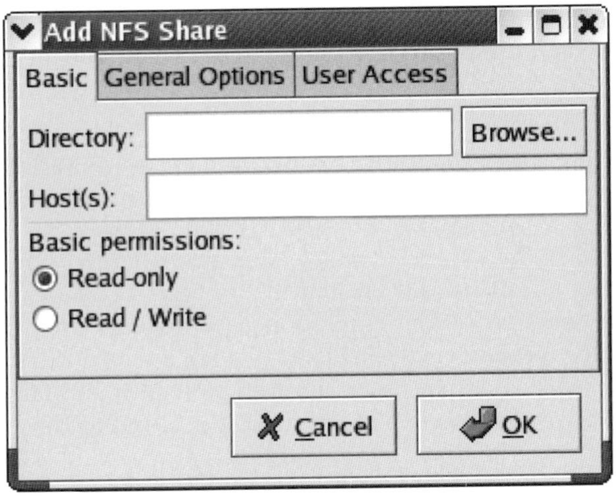

Figure 5-24 Add NFS Share dialog box

4. In the Host(s) text box, type the network portion of your IP address to allow only computers on your network to access the directory. For example, if your IP address was 192.168.0.100, you would type **192.168.0.0/24**. The "24" means that there are 24 bits in the subnet mask of this network, which is equivalent to 255.255.255.0.

5. Click **OK** to add the NFS share. Now the NFS Server Configuration window has an entry for the directory that you just shared.
6. Click **Apply** to save the changes. A warning message box opens stating, "The NFS service is not currently running. Do you wish to start it?" Click **Yes** to start the NFS service.

Now that you have the NFS server running, you can mount the directory from any other Linux computer on the same network. If another Linux computer is not available, you can use the same computer to configure an NFS client.

To connect to an NFS share in Linux:

1. Create a directory that you will use to mount the NFS share. Because the directory called mnt already exists, you will use it to add a reference to the var directory. Open a terminal window and, at the shell prompt, type **mkdir /mnt/var** (be sure to insert a space after "mkdir").
2. Now that you have a new directory, you want to associate it with the NFS share. In the following, replace the IP address with the address of your NFS server. Type **mount 192.168.0.100:/var /mnt/var**, and then press **Enter**. (Note that there is a space after mount and another space before /mnt/var.)
3. Now the contents of the /mnt/var directory are actually /var on the NFS server. Type **ls /mnt/var**, and then press **Enter**. You now see the contents of the /var directory on the NFS server. Type **ls /mnt/var/www**, and you will see the contents of the /var/www directory on the NFS server.
4. To stop using the NFS share, type **umount /mnt/var**, and then press **Enter**.

Project 5-8

Change the properties for lcamoes that you created in Project 5-5. You can modify a number of settings for users, such as setting expiration dates for accounts and forcing users to change passwords. If you set expiration dates or lock an account, it is a good idea to know what the user will see when he or she tries to log on and fails. The user does not always get a descriptive message explaining what happened to the account.

To modify user properties for lcamoes and test their effects in Linux:

1. In the User and Groups utility, highlight **lcamoes** and click **Properties**.
2. Click the **Account Info** tab. See Figure 5-25.
3. Select the **Enable account expiration** check box. Enter a date before today's date to force an expiration.
4. Click **OK** to save the change to the properties for lcamoes.

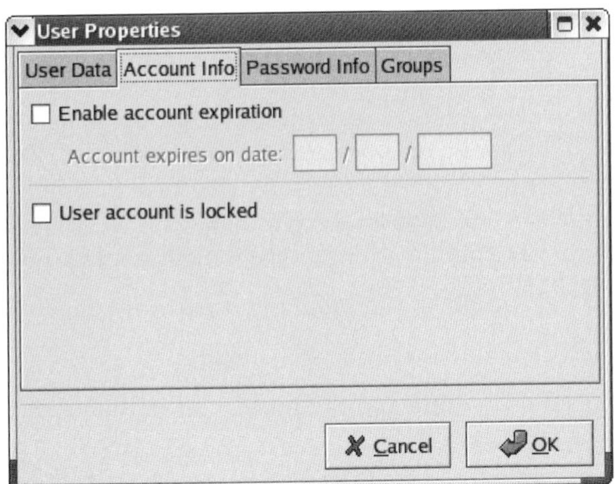

Figure 5-25 Account Info tab of the User Properties dialog box

5. Log out and log back on as lcamoes. Were you successful? What was the message?
6. Log on as root. In the Account Info tab of the properties for lcamoes, clear the **Enable account expiration** check box and select the **User account is locked** check box.
7. Log out and log back on as lcamoes. Were you successful? What was the message?
8. Log on as root. In the Account Info tab of the properties for lcamoes, disable the **User account is locked** check box.

CASE PROJECTS

Case Project 5-1

You have just hired an assistant administrator for your Linux server. For now, you will not allow him to log on as root. Create a user account for him.

A newly installed application will need a text file called netapp.conf in the /usr directory. Create the text file. Give ownership of the file to the new user. Linux has a utility called chown that you can use for this purpose. At a shell prompt, type `man chown` to display the manual pages for the chown utility. Allow the assistant (owner) full access, the group full access, and other users just read access. Test the system by logging on as the assistant administrator. As assistant administrator, can you create a file in /usr? Describe why you can or cannot do so.

Case Project 5-2

You have decided that it might be a good idea to provide some Windows technical support. Your new boss asks whether you have ever heard of group policies in Active Directory. You have, but are a bit weak on the details. Your boss wants you to write detailed, step-by-step instructions to implement the following plan. It will be e-mailed to a branch office to be handled by the support person there. You are to describe how to set up security for the computer configuration for the default domain policy.

- Set the maximum password age to 90 and the minimum password age to 10.
- Make the user account lock after three unsuccessful attempts.
- Make both the account lockout duration and the number of minutes before resetting the lockout counter 30 minutes.
- When users log on, the following message should appear: "Welcome to TechnoWidgets."

Case Project 5-3

Your objective is to create a secure area on the Windows server for a group called acctg. Create two users, ajones and mnoia. Put them in the acctg group. From the root of your Windows drive, create a folder called reports. In the reports folder, give the acctg group Full Control over the contents of the folder and remove the Users group from the folder.

CHAPTER

6

CONFIGURING A WEB SERVER

In this chapter, you will:

- Understand how a Web server works
- Install the Internet Information Services (IIS) and Apache Web servers
- Examine the IIS and Apache properties
- Host multiple Web sites
- Configure new Web sites in IIS and Apache
- Understand virtual directories

All Web servers are based on the Hypertext Transfer Protocol (HTTP), which governs the way Web servers communicate with browsers and other client software. When you install a Web server, it is configured to perform most common tasks by default, such as display simple Web pages. Although you can configure Microsoft's Internet Information Services (IIS) Web server and the Apache Web server in a similar manner, IIS and Apache use different approaches to configuration. For IIS, you use a GUI, often with wizards, to configure the Web server. For Apache, you typically use a text file called httpd.conf.

Often a Web server is not what it appears to be. A Web site such as *Microsoft.com* uses URLs that appear to have a structure of folders similar to those on a hard disk. In reality, that structure doesn't always reflect the organization of the folders on the Web server's hard disk. You can create virtual directories that are part of the Web site yet physically located outside of the Web site. Conversely, you may think that sites such as *www.MyFavoriteWidgets.com* and *www.WidgetSupplies.com* must represent different servers, or at least different IP addresses. However, you can use virtual servers to configure a Web server to host multiple sites. An extreme example is *www.freeserve.net*, which hosts about 150,000 sites using only four IP addresses.

Understanding How a Web Server Works

Although Web servers have evolved substantially since their introduction, the main purpose of a Web server is to send HTML documents to a browser. HTML is the formatting language that browsers use to display text and graphics. All Web servers support the **Hypertext Transfer Protocol (HTTP)**, which defines how information is passed between the browser and the Web server. Web servers and browsers must follow the same rules defined by HTTP. This consistency allows someone using a Netscape browser or an Internet Explorer browser, for example, to see the same pages on any server. Netscape, Internet Explorer, Konqueror, and other browsers may differ in terms of the HTML that the Web designers use to create Web pages, but the Web server always provides the same HTML to the browser.

The two most popular Web servers are Apache from the Apache Software Foundation and Internet Information Services (IIS) from Microsoft. Prior to the introduction of IIS 5.0, IIS stood for Internet Information Server. According to Netcraft (*www.netcraft.com*), nearly two-thirds of all Web servers use Apache and less than one-third use IIS. Both servers publish HTML pages and perform other tasks necessary for producing interactive Web pages. Chapter 7 explores the use of programming languages and databases on Web servers to produce interactive Web pages.

After you install a Web server, you can configure it to change the port number on which it listens for Web requests, the location to which the Web server retrieves HTML files (called the root of the server), and the settings that determine the performance of the computer depending on levels of traffic. You can expand the Web server to accept requests from multiple domains, thereby creating virtual servers. You can also store HTML documents that are not part of the root file structure by using virtual directories. This chapter explores these configurations in detail.

Like DNS servers, Web servers are services (often called daemons in Linux) that listen for requests at ports. Most listen at port 80 for incoming requests, though they can use any port beyond 1023. Ports up to and including 1023 are reserved for other uses. Often, if a Web server is not running on port 80, it runs on port 8080 or 8000, but using these ports is simply convention. Web server administrators sometimes take advantage of this technique when two Web servers are running on the same computer.

Each Web server has a **root**, which is where you store the HTML documents and subfolders for your site. If you install IIS on the C: drive, the root is c:\inetpub\wwwroot. For example, if you used this root for the *www.technowidgets.com* Web site, and you stored a file named hello.htm in d:\inetpub\wwwroot, you could display it from a browser by entering *http://www.technowidgets.com/hello.htm* as the URL.

Understanding HTTP

The current version of HTTP, version 1.1, describes how to format messages that are sent from the browser to the Web server and back. The messages contain specific commands that instruct the server to retrieve certain Web pages. Because all popular Web servers and browsers have been supporting HTTP version 1.1 for years, this section focuses on this version. When the *GoCertify.com* Web site analyzed which protocol approximately 43,000 visitors use, it found that only about 0.01 percent of the browsers that accessed the site used HTTP/1.0. Of these visitors, 78 used Netscape 3, 4 used Internet Explorer 2, and 77 used Internet Explorer 3.

HTTP is a **stateless** protocol, meaning that each Web page sent to the user is independent of every other Web page the server sends. As a consequence, you cannot use the protocol to keep track of users who are viewing Web pages on your site. For example, if you have an e-commerce site where people buy books, you need to use programming techniques instead of HTTP features to track visitors and the books they buy.

One of the most important characteristics of HTTP 1.1 is its support for **persistent connections**. This capability allows the browser to receive multiple files in one TCP connection. Without a persistent connection, each file sent would require an independent TCP connection, which takes extra processing on the Web server to set up and release. Such extra processing can decrease performance. This potential problem becomes even more significant when you realize that most Web pages contain multiple files. Besides the main file that contains text, the Web page may contain graphic images. Each image must be sent to your browser separately.

The following procedure shows the communication between a browser and a Web server that displays a simple page containing the text "Hello, World." The procedure assumes that a host called *www.technowidgets.com* resolves to an IP address of 192.168.0.100.

1. You type http://www.technowidgets.com/hello.htm in the Web browser.
2. The Web browser contacts the DNS server to find the IP address for *www.technowidgets.com*. The DNS server returns 192.168.0.100.
3. The browser composes the following message and sends it to port 80 on 192.168.0.100:

   ```
   GET /hello.htm HTTP/1.1
   Host: www.technowidgets.com
   ```

4. In this example, the Web server is a Microsoft Web server and responds to the browser with the following message:

   ```
   HTTP/1.1 200 OK
   Server: Microsoft-IIS/5.0
   Date: Fri, 17 May 2005 18:47:30 GMT
   Content-Type: text/html
   Accept-Ranges: bytes
   Last-Modified: Fri, 17 May 2005 18:21:25 GMT
   ETag: "90cbb2a7cffdc11:b50"
   Content-Length: 43

   <html><body>
   Hello, World
   </body></html>
   ```

5. The browser retrieves the message and reads its **header**, which contains information about the page. Each header starts with the header name, followed by a colon. The data associated with the header follow the colon. At the bottom of the message, you see that the page displays the text "Hello, World."

Step 3 is an important one for configuring servers. Notice that when the message is sent to IP address 192.168.0.100, the host name is *www.technowidgets.com*. The host name is separate from the IP address, meaning that the Web server at 192.168.0.100 can look at the host name and then display pages on a different Web site. You will see how to apply this technique later in the chapter.

In Step 5, the headers contain the following information for the browser: the Web server's use of IIS version 5.0 (Microsoft Windows 2000), the current date and time on the server, and the last time the file was updated. The other important information in one header is that the content type is text/html, which defines it as a typical Web page.

Understanding Features in Apache Web Server

Apache Web server was available only in version 1.3 for many years. In 2001, the Apache Software Foundation released version 2.0. Linux 8 comes with version 2, so that is the focus of this chapter.

Apache's philosophy is to start with minimal features and then expand the server as necessary. For example, Apache doesn't support programming languages besides the default languages supported by CGI scripts (described in Chapter 7). However, you can easily add languages to the Apache setup, sometimes with a single line in a configuration file. When you install Apache, a directory is set up for an online manual and icons used on Web pages. The only sample HTML document is a single sample test page. This modularity allows you to optimize Apache for the required tasks without wasting processing time and memory on unneeded tasks. You can even use Apache to help secure your Web environment by configuring it as a **proxy server**, which isolates your real Web server from the Internet. A proxy server takes requests for pages from the Internet and transfers them to the real Web server inside your network.

Following are some of the major improvements in Apache 2.0:

- *Better support for Windows*—Running Apache 1.3 under Windows often produced malfunctions, but version 2.0 provides improved reliability.
- *Support for IPv6, the future version of IP addressing*—The current method of IP addressing uses 32 bits, which does not provide enough addresses to meet demand as the Internet grows. Internet protocol version 6 (IPv6) uses 128 bits, which greatly expands the number of available addresses.
- *Simplified configuration*—Apache 1.3 provides multiple ways to set the port number and IP address that the server would use for listening. Version 2.0 provides only a single way, which simplifies the setup.

- *Unicode support in Windows NT, 2000, and 2003*—Apache 2.0 supports Unicode in Windows, which allows you to use foreign-language character sets in Web pages.
- *Multilanguage error responses*—Apache 2.0 provides error messages in a number of languages.

Understanding Features in Internet Information Services

For many Web sites, any version of IIS provides the needed functionality of publishing Web pages. Windows 2000 comes with IIS 5.0, and Windows Server 2003 uses IIS 6.0. All versions of IIS support HTML and **Active Server Pages (ASP)**, which you use to create dynamic pages. ASP.NET is available on both Windows 2000 and Windows 2003. You will learn about ASP and ASP.NET in Chapter 7.

IIS 5.0 is installed with many options and samples to make it easy to get started. For example, an administrative interface allows you to use a browser to manage IIS. Sample applications show you how to create ASP pages. The SMTP protocol is also installed, enabling you to send e-mail from your Web pages. Unfortunately, this user-friendly approach gives malicious users more ways to attack your site. For example, in late 2002, Microsoft announced a patch to update the Microsoft Data Access Component (MDAC). According to security bulletin MS02-065, an attacker could compromise any Windows NT or Windows 2000 Web server and not only change Web pages, but even format the disk.

IIS 6.0 does not install as many default features, although they can be added later. This version even provides an IIS Lockdown Wizard to restrict the functionality to only those capabilities that you really need. This approach helps prevent Web administrators from accidentally including features that attackers can exploit.

Following are key features in IIS 5.0:

- *Web Distributed Authoring and Versioning (WebDAV)*—WebDAV allows the server to share Web-based files.
- *Web folders*—Web folders use the WebDAV technology, allowing the user to drag files between the local system and the Web server.
- *Named virtual hosting*—If you are running more than one physical Web server, virtual hosting lets them all use single IP address.
- *Multiple user domains*—IIS lets you set up more than one domain for a user, which in turn supports multiple user databases through the use of Active Directory.
- *Per Web site bandwidth throttling*—This feature allows you to control the amount of bandwidth that each site on your server consumes.
- *Kerberos*—The Kerberos authentication protocol is integrated with the Web server, which allows you to implement more secure authentication.

- *Secure Sockets Layer 3.0*—This technology supports encrypted communication between a Web server and a browser, increasing the security of a Web site.

Some of the features new to IIS 6.0 include the following:

- *Increased security*—The default installation for IIS 6.0 is the "locked down" mode, which permits only HTML files to be used. IIS 5.0, by default, supports ASP and other methods of creating dynamic pages. Allowing only HTML files significantly reduces attackers' ability to extract important data.
- *Expanded language support*—**XML** and **SOAP** are important components used in application development. You will learn about both in Chapter 7.
- *Support for IPv6, the future version of IP addressing*—As mentioned in the "Understanding Features in Apache Web Server" section, the current method of IP addressing uses 32 bits, which does not provide enough addresses to meet demand as the Internet grows. Internet protocol version 6 (IPv6) uses 128 bits, which greatly expands the number of available addresses.
- *Increased dependability*—IIS 6.0 increases dependability through **kernel-mode** HTTP service and a self-healing mechanism. A kernel-mode service is protected from being corrupted by another program.

Installing Web Servers

Each version of Windows or Linux provides a Web server that is easy to install and runs without any extra configuration. However, you use a different procedure to install each Web server. In Windows 2000, you can install the Web server while you install the operating system. In Windows 2003, you can install it only after you have installed the operating system. In Linux, it is easiest to install Apache Web server when you install the operating system. Recall that when you installed Linux and selected the server installation type, Apache was one of the packages available. Although Apache is by far the most popular Web server available for Linux, you can also install Apache on Windows 2000 or Windows 2003.

Windows 2003 provides a Configure Your Server Wizard that allows you to more easily install a Web server and associated components. For example, you can install IIS and the following components using this wizard:

- *FrontPage Server Extensions*—Allows applications such as FrontPage and Visual Studio to upload files to the Web server and is needed for Web folders.
- *Microsoft Data Engine (MSDE)*—A scaled-down version of SQL Server 2000 that supports as many as five simultaneous connections.
- *ASP.NET*—A programming environment that allows programmers to develop dynamic Web pages.

Installing IIS on Microsoft Windows 2000 or Windows Server 2003

This section shows you how to install IIS on Windows 2003 using the Configure Your Server Wizard. Note that you can also install IIS on Windows 2003 without its components in the same way you install IIS in Windows 2000. Before you perform the following steps, insert the main Windows Setup CD in the CD drive and log on as an administrator.

To install IIS 6.0 in Windows 2003:

1. Click **Start** and then click **Manage Your Server**. The Manage Your Server window opens. See Figure 6-1. Your window might not list the WINS server, which was installed in Chapter 5. WINS is not needed for any of the tutorials or projects.

6

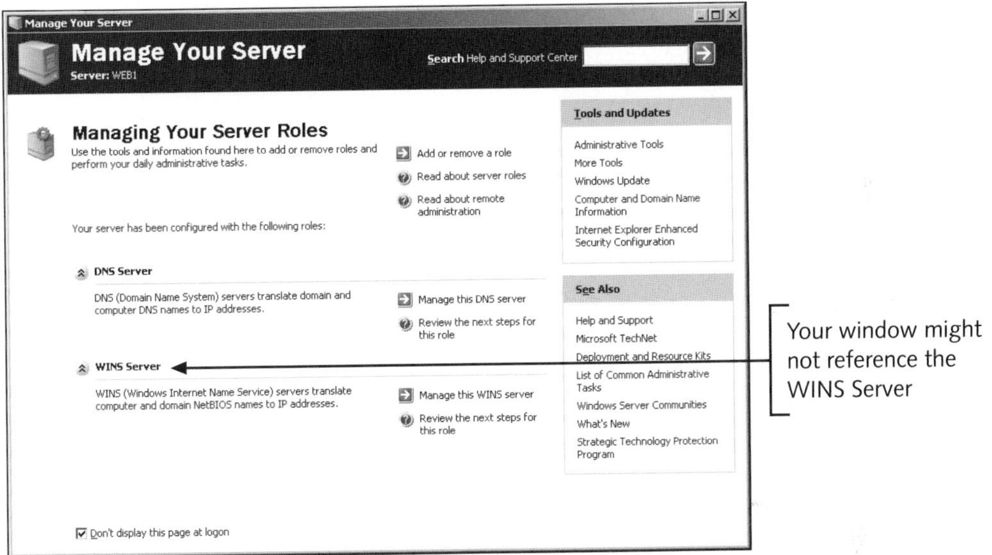

Figure 6-1 Manage Your Server window

2. Click **Add or remove a role** to select a role for your server. For example, your server can perform the roles of file server and Web server. The Preliminary Steps dialog box opens, reminding you to make sure that you have installed a NIC and have the Setup CD.

3. Click **Next**. The Server Role dialog box opens. See Figure 6-2. Notice that the role of DNS server is already configured. If you already installed Active Directory, that service would appear in the Server Role list as well.

4. Click **Application server (IIS, ASP.NET)** and then click **Next**. The Application Server Options dialog box opens. See Figure 6-3. Select the **Enable ASP.NET** check box to install this popular programming environment. FrontPage Server Extensions allow you to remotely manipulate files on your Web server through software products such as FrontPage and Visual Studio.

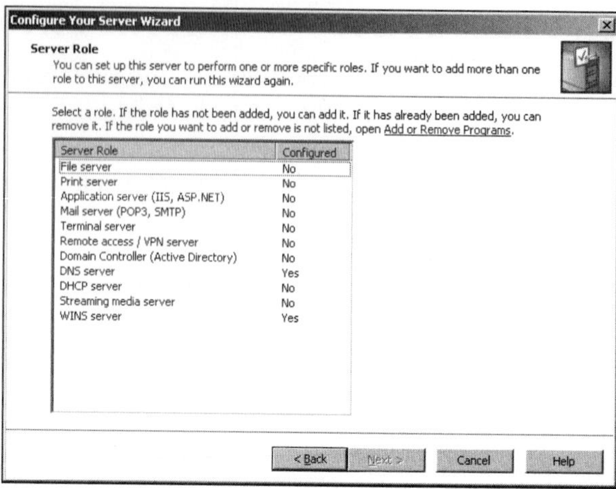

Figure 6-2 Server Role dialog box

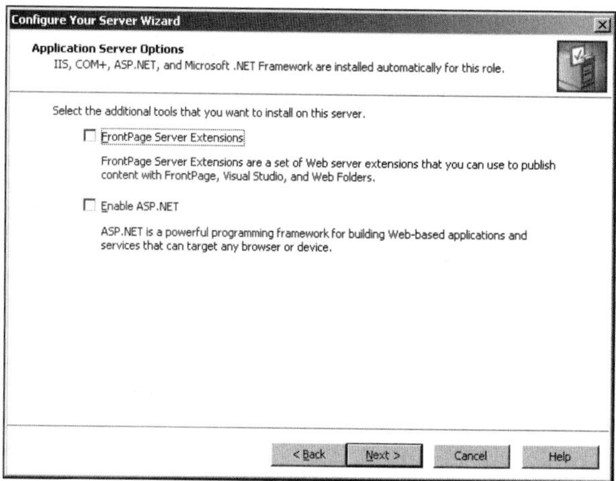

Figure 6-3 Application Server Options dialog box

5. Click **Next**. The Summary of Selections dialog box opens, listing those items that will be installed. Besides IIS and ASP.NET, this wizard automatically installs the Microsoft Distributed Transaction Coordinator and COM+.

6. Click **Next** to begin installing IIS 6.0. When a dialog box opens requesting the Setup CD, insert the CD, and then click **OK**. When the Server Setup Window opens, click **Exit**. A few windows describe the installation, and then a dialog box notifies you that the procedure is complete. See Figure 6-4.

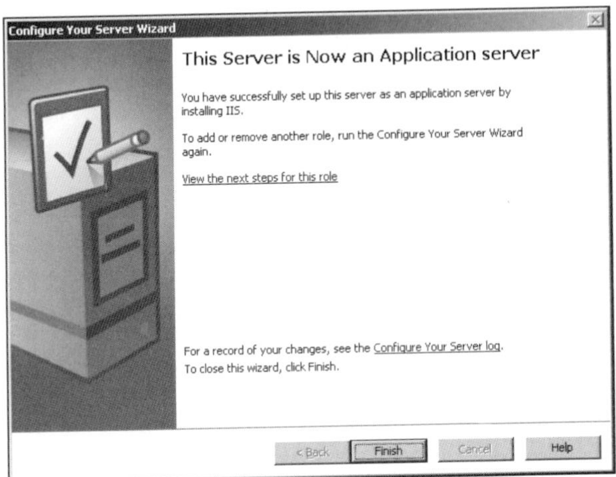

Figure 6-4 This Server is Now an Application server dialog box

7. To view help screens related to IIS, you could click **View the next steps for this role**. To make sure that IIS was installed correctly, you could click **Configure Your Server log**. Click **Finish** to exit the wizard.

After installing IIS in Windows 2003, an extra menu item appears in Administrative Tools called Internet Information Services (IIS). Also stored in the root of your drive is a folder called Inetpub, which contains two subfolders. The AdminScripts folder contains scripts to allow you to manage your Web server remotely. The wwwroot folder is where you store your Web pages.

Although you can use the Windows 2000 Configure Your Server Wizard to install IIS 5.0 in Windows 2000, when you select the Web server option, it opens the Windows Component dialog box so you can select appropriate options. It is just as easy to use the Control Panel to add IIS.

To install IIS 5.0 in Windows 2000:

1. In the Control Panel, double-click **Add/Remove Programs** to open the Add/Remove Programs window. See Figure 6-5. (Your window might contain different programs.)
2. In the left pane of the Add/Remove Programs window, click **Add/Remove Windows Components** to start the Windows Components Wizard. See Figure 6-6.

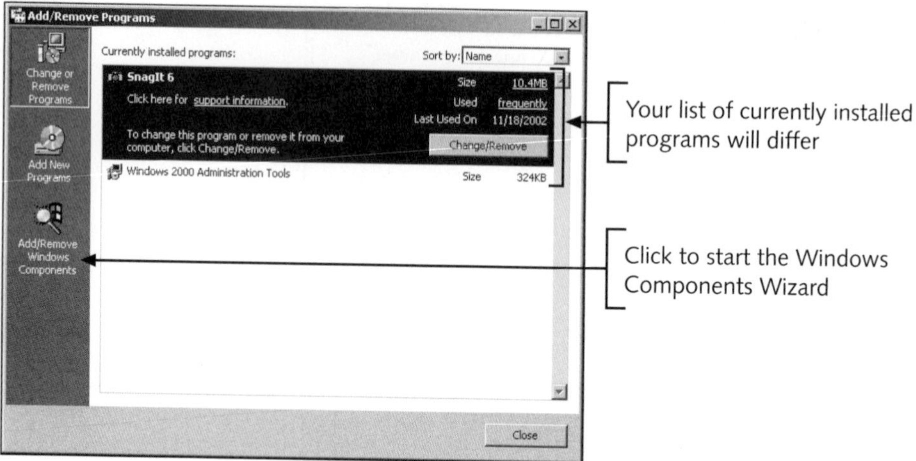

Figure 6-5 Add/Remove Programs window

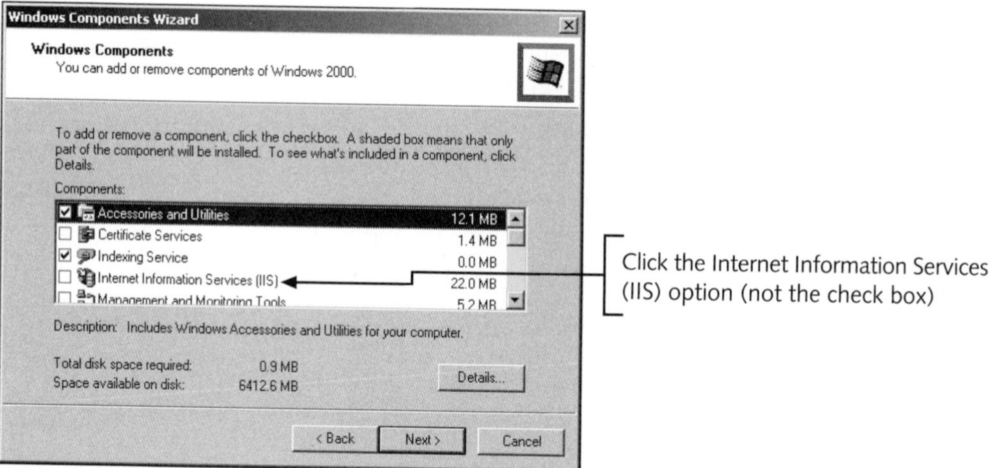

Figure 6-6 Windows Components dialog box

3. Click **Internet Information Services (IIS)** to highlight that option. Be sure to click the text, not the check box, so that you select only the Web server, not all of the components of IIS. See Figure 6-7.

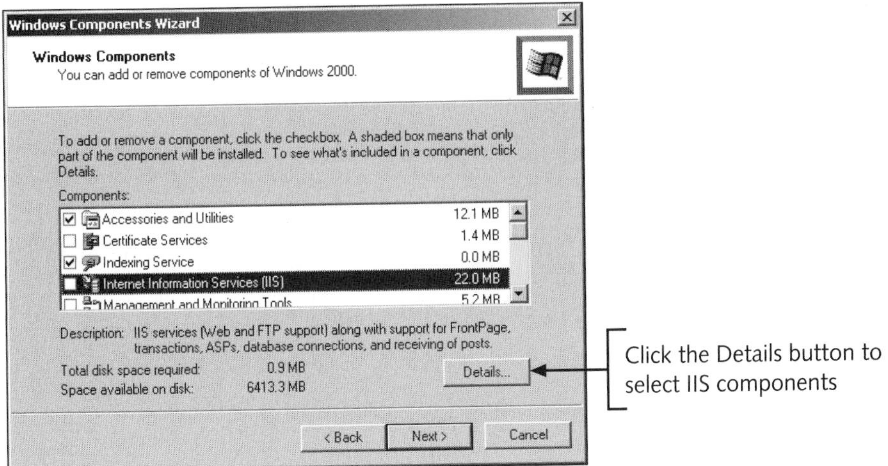

Figure 6-7 Selecting Internet Information Services (IIS)

4. With Internet Information Services (IIS) highlighted, click the **Details** button. The Internet Information Services (IIS) dialog box opens, listing available IIS components. See Figure 6-8.

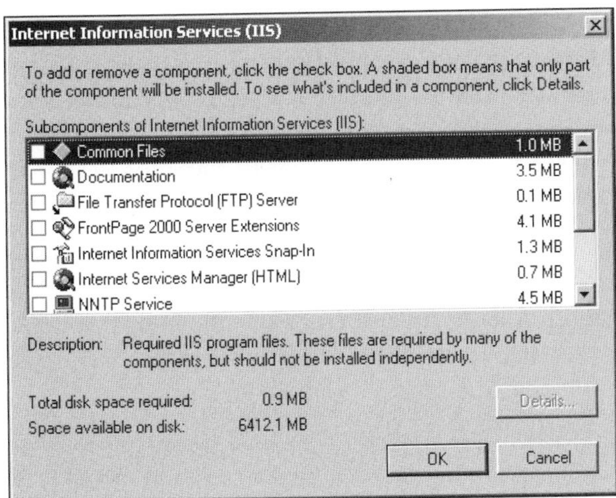

Figure 6-8 IIS components

The major components available include the following:

- *File Transfer Protocol (FTP) Server*—Used to transfer files. FTP is discussed in Chapter 9.
- *FrontPage 2000 Server Extensions*—Used by programs such as FrontPage to transfer files to the Web server for Web development.
- *NNTP Service*—Used to create user forums.

- *SMTP Service*—Used to send e-mail messages directly from Web pages.
- *World Wide Web Server*—Used as the service for the Web server.

5. Scroll and then click **World Wide Web Server** to select it. Notice that selecting this check box automatically checks the boxes for **Internet Information Services Snap-In**, which allows you to configure the server, and **Common Files**, which are used by more than one of the services.
6. Click the **Documentation** check box to install the online Help for IIS. You have now selected all of the IIS components you need for this chapter. You will install other components as you need them.
7. Click **OK** to return to the Windows Components dialog box.
8. Click **Next** to have Windows copy files and install them on your server.
9. When Windows is finished installing IIS, the Completing the Windows Components Wizard dialog box opens. Click **Finish**, and then close the Add or Remove Programs window and the Control Panel window.

After installing IIS in Windows 2000, you have an extra menu item in Administrative Tools called Internet Services Manager. The root of your drive contains a folder called Inetpub, which contains a number of subfolders. The AdminScripts folder contains scripts to allow you to manage your Web server remotely. The iissamples folder contains many sample Web applications to show you the variety of tasks that can be accomplished through the Web server. The scripts folder can hold special files, called CGI scripts, that can add functionality to your Web server. Unfortunately, these folders (especially the iissamples folder) create an insecure Web server because attackers can readily exploit the files they contain. You will see how to restrict access to these folders when you configure the server. The last folder, wwwroot, is where you put your Web pages.

To test the installation, you can use Notepad to create an HTML document called default.htm and store it in the \inetpub\wwwroot folder. You can use the name default.htm because when the URL does not contain a specific filename, it automatically looks for and then displays the contents of default.htm. You can use the default.htm file in \inetpub\wwwroot to create the home page for your Web site.

To create a default Web page for IIS:

1. Start Notepad.
   In Windows 2003: Click **Start**, and then click **Notepad**.
   In Windows 2000: Click **Start**, point to **Programs**, point to **Accessories**, and then click **Notepad**.
2. Type the following HTML code:

```
<html><body>
This is the default Web page in Windows
</body></html>
```

3. Click **File** on the menu bar, and then click **Save**. The Save As dialog box opens.
4. Click the **Save as type** list arrow, and then click **All Files**. If you accept the default text format, Notepad automatically adds .txt to your filename. Thus, although you type default.htm as a filename, it would be saved as default.htm.txt.
5. Click the **Save in** list arrow, and then navigate to the \inetpub\wwwroot folder on the drive where you installed Windows.
6. In the File name text box, type **default.htm** and then click **Save**. See Figure 6-9. Your file list is different in Windows 2000.

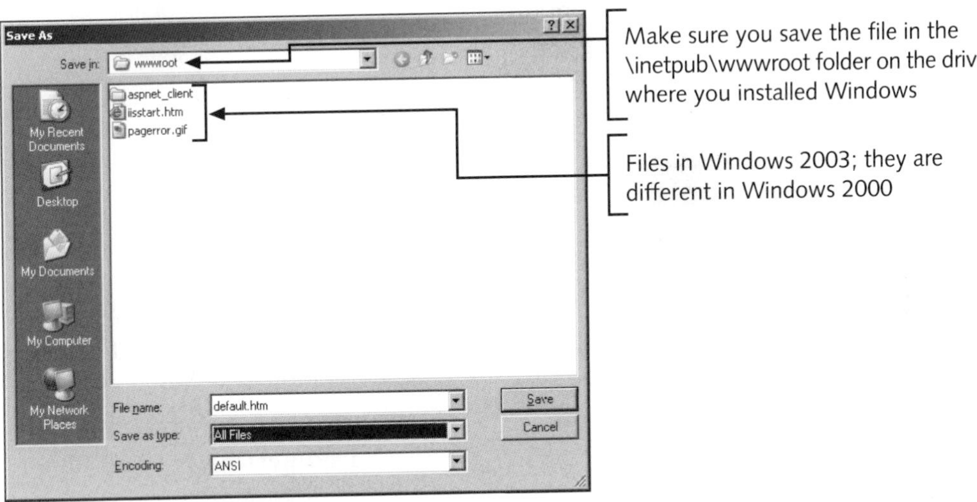

Figure 6-9 Saving default.htm

7. Close the Notepad window.

Now you should confirm that your browser will display the Web page that you just created. You can use Internet Explorer to display the default page for your Web site. If the default.htm page does not appear when you start Internet Explorer, make sure that the file you created has an .htm extension, and that you stored it in the \inetpub\wwwroot folder on the same drive where you installed Windows.

To display the default Web page in Windows 2003:

1. Click the **Internet Explorer** icon on the Quick Launch toolbar on the desktop.
2. Because this is the first time that you have used Internet Explorer, a dialog box opens stating that enhanced security is enabled on the server. Select the **In the future, do not show this message** check box, and click **OK**.
3. In the Address text box, type **http://localhost/** and then press **Enter**. The name "localhost" represents the IP address of 127.0.0.1, which always refers to

the computer you are currently using. The browser displays the default.htm Web page you created. See Figure 6-10.

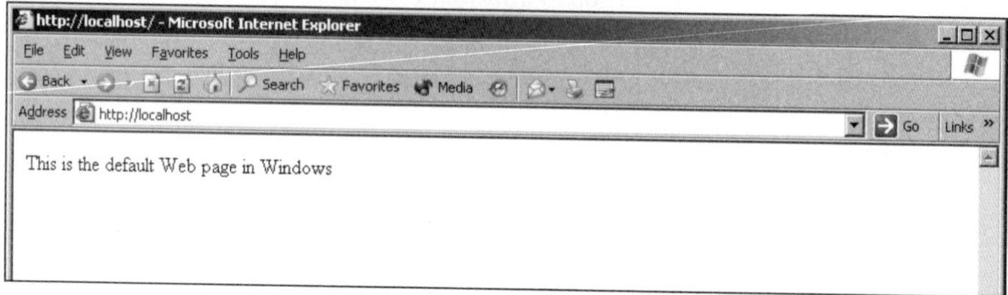

Figure 6-10 default.htm in Internet Explorer in Windows 2003

4. Close Internet Explorer.

You can also display the default Web page in Windows 2000.

To display the default Web page in Windows 2000:

1. Click the **Internet Explorer** icon on the Quick Launch toolbar on the desktop.

   Because this is the first time that you have used Internet Explorer, the Internet Connection Wizard opens. The first time you use Internet Explorer, the Internet Connection Wizard guides you through setting up Internet Explorer.

2. Click the **I want to set up my Internet connections manually, or I want to connect through a local area network (LAN)** option button, and then click **Next**.

3. The Setting up your Internet connection dialog box opens. Click the **I connect through a local area network (LAN)** option button, and then click **Next**.

4. The Local area network Internet configuration dialog box opens. You have the opportunity to configure it to connect through a proxy server. Proxy servers isolate the internal network from the Internet. Click **Next** to accept the default of no proxy settings.

5. The Set Up Your Internet Mail Account dialog box opens. Click the **No** option button, and then click **Next**.

6. The Completing the Internet Connection Wizard dialog box opens. Click **Finish** to exit the wizard and start the Internet Explorer. If the Work offline message box opens, click **Try Again**. Internet Explorer tries to access *www.msn.com*.

7. In the Address text box, type **http://localhost** and then press **Enter**. The name "localhost" represents the IP address of 127.0.0.1, which always refers to the computer you are currently using.

   The browser displays the default.htm Web page you created. See Figure 6-11.

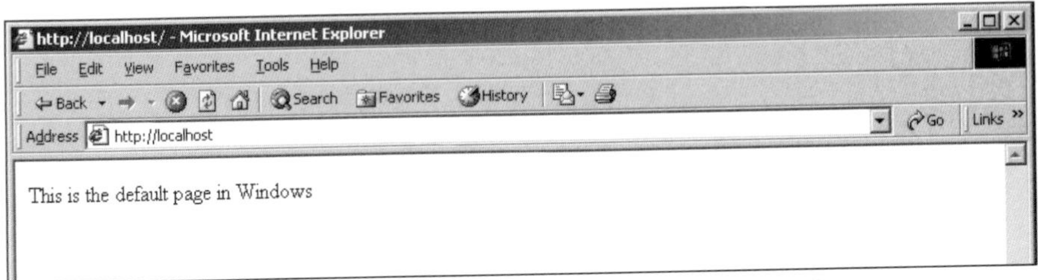

Figure 6-11 default.htm in Internet Explorer in Windows 2000

If you installed the DNS server in Chapter 4, you should be able to use DNS to resolve IP addresses. For example, if your domain is *technowidgets.com*, you should be able to type *http://www.technowidgets.com* in your browser to access the Web site.

Installing Apache on Red Hat Linux

If you have installed Linux on your Web server, you can install Apache in one of three ways. First, you can have Linux automatically install Apache when you install Linux. Second, you can install the version of Apache provided on the Red Hat CD 2. Using this method is easy because you use the rpm method that you used to install DNS in Chapter 4. Third, you can download a program from the Web that is designed to work with any Linux distribution. When you use this method, you download the source code for Apache and then compile it yourself. This chapter guides you through installing Apache from the Red Hat CD. You need to log on as root to install and configure Apache.

You installed Apache in Chapter 3 when you installed Linux and selected Web Server as a package to install. The following steps are for reference only—you should not perform them now.

To install Apache from the Red Hat CD:

1. Insert your Red Hat installation CD 2 in the CD drive.
2. On the desktop, double-click **CD/DVD-ROM** to mount the CD and open the Konqueror Web browser.
3. Double-click the **RedHat** directory icon in the right pane. The contents of the RedHat directory appear in the Konqueror window.
4. Double-click the **RPMS** directory icon to display the packages that you can install.
5. Scroll down until you see a package that begins with "httpd-2.0." As enhancements are added, the rest of the filename will vary. Double-click the package icon associated with this name to install the Apache Web server.
6. Close the Konqueror window.
7. Right-click the **CD/DVD-ROM** icon on the desktop, and then click **Eject** to eject the CD.

Starting the Apache Web Server

By default, Linux does not start the Apache Web server after you install it. Once you learn how to start Apache, however, make sure it starts every time you reboot the computer. You will use the same technique to start the Web server as you used to start DNS.

Table 6-1 shows you how to start, stop, and restart the Apache Web server. No one can see your Web pages until you start the Web server. If you change the Web server configuration, you need to restart the Web server so that it will recognize the changes. You stop the server when you do not want anyone to view your Web site. The root of the Web server is in the /var/www/html directory. Remember that the root of the Web server is where you store your Web pages.

Table 6-1 Starting, stopping, and restarting Apache

Procedure	Command
Start Apache	`apachectl start`
Stop Apache	`apachectl stop`
Restart Apache	`apachectl restart`

To start the server, open a terminal window and type **apachectl start** (with a lowercase letter "l" at the end). After you press Enter, you see the following warning: "Could not determine the server's fully qualified domain name, using 127.0.0.1 for ServerName." This message means that you have not configured the name of the server yet, but the Web server will run anyway.

To configure the name of the server in Apache:

1. In a terminal window, type **kedit /etc/httpd/conf/httpd.conf** and press **Enter**.
2. Type **Ctrl+F** to open the Find dialog box. Type **ServerName** and then click **Find** to move the insertion point to the beginning of the ServerName explanation. Click **Find** again to move the insertion point to a sample of the ServerName configuration.
3. Create a blank line after the ServerName configuration sample and then type **ServerName web1.technowidgets.com:80**. The :80 at the end indicates that the Web server listens at the default of port 80.
4. Save the file and exit kedit.
5. Type **apachectl restart** and press **Enter**. Notice that no warning appears about the name of the server.

To make sure that the Apache Web server starts every time you start the computer, you need to include the command to start the Web server in the /etc/rc.d/rc.local directory, as you did with the daemon to start DNS.

To start Apache automatically when the computer is started:

1. In a Linux terminal window, type **kedit /etc/rc.d/rc.local** and then press **Enter**.
2. At the bottom of the file, type **apachectl start**.
3. Click the **Save** icon on the kedit toolbar, and then close the terminal window.

To test the installation, you can use kedit to create an HTML document called index.html and then store this document in the /var/www/html directory. You use the name index.html because when the URL does not contain a specific filename, it automatically looks for and then displays the contents of index.html. You can use the index.html file in /var/www/html to create the home page for your Web site.

To create a default Web page for Apache:

1. In a terminal window, type **kedit /var/www/html/index.html** and then press **Enter**.
2. Type the following HTML code:

```
<html><body>
This is the default Web page in Apache
</body></html>
```

3. Click the **Save** icon on the kedit toolbar, and then close the terminal window.

To display the default Web page in Linux:

1. Make sure that Apache is started by opening a terminal window and typing **apachectl start**.
2. On the desktop, click the **Konqueror** icon, the icon next to the red hat on the bottom toolbar. The Konqueror Web browser opens. See Figure 6-12. You use Konqueror as both a file manager and a Web browser.
3. In the Location text box, type **http://localhost** and then press **Enter**. Linux uses the name "localhost" for the computer you are using. Konqueror displays the default index.html Web page. See Figure 6-13.

   If the index.html Web page appears in Konqueror, it means that Apache is correctly installed on your computer.

If you installed Apache and DNS properly, you should be able to use DNS to resolve IP addresses. In Step 3, if your domain is *technowidgets.com*, for example, you should be able to type *http://www.technowidgets.com* instead of *http://localhost* in the browser to access the Web site.

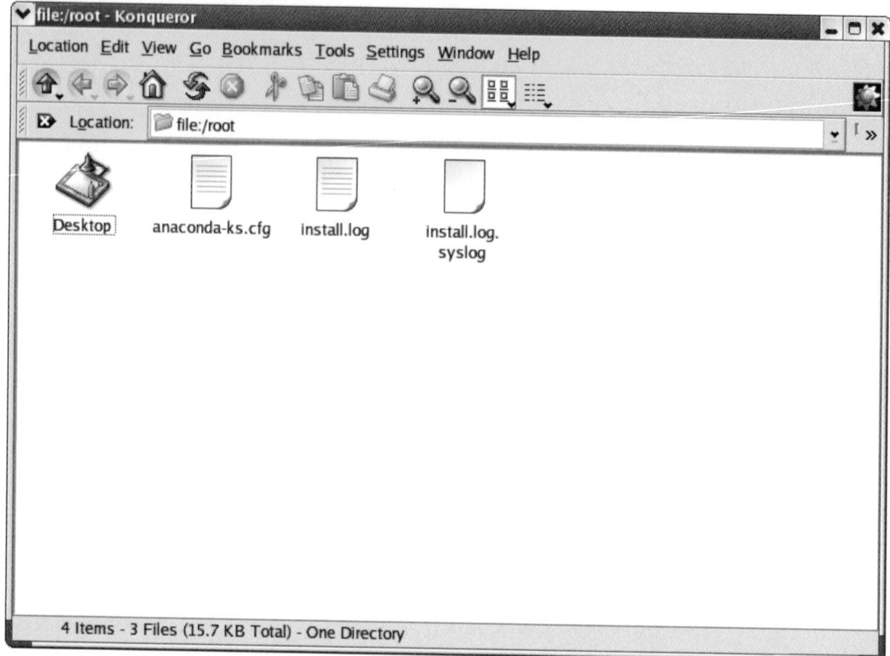

Figure 6-12 Konqueror Web browser

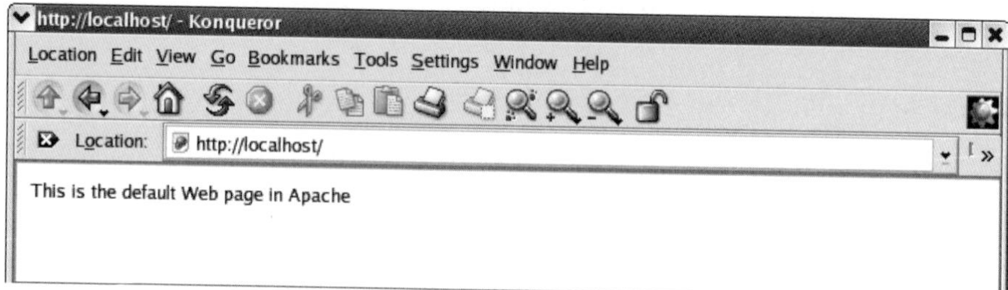

Figure 6-13 Default index.html in Konqueror

EXAMINING INTERNET INFORMATION SERVICES PROPERTIES

The Windows Setup program configures settings in IIS that meet the demands of most Web sites. In many cases, you do not need to make any changes. As installed, IIS supports HTML and ASP in Windows 2000. In Windows 2003, IIS supports HTML and ASP.NET. However, as your Web site grows and changes, you will probably need to adjust the settings and other properties of IIS. This section defines those properties. You will find out why and how you change these properties later in this chapter and in subsequent chapters.

To display the properties of the default Web site on IIS:

1. *In Windows 2003:* In Administrative Tools, click **Internet Information Services (IIS) Manager**. The Internet Information Services (IIS) Manager window opens. See Figure 6-14.
   In Windows 2000: In Administrative Tools, double-click **Internet Services Manager**.

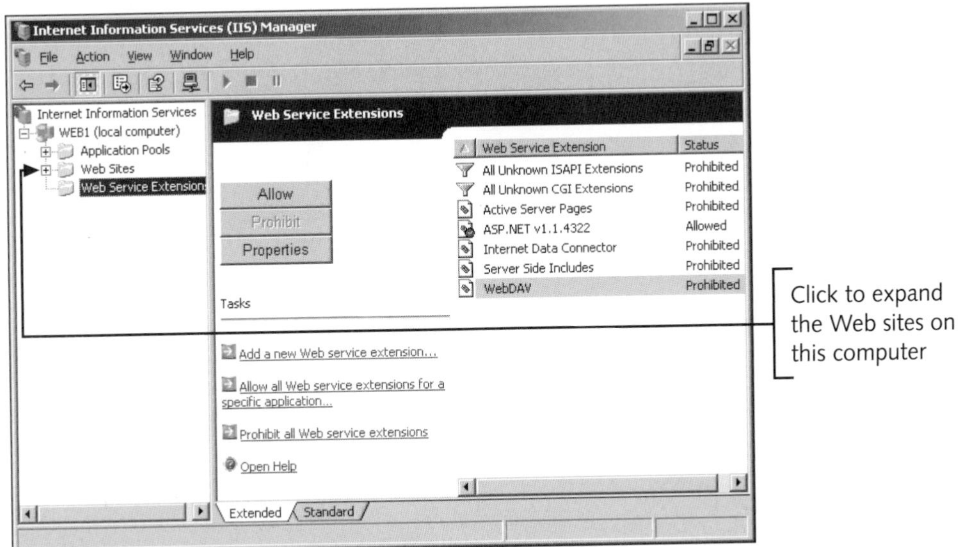

Figure 6-14 Internet Information Services (IIS) Manager window

2. *In Windows 2003:* Expand your **Web Sites** folder.
   In Windows 2000: Double-click the name of your computer in the left pane.

3. Right-click **Default Web Site** to open its shortcut menu. The shortcut menu includes commands that let you stop the server or pause it, which prevents new connections. The selection to start the server is disabled because the Web server is already started.

4. Click **Properties** on the shortcut menu to open the Default Web Site Properties dialog box. Figure 6-15 shows this dialog box in Windows 2003. The Properties dialog box for Windows 2000 is almost identical.

The default Web site properties show you the main settings for IIS. The Web site identification area in this dialog box includes a description of the Web site, which you can use to enter a more meaningful name for your server. The IP address text box defaults to all the IP addresses on the computer that are not assigned to other IIS services, and the TCP port indicates which port the Web server is using. In the section on virtual hosting later in this chapter, you will examine the Web site identification settings in detail and configure multiple Web sites, which will have different Web site identifications.

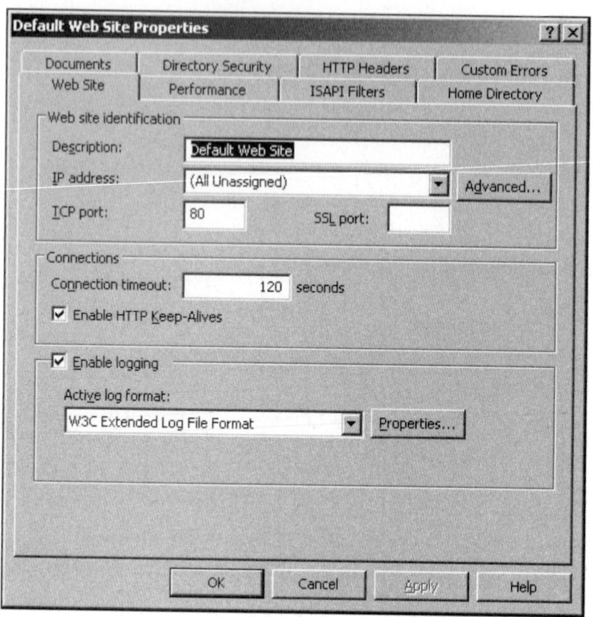

Figure 6-15 Default Web Site Properties dialog box in Windows 2003

The Connection timeout text box in the Connections area shows that any Web site user is disconnected from your Web server after 120 seconds (900 seconds in Windows 2000) of inactivity. This is done to conserve resources. If you check the Enable HTTP Keep-Alives box, a browser can request that a connection stay open while multiple items on a page such as graphics are transferred, instead of closing the TCP connection after transferring each image on the page.

If you check the Enable logging box, IIS creates and stores log files, which are text files of information that you can use to monitor performance and events, such as shutting down the Web server, and even information about who has visited your site. It is a good idea to enable logging—but only if you actually read the logs. By default, the logs are stored in the \windows\system32\LogFiles directory on the drive where you installed Windows. If you partitioned your drive, the files are stored on the smaller partition along with the operating system files. Over time, the partition can fill up with log files and cause the server to shut down. Logs will be fully explored in Chapter 11.

Next, you can explore the IIS security settings that allow you to control access to your Web server. The Directory Security tab in the Default Web Site Properties dialog box contains these security settings. In the Default Web Site Properties dialog box, click the Directory Security tab to open this property sheet. See Figure 6-16.

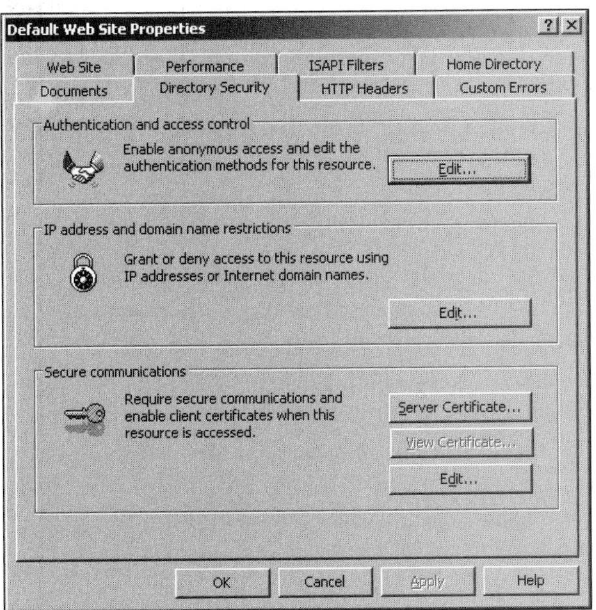

Figure 6-16 Directory Security Properties for IIS in Windows 2003

The first section of this property sheet dialog box controls anonymous access. When you installed IIS, a user was created based on the name of your computer. For example, if the name of your computer is WEB1, this user is called IUSR_WEB1. This guest account only has access to your Web site. When people request a Web page, they are logged on to the server using this account. If you delete this user or change its password, then anonymous users cannot view Web pages on your Web site. For a private site, you can disable anonymous access and have users log on using their own accounts.

You can also control access to the Web site based on IP address. You can either start by denying all connections except the ones you allow or allow all connections except the ones you deny.

To set up secure communications, a server certificate is required that verifies the name of the organization that is hosting the Web site. You can also enable client certificates to verify the identity of the person connecting to your site. With certificates, communication is encrypted.

Click each of the other tabs in the Default Web Site Properties dialog box. Each tab is explained in the following list.

- *Operators (Windows 2000 only)*—This property sheet lists users who can administer the site. It can be useful if you want to permit specific users to help you administer the Web site.
- *Performance*—Use the Performance property sheet to limit the total amount of network bandwidth available to this Web site as measured in kilobytes (KB)

per second. It is useful when a single computer supports multiple Web sites. You can also limit the number of simultaneous connections that the server allows in Windows 2003.

- *ISAPI Filters*—Use this property sheet to specify applications that process HTTP requests, known as ISAPI filters. For example, Microsoft Exchange installs an ISAPI filter to process Web e-mail.
- *Home Directory*—This property sheet specifies the location and properties of the home directory. You can determine whether to log information about anyone who accesses this site, and whether execute permissions cover only scripts (the default) or cover executable programs as well.
- *Documents*—When a URL does not reference the name of a page, you can use the Documents property sheet to configure the name of the page that the Web site displays. By default, the Web server looks for the following pages: default.htm, default.asp, index.htm (Windows 2003 only), iisstart.htm, and default.aspx (Windows 2003 only). You can add and remove pages, and alter the order in which the Web server checks for pages.
- *HTTP Headers*—Recall that the Web server sends headers along with the Web page to the user. You can use the HTTP Headers property sheet to add your own custom header for a special browser-based application, enable content expiration on a particular date, and even set a content rating such as violence, sex, nudity, and language for your site.
- *Custom Errors*—Use this property sheet to specify the HTML files that display HTTP errors to the Web site user. For example, by default, error 404 is "File not found." Instead of displaying this standard message, you could display a different HTML document, such as one containing a site map that would help the user find the correct page.

Examining Apache Properties

Apache uses a configuration file called httpd.conf, which does the same work as the GUI interface does for IIS. The httpd.conf configuration file, located in /etc/httpd/conf, contains more than 1,000 lines of code, which may seem overwhelming. In reality, more than 60 percent of the lines in the file are comments that help explain changes or provide examples of changes. Also, the typical Web site administrator would use only a few sections of this configuration file. Just as with IIS, the default configuration is acceptable for most Web sites.

A number of organizations have created GUI interfaces for Apache. However, once you select a GUI interface and use it to modify the Apache configuration, you cannot modify the configuration file manually and then go back to the GUI. Another advantage to using httpd.conf instead of the GUI is that it is consistent across all distributions and there are very few differences between the configuration file for Apache 2.0 and Apache 1.3.

To examine the properties in the httpd.conf file, you can open it in a text editor. In a terminal window, you type **`kedit /etc/httpd/conf/httpd.conf.`** See Figure 6-17.

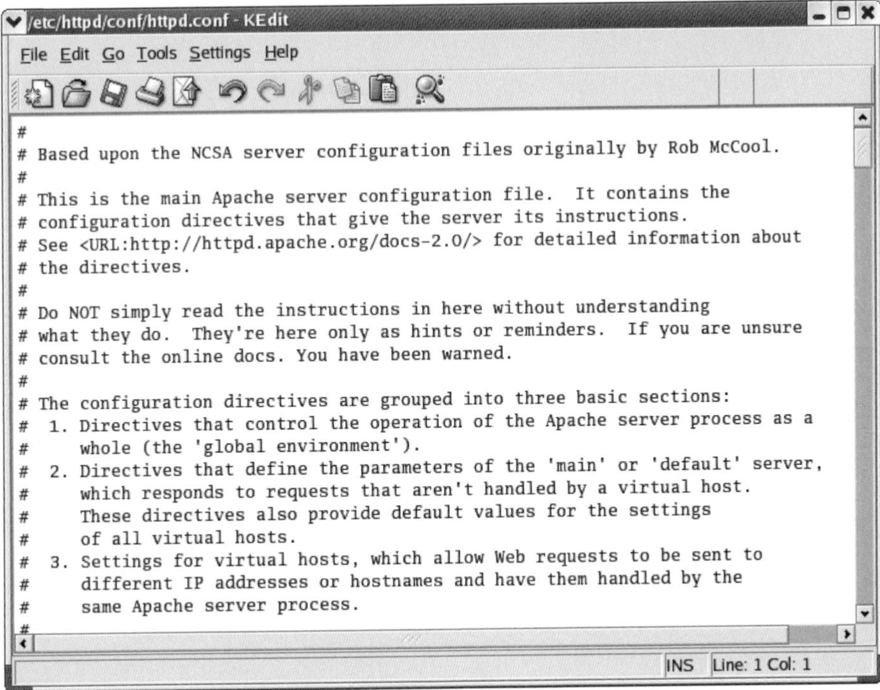

/etc/httpd/conf/httpd.conf - KEdit
File Edit Go Tools Settings Help
#
Based upon the NCSA server configuration files originally by Rob McCool.
#
This is the main Apache server configuration file. It contains the
configuration directives that give the server its instructions.
See <URL:http://httpd.apache.org/docs-2.0/> for detailed information about
the directives.
#
Do NOT simply read the instructions in here without understanding
what they do. They're here only as hints or reminders. If you are unsure
consult the online docs. You have been warned.
#
The configuration directives are grouped into three basic sections:
1. Directives that control the operation of the Apache server process as a
whole (the 'global environment').
2. Directives that define the parameters of the 'main' or 'default' server,
which responds to requests that aren't handled by a virtual host.
These directives also provide default values for the settings
of all virtual hosts.
3. Settings for virtual hosts, which allow Web requests to be sent to
different IP addresses or hostnames and have them handled by the
same Apache server process.
#
INS Line: 1 Col: 1

Figure 6-17 The httpd.conf file

The Apache configuration file is divided into three sections: Global Environment, Main server configuration, and Virtual Hosts. The Global Environment section controls the server's overall operation. The Main server configuration section has configuration information for the default server. The Virtual Hosts section contains settings for virtual hosts, also known as virtual servers in IIS. You will learn about virtual hosts in a later section.

Apache Global Environment Settings

You will rarely modify the global settings in the Apache configuration file. Some of these settings focus on physical locations of directories during setup or standard settings common to most servers, such as the port number. The major change you will make in this section is changing the default of "KeepAlive Off" to "KeepAlive On." Recall that the KeepAlive property gives users to your site a persistent connection over a given number of seconds. It allows browsers to download a Web page with images without having to create a new connection for each image. You should change other settings only after your Web site has been in operation for a substantial time and you want to fine-tune the site. For example, you could triple the KeepAlive timeout if you find that users often click links within your site, but not within the default of 15 seconds, assuming that KeepAlive has been turned on.

Following is a list of the major global settings for configuring Apache:

- *ServerRoot*—Shows the directory location of the server files.
- *KeepAlive*—Indicates whether Apache should maintain a persistent connection for multiple files. Always leave it set to On unless your Web site has only text files and users rarely move from one page to another.
- *MaxKeepAliveRequests*—Determines how many files can be transferred in a single connection. The default is 100, which is acceptable for most sites.
- *KeepAliveTimeout*—Indicates the number of seconds that Apache maintains the connection. By default, it is set to 15 seconds, which provides enough time to maintain a connection for a single page.
- *Listen*—Determines the port number for the server. The default is 80.

Apache Main Server Configuration

The main server configuration in the Apache configuration file describes the default server. Approximately 70 percent of the Apache configuration information appears in this section. Again, you will rarely need to change these settings—only if your Web site changes significantly.

The settings in the main section determine the basic security configuration, default document description, error logging, and support for foreign languages. You might need to change one or more of the following main settings from time to time.

- *User*—Shows the user name that Apache employs when someone requests a Web page. This user cannot log on to the server and has very restricted access. By default, when Apache is installed, it creates a user called apache. This restricted user only has access to the Web site. The guest user name cannot be used to log on to the server.
- *ServerAdmin*—Lists the e-mail address of the administrator. Apache server error messages can be sent to this e-mail address. By default, it is root@localhost.
- *ServerName*—Shows either the DNS host name or the IP address. If you do not have an entry here, Apache displays a warning when you start the server.
- *DocumentRoot*—Identifies the directory where the Web pages are stored.

For a minimal Apache configuration:

1. In a terminal window, type **kedit /etc/httpd/conf/httpd.conf** and then press **Enter**.
2. Click the magnifying glass icon on the toolbar. The Find-KEdit dialog box opens. Type **ServerName**, and then click **Find**.

3. You see the beginning of some comments concerning ServerName. Click **Find** again.
4. You see the beginning of an example of how to use ServerName. On the next line, which is blank, type
ServerName www.technowidgets.com:80
5. Click the floppy disk icon on the KEdit toolbar to save the changes and close the kedit window.
6. To restart the Web server, type **apachectl restart** and then press **Enter**.

Hosting Multiple Web Sites

You can create multiple Web sites on a single server for a variety of purposes. These are known as virtual servers and virtual hosts. For example, you might work for an organization that sells products under different company names that require different Web sites. Each site might not be large enough to require its own Web server, so all the Web sites could share a single Web server. In a related manner, your boss might have an idea for a new domain name with a corresponding Web site and want to explore some marketing opportunities without the unneeded investment of a new server. In addition, your company might want to support some nonprofit organizations by hosting their Web sites on your server. Virtual servers are also used by Web hosting companies to host basic Web sites.

For multiple Web sites to exist on the same computer, you have to make each site distinct, which you can do by hosting Web sites by port number, by IP address, or based on host name. The following sections describe each method.

Hosting Web Sites by Port Number

One way to host multiple Web sites is to have each Web site listen at a different port. The first Web server you install listens at port 80, so any additional Web site must listen at a different port. In Chapter 5, you learned that the well-known ports are numbered from 1 to 1023. Because they are reserved, you should not use these port numbers for your additional Web sites. Recall that common choices are 8000 and 8080, because they are unreserved and easy to remember, but you could pick any port above 1023. When you configure a Web site to use a port other than 80, you must reference the alternate port number in the URL associated with the site because the browser otherwise assumes that a Web site uses port 80. For example, if the host *www.technowidgets.com* is listening at port 8080, and you want to display the document prod.htm, you would type *http://www.technowidgets.com:8080/prod.htm*.

Because entering a URL that specifies a port number is awkward and difficult to remember, creating Web sites by using an alternate port number is the least popular method. When you are creating your Web pages, your links have to reference the alternate port number, too.

The other two methods do not force the person requesting a Web page to alter the format of the URL. For example, users would not know whether *www.technowidgets.com* resides on its own high-performance server or is just one of many supported by a Web hosting company.

Hosting Web Sites by IP Address

You access a service such as a Web server by using a combination of an IP address and a port number. For example, when someone types *www.technowidgets.com* in a browser, the host name is translated into an IP address. The user does not know or care whether that IP address is one of many on the server or is the only IP address on the server.

As a Web server administrator, you configure two types of IP addresses on a computer. The first type of IP address corresponds to a physical NIC in the computer. The second type is a **virtual IP address**, which is added to the IP address for a NIC.

You use multiple NICs when you are connected to multiple networks. For example, one NIC may be connected through a router to the Internet. Another NIC may be connected to an internal LAN. In this case, you could set up a Web site that corresponds to the IP address connected to the Internet for potential customers of your products. You could also set up a Web site that corresponds to the IP address connected to your LAN for employee information such as department memos and information on benefits. From the Web server's perspective, the Web site for internal use by your organization exists on the **intranet**, which is a private network.

Virtual IP addresses are often used when you have multiple domain names. For example, when you set up the NIC on your Web server, you gave it an address of 192.168.0.100. You could then add virtual IP addresses to the same NIC of 192.168.0.150 and 192.168.0.200. When you configure DNS for the new domain, the host IP address for each Web server would be unique, based on each of the virtual IP addresses. However, to support this scheme, you need multiple IP addresses from your ISP. In the past, it was fairly easy to get a block of 254 addresses, but now it is more difficult because the Internet is more popular and fewer IP addresses are available. Virtual IP addresses can be used to reference e-mail servers and FTP servers that exist on the same server with your Web site when your Internet presence is minimal. When the site becomes so popular that you want to split it across three separate physical servers, the IP addresses are already set up and the ensuing conversion is relatively easy.

Hosting Web Sites Based on Host Name

The easiest and most common way to host Web sites is by host name. Early in the chapter, you learned that when the browser sends a request for a Web page to a server at a particular IP address, it also sends the host name, such as *www.technowidgets.com*, to the Web server. What if you also wanted another Web site at the same IP address called *www.widgetsofthefuture.com*? Given the way the browser requests a Web page, the Web server can read the host name and redirect the request to the appropriate Web site.

If you configure Web sites by host name, you need only one IP address from your ISP, making it the most economical method. When you configure the DNS, you have to remember just a single address. As opposed to changing the port number, which also requires only a single IP address, you do not have to change the URL for the Web site.

One slight drawback to this method is that it requires a browser that supports HTTP 1.1, the most recent version. However, only browsers predating Internet Explorer 3.0 or Netscape 2.0 do not support HTTP 1.1.

Configuring New Web Sites in IIS

In this section, you will learn how to configure the Web server so that you will have one Web site based on an IP address and a different site based on a host name. You will use the DNS configuration from Chapter 4 to test it. In Chapter 4, you created a DNS configuration based on a domain name such as *technowidgets.com*. In the example, *www.technowidgets.com* referred to 192.168.0.100 and *research.technowidgets.com* referred to 192.168.0.150. One of the new Web sites you will create here is for research. The DNS configuration also has *web1.technowidgets.com* at 192.168.0.100, which is the same as *www.technowidgets.com*. The site for *web1.technowidgets.com* will be distinguished by the host name. Refer to the actual IP addresses that you used in Chapter 4 along with your actual domain name.

Configuring a Web Site Using an IP Address

You need to complete two procedures to create a Web site using an IP address. First, you must add another IP address to your configuration. Second, you must add the new Web site based on the IP address. The figures shown here are for Windows 2003, and some differ slightly from the screens seen in Windows 2000; however, the steps are the same in either version.

To add an IP address to your NIC in Windows:

1. *In Windows 2003:* Click **Start**, point to **Control Panel**, point to **Network Connections**, and then click **Local Area Connection**.
   In Windows 2000: Click **Start**, point to **Settings**, click **Network and Dial-up Connections**, and then double-click **Local Area Connection**.
   The Local Area Connection Status dialog box opens.

2. Click **Properties** to open the Local Area Connection Properties dialog box shown in Figure 6-18. Your dialog box might not include the Network Load Balancing option.

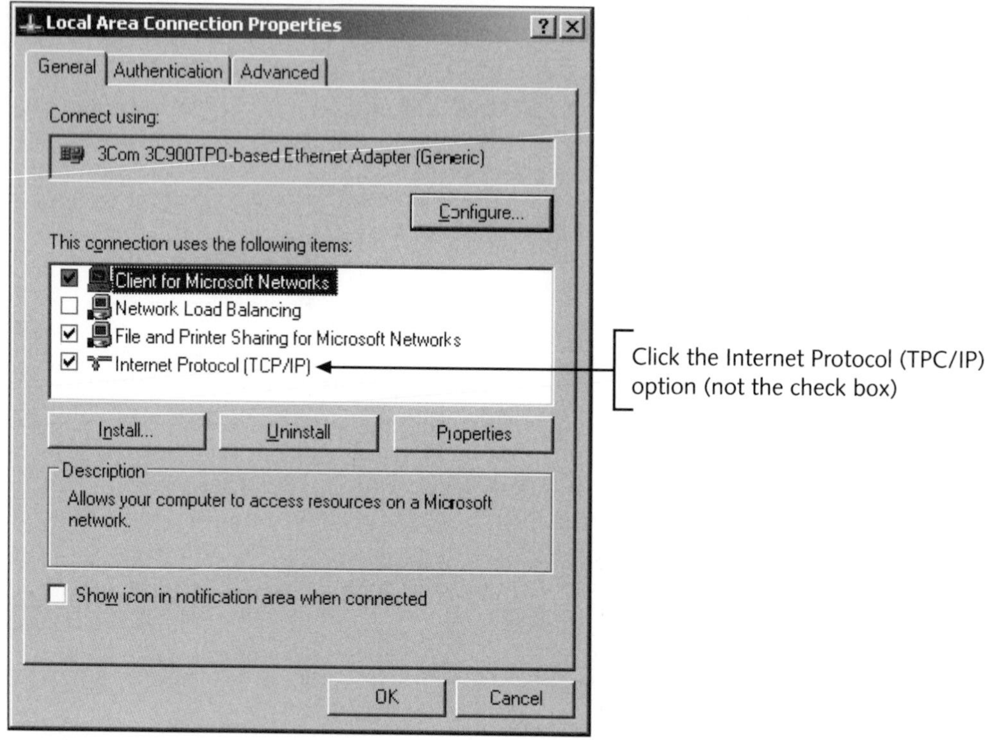

Figure 6-18 Local Area Connection Properties dialog box

3. In the list of connections, click **Internet Protocol (TCP/IP)** to select it, and then click the **Properties** button to open the Internet Protocol (TCP/IP) Properties dialog box shown in Figure 6-19.

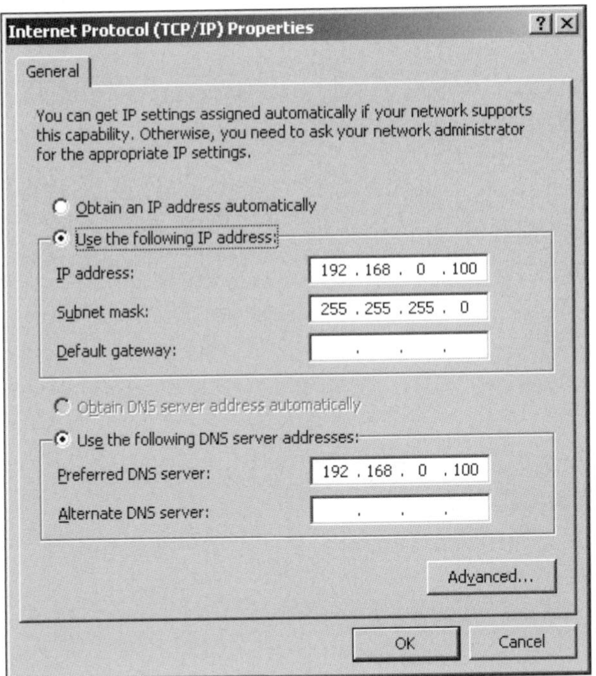

Figure 6-19 Internet Protocol (TCP/IP) Properties dialog box

4. Click the **Advanced** button to open the Advanced TCP/IP Settings dialog box. See Figure 6-20.
5. On the IP Settings tab, click the top **Add** button to add a new IP address.
6. In the TCP/IP address text box, type the IP address that corresponds to *research.technowidgets.com*. The example in Chapter 4 uses **192.168.0.150**.
7. Press **Tab** to have Windows provide the appropriate subnet mask.
8. Click **Add** to add the IP address you just entered. Notice that two IP addresses are now listed on the Advanced TCP/IP Settings dialog box.
9. Click **OK** twice to close the Advanced TCP/IP settings dialog box and the Internet Protocol (TCP/IP) Properties dialog box. To close the Local Area Connection Properties dialog box, click **Close** in Windows Server 2003 or click **OK** in Windows 2000. Click **Close** to close the Local Area Connection Status dialog box.

Before you create the new Web site based on the new IP address for *research.technowidgets.com*, it would be a good idea to test your configuration by pinging the host name at your domain. Open a command prompt, type *ping research.technowidgets.com*, and then press Enter. You should receive four messages that begin "Reply from 192.168.0.150:". If you do not receive these messages, check your DNS for the exact name and corresponding IP address for research. Then return to the Internet Protocol (TCP/IP) Properties dialog box to make sure that the IP address matches the one you configured in DNS.

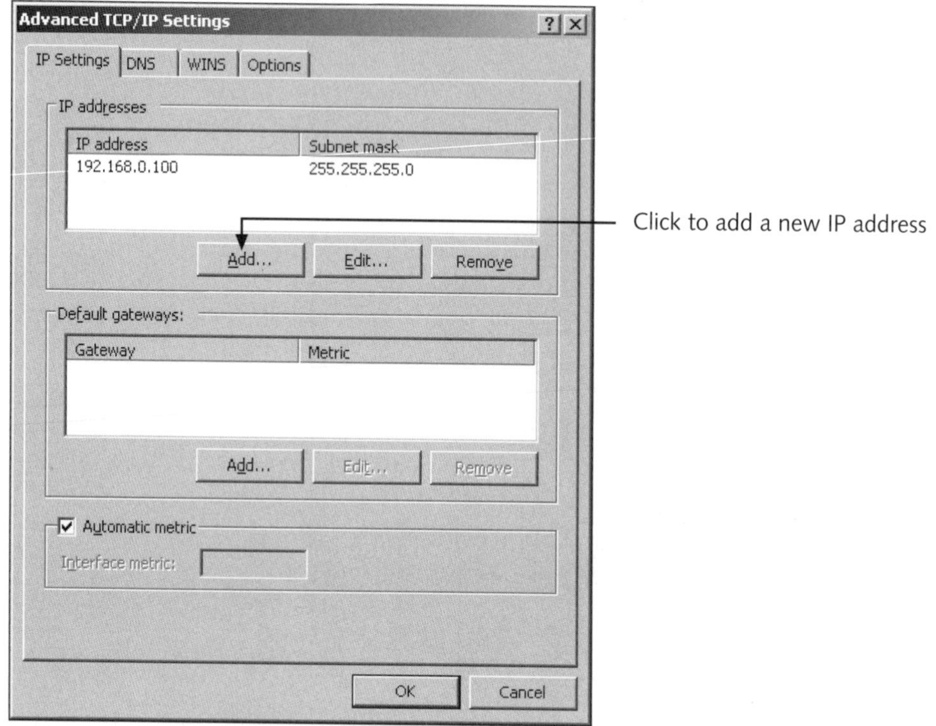

Figure 6-20 Advanced TCP/IP Settings dialog box

Now you can create a Web site based on the new IP address. Although the steps to get to the Web Site Creation Wizard are different in Windows 2000 and Windows 2003, the wizard is the same except for creating the folder for the new Web site.

To start the Web Site Creation Wizard in Windows 2003:

1. In Administrative Tools, click **Internet Information Services (IIS) Manager**.
2. Click the **plus icon** (+) next to the computer name.
3. Right-click **Web Sites**, point to **New**, and then click **Web Site**. The Web Site Creation Wizard Welcome dialog box opens.

If you are using Windows 2003, skip to the following "To start the Web site Creation Wizard" steps. In Windows 2000, the wizard does not allow you to create a folder for your new Web site, so it is easiest to create this folder before you start the wizard. Because the folder for the default Web site is in the Inetpub folder, it is a good idea to create your new Web site in that folder, too.

To create the research folder for the Web site in Windows 2000:

1. Right-click **Start**, and then click **Explore**.
2. In the left pane, click **Inetpub**.

3. In the right pane, right-click a blank area of the window, point to **New**, and then click **Folder**. A folder is created with the default name of New Folder.
4. Type **research** and then press **Enter**.

To start the Web Site Creation Wizard in Windows 2000:

1. In Administrative Tools, double-click **Internet Services Manager**.
2. Right-click the name of the computer, point to **New**, and then click **Web Site**. The Web Site Creation Wizard Welcome dialog box opens.

To create a Web site using the Web Site Creation Wizard:

1. In the Welcome to the Web Site Creation Wizard dialog box, click **Next** to continue.
   The Web Site Description dialog box opens, as shown in Figure 6-21. Type **research** in the text box, and then click **Next**.

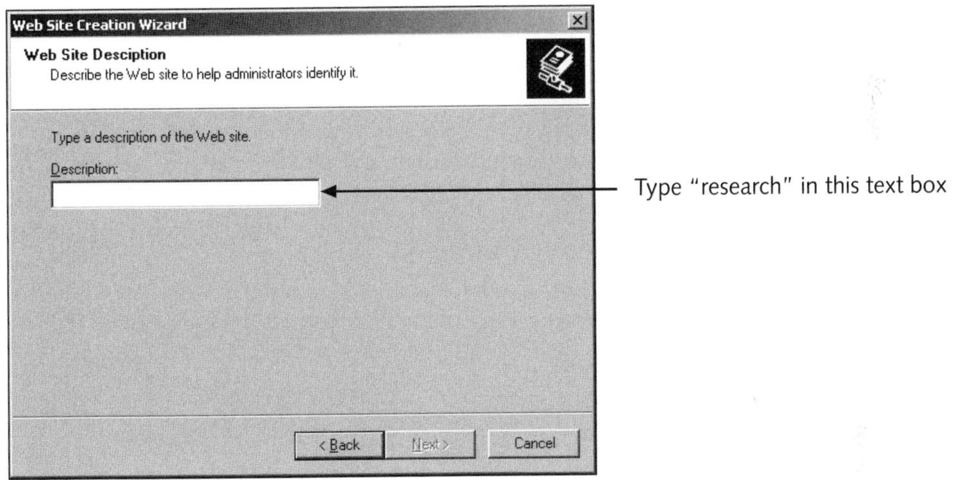

Figure 6-21 Web Site Description dialog box

2. The IP Address and Port Settings dialog box opens, as shown in Figure 6-22. This is the key dialog box that you use to distinguish Web sites.
   Click the **Enter the IP address to use for this Web site** list arrow, and then click the IP address for *research.technowidgets.com*. The default is 192.168.0.150. Click **Next**.

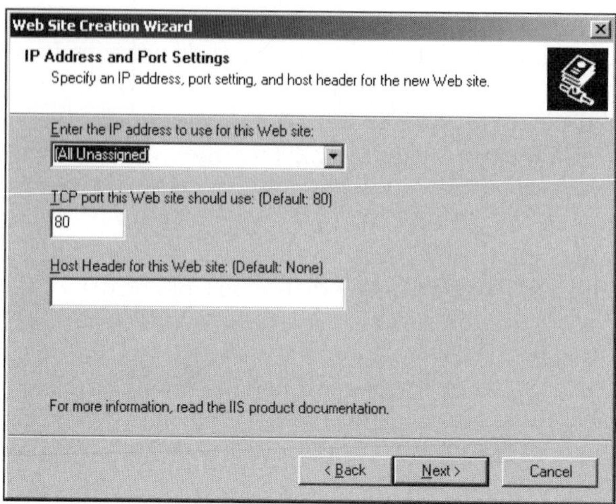

Figure 6-22 IP Address and Port Settings dialog box

3. The Web Site Home Directory dialog box opens. You use this dialog box to specify your home directory. Because the default Web site is in the Inetpub folder, it is a good idea to put your new site in Inetpub, too. Click the **Browse** button. Expand the drive letter that contains IIS, expand **Inetpub**, and then select it.
   In Windows 2003: Click the **Make New Folder** button. Type **research** as the folder name.
   In Windows 2000: You should already have created the folder, so click **research**.
   Click **OK**. The path to your new Web site now appears in the Path text box. See Figure 6-23. Click **Next**.

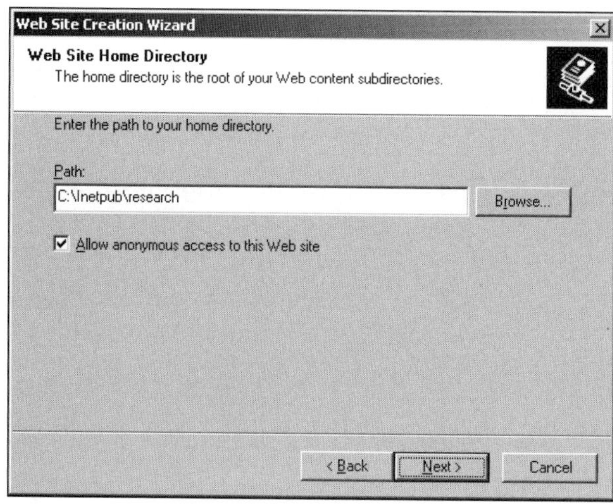

Figure 6-23 Web Site Home Directory dialog box

4. The Web Site Access Permissions dialog box opens. See Figure 6-24. This dialog box lists the default permissions for the home directory, which should match the properties for the default Web site. The Read permission allows visitors to your site to view HTML files. The Run scripts permission allows visitors to see dynamic pages created through programming languages such as Active Server Pages. The Execute permission would be used for actual applications that pose more of a security risk. The Write permission allows users to upload files to the Web site. The Browse permission allows visitors to see a list of all files in a directory if no default page exists. Click **Next** to accept the defaults.

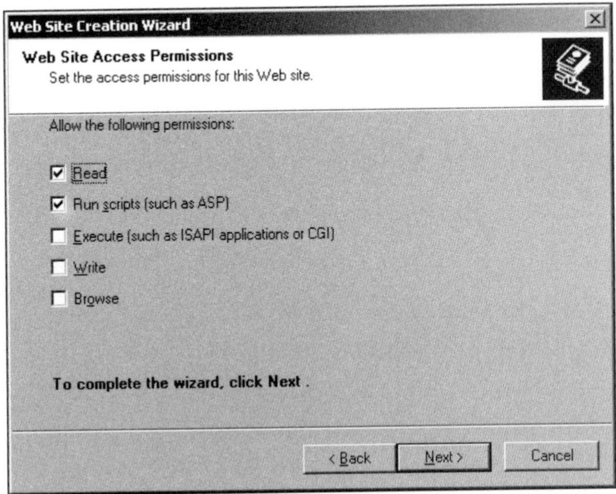

Figure 6-24 Web Site Access Permissions dialog box

5. A dialog box indicating successful completion of the wizard appears. Click **Finish** to exit the wizard.

Now you need to create a Web page to test the new Web site. Earlier in the chapter, you completed steps to create a file called default.htm. Now you can follow the same steps to create a default Web page that contains the statement: "This is the research site."

To create a default Web page for the new Web site:

1. In Notepad, type the following HTML code:

```
<html><body>
This is the research site
</body></html>
```

2. Save the document as **default.htm** in the folder you created in the wizard called \Inetpub\research on the drive where you installed Windows. Be sure to save the file with an .htm extension. For the Save as type, select **All Files**.

3. Open Internet Explorer, and type **research.technowidgets.com** in the Address text box. The default Web page with the "This is the research site" text should appear. You could also type the IP address of the new Web site in the browser and open the same page.

Configuring a Web Site Using a Host Name

Now that you have configured a Web site using an IP address, configuring one with a different host name is even easier. To test the functionality of the new Web site, DNS must be running on your Web server. You need to be able to ping *web1.technowidgets.com* (the Web site you set up in Chapter 4) to make sure it is working properly. The important difference between using a host name and using an IP address is that in the IP Address and Port Settings dialog box of the Web Site Creation Wizard, you enter a host name instead of an IP address.

To start the Web Site Creation Wizard in Windows 2003:

1. In Administrative Tools, click **Internet Information Services (IIS) Manager**.
2. Click the **plus icon** (+) next to the computer name.
3. Right-click **Web Sites**, point to **New**, and then click **Web Site**. The Web Site Creation Wizard Welcome dialog box appears.

In Windows 2000, the wizard does not allow you to create a folder for your new Web site, so it is easiest to create this folder before you start the wizard. Because the folder for the default Web site is in the Inetpub folder, it is a good idea to create your new Web site in that folder, too. If you are using Windows 2003, skip to the "To create a Web site using the Web Site Creation Wizard" section.

To create the research folder for the Web site in Windows 2000:

1. Right-click **Start**, and then click **Explore** to open Windows Explorer.
2. In the left pane, click **Inetpub**.
3. In the right pane, right-click a blank area of the window, point to **New**, and then click **Folder**. A folder is created with the default name of New Folder.
4. Type **web1** as the name of the new folder, and then press **Enter**.

To start the Web Site Creation Wizard in Windows 2000:

1. In Administrative Tools, double-click **Internet Services Manager**.
2. Right-click the name of the computer, point to **New**, and then click **Web Site**. The Web Site Creation Wizard Welcome dialog box appears.

To create a Web Site using the Web Site Creation Wizard:

1. At the Welcome to the Web Site Creation Wizard dialog box, click **Next** to continue.

2. Type **web1** in the text box, and then click **Next**.

3. The IP Address and Port Settings dialog box opens. It is the key dialog box that you use to distinguish Web sites. Click the **Enter the IP address to use for this Web site** list arrow, and then click the IP address for *web1.technowidgets.com*. The default is 192.168.0.100. This IP address is also associated with *www.technowidgets.com*. In the Host Header for this site text box, type **web1.technowidgets.com**. See Figure 6-25. Click **Next**.

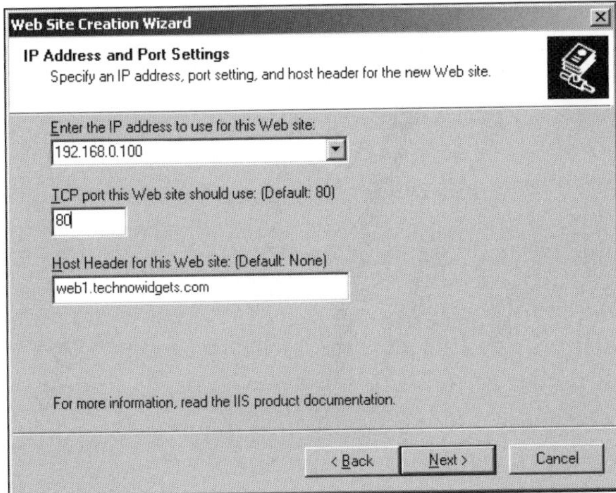

Figure 6-25 IP Address and Port Settings dialog box

4. The Web Site Home Directory dialog box opens. You use this dialog box to specify your home directory. Because the default Web site is in the Inetpub folder, it is a good idea to put your new site in Inetpub, too. Click the **Browse** button. Expand the drive letter that contains IIS, expand **Inetpub**, and then select it.

5. *In Windows 2003:* Click the **Make New Folder** button. Type **web1** as the folder name.
   In Windows 2000: You should have already created the folder, so click **web1**. Click **OK**. The path to your new Web site now appears in the Path text box. See Figure 6-26. Click **Next**.

6. The Web Site Access Permissions dialog box opens. It lists the default permissions for the home directory, which should match the properties for the default Web site. Click **Next** to accept the defaults.

7. A dialog box indicating successful completion of the wizard appears. Click **Finish** to exit the wizard.

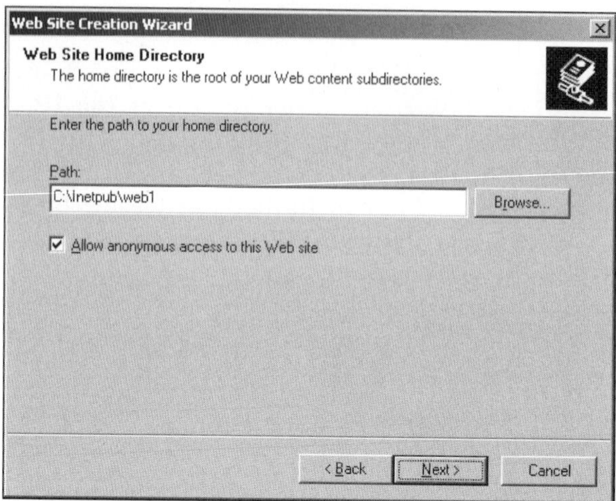

Figure 6-26 Web Site Home Directory dialog box

As in the previous section, create a Web page that now refers to web1 and says "Welcome to the web1 site." Save the document as default.htm in the \Inetpub\web1 folder. Open your browser and type *web1.technowidgets.com* to see the Web page for your new site.

Configuring New Web Sites (Virtual Hosts) in Apache

When you create a new Web site in Apache, you are creating a **virtual host**. In this case, you need to create a directory for each new Web site. To make sure that each Web site works correctly, you will create and save a Web page in each Apache directory for testing. Based on information from the DNS server you created in Chapter 4, you will create virtual hosts based on IP addresses and host names.

The Apache configuration file uses tags, which are related to the tags in HTML. For example, in the sample Web page created for the new Web sites in IIS, a tag called <body> tells the browser that what follows is the body of the page. The </body> tag tells the browser that the end of the body has been reached.

In this section, you will create virtual hosts with a tag that looks something like <VirtualHost 192.168.0.150> and end the description of the virtual host with </VirtualHost>. One important concept to remember is that nearly all text is case-sensitive in Apache configuration files. If you accidentally type </Virtualhost>, Apache will not recognize the new Web site because the "H" in the <VirtualHost> tag is not capitalized. Apache does not display a message for capitalization errors when you restart the Web server, so you must enter tags in the configuration file carefully.

Between the opening and closing tags, you can specify many configuration options. In fact, most of the configuration options for the default server can be put between the opening and closing tags. The items you will enter in this section have already been specified for the default site elsewhere in the configuration file. You will begin with the minimum needed to make the Web sites functional. In later chapters, you will add and refine these options.

The first item Apache needs to know is the host name of the server. You need to add the key word ServerName, followed by a space, and then the host name of the Web site. In the case of the host name of *research.technowidgets.com*, you would add the following line:

```
ServerName research.technowidgets.com
```

The other configuration line that you need names the directory where you will store the Web pages. You need to add the key word DocumentRoot, followed by a space, and then the location of the Web site. For example, if this directory is /var/www/research, you would add the following line:


```
DocumentRoot /var/www/research
```

Creating Directories and Web Pages for Virtual Hosts

Before you can create a virtual host, you must create a directory where you will store the site. You can place Web pages for virtual hosts anywhere in the Linux system. If you have multiple disk drives, you can put the Web pages for each virtual host on separate disk drives. In the following steps, you will create directories next to the existing Web site for ease of maintenance. In Red Hat Linux, the default Web site is found in the /var/www/html directory. A logical place to create the new Web sites is beneath the /var/www directory, but you could put them on other places on the server as well. The following steps show how to create a directory called research for the IP address-based virtual host, and a directory called web1 for the name-based virtual host. Recall that the name of the file used for the default Web page in Apache is index.html, which is different from the name used in IIS.

To create the directories for the virtual hosts in Linux:

1. In a terminal window, change to the directory where you are creating the new subdirectories by typing **cd /var/www** and then pressing **Enter**. Remember to insert a space after cd.
2. Type **mkdir research** and then press **Enter** to create the directory for the research Web site.
3. Type **mkdir web1** and then press **Enter** to create the directory for the web1 Web site.

To create Web pages for the new Web sites:

1. Assuming that you just created the directories in the previous steps and are still in the /var/www directory, type **kedit research/index.html** and press **Enter** to create the default page for the research Web site.

2. Type the following to identify the research site:
   <html><body>
   This is the research site
   </body></html>
3. Click the floppy disk icon to save the file.
4. Change the word "research" to **web1**.
5. Click **File** and then click **Save As** to open the Save File As dialog box.
6. In the Location text box, type **/var/www/web1/index.html**, click **OK**, and then click the floppy disk icon to save the new Web page as the default Web page for the web1 Web site. Close KEdit.

Configuring a Virtual Host in Apache Using an IP Address

Before you can create a virtual host based on a different IP address, you must associate a new IP address with the existing NIC. Next, you must modify the configuration file, httpd.conf, to create the new virtual host. Finally, you must restart the Web server so that Apache will recognize the changes.

To associate a new IP address with the NIC:

1. In a terminal window, type **kedit /etc/rc.d/rc.local**.
   This is the same file you edited to make sure that Apache starts automatically when you start Linux.
2. At the bottom of the file, add a line that contains the IP address for the research host in the DNS file you created in Chapter 4. The example in Chapter 4 uses 192.168.0.150, so you type **/sbin/ifconfig eth0:0 192.168.0.150**.
   The utility to create the IP address is ifconfig, which is located in the /sbin directory. The first Ethernet NIC is referred to as eth0:0.
3. Click the floppy disk icon to save the file, and then close the window.
4. Because the command in Step 2 will not be recognized until you restart the computer, type **/sbin/ifconfig eth0:0 192.168.0.150** to create the new IP address.

Before you modify the httpd.conf file, it is a good idea to make a backup copy of it. A common technique is to have the file extension match today's date. For example, if today was July 21, you would type `cp /etc/httpd/conf/httpd.conf /etc/httpd/conf/httpd.721` in a terminal window. Note the space before "/etc" in both commands.

To create a virtual host using an IP address:

1. Open the httpd.conf file using kedit in a terminal window.
   Type **kedit /etc/httpd/conf/httpd.conf** and then press **Enter**.

2. The section for adding virtual hosts is at the end of the file, so move the cursor to the beginning of the last line in the file. This line is blank.
3. Type the following, remembering to replace the IP address with the one you created in the previous steps and the given domain with your domain:
   <VirtualHost 192.168.0.150>
   ServerName research.technowidgets.com
   DocumentRoot /var/www/research
   </VirtualHost>
4. Save the changes and exit KEdit by clicking the **Save** icon and then closing the window.
5. Restart Apache by typing **apachectl restart** and then pressing **Enter**.
6. Open the Konqueror Web browser, type **research.technowidgets.com** for the URL, and then press **Enter**. You should see the Web page you created.

Configuring a Virtual Host in Apache Using a Host Name

To configure a single IP address to host multiple Web sites, you first have to declare the IP address that you will use for the virtual host names. You then configure each Web site, being careful to use the same IP address, but a different host name.

For example, you could configure the two hosts that you set up in Chapter 4, *www.technowidgets.com* and *web1.technowidgets.com*, to share a single IP address, 192.168.0.100. You first have to configure the IP address so that Apache will recognize it as one used for host names. For example, you could add "NameVirtualHost 192.168.0.100" to the configuration in the Virtual Host section at the bottom of the file. The actual configuration of the two Web sites would be exactly like the one for a virtual host using an IP address, except that you use the same IP address for both configurations.

To create a virtual host using host names:

1. Open a terminal window, type **kedit etc/httpd/conf/httpd.conf**, and then press **Enter**.
2. Create a blank line at the end of the file. Type **NameVirtualHost 192.168.0.100** and then press **Enter** to create a line that states that this IP address will contain multiple virtual hosts.
3. Create the configuration for *www.technowidgets.com* and *web1.technowidgets.com*. Type the following text:
   <VirtualHost 192.168.0.100>
   ServerName www.technowidgets.com
   DocumentRoot /var/www/html
   </VirtualHost>
   <VirtualHost 192.168.0.100>
   ServerName web1.technowidgets.com

DocumentRoot /var/www/web1
</VirtualHost>
The bottom of the httpd.conf file should look like the one in Figure 6-27. Save your changes and exit KEdit by clicking the **Save** icon and then closing the window.

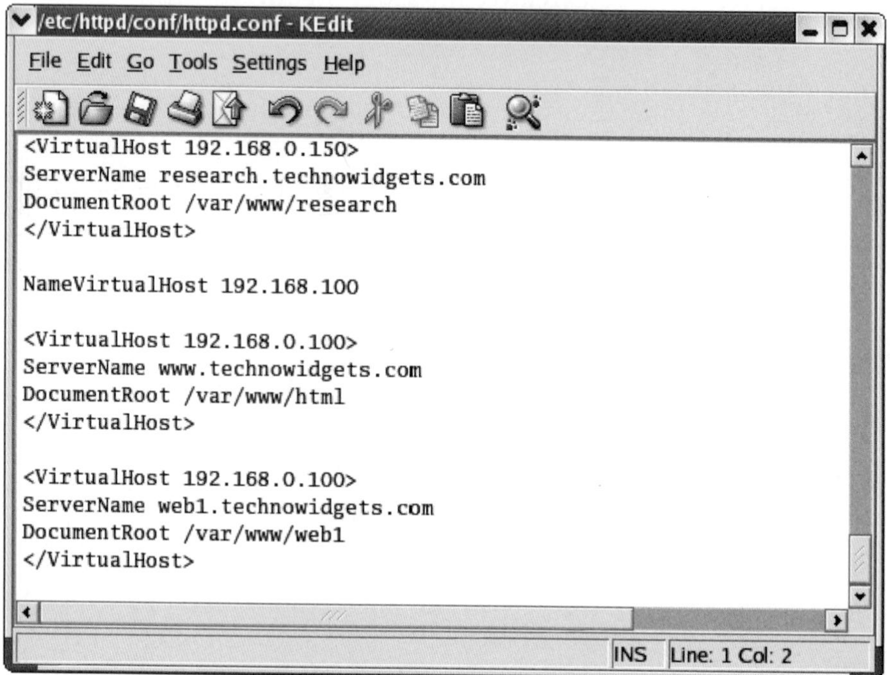
/etc/httpd/conf/httpd.conf - KEdit
File Edit Go Tools Settings Help
<VirtualHost 192.168.0.150>
ServerName research.technowidgets.com
DocumentRoot /var/www/research
</VirtualHost>
NameVirtualHost 192.168.100
<VirtualHost 192.168.0.100>
ServerName www.technowidgets.com
DocumentRoot /var/www/html
</VirtualHost>
<VirtualHost 192.168.0.100>
ServerName web1.technowidgets.com
DocumentRoot /var/www/web1
</VirtualHost>
INS
Line: 1 Col: 2

Figure 6-27 Creating a virtual host using a host name

4. Type **apachectl restart**, and then press **Enter**.
5. Open the Konqueror Web browser, type **www.technowidgets.com** for the URL, and then press **Enter**. You should see the default Web page. See Figure 6-28.
6. Type **web1.technowidgets.com** for the URL, and then press **Enter**. You should see the Web page you created. See Figure 6-29.

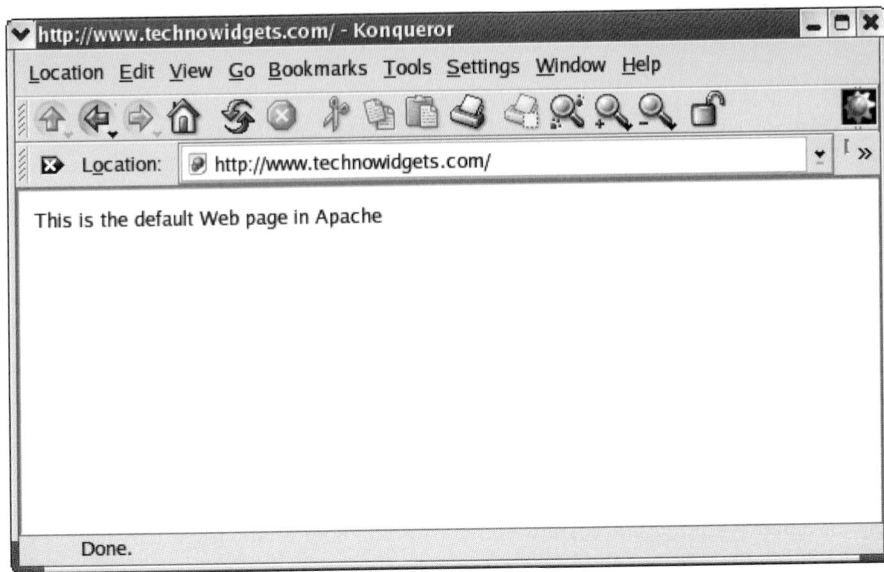

Figure 6-28 Default Web page for *www.technowidgets.com*

Figure 6-29 Default Web page for *web1.technowidgets.com*

6

Understanding Virtual Directories

A **virtual directory** is a Web directory that is not physically located beneath the Web root. For example, a URL of *www.technowidgets.com/prod* does not necessarily mean that a directory called prod is below either \inetpub\wwwroot or the corresponding root directory.

Instead, the directory prod could be one of the following locations:

- Another directory on the computer such as \categories\products
- A directory located on another computer
- A URL on another Web server

Allowing the Web directory to refer to another physical directory on the computer could make it easier to organize the Web site based on directory permissions. For example, the marketing manager could be in charge of updating product information. In Linux, that manager could log on and have the directory that corresponds to the prod virtual directory be her default home directory, which would facilitate updating the pages. The physical directory for the root of the Web server would also be less cluttered with directories. On the other hand, creating a virtual directory in this case would make it more difficult to keep track of where the Web pages for the site actually reside.

When you use a directory that is physically stored on another computer, you are typically connected by a LAN. The marketing manager updating the product Web pages may have access to another computer on the LAN. The Web server can use the directory on the other computer through a share in the Windows environment or NFS in a Linux environment.

The ability to have a directory actually be a URL on another Web server is a very powerful option. It allows you to balance the load of the Web server by letting other Web servers process certain Web pages. Suppose you used the prod directory to hold pages containing thousands of images. By having the pages reside on another Web server, you could dedicate a whole Web server to retrieving large image files. Virtual directories can also be used to organize corporate Web sites. For example, your company may have Web sites in various regions around the world. You can make them appear to exist on a single server by creating directories that correspond to your regional Web servers.

Configuring Virtual Directories in IIS

To create a virtual directory in IIS, you use a wizard in both Windows 2000 and Windows 2003. You start the wizard for the virtual directory in the same place that you started the wizard for the new Web site.

To create a virtual directory in IIS:

1. *In Windows 2003:* Open **Internet Information Services (IIS) Manager**. *In Windows 2000:* Open **Internet Services Manager**.
2. Expand the items in the left pane until you see **Default Web Site**.

3. Right-click **Default Web Site**, point to **New**, and then click **Virtual Directory**.
4. The Virtual Directory Creation Wizard Welcome dialog box opens. Click **Next**.
5. The Virtual Directory Alias dialog box opens. See in Figure 6-30. Here is where you enter the name of the directory as it will appear in a URL.

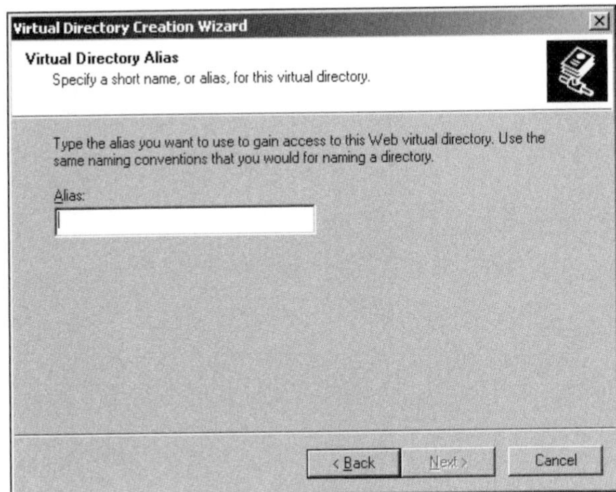

Figure 6-30 Virtual Directory Alias dialog box

In the Alias text box, type **prod** and then click **Next**.

6. The Web Site Content Directory dialog box opens. You use this dialog box to specify the location of your virtual directory. See Figure 6-31.

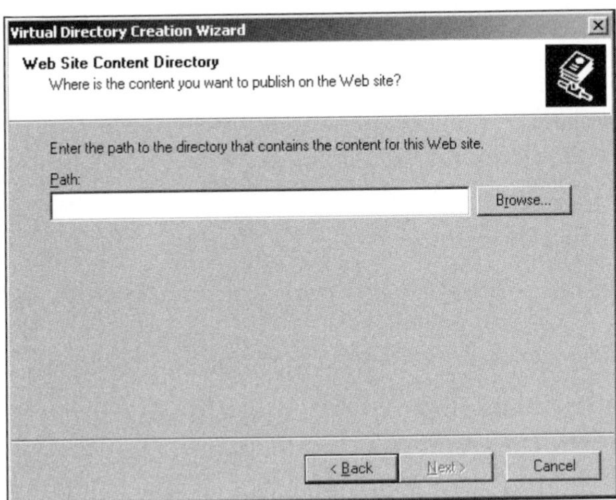

Figure 6-31 Web Site Content Directory dialog box

Click **Browse**, click the drive that corresponds to your installation of Windows, and then click **Inetpub**. Click the **Make New Folder** icon, and then type **VirtProd** as the name of the new folder.

7. *In Windows 2003:* Click **OK** to create the folder \Inetpub\VirtProd as the physical location of your virtual directory.
   In Windows 2000: The folder has already been created, so you can select **VirtProd** in the list. Click **Next**.
8. The Virtual Directory Access Permissions dialog box opens. See Figure 6-32. This dialog box lists the default permissions for reading Web pages and running scripts such as Active Server Pages. The permissions are the same as the ones for creating new Web sites.

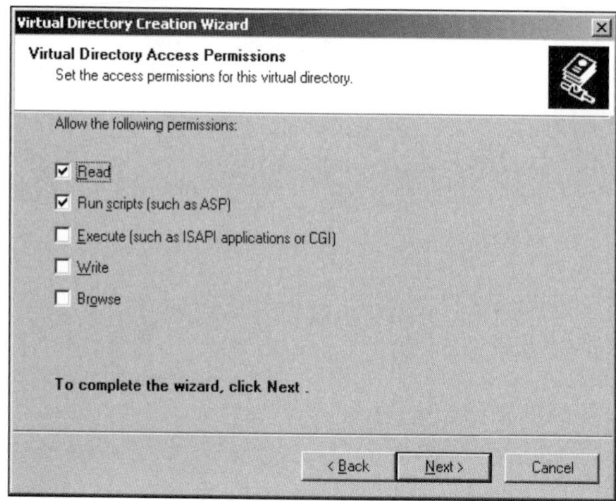

Figure 6-32 Virtual Directory Access Permissions dialog box

9. Click **Next** to accept the defaults, and then click **Finish** to complete the wizard.

Note that the wizard did not provide an option to create a virtual directory that referenced a share on another computer or a URL. To do that, you have to modify the properties of the virtual directory.

To display the properties of the virtual directory:

1. *In Windows 2003:* If necessary, open **Internet Information Services (IIS) Manager**.
   In Windows 2000: If necessary, open **Internet Services Manager**.
2. If necessary, expand the items in the left pane until you see the contents of the **Default Web Site**. See Figure 6-33.
3. Right-click **prod**, and then click **Properties** to open the Properties dialog box for this directory. See Figure 6-34.

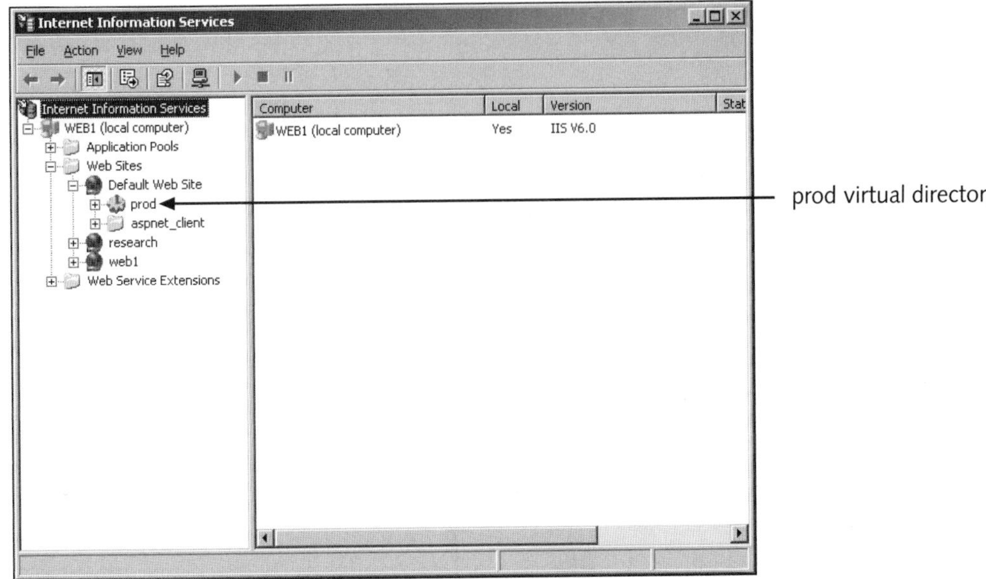

Figure 6-33 IIS window showing prod virtual directory

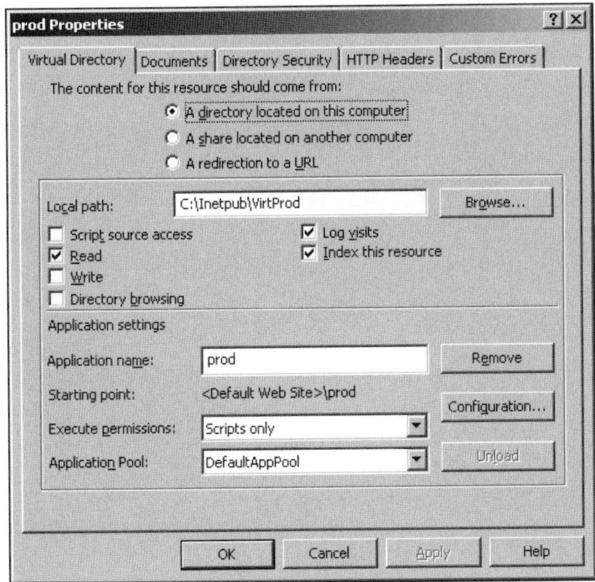

Figure 6-34 Properties dialog box for the prod virtual directory

As you can see in Figure 6-34, the option button at the top of the Virtual Directory tab is set to "A directory located on this computer." If you click the "A share located on another computer" option button, the dialog box changes to the one shown in Figure 6-35. Notice that the text box for Local path changed to Network directory. The default shows the structure of inserting the name of the server and the name of the share. If you click the "A redirection to a URL" option button, the dialog box changes to the one shown in Figure 6-36. If you check the "The exact URL entered above" box, all requests for any files in the virtual directory are directed to a single file that you entered in the text box, such as /msgs/notavail.htm. If you check the "A directory below URL entered" box, the virtual directory is associated with a URL that contains a directory such as /newprods. If you check the "A permanent redirection for this resource" box, a message is sent to the client so that some browsers will update bookmarks.

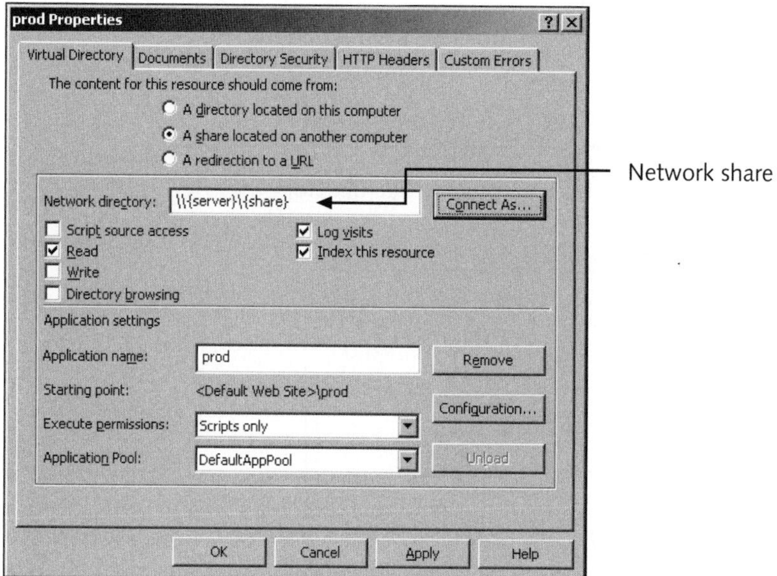

Figure 6-35 Share located on another computer

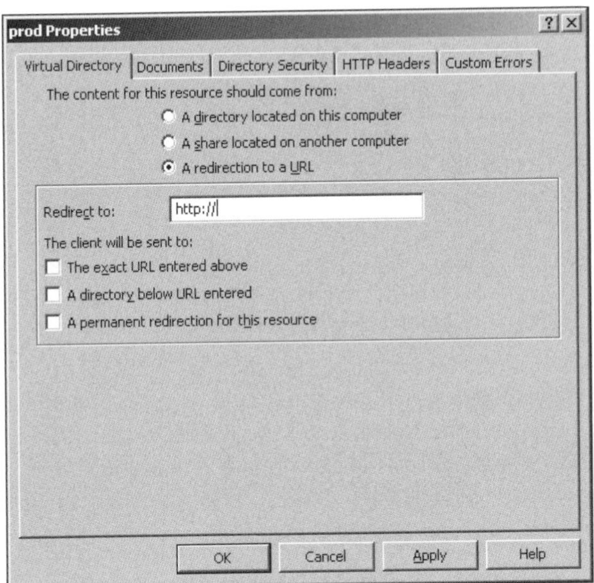

Figure 6-36 A redirection to a URL

Configuring Virtual Directories in Apache

As you have already seen, you need to modify the httpd.conf file to configure a Web site that you are administering on an Apache Web server. As in IIS, a virtual directory in Apache has two components. First, you need to associate the physical location where the Web pages will reside with the name of the directory as the browser would reference it. Second, you need to configure the properties for the virtual directory. For example, Apache has an icons directory where small images are stored. These images are used on Web pages. In a browser on the Apache server, if you type *http://localhost/icons/world1.gif*, a small image of the world appears. Based on the URL, the directory icons is located beneath the root of the Web server. If it were physically part of the Web server directory structure, it would be located at /var/www/html/icons because /var/www/html is the root of the Web server. However, the developers of Apache decided to put the icons directory in another location—namely, /var/www/icons. To associate the name of the virtual directory with its physical location, you use the `Alias` command. In httpd.conf, you can see the following line:

```
Alias /icons/  "/var/www/icons/"
```

This code states that when /icons/ is detected in a URL, the request should be sent to the /var/www/icons directory.

In the second step, you define the virtual directory's properties. The properties for a directory are similar to the properties for a virtual host. For the icons virtual directory, httpd.conf contains the following information:

```
<Directory "/var/www/icons">
        Options Indexes MultiViews
        AllowOverride None
        Order allow, deny
        Allow from all
</Directory>
```

The preceding example shows two option properties. The Indexes option states that if there is no index.html default file in the directory, then Apache will display a list of files in the directory. This feature corresponds to the browsing option in IIS. The second option, MultiViews, allows for a language-specific response to a request. That is, if the browser has been configured to prefer Italian, and there is an associated Italian page, it is sent to the browser. The rest of the properties are related to security. The following list describes the default security properties of the icons directory:

- *AllowOverride None*—Directories beneath this directory cannot alter the access permissions.
- *Order allow, deny*—First apply the "allow" permissions, and then apply the "deny" permissions.
- *Allow from all*—Set no restrictions.

Virtual directories in IIS are different from virtual directories in Apache. In IIS, a virtual directory is always associated with an individual Web site. For example, earlier in this chapter, you created a virtual directory called prod that you associated with the *www.technowidgets.com* Web site. That virtual directory can be used only with *www.technowidgets.com*, but no other Web site. In Apache, the icons virtual directory can be used by all of the virtual hosts, because it was defined in the main server configuration area and not within any of the virtual hosts. As a contrast, you will create the prod virtual directory so it can be used only from the *web1.technowidgets.com* Web site in Apache. The physical location of the prod virtual directory will be /var/www/prod.

To create a virtual directory called prod on the Apache Web server:

1. Open a terminal window and change to the directory where you are creating new subdirectories. Type **cd /var/www** and then press **Enter**.
2. Type **mkdir prod** and then press **Enter** to create the directory for the prod virtual directory.

To create Web pages for the new Web sites:

1. Type **kedit prod/index.html** and then press **Enter** to create the default page for the research Web site.

2. Type the following HTML code to identify the research site:

```
<html><body>
This is the prod virtual directory
</body></html>
```

3. Click the floppy disk icon on the toolbar of kedit to save the file.

4. Close the window.

To configure httpd.conf to add a virtual directory for the *web1.technowidgets.com* Web site:

1. In a terminal window, open the httpd.conf file by typing **kedit /etc/httpd/conf/httpd.conf** and then pressing **Enter**.
   Recall that the virtual hosts are found at the bottom of the file.

2. Add the virtual directory information, which is shown in bold in the following text:

```
<VirtualHost 192.168.0.100>
ServerName web1.technowidgets.com
DocumentRoot /var/www/web1
Alias /prod/ "/var/www/prod/"
<Directory "/var/www/prod">
    AllowOverride None
    Order allow, deny
    Allow from all
</Directory>
</VirtualHost>
```

Now you can test your virtual directory by opening the Konqueror browser and typing the URL *web1.technowidgets.com/prod*. Because you did not type the name of the Web page, Apache sends the default Web page of index.html, which you created earlier with the text of "This is the prod virtual directory."

Chapter Summary

- The primary purpose of a Web server is to produce pages of HTML. The protocol used to communicate between the Web server and the browser is HTTP. The two most popular Web servers are Apache from the Apache Software Foundation and Internet Information Services (IIS) from Microsoft. Web servers typically listen at port 80, but you can modify this setting to have them listen at any port higher than 1024.
- You install the IIS Web server software as a Windows component in both Windows 2000 and Windows 2003. You install Apache 2.0, which is part of the Red Hat Linux installation, as you would any other software.
- IIS properties can be configured globally so that all new sites will share the new configuration. You can also change the properties for individual sites. Most IIS properties are related to the location of files, characteristics of files, and security settings. You can view and change them using a GUI.

- To configure an Apache Web server, you modify a text file called httpd.conf. The properties are separated among the global configuration, main configuration, and virtual hosts. Although the httpd.conf file has more than 1,000 lines of codes, most of them consist of comments and properties that are rarely changed.
- You can create more than one Web site on a single server. For multiple Web sites to exist on the same computer, you have to make each one distinct. You can create a distinct Web site by configuring it with a different port number, a different IP address, or a different host name.
- In IIS, you use a wizard to create a Web site. You need to configure the folder where you will create the root of the Web site. One wizard dialog box allows you to make the Web site distinct from the other Web sites that you have configured previously. You also have to determine the basic access permissions and file types that you will allow on the site.
- New Web sites in Apache are called virtual hosts. You configure the virtual hosts in httpd.conf by using tags similar to those found in HTML. To define a virtual host, you configure the IP address, the location of the root, and the host name of the site.
- Virtual directories are directories that appear to be located beneath the root of the Web server, yet are physically located elsewhere. A virtual directory can correspond to another directory on the same computer as the Web server, a directory located on another computer, or a URL on another Web server.

Review Questions

1. The primary purpose of a Web server is to produce files using the following formatting language:
   a. HTTP
   b. HTML
   c. PORT 80
   d. FTP
2. Which protocol is used to communicate between the Web server and the browser?
   a. HTTP
   b. HTML
   c. PORT 80
   d. FTP
3. What does IIS stand for?
   a. Internal Internet Server
   b. Internet Informal Server
   c. Internet Information Service
   d. Internet Information Services

4. Web servers typically listen at port ______________.
5. Which of the following ports is the worst choice for a Web server?
   a. 88
   b. 8080
   c. 8000
   d. 8888
6. More Web servers use Apache than IIS. True or False?
7. What is the current version of HTTP?
   a. 1.0
   b. 1.1
   c. 2.0
   d. 2.1
8. One of the most important characteristics of the current version of HTTP is ______________ ______________.
9. The Internet Explorer browser can view pages on an Apache Web server, and the Konqueror browser can see pages on an IIS Web server. True or False?
10. Which of the following describes WebDAV?
    a. It is an Apache configuration for virtual hosts.
    b. It allows you to share Web-based files in IIS.
    c. It allows high-speed Digital Audio/Video.
    d. It is an IIS virtual directory setting.
11. Which of the following is *not* one of the components available when installing IIS?
    a. SMTP Service
    b. FTP Service
    c. NNTP Service
    d. DNS Service
12. What is the current version of the Apache Web server?
    a. 1.3
    b. 2.0
    c. 3.x
    d. 4.x

13. What is the name of the file used to start and stop Apache?
    a. apachectl
    b. httpd.conf
    c. HTML
    d. http
14. Apache has a configuration for ISAPI filters. True or False?
15. Which of the following describes the KeepAlive setting?
    a. It shuts down the server after a certain number of seconds.
    b. It prevents the server from shutting down.
    c. It determines whether to maintain a persistent connection for multiple files.
    d. It determines how long someone can view a Web page.
16. What is the syntax for displaying a Web site at port 8080?
    a. www.technowidgets.com/8080
    b. www.technowidgets.com:8080
    c. www.technowidgts.com8080
    d. You cannot display a Web site at port 8080.
17. In Apache, if you want the root of your virtual host to be in /var/www/intranet, you would type the following:
    a. DocumentRoot /var/www/intranet
    b. Root / var/www /intranet
    c. WebRoot / var/www /intranet
    d. SiteRoot / var/www /intranet
18. To name the virtual host *intranet.technowidgets.com* in Apache, you would type the following:
    a. VirtualHost intranet.technowidgets.com
    b. ServerName intranet.technowidgets.com
    c. HostName intranet.technowidgets.com
    d. WebName intranet.technowidgets.com
19. A virtual directory in IIS can refer to a URL on another Web server. True or False?
20. In Apache, when associating a virtual directory with the physical location, what is the first word on the line?
    a. Cname
    b. Map
    c. Alias
    d. Associate

Hands-on Projects

Project 6-1

In this project, you will explore the effects of setting connection properties in IIS. You will use a Telnet session to simulate a browser connecting to a Web server. A block of text that you paste into the Telnet session requests a Web page from the Web server. The response after the page is sent depends on the properties that are set.

To determine the effect of requesting a Web page using Telnet:

1. Create a Web page called **hello.htm** that displays "Hello, World" and store it in \inetpub\wwwroot.
2. In Notepad, type the following lines and then press **Enter** twice. Make sure that you do not insert a blank line between the two lines *and that you add two blank lines at the end*. The blank lines mean that the request is sent to the Web server. You should replace *www.technowidgets.com* with the name of one of your hosts:
   GET /hello.htm HTTP/1.1
   HOST: www.technowidgets.com
3. Press **Ctrl+A**, and then press **Ctrl+C** to copy all of the text to the Clipboard.
4. At a command prompt, type **telnet localhost 80** and then press **Enter** to connect to the Web server at port 80. If you tried to type text now, you could not see it so it is much easier to paste text from the Clipboard. However, because this is a command prompt, a special technique is needed to paste text.
5. In the upper-left corner, click **C:**, point to **Edit**, and then click **Paste**. You see the response from the Web server. If nothing happens, you probably forgot to add the blank lines to the end of the text in Step 2, so press **Enter** a couple of times. What response did you get?
6. Wait about one minute and repeat Step 5. Were you successful?
7. Press **Ctrl+C** to end the Telnet session.

To modify the connection timeout property and try connecting again:

1. Open the Internet Information Services window.
2. Expand the items in the left pane until you see **Default Web Site**.
3. Right-click **Default Web Site**, and then click **Properties**.
4. Change the Connection Timeout to **9** seconds.
5. Click **Apply** to change the connection timeout.
6. Repeat Steps 4 and 5 in the previous set of steps to use Telnet to display a page. How many seconds does it take until you lose the connection?

To disable Keep-Alives and test the configuration again:

1. If necessary, open the Internet Information Services window.

2. If necessary, expand the items in the left pane until you see **Default Web Site**.
3. Right-click **Default Web Site**, and then click **Properties**.
4. Change the Connection Timeout to **120** seconds.
5. Clear the **Enable HTTP Keep-Alives** check box to disable Keep-Alives.
6. Click **Apply** to accept the changes.
7. Repeat Steps 4 and 5 in the first set of steps to use Telnet to display a page. How many seconds does it take until you lose the connection?

Project 6-2

In Project 6-1, you noticed that when you request a page, much more data is actually received. This extra information takes the form of headers, such as Content-Type: text/html. A header has two parts: the name, which is followed by a ":", and the value. Sometimes a Web site wants to send a custom header to each browser that connects. Programmers could use this information to build custom responses based on header information.

To add a custom header and determine the effect on a Web page response:

1. Open the Internet Information Services window.
2. Expand the items in the left pane until you see **Default Web Site**.
3. Right-click **Default Web Site**, and then click **Properties**.
4. Select the **HTTP Headers** tab.
5. Click **Add** to add a custom HTTP header. The Add/Edit Custom HTTP Header dialog box opens.
6. For the Custom header name, type **Technowidgets**.
7. For the Custom Header Value, type **Version 5**.
8. Click **OK** to accept the header.
9. Click **Apply** to change the configuration. Then click **OK**.
10. Repeat the steps in Project 6-1 to determine the effect of requesting a Web page using Telnet. Do you see the header that you created? Where is it?

Project 6-3

In Windows, each HTTP error corresponds to a file that is sent to the browser in response to the error. You can customize these files. For example, you can change a "Not Found" error page to display a more descriptive message. However, by default, Internet Explorer overrides the error file on the server, which reduces the usefulness of custom error pages. In this project, you will create a custom page for error 404 (Not Found) and test it.

To create a custom page for error 404:

1. In Notepad, type the following HTML code:

```
<html><body>
<H1>The file you requested was not found</H1>
</body></html>
```

2. Save the file as **404.htm**. Remember to set the Save as type to All Files.
   In Windows 2003: Save the file in \WINDOWS\Help\iisHelp\common.
   In Windows 2000: Save the file in \WINNT\help\iisHelp\common.
3. Open the Internet Information Services window.
4. Expand the items in the left pane until you see **Default Web Site**.
5. Right-click **Default Web Site**, and then click **Properties**.
6. Select the **Custom Errors** tab.
7. Click **404** under the HTTP Error heading.
8. Click **Edit** (**Edit Properties** in Windows 2000) to edit the filename for error 404. The Edit Custom Error Properties (Error Mapping Properties in Windows 2000) dialog box opens.
9. Change the file to point to the one you created in Step 2. Click **OK**.
10. *Windows 2000 only*: Click **OK** to change the file designation. The Inheritance Overrides dialog box opens. Click **Select All**, and then click **OK** to allow property inheritance.
11. Click **OK** to make the change permanent.

To test the configuration:

1. Open your browser, type **localhost/xyz.htm**, and then press **Enter**. What was the response? If the browser did not use the new page you created, the problem is not with the server. Internet Explorer has a default setting to "show friendly HTTP error messages." Each type of Web server may have a different error page format, so to keep messages consistent, the browser pays no attention to what you did on the server. To see the file you created, you need to adjust the properties of the browser.
2. In Internet Explorer, click **Tools** on the menu bar, and then click **Internet Options**.
3. Select the **Advanced** tab.
4. Scroll down and click the **Show friendly HTTP error messages** check box to unselect it.
5. Click **OK** to save the setting.
6. Enter the URL of **localhost/xyz.htm** again or click **Refresh**. Now you should see the page you created.

You can also create custom HTTP error messages in Apache. The details are in httpd.conf. You can create an error message based on plain text, create an HTML file, or process a script. In this project, you will create a text message.

To add an error message for "file not found" and test it:

1. Open **httpd.conf** in kedit.
2. Search for HTTP_NOT_FOUND.
   The resulting line should be "ErrorDocument 404 /error/HTTP_NOT_FOUND.html.var." Insert a pound sign (#) at the beginning of the line to make a comment out of it, thereby disabling the line.
3. Create a blank line, and then type **ErrorDocument 404 "The page was not found"**.
4. Save the file, and then close the kedit window.
5. Restart the Web server.
6. Open the browser.
7. For the URL, type **localhost/h.htm** or any other request for a nonexistent page. Did the server respond with your custom error document? The Konqueror browser works differently from Internet Explorer in that it allows error messages from Web servers to be displayed by default.

Project 6-4

In this project, you will explore the effects of setting connection properties in Apache. You will use a Telnet session to simulate a browser connecting to a Web server. The response after the page is sent depends on the properties that are set.

To determine the effect of requesting a Web page using Telnet:

1. Create a Web page called **hello.htm** that displays "Hello, World." Store the page in the root of your Apache Web server.
2. Open a terminal window, type **telnet localhost 80**, and then press **Enter**.
3. Type the following:
   GET /hello.htm HTTP/1.1
   HOST: www.technowidgets.com
4. Press **Enter** to create a blank line. It tells the server that there are no more headers and that it should respond. What is the response? At the end of the response, the server states "Connection closed by foreign host." This is the opposite of IIS, which has KeepAlive enabled.

To determine the effect of enabling KeepAlive:

1. Open **httpd.conf** in kedit.
2. Press **Ctrl+F** to find KeepAlive. Notice that KeepAlive is set to Off.
3. Change KeepAlive Off to **KeepAlive On**.
4. Save the file and then exit.
5. Restart the Web server.

6. Repeat Steps 1 through 4 in the first section of this project. Did the server respond in the same way?
7. Immediately request the page again. What happened?
8. Wait about 30 seconds and then request the page again. What happened?
9. In httpd.conf, search for **KeepAliveTimeout**. What is the current setting?

The previous steps show the effect of not only KeepAlive but also KeepAliveTimeout. Even with KeepAlive turned on, the connection will stay open only the number of seconds determined by KeepAliveTimeout.

Project 6-5

Imagine a very large site where pages are split among servers maintained by separate personnel, but where you want the appearance of a single, seamless site. In this case, you can have a virtual directory point to a URL instead of a folder on the Web server. In this project, you will create a virtual directory called products and redirect it to another student's Web site.

To create a virtual site that corresponds to a URL in Windows:

1. Create a virtual directory called **products** that corresponds to any folder on your computer. It doesn't matter which folder it is because you will change it. When you create a virtual directory, you cannot have it point to a URL.
2. Open Internet Information Services.
3. View the properties of the products virtual directory.
4. Click the **A redirection to a URL** option button.
5. For the URL, type the IP address of another student's Web server, followed by a slash. For example, type **192.168.0.200/**. The Web server could be either Apache or IIS.
6. Select **The exact URL entered above** check box.
7. Click **Apply**.
8. On the other student's Web server, create two Web pages. Name the first page **default.htm** if it is a Windows server or **index.html** if it is an Apache server. Name the second page **hello.htm**. Store the pages in the root of the Web server. Create simple content for the pages to distinguish them.
9. In your browser, type **localhost/products** as the URL. Which page is displayed?
10. In your browser, type **localhost/products/hello.htm** as the URL. Which page is displayed? You probably didn't get the result you expected. The setting you gave the virtual directory told it to go to a single page, no matter what URL you typed. You could even type a nonexistent page, and the server would still display the default page. This capability is useful when a portion of a site is down and you want to display a single page for all requests.

11. View the properties for the products virtual directory again. Unselect the check box for **The exact URL entered above**, and then select **A directory below this one**.
12. Click **OK** to save the changes.
13. Stop the Web server, and then restart it.
14. In your browser, type **localhost/products/hello.htm** as the URL. Which page is displayed? You probably got the result you expected. Now type **localhost/products**. You should see the default page.

Project 6-6

Sometimes you want to allow users to have their own Web pages. For example, if you had a user account of cbranco at *www.technowidgets.com*, you could type *www.technowidgets.com/~cbranco/* and get the home page. For a large site, you would probably have a script to automate this process, but it is easy to set up a sample site.

To set up Apache to allow user Web sites:

1. Open **httpd.conf** in kedit.
2. Search for **UserDir:** (be sure to include the colon (:) at the end.) You see the lines shown in Figure 6-37.
3. Insert # before "UserDir disable" to enable it.
4. Delete the # before "UserDir public_html" to allow each user's public_html directory to be used to store Web pages.
5. Starting with the line that states "#<Directory /home/*/public_html>," delete the # at the beginning of the line and the rest of the lines starting with # down to "</Directory>". This configures the directory structure.
6. Save the file and then exit.
7. Restart the Web server.

To create a user who can create Web pages:

1. Open a terminal window.
2. Type **adduser cbranco** and then press **Enter.**
3. Type **passwd cbranco** and then press **Enter**. When the system prompts you for a new password, type **password**. You will get a warning that your choice is a bad password but the system will still accept it. The user has a home directory but Apache needs execute permissions. Retype the new password when prompted.
4. Type **chmod 711 /home/cbranco** and then press **Enter**.
5. To create the public_html directory for cbranco, type **mkdir /home/cbranco/public_html** and then press **Enter**.
6. To give cbranco ownership of public_html, type **chown cbranco /home/cbranco/public_html** and then press **Enter**.

```
# UserDir: The name of the directory that is appended onto a user's home
# directory if a ~user request is received.
#
# The path to the end user account 'public_html' directory must be
# accessible to the webserver userid. This usually means that ~userid
# must have permissions of 711, ~userid/public_html must have permissions
# of 755, and documents contained therein must be world-readable.
# Otherwise, the client will only receive a "403 Forbidden" message.
#
# See also: http://httpd.apache.org/docs/misc/FAQ.html#forbidden
#
<IfModule mod_userdir.c>
    #
    # UserDir is disabled by default since it can confirm the presence
    # of a username on the system (depending on home directory
    # permissions).
    #
    UserDir disable
    #
    # To enable requests to /~user/ to serve the user's public_html
    # directory, remove the "UserDir disable" line above, and uncomment
    # the following line instead:
    #
    #UserDir public_html
</IfModule>
#
# Control access to UserDir directories. The following is an example
# for a site where these directories are restricted to read-only.
#
#<Directory /home/*/public_html>
#    AllowOverride FileInfo AuthConfig Limit
#    Options MultiViews Indexes SymLinksIfOwnerMatch IncludesNoExec
#    <Limit GET POST OPTIONS>
#        Order allow,deny
#        Allow from all
#    </Limit>
#    <LimitExcept GET POST OPTIONS>
#        Order deny,allow
#        Deny from all
#    </LimitExcept>
#</Directory>
```

Figure 6-37

7. Apache needs to read from this directory, so type **chmod 755 /home/cbranco/public_html** and then press **Enter**.

To create a Web page and test the configuration:

1. Log off as root, and then log on as cbranco.
2. Open a terminal window.

3. Type **kedit public_html/index.html** and then press **Enter**. The file index.html is the default page for a directory. That is, if you do not reference a page, the system will display the contents of index.html.
4. Create a simple Web page of your choice.
5. Save the file and then exit.
6. Open the browser.
7. For the URL, type **http://localhost/~cbranco/**. The browser displays your Web page.

Project 6-7

In this project, you test virtual directories and note the difference between Apache and IIS.

To test a virtual directory in Windows:

1. Make sure that you have completed the "To create a virtual directory in IIS" steps in the chapter.
2. Use a text editor to create a Web page with the text "This is a virtual directory" and store the page in \Inetpub\VirtProd.
3. Start Internet Explorer, type **localhost/prod** as the URL, and then press **Enter**. Did the Web page you created in Step 2 appear?
4. Delete the text in the Address text box, type **localhost/prod/** as the URL, and then press **Enter**. Did the Web page appear? Explain why or why not.

To test a virtual directory in Apache:

1. Make sure that you have completed the "To create a virtual directory called prod on the Apache Web server," "To create Web pages for the new Web sites," and "To configure httpd.conf to add a virtual directory for the web1.technowidgets.com Web site" steps in the chapter.
2. Start Konqueror, type **localhost/prod** for the URL, and then press **Enter**. Does a Web page appear?
3. Delete the text in the Address text box, type **localhost/prod/** as the URL, and then press **Enter**. Did the Web page appear? Explain why or why not. Compare this to the results you found when you performed these steps with IIS and Internet Explorer.

CASE PROJECTS

Project 6-1

Create another site on your IIS Web server based on a new host name. If you did not create the intranet host in Chapter 4, do so now and add the associated IP address. Create a Web site based on the intranet host. Create a folder beneath Inetpub for the Web site. Create a Web page to test the functionality of your new Web site.

Project 6-2

Create a new Web site in IIS based on a new IP address. Create a new host address that is compatible with your existing IP address. Create a Web site based on that address. Create a Web page to test the Web site. You do not have to create an entry in the DNS server. If the IP address you created was 192.168.0.200, for example, in Internet Explorer you could type a URL of *http://192.168.0.200*.

Project 6-3

Create a Web site in Apache based on a new host name. If you did not create the intranet host in Chapter 4, do so now and add the associated IP address. Create a Web site based on the intranet host. Create a Web page to test the functionality of your new Web site.

Project 6-4

Create a new Web site in Apache based on a new IP address. Create a new host address that is compatible with your existing IP address. Create a Web site based on that address. Create a Web page to test the Web site. You do not have to create an entry in the DNS server. If the IP address you created was 192.168.0.200, for example, in Konqueror you could type a URL of *http://192.168.0.200*.

Project 6-5

Create a virtual directory for one of the IIS Web sites you created in Project 6-1 or 6-2. Create a page to test the directory.

Project 6-6

Create a virtual directory for one of the Apache Web sites you created in Project 6-3 or 6-4. Create a page to test the directory.

CHAPTER

7

INSTALLING AND TESTING A PROGRAMMING ENVIRONMENT

In this chapter, you will:

- Understand the need for programming languages
- Understand database management systems (DBMSs)
- Install and test DBMSs
- Understand the Web-based programming environment
- Program with databases

As you learned in Chapter 6, all Web servers are based on the HTTP protocol and primarily use pages built with HTML. These pages are often created with a text editor. To produce an e-commerce Web site where the user enters information and the Web site produces individualized Web pages, however, you need both a programming language and a database. A programming language processes information from the user and from data stored in a database. The result of the processing can consist of a report sent to the user or data returned to the database.

You can use many programming languages for creating interactive Web pages. For IIS, the most common languages are Active Server Pages (ASP), which has been available for all versions of IIS, and ASP.NET, which first became available with IIS 5.0 as an add-on. For Apache, PHP is a popular choice; it has a structure similar to that of ASP. Older, but still popular programming languages such as Perl are used with both IIS and Apache.

Central to most Web sites that use programming languages are database management systems (DBMSs) that allow you to store data gathered from users and then produce a variety of reports. For IIS, the most common DBMS is Microsoft SQL Server. For Apache, the preferred option is MySQL, a powerful, open-source DBMS. Another DBMS, Oracle, is used in both environments.

Understanding the Need for Programming Languages

When you view a Web page, it may correspond to an HTML file that someone created and published, or it may contain text, graphics, and other elements that were generated by a programming language. Web pages that contain only HTML statements, such as the ones you created in Chapter 6, are called **static** pages. Pages that contain programming statements allow the content to change, so they are called **dynamic** pages. You encounter dynamic pages whenever you use a search engine on the Web or purchase something online. You can also use dynamic pages to create personalized pages such as those available at *my.yahoo.com*.

You can use programming languages to create not only dynamic Web pages, but those specifically designed to run on Web servers and update databases. For example, when you order a book online, much of the programming creates the order information in a database. The Web site has to store your name, address, books that you want to purchase, credit card information, and other related data. Programming languages can also be used to communicate with other systems. For example, when you fill out a form on a Web page and then submit it, the contents are e-mailed to the recipient.

Understanding Programming Languages

A programming language processes data. The data can come from a variety of sources, including a user who typed information on a Web page or a database on a computer. The programming language can then extract user information from the data and store it in a database or use the information to search a database and produce a report.

The program performs three basic steps: input, processing, and output. For example, suppose you want to search a book seller's Web site for books on Portugal. You enter the information on the Web page and click a button to submit the form to the Web server (input). Based on your input, the program on the Web server searches a database for books (processing). Based on the results, a Web page is produced and sent to your browser (output).

In the same way that a human language can be used to give instructions, a programming language processes data in three ways. First, one instruction after another is processed; this is simply called **sequence**. Second, based on data, more than one option is possible; this is called **logic**. For example, if someone purchases more than $500 in merchandise, shipping might be free; otherwise, it might cost $20. A program uses logic to check whether the purchase exceeds $500 and to determine what to do based on the results. The third way a program processes data is **iteration**, or processing the same instructions multiple times. For example, when you produce an employee report with 100 employees, you process the instructions to display a single employee 100 times.

You use a programming language to create something as simple as a counter on a Web page to display how many times someone has viewed your site. An e-commerce site such as *Amazon.com* uses programming to display a list of books based on search criteria, maintain your purchase history, and display personalized advertisements. Behind the scenes, an e-commerce site uses programming to update the inventory system and process credit card information.

Understanding the E-Commerce Environment

The primary purpose of an e-commerce site is to allow visitors to find a product and purchase it—the public side of an e-commerce site. A Web server administrator, however, must also consider the administrative side of the site. You need to add, update, delete, and report on the products you have available for sale. Likewise, you need to track customers, payments, shipping, and returned products and to perform other tasks, such as maintaining security.

As an e-commerce site expands, so does its complexity. A Web site might offer a hierarchy of products with sale prices on some categories for a certain number of days or for a certain category of customer. You may need to produce targeted advertisements based on customer preferences and then track how often the advertisements work so as to fine-tune the system. Many products, such as Microsoft Commerce Server, can be used to build the foundation for a Web site, allowing companies to create an e-commerce site more quickly than by doing all the programming themselves. Products such as Microsoft Commerce Server are not separate server programs, but rather programming environments that are added to an existing Web server. These environments include tools that help automate the creation and maintenance of an e-commerce site.

Understanding Internal Business Applications

Another area of program development involves applications that automate business processes such as order processing. In this area, companies typically control their internal networks and can specifically define the entire computing environment. A company can base its Web-based applications on a clear understanding of the speed of the connections, the number of connections, and the brand and version of a browser. For these reasons, Web-based applications on an intranet can be much more focused than those on the Internet.

Understanding Database Management Systems

Databases are an integral part of most Web environments because Web environments have evolved significantly from just offering simple, static pages. A Web site without any database connectivity is probably so simplistic that it would have little need for a full-time Web administrator.

The purpose of a DBMS is to store data in an organized manner for further processing. Web server administrators can learn one method of organizing data and one language (SQL) to define and manipulate the data. From the free DBMSs such as MySQL to the more costly DBMSs such as Oracle, the basic functionality remains the same–a DBMS stores data in an organized structure so that it can be easily retrieved.

While some hierarchical DBMSs organize data into a structure similar to an organization chart, most DBMSs are relational databases that organize data into tables. These tables are then grouped into a database according to common characteristics. For example, employee information is stored in one table, while product information is stored in another table. Each table contains columns and rows similar to a spreadsheet. Each column describes a characteristic of a table. For example, an employee table would include characteristics such as Social Security number (SSN), first name, last name, department number, and salary. Each of these characteristics would be a column in the employee table. Each row contains data for an employee corresponding to one or more of the columns. As an example, Table 7-1 shows a table with three employees. Each row has one employee, and each column lists a characteristic of the employee.

Table 7-1 Employee table with three employees

SSN	First name	Last name	Department number	Salary
553879098	Lynn	Gweeny	10	55000
623827368	Elark	Kaboom	10	60000
756838998	John	Doh	20	45000

Furthermore, each table has one or more columns that represent a **primary key**. A value of a primary key uniquely defines a row of data. For example, in Table 7-1, the SSN would be the primary key because each number is unique and therefore corresponds to a single row. In Table 7-2, the primary key would be the department number.

Table 7-2 Department table with two departments

Department number	Department name	Manager
10	Accounting	553879098
20	Manufacturing	756838998

The tables in a relational database are related in such a way that the data remains reliable. For example, you could have stored the department name and the SSN of the manager in the employee table. This would make processing data faster. But what if the department name changed? You would have to remember that the department name is found in more than one place and make sure that you change it everywhere it appears. This problem may seem like a minor point but as your database gets larger and more complex, you need specific rules governing how to design your tables. You relate data in tables through a **foreign key**, or a column in one table that is related to a primary key in another table. For example, in Table 7-1, the department number is a foreign key that is related to the department number in the Department table. This relationship is useful when you want to find the name of the department of a given employee. You use the department number of the employee to look up the department name in the Department table. The benefit of organizing data in a relational structure is obvious: If you need to change the department name, you simply change it in just one place. The same department will then have the same name in another table, making the data reliable. Table 7-2 also has a foreign key—the Manager column in the department table. The Manager column is related to the SSN column in the Employee table.

The series of rules for organizing data into tables is called **normalization**. Basically, tables are normalized when all columns that are not part of the primary key are related solely to the primary key, and not to each other.

Related tables are organized into individual databases. For example, the Employee and Department tables could be organized into a Human Resources database. Tables related to inventory could be organized into a Manufacturing database. Both the Human Resources and Manufacturing databases could exist within the same DBMS.

Understanding Structured Query Language, the Language of Databases

Structured Query Language (SQL, pronounced "sequel") is the language used by virtually all DBMSs. It uses English-like statements to interact with the database. Three categories of SQL statements exist: the Data Manipulation Language (DML), the Data Definition Language (DDL), and the Data Control Language (DCL).

Only the DML is commonly used in programming. This language controls the inserting, updating, deleting, and retrieval of data. For example, if you wanted to retrieve the last names and first names from the Employee table, the SQL statement would be "select lastname, firstname from employee" in any relational DBMS. Likewise, to insert a row of data into the Employee table, any DBMS would recognize the SQL statement "insert into employee values ('667589898','Elark', 'Kaboom',10,60000)."

The DDL assists you in defining tables and other related structures in a database. For example, to create the Employee table shown earlier in Table 7-1, you could use the following SQL statement:

```
Create table employee (
ssn char(9) primary key,
firstname varchar(20),
lastname varchar(30),
depno char(2),
salary numeric(6));
```

The column names (ssn, firstname, lastname, depno, salary) are followed by the type of data that will be stored in the table for the particular column. The char data type defines the number of characters that will be stored for this column value as stated in parentheses. For example, the ssn column can contain nine characters. The varchar data type is similar, but with one important exception: It takes up only the space needed for data, whereas the char data type always takes up the maximum allowed by the definition. For example, if you used the char data type for the first name and defined it as containing up to 20 characters, even if the first name had only 5 characters, it would still use 20 characters in the column. When you define the column using the varchar data type, a five-character name takes up only 5 characters. The char data type is typically used for data that is of a consistent length, such as state postal codes, phone numbers, and ZIP codes.

In the preceding code, the salary is defined as a number that can be up to six digits. It is accepted practice to use numeric data types only for numbers that can be manipulated in calculations. Numeric data such as Social Security numbers, phone numbers, and zip codes cannot be used in calculations, so they are often assigned to the char data type.

The last data type, numeric, is not common to all databases. With Microsoft SQL Server, you would use the money data type. In Access, you would use the currency data type instead. Other DBMSs, such as Oracle, use the number data type.

The DML is often simplified through use of a GUI. For example, in Microsoft database products, you typically create a table by filling in a form and selecting the data types from a list box. You can also create reports in Microsoft Access by selecting the columns you want on the report and many other criteria from an easy-to-use GUI or one of the many wizards available. In fact, you can create sophisticated applications in Access without working directly with SQL.

The DCL allows you to control access to your tables and determine which operations users can perform on your tables, but it is not included in all DBMSs. For example, Microsoft Access does not have a DCL. The grant command, for example, allows you to give access to your tables while the revoke command stops users from accessing your tables. The DCL is an administrative language that is not used in programming.

Using Microsoft Access Files with IIS

Microsoft Access, a DBMS that is part of the Microsoft Office suite of products, is known for its ease of use. Although Microsoft Access is not included with Microsoft Windows 2000 or Windows Server 2003, the software needed to manipulate Access files is included. Microsoft Access is a file-based DBMS, meaning that each database is stored in a file that can be copied from computer to computer. While Access is an appropriate choice for Web sites with minimal data requirements, it is not designed to handle large databases. Furthermore, Access does not provide the security, disaster recovery, or undo capability (called a rollback in SQL) that more sophisticated database software offers.

You will explore using Access with IIS in Hands-on Project 7-1. You will also have the option of using Access in Hands-on Projects 7-3 and 7-4. As you will see, the difference between using Access and using Microsoft SQL Server is a single line of code in these programs.

INSTALLING AND TESTING DBMSs

In this section, you will learn how to install Microsoft SQL Server on Windows 2003 and Windows 2000. On your Linux server, you will install MySQL, which Red Hat includes on CD 3.

Installing and Testing Microsoft SQL Server

The following steps explain how to install SQL Server 2000 on a Windows computer, create a database of employee information, create a table named employee, add data to the employee table, and retrieve data from the employee table.

To install SQL Server 2000 from the MSDN CD in Windows:

1. *In Windows 2003:* Log on as the administrator, and then insert the SQL Server 2000 CD in the CD drive. If a dialog box appears asking what should be done with the CD, click **Open folder to view files using Windows Explorer**, and then click **OK**. If a dialog box does not appear, open Windows Explorer. If the Setup program starts automatically, skip to Step 5.

   In Windows 2000: Log on as the administrator, and then insert the SQL Server 2000 CD in the CD drive. Open Windows Explorer.

2. Navigate to the \ENGLISH\ENT folder on the developer's CD, or \Standard on the full version of the CD.

3. Double-click **SETUP.BAT** to start the installation wizard. In Windows 2003, if a dialog box opens stating that SQL Server 2000 SP2 is not supported, click the **Continue** button.

   When the Welcome screen appears, click **Next**. The Computer Name dialog box opens. See Figure 7-1.

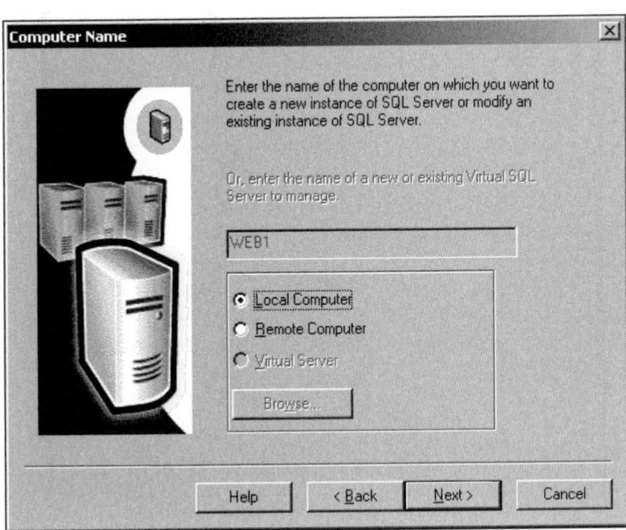

Figure 7-1 Computer Name dialog box

4. Click **Next** to accept the default of installing SQL Server 2000 on the Local Computer.

   Note that you could also install SQL on a remote computer. In this case, the text box would become active so that you could enter the name of the remote computer. The Installation Selection dialog box opens, allowing you to choose whether to install a new instance of SQL Server or work with advanced options. Microsoft uses the term "instance" to mean the SQL Server programs necessary to create the DBMS. See Figure 7-2.

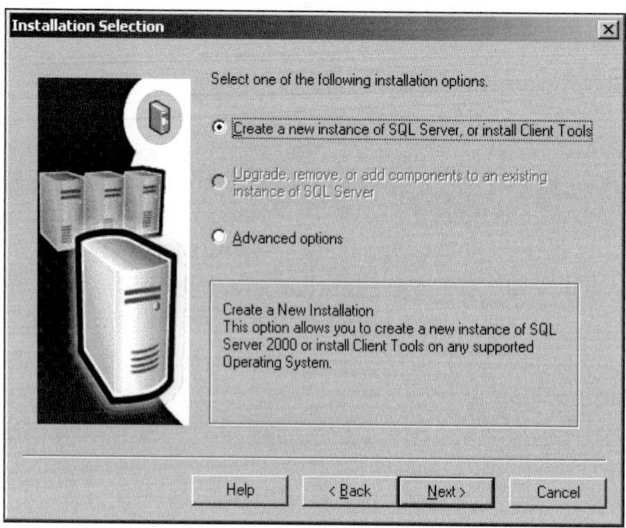

Figure 7-2 Installation Selection dialog box

5. Click **Next** to accept the default of creating a new instance of SQL Server. The User Information dialog box opens. See Figure 7-3. This dialog box contains the name and company information that you supplied when you installed the operating system.
6. Click **Next**. The Software License Agreement dialog box opens. In an educational environment, the licensing has been taken handled previously, but in a production environment, you must make sure that you have paid for the correct license(s).
7. Click **Yes** to accept the license agreement. The Installation Definition dialog box opens. See Figure 7-4. Make sure that the **Server and Client Tools** option button is selected.

   If you were working on a workstation and wanted the software to connect to an existing server, you would select Client Tools Only. If you wanted to install the software that allows the programming languages to interact with SQL Server, you would select Connectivity Only.

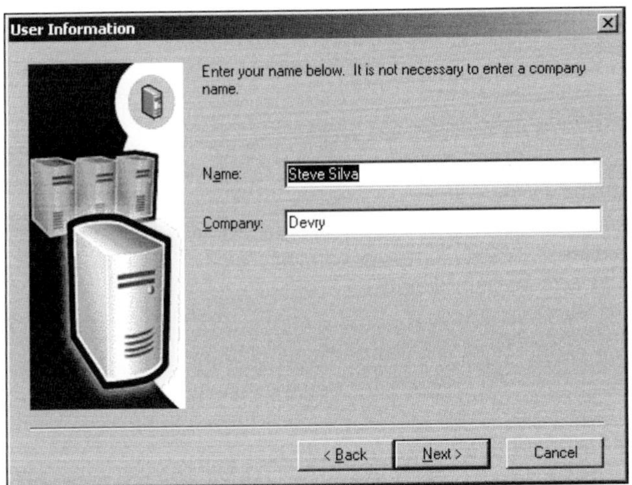

Figure 7-3 User Information dialog box

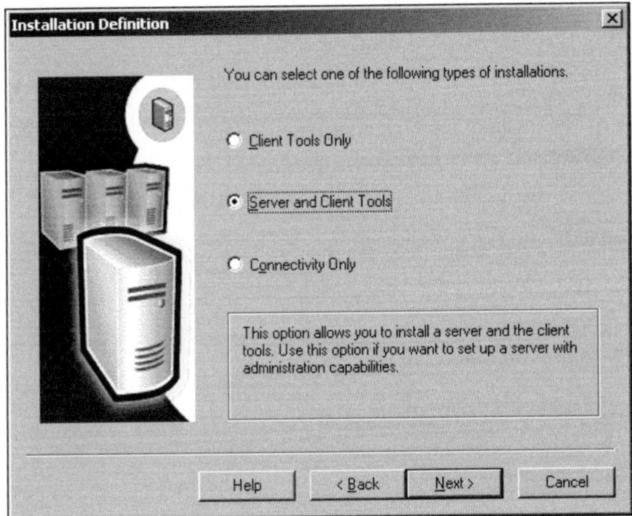

Figure 7-4 Installation Definition dialog box

8. Click **Next**. The Instance Name dialog box opens. See Figure 7-5. Because you are installing a new instance of SQL Server, make sure that the Default check box is selected.

   If you wanted to maintain an instance of SQL Server or add another instance, you could clear the check box and enter the instance name.

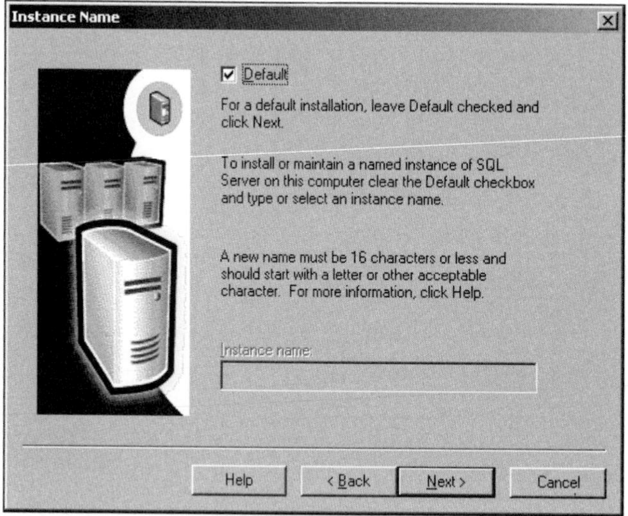

Figure 7-5 Instance Name dialog box

9. Click **Next**. The Setup Type dialog box opens. See Figure 7-6. Make sure that the **Typical** option button is selected. The drive letters that appear in your dialog box will probably differ from the ones shown in Figure 7-6, depending on the operating systems you installed.

   You would choose the Custom option button to include items more appropriate for developers.

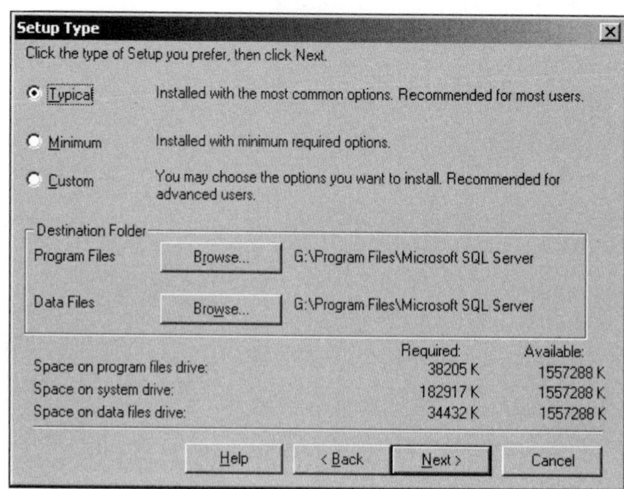

Figure 7-6 Setup Type dialog box

10. Click **Next**. The Services Accounts dialog box opens. See Figure 7-7.

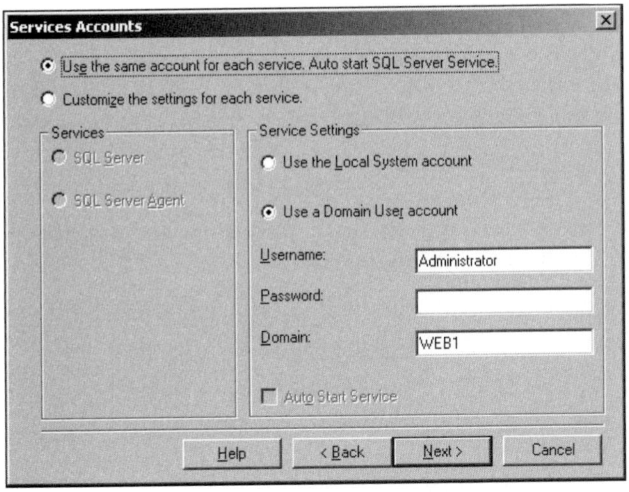

Figure 7-7 Services Accounts dialog box

11. Click the **Use the Local System account** option button.

    If you accept the default as the administrator account and change the password on the administrator account, SQL Server will not run. A domain user account is necessary when SQL Server needs to communicate with an instance of SQL server on another computer. In such a case, you typically would have created a special user account just for SQL Server.

12. Click **Next**. The Authentication Mode dialog box opens. See Figure 7-8.

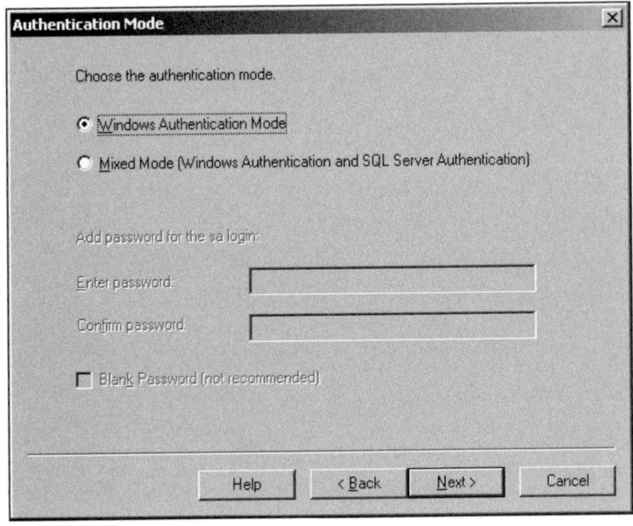

Figure 7-8 Authentication Mode dialog box

13. Click the **Mixed Mode** option button. When you click this button, the text boxes under "Add password for the sa login" are enabled. The sa (system administrator) login allows full access to SQL Server. Click the **Blank Password** check box because the sample files assume a blank sa password. In a production environment, however, you should not use a blank password because it would allow anyone full access to your database.

    Note that if you select the Windows Authentication Mode option button, the sample files for this chapter will not work.

14. Click **Next**. The Start Copying Files dialog box opens. Click **Next** to begin copying files from the CD to your hard disk. The Choose Licensing Mode dialog box opens. See Figure 7-9.

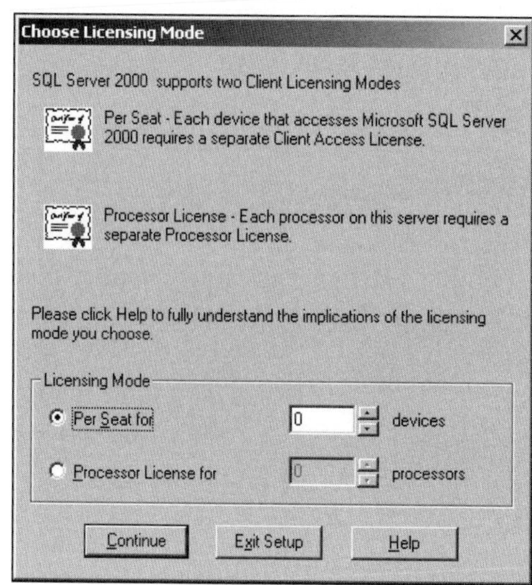

Figure 7-9 Choose Licensing Mode dialog box

    Because you are simulating an installation for use on the Internet, click the **Processor License for** option button and enter **1** for the number of processors.

15. Click **Continue** to install SQL Server. When the Setup Complete dialog box opens, click **Finish** to exit the wizard. Close the Windows Explorer window.

Once you have installed SQL Server, your first task is to create a database.

To create a database in SQL Server for Windows:

1. Open Enterprise Manager.

    In Windows 2003: Click **Start**, and then click **Enterprise Manager**. The SQL Server Enterprise Manager window opens.

    In Windows 2000: Click **Start**, point to **Programs**, point to **Microsoft SQL Server**, and then click **Enterprise Manager**.

2. In the left pane, click the **plus sign** (+) next to Microsoft SQL Servers, next to the SQL Server Group, and then next to (local) (Windows NT) on Windows 2003. In Windows 2000, instead of (local), you see the name of your computer.

   A series of folders opens, as shown in Figure 7-10. Notice that the left pane displays Windows NT in the name of the local computer, which is the version of Windows that came before Windows 2000. The properties for SQL Server define Windows 2000 as Windows NT 5.0, and Windows 2003 as Windows NT 5.2.

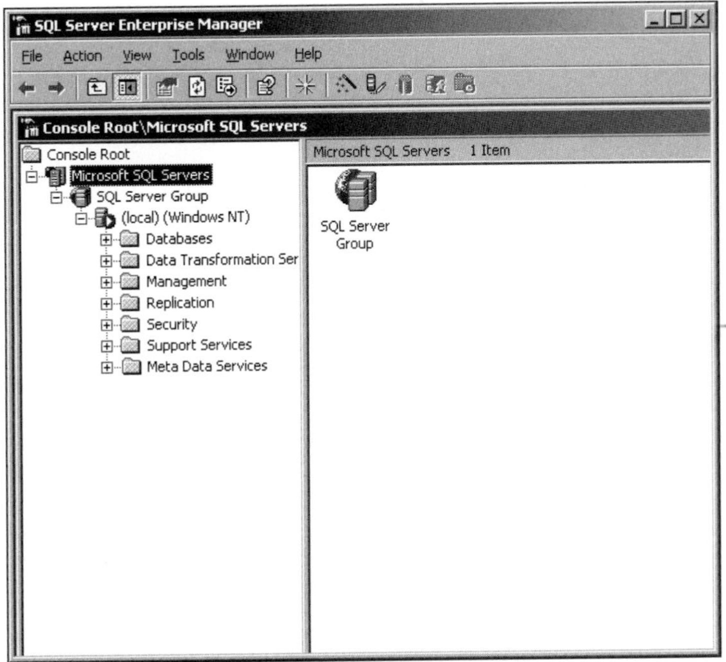

Figure 7-10 SQL Server Enterprise Manager window

3. In the left pane of the SQL Server Enterprise Manager window, right-click **Databases** and then click **New Database** to create a SQL Server database. You are creating the human resources database. To make it easier to type, you will abbreviate the name of the database to simply hr.

4. In the Name text box, type **hr** and then click **OK** to create the human resources database.

5. Keep the SQL Server Enterprise Manager window open for the next series of steps.

Now that you have created the hr database, your next step is to create the tables and then enter data into them. You can create tables in SQL Server by using either a wizard or the SQL `create table` statement. To load data into the table, you can also use a GUI or SQL `insert` statement. In the following steps, you fill in GUI forms to create the employee table and add data.

To create the employee table and load three rows of data in SQL Server for Windows:

1. In the left pane of the SQL Server Enterprise Manager window, expand the **Databases** folder.
2. Right-click **hr**, point to **New**, and then click **Table**. The New Table window opens.
3. Your objective is to create the employee table as described in Table 7-1. Complete the form so that it matches Figure 7-11. (You might need to expand the top pane.)

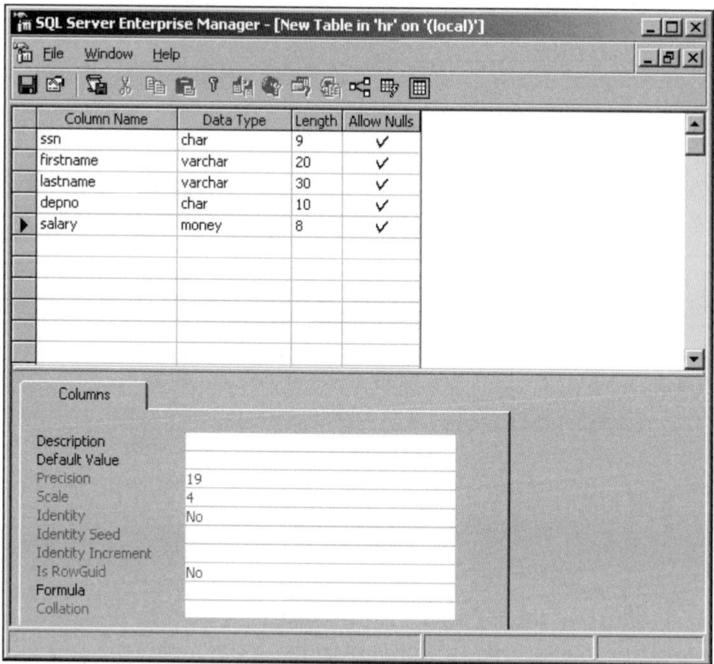

Figure 7-11 Create the employee table

4. To make the ssn column become the primary key, click the unnamed button to the left of ssn and then click the **Set primary key** icon on the toolbar. (Point to the toolbar buttons to display their names.) The key icon appears to the left of ssn.

5. Click the **Save** icon on the toolbar to save the table. The Choose Name dialog box opens.
6. Enter **employee** in the text box, and then click **OK** to save the table.
7. Close the New Table window, but leave the SQL Server Enterprise Manager open for the next series of steps.

Now that you have created the employee table, you need to add data to it. The easiest way is to open the table and type the data.

To add data to the employee table in SQL Server for Windows:

1. In the left pane of the SQL Server Enterprise Manager window, expand **Databases**, if necessary, and within Databases, expand **hr**. Click **Tables**. The list of tables in the hr database is displayed in the right pane. See Figure 7-12.

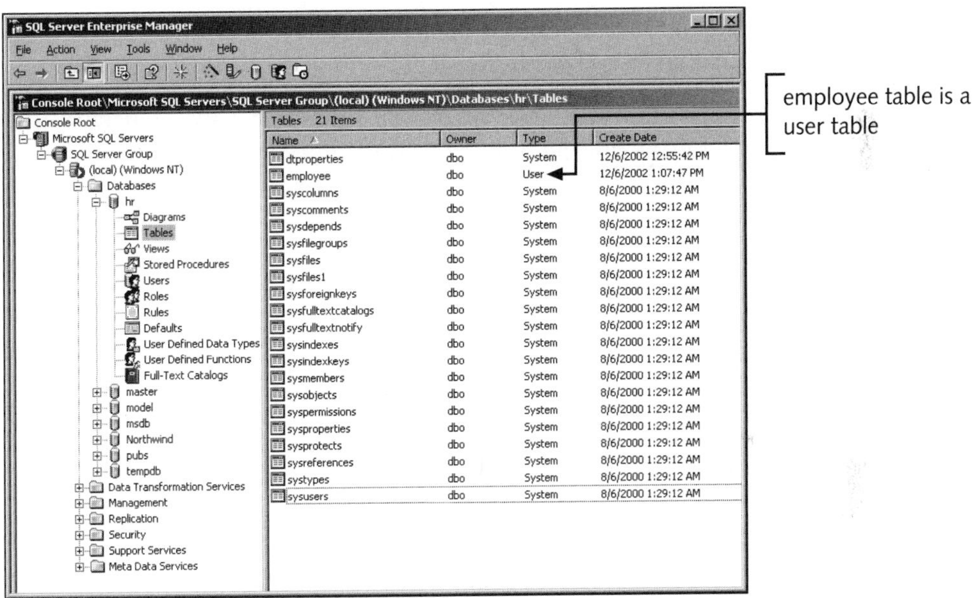

Figure 7-12 List of tables in the hr database

Note that all the tables that appear are system tables except the employee table, which is a user table.

2. Right-click **employee**, point to **Open Table**, and click **Return all rows**. The Data in Table window opens. Complete the table so it matches Figure 7-13.
3. Close the SQL Server Enterprise Manger window.

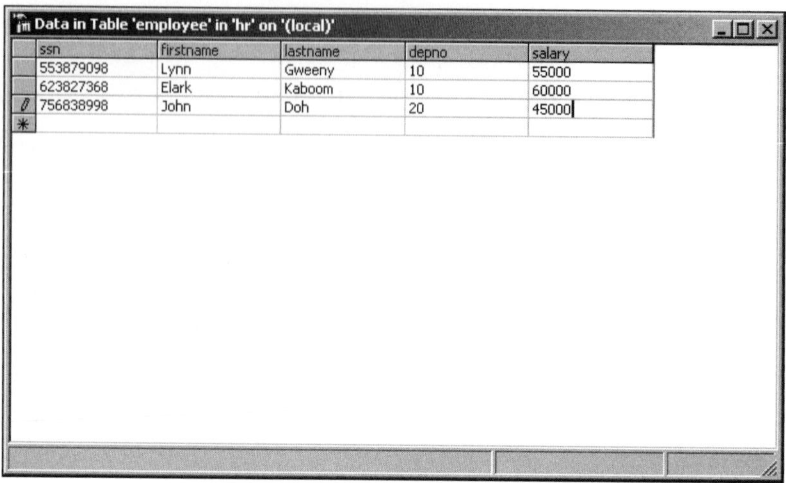

Figure 7-13 Adding data to the table

You have installed SQL Server, created the human resources database, created the employee table, and added data to it. Now you are ready to write programs to access the data. In a later section, you will learn how to write an ASP program and an ASP.NET program to display employee data and add new data to the table.

Installing and Testing MySQL in Red Hat Linux

On a Linux Web server, you can use MySQL instead of SQL Server to perform database operations. MySQL is a high-performance database similar to SQL Server. Although you will use the default text-based interface for MySQL, many GUI-based interfaces are available to make MySQL administration easier.

To install MySQL on Linux:

1. Insert Red Hat CD 3 in the CD drive.
2. Double-click the **CD/DVD-ROM** icon on the desktop. Konqueror opens, with the directories of the CD shown in the right panel.
3. Double-click the **RedHat** directory icon in the right panel. This displays the contents of the RedHat directory.
4. Double-click the **RPMS** directory icon in the right panel. This displays the contents of the RPMS directory.
5. Scroll down to the **mysql-3.23.52-3.i386.rpm** package and double-click it. A dialog box opens and, after a short while, states that it has completed system preparation. Click **Continue** to install MySQL.
6. The installation program installs two associated Perl packages. A dialog box opens requesting Red Hat CD 2. Insert the CD and then click **OK**.

7. A dialog box opens requesting Red Hat CD 3. Insert the CD and then click **OK**.
8. The Completed System Preparation dialog box opens. Click **OK** to finish the installation.
9. Repeat Steps 2, 3, and 4.
10. In the right panel of the Konqueror window, double-click **mysql-server-3.23.52-3.i386.rpm**. The Completed System Preparation dialog box opens. Click **Continue**. The package is installed. Close the Konqueror window.

Although MySQL is installed, it is not running, so you cannot use it. As with DNS and Apache, you need to learn how to start the server and edit rc.local to make MySQL start whenever the computer starts.

To start MySQL:

1. To start MySQL manually, type **/etc/rc.d/init.d/mysqld start** in a terminal window.
2. To have MySQL start when Linux starts, you must change the rc.local file. Open a terminal window, type **kedit /etc/rc.d/rc.local**, and then press **Enter**.
3. At the bottom of the file, add the following line:
   /etc/rc.d/init.d/mysqld start
4. Click the **floppy disk** icon to save the changes, and then close the kedit window.

Now MySQL is installed and running in the background. You can use a program called MySQL monitor to run SQL statements and other utilities. Because MySQL is installed without a password, the first time you run the MySQL monitor, you do not have to log on to it. After you set the password for the root account of MySQL, however, you must log on to the MySQL monitor. Remember the password for MySQL because you will need it for the MySQL monitor and when you test Web programs that you will write.

To set the password for the root account for MySQL in Linux:

1. In a Linux terminal window, type **mysql** and then press **Enter** to start the MySQL monitor.
2. Type **SET PASSWORD FOR root = PASSWORD('password');** and then press **Enter** to create a password of "password." Be sure to type the text exactly as shown, including the semicolon at the end. You should receive a response that states "Query OK."
3. Type **exit** and then press **Enter** to exit the MySQL monitor.

Much as with Microsoft SQL Server, you have to create the human resources database, create the employee table, and then add data to the table in MySQL. With MySQL, you will run a script that contains the SQL commands necessary to create the table and add the data instead of typing the information into a form. Running a script is also common practice in SQL Server. To run the script, you must know the path to the Chapter7 directory on your Data Disk, which is assumed to be /mnt/floppy/chapter7. The following procedure should look like Figure 7-14.

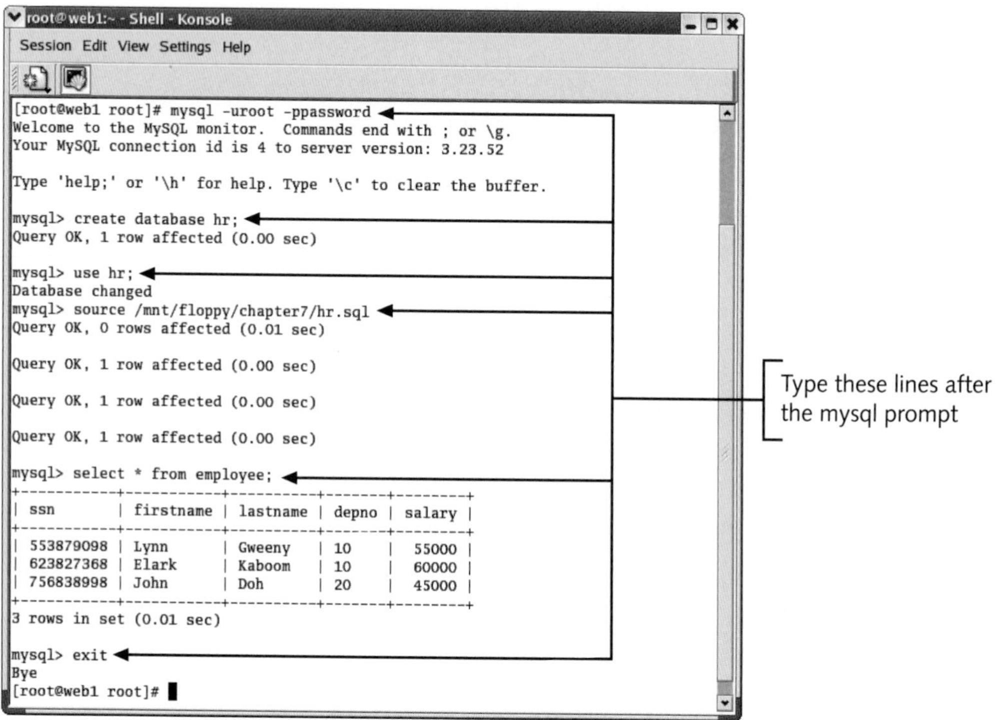

Figure 7-14 Create MySQL database, add data, and display contents

To create the employee database and run the script to create the employee table and add data with MySQL in Linux:

1. In a terminal window, type **mount /mnt/floppy** and then press **Enter** to make the floppy disk accessible. (Be sure to insert a space after you type "mount.")
2. Type **mysql -uroot -ppassword** and then press **Enter**. The -u stands for "user name," and it is followed by "root." The -p stands for "password," and it is followed by the actual password, which is "password."
3. Type **create database hr;** and then press **Enter** to create a database named hr.
4. Type **use hr;** and then press **Enter** to make the hr database become the default database.

5. Type **source /mnt/floppy/chapter7/hr.sql** and then press **Enter** to run the following script:

```
create table employee (
ssn char(9) primary key,
firstname varchar(20),
lastname varchar(30),
depno char(2),
salary numeric(6));

insert into employee values('553879098','Lynn','Gweeny','10',55000);
insert into employee values('623827368','Elark','Kaboom','10',60000);
insert into employee values('756838998','John','Doh','20',45000);
```

6. Type **select * from employee;** and then press **Enter** to display the contents of the employee table. The "*" (asterisk) tells the utility to display all the columns.

7. Type **exit** and then press **Enter** to exit MySQL monitor.

UNDERSTANDING THE WEB-BASED PROGRAMMING ENVIRONMENT

Web programming is often based on an input-process-output model as described in a previous section. When a Web server receives a request for a dynamic Web page, it receives input from the user's browser, processes the information, and then produces output. For example, when you click a link on a Web page to display a category of products, the browser sends a request for category information to the page that contains the list of products. This request provides the input. The page that receives the category contains a program, which directs the Web server to look up the product data in a database (process) and shows the product list (output). The input for the program in the Web page can come from the URL link that the user clicks, information that the user supplies in a form in the browser, a cookie stored on your disk, or information contained within the program in the Web page. A **cookie** is text that a Web site stores on your disk that can be retrieved by the Web server when you visit the site. Often a cookie provides personalization information to the Web site. For example, sites such as *my.yahoo.com* allow you to personalize the type of news and other information that your browser displays by default. You can log on to the site when you visit it, or you can allow the site to store a cookie containing logon information on your disk.

The original environment for Web programming is the **Common Gateway Interface** (**CGI**), a protocol that allows the operating system to interact with the Web server. CGI is powerful and flexible, but it also creates a favorite entry point for hackers. Using CGI can leave your system vulnerable to attack because programs written to the CGI specification can access system utilities that can, in turn, be used to compromise the server. Among the most common languages used for CGI are **Practical extraction and reporting language** (**Perl**), C, and shell scripts. Because these languages were created before the Web environment existed, they were not designed for Web security. Instead, they depend on the skills of the programmer to make sure that the applications are secure.

Programmers often create Web programs with a text editor. Alternatively, they can use many sophisticated products to become more productive. Products such as Microsoft Visual Studio .NET and Borland JBuilder, for example, help programmers organize, develop, test, and deploy Web-based programs.

Apache makes adding programming languages relatively easy and provides good support for databases. It gives you the flexibility to create a Web environment that is tailored to the specific needs of your organization.

With IIS, the most common programming languages are ASP and ASP.NET, both of which are Microsoft creations. ASP was the first Web-based programming language from Microsoft available for IIS. ASP.NET is available for IIS 5.0 (Windows 2000) if you also install the .NET Framework, which is available for free from Microsoft. ASP.NET is the primary programming language for IIS 6.0 (Windows 2003), although you can also use ASP in IIS 6.0.

ASP.NET represents a significant improvement over ASP. To see how, suppose you want to create a form to enter employee information, including salary information. In ASP, you must have HTML expertise because you must write all the tags needed to format the employee form and include all the programming commands for the browser to make sure that the form was filled in correctly. In ASP.NET, in contrast, you can simply state that a text box should contain a valid phone number and let ASP.NET actually write the code. Another difference between ASP and ASP.NET relates to performance. Each time a browser requests an ASP page on a Web server, the text in the page must be converted to a format that the server can understand, which takes extra time. With ASP.NET, the Web page is most likely already converted to the correct format, so the page can be processed much faster.

Using the Programming Examples

A programming environment includes both the programming languages and the databases that you support. To verify that your programming environment works correctly, you can create a comparable test across the languages. In this section, you will create an application to enter employee information in a form and then display the contents of the form. In a later section, you will test the database connectivity.

The application contains two pages, which belong in the root directory of the Web server. The first page is written in HTML, a language that allows you to create a form and format it in a browser. The form records an employee's Social Security number, first name, last name, and salary. A second page processes the form so that it produces output such as "Hello, Lynn Gweeny.Your Social Security Number is 553879098 and you make $55000." The contents of the page that produces the form resembles Figure 7-15 with one important exception. After the "action=" statement in the form, you insert the name of the file that will process the form, such as ProcessForm.asp. The second page must be written in a programming language supported by your Web server. The extension of the filename usually identifies the language in which it was written. For example, ProcessForm.asp would contain ASP programming instructions (code). ProcessForm.aspx would contain ASP.NET code, and ProcessForm.php would contain PHP code.

Figure 7-15 shows the HTML code for creating the employee form.

```
<HTML>
<BODY>
Please enter the following information and then click Submit:<BR>
<FORM action=filename>
SSN: <input type=text name=ssn><BR>
First Name: <input type=text name=first><BR>
Last Name: <input type=text name=last><BR>
Salary: <input type=text name=salary><BR>
<input type=submit name=submit value=Submit>
</FORM>
</BODY>
</HTML>
```


Figure 7-15 form.htm—the form used for processing

In Figure 7-15, the information between the angle brackets < > consists of HTML statements that aid in formatting text within the browser. HTML statements are not case-sensitive, which means that they can be written in uppercase or lowercase text. The <FORM...> statement signals the start of the form, and the </FORM> statement identifies the end of the form. The <BR> tag causes subsequent text to appear at the beginning of the next line. The <input type=text name=first> statement opens a text box. When the information from the form is processed by Active Server Pages or another language, each text box is distinguished by its name. Thus what you enter in the text box for Social Security Number will be associated with ssn, the text box for the first name will be associated with first, and so on. The <input type=submit name=submit value=Submit> statement displays a button that, when pressed, sends the form to the page that processes it.

Programming Languages on IIS

By far, the most popular Web programming languages are the ones produced by Microsoft. As noted earlier, ASP was the original Web-based programming language for IIS. Today's IIS also supports ASP.NET, which represents a new generation of programming languages for the Web.

Understanding Active Server Pages

ASP is a scripted language that is included with all versions of IIS. With a scripted language, you include commands in a script—a text file—that the Web server processes.

When you configured new Web sites and virtual directories in Chapter 6, one of the settings you chose was to allow scripts to be processed by the Web server. If you did not allow scripts, your ASP files would not work.

By default, ASP is not installed in Windows 2003, but it is installed on Windows 2000.

To install ASP in Windows 2003:

1. In the Control Panel, click **Add or Remove Programs**. The Add or Remove Programs window opens.
2. Click **Add/Remove Windows Components**. The Windows Components Wizard dialog box opens.
3. Scroll to and click **Application Server**, and then click **Details**. The Application Server dialog box opens.
4. Click **Internet Information Services (IIS)**, and then click **Details**. The Internet Information Services (IIS) dialog box opens.
5. Click **World Wide Web Service**, and then click **Details**. The World Wide Web Service dialog box opens.
6. Click the **Active Server Pages** check box.
7. Click **OK** three times to return to the Windows Components Wizard dialog box. Click **Next** to install ASP. After a few moments the Completing the Windows Components Wizard dialog box opens. Click **Finish** to exit the wizard. Close the Add or Remove Programs window.

To process the form.htm form shown earlier in Figure 7-15, you would change the fourth line from <form action=> to <form action=ProcessForm.asp>. ProcessForm.asp, which is a script that you can create in any text editor, is shown in Figure 7-16.

```
<%@ Language=VBScript %>
<HTML><BODY>
Hello, <%=request("first")%> <%=request("last")%>.<BR>
Your Social Security Number is <%=request("ssn")%> and you make
$<%=request("salary")%>.
</BODY></HTML>
```

Figure 7-16 Process form using Active Server Pages

The first line in Figure 7-16 states that the ASP code in the file uses a programming language called VBScript, which is based on Visual Basic, a language that is commonly used in desktop applications. (The other choice is JScript, which is related to the Java programming language.) Just as HTML code is enclosed in angle brackets (< >), so ASP code is enclosed in <% %>. The important part of the code takes information received from the form and displays it. The <%=request("first")%> code performs this task. Notice how the text between the quotation marks matches the text box names specified in form.htm.

Before you test the application, you should understand all the steps involved in processing the pages from a conceptual point of view. A form is processed as follows:

1. In a browser, the user requests the page that contains the form, such as form.htm. Because the filename ends in .htm, the Web server sends the file to the browser without processing it.
2. The user enters data in three text boxes.
3. The user clicks the Submit button, which sends the information in the form, such as Social Security number, first name, last name, and salary, to a Web page called ProcessForm.asp.
4. ProcessForm.asp takes the information sent from the form and processes it. Because the filename ends in .asp, the Web server sends the file to a program that can process ASP code. In this case, processing involves formatting the information and sending it back to the user. Other forms are processed by connecting to a database and updating it or extracting information from it and then producing a report.

To create the form test application in IIS in Windows:

1. Start Notepad as you usually do. Click **File** on the menu bar, and then click **Open**. In the Open dialog box, click the **Files of type** list arrow, click **All Files**, navigate to the Chapter7 folder on your Data Disk, and then open **form.htm**.
2. Replace the fourth line with the following statement:
   <form action=ProcessForm.asp>
3. Click **File** on the menu bar, and then click **Save As** to save the file.
4. Navigate to the root of your Web server, which is \inetpub\wwwroot. Change the file type to ***.*** (or **All Files**), and then click **Save**.
5. Close Notepad.
6. Use Windows Explorer to copy **ProcessForm.asp** from the Chapter7 folder on your Data Disk to \inetpub\wwwroot.

To test the ASP application in Windows:

1. Start Internet Explorer.
2. In the Address text box, type **http://localhost/form.htm** and then press **Enter**. If a dialog box opens containing a Try Again button, click the **Try Again** button.
3. The form opens. Fill in the form as shown in Figure 7-17 and then click **Submit**. Figure 7-18 shows the resulting Web page.

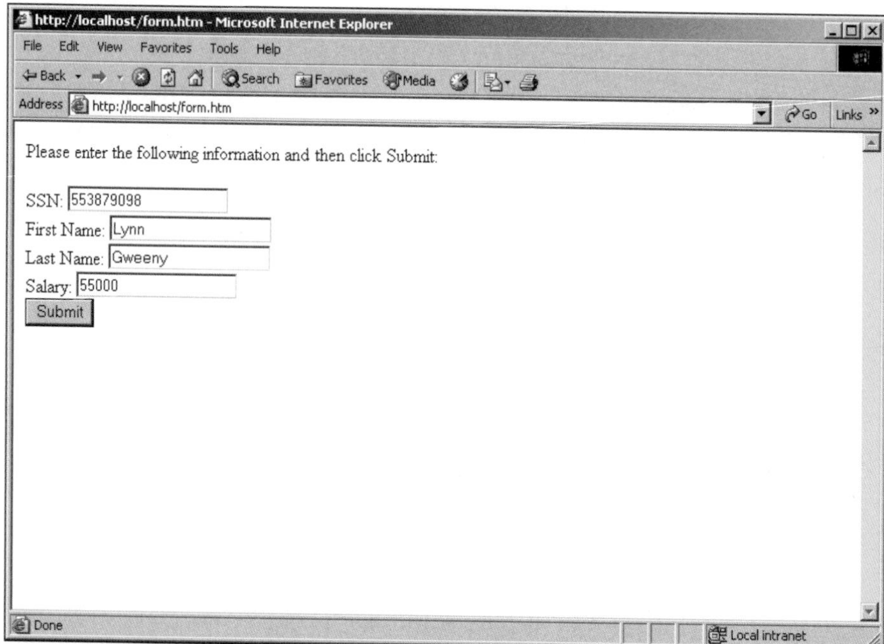

Figure 7-17 Employee form

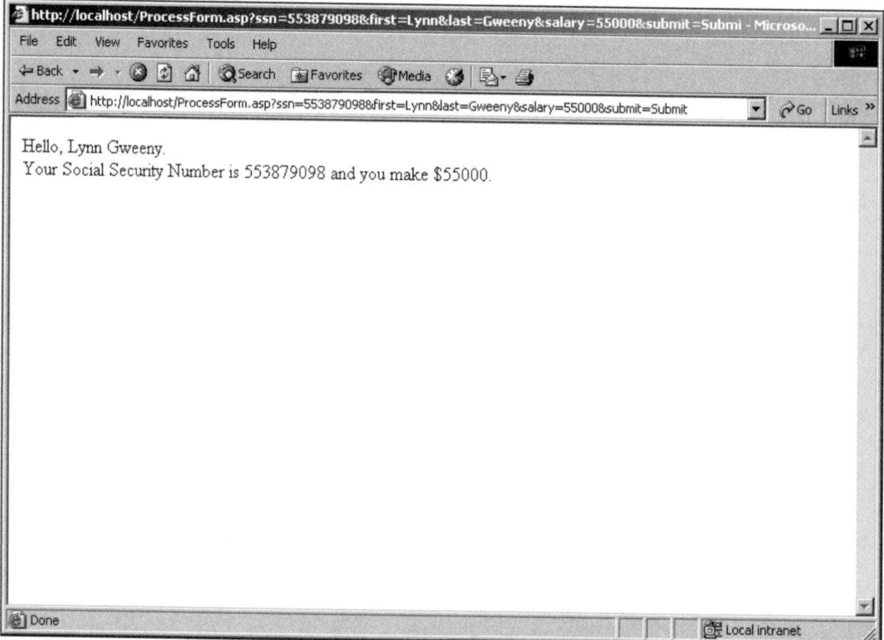

Figure 7-18 Output of form after clicking Submit

The Address text box in Figure 7-18 shows how browsers communicate with Web servers. When you click the Submit button on the form, the browser pairs the text box names in form.htm with the data you entered in the form, such as Lynn Gweeny's name and Social Security number. In the Address text box, the browser adds the text box name and data pairs to the file that form.htm indicates should process the form, separating the pairs with an ampersand (&). Then the browser sends this information to the Web server so it can process the information and return the results, which the browser displays. No matter how complex a form, the browser always uses name/value pairs to transmit the form information to the Web server to be processed. You can simulate the use of the form by mimicking how the browser communicates with the Web server. If you typed the following into the browser, the Web server would return the information shown in Figure 7-19:

```
http://localhost/ProcessForm.asp?first=Bob&ssn=5&salary=23
```


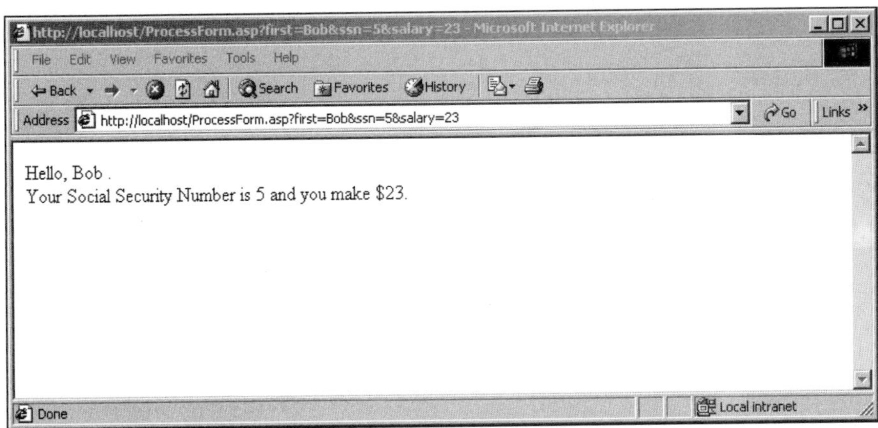

Figure 7-19 Output based on manual input

Note that the order of the name/value pairs in the Address text box has changed. The pairs can appear in any order.

Not all forms process data by sending it to a Web server as part of the URL. In Chapter 6, you learned how the browser communicates with the Web server. In the default method, the browser uses a **GET** command to request an HTML file. If the browser uses **GET**, it adds the name/value pairs to the URL. However, a URL can contain no more than about 2,000 characters, so the **GET** command is not useful for long or complex forms. In such cases, a browser can instead use the **POST** command, which stores the name/value pairs in a file that is sent back to the Web server instead of being added to the URL. No limitation applies to the size of the form if you use the **POST** command. To cause the form to use the **POST** command, you would change the fourth line in form.htm to the following statement:

```
<form method=post action=ProcessForm.asp>
```

Note that Web servers can process forms slightly faster using the default **GET** command. Also, because the **GET** command is limited as to the length of input, it avoids one problem associated with the **POST** command—an attacker cannot send an unusually long request to the Web server in an effort to penetrate it. Because of the potential problem with the **POST** command, many Web hosting companies allow only the **GET** command to be used with their systems.

Active Server Pages.NET

In 2001, ASP.NET became available through the release of .NET Framework, a new-generation programming environment for IIS. .NET Framework can be added to Windows 2000 and is already integrated into Windows 2003 Server.

ASP.NET generates Web pages much faster than does ASP. Whereas ASP executes a script that you write, ASP.NET compiles a script before running it. Compiling the script converts it into an executable file, which the computer can process more quickly. ASP.NET also takes the extra step of caching the output, which improves the response time of the Web server. As an example, suppose a Web application produces a Web page for company employees that lists today's important events. These events are stored in a database. If the page is accessed 100 times per day, it would be inefficient to search the database and reproduce the Web page 100 times. Instead, ASP.NET produces the page from the database and saves it. The next time someone requests it, the Web server can send the page directly from the cache instead of processing the request each time. ASP applications converted to run as ASP.NET applications typically serve three to five times as many pages.

The programming model of ASP.NET is also superior to that of ASP. In ASP, you must explicitly state every minor detail of programming. In ASP.NET, the language helps you with the program. As an example, suppose you want to produce a report. As you will see in the section on database connectivity, ASP.NET lets you produce a detailed report with a single command. It also helps you avoid the problem of code that runs well in one browser, but not another. Because Internet Explorer, Netscape, AOL, Opera, Konqueror, and other browsers are different, it can be difficult to produce pages that act the same no matter which browser is used. Suppose you want to display a calendar so a user can select a date. In ASP, you must write a script that will be compatible with all the browsers. In ASP.NET, you simply state that you want to include a calendar component. ASP.NET determines which browser the user has and generates code that is compatible with that particular browser. Also, you may want to validate data in a form, such as by restricting input on a text box to a number between 100 and 5,000. For data validation in ASP, programmers often had to create complex and detailed JavaScript code that was tested across multiple browsers. With ASP.NET, you just describe the type of validation you want and ASP.NET ensures that the form is validated correctly.

The downside to ASP.NET is that with increased capabilities comes increased complexity in many areas. Although you can specify a report in a single line, the overall program still takes quite a few lines of code. Learning to program in ASP.NET can also be more difficult than programming in ASP. However, ASP.NET programs can be more easily created with Visual Studio.NET, a product from Microsoft. Such programs also do not reflect exactly the communication between the Web server and the browser. This characteristic can be advantageous in that ASP.NET hides standard operations that must be explicitly stated in ASP, but it makes it more difficult for programmers to write code that performs very specific tasks. Indeed, you will see more similarities between ASP, PHP, and Perl than between ASP and ASP.NET.

ASP.NET supports more than 25 languages, including VB .NET, C# (similar to C++), and J# (similar to Java). An experienced ASP.NET programmer can easily move from one language to another because you perform tasks the same way in each language. For example, the command to validate a text box on a form or to produce a report is the same whether you are using VB .NET or J# .NET.

Figure 7-20 shows an ASP.NET application that processes employee information in a form. Although in ASP you describe in detail what is sent to the browser, in ASP.NET it is more accurate to say that you are describing what you want processed. When a user requests the page, ASP.NET produces a form that is sent to the browser. Notice that the form statement in ASP.NET differs from the one in ASP because it does not contain `action=`. The text boxes are also different. ASP.NET generates the HTML necessary to turn the description of the form into something that is understandable by all browsers.

The bottom of the page contains the code **<span id="Message" runat="server"/>**. This statement indicates where the output will be placed. When a user clicks the Submit button, processing starts with the code at the top of the page. The line below **Sub Submit_Click**... begins with **Message.InnerHtml**. This reference is related to **id="Message"** in the HTML span statement. This code also displays the same message as produced by ProcessForm.asp (such as "Hello, Lynn Gweeny. Your Social Security Number is 553879098 and you make $55000").

```
<HTML>
<script language="VB" runat="server">
   Sub Submit_Click(Sender As Object, E As EventArgs)
      Message.InnerHtml = "Hello, " & first.text & " " & last.text & _
      ". Your Social Security Number is " & ssn.text & _
      " and you make $" & salary.text
    End Sub
</script>
<BODY>
Please enter the following information and then click Submit:<BR>
  <form runat="server">
SSN: <asp:TextBox id=ssn runat=server/><BR>
First Name: <asp:TextBox id=first runat=server/><BR>
Last Name: <asp:TextBox id=last runat=server/><BR>
Salary: <asp:TextBox id=salary runat=server/><BR>
<input type=submit OnServerClick="Submit_Click" value="Submit"
runat=server>
</form>
<BR>
<span id="Message" runat="server"/>
</BODY>
</HTML>
```

Figure 7-20 Form and output using ASP.NET

Figure 7-21 begins to show the true power of ASP.NET. This ASP.NET file includes validation statements so you can verify that users enter something in the text box for the first name, and it indicates that an acceptable salary value is in the range of 12000 to 85000. In the validation modules, you describe how you want to validate data and let ASP.NET determine how it will achieve the results across different browsers. In Figure 7-21, the validation statements are shaded. The first shaded statement begins with `<asp:RequiredFieldValidator`, which indicates that you are describing a text box that needs to have some text in it. The statement `id="rfvfirst"` uniquely identifies this validator. The statement `runat="server"`, seen in many areas, basically states that ASP.NET will control the code. The statement `ControlToValidate="first"` notifies ASP.NET that the text box called "first" is to be validated. The statement `Display="Dynamic"` states that the error will be displayed where it occurred. The statement `* You must enter a first name` is the actual error message. The statement `</asp:RequiredFieldValidator>` ends the description of the validation. As you can see in the second validation, it is a `RangeValidator`. With such a validator, you specify a minimum value and a maximum value.

```
<HTML>
<script language="VB" runat="server">
Sub Submit_Click(Sender As Object, E As EventArgs)
    Message.InnerHtml = "Hello, " & first.text & " " & last.text & _
    ". Your Social Security Number is " & ssn.text & _
    " and you make $" & salary.text
    End Sub
</script>

<BODY>
Please enter the following information and then click Submit:<BR>
  <form runat="server">
SSN: <asp:TextBox id=ssn runat=server/><BR>
First Name: <asp:TextBox id=first runat=server/>
<asp:RequiredFieldValidator id="rfvfirst" runat="server"
  ControlToValidate="first" Display="Dynamic">
  * You must enter a first name</asp:RequiredFieldValidator><BR>
Last Name: <asp:TextBox id=last runat=server/><BR>
Salary: <asp:TextBox id=salary runat=server/>
<asp:RangeValidator id="rvsalary" runat="server"
  ControlToValidate="salary" Type="Integer"
  MinimumValue="12000"  MaximumValue="85000" Display="Dynamic">
  * Salary must be between 12000 and 85000</asp:RangeValidator><BR>
<input type=submit OnServerClick="Submit_Click" value="Submit"
runat=server>
</form>
<BR>
<span id="Message" runat="server"/>
</BODY>
</HTML>
```

Figure 7-21 Form validation using ASP.NET

Installing .NET Framework in Windows 2000

Although .NET Framework is an integral part of Windows 2003, in Windows 2000 you must install it by using the .NET Framework SDK. Before you work with an ASP.NET example in Windows 2000 in this chapter, you will install .NET Framework. To install .NET Framework, you need to install the latest Service Pack as described in Chapter 3.

To install .NET Framework on Windows 2000:

1. Insert the .NET Framework SDK CD into the CD drive. The Welcome to the Microsoft .NET Framework SDK HTML page opens in your browser. See Figure 7-22. This HTML page is read directly from the CD. (If not, open default.htm on the CD.) A Web server or connection to the Internet is not required.

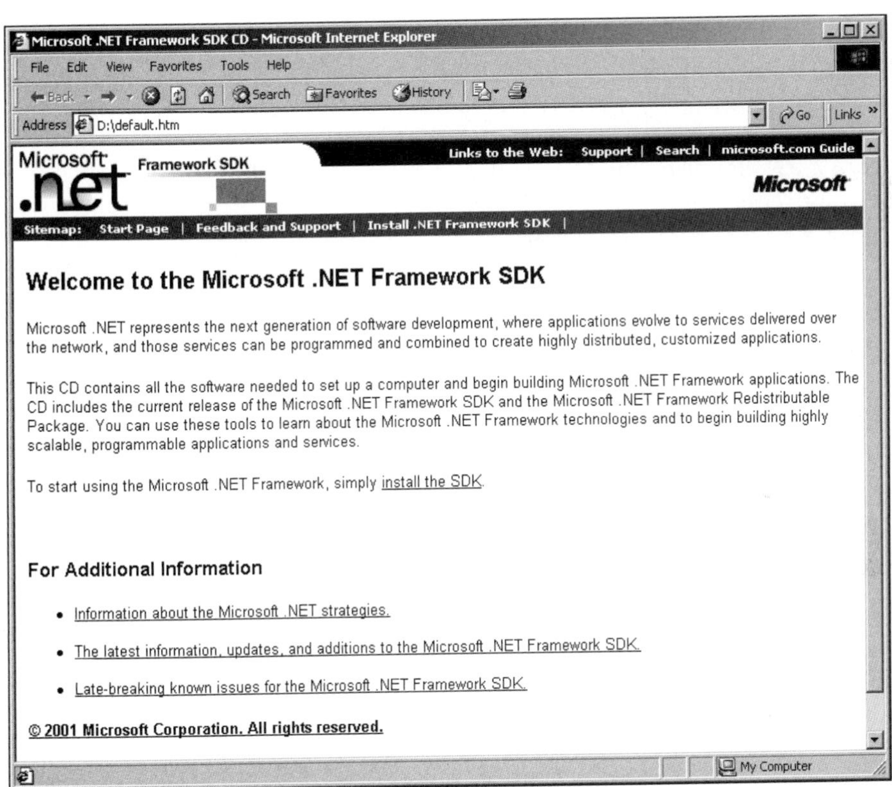

Figure 7-22 Microsoft .NET Framework SDK Web page

2. Click the **install the SDK** link to start the installation process. The Installing the Microsoft .NET Framework SDK HTML page opens, listing the items you need to install the SDK. You should have already installed IIS. You have not installed Internet Explorer 6.0, however, so you can start with Step 3. See Figure 7-23.

3. Click **\IE60**. A folder opens that contains the setup program for Internet Explorer. See Figure 7-24.

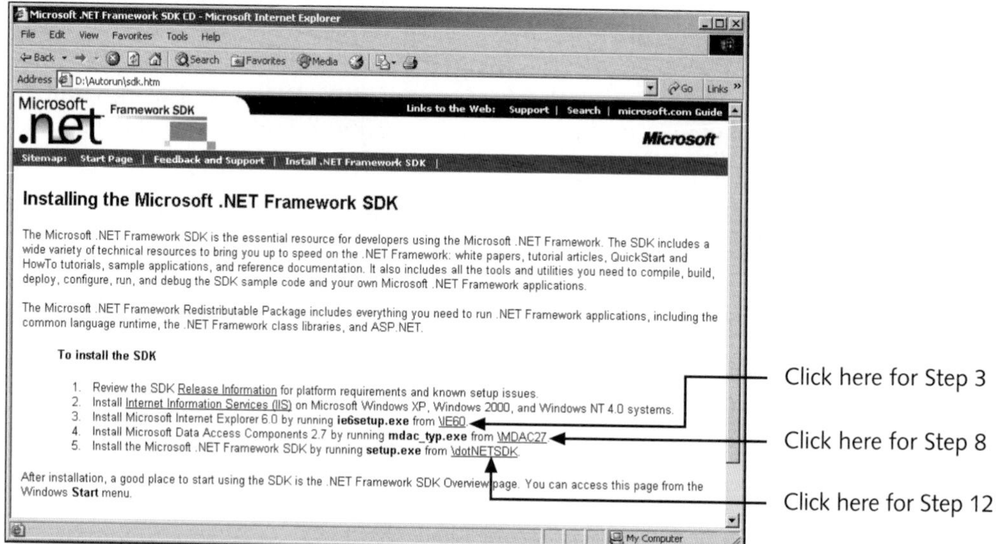

Figure 7-23 Installing the Microsoft .NET Framework SDK HTML page

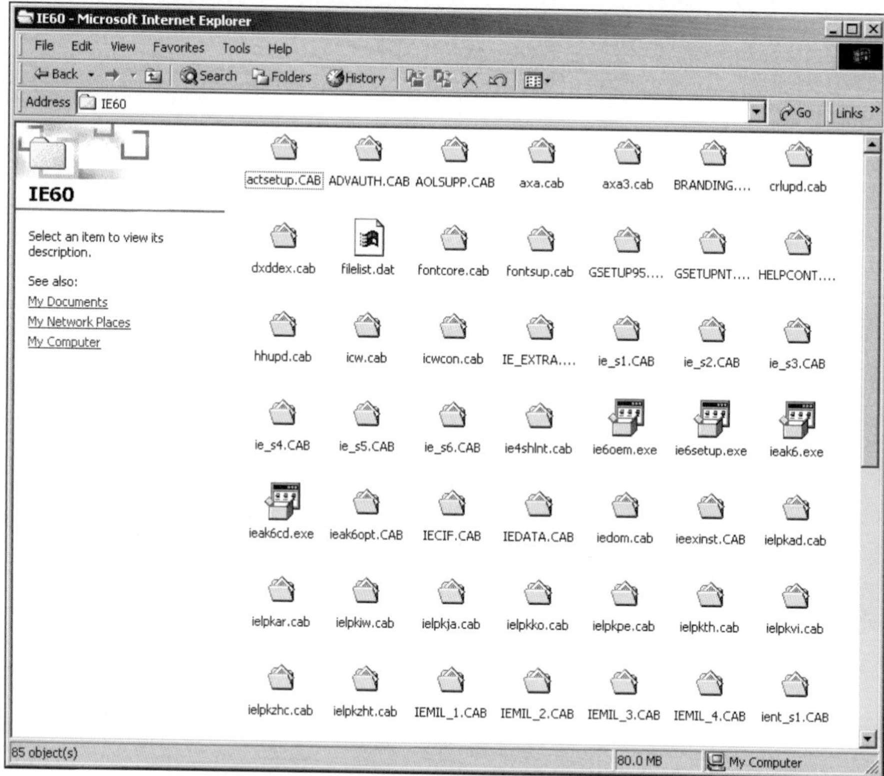

Figure 7-24 \IE60 folder in Windows Explorer

4. Double-click **ie6setup.exe**. The Welcome to Setup for Internet Explorer and Internet Tools dialog box opens.
5. Click the **I accept the agreement** option button, and then click **Next**. The Windows Update: Internet Explorer and Internet Tools dialog box opens.
6. Click **Next**. After a few minutes, the Progress dialog box opens, showing you what is being installed and how much of the installation is complete. The Restart Computer dialog box opens. Click **Finish** to exit the wizard and restart your computer. When the computer restarts and you log on as the administrator, a message box states that it is updating Windows and completes three steps: Browsing Services, Internet Tools, and System Services.
7. Resume the installation process by opening Windows Explorer, navigating to the root of the .NET Framework CD, and double-clicking **default.htm**. The HTML page in Figure 7-22 opens again. Click **install the SDK**. You return to Step 4 in the installation process shown earlier in Figure 7-23.
8. Click **\MDAC27** to install Microsoft Data Access Components. A Windows Explorer window opens containing a single file. Double-click the **mdac_typ** icon to install the components. The Microsoft Data Access Components 2.7 Setup dialog box opens.
9. Click the **I accept all of the terms of the preceding license agreement** check box, and then click **Next**. After a few moments, the Detecting in-use Files dialog box opens, stating that it needs to shut down the SQL Server tasks. Click **Next** to shut down the tasks and let the installation proceed.
10. Click **Finish** to install the Microsoft Data Access Components software. This process may take a minute or so. The Restarting the System dialog box opens. Accept the default of Let setup restart the system now by clicking **Finish**.
11. When the computer restarts and you log on, open Windows Explorer, navigate to the root of the .NET Framework CD, double-click **default.htm**, and then click **install the SDK**.
12. Click **\dotNETSDK** to install the .NET Framework. Windows Explorer opens to display the contents of the dotNETSDK folder.
13. Double-click the **setup** file icon to start the .NET Framework SDK installation. When the Microsoft .NET Framework SDK Setup dialog box opens, click **Yes** to install the SDK. If a dialog box asks you to allow it to update the Windows installer components, click **Yes** to update the components. The .NET Framework SDK wizard starts.
14. Click **Next** to continue with the wizard. The License Agreement dialog box opens. Click the **I accept the agreement** option button, and then click **Next**. The Install Options dialog box opens. See Figure 7-25.

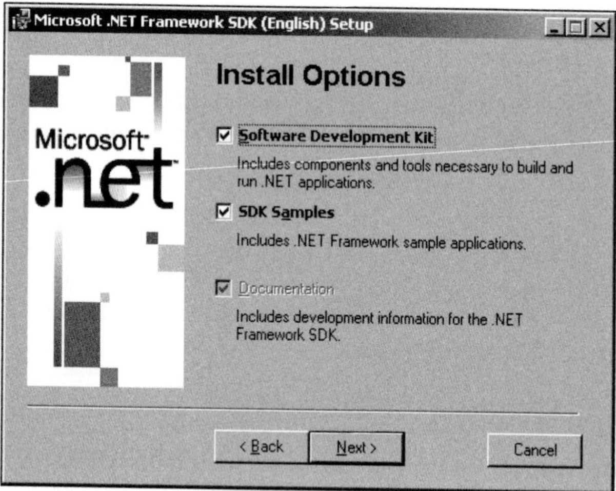

Figure 7-25 Install Options dialog box

15. Click **Next** to accept the defaults of installing the SDK and samples. The Destination Folder dialog box opens.
16. Click **Next** to accept the default location. The Installing Components dialog box opens and displays the progress of the installation. This process may take a few minutes. When the setup is finished and a dialog box opens, click **OK** to exit the wizard.
17. Restart the computer.

Now that you have installed .NET Framework, you can use ASP.NET to perform programming tasks on your IIS Web server.

To show the effects of validation in ASP.NET in Windows:

1. Use Windows Explorer to copy **ProcessFormVal.aspx** from the Chapter7 folder of your Data Disk to **\inetpub\wwwroot**.
2. In Internet Explorer, type **http://localhost/ProcessFormVal.aspx** as the URL, and then press **Enter**.
3. In the SSN text box, type **553879098**. Leave the First Name text box blank. In The Last Name text box, type **Gweeny**. In the Salary text box, type **10000**. Click **Submit**. Your browser should resemble Figure 7-26.

Programming for Apache

Two of the most popular programming languages available for Apache are Perl and **PHP Hypertext Protocol** (**PHP**). The original Web programming language, Perl is still used today. PHP is a relative newcomer but its ease of use has helped it gain market share over the years. Overall, PHP is easier to learn than Perl, and it lets you quickly create sophisticated applications.

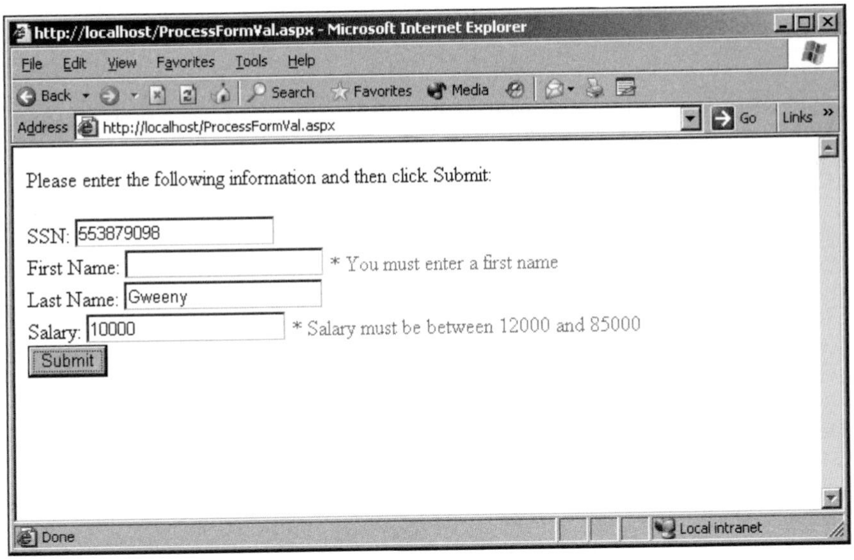

Figure 7-26 Form validation in ASP.NET

The Java-based programming languages let you work in both a desktop environment and the Web environment. **JavaServer Pages (JSP)**, for example, is similar in structure to ASP. However, with ASP, the same text scripts are processed every time the page is requested. With JSP, the pages are converted to Java servlets and compiled. When code is compiled, the resulting file can be processed more quickly by the computer.

CGI and Perl Programming

CGI allows you to use any language compatible with the protocol, such as Perl, shell scripts, or C. Figure 7-27 shows the contents of a shell script named hello.cgi, which displays "Hello, World" on a browser.

```
#!/bin/sh
echo "Content-Type: text/html"
echo
echo "<html><body>"
echo "Hello, World"
echo "</body></html>"
```

Figure 7-27 Displaying "Hello, World" with a shell script

The first line of the code identifies the program that will process the file. The location of the shell script program "/bin/sh" follows the "#!" (pronounced "she-bang"). The next line tells the browser what to expect—in this case, "text/HTML." The following blank line is important because it separates the header information from the actual HTML to be displayed by the browser.

Now you can learn about the CGI configuration of the Web server. Because CGI scripts can potentially access the operating system, you want to isolate the directories that can process scripts. Apache installs a virtual directory called /cgi-bin by default. Figure 7-28 shows the lines in the httpd.conf file that specify the /cgi-bin virtual directory, which is isolated from other directories and is designed to run scripts, as indicated in the line that begins `ScriptAlias /cgi-bin/` and is followed by the location of the directory.

```
ScriptAlias /cgi-bin/ "/var/www/cgi-bin/"
<Directory "/var/www/cgi-bin">
    AllowOverride None
    Options None
    Order allow,deny
    Allow from all
</Directory>
```

Figure 7-28 CGI configuration in httpd.conf

In addition to isolating the CGI script directory, you must set the file permissions of the CGI scripts. Recall that users connect to the Apache Web server by using apache as the user name. The apache user is allowed to access HTML pages on the Web site. For CGI scripts, you must manually set the file permissions to allow the apache user to execute them. Recall from Chapter 5 that you can use the `chmod` command to alter the file permissions. By default, when you create a file such as hello.cgi, the file permissions are 644 (rw-r—r—). This means that although you can read and write to the file, no one—including you—can execute the script. To allow Web users to execute the script (but not write to the file), you can change the permissions to 755 (rwxr-xr-x), which you do in the following steps.

To display "Hello, World" using a shell script in Apache on Linux:

1. Copy the **hello.cgi** file from the Chapter7 directory of the Data Disk to the **/var/www/cgi-bin** directory using Konqueror.
2. In a terminal window, type **cd /var/www/cgi-bin** and then press **Enter** to access the cgi-bin directory. Type **chmod 755 hello.cgi** and then press **Enter** to allow the script to be executed.
3. To display the contents of the CGI script, open the Konqueror Web browser, enter **http://localhost/cgi-bin/hello.cgi** as the URL, and then press **Enter**. The browser displays "Hello, World."

Perl is a useful language because its strength lies in processing files, which is what a Web server needs to do. For many years, Perl was one of the few languages to run well on any server, which made it a good choice for creating applications that can be run on Microsoft, Linux, and UNIX servers. Many large, Web-based applications that support multiple servers use Perl.

Figure 7-29 shows a Perl script that processes the form.htm shown earlier in Figure 7-15.

```
#!/usr/bin/perl
use CGI;
my $cgi=new CGI;
print "Content-Type: text/html\n\n";
print "<html><body>";
print "Hello ",$cgi->param("first")," ",$cgi->param("last"),".<BR>\n";
print "Your Social Security Number is ",$cgi->param("ssn")," \n";
print " and you make \$",$cgi->param("salary");
print "</body></html>";
```

Figure 7-29 Perl script to display contents of form

The first line, `#!/usr/bin/perl`, indicates that the Perl program that processes the script is located in the /usr/bin directory. The first line turns the code into a Perl script, so that everything after the first line must be based on the Perl language. Perl statements end in semicolons. Lines 2 and 3—`use CGI;` and `my $cgi=new CGI;`—tell Perl to use the CGI interface to process forms. The fourth line—`print "Content-Type: text/html\n\n";`—indicates that the content is HTML text, meaning the information to process is an HTML page. The `\n` stands for new line and causes the output to advance to the next line. The two `\n` codes in line 4 create a blank line that is needed to separate headers from HTML. Line 6 includes the Perl command `$cgi->param`, which corresponds to `request` in ASP.

To create a Perl script to process form.htm in Apache in Linux:

1. Copy **form.htm** from the Chapter7 directory of the Data Disk to the root directory of your Web server, which is /var/www/html.
2. Use KEdit to change the fourth line to **<form action=/cgi-bin/ProcessForm.cgi>**, and then save the **form.htm** file.
3. Use Konqueror to copy **ProcessForm.cgi** from the Chapter7 directory of the Data Disk to the /var/www/cgi-bin directory.
4. Change the file permissions to give the file execute permissions. In a terminal window, type **cd /var/www/cgi-bin** and then press **Enter** to change to the cgi-bin directory. Type **chmod 755 ProcessForm.cgi** and then press **Enter** to allow the script to be executed.
5. Open a browser, type **http://localhost/form.htm**, and then press **Enter**.
6. Complete the form with the following text:

   SSN: **553879098**
   First Name: **Lynn**
   Last Name: **Gweeny**
   Salary: **55000**
7. Click **Submit** to see the resulting Web page, shown in Figure 7-30.

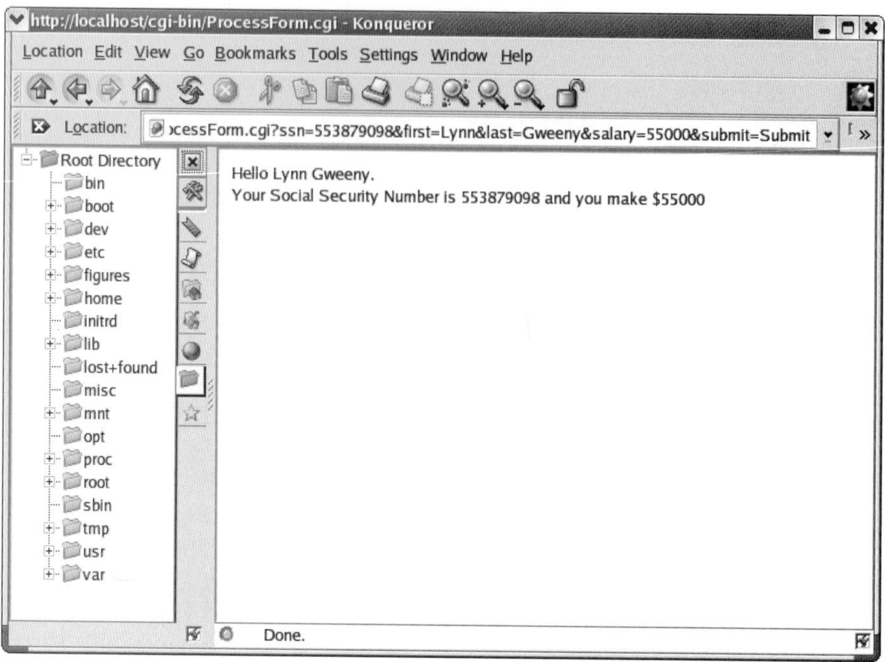

Figure 7-30 Results of Perl script

Programming with Databases

When you use a program to work with the data in a database, such as to retrieve the information and then display it, the first step is to connect to the database. The second step is to send a command to the database in the form of an SQL statement. If the SQL statement is used to add or change data, you do not need to perform any other database steps. If the SQL statement retrieves data, then the third step is to process the data. Each step is described in detail in the following sections.

Connecting to the Database

With so many DBMSs and programming languages, operating systems need a common way to bring them together. Microsoft uses **Open Database Connectivity** (**ODBC**) and its modern relative **OLE DB (Object Linking and Embedding Database)**. ODBC acts as an intermediary between the DBMSs and the programming languages. The producer of each DBMS creates software that adheres to the ODBC standard. Programming languages can then incorporate commands to connect to ODBC instead of commands to connect to each individual DBMS. If a programming language is compatible with ODBC, it can use any DBMS that has ODBC drivers. ODBC drivers are also available for Microsoft Excel and text files. The advantage of ODBC and OLE DB is that, as a programmer, you just have to learn one, simplified way to connect to and use a database, whether it is based on Microsoft Access, Microsoft SQL Server, or Oracle.

Linux uses **Java Database Connectivity** (**JDBC**) for the Java programming environment (you can also use JDBC on a Windows server). JDBC works in much the same way as ODBC. When JDBC is used in a Windows environment, you can use a JDBC-ODBC bridge to allow Java programs to access the DBMSs supported by ODBC.

The main disadvantage of both ODBC and JDBC is that the extra layer of software between the DBMS and programming language decreases performance. Some major DBMS producers, such as SQL Server and Oracle, also produce software that is specifically designed for particular programming environments. You will see an example of it when you install special drivers to allow PHP to access MySQL databases in the "Database Programming with PHP" section.

Sending SQL Commands to the Database

You typically use two types of SQL commands in programming. The first type receives data from one or more tables in a database. For example, you can use the `select` SQL statement to request a list of all employees or only those employees with a last name of Sampaio; the latter statement would be `select * from employee with lastname='Sampaio'`. You can use the result of such a SQL statement to produce a report, make calculations, or update another table in the same database or in another database.

The second type of SQL command changes data in a database. You can use such commands to insert, update, and delete data. Often, you will use HTML to create a form to focus on what needs to be changed. For example, you could create a form to prompt users for the Social Security number of the employee whom they want to delete. Instead of displaying the Social Security number as you did in a previous example, however, you would use this number in a SQL command to delete the employee information from the employee table. The following statement deletes an employee with a Social Security number of 345345433: `delete from employee where ssn= '345345433'`. Forms are commonly used when you register at a Web site. That is, you fill out a form, click a button, and send your registration information to the Web server. The Web server takes this information, embeds it into SQL statements, and then executes the statements to add the contents of the form to a table.

Processing Data from a Database

Processing data from a database is similar to processing data from a form except that a form gives you just one set of data. With a database, the SQL statement could retrieve thousands, or even millions, of sets of data, called **records** or, more appropriately, **rows**. To process each row of data in a similar manner, you use a loop in your program. A **loop** performs a sequence of instructions until a particular condition occurs. The sequence of instructions describes how to process each row. The particular condition is most often reaching the last of the rows retrieved.

Database Programming with ASP

Now that you are familiar with how to use SQL statements in programs to process data from a database, you are ready to write a program in ASP to produce a report. Figure 7-31 shows a report based on the SQL Server table that you created earlier in the chapter. Figure 7-32 shows the report.asp file, which contains the ASP code necessary to create the report. Notice that the report does not have information on the department number of the employee. This example demonstrates that you can easily select the information that you want to display.

SSN	First	Last	Salary
553879098	Lynn	Gweeny	55000
623827368	Elark	Kaboom	60000
756838998	John	Doh	45000

Figure 7-31 Employee report

```
<%<\@> Language=VBScript %>
<%
set conn = server.CreateObject("adodb.connection")
Conn.open "database=hr;driver={SQL Server};server=(local);uid=sa"
set rs = conn.Execute("select ssn,firstname,lastname,salary from employee")
%>
<HTML>
<BODY>
<TABLE>
 <TR>
  <TD>SSN</TD><TD>First</TD><TD>Last</TD><TD>Salary</TD>
 </TR>
 <% do while not rs.eof%>
 <TR>
  <TD><%=rs("ssn")%></TD>
  <TD><%=rs("firstname")%></TD>
  <TD><%=rs("lastname")%></TD>
  <TD><%=rs("salary")%></TD>
 </TR>
<%
 rs.movenext 'Go to the next employee record
 loop 'Go back to the "do while" statement
%>
</TABLE>
</BODY>
</HTML>
```

Figure 7-32 ASP code to produce the employee report

The following statement creates an object variable called conn that allows you to create a connection:

```
set conn = server.CreateObject("adodb.connection")
```

A variable is a storage container for data. You can put data into the variable and then use the variable to reference the data in it. An object variable can have a large and varied amount of data associated with it. For example, the variable conn is filled with information related to creating connections. The following statement opens a connection to the employee database in SQL Server on the same server as the Web server (local) and gives it a user ID (uid) of "sa":

```
Conn.open "database=hr;driver={SQL Server};server=(local);uid=sa"
```

The following statement sends the connection a SQL statement that retrieves all the data in the table called employee. Its result is stored in an object variable called rs. This type of variable is also called a collection because it holds a collection of data. The rs object variable is used to retrieve each row of data.

```
set rs = conn.Execute("select ssn,firstname,lastname,salary from
employee")
```


The next statement begins the loop and specifies that the next statements will be processed until the end of the data is reached. Notice that you use the rs object variable. Within rs, `eof` stands for "end of file." The statement means that the program should execute the following statements if you have not reached the end of the file.

```
<% do while not rs.eof %>
```

The `rs("ssn")` line displays the Social Security number for the current employee record. Notice its similarity to the ASP command `request("ssn")` that was used to display data from the form. The rest of the statements are HTML tags used to format the report. The `<TABLE>` statement creates a table. The `<TR>` statement creates a new row in the table. The `<TD>` statement creates a new cell in the row of the table.

The following line tells the program to move to the next employee record:

```
rs.movenext 'Go to the next employee record
```

The next line indicates the end of the loop:

```
loop 'Go back to the "do while" statement
```

To produce the employee report using ASP in Windows:

1. Use Windows Explorer to copy **report.asp** from the Chapter7 folder of your Data Disk to \inetpub\wwwroot.
2. In Internet Explorer, type **http://localhost/report.asp** as the URL, and then press **Enter** to display the report. The results should resemble Figure 7-31.

Using Data Source Names

Data source names (DSNs) are connections to databases that an administrator creates on the server. Many programmers use DSNs in their ASP code. Often, programmers are not allowed physical access to the Web server. Instead, they work remotely and use a variety of techniques to send the ASP code to the Web server. When they want a connection to a database, they ask the Web administrator to create a DSN. By defining connections centrally, the administrator can change the configuration without forcing the programmers to change their ASP code.

DSNs are created in the Windows Control Panel. Their use allows detailed information about the databases, such as the IP address of the DBMS server and the passwords used, to remain isolated. However, to keep the examples in this chapter simple, you will not be using passwords to access the DBMS.

To create a DSN named humanresources in Windows:

1. In Administrative Tools, click **Data Sources (ODBC)**. The ODBC Data Source Administrator dialog box opens. See Figure 7-33. (In Windows 2000, this dialog box includes a driver for SQL Server.)

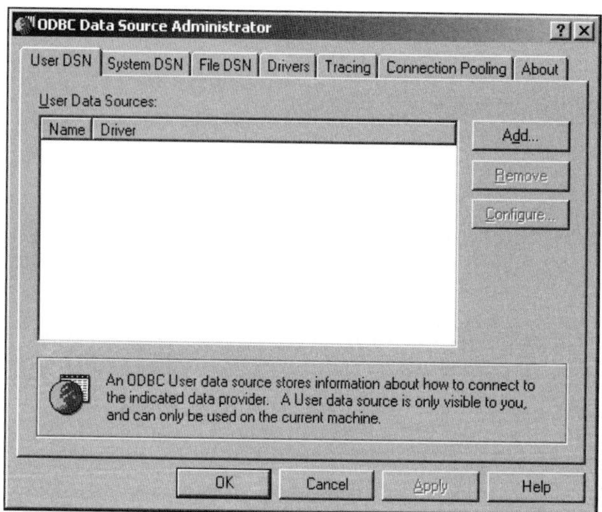

Figure 7-33 ODBC Data Source Administrator dialog box

2. Click the **System DSN** tab, and then click the **Add** button to add a System DSN so that an ASP program can use it. The Create New Data Source dialog box opens. See Figure 7-34. (The options in your dialog box might be different.)
3. You use the Create New Data Source dialog box to select the name of the database driver. Scroll down to the bottom of the list, and then click **SQL Server**. Click **Finish**.
4. The Create a New Data Source to SQL Server dialog box opens. You use this dialog box to create the name that programs accessing the DSN will recognize. In the Name text box, type **humanresources**. The Server text box associates the DSN with an instance of SQL Server. For the server, click the **Server** list arrow, and make sure **(local)** is selected. See Figure 7-35.

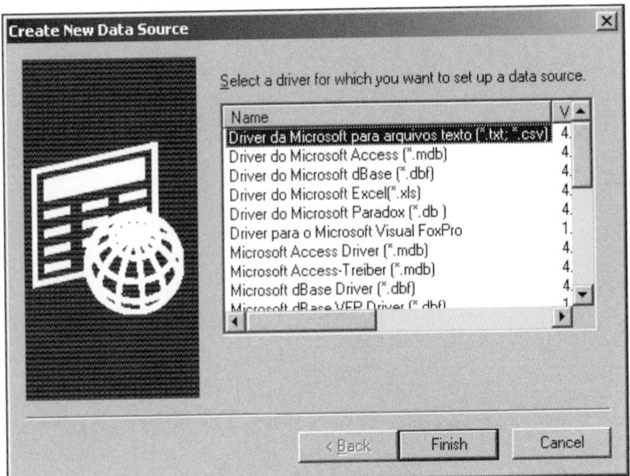

Figure 7-34 Create New Data Source dialog box

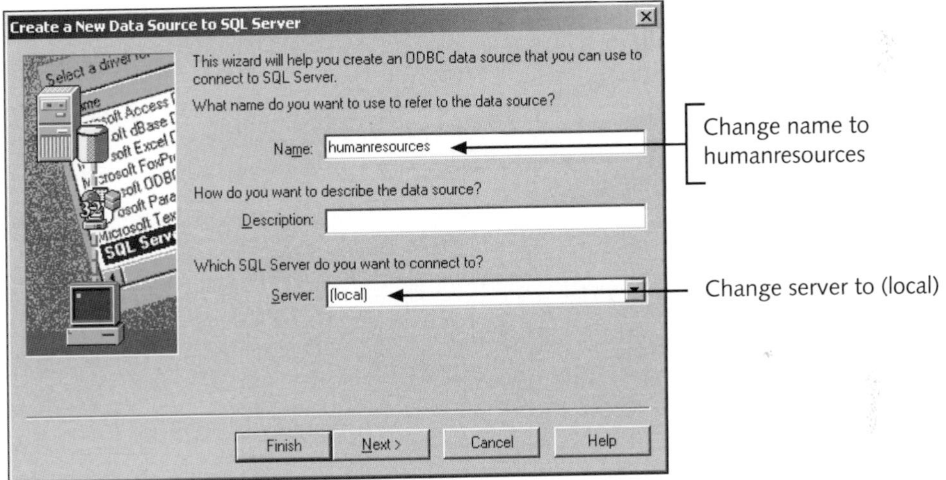

Figure 7-35 Create a New Data Source to SQL Server dialog box

5. Click **Next**. The dialog box to verify the authenticity of the login ID appears. Click the **With SQL Server authentication using a login ID and password entered by the user** option button. In the Login ID text box, type **sa**. See Figure 7-36.

6. Click **Next**. In the next Create a New Data Source to SQL Server dialog box, you specify the name of the default database. Click the **Change the default database to:** check box, click the corresponding list arrow, scroll up, and then click **hr** to select the hr database. See Figure 7-37.

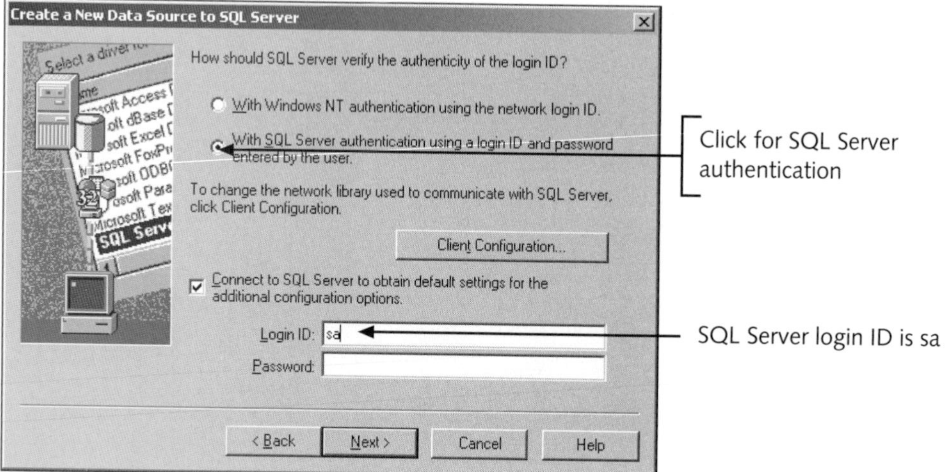

Figure 7-36 Verify authenticity of the login ID

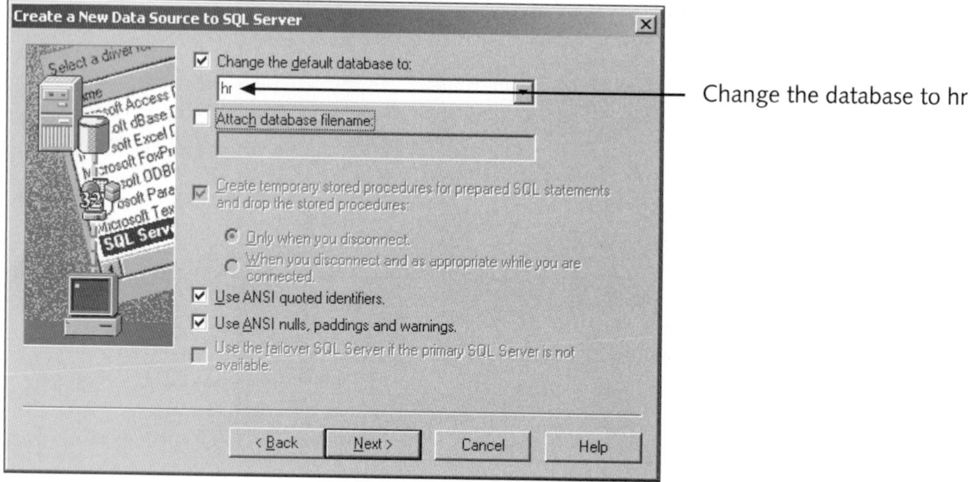

Figure 7-37 Specifying the name of the database

7. Click **Next**. You can change the language of system messages, set log options, use strong encryption for data, and use regional settings, but you typically should keep the defaults.
8. Click **Finish** to save the changes. A summary of the configuration appears, as shown in Figure 7-38. Your configuration information might be different.
9. Click **Test Data Source** to test the connection. You should see something similar to Figure 7-39.

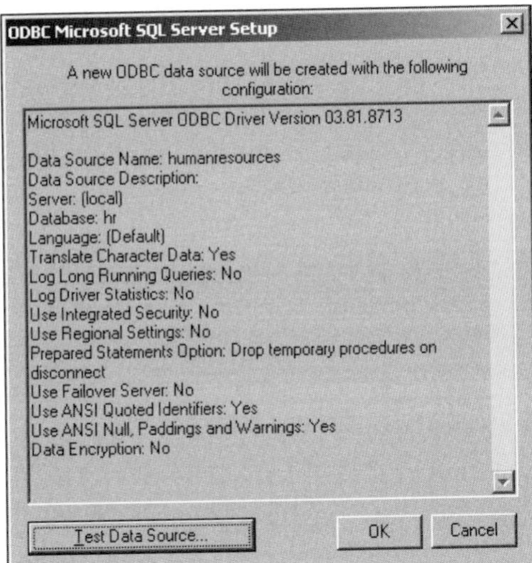

Figure 7-38 Configuration summary

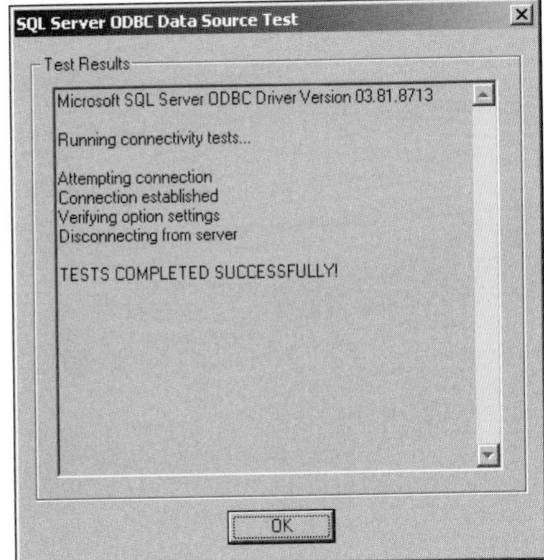

Figure 7-39 Results of testing the DSN

10. Click **OK** to close the dialog box, click **OK** to close the ODBC setup, and then click **OK** to close the ODBC Data Source Administrator dialog box.
11. Now that you have a DSN, you can change the fourth line in report.asp (shown earlier in Figure 7-32) to the following:

```
Conn.open "DSN=humanresources;uid=sa"
```

12. In Internet Explorer, type **http://localhost/report.asp** as the URL, and then press **Enter** to display the report.

The report.asp file then creates the same report as before. Now if the hr database changes to a different server, you do not have to change report.asp, just the DSN configuration. This simplicity can be a significant advantage because many files could contain a reference to the hr database.

Although DSNs make life easier for the programmer and give more control to the administrator, they do have two disadvantages. First, opening a connection is slower when you have a DSN because it introduces another layer of software. Second, DSNs can cause administrative problems. For example, a programmer may need to create a new DSN or change a DSN outside your normal working hours.

Database Programming with ASP.NET

As you have learned, ASP.NET makes common tasks, such as producing reports, easier to perform. Although you complete more steps in ASP.NET when specifying the data for the report, the report itself can be reduced to a single statement. The code in Figure 7-40 produces a report similar to the one shown in Figure 7-31.

```
<%@ Import Namespace="System.Data" %>
<%@ Import Namespace="System.Data.SqlClient" %>
<html>
<script language="VB" runat="server">
Sub Page_Load(Sender As Object, E As EventArgs)
Dim ds As DataSet
Dim conn As SqlConnection
Dim cmd As SqlDataAdapter
ds = new DataSet()
conn = New SqlConnection("server=(local);database=hr;uid=sa")
cmd = New SqlDataAdapter("select * from employee", conn)
cmd.Fill(ds, "Employees")
DG1.DataSource=ds.Tables("Employees").DefaultView
DG1.DataBind()
End Sub
</script>
<body>
<ASP:DataGrid id="DG1" runat="server"/>
</body>
</html>
```

Figure 7-40 ASP.NET code to create an employee report

The code following `Page_Load` is processed when the browser requests the page. Although the syntax is different from ASP, some similarities are apparent. The line `conn = New SqlConnection("server=(local);database=hr;uid=sa")` defines the connection. The line `cmd = New SqlDataAdapter("select * from employee", conn)` defines the data to be retrieved from the database.

The following two lines fill the report (DataGrid) with data:

```
cmd.Fill(ds,"Employees")
DG1.DataSource=ds.Tables("Employees").DefaultView
```

The next line displays the report:

```
DG1.DataBind()
```

So far, it is difficult to see the advantage of ASP.NET. The real advantage in this program actually comes in the definition of the report: `<ASP:DataGrid id="DG1" runat="server"/>`. That single line replaces the 16 lines in Figure 7-31 between <BODY> and </BODY> and eliminates the possibility of making errors in those 16 lines. Using ASP.NET offers other advantages as well. For example, if you change the `select` statement to retrieve everything except the salary, ASP.NET would automatically adjust the report. The DataGrid control also offers many options to alter headings, fonts, colors, columns, and other attributes. If you were using Visual Studio.NET to create this report, you could drag components from a toolbox and complete some wizards without using any coding skills.

7

A sample file on your Data Disk was created with ASP.NET and contains the employee report information. You can produce this report by displaying it in your browser.

To produce the employee report with ASP.NET on Windows:

1. Use Windows Explorer to copy **report.aspx** from the Chapter7 folder of your Data Disk to the \inetpub\wwwroot folder on your IIS server.
2. In Internet Explorer, type **http://localhost/report.aspx** and then press **Enter** to display the report. See Figure 7-41.

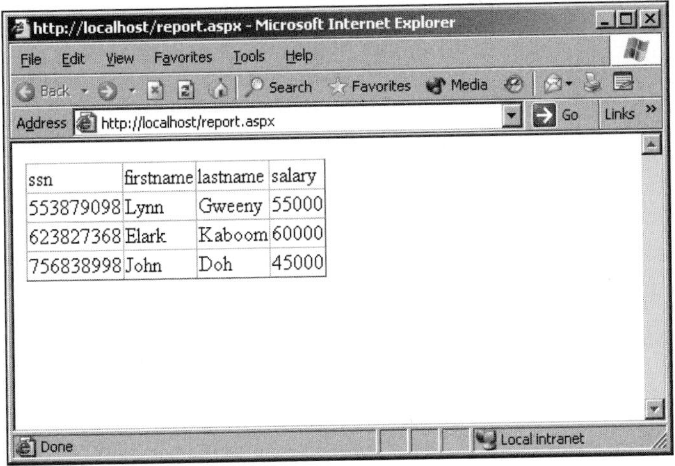

ssn	firstname	lastname	salary
553879098	Lynn	Gweeny	55000
623827368	Elark	Kaboom	60000
756838998	John	Doh	45000

Figure 7-41 Employee report created with ASP.NET

Database Programming with PHP

PHP is one of the most useful languages available for Apache and is easy to configure because it is almost ready to use when you install Apache. Although you cannot see the PHP configuration in httpd.conf, the configuration files in /etc/httpd/conf.d are included when httpd.conf is processed. One of the files in the /etc/httpd/conf.d directory is php.conf, which loads the php module and configures it. There are also configuration files for PERL and another language called Python.

Although files with a PHP extension will be processed, the tags that PHP uses are not the ones often associated with PHP. By default, only the <?php tag is allowed, though programmers frequently prefer to use the <? tag.

To allow the <? tag in PHP in Linux:

1. At the terminal prompt, type **kedit /etc/php.ini** and then press **Enter**.
2. Press **Ctrl+F** to open the Find dialog box. Type **short_open_tag**, and then click **Find**.
3. The setting to the right of the "=" shows "Off". Change Off to **On**.
4. Save the file and then exit.

Now the Apache Web server will recognize PHP files. However, PHP does not recognize a MySQL database. To force it to do so, you need to install drivers specifically for MySQL.

To add MySQL support to PHP in Linux:

1. Insert Red Hat Linux CD 3 in the CD drive.
2. In Konqueror, navigate to the **/mnt/cdrom/RedHat/RPMS** directory.
3. Scroll to and then double-click **php-mysql-4.2.2-8.0.5.i386**. Your filename may be slightly different, but should include "php-mysql."
4. A dialog box opens and displays "Completed System Preparation" after a few moments. Click **Continue**.
5. In a terminal window, restart MySQL by typing **/etc/rc.d/init.d/mysqld restart** and then pressing **Enter**.
6. Type **apachectl restart** to restart Apache.

Now you can copy the report.php file from the Chapter7 directory to /var/www/html and display it in the browser. Figure 7-42 shows the contents of the report.php file.

```
<?
$conn=mysql_connect("localhost","root","password");
$db = mysql_select_db("hr");
$ResultSet = mysql_query("select ssn,firstname,lastname,salary from emp");
?>

<html>
<body>
<TABLE>
 <TR>
  <TD>SSN</TD><TD>First</TD><TD>Last</TD><TD>Salary</TD>
 </TR>
 <? while($rs = mysql_fetch_array($ResultSet, MYSQL_ASSOC)){ ?>
 <TR>
  <TD><? echo $rs["ssn"] ?></TD>
  <TD><? echo $rs["firstname"] ?></TD>
  <TD><? echo $rs["lastname"] ?></TD>
  <TD><? echo $rs["salary"] ?></TD>
 </TR>
 <? } ?>
</table>
</body>
</html>
```


Figure 7-42 report.php tests database connectivity

Notice how similar the report.php file is to the ASP code shown in Figure 7-32. It still provides the basics of connecting to the database in lines 2 and 3, sending a query to the database in line 4, and looping through the data in lines 13 through 20.

PHP is case-sensitive, so you must match the case of database names, column names, and other text. For example, if you created the column name for first name in MySQL as "First" instead of "first", then you would have to change the line referencing it to the following:

```
<TD><? echo $rs["First"] ?></TD>
```

Chapter Summary

- Programming languages process data, allow you to create dynamic Web pages that allow their content to change, and can produce features as simple as a counter that displays the number of visitors to a Web page or as complex as a sophisticated e-commerce site. Many Web sites use programming languages to create internal business applications such as those that perform order processing.
- Database management systems organize data for processing. Relational DBMSs organize data in tables. Tables have columns that describe the characteristics of the table, such as Social Security number and salary. A primary key refers to the column or columns that uniquely define a row of data in a table. A foreign key refers to a column whose values correspond to the values of a primary key.

- The language used to communicate with DBMSs is SQL. You can use SQL commands to insert, update, and delete rows. The command to retrieve rows from a table is `select`.
- In Windows, data source names (DSNs) allow you to create an interface between the programs that access databases and the actual databases. The advantage of this approach is that you can keep the same DSN but readily change the location of the actual database.
- Although Microsoft SQL Server is a commercial product that is rather costly, MySQL is an open-source product, which means it is available for free. SQL Server uses GUIs to create databases and tables, insert data, and display data. MySQL has an interactive administrative tool that allows you to perform similar tasks.
- Web-based programming relies on browsers to display HTML forms. A programming language on the Web server processes these forms. Typical Web-based processing is simpler than the typical event-driven, client-based application.
- The original environment for Web programming is CGI. Perl is often used as the scripting language for CGI. ASP and the newer ASP.NET are designed to run very efficiently on IIS. The .NET Framework needs to be installed before you can use ASP.NET on Windows 2000.
- When Web-based programming environments access a database, their first step is to connect to the database. Their second step is to send a command, in the form of a SQL statement, to the database. If the SQL statement produces data, then the third step is to process the data. These steps are the same for virtually all DBMSs and programming languages. For DBMSs and programming languages to work together, however, you need software drivers. ODBC and JDBC are common technologies that act as go-betweens for DBMSs and programming languages.
- PHP is an easy-to-use language that is somewhat similar in structure to ASP. To make PHP available on an Apache Web server, a single line must be added to httpd.conf. To change the default <?php tag to a simpler <? tag, you must change the php.ini file. To get PHP to work with MySQL, you must install a special module called php-mysql.

REVIEW QUESTIONS

1. A Web page that has an .htm or .html extension is called a ________________ page.
2. Dynamic pages contain ________________.
   a. HTML statements
   b. programming statements
   c. both a and b
   d. neither a nor b

3. Which of the following tasks typically does not require programming?
   a. update inventory
   b. display the number of Web site visitors
   c. display a heading for a report
   d. retrieve employee information
4. SQL is one of many languages you can use to communicate with DBMSs. True or False?
5. A relational DBMS organizes data into ____________.
   a. tables
   b. trees
   c. a mesh
   d. networks
6. What is a primary key?
   a. a security mechanism to protect tables
   b. a security mechanism to protect columns
   c. the column or columns that uniquely define a row of data
   d. none of the above
7. What is a foreign key?
   a. a column in one table that is related to a primary key in another table
   b. a security mechanism to protect tables
   c. a security mechanism to protect columns
   d. the column or columns that uniquely define a row of data
8. The series of rules for organizing data into tables is called ____________.
9. What does SQL stand for?
   a. Standard Query Language
   b. Super Query Language
   c. Structured Quantifiable Language
   d. Structured Query Language
10. The ____________ data type is useful for storing text such as last names, where the number of characters can vary significantly.
11. An example of a DML statement is ____________.
12. The only real difference between a database created with SQL Server 2000 and Access is that SQL Server 2000 can handle larger databases. True or False?

13. What is the statement to display just the first name of all employees in the employee table?
    a. `select from employee firstname`
    b. `select firstname from employee`
    c. `select firstname employee`
    d. `select column firstname from table employee`
14. An open-source database available for Linux is ________________.
    a. SQL Server 2000/Linux
    b. Linux SQL
    c. MySQL
    d. Red Hat DBMS
15. A disadvantage with the DBMS you installed in Linux is that it has no security. True or False?
16. Which of the following is not a programming language?
    a. CGI
    b. ASP
    c. JSP
    d. PHP
17. Which of the following is compiled into a servlet before it is executed?
    a. ASP
    b. PHP
    c. Perl
    d. JSP
18. SQL Server 2000 only runs on Windows 2000. For Windows 2003, you need SQL Server .NET. True or False?
19. What does DSN stand for?
    a. database solution number
    b. data source number
    c. data source name
    d. data system name
20. What is the opening tag in PHP?
    a. <%
    b. <?
    c. <*
    d. <$

HANDS-ON PROJECTS

Project 7-1

Create a report for a database application using a Microsoft Access database. You will use an Access file from the Data Disk files for Chapter 7 called hr.mdb. This database has the same format that you used earlier in the chapter, so you can use the same ASP file and simply change the DSN name.

To create the hrMDB DSN in Windows:

1. In Windows Explorer, copy **hr.mdb** from the Chapter7\Projects folder of the Data Disk to the \inetpub folder on your Windows server.
2. In Administrative Tools, click **Data Sources (ODBC)**. The ODBC Data Source Administrator dialog box opens.
3. Click the **System DSN** tab, and then click **Add** to add a system DSN. You need a system DSN so that an ASP program can use it. The Create New Data Source dialog box opens.
4. Click **Microsoft Access Driver (*.mdb)** to select the Microsoft Access driver.
5. Click **Finish**. The ODBC Microsoft Access Setup dialog box opens.
6. In the Data Source Name text box, type **hrMDB**, and then click **Select**. The Select Database dialog box opens.
7. For the database name, navigate to \inetpub and then click **hr.mdb**.
8. Click **OK** to return to the ODBC Microsoft Access Setup dialog box.
9. Click **OK** twice to exit the Data Sources (ODBC) application.

To change report.asp to display the report from Access:

1. In a text editor, change the line in report.asp

   ```
   Conn.open "database=hr;driver={SQL Server};server=(local);uid=sa"
   ```

   to

   ```
   Conn.open "DSN=hrMDB"
   ```

2. Open the browser, type **http://localhost/report.asp**, and then press **Enter** to display the same report that you produced when you used SQL Server. Refer back to Figure 7-31.

Project 7-2

Modify the ASP.NET program called report.aspx (shown in Figure 7-41) to have more functionality as shown in Figure 7-43. The column headings have a blue background color with a white text font, and they are not simply the names of the columns in the table. Instead of ssn, for example, the heading is SocSecNum. Instead of two columns for first name and last name, they are combined into a single column called Emp Name.

To modify report.aspx:

1. In a text editor, edit **report.aspx** by changing the line

```
<ASP:DataGrid id="DG1" runat="server"/>
```

to

```
<ASP:DataGrid id="DG1" runat="server" AutoGenerateColumns=false>
<HeaderStyle Font-Bold="True" ForeColor="white" BackColor="blue"/>
<ItemStyle ForeColor="black" BackColor="yellow"/>
<AlternatingItemStyle ForeColor="yellow" BackColor="black"/>
<Columns>
  <asp:BoundColumn DataField="ssn" HeaderText="SocSecNum"/>
  <asp:TemplateColumn HeaderText="Emp Name">
    <ItemTemplate>
      <%# Container.DataItem("firstname")%>
      <%# Container.DataItem("lastname")%>
    </ItemTemplate>
  </asp:TemplateColumn>
  <asp:BoundColumn DataField="salary" HeaderText="Salary"/>
</Columns>
</asp:DataGrid>
```

2. Save **report.aspx** and display it in the browser.

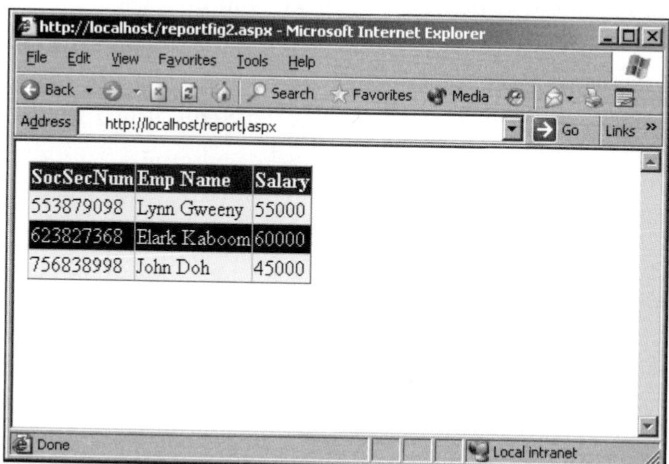

Figure 7-43 Results of changing report.aspx

Project 7-3

Create an ASP application to add an employee. Modify form.htm so that when you submit the form, a SQL insert statement is created and sent to the employee table. If you plan to use the Microsoft Access table, you must change the security on the file to allow data to be added. If you use SQL Server, no changes are needed.

To change the security on the Access file:

1. In Windows Explorer, navigate to \inetpub, right-click **hr.mdb**, and then click **Properties**. The hr.mdb Properties dialog box opens.
2. Click the **Security** tab. See Figure 7-44. Your objective is to give the anonymous guest account, which is IUSR_ followed by the name of your computer, read and write access to the file.

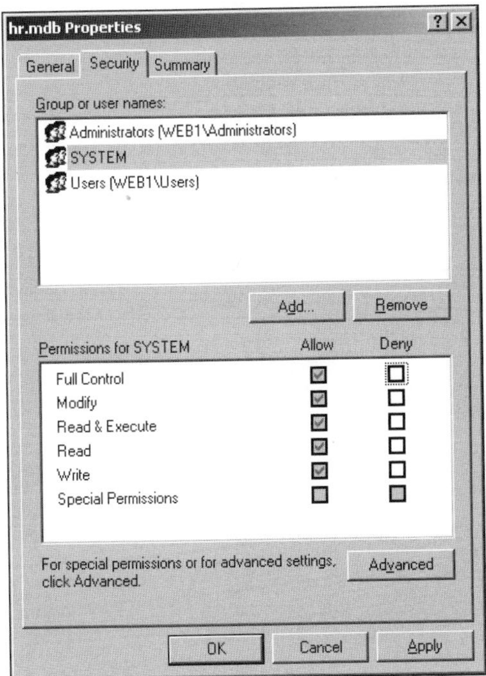

Figure 7-44 Security tab in hr.mdb Properties dialog box

3. Click **Add** to add a user to the list. The Select Users or Groups dialog box opens. See Figure 7-45.
4. Click **Advanced**. In this dialog box, you can list the users so you can select by name. Click **Find Now**. A list of users and groups appears in the dialog box. See Figure 7-46. At the bottom of the figure, you can see IUSR_WEB1. Although yours will begin with IUSR_, the rest of the user name may be different. Click this user, and then click **OK**.

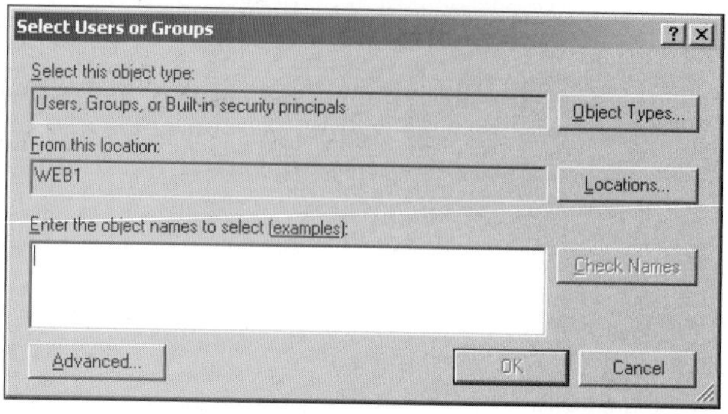

Figure 7-45 Select Users or Groups dialog box

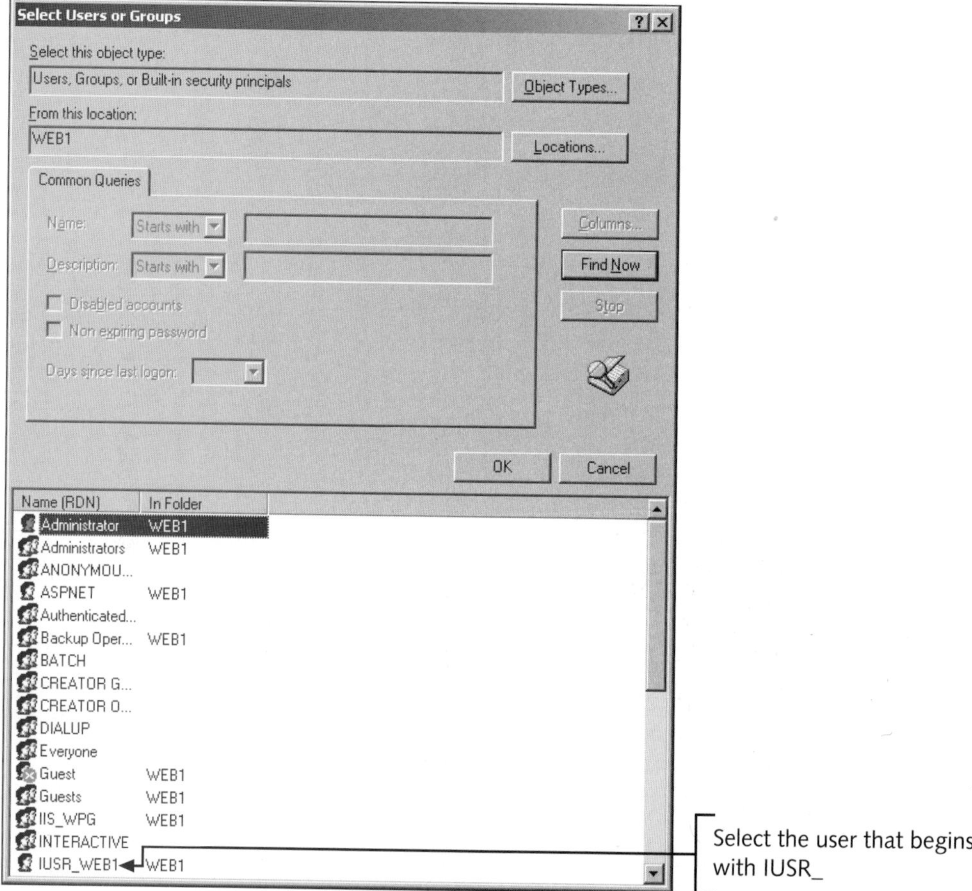

Figure 7-46 Find the IUSR guest account

5. Click **OK** again to return to the hr.mdb Properties dialog box.

6. Click the **Write** check box in the Allow column to allow write permission.
7. Click **OK** to close the hr.mdb Properties dialog box.

To create an application to insert an employee record:

1. In a text editor, open **form.htm** from the Chapter7\Projects folder, and then save it in \inetpub\wwwroot. Click **Yes** to confirm that you want to replace form.htm. Change the line

   ```
   <form action=>
   ```

   to

   ```
   <form action=insertaction.asp>
   ```

2. After the `Last Name: <input type=text name=last><BR>` line, insert the following line:

   ```
   Department: <input type=text name=depno><BR>
   ```

3. Save and close **form.htm**.
4. In \inetpub\wwwroot, create a file named **insertaction.asp** and type the following, which uses the Access database:

   ```
   <%@ Language=VBScript %>
   <%
   Set conn = server.createobject("ADODB.connection")
   Conn.open ="DSN=hrMDB"
   sql="insert into employee values ('" & _
      request("ssn")    & "', '" & _
      request("first")   & "', '" & _
      request("last")  & "', '" & _
      request("depno")  & "', " & _
      request("salary") & ")"
   Conn.execute sql
   Conn.close
   Set conn = nothing
   %>
   <html><body>
   The employee record was added!
   </body></html>
   ```

5. If you prefer to use the SQL Server database, change the fourth line as follows:

   ```
   Conn.open "database=hr;driver={SQL Server};server=(local);uid=sa"
   ```

Be careful with the quotation marks and the apostrophes. For example, the sixth line is

```
request("ssn") & quotation apostrophe, apostrophe quotation & _
```

However, the line that contains depno does not have the apostrophe after the comma.

7

The information coming from the form is combined to create an insert statement in SQL. For example, suppose you typed the following information for the data on the form: ssn: 667879898

First name: Mary
Last name: Noia
Depno: 20
Salary: 30000

This data would be combined to create the following string of characters:

```
Insert into employee values ('667879898','Mary','Noia','20',30000)
```

The text in parentheses would be inserted in the sql variable on line 5. The sql variable would be sent to the database on line 11.

To test the file:

1. Open a browser, type **localhost/form.htm**, and then press **Enter** to display the form.
2. Fill in the form with Mary Noia's information, and then click **Submit** to add the record to the table.
3. In the browser, type **localhost/report.asp** and then press **Enter** to see the report with the new employee. If a report with the new employee does not appear, check line 4 of report.asp and make sure that it matches line 4 of insertaction.asp.

Project 7-4

Write a program to update the employee's salary in ASP. In SQL, to change the salary of the employee with a ssn of 553879098 to 70000, you would create the following statements:

```
update employee
set salary=70000
where ssn='553879098'
```

First, you must create a form that prompts for the employee's ssn and salary. Next, you would send the information to an ASP page to create the update statement, and finally you would send it to the database.

To modify form.htm for the update:

1. In a text editor, open **form.htm** from the Chapter7\Projects folder, and then save it in \inetpub\wwwroot. Click **Yes** to confirm that you want to replace form.htm. Change the line

   ```
   <form action=>
   ```

   to

   ```
   <form action=updateaction.asp>
   ```
2. Delete the lines with the first name and last name.

3. Save **form.htm**, and then close the text editor.
4. Create a file called **updateaction.asp** and put it in \inetpub\wwwroot. It should contain the following statements for Access:

```
<%@ Language=VBScript %>
<%
Set conn = server.createobject("ADODB.connection")
Conn.open ="DSN=hrMDB"
sql="update employee set salary= " & _
   request("salary")    & " where ssn = '" & _
   request("ssn")   & "'"
Conn.execute sql
Conn.close
Set conn = nothing
%>
<html><body>
The employee record was changed!
</body></html>
```

5. If you prefer to use SQL Server, change the fourth line as follows:

```
Conn.open "database=hr;driver={SQL Server};server=(local);uid=sa"
```

6. In the browser, open **form.htm** and fill in a Social Security number of 553879098 and a salary of 70000. Click **Submit** to change the salary of Lynn Gweeny to 70000.
7. In the browser, open **report.asp** to see the change to Lynn Gweeny's salary.

Project 7-5

Create a PHP program to process the form.htm form shown in Figure 7-15. The form.htm Web page prompts the user for a Social Security number, first name, last name, and salary. The action page is set to ProcessForm.php. In this file, you display the information entered in the form.

To process form.htm using PHP:

1. In a text editor, open **form.htm** from the Chapter7\Projects folder, and then save it in the /var/www/HTML folder. Change the line in form.htm

```
<form action=>
```

to

```
<form action=ProcessForm.php>
```

2. Save and close **form.htm**.
3. In /var/www/HTML, use kedit to create a file named **ProcessForm.php**, and then type the following:

```
<?
$request = $HTTP_GET_VARS;
?>
```

```
<html><body>
<?
echo "Hello $request[first] $request[last].<BR>";
echo "Your Social Security Number is $request[ssn], ";
echo "and you make \$$request[salary]";
?>
</body></html>
```

4. Save and close **ProcessForm.php**.
5. Open a browser, type **localhost/form.htm**, and then press **Enter** to display the form.
6. Complete the form as shown in Figure 7-17, and then click **Submit**. The output should appear as shown in Figure 7-18.

Project 7-6

Create a PHP application to add an employee. Modify form.htm so that when you submit the form, a SQL insert statement is created and sent to the employee table.

To create an application to insert an employee record:

1. In a text editor, open **form.htm** from the Chapter7\Projects folder, and then save it in /var/www/html, overwriting the existing form.htm. Change the line

```
<form action=>
```

to

```
<form action=insertaction.php>
```

2. Find the following line:

```
Last Name: <input type=text name=last><BR>
```

After this line, insert the following line:

```
Department: <input type=text name=depno><BR>
```

3. Save and close **form.htm**.
4. In /var/www/html, create a file named **insertaction.php** and type the following code, which uses the MySQL database. The lines of code to make sure that no errors in the database connection occur have been deleted for clarity. In Project 7-5, $request was used for the form variable. In insertaction.php, $r is used to shorten the line used to create the insert statement.

```
<?
$r = $HTTP_GET_VARS;
$conn=mysql_connect("localhost","root","password");
$db = mysql_select_db("hr");
$sql = "insert into employee values
('$r[ssn]','$r[first]','$r[last]','$r[depno]',$r[salary])";
$Ret = mysql_query($sql);
```

```
?>
<html><body>
The employee has been added!
</body></html>
```

The information coming from the form is combined to create an insert statement in SQL. For example, suppose you typed the following information for the data on the form: SSN: 667879898

First name: Mary
Last name: Noia
Deptno: 20
Salary: 30000

It would be combined to create the following string of characters:

```
Insert into employee values ('667879898','Mary','Noia','20',30000)
```


The string of characters would be inserted in the sql variable on line 5. The sql variable would be sent to the database on line 6.

5. Open a browser, type **localhost/form.htm**, and then press **Enter** to display the form.
6. Fill in the form with Mary Noia's information, and then click **Submit** to add the record to the table.
7. In the browser, type **localhost/report.php** and then press **Enter** to see the report with the new employee.

Project 7-7

Write a program to update an employee's salary in PHP. In SQL, to change the employee with a ssn of 553879098 to 70000, you would include the following statements:

```
update employee
set salary=70000
where ssn='553879098'
```

First, you must create a form that prompts for the employee's ssn and salary. Next, you would send the information to a PHP page to create the update statement, and finally you would send it to the database.

To modify form.htm for the update:

1. In a text editor, open **form.htm** from the Chapter7\Projects folder, and then save it in /var/www/html, overwriting the existing file. Change the line

   ```
   <form action=>
   ```

   to

   ```
   <form action=updateaction.php>
   ```

2. Delete the lines with the first name and last name.
3. Save **form.htm**, and then close the text editor.
4. Create a file called **updateaction.php** and store it in /var/www/html. Type the following code in the file:

```
<?
$r = $HTTP_GET_VARS;
$conn=mysql_connect("localhost","root","password");
$db = mysql_select_db("hr");
$sql = "update employee set salary=$r[salary] where ssn='$r[ssn]'";
$Ret = mysql_query($sql);
?>
<html><body>
The employee salary has been updated!
</body></html>
```

5. In the browser, open **form.htm**, and fill in a Social Security number of 553879098 and a salary of 70000. Click **Submit** to change the salary of Lynn Gweeny to 70000.
6. In the browser, open **report.php** to see the change to Lynn Gweeny's salary.

Project 7-8

The existing report.php page produces a report for all employees. Often it is useful to create a report for a subset of the employees. In this project, you will create a form that requests a department number. When it is submitted, it will generate a report for all employees from that department. In SQL, you modify the select statement to retrieve rows that meet a certain criterion. For example, to retrieve all employee information for employees in department 10, you would write the following:

```
select *
from employee
where depno='10'
```

To create a custom report based on department number:

1. Create a Web page called **formdepno.htm** and store it in /var/www/html. It should contain the following:

```
<HTML>
<BODY>
Please enter the department number and click Submit:<BR>
<FORM action=reportdepno.php>
Department: <input type=text name=depno><BR>
<input type=submit name=submit value=Submit>
</FORM>
</BODY>
</HTML>
```

2. Create a file called **reportdepno.php** and save it in /var/www/html. It should contain the following code. Be careful to include the space after "employee" on line 5. On line 6, there is a "." before the "=", which appends the characters on the previous line to the $sql variable. This report is very similar to report.php. The tests for database errors have been removed for clarity.

```
<?
$request = $HTTP_GET_VARS;
$conn=mysql_connect("localhost","root","password");
$db = mysql_select_db("hr");
$sql = "select ssn,firstname,lastname,salary from employee ";
$sql .= "where depno = '$request[depno]'";
$ResultSet = mysql_query($sql);
?>
<html><body>
<?
echo "<h2>Report for Department $request[depno]</h2><BR>";
echo "<TABLE><tr><th>ssn</th><th>First</th><th>Last</th>
<th>Salary</th></tr>";
while($rs = mysql_fetch_array($ResultSet, MYSQL_ASSOC))
{
echo "<tr>";
echo "<td>".$rs["ssn"]."</td>";
echo "<td>".$rs["firstname"]."</td>";
echo "<td>".$rs["lastname"]."</td>";
echo "<td>".$rs["salary"]."</td>";
echo "</tr>";
}
 echo "</table>"; ?>
</body></html>
```

3. In the browser, open **formdepno.htm**, and then enter a department number of **10**. Click **Submit** to view the report of employees from department 10.

CASE PROJECTS

The following case projects are based on an inventory database that contains a table called parts with a four-character item ID called itemid, a description of up to 20 characters, cost, and a quantity. The primary key is itemid. The table should contain the data shown in Table 7-3.

Table 7-3

Itemid	Description	Cost	Quantity
A15	Widget	10	50
A20	SuperWidget	15	20
C53	EconoWidget	5	18

Case Project 7-1

Create an ASP application for inventory information. Create the inventory database in SQL Server. Create the parts table and add the information. Create a report to display the information in the table.

Case Project 7-2

Create an ASP application to add new inventory records and update inventory quantities. For the update form, prompt the user for the itemid and quantity. When you are done, display the report you created in Case Project 7-1.

Case Project 7-3

Create a form to prompt for an itemid. Create a page to delete the row based on the itemid entered. For example, the following SQL command would delete item G65:

```
delete from parts
where itemid = 'G65'
```

Display the report from Case Project 7-1 to make sure that it worked.

Case Project 7-4

Create an ASP.NET application to display the contents of the table you created in Case Project 7-1.

Case Project 7-5

Perform the tasks outlined in Case Project 7-1 using MySQL and PHP instead of SQL Server and ASP.

Case Project 7-6

Perform the tasks outlined in Case Project 7-2 using MySQL and PHP instead of SQL Server and ASP.

Case Project 7-7

Perform the tasks outlined in Case Project 7-3 using MySQL and PHP instead of SQL Server and ASP.

CHAPTER

8

PROVIDING E-MAIL SERVICES

In this chapter, you will:

- Understand the e-mail environment
- Understand e-mail protocols
- Install and administer Microsoft Exchange 2000
- Install and administer sendmail for Linux
- Install and configure IMAP4 and POP3 servers for Linux
- Configure e-mail clients
- Understand Web-based e-mail clients

Although most e-mail today works via standard Internet protocols, e-mail services have historically used many methods with varying levels of popularity. Until the late 1990s, e-mail was based on proprietary systems. As the popularity of the Internet grew, standards became more widespread, allowing different e-mail systems to communicate with each other. The standard for current e-mail services is to use DNS with a special Mail Exchange record that contains the IP address of the mail server for a domain. The e-mail systems use as many as three standard protocols to communicate: **Simple Mail Transfer Protocol** (**SMTP**), for sending e-mail, and **Post Office Protocol** (**POP3**) or **Internet Mail Access Protocol** (**IMAP4**), for retrieving e-mail from electronic mailboxes.

The two most common e-mail packages are sendmail for Linux and Microsoft Exchange 2000 for Windows. Sendmail implements SMTP, while Exchange 2000 implements SMTP, POP3, and IMAP4. In addition, Exchange 2000 has a Web-based client called **Outlook Web Access (OWA)**. To add POP3 and IMAP4 capabilities to Linux, you can use the imap-2001 package. You configure e-mail clients in similar ways, no matter what the software. To do so, you supply the IP address for the outgoing server (SMTP) and the incoming server (POP3 or IMAP4), and you supply your e-mail address and the account information necessary to retrieve e-mail.

UNDERSTANDING THE E-MAIL ENVIRONMENT

Over the years, e-mail has evolved from a variety of proprietary systems to the current system, which is based on Internet standards. In the 1980s and 1990s, people who depended on e-mail may have had three or more e-mail addresses, one for each major e-mail system. For example, in the 1980s, CompuServe was one of the most popular online services, and companies such as Microsoft, Borland, and Lotus conducted forums on CompuServe. You could use CompuServe to send e-mail, but only to other users on CompuServe. CompuServe eventually offered gateways to other e-mail systems, including Internet-based e-mail.

Even in the 1990s, e-mail was commonly used only within individual companies, without any connections to the Internet. The version of Microsoft's e-mail server available in the mid- to late 1990s was designed primarily to exchange mail within a company. Doing so represented a challenging task because large corporations often had a number of e-mail systems, including the once-popular Lotus cc:Mail. Also, one site could connect to another site within the company using a variety of methods. That situation changed with the 1997 release of Microsoft Exchange 5.5, which included add-on software that allowed Exchange to send and receive e-mail across the Internet. Sendmail, the most common e-mail system available for UNIX and Linux, can still accept and relay e-mail based on previous addressing standards such as BITNET and DECNET.

Although this chapter focuses on configuring a single e-mail server for use on the Internet, a large company needs to consider other aspects of administering an e-mail system. Often, a company uses many e-mail servers that need to exchange messages, with a single server acting as a gateway to the Internet.

For Windows, Microsoft Exchange 2000 represents the standard for e-mail service. Microsoft Exchange 2000 has capabilities far beyond simple e-mail, including the following features:

- *Instant messaging*—Send messages instantly using secure architecture.
- *Unified messaging platform*—Use a single inbox for e-mail, voicemail, fax, and pages.
- *Chat service*—Communicate online with others who share similar interests. The chat service is based on the Internet Relay Chat (IRC) protocol, which makes it compatible with any chat client. This service requires Active Directory and the Conferencing server add-on.
- *URL addressing*—Use a single URL to access stored data.
- *Audio and video conferencing*—Meet with others online by speaking to and viewing images of one another. This service uses the Telephony 3.0 (TAPI) protocol, which supports the use of multicast technology. With **multicast**

technology, a single IP packet can be sent to multiple recipients as opposed to having to send IP packets to each individual recipient.

- *Collaborative development*—Work with others to develop applications.
- *Integration with Outlook*—Use Microsoft Outlook features such as scheduling, contacts, and shared documents.

Although both Microsoft Windows 2000 and Windows Server 2003 include SMTP as a Windows component, Windows 2003 adds a POP3 Windows component. The POP3 component lets you provide basic e-mail services on your Windows 2003 server without purchasing other software such as Exchange 2000. In Hands-on Project 8-9, you install and administer POP3.

An e-mail system must balance simplicity and functionality. The basic protocols used for e-mail systems must be simple enough so that all Internet systems can send and receive messages. Unfortunately, the original specifications for e-mail did not address some areas of functionality. For example, only text messages were originally supported. To allow users to send pictures and sound via e-mail, the **Multipurpose Internet Mail Extensions (MIME)** specification was developed. MIME formats allow pictures, sound, and other binary data to be converted into text formats. When the message is delivered, the text is converted into the correct binary format. Formats that MIME can handle include the following:

- *Applications*—Data can be formatted as Postscript or octet-stream files. Octet-stream is commonly used by Microsoft for sending application data such as Word documents.
- *Images*—Graphics can be sent in a variety of formats, such as .jpg or .gif files.
- *Video*—Videos can be sent in formats such as .mpeg.

Understanding the Role of DNS in E-mail Systems

Recall from Chapter 4 that the purpose of DNS is to map host names to IP addresses. For example, *www.technowidgets.com* represents a host that corresponds to the IP address 192.168.0.100. Typically, a host corresponds to a single IP address. A domain name often corresponds to the IP address of its Web site. For example, if you type *redhat.com* in a browser, the Red Hat Web site appears. In an e-mail address such as *info@technowidgets.com*, *technowidgets.com* represents the IP address of the e-mail server, which is probably different from the IP address of the Web server. Because a domain name such as *RedHat.com* or *technowidgets.com* can represent the IP addresses of both a Web site and an e-mail server, you need a way to distinguish between the two. In DNS, you configure the IP address of your domain name to be used for a Web site by using an "A" record, as in `IN A`

`192.168.0.100`. You configure DNS to associate the domain name with the IP address of your e-mail server through a **Mail Exchange** (**MX**) record, as in:

```
IN      MX  10  mail.technowidgets.com.
```

Figure 8-1 contains a DNS file based on the one in Chapter 4.

```
@       IN     SOA    Web1.technowidgets.com. admn.technowidgets.com. (
                                        2002072100 ; Serial
                                        28800      ; Refresh
                                        14400      ; Retry
                                        3600000    ; Expire
                                        86400 )    ; Minimum
               IN     NS       Web1
               IN     A        192.168.0.100
               IN     MX   10  mail.technowidgets.com.

Web1           IN     A        192.168.0.100
www            IN     CNAME    Web1
www.support    IN     CNAME    Web1
research       IN     A        192.168.0.150
               IN     MX   10  mail
mail           IN     A        192.168.0.200
```

Figure 8-1 DNS file with MX records

Recall from Chapter 4 that the @ ("at" symbol) at the beginning of the figure represents the name of the domain, which is *technowidgets.com*, and that the first three IN records refer to the domain name. The third IN record could be rewritten as follows:

```
technowidgets.com. IN  MX  10  mail.technowidgets.com.
```

This record means that if an e-mail system is looking up the domain name, it should be referred to the address at *mail.technowidgets.com*. Later in the definition, you see that the mail host corresponds to 192.168.0.200. One MX record is associated with *research.technowidgets.com* and with *mail.technowidgets.com*. Thus, if someone sent an e-mail message to *jsampaio@research.technowidgets.com*, the e-mail server would look up the MX record for *research.technowidgets.com* and find that the IP address for *mail.technowidgets.com* is 192.168.0.200. However, you could not successfully send an e-mail message to *mnoia@www.technowidgets.com* or *mnoia@Web1.technowidgets.com* because no MX record is associated with them.

In the MX record, a number from 1 to 99 is included to show the priority of the associated mail server. By convention, the default number is set to 10, but you could use any other number in the range. The lower the number, the higher the priority. If you had multiple e-mail servers, you could change your DNS configuration to the one shown in Figure 8-2.

```
@      IN     SOA    Web1.technowidgets.com. admn.technowidgets.com. (
                                         2002072100 ; Serial
                                         28800      ; Refresh
                                         14400      ; Retry
                                         3600000    ; Expire
                                         86400 )    ; Minimum
               IN      NS      Web1
               IN      A       192.168.0.100
               IN      MX  10  mail.technowidgets.com.
               IN      MX  20  mail2.technowidgets.com.

Web1         IN     A      192.168.0.100
www          IN     CNAME Web1
www.support  IN     CNAME Web1
research     IN     A      192.168.0.150
             IN     MX 10 mail
mail         IN     A      192.168.0.200
mail2        IN     A      192.168.0.202
```

Figure 8-2 DNS file with MX records for two e-mail servers

When you send an e-mail message to *technowidgets.com*, the message first goes to *mail.technowidgets.com* because it has the lowest number associated with the MX record. If that e-mail server is not available, the message goes to *mail2.technowidgets.com*.

Understanding E-mail System Terminology

E-mail systems have to perform more than one task. First, an e-mail server must accept e-mail messages from clients and send the messages to other e-mail servers. An e-mail server must also accept e-mail messages from other e-mail servers. The component involved in the transfer of the e-mail messages is the **Mail Transfer Agent** (**MTA**), which accepts e-mail from clients and then sends the e-mail to another MTA for storage. The MTA might store the messages in a sophisticated database or in simple text files.

To send e-mail to the MTA, an e-mail user must have a **Mail User Agent** (**MUA**), sometimes simply referred to as a **UA**. The MUA is client software that correctly formats messages and sends them to the MTA, which in turn sends the e-mail to the MTA of the recipient. The MUA also retrieves e-mail from a **Mail Delivery Agent** (**MDA**), which is responsible for delivering e-mail from the e-mail system to the MUA. The MDA is part of the e-mail server. Figure 8-3 illustrates the flow of e-mail.

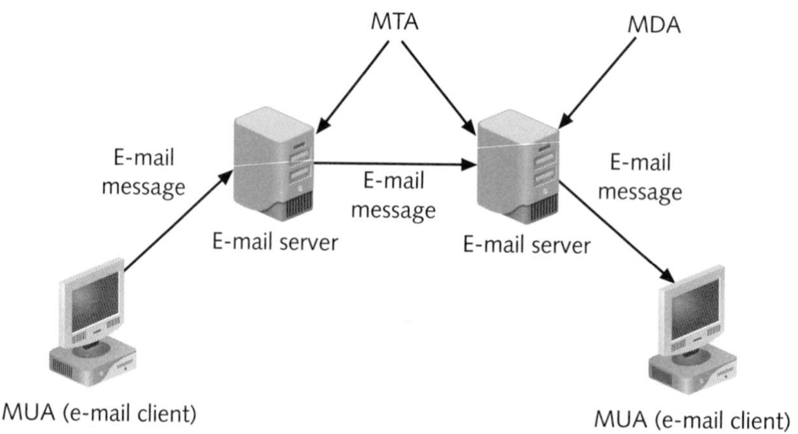

Figure 8-3 Flow of e-mail

When configuring e-mail systems, you need to know the meaning of specialized terms, such as **masquerading**. When you are sending mail from *mail.technowidgets.com* or *mail2.technowidgets.com*, you do not want the full host name to appear on the return address, as in *mnoia@mail.technowidgets.com*, because that is not the standard format for e-mail addresses. Instead, you should mask the actual host name and replace it with *technowidgets.com* so that the return address is *mnoia@technowidgets.com*. Some e-mail systems, such as Microsoft Exchange 2000, automatically provide masquerading. Others, such as sendmail, require you to specifically state the domain portion of the return address when you configure your e-mail server.

Relaying is the process of sending e-mail to an intermediate MTA before the message is transmitted to its final destination. Organizations use relaying when a number of MTAs gather e-mail before it is sent to the one MTA in the organization that has a connection to the Internet. However, relaying should not be allowed on single MTAs connected to the Internet, because spammers can route almost unlimited e-mails through your MTA. A **spammer** is someone who sends unsolicited e-mail, typically to try to sell something. As a benefit to the spammers, the return address is often masqueraded so that it appears to have come from your organization. As a consequence, a spammer could market a "miracle" weight-loss device via e-mail and make it appear as if the message was coming from a respected company such as TechnoWidgets.

Sometimes it is appropriate to have an e-mail address that is not related to a specific user. For example, you may want an e-mail address for *info@technowidgets.com* or *sales@technowidgets.com*. To make it easier to retrieve e-mail for these addresses, you can set up an **alias** whereby e-mail sent to info or sales is routed to a specific address, such as *lcamoes@technowidgets.com*. In actuality, no e-mail account for info or sales exists. Both simply represent other addresses associated with lcamoes. If lcamoes leaves TechnoWidgets, then you could reassign the aliases to the new person, such as *fpessoa@technowidgets.com*. An alias can also be useful when employees leave a company, but their jobs require that someone still read and respond to their e-mail messages. For example, if an employee with an e-mail address of *jdesena@technowidgets.com* leaves TechnoWidgets, but the owner of the edequeroz account will handle the jdesena e-mail, then the jdesena account can be deleted and a jdesena alias created for edequeroz so that edequeroz will receive e-mail destined for jdesena.

UNDERSTANDING E-MAIL PROTOCOLS

As the previous section explained, MTAs and MDAs perform different jobs. The MTA transfers e-mail from one server to another, and the MDA delivers mail to the user. These agents use different protocols to do each job. Just as the Web server depends on the HTTP protocol to communicate, so the MTA depends on SMTP, and the MDA depends on POP3 or IMAP4. Some e-mail systems, such as Microsoft Exchange 2000, include all the protocols in one package. Other e-mail systems supply communication for a single protocol. For example, sendmail is simply an MTA that uses SMTP. To deliver e-mail messages to client software packages, you would have to install another server program that supports POP3 or IMAP4.

Each protocol requires its own server software. For example, the SMTP protocol is used by an SMTP server, the POP3 protocol is used by a POP3 server, and the IMAP4 protocol is used by an IMAP4 server. Just as a Web server listens at port 80, so an SMTP server listens at port 25, a POP3 server listens at port 110, and an IMAP4 server listens at port 143. In essence, Exchange 2000 contains multiple servers.

You should recognize how the e-mail protocols operate for two reasons. First, you need to understand how e-mail servers work and to respect their capabilities and limitations. Second, as you will see in the Hands-on Projects, you can use your knowledge of protocols along with the Telnet utility to connect to an e-mail server and test the components. These techniques can prove very useful in testing new servers and providing solutions to user e-mail problems.

Understanding SMTP

SMTP is a text-based protocol that e-mail clients and servers use to send e-mail messages. Both Microsoft Exchange 2000 and sendmail support SMTP. Just as you can simulate accessing a Web page using Telnet instead of a browser, so you can send an e-mail message using Telnet and your knowledge of the SMTP protocol instead of an e-mail client. As is true with other TCP/IP text-based protocols, SMTP has commands and headers. Commands divide communication into distinct parts; **headers** add descriptive information. SMTP uses only a few commands to do its work. Table 8-1 describes the common commands associated the SMTP protocol. Table 8-2 describes the common SMTP headers.

Table 8-1 Common SMTP commands

Command	Purpose
HELO	Identifies the domain sending the message
DATA	Indicates the body of the message
VRFY	Verifies the e-mail user
QUIT	Ends the SMTP session

Table 8-2 Common SMTP headers

Header	Description
MAIL FROM:	Identifies who is sending the message (required)
RCPT TO:	Identifies the recipient of the message (required)
RECEIVED:	Identifies the e-mail server that processed the message; multiple instances of this header can be provided
DATE:	Indicates the date of the e-mail
FROM:	Shows the e-mail address of sender as it is typically displayed in an e-mail client
SUBJECT:	Shows the subject of the e-mail message
TO:	Shows the recipient of the e-mail message as it is typically displayed in an e-mail client
CC:	Sends copies of the message to a list of e-mail addresses
BCC:	Sends copies of the message to a list of e-mail addresses but does not display the e-mail addresses

Figure 8-4 shows an example of the minimal communication necessary between the client and the server to produce a simple e-mail message. The first command is **HELO**, which is sent by the client (in this case, from the keyboard) and is followed by responses from the server. These basic commands have many extensions. For example, instead of the **HELO** command, e-mail clients and servers can use **EHLO**, which is the extended **HELO** command that allows for more robust communication. This chapter covers only communication based on the **HELO** command.

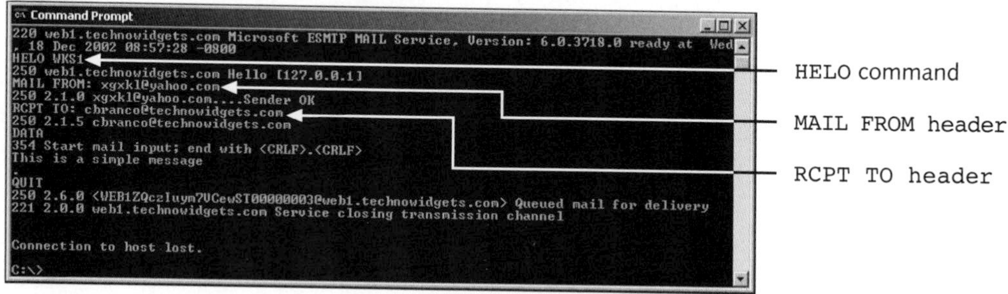

Figure 8-4 SMTP communication to produce a message

Note that each response from the server begins with a number that has a specific meaning. An e-mail client would read these numbers to determine how to respond. For example, a response of 254 indicates that the statement you typed was correct, 220 opens a connection, and 221 closes a connection. Message 354 states that the e-mail server is ready to accept an e-mail message and to end the message with the equivalent of pressing Enter, typing a dot, and pressing Enter again.

HELO Command

The `HELO` command signifies the beginning of a message. It sends the name of the host or domain that is sending the message. For example:

```
HELO WKS1
```

The SMTP protocol was developed without addressing any concerns related to security. Generally, the identifying name is not checked for accuracy. However, the receiving e-mail server can use DNS to do a reverse lookup on the IP address of the sending e-mail server. That is, the receiving e-mail server can find the host corresponding to the IP address. Then the e-mail server can match the domain from the lookup with the domain in the `HELO` command.

MAIL FROM Header

E-mail clients and servers use the `MAIL FROM` header to describe who is sending the e-mail message. You use the `MAIL FROM` header in the following format from Figure 8-4:

```
MAIL FROM: mnoia@technowidgets.com
```

As with the `HELO` command, SMTP does not usually verify the validity of the sender. Because e-mail addresses are readily available, spammers often use valid temporary e-mail addresses to send their messages to thousands of recipients at a time. Checking whether an e-mail address is valid would require a significant increase in processing, which is not worth the amount of spam this validity check would prevent.

RCPT TO Header

You use the `RCPT TO` header to describe the recipient of the e-mail message. This header has the following format:

```
RCPT TO: cbranco@technowidgets.com
```

How the server responds to this header depends on where the message originates. If the message is coming from within your network (domain), you should be able to send your message to any user on the Internet. Responding with `250 2.1.5 cbranco@technowidgets.com`, for example, means that this e-mail address is acceptable to the server because it recognizes cbranco. However, if the message is coming from the Internet and the recipient is not a member of the e-mail server's domain, the e-mail message will probably be rejected. For example, if the e-mail server being accessed belonged to *technowidgets.com*, and a message from the Internet was being sent to *test@xyz.com*, the e-mail server would probably respond with a message such as `550 5.7.1 Unable to relay for test@xzy.com`. If this message were allowed, spammers could use your e-mail server to send messages to others.

DATA Command

The body of the message follows the **DATA** command. The e-mail message must be in text format. Any binary data has to be converted using an accepted MIME format. Although the SMTP protocol sets no practical limit on the size of the message, in reality e-mail servers often limit the size of the messages that they accept. The protocol senses the end of the message by detecting a period at the beginning of a line, followed by a blank line. Once the blank line is detected, the message is sent. At this point, processing can start over with another **MAIL FROM** header, or processing can be stopped with the **QUIT** command.

Your e-mail client hides the details of how this protocol works. You simply type the message, and the e-mail client provides the extra dot and a blank line as required by the protocol.

Recall from Figure 8-4 that the response to the **DATA** command is `354 Start mail input; end with <CRLF>.<CRLF>`, which means that the client is ready to receive the e-mail message. The reference to `<CRLF>` means carriage return/line feed, a dated terminology based on devices that looked like typewriters. With these devices, a carriage return physically brought the printing head to the beginning of the line and the line feed advanced the paper to the next line. `<CRLF>` simply means the beginning of the next line.

In Figure 8-4, the e-mail message sent is "This is a simple message." A line containing only a dot followed by a blank line allows the e-mail server to detect the end of the message. When the e-mail server detects the blank line, it responds with `250 2.6.0 <WEB1WS9ygybHdtf79In00000002@Web1.technowidgets.com> Queued mail for delivery`, which means that the message was accepted.

VRFY Command

The **VRFY** command was designed to verify a user. The e-mail server can use this command to test whether an e-mail message is coming from a valid user, one who actually exists on the e-mail server of the sender. For example, suppose you receive a message that indicates it is from *jsmith@nogrlam.com*. The **VRFY** command could find out whether there really is a jsmith at *nogrlam.com*. The e-mail server can also use the **VRFY** command to verify a user before sending a message.

E-mail administrators do not usually allow this command to respond as it was designed to do, because unscrupulous people could easily use **VRFY** to build lists of e-mail addresses. For example, in Microsoft Exchange 2000, whether you request the verification of a valid e-mail account or an invalid e-mail account, Exchange 2000 responds with a message similar to the one below:

```
252 2.1.5 Cannot VRFY user, but will take message for
cbranco@technowidgets.com
```

Other SMTP Headers

As you have seen, headers provide specific information concerning the e-mail message, such as who sent the message and who should receive it. Other headers describe more information about the message that can be used by e-mail clients and servers. When you fill in the subject line in an e-mail client such as Microsoft Outlook and send the message, the client software inserts the text for the subject of the message in the subject header. For example, if you type "Important Meeting" in the subject line, when the client software sends the message, it includes "Subject: Important Meeting." When the client software of the recipient detects the subject header, it uses this information to format the message that the recipient reads.

You probably recognize the headers shown earlier in Table 8-2 from working with e-mail client software. For example, the `FROM:` header can be used for a more user-friendly name. Even though the `MAIL FROM:` header must have a specific e-mail address, such as `mnoia@technowidgets.com`, the `FROM:` header can contain `Mary Noia mnoia@technowidgets.com`. If the client software detects the `FROM:` header, it can use that information instead of the information in the `MAIL FROM:` header.

Some headers are usually not displayed in client software, but can be used by e-mail administrators to gain more detailed information about the e-mail message. You use the `RECEIVED:` header to trace the route of a message as it was passed from server to server and to discover the date and time on which the message was received. For example, suppose you decide to send a musical birthday e-mail to a friend from a greeting card site on the Internet. The message that your friend receives probably has two `RECEIVED:` headers: one with information about the message accepted by the greeting card site, and another with information about the message being accepted by your e-mail server from the greeting card site. This information can be useful in finding out whether an e-mail message was delayed on its route to one of your users.

Understanding POP3

E-mail client software can use the POP3 protocol to list, read, and delete e-mail messages. Microsoft Exchange 2000, for example, contains a POP3 server. The first step in retrieving your e-mail is to log on to the POP3 server, typically through an e-mail client. Although some POP3 servers accept secure logons, your e-mail client software usually sends the user name and password as unencrypted text. This software can list all e-mail headers so that you can view the subject of the e-mail message, the size of the message, and the sender's identity before deciding whether to download and read the e-mail. This ability can be useful if you receive large messages but have a slow connection to your POP3 server. Although you can leave e-mail messages on a POP3 server, the e-mail service is designed so that messages downloaded to the client are deleted from the server at the same time.

Table 8-3 lists some POP3 commands that are commonly sent by e-mail client software to the POP3 server.

Table 8-3 Common POP3 commands

Command	Description
`USER` *`username`*	Connects to POP3 server based on user name, as in `USER mnoia`
`PASS` *`password`*	Enters the password for the user, as in `PASS: Ax6yy`
`LIST`	Displays the message number followed by the number of characters in the message; the message number starts at 1 for each session
`UIDL`	Displays the unique ID for each message, which can be used by the client software to determine which messages have been read
`RETR` *`n`*	Replaces the *n* with a message number to retrieve that message
`TOP` *`n`* `lines`	Instead of retrieving the whole message, retrieves the number of lines designated by the *lines* parameter for message number *n*
`DELE` *`n`*	Deletes message number *n* from the server
`QUIT`	Ends the session

Figure 8-5 shows a sample POP3 session. The session begins with the e-mail client sending the user name and password to the e-mail server via the `USER` and `PASS` commands. Then the e-mail client either uses the `LIST` or `UIDL` command to retrieve a list of the e-mail messages available. With `UIDL`, the client software can track which e-mail messages have been read because it assigns a unique ID to each message and tracks those that have been read so they are not downloaded again.

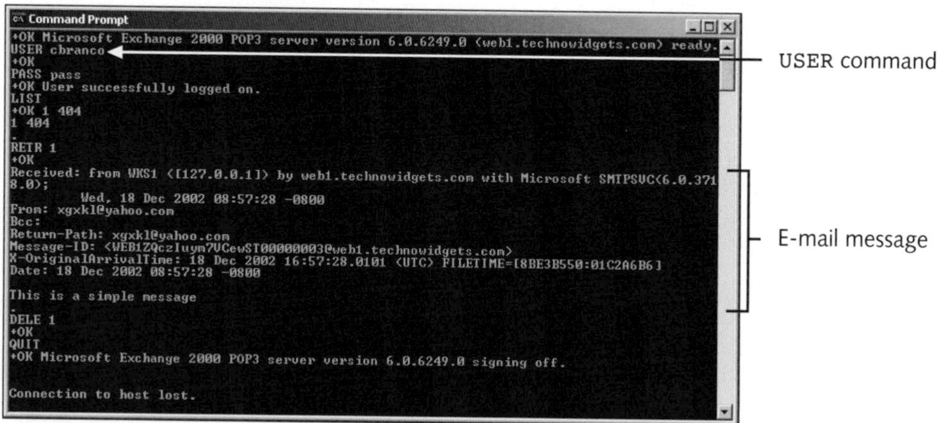

Figure 8-5 Example of a POP3 session

In the simplest situation, the client software retrieves all messages with the `RETR` command and deletes all retrieved messages with the `DELE` command. In some cases, the client software uses the `TOP` command to retrieve the first few lines of the message that contain the headers and part of the message. This strategy allows the user to find out information such as the message sender's identity, the size of the message, and the subject before determining whether to retrieve it or even to delete the message without reading it. The `QUIT` command ends the POP3 session.

Understanding IMAP4

IMAP4 is a much more complex protocol than POP3. It allows the user to organize folders on the server and permanently store messages in those folders. Because messages stay on the server, the user can access messages from any computer that has an e-mail client that supports the protocol. The trade-off for the organization with the IMAP4 server is that because all messages remain on the server instead of being downloaded to the client, messages can consume a lot of storage space on the server. This concern is especially problematic if users receive large files, such as images, video, and music files.

To keep track of the status of messages, IMAP4 uses **flags** to determine whether the message is new to the mailbox, read, answered, urgent, deleted, or a draft. A flag is a simple characteristic that can equate to true or false. The flags are `\Recent`, `\Seen`, `\Answered`, `\Flagged`, `\Deleted`, and `\Draft`, respectively.

IMAP4 provides many commands for managing multiple mailboxes and for managing e-mail messages. Of the commands for managing messages, `FETCH` is the most complex. Because IMAP4 does not provide a single command to retrieve both the header information and the body of the message, the e-mail client must use `FETCH` in a series of commands. To retrieve all header information for the first message, the e-mail client issues the following command to the IMAP4 server:

```
FETCH 1 BODY[HEADER]
```

To retrieve the body of the message, the e-mail server then issues the following command:

```
FETCH 1 BODY[TEXT]
```

To retrieve the first 60 characters of a message, the e-mail server uses the following command:

```
FETCH 1 BODY[TEXT]<0.60>
```

The zero in the previous example gives the starting position, and 60 is the number of characters to be retrieved. If the e-mail client wanted to retrieve the first ten messages in the previous commands, it would replace the 1 with 1:10.

Although IMAP4 has a `DELETE` command, it is used for deleting mailboxes, not messages. Fortunately, you cannot delete your default inbox—only the mailboxes that you have created. To delete a message, you add the `\Deleted` flag to the message. When you log out, the message is actually deleted. The e-mail client uses the following command to delete the first message:

```
STORE 1 +FLAGS (\Deleted)
```

The command to undo the deletion is the same as in the previous command, except that you replace `+FLAGS` with `-FLAGS`, as in the following example:

```
STORE 1 -FLAGS (\Deleted)
```

Table 8-4 lists some common IMAP4 commands.

Table 8-4 Common IMAP4 commands

Command	Description
LOGIN *username password*	Log on to the server with your user name and password, which are unencrypted.
SELECT *mailbox*	Select a mailbox before you perform mail tasks. The default mailbox is called inbox. The response gives a summary of mailbox information, such as the number of unread messages and the total number of messages.
FETCH *message(s) item(s)*	Retrieve messages. The *message(s)* parameter gives the message number. Optionally, you can specify a range of messages, such as 1:8. The *item(s)* parameter determines what part of the message is fetched—that is, individual header items or the body of the text.
STORE *message(s) flags*	Change the flags associated with a message. Typically, this command is used to mark messages to be deleted, undeleted, or identified as unread.
LOGOUT	End the IMAP4 session.

Installing and Administering Microsoft Exchange 2000

Microsoft Exchange Server 2000 can be much more than a simple e-mail server. As noted earlier, it supports the SMTP, POP3, and IMAP4 protocols, making Exchange Server 2000 a complete e-mail messaging solution. It also supports the **Lightweight Directory Access Protocol (LDAP)**, which is often used in LAN environments for communications between e-mail clients such as Microsoft Outlook and Exchange. In addition, Microsoft Exchange Server 2000 supports collaboration in the form of chat services and instant messaging. Microsoft designed Exchange Server 2000 to be very easy to install and maintain in a simple environment, yet expandable to support a very large organization. According to Microsoft, as of 2002, its Exchange infrastructure supported more than 71,000 mailboxes and 4.5 million messages per day, with 1.5 million messages going to and coming from the Internet.

Microsoft Exchange 2000 Architecture

Exchange 2000 is tightly integrated with Active Directory services. As a result, administrators can manage all aspects of the network, including Exchange 2000 users, from the Active Directory Users and Computers console. Once Exchange 2000 is installed, a new tab called Exchange Features appears in the user properties dialog box available from the Active Directory Users and Computers console.

Active Directory uses Dynamic DNS for name resolution, which Exchange 2000 needs to service users. DNS must also be available to resolve domain names on the Internet so that SMTP will function correctly and can deliver mail. Although the Microsoft DNS server can supply a domain naming service that handles both functions, you can also use two DNS servers.

Exchange 2000 can interact with e-mail servers such as Lotus Notes and Novell Groupwise through the use of connectors, which translate messages from one system to another. In Exchange 5.5, the version previous to Exchange 2000, the focus of Exchange was sending e-mail messages within an organization, including between incompatible systems. Although Exchange 5.5 was released in 1997, it was not closely tied to the Internet protocols. In fact, to send and receive Internet e-mail, you had to install **Internet Mail Service** (**IMS**), a software add-on that provided the SMTP, POP3, and IMAP4 protocols.

Because Exchange was designed to handle e-mail within large organizations, Microsoft created an architecture that included multiple servers. You can configure these servers to provide specific services. For example, you can install a server dedicated to providing connector services for Novell Groupwise. A single server connected to the Internet can accept e-mail from other Exchange servers, including Exchange 5.5 and Exchange 2000 servers, located within your organization.

Because organizations rely on e-mail, they want to make sure that if one part of the system fails, e-mail will continue to function. To meet this need, multiple Exchange 2000 servers can share a single disk subsystem. Along with an active server that processes the e-mail, you can use a passive server that is ready to start functioning in case the active server malfunctions or is taken off the network for maintenance. You can separate the servers that handle the HTTP (Web-based e-mail), SMTP, POP3, and IMAP4 protocols from the servers that store the e-mail. This isolation can be important if, for example, hackers attack the server that handles SMTP. The SMTP server may be disabled, but users can still retrieve their e-mail because it resides on a different server.

Understanding the Extra Features of Microsoft Exchange 2000

Exchange 2000 has extra features that enhance communication, including the Unified Messaging Platform, Exchange 2000 Conferencing server, chat services, and instant messaging. Some of these features are integrated with client products such as Outlook 2000 (and later) and NetMeeting.

Unified Messaging Platform

The mailbox in Exchange 2000 can be used for more than simple text. It supports **Voice Profile for Internet Mail (VPIM)**, which allows for interoperability between voicemail systems. VPIM enables you to listen to voicemail through an e-mail client. The mailbox can also store faxes and pager messages. These capabilities are not built into Exchange 2000, but rather are provided by third-party companies that supply modules supporting these capabilities.

Microsoft Exchange 2000 Conferencing Server

The Exchange 2000 Conferencing server is an add-on product to Exchange 2000 that allows audio and video conferencing. During an audio conference, for example, you can speak and listen to others. During a video conference, you can speak to, listen to, and see others. The Conferencing server provides high performance through **Telephony API 3.0**, a programming interface that allows efficient multicasting.

Chat Services

A chat service allows two or more users to communicate simultaneously. Microsoft includes a chat service based on the **Internet Relay Chat** (**IRC**) protocol, which is a common standard. The company's implementation supports up to 20,000 users on a single server. During a chat, text messages are generally sent among users. When you type and send a message, it is displayed on the screens of all the other users who are part of the chat group. Your message is prefaced by your name. Chat services also include an Auditorium mode whereby only the central speaker and moderator can send messages to all participants. The participants can send messages only to the moderator, thereby keeping the central speaker from being inundated with messages.

Instant Messaging

Instant messaging allows users to send messages directly to other users, who are immediately notified of their receipt. This system allows for much quicker collaboration than e-mail. In recent years, instant messaging has become a significant Internet application. Microsoft's version is built on a secure, standards-oriented architecture and is designed to allow users within an organization to communicate with each other.

Installing Microsoft Exchange 2000

Before you can install Exchange 2000, you must install a number of components, particularly Active Directory services. Exchange 2000 is the only product covered in this book that requires AD. If you have not installed AD yet, follow the installation instructions in Chapter 5. IIS is also required because one of the IIS components is SMTP, which is installed by default when you install IIS in Windows 2000, although you need to add support for SMTP in Windows 2003. Exchange 2000 also requires **Network News Transport Protocol** (**NNTP**), a protocol used for newsgroups. (NNTP is discussed in detail in Chapter 9.) NNTP is not installed by default when you install IIS, so you must install it separately.

To install NNTP on Windows 2003 and 2000, and SMTP in Windows 2003:

1. Insert the Windows installation CD. Click **Exit** in the installation dialog box, if necessary.
2. *In Windows 2003:* In the Control Panel, click **Add or Remove Programs**. The Add or Remove Programs dialog box opens.

In Windows 2000: In the Control Panel, double-click **Add/Remove Programs**. The Add/Remove Programs dialog box opens.

3. Click **Add/Remove Windows Components**. The Windows Components dialog box opens.
4. *In Windows 2003 only:* Highlight **Application Server** and then click **Details**.
5. Highlight **Internet Information Services (IIS)** and then click **Details**. The Internet Information Services (IIS) dialog box opens, allowing you to change IIS subcomponents.
6. Click the **NNTP Service** check box to add the NNTP protocol to IIS, which is needed for Microsoft Exchange 2000. Click the **SMTP Service** check box in Windows 2003 to add the SMTP protocol to IIS.
7. Click **OK** to accept the list of subcomponents. *In Windows 2003 only:* Click **OK** again to close the Application Server dialog box.
   You return to the Windows Components dialog box.
8. Click **Next**. The Configuring Components dialog box opens. Windows installs the NNTP protocol, which might take a few minutes. The Completing the Windows Components Wizard dialog box opens.
9. Click **Finish** to exit the wizard, and then close the window.
10. Close the Control Panel.

After installing Exchange 2000, you must install Service Pack 3 if you are using Windows 2003, because Exchange 2000 will not run without it. If you are using Windows 2000, it is a good idea to install the service pack, even though it is not strictly necessary for completing the step-by-step procedures.

Although the hardware requirements of Exchange 2000 are the same as those for Windows 2000 (a Pentium 166 with 128 MB of RAM and up to 700 MB of free disk space), you often need more power and storage space for Exchange 2000. Microsoft uses three Exchange 2000 Server configurations. For a server with 250 mailboxes, it recommends a computer with two 900-MHz Xeon processors, 512 MB of RAM, and eight 18-GB disk drives. Most Exchange 2000 servers at Microsoft handle about 3,750 mailboxes stored on servers with eight 700-MHz PIII processors with 4 GB of RAM and a shared Storage Area Network disk subsystem with 42 18-GB disk drives.

To install Microsoft Exchange Server 2000:

1. Refer to "Installing Active Directory Service in Windows" in Chapter 5 to install Active Directory, if necessary. Active Directory must be installed before you install Microsoft Exchange 2000.
2. Insert the Microsoft Exchange 2000 CD.

3. If the Setup program does not start automatically and open the Microsoft Exchange 2000 Enterprise Server dialog box shown in Figure 8-6, do the following:

   In Windows 2003: A dialog box opens with the default option to "Open folder to view files using Windows Explorer." Click **OK** and navigate to the \ENGLISH\EXCH2000\ENT folder on the CD.

   In Windows 2000: Use Windows Explorer to navigate to the \ENGLISH\EXCH2000\ENT folder on the CD.

   Double-click **LAUNCH.EXE** to begin the installation. The Microsoft Exchange 2000 Enterprise Server dialog box opens.

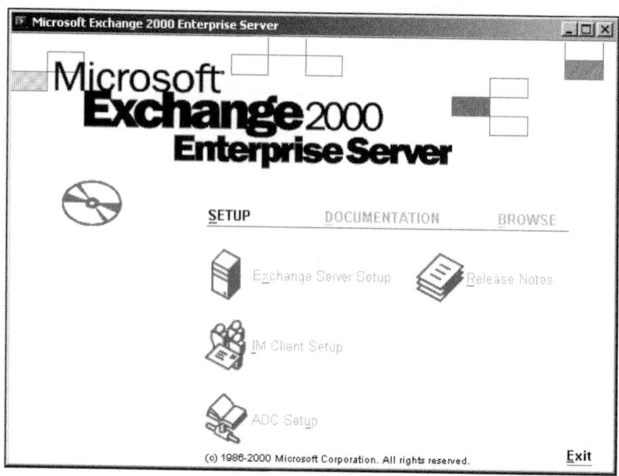

Figure 8-6 Microsoft Exchange 2000 Enterprise Server dialog box

4. Click **Exchange Server Setup** to start the installation wizard. In Windows 2003, a dialog box opens stating that Exchange Server 2000 is not supported by this version of Windows. Click **Continue**.

   The Welcome to the Microsoft Exchange 2000 Installation Wizard dialog box opens, warning you to close all open applications.

5. Close any open applications, and then click **Next**. The End-User License Agreement dialog box opens.

6. Click the **I agree** option button to accept the license agreement, and then click **Next**. The Product Identification dialog box opens. Enter your 25-digit identification number, and then click **Next**. The Component Selection dialog box opens. See Figure 8-7.

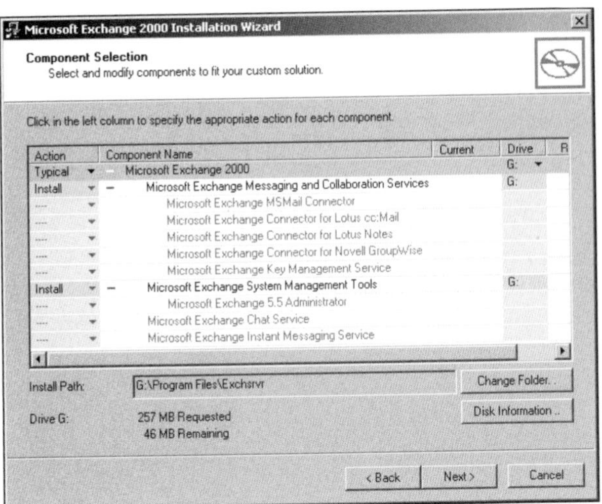

Figure 8-7 Component Selection dialog box

The default action is set to Typical. A typical installation installs both Microsoft Exchange Messaging and Collaboration Services, which is the actual server product, and Microsoft Exchange System Management Tools, which allows you to manage the server. Your install drive may be different from the one shown in Figure 8-7. Keep the default location that you have.

7. Click **Next** to perform a typical installation. The Installation Type dialog box opens. See Figure 8-8. Because this is a new installation, make sure the Create a new Exchange Organization option button is selected.

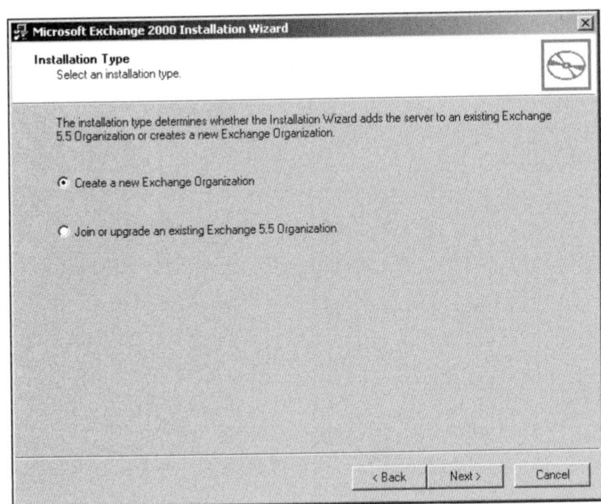

Figure 8-8 Installation Type dialog box

8. Click **Next**. The Organization Name dialog box opens. Change the name of the organization to **TechnoWidgets**, as shown in Figure 8-9.

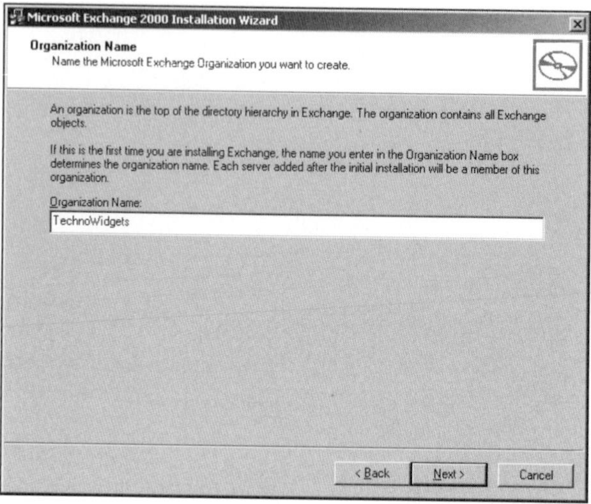

Figure 8-9 Organization Name dialog box

9. Click **Next**. The Licensing Agreement dialog box opens. Click the **I agree that: I have read and agree to be bound by the license agreements for this product** option button to accept the licensing agreement, and then click **Next**. The Component Summary dialog box opens, which shows that you are about to install the server and system management software. See Figure 8-10. Details such as the drive letter for your installation might vary.

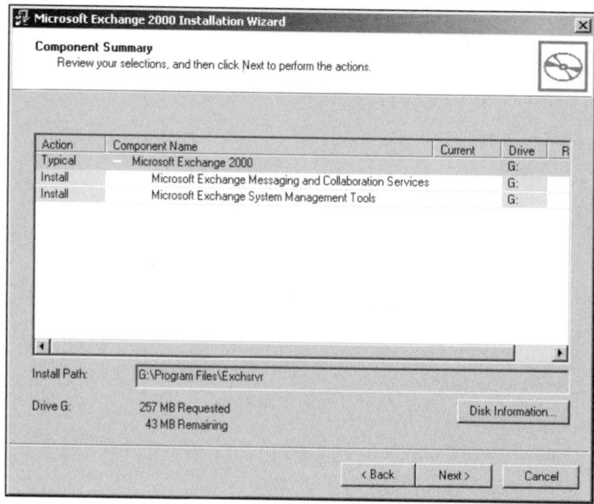

Figure 8-10 Component Summary dialog box

10. Click **Next** to install the software. If you receive a warning about an insecure domain, click **OK**. The Component Progress dialog box opens and shows the actions that the installation wizard performs. This process takes a while.
11. Click **Finish**. If you are using Windows 2003, a message might appear concerning the inability to install the Exchange 2000 IFS driver. This problem will be fixed when you install Exchange Service Pack 3.
12. Close the Microsoft Exchange 2000 Enterprise Server window.
13. Restart the server. In Windows 2003, a dialog box opens stating that a service did not start. Click **OK**. This problem will be solved when you install Service Pack 3 in the next set of steps.

To install Exchange 2000 Service Pack 3:

1. The Service Pack is usually provided on the Microsoft Web site as a compressed file called EX2KSP3_server.exe. You can download this file from *www.microsoft.com/exchange/downloads/2000/sp3/english.asp*.
2. Create a folder on C:\ called **SP3**.
3. On the Microsoft Web page, right-click **EX2KSP3_server.exe** and save it in the SP3 folder.
4. Navigate to the SP3 folder and double-click **EX2KSP3_server.exe** to uncompress it. The WinZip Self-Extractor dialog box opens.
5. In the "Unzip to folder" text box, type **C:\SP3** or any other drive with at least 325 MB available.
6. Click **Unzip** to unzip the more than 9,000 files into a directory called server on your hard disk. The WinZip program creates the folder called server, as well as many other folders.
7. After the files finish unzipping, click **OK**, and close the WinZip dialog box.
8. Use Windows Explorer to navigate to \server\setup\i386. Double-click **update.exe**.

   In Windows 2003 only: A dialog box opens stating that Exchange 2000 is not supported. Click **Continue**.
9. The Welcome to the Microsoft Exchange 2000 Service Pack Installation Wizard dialog box opens. Click **Next**.
10. The Component Selection dialog box opens, with Update listed under the Action heading. Click **Next**.
11. The Component Summary dialog box opens, describing what will be updated. Click **Next**.
12. The Component Progress dialog box opens and shows the progress of the update. This process takes a few minutes.
13. The Completing the Microsoft Exchange 2000 Wizard dialog box opens. Click **Finish** to exit the wizard.

Administering Microsoft Exchange 2000

You use two software components to administer Exchange 2000. The first is the Exchange System Manager, shown in Figure 8-11. You open the Exchange System Manager by clicking **Start**, pointing to **All Programs** (**Programs** in Windows 2000), pointing to **Microsoft Exchange**, and then clicking **System Manager**. The other is the Active Directory Users and Computers, which has been modified to integrate user management and Exchange 2000 management.

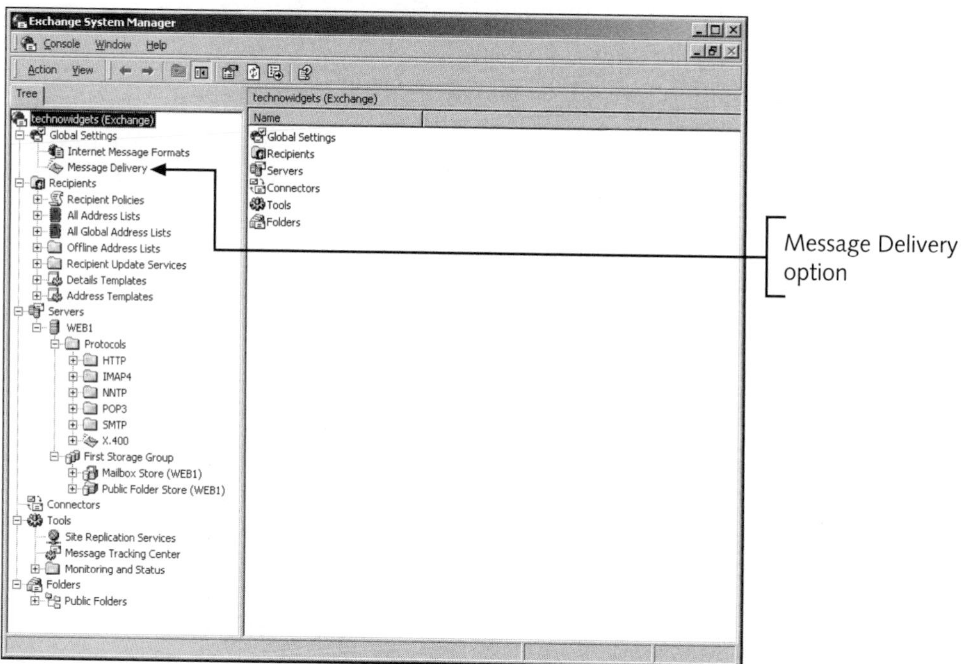

Figure 8-11 Exchange System Manager window

The Exchange System Manager allows you to administer many aspects of the server. Some settings are rarely accessed and are mostly used for reference. However, you need to understand the settings discussed in the following paragraphs because most organizations configure these settings.

Listed under Global Settings on the Exchange System Manager window, the Internet Message Formats contain the standard MIME associations, such as associating the text/HTML format with files that have .htm or .html extensions. Another global setting specifies the properties for message delivery. When you double-click the Message Delivery icon in the Exchange System Manager window, the Message Delivery Properties dialog box opens. Figure 8-12 shows three restrictions you can set for messages in this dialog box—outgoing message size, incoming message size, and recipient limits.

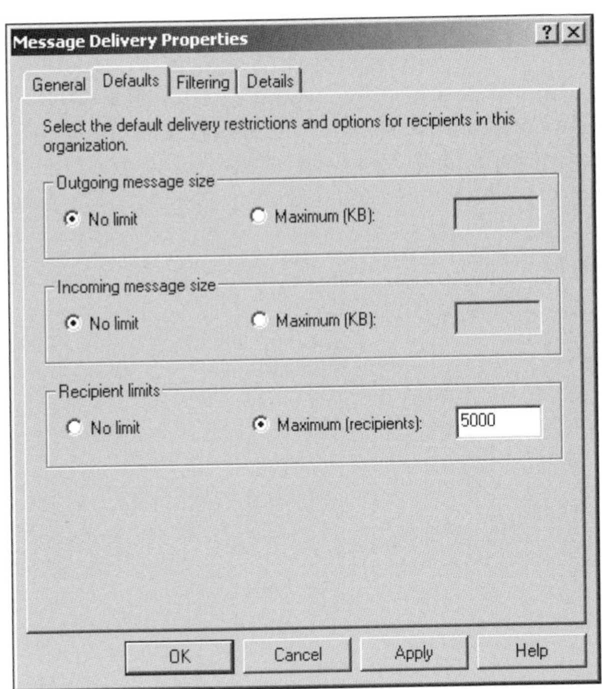

Figure 8-12 Defaults for the Message Delivery Properties dialog box

Setting these restrictions can be useful, especially when you need to find people who are sending inappropriate e-mail messages. For example, an angry user could send messages with 20 MB attachments that may significantly slow down your server. In such a case, you may want to limit the size of incoming messages. A limit of 2 MB is adequate in most circumstances. You could set the outgoing message size if your organization has a policy of sending only short text messages, yet some users send messages with large file attachments, such as images and music files, that can also slow down the system. Determining the default message sizes can be challenging. If your users send only text messages and very small attachments, then a limit of about 50 K is reasonable. If you have users who need to send larger messages, the outgoing message size can be increased on an individual basis. For organizations that send Microsoft Word documents and PowerPoint presentations with graphics, for example, an outgoing message size of 2 MB or more may be appropriate. A limit of 50 recipients is enough for most organizations, although specific users who need to send company announcements to all employees need a recipient limit equal to the number of employees.

The Filtering tab of the Message Delivery Properties, shown in Figure 8-13, allows you to filter e-mail that you do not want to deliver. E-mail can be filtered based on a specific e-mail address such as *deals@superspammers.com* or based on everyone at a specific domain name such as **@superspammers.com*. You can select the "Accept messages without notifying sender of filtering" check box to reduce the amount of traffic needed to return a message to the offending sender. This option is useful if someone is sending unwanted e-mails with a commercial message to many of your users. By default, all of the messages that are filtered are deleted, but if you want to archive them, you can select the "Archive filtered messages" check box. Because an archive can grow rapidly if many users receive filtered e-mail messages, you should monitor the size of the archive file. Generally, you should select the "Filter messages with blank sender" check box because legitimate e-mail messages have a sender.

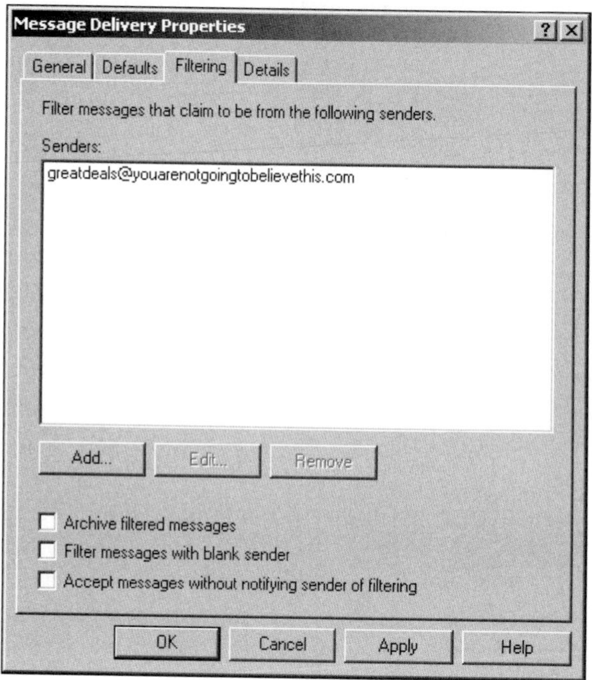

Figure 8-13 Filtering tab of the Message Delivery Properties dialog box

In the Exchange System Manager window, you use the Recipients folder to set up new policies for accepting e-mail addresses from other e-mail systems, such as Lotus Notes, in addition to the Internet. You can create specific address lists such as those for e-mail users with **external e-mail addresses** or people in a particular department. An external e-mail address is used when you accept email for *jdesena@technowidgets.com*, even if he has no mailbox in Exchange 2000. The messages are sent to an external e-mail server such as *jdesena5323@yahoo.com*. The Recipients folder contains Templates subfolders, which allow you to modify foreign language templates for users.

You use the Servers folder in the Exchange System Manager window to monitor and occasionally configure server-related components. For example, you can use the subfolders in the Protocols folder to view current sessions for SMTP, IMAP4, and POP3, which permits you to discover whether a significant backlog of messages is related to a particular protocol. You use the First Storage Group subfolder for advanced configuration, such as adding a storage group to balance the load of mailboxes and public folders.

The Tools folder in the Exchange System Manager window contains the Message Tracking Center folder, where you track messages. You can track messages in a variety of ways, including by recipient, by sender, and by date the message is sent. If you know that the system slows significantly between certain hours, for example, you can track the messages for those hours. The Message Tracking Center monitors the time of the message, the size of the message, the number of recipients of the message, and the e-mail addresses of the recipients.

Administering Microsoft Exchange 2000 Users

When you add a user to an Exchange 2000 server, you create a mailbox for that user from the Active Directory Users and Computers console. By default, you use the New Object – User dialog box shown in Figure 8-14 to create a mailbox for each new user. When you create a new user, the third dialog box allows you to create a mailbox.

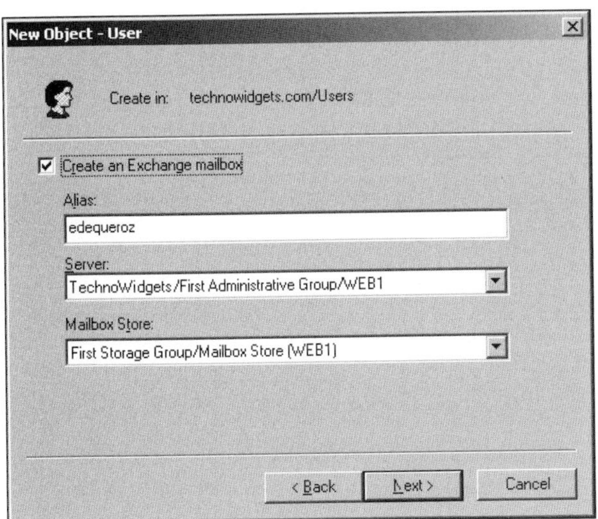

Figure 8-14 New Object - User dialog box

After you add a new user, you can configure his or her mailbox. To do so, you use the Properties dialog box for that user, which is available from the Active Directory Users and Computers console. Exchange 2000 adds three tabs to this Properties dialog box for users who have mailboxes. You use the Exchange Features tab to enable and disable instant messaging. The E-mail Addresses tab allows you to add e-mail addresses for a particular user. See Figure 8-15.

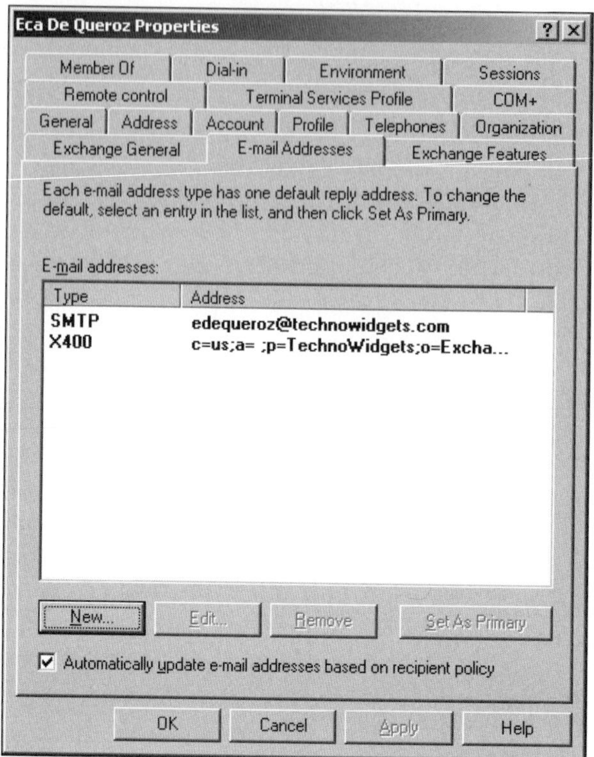

Figure 8-15 E-mail Addresses tab on the user Properties dialog box

You can use the New button in this dialog box to add a new e-mail address, such as *info@technowidgets.com*, which would allow edequeroz to retrieve all the e-mail messages directed to *info@technowidgets.com*. This also shows you how to create an e-mail address without creating an associated user. In this case, there is no user called info, yet e-mail can be sent to info.

You use the Exchange General tab shown in Figure 8-16 to configure a variety of options for a single user.

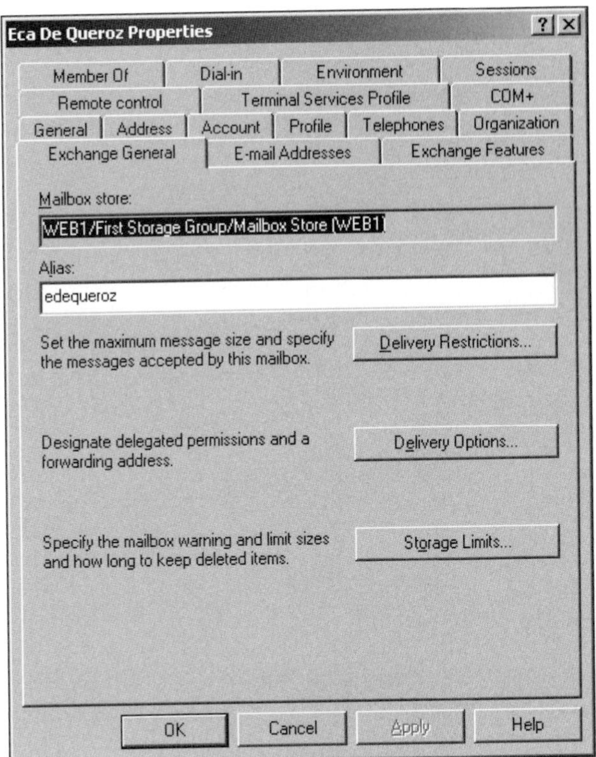

Figure 8-16 Exchange General tab on the user Properties dialog box

8

You use the Delivery Restrictions button to open the Delivery Restrictions dialog box shown in Figure 8-17. There you can limit the size of outgoing messages and incoming messages, thereby overriding the defaults set in the Exchange System Manager. You can also restrict e-mail messages based on the e-mail address of the sender.

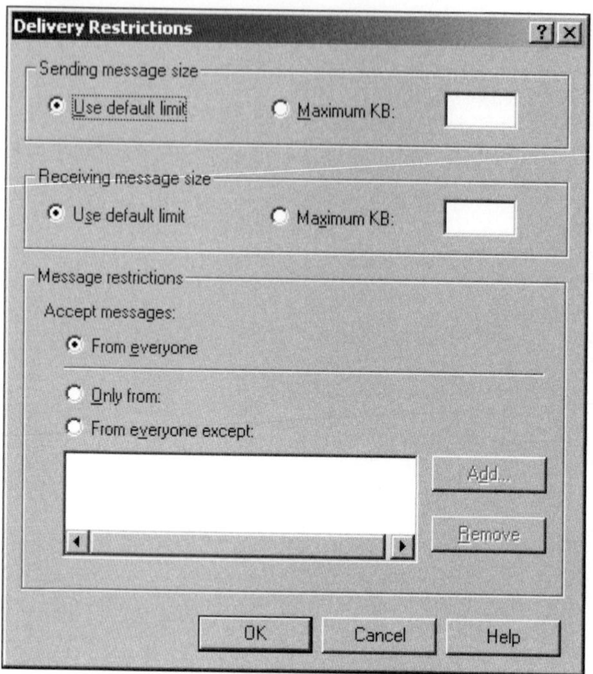

Figure 8-17 Delivery Restrictions dialog box

You use the Delivery Options button to open the Delivery Options dialog box shown in Figure 8-18. There you can grant permission to another user to send messages on behalf of the current user. For example, an executive might grant permission to an assistant who typically handles the executive's e-mail. If Eca de Queroz was an executive, you could click Add to add a user who could send e-mail with a return address of *edequeroz@technowidgets.com*. You can also use the Delivery Options dialog box to specify a forwarding address, which can be useful if a person is no longer with the organization, yet you still want to accept his or her e-mail. For example, if a salesperson left the company, you could transfer her clients to another user. You can also change the number of recipients for the user. The default for all users was set in the Exchange System Manager.

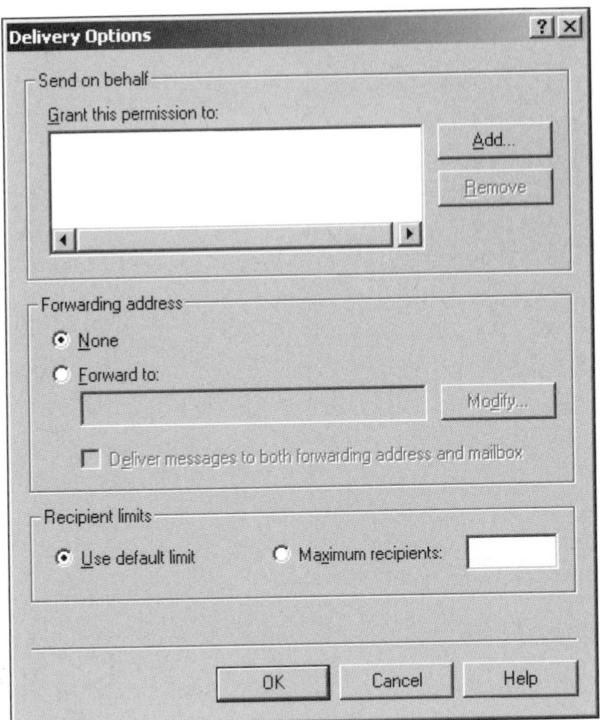

Figure 8-18 Delivery Options dialog box

Although you also can set default storage limits for all users, you can override these limits in the Storage Limits dialog box, shown in Figure 8-19. Notice that you can set three different limits. The "Issue warning at (KB)" text box allows you to warn the user that his or her mailbox is filling up. The "Prohibit send at (KB)" text box prevents the user from sending e-mail when the limit is reached but still allows that person to receive e-mail. This option is a good choice because, although you want to manage storage limits, normally you do not want to refuse potentially important e-mail messages. Setting this option encourages users to delete old messages so that new messages can be sent. Use the "Prohibit send and receive at (KB)" option when a user either does not check e-mail or leaves the organization without deleting the user name. In such a case, messages could be sent to the mailbox indefinitely and the mailbox could grow very large.

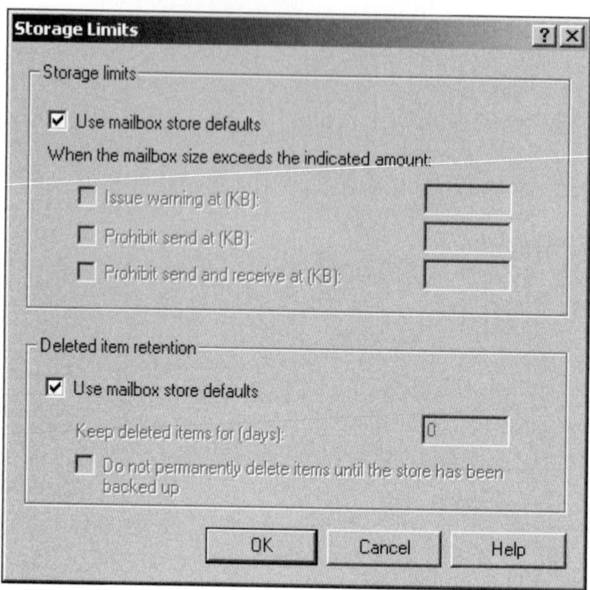

Figure 8-19 Storage Limits dialog box

When users delete e-mail messages, the messages are not actually deleted from the system, but rather are stored in a temporary location, which can consume a lot of storage space. You can limit the space consumed by the deleted messages by entering a value in the "Keep deleted items for (days)" text box. However, some organizations have a policy to retain all e-mail messages. In this case, you can check the box next to "Do not permanently delete items until the store has been backed up."

INSTALLING AND ADMINISTERING SENDMAIL FOR LINUX

Sendmail only accepts and sends e-mail. It is an MTA, and does not include an MDA as Exchange 2000 does. Thus the only protocol sendmail understands is SMTP. If you want to retrieve mail using POP3 or IMAP4, you must install other server software. You can use sendmail only if your users can log on to the sendmail server. In this case, they are retrieving mail as local clients. The e-mail resides on the same computer to which they logged on, so no other protocols are needed—just a client package to retrieve e-mail. To avoid using e-mail software other than sendmail, you can also use Web-based e-mail. When you do so, the Web server is the client connecting to the sendmail server on the same computer.

Installing Sendmail

As with other Linux applications, to install sendmail, you use the rpm utility. If you selected the check box for mail server when you installed Linux, sendmail is already installed. Otherwise, you need Red Hat Linux CDs 1 and 3 to install sendmail. There are two parts to the sendmail installation. The sendmail-8.12.5-7.i386.rpm package is the actual sendmail program. However, because the default method of configuring sendmail is difficult for beginners, you can use sendmail-cf-8.11.6-3.i386.rpm, a software package designed to help you configure sendmail. This package contains the m4 macro processor, which you will use to configure sendmail here. A third file, sendmail-doc-8.11.6-3.i386.rpm, installs the documentation for sendmail.

To install sendmail and the m4 macro processor in Linux:

1. Insert Red Hat Linux CD 1 in the CD drive.
2. On the desktop, double-click **CD/DVD-ROM**.
3. Navigate to the \RedHat\RPMS directory.
4. Double-click the file that begins with **sendmail-8** to install the sendmail program. If the program is already installed, a dialog box notifies you that you do not need to install sendmail. However, you still need to continue with the following steps. If sendmail is not installed, the Completed System Preparation dialog box opens. Click **Continue**.
5. Close the Konqueror window. Open a terminal window, type **umount /mnt/cdrom**, and then press **Enter**. (Be sure to insert a space after typing "umount".) Replace Linux CD 1 with CD 3.
6. On the desktop, double-click **CD/DVD-ROM**.
7. Navigate to the \RedHat\RPMS directory.
8. Double-click the file that begins with **sendmail-cf** to install the m4 macro processor.
9. The Completed System Preparation dialog box opens. Click **Continue**. If you are using Linux 8.0, the dialog box may stop responding. If it has not finished after two minutes, open a terminal window, type **shutdown –r now**, and then press **Enter**. You installed sendmail, and can continue with the configuration.

After installing sendmail, you do not have to start the e-mail service as you did with the DNS server (using named) or the Apache Web server (using httpd). This is because sendmail uses xinetd to listen at port 25. When xinetd receives a message on port 25, it starts sendmail, which processes the message. When sendmail finishes processing the message, the software stops and frees the memory that it was using. This approach is very different from that used with DNS or a Web server, both of which run in the background waiting for communication so they can respond quickly to client requests. An e-mail server does not need to run in the background and respond quickly to client requests when users send e-mail messages that remain on the e-mail server until they are retrieved. However, some e-mail software for Linux does not use xinetd; these packages remain running in the background so as to provide improved performance in systems that exchange a lot of e-mail.

Configuring Sendmail

Unless you are an experienced sendmail administrator, you need to know how to configure sendmail using the m4 macro processor. A macro is a command that can represent many lines of code in a configuration file. You first create a text file that defines all the macros you want to use. Then you use the m4 program to translate the macros into the configuration file that sendmail uses. Clearly, a file with 12 lines of macros is easier to understand than a configuration file containing more than 1,000 lines of code.

Some macros are required to configure sendmail. Others make sendmail more secure and activate the options you need. Both the required macros and some of the optional macros are stored in /etc/mail/sendmail.mc. Most of the optional macros start with "dnl," which tells the macro processor not to process the macro. When you are finished with the configuration, you must type the following line in a terminal window to process the macro file and create sendmail.cf:

```
m4 /etc/mail/sendmail.mc > /etc/mail/sendmail.cf
```

When you describe a string of characters in the macro configuration file, be sure to begin the string with a single opening quote, or back tick character (`), not an apostrophe ('). (The back tick symbol key is typically located under the Esc key on your keyboard.) For example, look closely at the following macro:

```
FEATURE(`smrsh',`/usr/sbin/smrsh')
```

The symbol before the "s" in smrsh is the back tick and signals the beginning of a string in the macro, yet the "h" in smrsh is followed by an apostrophe. An exception is a macro that contains just a single string of characters. In such a case, the back tick and the apostrophe are optional. For example, the following two macros are legal:

```
FEATURE(`accept_unresolvable_domains')
FEATURE(accept_unresolvable_domains)
```

Figure 8-20 shows a minimal configuration file named sendmail.mc. The first line in the sendmail.mc file is `divert(-1)`. This command forces sendmail to start the macro processing from the beginning and clears out any entries in the buffer. The `include(`/usr/share/sendmail-cf/m4/cf.m4')` line describes where to find the file necessary to translate the macros into the actual configuration. The `OSTYPE(`linux')` line describes the operating system; it is used to generate configuration information specific to Linux. The references to procmail in `define(`PROCMAIL_MAILER_PATH',`/usr/bin/procmail')` and `FEATURE(local_procmail,`',`procmail -t -Y -a $h -d $u')` describe the local mail application responsible for putting the e-mail messages in the correct user directories and other related activities. The MAILER macros, `MAILER(smtp)` and `MAILER(procmail)`, define the methods used to transfer e-mail messages. The last command describes the domain that is using sendmail. If *technowidgets.com* is the domain, you would add `Cwtechnowidgets.com`.

```
divert(-1)
include(`/usr/share/sendmail-cf/m4/cf.m4')
OSTYPE(`linux')
define(`PROCMAIL_MAILER_PATH',`/usr/bin/procmail')dnl
FEATURE(local_procmail,`',`procmail -t -Y -a $h -d $u')dnl
MAILER(smtp)dnl
MAILER(procmail)dnl
Cwtechnowidgets.com
```

Figure 8-20 Minimal sendmail.mc file

Other macros make sendmail more useful and secure. Some of the most popular ones include the following macro:

```
FEATURE(`smrsh',`/usr/sbin/smrsh')
```


This macro forces sendmail to use a restricted shell called smrsh instead of the default /bin/sh shell. This choice makes sendmail less vulnerable to hackers who try to access commands that are not part of sendmail.

The following macro contains e-mail addresses to be sent to other users:

```
FEATURE(`virtusertable',`hash -o /etc/mail/virtusertable.db')
```

Because this macro is a hash file, the makemap utility must translate it from a simple text file to the virtual user table. The text file contains two entries on each line. The first entry represents the e-mail message that is read by sendmail. The second entry describes how to process the e-mail message. The most common use of this feature is to send a generic e-mail message to a specific user. For example, suppose you ask prospective clients to send inquiries to *info@technowidgets.com*, but the person who reads the e-mail uses the *fpessoa@technowidgets.com* account. You can type the following line into /etc/mail/virtusertable.db to route e-mail sent to info to fpessoa:

```
info@technowidgets.com fpessoa@technowidgets.com
```

You can also use this macro when you have a number of domains but only a single set of users. All the mail from the other domains can be routed to e-mail addresses in a single domain. Suppose that besides *technowidgets.com*, you have other domains such as *bestwidgets.com* and a company you purchased, *buggywhipstoday.com*. To send all the e-mail to a single set of users, you would add the following lines to /etc/mail/virtusertable.db:

```
@bestwidgets.com %1technowidgets.com
@buggywhipstoday.com %1technowidgets.com
```

If you saved the previous two lines plus the line that begins "info@technowidgets.com" in a file called virtusertable.txt, you could convert it to the hash file with the following command:

```
makemap  /etc/mail/virtusertable.db  <virtusertable.txt>
```

A useful feature to control access to sendmail is the access feature, which has the following syntax:

```
FEATURE(`access_db',`hash -o /etc/mail/access.db')
```

The file /etc/mail/access.db refers to a hash file, as virtusertable.db does, so you would have to create a text file first and then process it with the makemap command. The text file would contain a list of addresses and settings that specify whether to accept or reject e-mail from these addresses.

You can reject an e-mail message in two ways. The **REJECT** option prevents the e-mail from being received, but sends a message to the sender stating that the original message has been rejected. With the **DISCARD** option, sendmail does not send a message to the sender. Another option relays e-mail messages to or from a specific domain. By default, only e-mail coming from your domain or being sent to your domain is accepted. You could use this option to allow parts of your organization that have different domain names to use your sendmail server. Following are two examples of these options:

```
greatdeals@wonderfulproducts.com REJECT
bestwidgets.com                  RELAY
```

Some configuration options can create security problems, but might be necessary under some circumstances. The **FEATURE(`accept_unresolvable_domains')** macro allows sendmail to accept e-mail from users where the domain cannot be verified through DNS. The **FEATURE(`promiscuous_relay')** macro allows sendmail to accept e-mail from any domain and then send the message to any domain. It enables spammers to use your e-mail server to send unlimited e-mail messages to other domains.

Installing and Configuring IMAP4 and POP3 for Linux

Although sendmail implements only SMTP, the University of Washington has created the software necessary to implement both IMAP4 and POP3 in sendmail. Red Hat Linux has a copy of the software on Red Hat CD 2. You must first install the software, and then enable it.

To install IMAP4 and POP3 servers in Linux:

1. Insert Red Hat Linux CD 2 in the CD drive.
2. On the desktop, double-click **CD/DVD-ROM**.
3. Navigate to the \RedHat\RPMS directory.
4. Double-click the file that begins with **imap-2001**. The Completed System Preparation dialog box opens. Click **Continue**. After a few moments, the next dialog box closes, and both the IMAP4 and POP3 servers are installed.

After installing the software, you must enable it. IMAP4 and POP3 each have a file in the /etc/xinetd.d directory. For example, if you open the imap file after installing the

IMAP4 and POP3 software, one line shows that `disable = yes`, meaning that IMAP4 is disabled. See Figure 8-21.

```
# default: off
# description: The IMAP service allows remote users to access their mail using \
#              an IMAP client such as Mutt, Pine, fetchmail, or Netscape \
#              Communicator.
service imap
{
        socket_type         = stream
        wait                = no
        user                = root
        server                    = /usr/sbin/imapd
        log_on_success            += DURATION USERID
        log_on_failure            += USERID
        disable                   = yes
}
```

Figure 8-21 Contents of /etc/xinetd.d/imapd

To enable IMAP4, you must edit the file to change `disable = yes` to `disable = no`. Then you do the same for the POP3 file.

To enable IMAP4 and POP3 in Linux:

1. Open a terminal window in Linux.
2. Type **kedit /etc/xinetd.d/imap**, and then press **Enter**.
3. On the last line, change **disable = yes** to **disable = no**.
4. Save the file, and then exit the editor.
5. Although you can repeat the same commands in Steps 2–4 to enable POP3 as you did for IMAP4, it is easier to type the following command and then press **Enter**:

   chkconfig ipop3 on
6. Restart xinetd to recognize the changes you made by typing the following command and then pressing **Enter**:

   service xinetd restart

Configuring E-mail Clients

Many software developers offer e-mail clients. Microsoft Outlook (2000 or 2002), for example, is a comprehensive e-mail package that is part of the Microsoft Office suite. Unlike some other e-mail clients, which are free, you must purchase Outlook. Microsoft Outlook Express provides e-mail connectivity and support for newsgroups. Netscape

Communicator combines a browser with Netscape Messenger, an e-mail client. Mozilla, another browser related to Netscape, also has an e-mail client. The KDE environment has KMail, a standalone e-mail client.

An alternative to configuring an e-mail client is to use a browser to access e-mail. Exchange 2000 has Outlook Web Access, which offers many of the capabilities of Outlook in a Web-based environment.

All e-mail clients have similar configuration options, with the exception of Outlook 2002, which allows you to connect directly to the Exchange 2000 server over a LAN.

You typically need to provide the following information to configure e-mail clients:

- *SMTP server address*—This address is also called the outgoing server address.
- *E-mail address*—This is your address for retrieving e-mail from a POP3 or IMAP4 server.
- *E-mail password*—This password allows you to retrieve e-mail from the POP3 or IMAP4 server.
- *Server address*—This address is for either a POP3 server or an IMAP4 server. Remember that servers such as Exchange 2000 and the University of Washington IMAP4 server implement both protocols.

It is common practice to have both a computer at your workplace and a home computer configured to receive business e-mail. You have already learned that your SMTP server should be accessed only by users in your own domain. If you allowed users outside your domain to access your SMTP server, spammers could use it to send e-mail. For this reason, when you use your home computer, you connect to the domain of your ISP, such as *econoisp.com*. You then set your SMTP server to the ISP's SMTP server at *econoisp.com*, not your business's SMTP server at *technowidgets.com*. When you configure your computer at your workplace, you set your SMTP server to the one at *technowidgets.com*. However, whether your computer is located at your workplace or your home, the POP3 or IMAP4 server address is the same because your e-mail is stored on a single server at your organization.

Configuring an E-mail Client in Linux

KMail is an e-mail client available in the KDE environment (you can also install the Mozilla browser, which includes the Mozilla e-mail client). KMail is installed automatically when you install KDE.

To configure KMail in Linux:

1. Log on as one of the users that you created in previous chapters, such as cbranco.
2. In Linux, click the **Red Hat** icon, point to **Extras**, point to **Internet**, and then drag **KMail** to the panel at the bottom of the desktop. This will make it easier to start KMail.

3. Click **KMail**. The first time you start KMail, a dialog box notifies you that it will create a mail directory. Click **OK**. The KDE Mail Client - KMail window opens. See Figure 8-22.

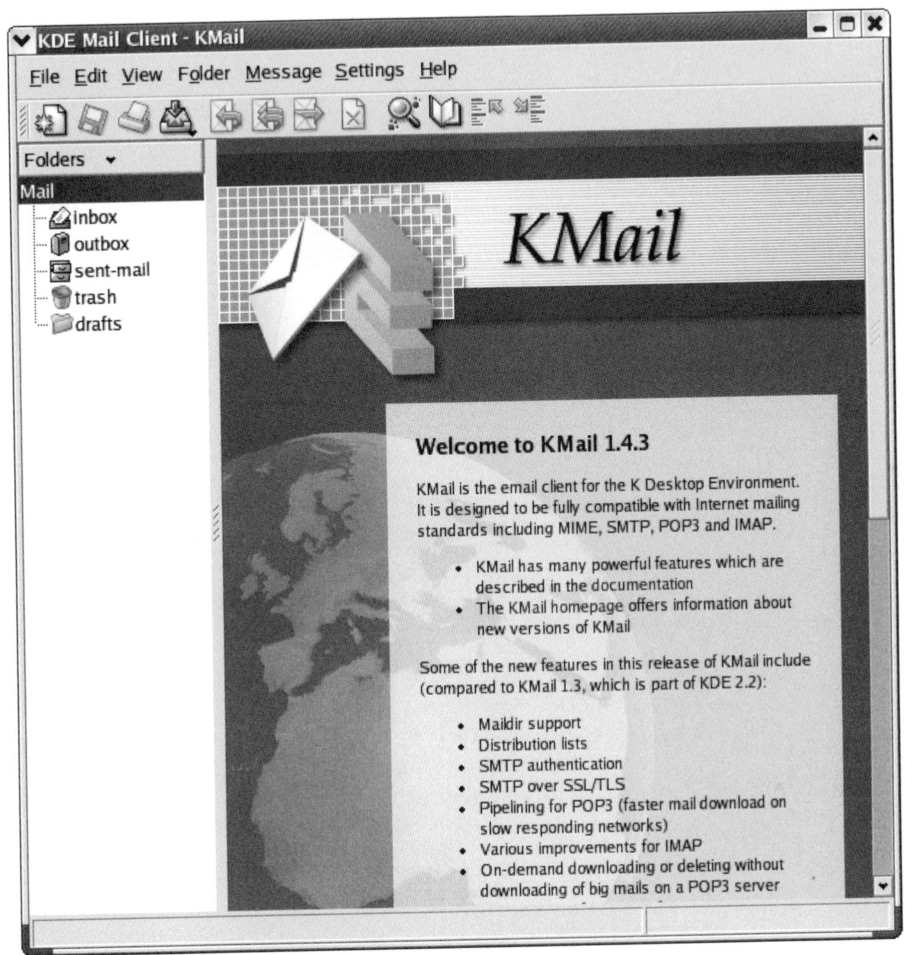

Figure 8-22 KDE Mail Client - KMail window

4. Click **Settings** on the menu bar, and then click **Configure KMail**. The Configure-KMail window opens, shown in Figure 8-23. You use this window to specify information about yourself and the e-mail servers that you use.

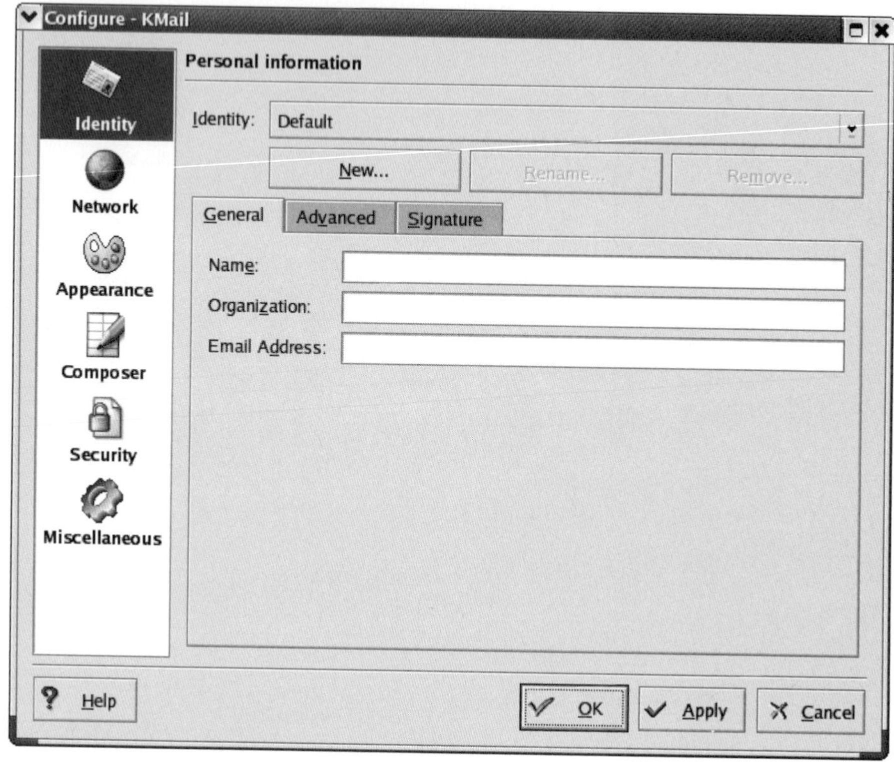

Figure 8-23 Configure window for KMail

5. Enter the name **Cristina Branco**, the organization **TechnoWidgets**, and the e-mail address **cbranco@technowidgets.com**. This choice determines the e-mail address that you will use when sending e-mail and the user-friendly name of Cristina Branco that will be sent with the e-mail address.
6. Click **Network** in the left panel. The Setup for sending and receiving messages window opens, as shown in Figure 8-24. Notice that the right panel is on the Sending tab. The window shows the default outgoing account of sendmail. However, you should configure this setting as if your SMTP server controlled all your e-mail communication.
7. Click **Add** to add a server. The Add Transport dialog box opens asking how the e-mail should be sent. See Figure 8-25.

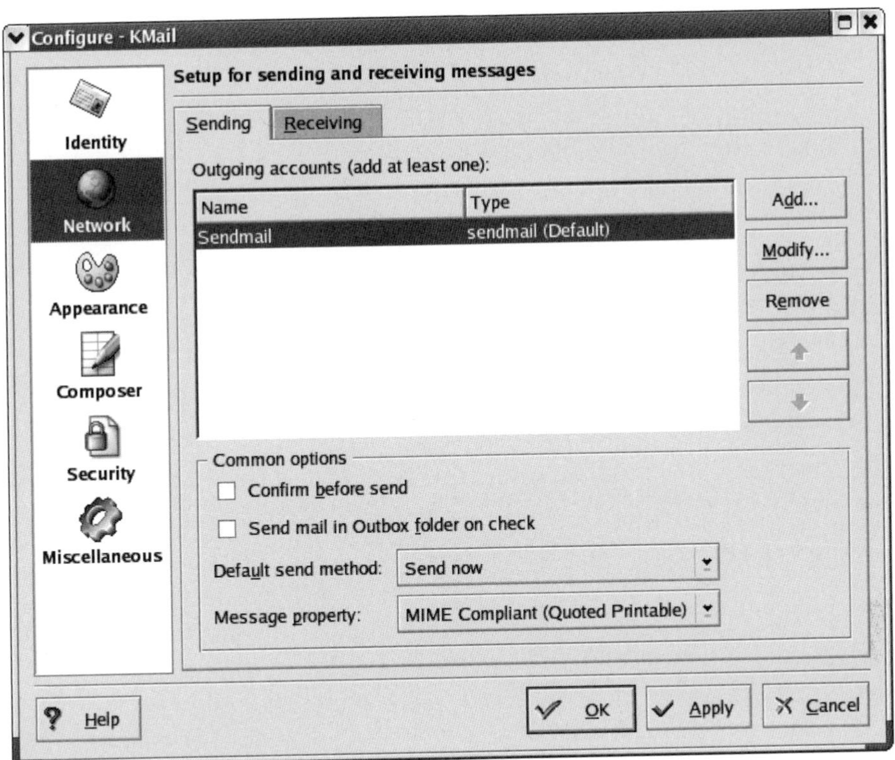

Figure 8-24 Setup for sending and receiving messages window

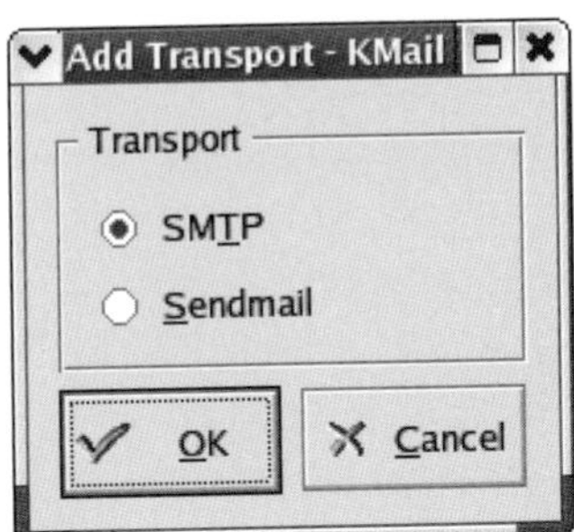

Figure 8-25 Add Transport - KMail dialog box

8

8. Accept the default of SMTP by clicking **OK**. The Transport: SMTP dialog box opens, as shown in Figure 8-26. In the Name text box, type **TechnoWidgets**. This name is displayed in the list of SMTP servers. In the Host text box, type **mail.technowidgets.com**. Click **OK** to save the configuration.

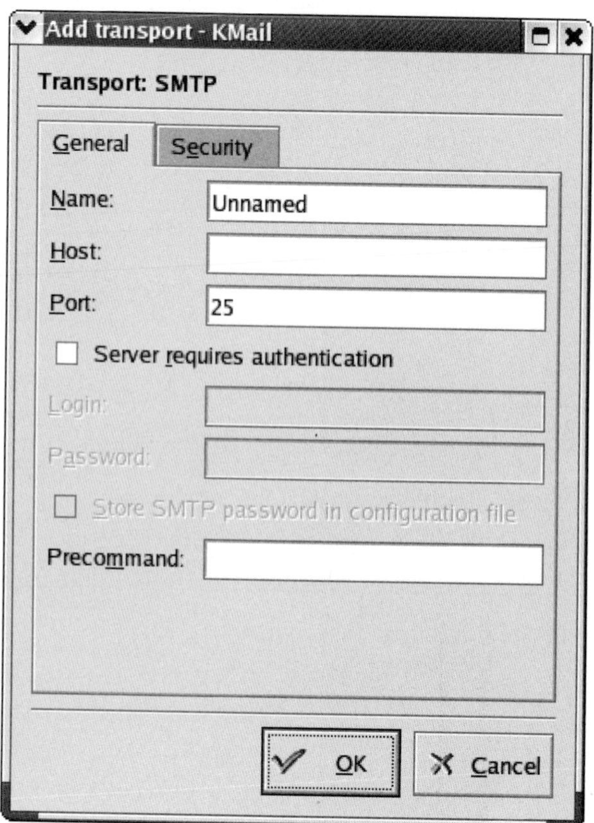

Figure 8-26 Transport: SMTP dialog box

9. Now you need to configure the incoming accounts, which correspond to the server or servers that store your e-mail. Click the **Receiving** tab in the right panel. The Receiving tab opens, as shown in Figure 8-27.

10. Click the **Add** button to add an incoming account. The Add Account – KMail dialog box opens, as shown in Figure 8-28.

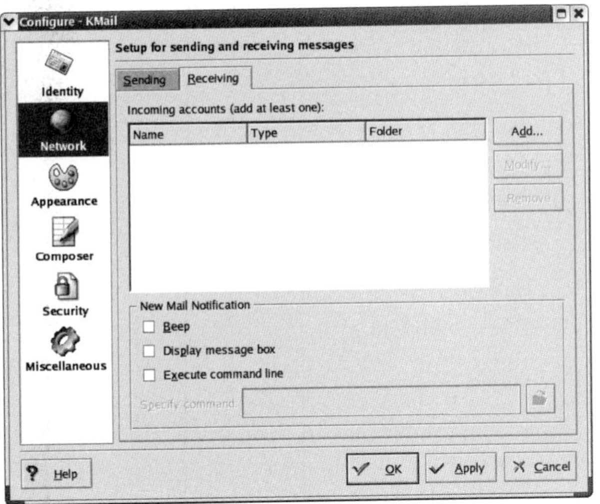

Figure 8-27 Configure - KMail dialog box with the Receiving tab selected

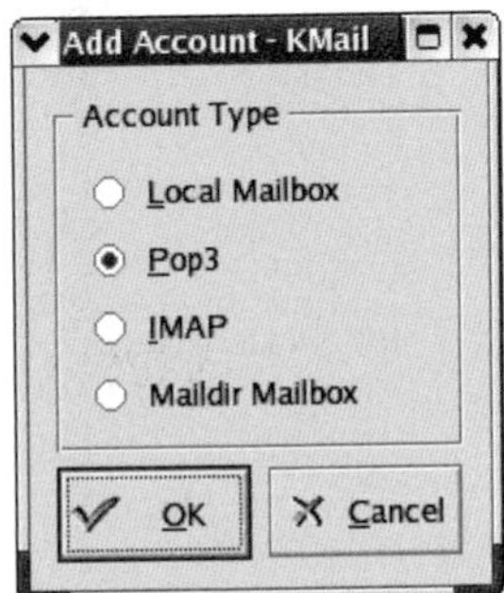

Figure 8-28 Add Account – KMail dialog box

11. Click the **IMAP** option button, and then click **OK**. The Account type: Imap Account dialog box opens, as shown in Figure 8-29. You use this dialog box to enter your account logon information.
12. Type **Business** in the Name text box, type **cbranco** in the Login text box, type **password** in the Password text box, and type **mail.technowidgets.com** in the Host text box. Entering the password here makes it easier to receive e-mail because you do not need to enter your password each time you use KMail to retrieve your e-mail. However, anyone else could retrieve your e-mail if you left your computer when you were logged on.
13. Click **OK** to save the account information.
14. Click **OK** to save the configuration information.

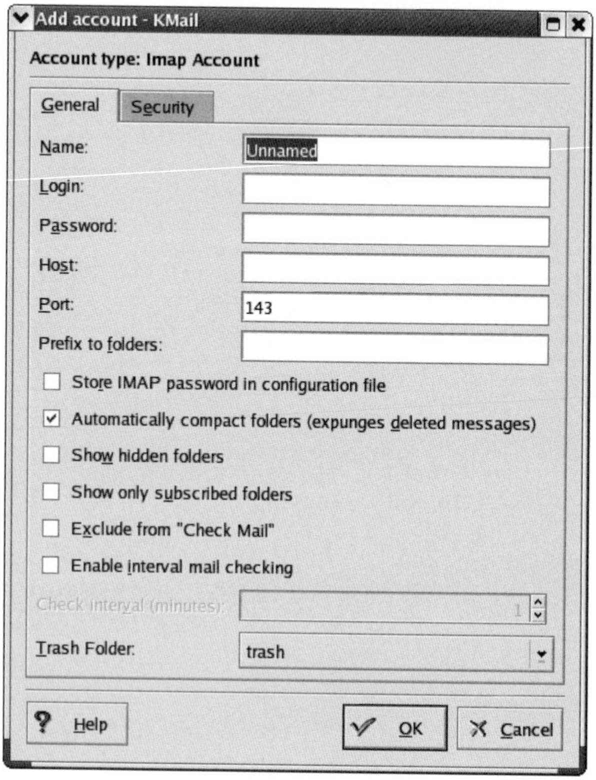

Figure 8-29 Account type: Imap Account dialog box

Configuring an E-mail Client in Microsoft Windows

The Outlook Express e-mail client is available in both Windows 2000 and Windows 2003. You can also purchase a more comprehensive e-mail client and collaboration tool called Outlook 2002.

Normally, you configure each user's computer individually. However, in the following steps, you will work with a single computer, which is the server. By default, only administrators can log on to a server. Before you can configure Outlook Express in Windows, you must allow another user to log on to the server.

To allow users to log on to the server in Windows:

1. Open the Administrative Tools window, and then click **Domain Controller Security Policy** (double-click in Windows 2000). The Default Domain Controller Security Settings window opens.
2. *In Windows 2003*: Expand the folders in the left pane as shown in Figure 8-30, and then click **User Rights Assignment**.

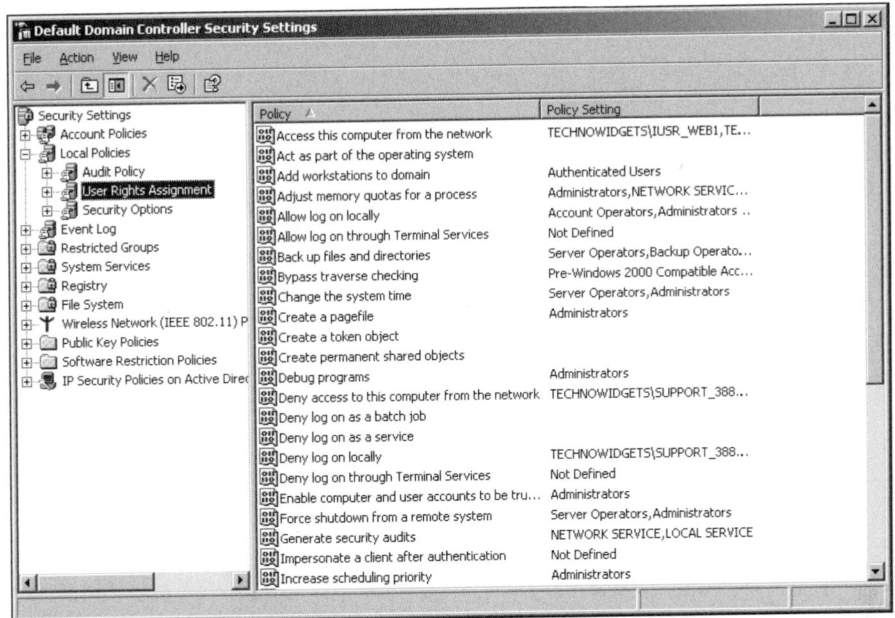

Figure 8-30 Default Domain Controller Security Settings expanded to show User Rights Assignment

In Windows 2000: Click the **plus sign** (+) next to **Security Settings** (Domain Controller Security Policy in Windows 2000) in the left pane. Click the **plus sign** (+) next to **Local Policies**, and then click **User Rights Assignment**.

3. *In Windows 2003:* Double-click **Allow log on locally** in the right pane. The Security Policy Setting dialog box for Allow log on locally Properties opens.

   In Windows 2000: Double-click **Log on locally** in the right pane. The Security Policy Setting dialog box for Log on locally opens.

4. Click **Add User or Group** (Add User in Windows 2000). The Add User or Group dialog box opens.
5. In the User and group names text box, type **Everyone**, and then click **OK**. The Everyone group allows any user you create on the server to log on at the server.
6. Click **OK** to close the Security Policy Setting dialog box.
7. Close all open windows.

To create a user to be used for e-mail:

1. In Administrative Tools, click (double-click in Windows 2000) **Active Directory Users and Computers**.
2. Right-click the **Users** folder in the left pane, point to **New**, and then click **User**. The New Object – User dialog box opens. Complete this dialog box using Cris Branco as the user, as shown in Figure 8-31.

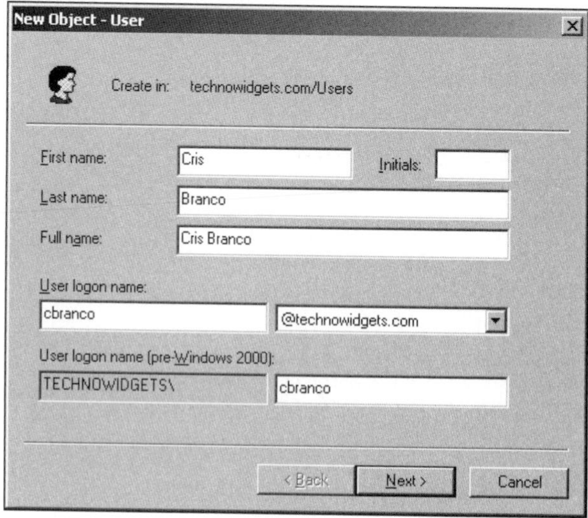

Figure 8-31 New Object – User dialog box for Cris Branco

3. Click **Next**. In the Password text box, type **Azore$3B**, and type it again in the Confirm Password text box. If the **User must change password at next logon** check box is selected, click it to remove the check mark.
4. Click **Next**. The dialog box shows Create an Exchange mailbox selected as the default. Although you would normally leave the check box for Create an Exchange mailbox selected, you will add a mailbox for Cris Branco in Hands-on Project 8-4. Therefore, click the **Create an Exchange mailbox** check box now to remove the check mark.
5. Click **Next**. A dialog box with a summary of the configuration information opens.
6. Click **Finish** to create the user, and then close the window.

Now you are ready to configure Outlook Express as your e-mail client.

To configure Outlook Express in Windows:

1. Log on to the Windows server as the user **cbranco**.
2. Start Outlook Express.

   In Windows 2003: Click **Start**, and then click **Outlook Express**.

In Windows 2000: Click the **Outlook Express** icon on the Quick Launch toolbar. (Point to the buttons on this toolbar to see the names of the icons.)

3. *In Windows 2000 only:* The first time you use Outlook Express, a dialog box might open asking if you want to make Outlook Express be your default mail client. Click **Yes**.
4. The Internet Connection Wizard opens, requesting your name. See Figure 8-32.

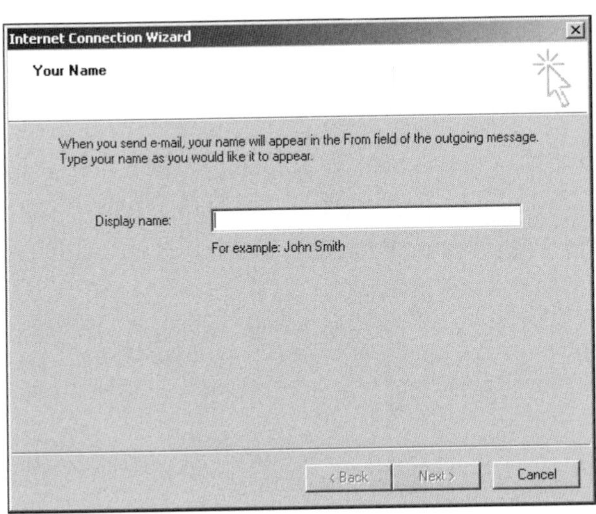

Figure 8-32 Internet Connection Wizard

5. Type **Cris Branco** in the Display name text box.
6. Click **Next.** The Internet E-mail Address dialog box opens. You use this dialog box to enter your e-mail address. Type **cbranco@technowidgets.com** in the E-mail address text box.
7. Click **Next.** The E-mail Server Names dialog box opens, as shown in Figure 8-33. In this dialog box, you select the type of server you want to use for incoming mail, enter the address of the incoming mail server, and then enter the address of the SMTP server for outgoing mail. Keep the default mail server as a POP3 server. Type **mail.technowidgets.com** in the Incoming mail (POP3, IMAP or HTTP) server text box. Type **mail.technowidgets.com** in the Outgoing mail (SMTP) server text box.

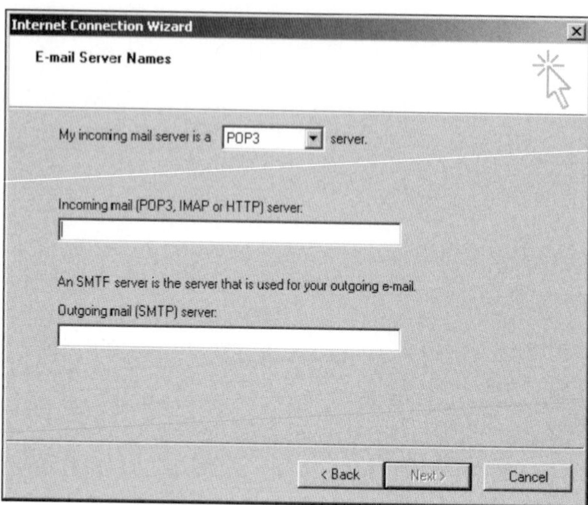

Figure 8-33 E-mail Server Names dialog box

8. Click **Next**. The Internet Mail Logon dialog box opens, allowing you to enter your account name and password. See Figure 8-34. For the password, type **password**.

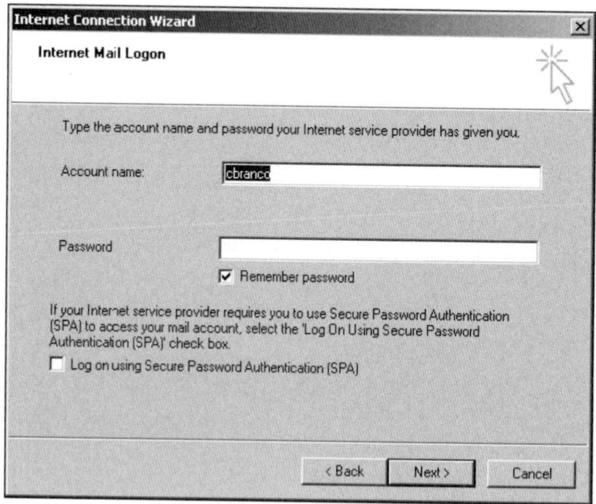

Figure 8-34 Internet Mail Logon dialog box

9. Click **Next**. The Congratulations window opens. You have finished setting up Outlook Express as your e-mail client.
10. Click **Finish** to exit the wizard.

Understanding Web-Based E-mail Clients

Web-based E-mail clients allow you to access your e-mail by using a browser. Microsoft Hotmail, Yahoo! Mail, and others have made Web-based e-mail very popular. Advantages of Web-based e-mail include the following:

- Because a browser is used, no client configuration is needed.
- The lack of configuration can significantly reduce support costs.
- No specialized client software is needed.
- Users are not required to retrieve e-mail from specific computers that have been configured for them.
- POP3 or IMAP4 protocols are not required, which reduces server-side support.
- Because Web-based e-mail is not constrained by POP3 or IMAP4 protocols, a richer environment can be developed that extends beyond basic e-mail.

Recall that Microsoft's Web-based e-mail product is OWA. When you installed Exchange 2000, OWA was also installed by default. Although you can use any browser to connect to OWA, Microsoft designed it to be used with Internet Explorer 5.0 and later. By using current versions of IE, OWA can use DHTML and XML to transfer format processing from the server to the browser. This approach reduces the load on the server, thereby allowing faster response times or more users on a single server.

OWA shares some features with Outlook 2002. Not only can it handle the e-mail chores, but you can also use it for calendar and contact tasks, such as scheduling activities and maintaining contact information. However, some Outlook 2002 features, such as tasks, journals, offline use, printing templates, reminders, spelling checker, and timed delivery, are not available with OWA.

The architecture of OWA uses the **Microsoft Web Storage System**, which allows direct access to all the OWA information needed by users. The previous version of OWA available with Exchange 5.5 used Active Server Pages, Collaboration Data Objects (CDO), and Messaging Application Programming Interface (MAPI). In Chapter 7, when you used SQL Server to access data and produce a report, these technologies allowed OWA to access e-mail messages and other related information. The problem with this older method is that it imposed a processing burden on IIS because ASP is an interpreted language and the coding was rather complex. With the current version of OWA, IIS simply passes user requests to the Web Storage System and receives information to be sent to the user.

To authenticate users, you can choose from a variety of approaches. The most basic method involves sending your user name and password to the server in text form. However, any hacker could read this information. By using the integrated Windows method with Windows 2000 and Internet Explorer 5 or later, you can use Kerberos, which encrypts the user's password. **Secure Sockets Layer** (**SSL**) is a method of encrypting all traffic to a site or a portion of a site. You can use SSL, but the extra processing required to support it can degrade performance.

Although no real configuration is required, you can prevent certain users from using OWA and force particular authentication mechanisms to be used. For example, if you required integrated Windows authentication, you could make sure that users only accessed OWA by using a Windows 2000 or newer operating system. By default, these operating systems would have the appropriate version of Internet Explorer for Kerberos authentication.

To prevent a user named Cris Branco from using OWA in Windows:

1. Log on as administrator. Open the Administrative Tools window, if necessary, and then click **Active Directory Users and Computers** (double-click in Windows 2000).
2. Click **View** on the menu bar, and then click **Advanced Features**. This adds tabs to the Properties dialog box for each user.
3. Click the **Users** folder. Right-click **Cris Branco**, and then click **Properties**.
4. Click the **Exchange Advanced** tab. You use this property sheet to configure Exchange settings, such as the protocols used to access your mailbox. See Figure 8-35.

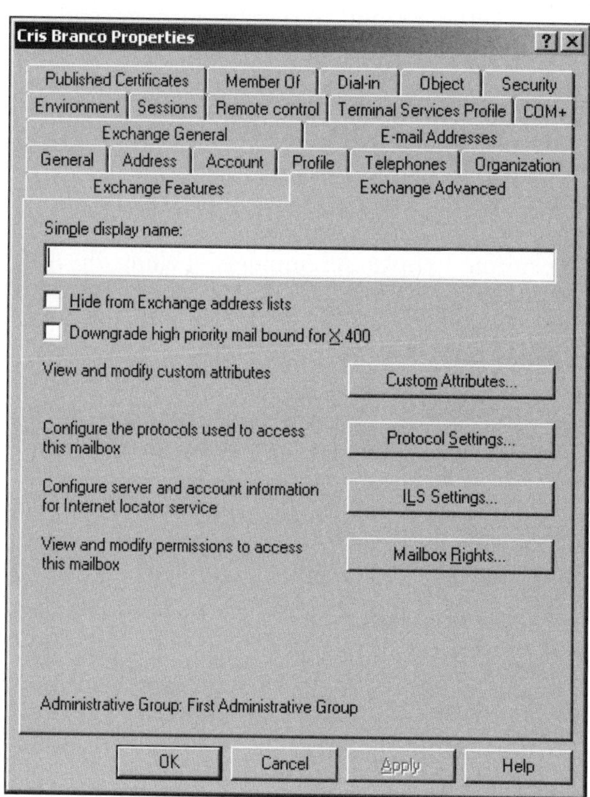

Figure 8-35 Exchange Advanced tab

5. Click **Protocol Settings**. The Protocols dialog box opens, listing the protocols available to access your mailbox. See Figure 8-36. You could prevent Cris Branco from using any of the three protocols, but here you decide to prevent her from using HTTP, which is the protocol that supports OWA.

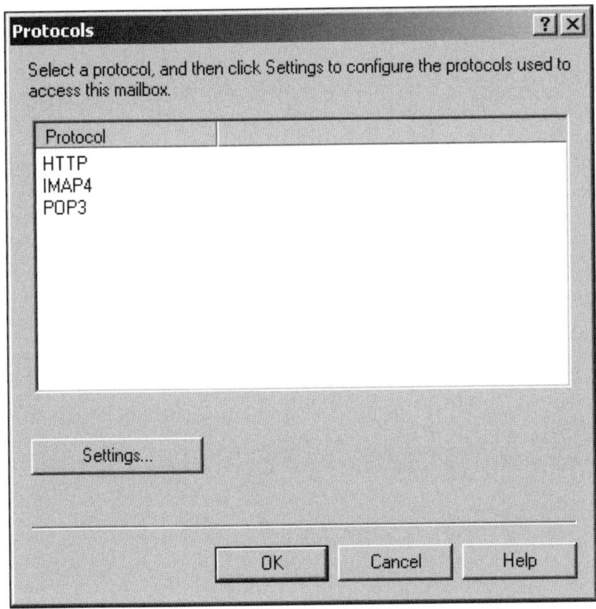

Figure 8-36 Protocols dialog box

6. Click **HTTP**, and then click **Settings**. The HTTP Protocol Details dialog box opens. This dialog box contains only a check box to enable or disable the protocol for the mailbox.
7. Click the check box to clear it, which disables HTTP for the mailbox.
8. Click **OK** to accept the changes until you return to the Active Directory Users and Computers window.
9. Close the Active Directory Users and Computers window.

Chapter Summary

- Over the years, e-mail has evolved from a variety of proprietary systems to a system based on Internet standards. Microsoft Exchange 2000 and sendmail are two of the most popular e-mail server products. Exchange 2000 goes beyond e-mail to provide instant messaging, public folders, a chat server, conferencing, and the ability to store voicemails and faxes. The MIME specification is used to translate between text and binary data such as pictures and sound.

- DNS plays a central role in messaging. In the DNS configuration, a Mail Exchange (MX) record associates a name with an IP address for an e-mail server. This way you can have one IP address associated with *technowidgets.com* to access a Web site based on the domain name, yet associate a different IP address with *technowidgets.com* when it is part of an e-mail address, as in *info@technowidgets.com*.
- A Mail Transfer Agent (MTA) accepts e-mail and sends it to the recipient's e-mail server. A Mail Delivery Agent (MDA) takes the e-mail from the server and sends it to the recipient. A Mail User Agent (MUA) is the client software that receives the e-mail.
- Three major protocols are involved in e-mail. Simple Mail Transfer Protocol (SMTP) is used to send e-mail from the client to the e-mail server and between e-mail servers. Post Office Protocol (POP3) is an MDA that retrieves e-mail from the e-mail server and typically deletes the existing e-mail messages on the server. Internet Mail Access Protocol (IMAP4) provides more robust support than POP3. You can keep messages on the server and store them in folders.
- The installation and administration of Exchange 2000 is straightforward in a single-server environment. Exchange 2000 supports SMTP, POP3, IMAP4, and LDAP. Once it is installed, you use Active Directory Users and Computers to administer Exchange 2000 users, and Exchange System Manager to administer the overall configuration of Exchange. You can alter the size of outgoing messages, change the number of recipients in a single message, and modify many other attributes.
- Sendmail is a product that implements SMTP. It offers the ability to fine-tune the e-mail environment but it can be challenging to configure. To simplify the configuration of sendmail, most users write macros that are processed and placed into the actual configuration file that is used by sendmail. Although hundreds of macros are possible, only a couple dozen are widely used.
- To implement IMAP4 and POP3 in a sendmail environment, you have to add other server software. One of the most popular packages comes from the University of Washington, the originators of the IMAP4 protocol. It is easy to install and requires very little configuration except remembering to enable the protocols.
- The configuration of e-mail clients focuses on entering common information. All clients will ask for your e-mail address, the address of your SMTP server for sending e-mail, the address of the POP3 or IMAP4 server, and the account and (optionally) the password necessary to retrieve e-mail.
- Web-based e-mail clients are very popular. With this approach, all you need is access to a browser to send and receive e-mail. This strategy eliminates the client-side configuration necessary with regular e-mail clients. Web-based e-mail clients do not require POP3 or IMAP4. Outlook Web Access (OWA) is a popular product that is part of Exchange 2000.

Review Questions

1. Which of the following is not an old e-mail standard?
   a. BITNET
   b. Lotus cc:Mail
   c. ExpressMail
   d. DECNET
2. Which of the following is *not* a feature in Exchange 2000?
   a. chat service
   b. instant messaging
   c. conferencing
   d. All of the above are features.
3. The ability to send pictures depends primarily on ____________.
   a. POP3
   b. IMAP4
   c. MIME
   d. ASP
4. Which of the following is *not* a MIME format?
   a. sound
   b. application
   c. image
   d. video
5. What kind of DNS record associates a name with an e-mail server?
   a. A
   b. CNAME
   c. NS
   d. MX
6. When a DNS record for an e-mail server contains a number such as 10, what does it mean?
   a. a sequence number that must begin at 10
   b. a priority, with the smallest number being the highest priority
   c. a priority, with the largest number being the highest priority
   d. The records do not contain numbers.

7. An example of an MDA protocol is ______________.
   a. SMTP
   b. POP3
   c. IMAP
   d. both b and c
8. An example of an MTA protocol is ______________.
   a. SMTP
   b. POP3
   c. IMAP
   d. b and c only
9. An example of an MUA is ______________.
   a. Outlook Express
   b. Exchange 2000
   c. sendmail
   d. b and c
10. An example of an MDA is ______________.
    a. Outlook Express
    b. Exchange 2000
    c. sendmail
    d. both b and c
11. An example of an MTA is ______________.
    a. Outlook Express
    b. Exchange 2000
    c. sendmail
    d. both b and c
12. What is masquerading?
    a. replacing the actual host name of the mail server with a domain name such as *technowidgets.com* in return addresses
    b. impersonating a valid sender
    c. impersonating a valid recipient
    d. impersonating a valid e-mail server
13. Which protocol is *not* used to download e-mail to a client?
    a. SMTP
    b. POP3

c. IMAP4

d. HTML

14. `DATA` is a command from the ______________ protocol.

a. SMTP

b. POP3

c. IMAP4

d. HTML

15. `RETR` is a command from the ______________ protocol.

a. SMTP

b. POP3

c. IMAP4

d. HTML

16. Which protocol is *not* included in Exchange 2000?

a. SMTP

b. POP3

c. IMAP4

d. All are included.

17. What additional protocol is required to install Exchange 2000?

a. SMTP

b. NNTP

c. HTTP

d. HTML

18. According to Microsoft, what is the minimum processor required for Exchange 2000?

a. Pentium 166

b. Pentium II 233

c. Pentium III 550

d. any Pentium 4

19. Sendmail implements which of the following protocol(s)?

a. SMTP

b. POP3

c. IMAP4

d. all of the above

20. To make sendmail configuration easier, you typically use a(n):
    a. macro processor
    b. compiler
    c. interpreter
    d. GUI

Hands-on Projects

Project 8-1

To install sendmail in a test environment, you should allow relaying and access from any hosts. You will use such a configuration in this project to test it.

To configure sendmail for a test environment in Linux:

1. Make sure that DNS is running and an MX record exists that has an IP address of your computer.
2. Install sendmail, if necessary.
3. Rename the existing sendmail.mc configuration file by typing the following command and then pressing Enter:
   mv /etc/mail/sendmail.mc /etc/mail/sendmail.mc.original
4. Create the following file in /etc/mail and name it **sendmail.mc**. Be careful to use the back tick (` ) at the beginning of strings of characters. Replace *technowidgets.com* on the last line with the domain name that you used for your DNS, but keep the `Cw`. Type the following code exactly as shown with no extra spaces.

```
divert(-1)
include(`/usr/share/sendmail-cf/m4/cf.m4')
OSTYPE(`linux')
define(`PROCMAIL_MAILER_PATH',`/usr/bin/procmail')dnl
FEATURE(promiscuous_relay)dnl
FEATURE(always_add_domain)dnl
FEATURE(local_procmail,`',`procmail -t -Y -a $h -d $u')dnl
FEATURE(accept_unresolvable_domains)dnl
MAILER(smtp)dnl
MAILER(procmail)dnl
Cwtechnowidgets.com
```

5. Process the macro file by typing **m4 /etc/mail/sendmail.mc >/etc/sendmail.cf** in a terminal window and then pressing **Enter**.
6. A warning appears about the promiscuous_relay feature. Because this is a test environment that you want other students to use, you can disregard the warning.
7. To have sendmail recognize the changes, restart it by typing **service sendmail restart** and then pressing **Enter**.

Now you need to test your configuration. You will use Telnet to do so. Telnet lets you test any e-mail server from any computer and find out if it the server has problems sending or retrieving e-mail, and what the problems are.

Before you start testing, add a user named fpessoa with a password of "password" if you have not done so already. For help in adding users in Linux, refer to "Understanding Linux User and Group Accounts" in Chapter 5. You will use fpessoa for testing. You will simulate an e-mail client to send a message to fpessoa. In the following steps, replace *technowidgets.com* with your domain name.

To send a message to fpessoa using Telnet in Linux:

1. Open a terminal window in Linux.
2. Type **telnet localhost 25** to open a session with the e-mail server on port 25. Sendmail responds with a line beginning with 220.
3. Type **helo Web1** and then press **Enter**. This starts a session. (Note that the Telnet commands are not case-sensitive.)
4. Type **mail from:** ***info@xyz.com*** and then press **Enter**. This command identifies who is sending the e-mail. You can use any e-mail address here. There will be a pause while sendmail tries to verify the address, but it will accept it anyway.
5. Type **rcpt to: fpessoa@technowidgets.com** and then press **Enter**. This command identifies who should receive the message. Make sure that you replace the domain name with your own domain name.
6. Type **data** and then press **Enter**. This command starts the section where you type the message.
7. Type **This is a test message** and then press **Enter**.
8. Type **.** (period) and then press **Enter**. The period signifies the end of the message. By pressing Enter, you send the message.
9. Type **quit** and then press **Enter** to end the session.

   The session should resemble Figure 8-37.

   There are a few ways to make sure that the e-mail was sent. You could wait until a POP3 or IMAP4 server is installed, or log on as fpessoa and use a primitive software utility such as mail to display the message. The easiest way to display the message is to use the `cat` command.
10. At a command prompt, type **cat /var/spool/mail/fpessoa** and then press **Enter**.

    As message appears, similar to the one shown in Figure 8-38. Notice that although the header you used was `mail from:`, it was changed in the message stored by sendmail to `Return-Path:` and `From:`.

8

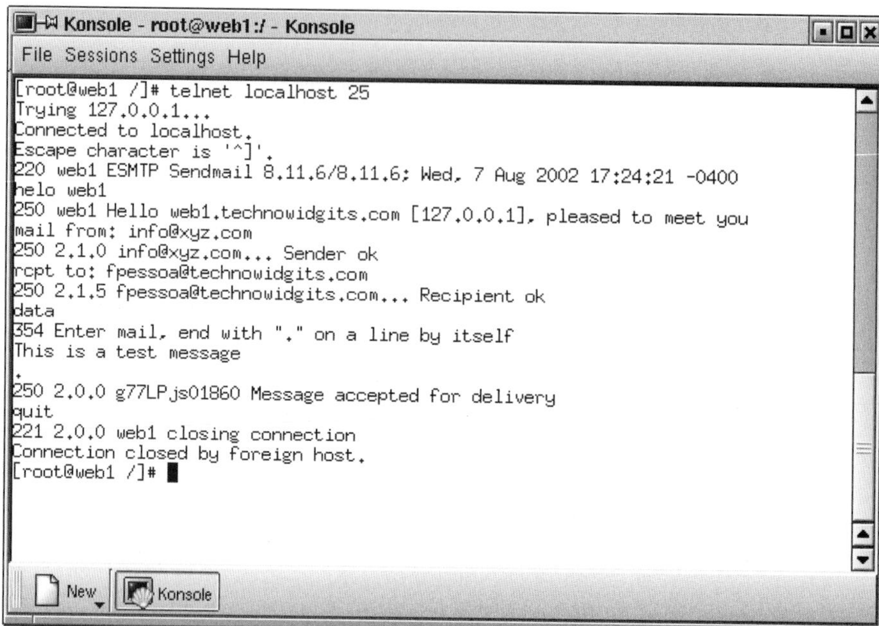

Figure 8-37 Telnet session to send e-mail

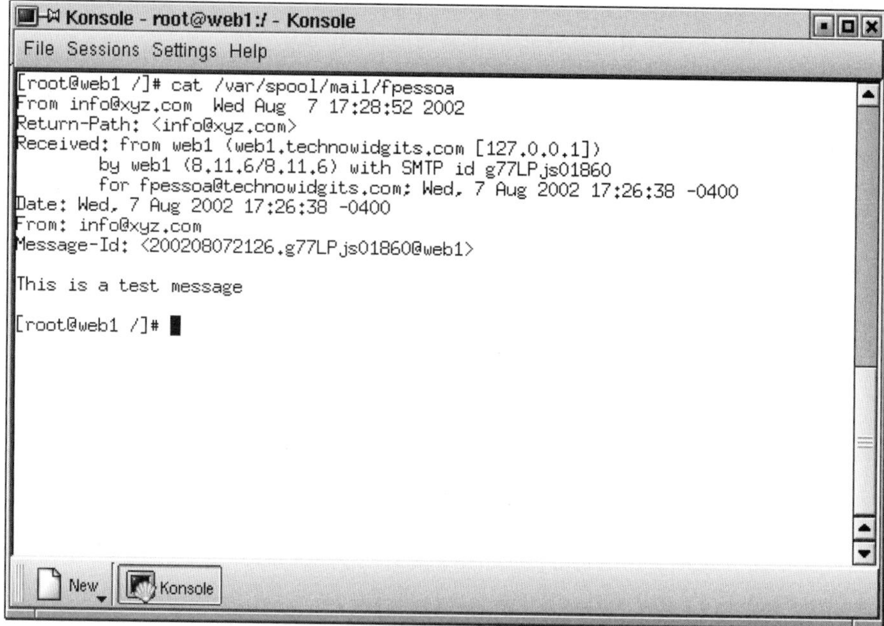

Figure 8-38 E-mail message for fpessoa

Project 8-2

Assuming that you have installed sendmail, it is a good idea to install and test an IMAP4/POP3 server, too.

To install and test an IMAP4 server using both the IMAP4 protocol and the POP3 protocol on a Linux server:

1. Install the IMAP4 server by following the steps in the chapter. Do not forget to enable it. See the steps titled "To install IMAP4 and POP3 servers in Linux."
2. If you have not restarted Linux since you enabled IMAP4, restart the xinetd service to enable it to recognize the changes by opening a terminal window, typing **service xinetd restart**, and then pressing **Enter**.
3. Type **telnet localhost 143** and then press **Enter**. This command opens a Telnet session with the IMAP4 server.
4. Type **a1 login fpessoa password** and then press **Enter**. This command authenticates you and allows a connection.
5. Type **a2 select inbox** and then press **Enter**. You have to select a mailbox before you can perform any mail-related operations. The default mailbox is inbox.
6. Type **a3 fetch 1 body[header]** and then press **Enter**. This command displays the header information for the first message.
7. Type **a4 fetch 1 body[text]** and then press **Enter**. This command displays the actual message.
8. Type **a5 logout** and then press **Enter** to end the session.

   The session should resemble Figure 8-39.

Next, you will retrieve the same e-mail using POP3.

To retrieve a message using POP3 on a Linux server:

1. Open a terminal window.
2. Type **telnet localhost 110** and then press **Enter**. This command connects you to the POP3 server.
3. Type **user fpessoa** and then press **Enter**. This command sends the user name to the server.
4. Type **pass password** and then press **Enter**. This command sends the password to the server.
5. Type **retr 1** and then press **Enter**. This command retrieves message 1.
6. Type **quit** and then press **Enter** to end the session.

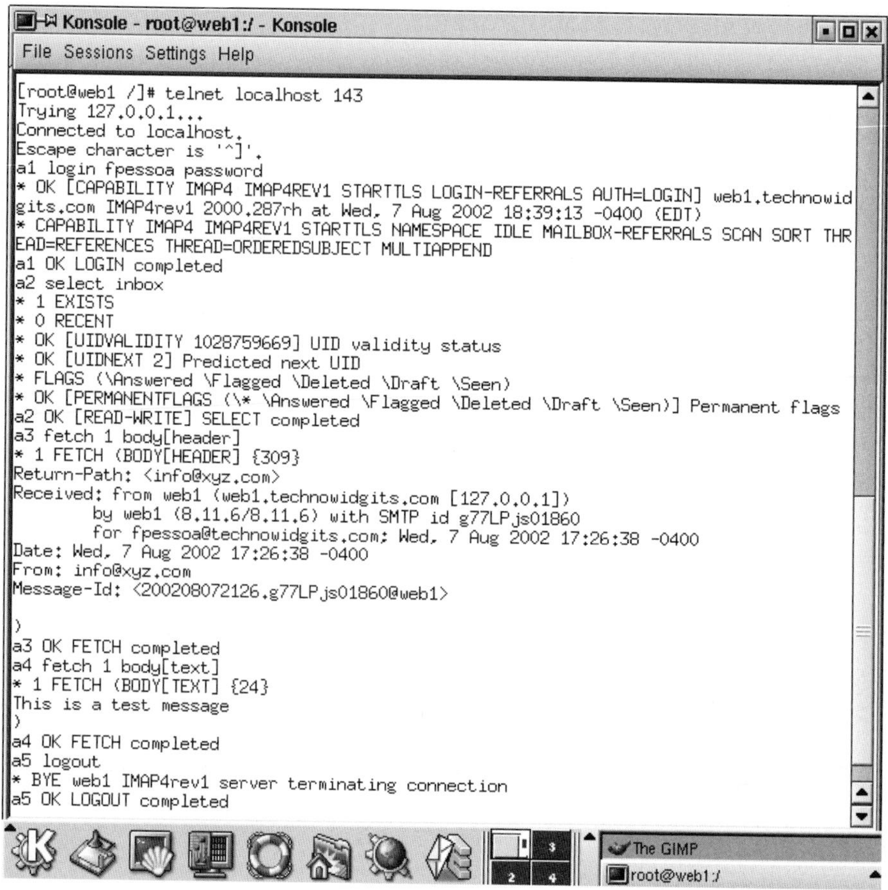

Figure 8-39 Telnet session to get e-mail message using IMAP4

The session should resemble Figure 8-40.

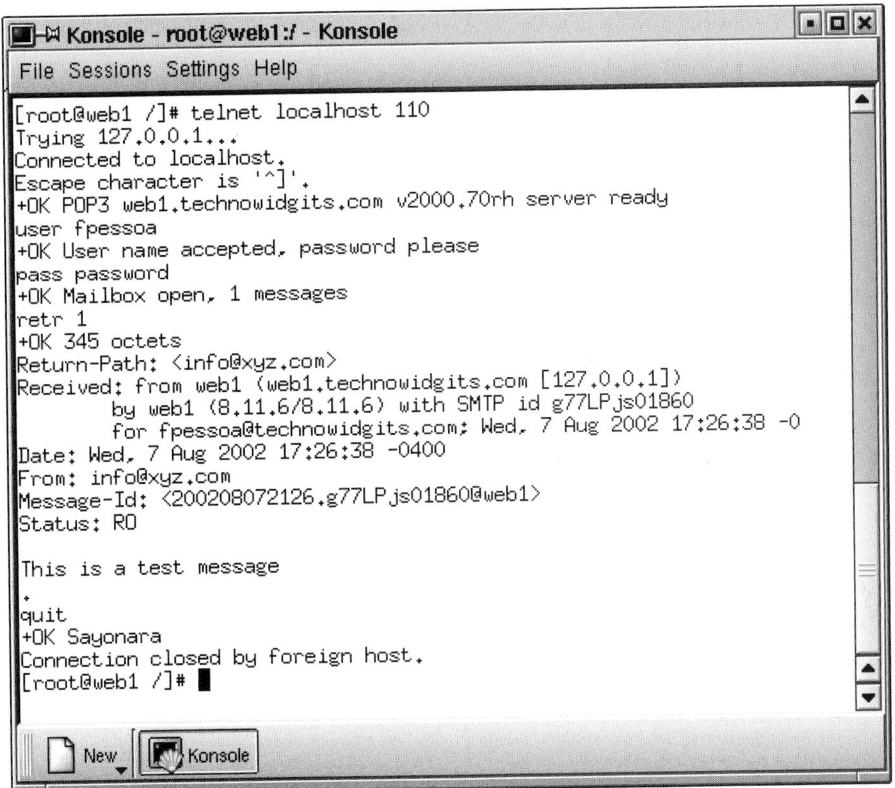

Figure 8-40 Telnet session to get e-mail message using POP3

Project 8-3

In this project, you will install Exchange 2000 and test it using Telnet. After installing Exchange 2000, you will add a user. Notice that an extra dialog box references the creation of an Exchange mailbox. You then use Telnet to create an e-mail message.

To install and test Exchange 2000 on a Windows server:

1. Make sure that DNS is working and you have an MX record that refers to your IP address. Make sure that you can ping *mail.technowidgets.com*.
2. Install Exchange 2000 as explained in the chapter. See the steps titled "To install Microsoft Exchange Server 2000."
3. Add a user named **Fernando Pessoa** with a logon name of **fpessoa** with a password of **password**. Create a mailbox.

4. Open Notepad and type the following, making sure that the line after "This is a test" is a single dot and there is one blank line after the dot. Refer to Project 8-1, Steps 2–9 in the steps to send e-mail using Telnet:

   telnet localhost 25
   helo web1
   mail from: info@xyz.com
   rcpt to: fpessoa@technowidgets.com
   data
   This is a test.
   .
   quit

5. Press **Ctrl+A** to select all the text, and then press **Ctrl+C** to copy the text to the Clipboard.
6. At the command prompt, click **C:** in the upper-left corner of the Command Prompt window to open a menu.
7. Point to **Edit**, and then click **Paste** to paste all the lines that you created in Notepad to Exchange 2000. After a pause, the server responds with "354 Start mail input; end with <CRLF>.<CRLF>." After a few moments, the server continues with "Queued mail for delivery."

These steps should generate a screen similar to the one shown in Figure 8-41.

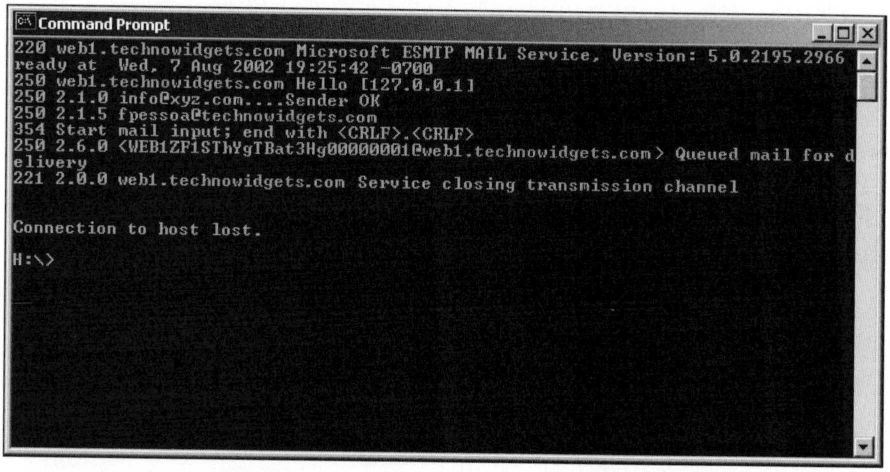

```
Command Prompt
220 web1.technowidgets.com Microsoft ESMTP MAIL Service, Version: 5.0.2195.2966
ready at  Wed, 7 Aug 2002 19:25:42 -0700
250 web1.technowidgets.com Hello [127.0.0.1]
250 2.1.0 info@xyz.com....Sender OK
250 2.1.5 fpessoa@technowidgets.com
354 Start mail input; end with <CRLF>.<CRLF>
250 2.6.0 <WEB1ZF1SThYgTBat3Hg00000001@web1.technowidgets.com> Queued mail for d
elivery
221 2.0.0 web1.technowidgets.com Service closing transmission channel


Connection to host lost.

H:\>
```

Figure 8-41 Telnet session to send a message to Exchange 2000

Project 8-4

In this project, you will configure and test Outlook Express and test Outlook Web Access. This project assumes that you have completed Project 8-3. You will use the user created in the chapter called cbranco. You will log on as fpessoa and send an e-mail message to cbranco.

To create a mailbox for cbranco:

1. In Administrative Tools, click **Active Directory Users and Computers**.
2. Click the **Users** folder in the left pane to display the list of users in the right pane.
3. Right-click **Cris Branco**, and then click **Exchange Tasks**. The Welcome to the Exchange Task Wizard opens.
4. Click **Next**. The Available Tasks dialog box opens. The default selection is to create a mailbox.
5. Click **Next** to create the mailbox for Cris Branco. The Create Mailbox dialog box opens. It contains the defaults for the e-mail name for Cris Branco and the location for the mailbox.
6. Click **Next**. The Completing the Exchange Task Wizard opens. The mailbox has been created.
7. Click **Finish** to exit the wizard. Close the Active Directory Users and Computers window.

To configure and test Outlook Express in Windows:

1. Log on as **fpessoa**.
2. Configure Outlook Express based on the steps in the chapter. (See the steps titled "To configure Outlook Express" in the "Configuring an E-mail Client in Windows" section.) Remember to change the domain name to the one that you created. Select **IMAP** as your incoming mail server.
3. Expand the folders in the upper-left pane, if necessary.
4. Click **Send/Recv** on the toolbar to retrieve e-mail. Click **Inbox**. In Windows 2000, use the Inbox under your domain name. You should see the message from *info@xyz.com* in the right pane, as in Figure 8-42.

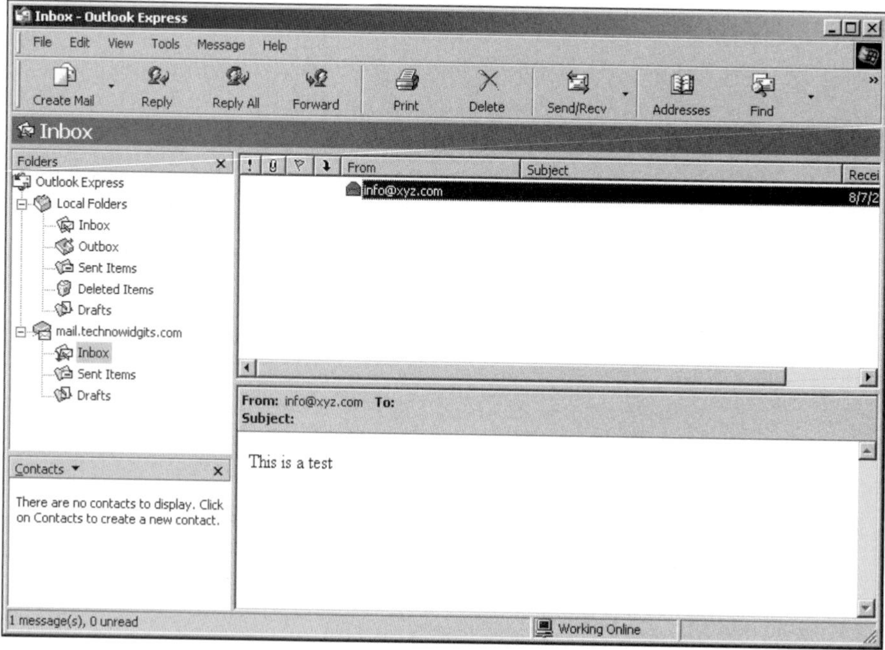

Figure 8-42 Inbox for Outlook Express

To send e-mail to cbranco using Outlook Express in Windows:

1. While logged on as fpessoa, start Outlook Express.
2. Click the **Create Mail** button on the toolbar.
3. Type **cbranco@technowidgets.com** in the To text box.
4. Type **Test 2** in the Subject text box.
5. Type **Another test** in the message area.
6. Click the **Send** button on the toolbar.
7. Exit Outlook Express and log out of Windows.

Project 8-5

In this project, you will configure and test KMail in Linux. This project assumes that you have completed Project 8-1 or that you have verified that sendmail is working and you have one user called fpessoa and another user called cbranco.

To configure and test e-mail clients in Linux:

1. Log on as **cbranco**.
2. Configure KMail for cbranco. Use the POP3 protocol.

   While logged on as cbranco, you can use KMail to send an e-mail message to fpessoa to make sure it is working.

3. Click **Message** on the KMail menu bar, and then click **New Message**.
4. Type **fpessoa@technowidgets.com** in the To text box.
5. Type a subject and message of your choice, and then click the **Send** button on the toolbar.
6. To check your mail, click the **Check Mail In** button on the toolbar.
7. Double-click the message in the right panel to view it.
8. Send an e-mail message to fpessoa. With e-mail set for SMTP, it may stay in the outbox for up to a minute before it is actually sent. Then you see the message transferred to the sent-mail folder.
9. Exit KMail, log out, and then log on again as **fpessoa**.
10. Configure KMail. Use the IMAP protocol. Give it a name of **Business**.
11. In KMail, retrieve the e-mail from cbranco by clicking **Business** in the left panel and then clicking **Inbox**.
12. Click the message in the upper-right panel. Click the **Reply** icon on the toolbar to reply to the message and create and send a reply. Then exit KMail and log out of Linux.
13. Log on again as **cbranco**, and check your e-mail to make sure that you received the message.

Project 8-6

The objective of this project is to send e-mail from one server to another. One server will use Linux and the other will use Windows. The Linux server will have the DNS server that will contain the domain information for both domains.

To test e-mail that is sent to another server:

1. In Linux, create a DNS server that contains not only the original domain on the Linux computer, but a domain from another student's Windows computer. Refer to Hands-on Project 4-3 for details.
2. Because this is a test environment, you need to allow relays. In the Exchange 2000 System Manager, expand the Servers, WEB1, Protocols, and SMTP folders. Right-click **Default SMTP Virtual Server** and then click **Properties**. The default SMTP Virtual Server Properties dialog box opens. Click the **Access** tab, and then click the **Relay** button. The Relay Restrictions dialog box opens. Click the **All except the list below** option button and then click **OK** to allow relaying. Click **OK** to close the Default SMTP Virtual Server Properties dialog box, and then close the Exchange System Manager window.
3. Make sure that you set the DNS entry in the TCP/IP configuration of the Windows computer to the IP address of the Linux server.
4. Ping the DNS entries for the mail servers on both computers.

5. If you haven't already created a user called fpessoa on the Windows server, do so now and create a mailbox for him.
6. If you haven't already completed Project 8-5, follow the steps in there to create a KMail account for cbranco.
7. Log on to Linux as **cbranco**, and use KMail to send a message to fpessoa.
8. Log on as **fpessoa**, and use Outlook Express to retrieve the message from cbranco.
9. Reply to the e-mail.
10. From the Linux computer, read the reply from fpessoa.

Project 8-7

You need to understand where e-mail goes when it is retrieved. You know that POP3 downloads the e-mail, but IMAP leaves it on the server. Sometimes users misplace e-mail when they switch from one computer to another. In this project, you will explore complete e-mail messages including headers. You need to have completed Project 8-5 or 8-6 so you will have messages to analyze.

To analyze e-mail messages in Linux:

1. In Linux, open a terminal window.
2. Type **cat /var/spool/mail/cbranco** and then press **Enter** to display all the e-mail messages that cbranco has on the server. As stated in Project 8-5, cbranco uses POP3, which by default downloads messages and deletes them from the server. If any messages were displayed, they are messages sent since the last time cbranco retrieved e-mail. Because fpessoa responded to her e-mail in Step 12 of Project 8-5, a message should be displayed.
3. Type **cat /var/spool/mail/fpessoa** and then press **Enter** to display all the e-mail messages that fpessoa has on the server. As stated in Project 8-5, fpessoa uses IMAP, which leaves messages on the server. You should find at least the message sent in Project 8-5.
4. Type **ls /home/cbranco/Mail/inbox/cur** and then press Enter to display the contents of the local inbox of cbranco. Although it is obviously on the same computer, in a real environment, cbranco mailbox would be on cbranco's computer. At least one message should appear here (the one created in Project 8-5), although the file names are difficult to read.
5. Type **ls /home/fpessoa/Mail/inbox/cur** and then press Enter to display the contents of the local inbox of fpessoa. There is no message here because IMAP left everything in the e-mail server directory.

Project 8-8

By default, Exchange 2000 allows any authentication method and anyone may connect to it. You will tighten security in a number of ways. More details on security are presented in Chapter 10.

To tighten security and implement other restrictions in Exchange 2000 in Windows:

1. Open the Exchange System Manager.
2. Click the **plus sign** (+) next to Servers.
3. Click the **plus sign** (+) next to Web1.
4. Click the **plus sign** (+) next to Protocols.
5. Click the **plus sign** (+) next to SMTP.
6. Right-click **Default SMTP Virtual Server**, and then click **Properties**. The Default SMTP Virtual Server Properties dialog box opens. See Figure 8-43. Here you can specify the IP address at which SMTP listens. By default, it listens at all IP addresses.

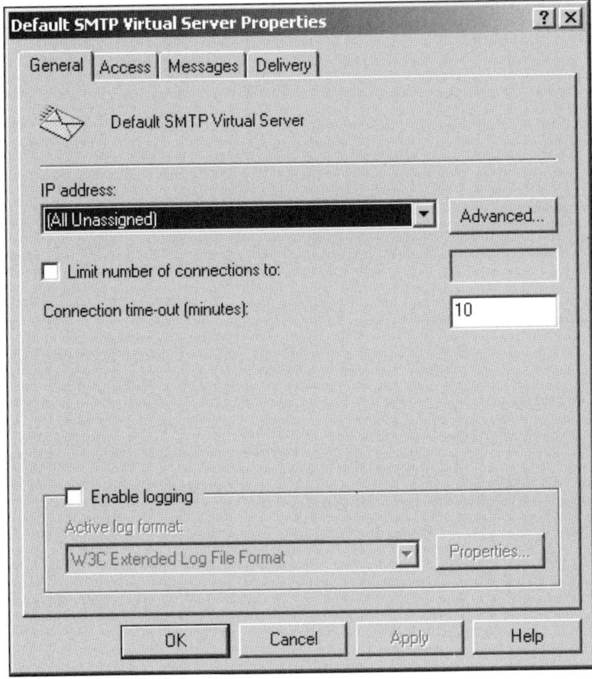

Figure 8-43 Default SMTP Virtual Server Properties dialog box

7. Check the **Limit number of connections to:** check box, and then type **100** in the corresponding text box. If you have a relatively slow server, you can limit the number of connections instead of using many slow connections.
8. Click the **Access** tab, as shown in Figure 8-44. Under Connection control, you can limit those who can use the SMTP server to only those users with internal addresses that begin with 192.168.0. This choice prevents users with other addresses from using your SMTP server.

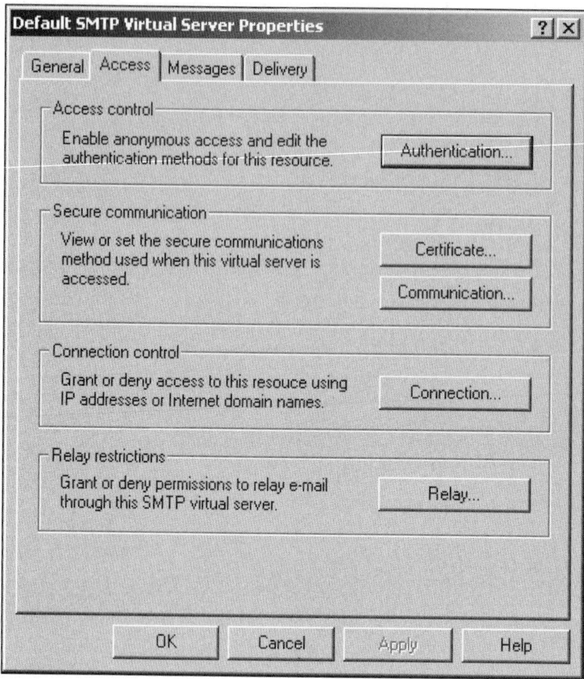

Figure 8-44 Access tab

9. Click **Connection**. The Connection dialog box opens, as shown in Figure 8-45.

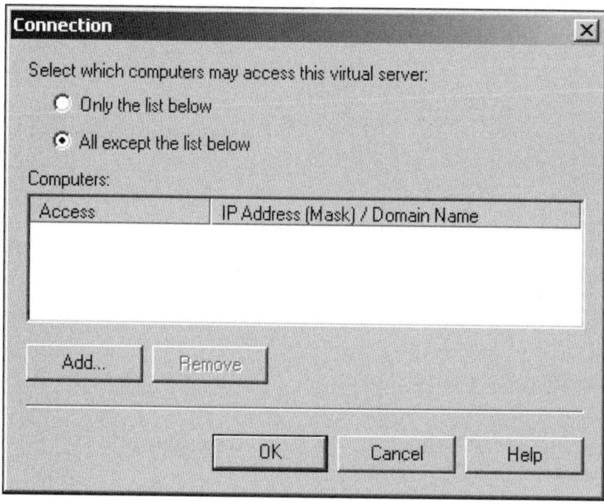

Figure 8-45 Connection dialog box

10. Click the **Only the list below** option button. This means that only the IP addresses in the box below can use SMTP.
11. Click **Add**. The Computer dialog box opens, as shown in Figure 8-46. Here you can define the computer or computers that you will allow to use your SMTP server.

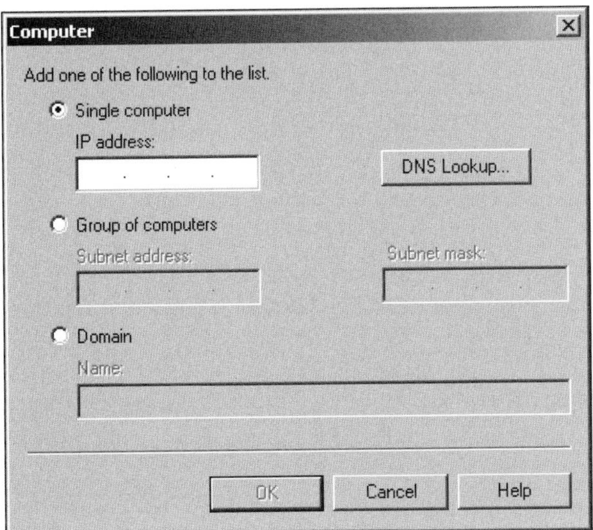

Figure 8-46 Computer dialog box

12. Click the **Group of computers** option button to allow everyone whose IP address begins with 192.168.0 to use your SMTP server.
13. In the Subnet address text box, type **192.168.0.0**.
14. In the Subnet mask text box, type **255.255.255.0**.
15. Click **OK** three times to return to the Exchange System Manager window.

Explain the difference between the properties for SMTP and the properties for POP3 and IMAP.

Project 8-9

Because Windows 2003 offers POP3 as a Windows service, you can create a minimal e-mail server without having to install Exhange.

However, if you installed Exchange 2000 already, and are running Windows 2003, do not uninstall Exchange 2000. (Exchange 2000 does not uninstall reliably on computers running Windows 2003.) This project is designed for those who have not yet installed Exchange 2000 or Active Directory.

You can create users for the POP3 service using Active Directory, local users, and an encrypted password file. In this project, you will use an encrypted password file. This is a good choice if you want to create many e-mail users who do not need user accounts for other purposes.

To install the POP3 service in Windows 2003:

1. Insert the Windows 2003 CD in the drive. When the Welcome screen opens, click **Exit**.
2. In the Control Panel, click **Add or Remove Programs**. The Add or Remove Programs window opens.
3. Click **Add/Remove Windows Components**. The Windows Components dialog box opens.
4. Click the **E-mail Services** check box, and then click **Next**. The POP3 service is installed along with the SMTP service, if necessary.
5. The Completing the Windows Components Wizard dialog box opens. Click **Finish** to exit the wizard. Close the Add or Remove Programs window.

Now that the POP3 service is installed, you have to administer it.

To configure the POP3 service for an Encrypted Password file:

1. In Administrative Tools, click **POP3 Service**. The POP3 Service window opens.
2. Right-click **WEB1** and then click **Properties**. The WEB1 Properties dialog box opens.
3. In the list box for Authentication Method, select **Encrypted Password File** and then click **OK**.

Now you need to add a domain for the POP3 service. Then you can add mailboxes for users.

To add a domain for the POP3 service:

1. In the POP3 Service window, right click **WEB1**, point to **New**, and then click **Domain**.
2. The Add Domain dialog box opens. In the text box, type **technowidgets.com** and then click **OK**. In the left pane, technowidgets.com is listed under WEB1.

To add a mailbox for a user:

1. In the POP3 Service window, right-click **technowidgets.com**, point to **New**, and then click **Mailbox**.
2. The Add Mailbox dialog box opens. For the Mailbox Name, type **fpessoa**. In the Password and Confirm Password dialog boxes, type **password**.
3. Click **OK** to add the mailbox.
4. The POP3 Service dialog box opens indicating that the mailbox was created. Click **OK**. If you click technowidgets.com in the left pane, fpessoa appears in the right pane. However, you cannot send mail until you allow your computer to relay messages.

To allow Windows 2003 to relay e-mail messages:

1. In Administrative Tools, click **Internet Information Services (IIS) Manager**.
2. Expand **WEB1** to display the Default SMTP Virtual Server in the left pane.
3. Right-click **Default SMTP Virtual Server** and then click **Properties**. The Default SMTP Virtual Server Properties dialog box opens.
4. Click the **Access** tab and then click the **Relay** button. The Relay Restrictions dialog box opens.
5. Click **Add** to add an IP address that can send e-mail. The Computer dialog box opens.
6. In the IP address text box, type **192.168.0.100** and then click **OK** three times to return to the Internet Information Services (IIS) Manager window. Close the window.

Now you can test the e-mail server. You can base your test on Hands-on Project 8-1 for sending mail (SMTP) and Hands-on Project 8-2 for retrieving mail (POP3). Although these projects refer to sendmail and Linux, the SMTP and POP3 commands are almost exactly the same, except you will be using Telnet in a Windows Command Prompt window and you need to reference the POP3 user in a slightly different way. First, follow the steps in "To send a message to fpessoa using Telnet in Linux" in Hands-on Project 8-1. Then follow the steps in "To retrieve a message using POP3 on a Linux server" in Hands-on Project 8-2. However, in Step 3, type user **fpessoa@technowidgets.com** instead of **user fpessoa**.

Case Projects

Case Project 8-1

On the Internet, research other e-mail clients for Linux. Download a trial version of an e-mail client. Configure the e-mail client and make sure that it works. In a one- to two-page written report, compare its functionality to that of KMail.

Case Project 8-2

On the Internet, research other e-mail clients for Windows. Download a trial version of an e-mail client. Configure the e-mail client and make sure that it works. In a written report, compare its functionality to that of Outlook Express.

Case Project 8-3

Find some Web-based e-mail packages for Apache. Compare and contrast the features of at least three. Install one of them and demonstrate its functionality. How does it compare to OWA?

Case Project 8-4

In Hands-on Project 8-6, you used a combination of a Linux server and a Windows server. In this project, use two Windows servers. You will have to alter the DNS in one of the servers to serve both domains. Send e-mail back and forth between the servers using OWA.

Case Project 8-5

In Hands-on Project 8-6, you used a combination of a Linux server and a Windows server. In this project, use two Linux servers. You will have to alter the DNS in one of the servers to serve both domains. Send e-mail back and forth between the servers using KMail.

CHAPTER

9

EXTENDING THE WEB ENVIRONMENT

In this chapter, you will:

- Understand File Transfer Protocol (FTP) services
- Install and configure an FTP server in Microsoft Windows
- Install and configure an FTP server in Linux
- Understand News servers
- Configure remote access to a server
- Understand streaming media servers
- Understand e-commerce software

Besides Web servers, you can use other server applications to enhance the functionality of the Web environment. You use a File Transfer Protocol (FTP) server to allow others to transfer files to and from your Web environment. You can configure an FTP server to allow anyone to log on and transfer files. Although users may be required to log on to an FTP server with a valid user name and password, this logon information is sent as clear text, which can be readily intercepted and understood. FTP can therefore pose a security problem. Browsers support both HTTP for Web pages and FTP for file transfer. Linux and Windows also include command-line FTP clients.

Another type of server you can use on the Web is a News server, which supports the Network News Transfer Protocol (NNTP). You use News servers to create threaded discussions in a newsgroup, in which participants exchange information on a topic of common interest.

Telnet is a protocol that allows you to remotely log on to a server. Although Windows administrators rarely employ Telnet, they can use many command-line utilities to administer servers remotely. Microsoft has added nearly 50 command-line utilities to Windows Server 2003. To support the Windows GUI remotely, Microsoft provides Terminal Services.

Other types of servers on the Web include streaming media servers and e-commerce servers. Streaming media servers support audio and video, which are useful for training and multimedia communication. E-commerce is an important and complex topic in the Web environment. Developers can also add specialized applications to the Web server to facilitate development, implementation, maintenance, and analysis functions.

UNDERSTANDING FTP SERVICES

File Transfer Protocol (FTP) is used to transfer files from a server to a client (download) and to transfer files from a client to a server (upload). FTP predates the Web by many years. Just as the Web is useful for reading information about topics, FTP can be used to download text files that you can then read. In addition, this protocol is designed to download programs, software patches, service packs, music, video, and other binary files. Because FTP is one of the protocols recognized by browsers, browser users do not always realize that they are using FTP to download a file. They simply know that a link starts a download and they are prompted for a location at which to save a file. HTTP is sometimes used to download binary files, although it is not as efficient as FTP for transferring large files. Occasionally users must use HTTP because security measures within their organization prevent them from using FTP.

FTP servers can operate as anonymous servers or they can require a valid logon. Typically, FTP servers are anonymous, meaning that anyone can download files. This approach is similar to a Web server where anyone can display pages. In both cases, the existence of special users allows the anonymous user to log on to the system and use FTP. In Linux, the anonymous user is called ftp. In Windows, the anonymous FTP user is the same one created for anonymous logon to the Web server: a guest account that begins with IUSR_ and is followed by the name of the computer. In both Linux and Windows, these user accounts are highly restricted so that the anonymous user connecting to the site can perform only tasks related to FTP.

Although you can allow users to upload files to an FTP server, doing so introduces risks to server security. As with other TCP/IP protocols, information that is passed to and from the FTP server is not secure. If you allow users to log on using valid user names and passwords, that information is not encrypted. Others can potentially capture that information and use it to penetrate your system. Also, simply allowing uploads can render your system vulnerable to unauthorized access. Recently, for example, Windows FTP servers were attacked by a simple utility that scanned a network for FTP servers. When it found one that used Windows and did not have the latest software patches, it penetrated the system and uploaded files until the hard disk on the FTP server was full. To make matters more frustrating for the administrator, many of the folders and files could not be deleted through Windows Explorer. Instead, the administrator had to use specific POSIX commands at the command line to clean up the disk.

The way FTP uses ports to communicate is different from the other protocols you have studied. For example, the Web server listens for requests at port 80 and then all pages pass through port 80 on their way to an unprivileged port on the client. An **unprivileged** port is any port above 1023. With FTP, the client connects to port 21, called the control port. This port is used for commands and general control of the data stream. Although port 20 is the data port, it is not actually used to transfer the data between the server and the client. Instead, the FTP server uses port 20 to tell the client which unprivileged port on the server it should use for the data transfer. The client then connects (through its own unprivileged port) to an unprivileged port on the server for the actual data transfer. This type of FTP transfer, called **passive mode**, is the most common data transmission method used today. The fact that FTP uses a number of unprivileged ports for data transfer is unique in the TCP/IP protocols. Using unprivileged ports for data transfer makes it more difficult to protect a server environment from attack. You will learn more about this problem in Chapter 10, which discusses security.

Communicating with FTP

Although the commands supported differ from one FTP server to another, in reality the servers use only a few essential commands. Because the most popular FTP client is the browser, in most cases these commands remain hidden from the user. However, in some cases, you might want to connect directly to an FTP server using a command-line or GUI-based FTP client, especially when you need to transfer multiple files. FTP clients are commonly used by administrators to move files from one place to another, especially in a Linux environment.

Table 9-1 describes the most common FTP commands. Some of the commands are normally not available when you log on as an anonymous user. Those commands would include any that add, delete, or modify files or the file structure of the FTP server, such as `put`, `mput`, `delete`, `mdelete`, `mkdir`, `rmdir`, and `rename`.

Table 9-1 FTP commands

Command	Description	Example
`ftp` *`host`*	Initiates a connection to an FTP server	`ftp ftp.technowidgets.com` `ftp 192.168.0.100`
`open` *`host`*	Once the FTP client has been started with the `ftp` command, opens a connection	`open ftp.technowidgets.com` `open 192.168.0.100`
`close`	Closes the connection but does not exit the FTP client	`close`
`quit` or `bye`	Closes the connection and exits the FTP client	`bye`
`ls` *`filenames`*	Displays filenames, and can use wildcards; if the command is used alone, all filenames are displayed	`ls *.rpm`

Table 9-1 FTP commands (continued)

Command	Description	Example
`dir` *`filenames`*	Displays the long listing of files and their properties, such as the size and date the file was created; if the command is used alone, all filenames are displayed	`dir *.rpm`
`binary`	Transfer the files following this command in binary mode; it is used for programs, images, sound, and related files	`binary`
`ascii`	Transfer the files following this command in text mode; it is used for text files	`ascii`
`get` *`filename`*	Downloads a single file; cannot be used with wildcards	`get sendmail-8.11.6-3.i386.rpm`
`put` *`filename`*	Uploads a single file; cannot be used with wildcards	`put testapp.zip`
`mget` *`filenames`*	Downloads multiple files, and can be used with wildcards; you are prompted as to whether you want each file downloaded	`mget sendmail*.rpm`
`mput` *`filenames`*	Uploads multiple files, and can be used with wildcards; you are prompted as to whether you want each file uploaded	`mput *.tif`
`prompt no`	Stops prompting; when used before you use `mget` or `mput`, you will not be prompted to accept every file that is transferred; also works with mdelete	`prompt no`
`prompt`	Starts prompting for each file when used with any command that allows for multiple files, which is the default	`prompt`
`hash`	Displays a hash symbol as files are being downloaded; allows you to determine more easily whether you have lost a connection with the FTP server because the hash symbol will no longer be displayed at regular intervals	`hash`
`cd` *`directory`*	Moves to another directory on the FTP server	`cd /software`

Table 9-1 FTP commands (continued)

Command	Description	Example
`lcd` *`directory`*	Moves to another directory on the client; the only way to download a file to a specific directory. When you use FTP commands such as `get` and `mget`, you are not prompted for a download directory; the command simply downloads the file to your current directory. If you used the command without a reference to a directory, it will display your current directory.	`lcd /docs`
`pwd`	Displays the current directory on the server; to display the current directory on the client, use `lcd`	`pwd`
`help` *`command`*	Finds very brief help on FTP commands; if used without a reference to a command, it will give you a list of commands available	`help mget`

Figure 9-1 shows a sample FTP session run from a command prompt. The user connects to the FTP server at *ftp.technowidgets.com*. The user name is anonymous. The password can be anything, although the program suggests that you type your e-mail address. This session displays a list of files on the server. The user wants to download all of the .tif image files without being prompted for each one. Because .tif files are binary files and the default is text, you need to enter the **`binary`** command first. Because you do not want to be prompted as to whether you want each file, you enter the **`prompt no`** command. In the code in Figure 9-1, text that the user enters is shown in bold.

```
C:\>ftp web1.technowidgets.com
Connected to ftp.technowidgets.com
220 ftpsrv1 Microsoft FTP Service (Version 5.0).
User (ftp.technowidgets.com:(none)): anonymous
331 Anonymous access allowed, send identity (e-mail name) as password.
Password:
230 Anonymous user logged in.
ftp> ls
200 PORT command successful.
150 Opening ASCII mode data connection for file list.
92010NT_Disk3.zip
readme.txt
FIG0320.tif
FIG0321.tif
FIG0322.tif
226 Transfer complete.
ftp: 172 bytes received in 0.03Seconds 9.07Kbytes/sec.
ftp> binary
200 Type set to I.
ftp> prompt no
Interactive mode Off.
ftp> mget *.tif
200 Type set to I.
200 PORT command successful.
150 Opening BINARY mode data connection for FIG0320.tif(602971 bytes).
226 Transfer complete.
ftp: 602971 bytes received in 0.10Seconds 6029.71Kbytes/sec.
200 PORT command successful.
150 Opening BINARY mode data connection for FIG0321.tif(377316 bytes).
226 Transfer complete.
ftp: 377316 bytes received in 0.05Seconds 7546.32Kbytes/sec.
200 PORT command successful.
150 Opening BINARY mode data connection for FIG0322.tif(567874 bytes).
226 Transfer complete.
ftp: 567874 bytes received in 0.11Seconds 5162.49Kbytes/sec.
ftp> quit
221

C:\>
```

Figure 9-1 An FTP session

Installing and Configuring an FTP Server in Microsoft Windows

By default, FTP is not installed when you install IIS, although it is one of the IIS components. It is as easy to install as the other components because a wizard guides you through the setup process.

To install FTP in Windows 2003:

1. Insert the Windows 2003 CD into the drive and click **Exit** when the Installation window opens.
2. In the Control Panel, click **Add or Remove Programs**.
3. Click **Add/Remove Windows Components** in the left pane. The Windows Components Wizard dialog box opens.
4. Highlight **Application Server**, and then click **Details**. The Application Server dialog box opens.
5. Highlight **Internet Information Services (IIS)**, and then click **Details**. The Internet Information Services (IIS) dialog box opens.
6. Click the **File Transfer Protocol (FTP) Service** check box, and then click **OK** twice to return to the Windows Components dialog box.
7. Click **Next**. The Configuring Components dialog box opens, showing the progress of the installation.
8. The Completing the Windows Components Wizard dialog box opens. Click **Finish** to exit the wizard.
9. Close both the Add or Remove Programs window and the Control Panel window.

To install FTP in Windows 2000:

1. Insert the Windows 2000 installation CD into the drive.
2. Click **Start**, point to **Settings**, and then click **Control Panel**.
3. Double-click **Add/Remove Programs**. The Add/Remove Programs window opens.
4. Click **Add/Remove Windows Components** in the left pane. The Windows Components Wizard dialog box opens.
5. Highlight **Internet Information Services (IIS)**, and then click **Details**. The Internet Information Services (IIS) dialog box opens.
6. Click the **File Transfer Protocol (FTP) Server** check box.
7. Click **OK** to accept the changes. You return to the Windows Components Wizard.
8. Click **Next**. The Configuring Components window opens, showing the status of the installation.
9. The Completing the Windows Components Wizard dialog box appears. Click **Finish** to exit the wizard.
10. Close both the Add/Remove Programs window and the Control Panel window.

Once you have installed FTP, it is ready to be used. The default content folder for FTP is \inetpub\ftproot. However, you can change the location of this folder and customize other settings.

To configure the FTP server:

1. *In Windows 2003:* In Administrative Tools, click **Internet Information Services (IIS) Manager**.
   In Windows 2000: In Administrative Tools, double-click **Internet Services Manager**.

   The Internet Information Services window opens.

2. *In Windows 2003:* Double-click the name of the computer in the left pane, and then double-click **FTP Sites**.
   In Windows 2000: Double-click the name of the computer in the left pane.

   The Default FTP Site appears in the right pane.

3. Right-click **Default FTP Site**, and then click **Properties**. The Default FTP Site Properties dialog box opens. See Figure 9-2.

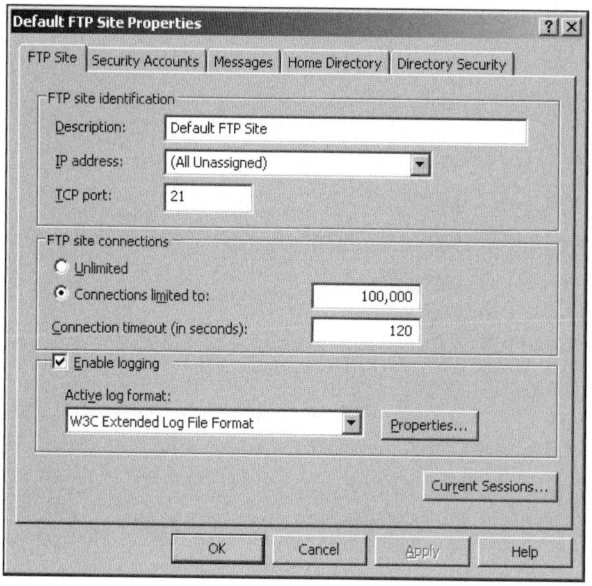

Figure 9-2 Default FTP Site Properties dialog box

The default number of connections is set to 100,000, an extremely high number. It would take multiple T3 (45 MB) lines along with a very high speed server to handle so many connections. A more reasonable number for small companies would be closer to 10.

4. In the Connections limited to text box, change the default number of connections from 100,000 to **10**.
5. Click the **Messages** tab. The FTP site messages dialog box is shown in Figure 9-3. The FTP Site Properties dialog box in Windows 2000 does not include the Banner text box.

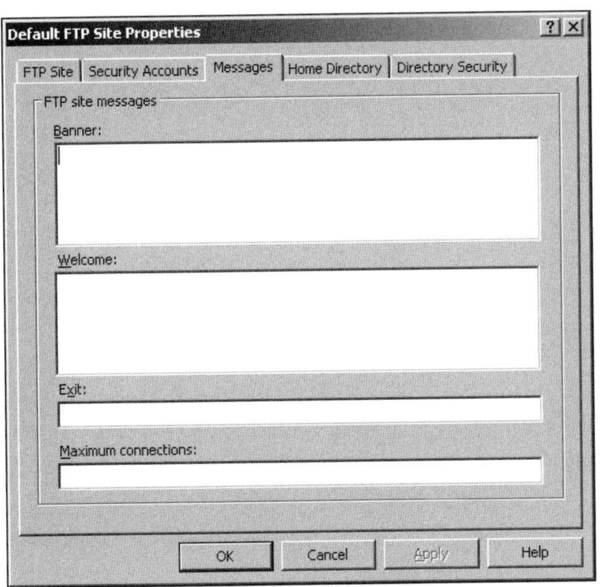

Figure 9-3 Messages tab in the Default FTP Site Properties dialog box

6. *In Windows 2003 only:* The text that you enter for the banner appears when you connect but before you log on. In the Banner text box, type **This is the Technowidgets.com FTP site.**
7. The text in the Welcome text box appears after you successfully log on. In the Welcome text box, type **Welcome to the Technowidgets.com FTP site. We hope that you like the files**.
8. The text in the Exit text box appears after you close the FTP connection. In the Exit text box, type **Thank you for using our site!**
9. The text in the Maximum connections text box appears after the maximum number of connections has been reached. In the Maximum connections text box, type **Sorry, the server is too busy. Try again later. Thanks!** Click **OK**.

After you change the settings as you did in the previous steps, the messages change to the ones in the sample session shown in Figure 9-4.

9

```
ftp web1.technowidgets.com
Connected ftp.technowidgets.com.
220-Microsoft FTP Service
220 This is the Technowidgets.com FTP site
User (web1.technowidgets.com:(none)): anonymous
331 Anonymous access allowed, send identity (e-mail name) as password.
Password:
230-Welcome to the Technowidgets.com FTP site. We hope you like the files.
230 Anonymous user logged in.
ftp> quit
221 Thank you for using our site!
```

Figure 9-4 FTP session with the messages changed

Other property sheets in the Default FTP Site Properties dialog box provide useful information, too. On the Security Accounts tab, you can configure who has access to FTP. See Figure 9-5. By default, anonymous connections are allowed. However, notice that the Allow only anonymous connections check box is cleared. It means that an administrator or some other user may connect. A good reason to allow only anonymous connections is that anonymous users do not send a user name and password to the server in clear text. Windows 2000 has an Operators text box that lists only administrators. In contrast, the option to configure operators is not available in Windows 2003; only administrators are allowed to administer the FTP server.

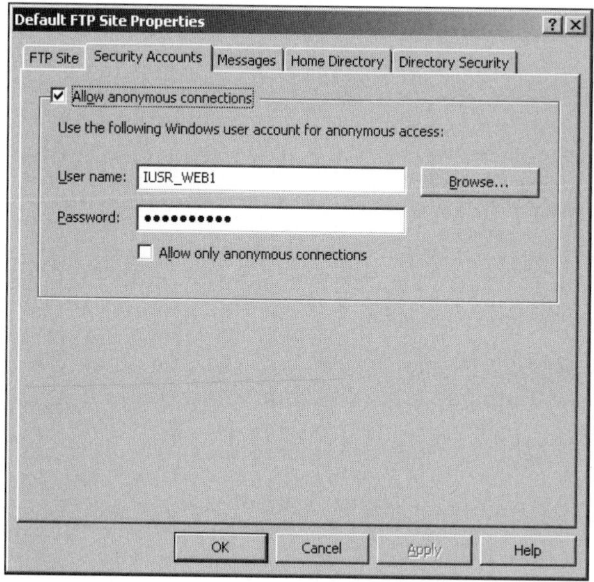

Figure 9-5 Security accounts for the default FTP site

The Home Directory tab shown in Figure 9-6 displays the directory configuration. By default, no one is allowed to write files to the FTP server.

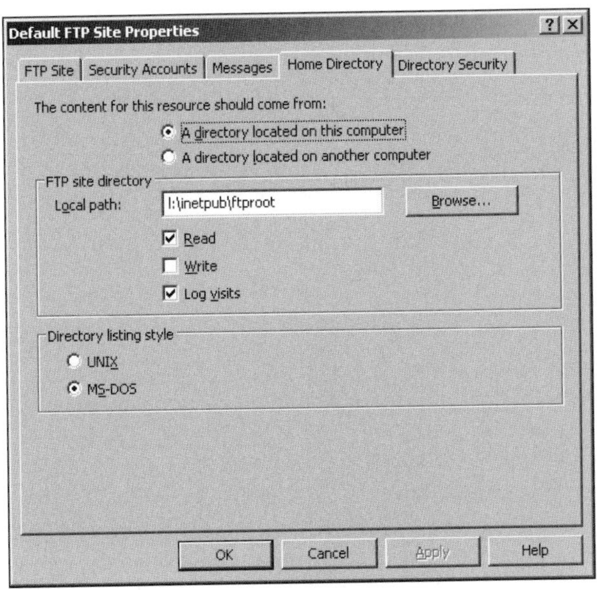

Figure 9-6 Home Directory tab of the Default FTP Site Properties dialog box

By default, FTP uses the MS-DOS approach to directory listing. See Figure 9-7. You can change this setting to display files according to the UNIX format. See Figure 9-8.

```
07-22-02  11:00AM              583326 FIG0423.tif
07-22-02  11:04AM              583326 FIG0424.tif
07-22-02  11:04AM              583326 FIG0425.tif
07-22-02  11:09AM              583326 FIG0426.tif
07-22-02  11:30AM              583848 FIG0427.tif
```

Figure 9-7 Long directory listing in the MS-DOS format

```
----------   1 owner    group        583326 Jul 22 11:00 FIG0423.tif
----------   1 owner    group        583326 Jul 22 11:04 FIG0424.tif
----------   1 owner    group        583326 Jul 22 11:04 FIG0425.tif
----------   1 owner    group        583326 Jul 22 11:09 FIG0426.tif
----------   1 owner    group        583848 Jul 22 11:30 FIG0427.tif
```

Figure 9-8 Long directory listing in the UNIX format

Some FTP clients can interpret only the UNIX format. If you want the broadest possible compatibility for your FTP server, you should change the directory listing style to UNIX.

Use the Directory Security tab shown in Figure 9-9 to control access by IP address. By default, all computers are allowed to connect. Any IP addresses listed in the window will be prevented from connecting. If you click the Denied access option button, everyone will be denied access except for the IP addresses listed in the window.

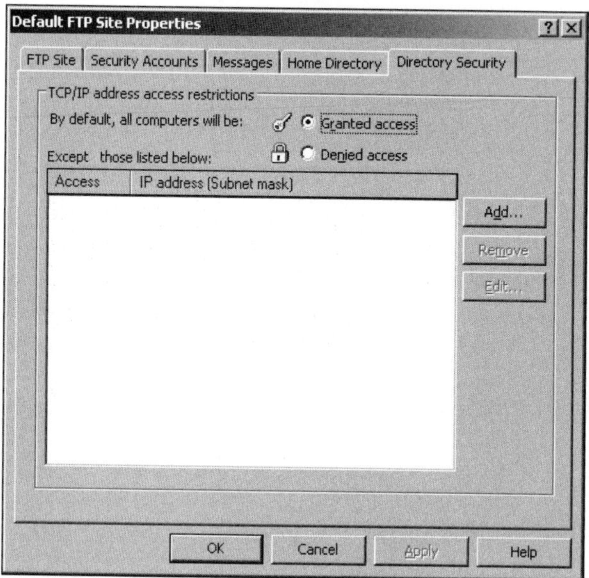

Figure 9-9 Directory Security tab of the Default FTP Site Properties dialog box

INSTALLING AND CONFIGURING FTP IN LINUX

Red Hat Linux comes with an FTP server developed by Washington University, called wu-ftpd. An additional software module allows anonymous access. When you installed Linux, you could have selected wu-ftpd along with other applications such as the Web server and DNS. If you did not install an FTP server in this way, you can find wu-ftpd on Red Hat Linux CD 1 in the /RedHat/RPMS directory.

To install FTP in Linux:

1. Insert Red Hat Linux CD 3 into the CD drive. On the desktop, double-click **CD/DVD-ROM** to mount the CD, and then open Konqueror.
2. Navigate to the RedHat/RPMS directory.

3. Double-click **wu-ftpd-2.6.2-8.i386.rpm** to install the server daemon. The version number in your filename may be slightly different.
4. The Completed System Preparation dialog box opens. Click **Continue** to install the FTP server. Close the Konqueror window.
5. In a terminal window, type **umount /mnt/cdrom** to prepare to eject the CD.
6. Insert Red Hat Linux CD 1 into the CD drive. On the desktop, double-click **CD/DVD-ROM** to mount the CD, and then open Konqueror.
7. Navigate to the RedHat/RPMS directory.
8. Double-click **anonftp-4.0-12.i386.rpm** to install the package that allows anonymous users to access the FTP server. The version number in your filename may be slightly different. If you selected FTP when you installed Linux, the Package already installed dialog box opens, and you can click **OK**. Otherwise, the Completed System Preparation dialog box opens. Click **Continue** to install the anonymous FTP server. Close the Konqueror window.

The wu-ftpd daemon is controlled by xinetd. In Chapter 8, you saw other daemons such as imap and pop3, which are also controlled by xinetd and do not run in the background like a Web server does. Xinetd monitors TCP packets for messages destined for the FTP server and starts wu-ftpd when it finds one. The other similarity with server daemons controlled by xinetd is that they are disabled by default. In previous chapters, you used a text editor to change the file, which in this case is /etc/rc.d/wu-ftpd. You can also enable wu-ftpd by typing the following command in a terminal window:

```
chkconfig wu-ftpd on
```

When you changed httpd.conf, which controls the Apache Web server, you had to restart the Apache daemon, httpd, so that the Web server would recognize the change. Because xinetd is the controlling daemon for wu-ftpd, once you change the configuration, you have to restart xinetd with the following command in a terminal window:

```
service xinetd restart
```

Now your FTP server is ready to accept anonymous connections. You put the files to download in /var/ftp.

Configuring the FTP Server

The /etc/ftpaccess file is the main configuration file. Figure 9-10 shows the default file without most of the comments and some of the less common configuration lines.

```
# Don't allow system accounts to log in over ftp
deny-uid %-99 %65534-
deny-gid %-99 %65534-
allow-uid ftp
allow-gid ftp
# User classes...
class   all   real,guest,anonymous  *
# Set this to your e-mail address
e-mail root@localhost
# Allow 5 mistyped passwords
loginfails 5
# Notify the users of README files at login and when
# changing to a different directory
readme  README*    login
readme  README*    cwd=*
# Messages displayed to the user
message /welcome.msg            login
message .message                cwd=*
# Allow on-the-fly compression and tarring
compress        yes             all
tar             yes             all
# Prevent anonymous users (and partially guest users)
# from executing dangerous commands
chmod       no          guest,anonymous
delete      no          anonymous
overwrite   no          anonymous
rename      no          anonymous
# If /etc/shutmsg exists, don't allow logins
shutdown /etc/shutmsg
passwd-check rfc822 warn
```

Figure 9-10 /etc/ftpaccess file

Most of the statements in the ftpaccess file relate to controlling access and configuring messages, which are described in subsequent sections. However, a few statements do not fit into those categories. As is true with applications such as Apache, FTP requests that you configure it with your e-mail address. As shown in Figure 9-10, by default the ftpaccess file has the following address:

```
e-mail root@localhost
```

You should change this line to your e-mail address so that you can receive system messages.

The mechanism for shutting down FTP is different than that employed with other server applications. Remember, the FTP server does not begin running until someone requests a connection—so you do not need to shut down a daemon that is not running. When you shut FTP down by typing **`ftpshut now`**, a text file called /etc/shutmsg is created. At this point, when someone tries to connect to the FTP server, xinetd checks for a message. If the message exists, xinetd does not start the FTP server. If the message does not exist, the FTP server starts and the user connects to the server. The names of the directory and file to check are determined by the following line in ftpaccess:

```
shutdown /etc/shutmsg
```

To allow connections again, you can delete the shutmsg file or type **ftprestart**, which deletes the file.

The two principal server utilities are ftpwho and ftpcount. As their names suggest, ftpwho displays a list indicating who is connected to your FTP server. This utility also provides information on the class of the user, the amount of processor time used, and the status of the connection. The ftpcount utility displays the number of users by class. Classes are described in the following section.

Controlling Access

The ftpaccess file starts by denying access to users and groups with IDs less than or equal to 99 and greater than or equal to 65535. (In other words, only users or groups with IDs 100–65534 are allowed access.) Recall from Chapter 5 that a uid or gid of less than 100 is reserved for system users and daemons. For example, root has a uid of zero, ftp has a uid of 14, and apache has a uid of 48. These users cannot log on to the FTP server. In Red Hat Linux, user uids normally start at 500. You can see the values for the uid and gid in /etc/passwd. The ftp user is the one system account that needs access to the FTP server, however, so the deny entries are overridden with the following commands:

```
allow-uid ftp
allow-gid ftp
```

Anyone who logs on anonymously uses the ftp user to gain access to the FTP server. This is done automatically when you use a browser, or when you use an FTP client and type a user name of anonymous. The approach is similar to that followed with a Web server that uses the apache user as the anonymous user when you request a Web page.

You can set up classes of users like the one in Figure 9-10, using a statement similar to the following:

```
class   all   real,guest,anonymous   *
```

You can use the class named `all` to control access. The `all` class consists of real users, guest users, and anonymous users. Real users, which you create, have home directories and standard local access. Guest users are based on accounts of real users that have been modified so as to restrict the accounts. The asterisk (*) at the end of the preceding line represents all IP addresses. You can, however, create classes for specific IP addresses. For example, you could create a class for all real users that access the FTP server locally with the following statements:

```
class local real 192.168.0.0/24
```

The /24 after the IP address states that the address has a 24-bit mask, which is equivalent to 255.255.255.0. Later in the ftpaccess file, you see where the class names are used in the following statements:

```
compress        yes        all
tar             yes        all
```

This code indicates that everyone who logs on to the server can compress files and use the `tar` command to group files together. Classes could also be used in the following access statements:

```
chmod       no      guest,anonymous
delete      no      anonymous
overwrite   no      anonymous
rename      no      anonymous
```

The preceding statements restrict the associated classes of users from potentially dangerous commands.

The following statement limits the user to a maximum of five failed logons before the server will disconnect the user. Because no specific password is required for the anonymous user, it is relevant only for real users and guests.

```
loginfails 5
```

The following statement does not really control access, but it does warn users who log on anonymously with a password that does not conform to an e-mail address that they should use. Even if they do use an e-mail address, however, it is not checked for accuracy so it probably should be deleted or at least commented out. To do so, you use the following command:

```
passwd-check rfc822 warn
```

If you want to limit the number of files that someone can transfer in a single session, you use the `file-limit` statement. You follow `file-limit` by either `in`, `out`, or `total` to describe the limitation depending on which direction the files are going. For example, the following lines limit anonymous users to a maximum of 25 files to download. Users from the class called local are allowed to upload only 10 files in a session.

```
file-limit   out   25   anonymous
file-limit   in    10   local
```

You can set the same type of limits on the number of bytes that users can transfer in a single session. The following statement limits anonymous users to 2 million bytes:

```
byte-limit   out   2000000   anonymous
```

In addition, you can limit the number of users who can be connected simultaneously. Because you can limit them by class, you can assure your local users that they can always log on. The following statement sets a limit of 200 anonymous users on any day of the week. If that number is exceeded, the file /etc/toomanyanon.txt is displayed.

```
limit   anonymous   200   Any   /etc/toomanyanon.txt
```

The /etc/ftphosts file is also used to control access. You use this file to allow or deny access to specific users from domains or IP addresses. You can use wildcards to match partial host names, domain names, or IP addresses. For example, Figure 9-11 allows mnoia to access the server from any IP address on the 192.168.0.0 network. She can also access it from 38.246.165.200. The anonymous user is denied logging in from 192.168.0.0 and hacker.net.

```
allow       mnoia 192.168.0.*
allow       mnoia 38.246.165.200
deny        anonymous 192.168.0.*
deny        anonymous hacker.net
```

Figure 9-11 /etc/ftphosts file

Configuring Messages

The wu-ftpd server allows you to configure messages in a variety of ways. For example, you can be notified of a readme file when you log on or move to a directory. All you have to do is make sure the file is either called readme or begins with README. That is, you could also put README.txt or README.doc in the directories because both names begin with README and would be recognized as readme files. Recall that the filenames are case-sensitive. Type the following code to receive notice of a readme file when you log on or move to a directory:

```
readme  README*    login
readme  README*    cwd=*
```

For the user to be notified of a readme file at logon, you have to put it in the root of the FTP server, which is /var/ftp. With the preceding reference to `cwd=*`, any directory that you change to that has a readme file that will cause the server to notify you. You could replace the asterisk (*) with a specific directory name relative to the root of the server, such as `cwd=/pub`. Then you would only be notified of a readme file in the pub directory, which is located at /var/ftp/pub.

You can also display a message after a user logs on or moves to a directory. To do so, use the following commands:

```
message /welcome.msg                login
message .message                    cwd=*
```

Because the welcome.msg file is located relative to the root of the FTP server, you must put it in /var/ftp. As with the configuration of the readme messages, if you want to display a message in any directory, name it .message. The filename must begin with a dot (.), which hides it from being displayed along with the other files in the directory when you use the `ls` command. As the root user, if you want to check whether a directory has a .message file, type `ls -a` to display hidden files.

If you want to display a message before the user logs on, you can add the following line with the full path to the banner file. Notice that the file path is given relative to the root of the system, not the root of the FTP server.

```
banner          /etc/banner.txt
```

UNDERSTANDING NEWS SERVERS

News servers allow **threaded discussions** on a variety of topics. Threaded discussions allow you to post messages in a **newsgroup** and have others respond. A newsgroup focuses on a specific topic. For example, comp.os.linux.security is a newsgroup devoted to Linux security issues, and alt.volkswagen.beetle is a newsgroup for Volkswagen Beetle owners and fans. Although you can create your own newsgroups on your server, you can also receive messages from other newsgroups that are part of Usenet. More than 40,000 newsgroups are currently in existence. You can find a complete listing of newsgroups at *ftp://ftp.isc.org/pub/usenet/CONFIG/newsgroups*. Very few organizations stay up-to-date on all the newsgroups because the effort can involve hundreds of gigabytes per day in newsfeeds, most of which involve to binary files. However, if the organization that delivers your newsfeeds allows you to select only the ones you need, the amount of resources needed to support a News server can be more reasonable.

It is common practice to set up a private News server only for topics that are relevant to the particular organization. For instance, you can share information on topics of interest such as brainstorming product information, management issues, and local software issues.

The News server uses the Network News Transfer Protocol (NNTP). Like the other text-based protocols, such as SMTP and POP3, NNTP does all of its work with relatively few commands. Table 9-2 lists the most common commands.

Table 9-2 News server commands

Command	Description
`ARTICLE`	Retrieves an article from the News server
`GROUP` *`name`*	Retrieves the article numbers of the first and last articles in the group, and estimates the number of articles in the group
`LIST`	Retrieves a list of valid newsgroups, along with the first and last article numbers in the newsgroup
`POST`	Posts (sends) an article to a newsgroup

Configuring a News Server in Windows

In Chapter 8, you installed NNTP, which created a News server. If you installed Exchange 2000 in Chapter 8, you configure the properties of NNTP News server through the Exchange System Manager. See Figure 9-12. If you did not install Exchange 2000, you would use Internet Information Services. See Figure 9-13.

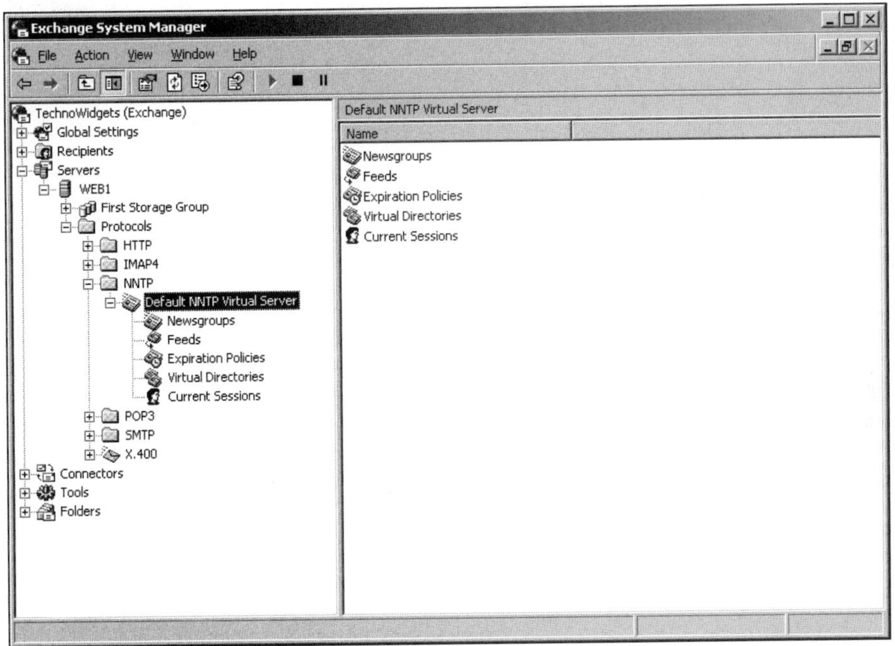

Figure 9-12 Exchange System Manager window

You have to configure only a few settings to get started using your News server. In the Settings property sheet of the NNTP Virtual Server properties dialog box, you can set up the SMTP server for moderated groups, and the domain name and the e-mail account of the News server administrator. See Figure 9-14 for an example of how the virtual server properties were set up for *technowidgets.com*.

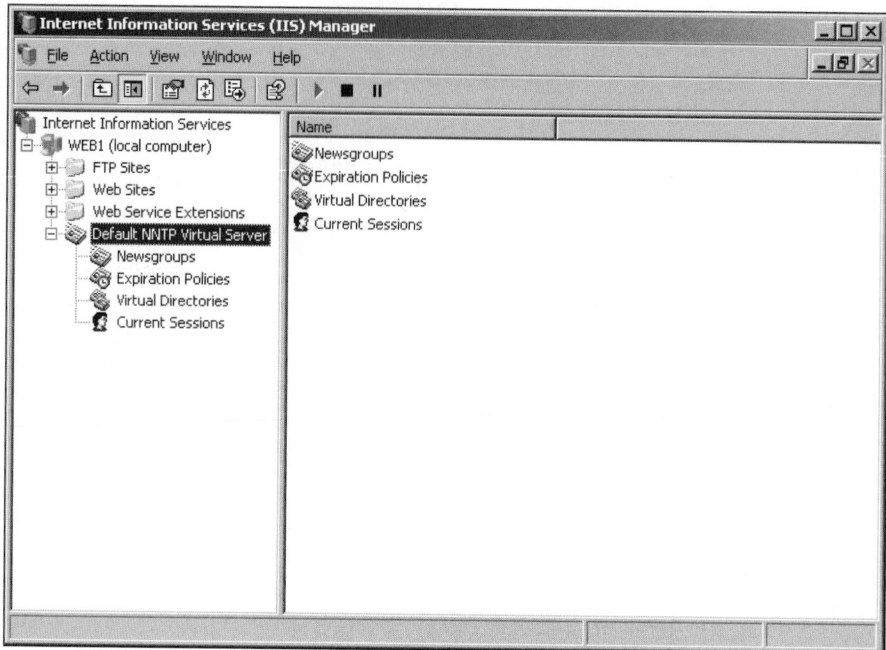

Figure 9-13 Internet Information Services window

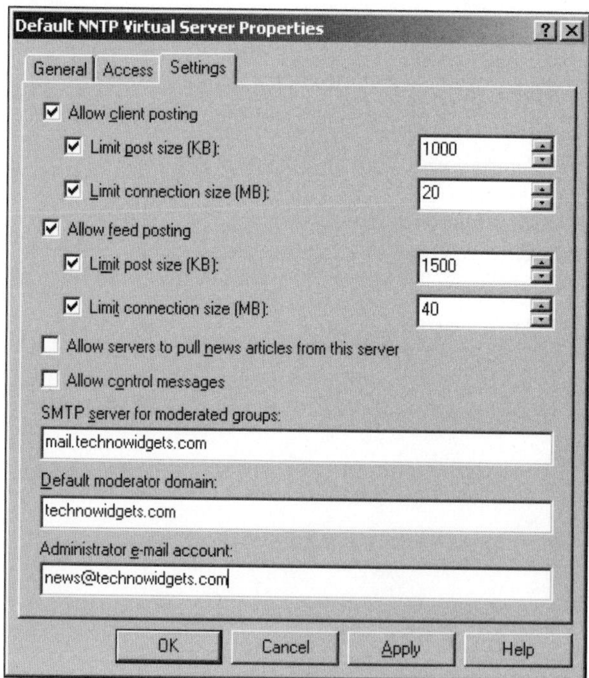

Figure 9-14 Default NNTP Virtual Server Properties dialog box

Now you can set up a newsgroup that is available locally. Two types of newsgroups exist: moderated and open. When a newsgroup is moderated, all postings go to the e-mail address of the moderator for the newsgroup. If the moderator determines that the posting is appropriate for the newsgroup, he or she posts it. With an open newsgroup, users post articles directly.

To create a newsgroup in Windows:

1. *If you installed Exchange 2000:* Click **Start**, point to **All Programs** (**Programs** in Windows 2000), point to **Microsoft Exchange**, and then click **System Manager**. Expand the left pane so that it looks like Figure 9-12.
   If you did not install Exchange 2000: In Chapter 8, follow the instructions to install the NNTP protocol. In Administrative Tools, click **Internet Information Services (IIS) Manager** (**Internet Services Manager** in Windows 2000). Expand the left pane so that it looks like Figure 9-13.
2. Right-click **Newsgroups** within the NNTP Virtual Server, point to **New**, and then click **Newsgroup**. The New Newsgroup Wizard opens. See Figure 9-15.

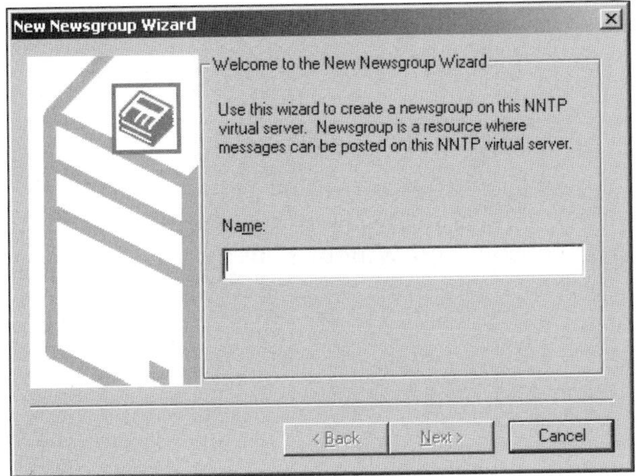

Figure 9-15 New Newsgroup Wizard

3. Type **technowidgets.products.suggestions** in the Name text box, and then click **Next**. A dialog box requesting a description and a Pretty name opens. See Figure 9-16. A Pretty name is a brief name that is used by the newsgroup.
4. Type **Employee suggestions for new products** in the Description text box.
5. Type **Product Suggestions** in the Pretty name text box.
6. Click **Finish** to complete the wizard.

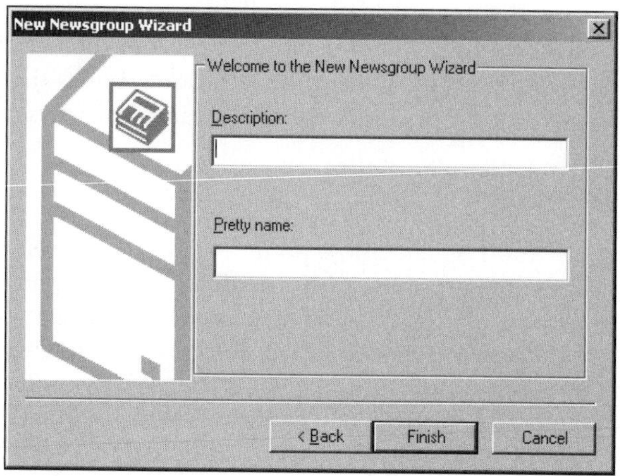

Figure 9-16 Description and Pretty name dialog box

Now you can double-click Newsgroups in the left pane and the new group will appear in the right pane. To make the newsgroup be a moderated newsgroup, you can double-click the name of the newsgroup, which opens its properties sheet . Click the Moderated check box, and then enter the e-mail address of the moderator. You can also make this newsgroup become read-only on this dialog box.

Once you have set up a newsgroup, you can configure a newsreader. Outlook Express includes a newsreader. If you have not configured Outlook Express as a mail reader, see "Configuring an E-mail Client in Microsoft Windows" in Chapter 8.

To configure Outlook Express as a newsreader in Windows:

1. Start Outlook Express.

   In Windows 2003: Click **Start**, point to **All Programs**, and then click **Outlook Express**.

   In Windows 2000: Click the **Outlook Express** icon on the taskbar, or click **Start** and then click **Outlook Express**.

2. Click the **Set up a Newsgroups account** link in the right pane under Newsgroups.
3. The Your Name dialog box should show your name, so click **Next**.
4. The Internet News E-mail Address dialog box should show your e-mail address, so click **Next**.
5. In the Internet News Server Name dialog box, type **web1.technowidgets.com** and then click **Next**.
6. Click **Finish** to complete the wizard.

7. When an Outlook Express dialog box asks if you want to download newsgroups from the news account you added, click **Yes**. The Newsgroup Subscriptions window opens. See Figure 9-17. Leave this window open for the next set of steps.

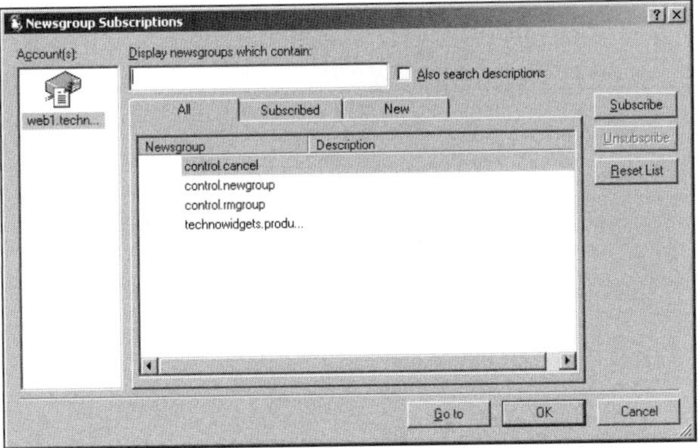

Figure 9-17 Newsgroup Subscriptions window

Notice the newsgroup whose name begins with "technowidgets." Before you can post to the newsgroup, you have to subscribe to it.

To subscribe to a newsgroup and post an article in Windows:

1. To subscribe, you can either double-click the **technowidgets.products.suggestions** newsgroup, or highlight it and then click **Subscribe**. An icon appears next to the newsgroup to show that you have subscribed to it.

2. With technowidgets.products.suggestions highlighted, click **Go to**. The technowidgets.products.suggestions - Outlook Express window opens. See Figure 9-18.

3. To post a message to the newsgroup, click the **New Post** button on the toolbar. The New Message window opens. See Figure 9-19.

4. Type **Super Size** for the subject and **Double the size** for the message. Click **Send** to post the message. If the Post News dialog box opens, click **OK**.

5. Double-click **web1.technowidgets.com** in the left pane to collapse the name of the News server, and then double-click it again to display the name of the newsgroup. Now the server will check for new postings. Click **technowidgets.products.suggestions** in the left pane to retrieve your message. It appears in the right pane.

6. Highlight the message in the upper-right pane. You see the complete message in the lower-right pane.

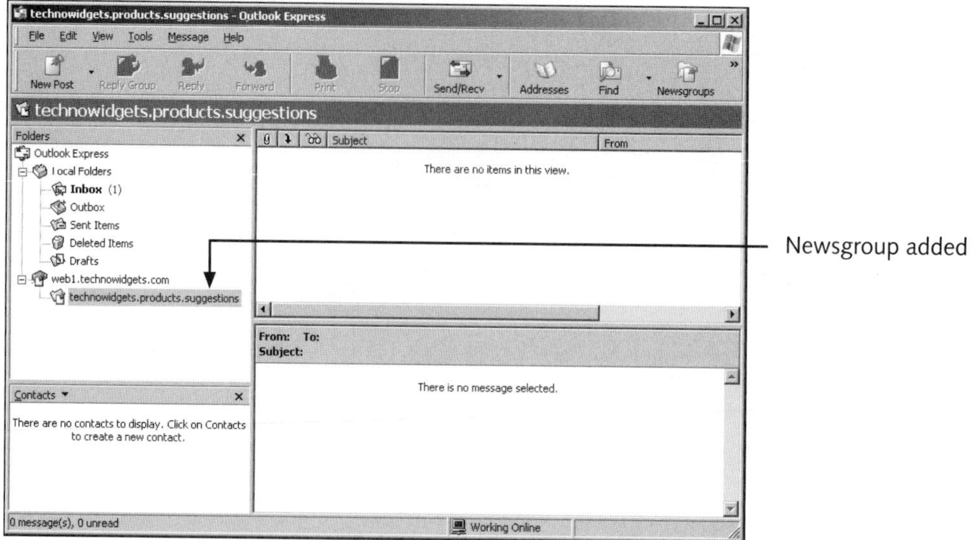

Figure 9-18 Newsgroup listed in Outlook Express

Installing and Configuring a News Server in Linux

The InterNetworkNews server is found on Red Hat Linux CD 2. Once you install the server, you must perform a few tasks to configure it. The InterNetworkNews server software includes about two dozen application files, plus more than a dozen configuration files. Fortunately, most of the configuration files are not needed to support local newsgroups, which is your objective.

Following is an overview of the tasks you need to perform to create a News server in Linux:

- Install the InterNetworkNews server.
- Enable the server.
- Alter the configuration in inn.conf.
- Make sure that there is a reference to your domain in /etc/resolve.conf.
- Create and rename the history files.
- Describe who can read and post to newsgroups in reader.conf.
- Set up the storage configuration in storage.conf.
- Create a newsgroup.
- Start the server.

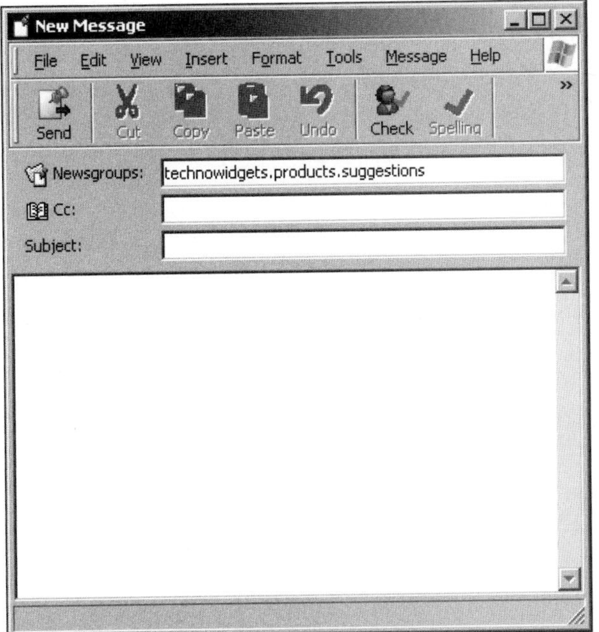

Figure 9-19 New Message window

9

The installation creates a variety of configuration files in /etc/news as well as a user called news. Remember that certain operations, such as creating history files and starting the server, must be done as the news user. The following installation needs to be performed only if you did not choose Network News when you installed Linux in Chapter 3.

To install InterNetworkNews in Linux:

1. Insert Red Hat Linux CD 2 into the CD drive. On the desktop, double-click **CD/DVD-ROM** to mount the CD, and then open Konqueror.
2. Navigate to the RedHat/RPMS directory.
3. Double-click **cleanfeed-0.95.7b-17.noarch.rpm**. The version number in your filename may be slightly different.
4. The Completed System Preparation dialog box opens. Click **Continue** to install cleanfeed.
5. Double-click **inn-2.3.3-5.i386.rpm**. The version number in your filename may be slightly different. The Completed System Preparation dialog box opens. Click **Continue** to install the News server. Close the Konqueror window.
6. In a terminal window, enable the News server by typing **chkconfig innd on** and then pressing **Enter**.

You must configure other settings before you start the server. First, you need to change entries in /etc/news/inn.conf. The format of the inn.conf file is <parameter>: <whitespace> <value>. A <whitespace> is created when you press the spacebar or Tab key. For example, you need to change the organization parameter to "The TechnoWidgets News site," so you would search the inn.conf file for the organization parameter and change it to the following:

```
organization:  The TechnoWidgets News site
```

You also need to change the pathhost parameter to the address of the News server, the domain parameter to the domain of the News server, and the server parameter to the address of the News server. For *technowidgets.com*, change the lines as follows:

```
pathhost:  web1.technowidgets.com
domain: technowidgets.com
server: web1.technowidgets.com
```

To have the News server start correctly, you need to make sure that the server is a member of the correct domain. Other applications are not as sensitive to this issue as innd. For *technowidgets.com*, you need to make sure that you have an entry in /etc/resolv.conf with the following command:

```
domain technowidgets.com
```

You must also configure the history files before you can start the News server. These history files must be created while working as the news user, which was created when you installed the News server. You must next rename the history files, and then you can start the News server.

To create history files and start the News server:

1. In a terminal window, type **su news** and then press **Enter** to switch to the news user.
2. Type **/usr/lib/news/bin/makehistory** and then press **Enter** to initialize the history text file.
3. Type **/usr/lib/news/bin/makedbz -i** and then press **Enter** to create the binary history files. (Be sure to insert a space before "-i" in the command.)
4. Type the following lines to rename the history files, pressing **Enter** at the end of each line:
   cd /var/lib/news
   mv history.n.dir history.dir
   mv history.n.hash history.hash
   mv history.n.index history.index
5. Type **/usr/lib/news/bin/inndstart** and then press **Enter** to start the server.
6. Type **exit** and then press **Enter** to return to the root account.

Now you can create a newsgroup.

To use the ctlinnd utility to create a newsgroup:

1. Type the following command to create a newsgroup called technowidgets.products.suggestions that is open for posting by everyone:

   /usr/lib/news/bin/ctlinnd newgroup technowidgets.products.suggestions y

2. To create the same group but have it moderated by mnoia, change the "y" to an "n" and add Mary Noia's e-mail name to the command:

   /usr/lib/news/bin/ctlinnd newgroup technowidgets.products.suggestions n mnoia@technowidgets.com

Even though the News server is fully functional now, you cannot post an article to a newsgroup until you configure the storage for the articles. By default, no storage is allowed. Fortunately, the basic configuration is simply commented out, so you can easily remove these comments to allow storage. The storage method for local articles is called timehash. Although you can configure the News server to allow any local newsgroup and not restrict storage, the News server can be readily modified based on the sample template at the beginning of the /etc/news/storage.conf file. The reference to "class" must be a unique class number within the storage.conf file.

9

To allow articles to be stored on the Linux server:

1. In a terminal window, type **kedit /etc/news/storage.conf** and then press **Enter**.
2. Delete the "#" at the beginning of the first "method timehash" and the three subsequent lines. The statements should match the following:

```
method timehash {
       newsgroups: *
       class: 0
}
```

3. Save and close the file.

Now that you have a newsgroup and the server is started, it is a good idea to use Telnet to confirm that it is running correctly. To do so, connect to the server and retrieve a list of the newsgroups, which will include control newsgroups.

To test the installation:

1. In a terminal window, type **telnet localhost 119** and then press **Enter** to connect to the News server at port 119.
2. Type **list** and then press **Enter** to retrieve a list of the newsgroups. The output of the Telnet session should appear similar to Figure 9-20.
3. Type **quit** and then press **Enter** to end the Telnet session.

If any problems arise when you test the installation, you can display critical errors by typing the following command:

```
cat /var/log/news/news.crit
```

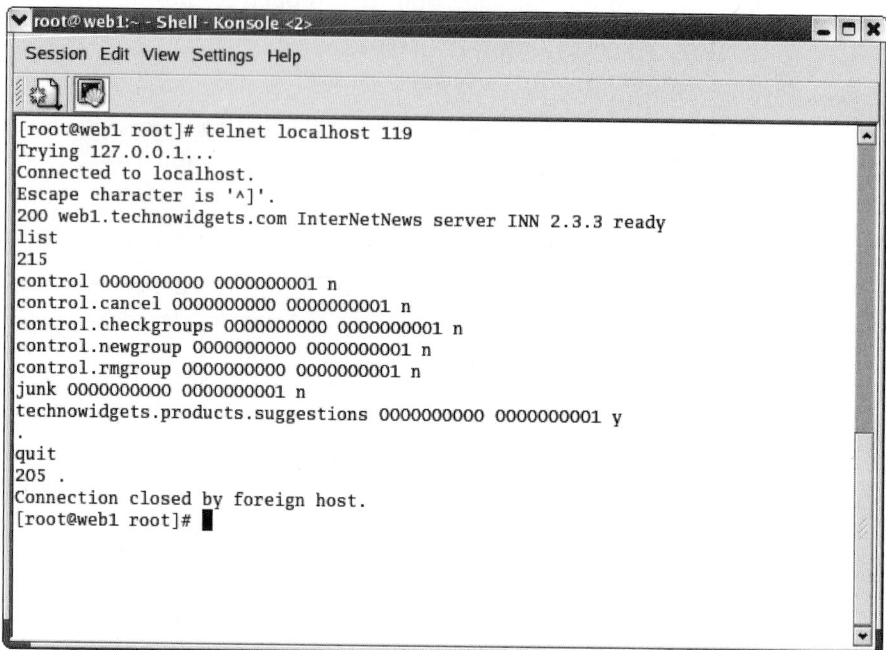

Figure 9-20 Telnet session to test installation

Now you can configure a newsreader, subscribe to the technowidgets.products.suggestions newsgroup, post a message, and then read the message. The KDE environment comes with a newsreader called KNode. However, all newsreaders use a similar configuration. Basically, you need to describe who you are and where the News server is located.

To install the KNode newsreader via a command-line installation:

1. Insert Red Hat Linux CD 3 into the CD drive.
2. Open a terminal window.
3. Type **mount /mnt/cdrom** and then press **Enter**.
4. Type **rpm -i /mnt/cdrom/RedHat/RPMS/knode*.rpm** and then press **Enter**. You may see a warning about the V3 DSA signature. It will not cause problems.

To configure the KNode newsreader in KDE:

1. In a terminal window, type **knode** and then press **Enter**. The Preferences window opens, as shown in Figure 9-21. You can also open the Preferences window by clicking **Configure KNode** in the Settings menu.

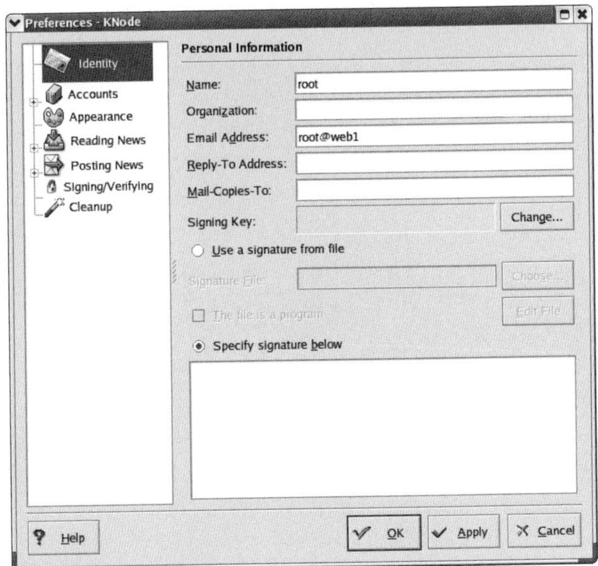

Figure 9-21 Preferences window for KNode

2. Change the name to **Cris Branco** and the e-mail address to **cbranco@technowidgets.com**.
3. Click **Accounts** in the left pane, and then click **News** to allow you to configure a connection to the News server.
4. Click **New** in the right pane to create a new News server account. The New Account dialog box opens. See Figure 9-22.
5. Type **TechnoWidgets News** as the name of the account, and then type **localhost** as the address for the server.
6. Click **OK** to save the changes. You now see TechnoWidgets News listed under Newsgroup Servers.
7. Click **OK** to exit the Preferences window. At the top of the left pane, TechnoWidgets News has been added to the list of names.

To subscribe to a newsgroup:

1. In KNode, click **TechnoWidgets News** at the top of the left pane.
2. Click **Account** on the menu bar, and then click **Subscribe to Newsgroups**.

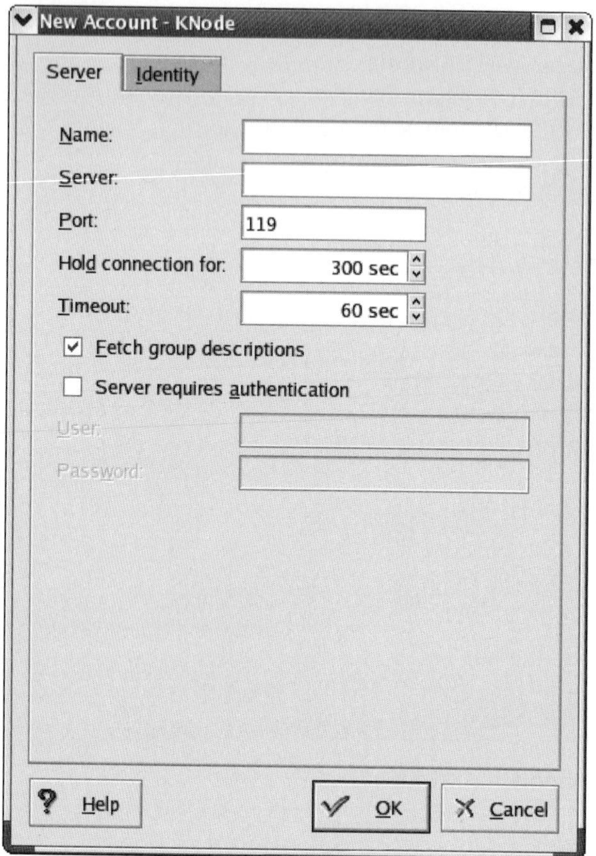

Figure 9-22 New Account dialog box

3. You are prompted with the following question: "You don't have any groups for this account. Do you want to fetch a current list?" Click **Yes**. The Subscribe to Newsgroups window opens.
4. Click the **technowidgets.products.suggestions** check box. Notice that it is now listed in the "subscribe to" pane.
5. Click **OK** to return to the main screen.

To post an article:

1. In KNode, if you do not see "t.p.suggestions" in the left pane, double-click **TechnoWidgets News** at the top of the left pane.
2. Click **t.p.suggestions**, click **Article** on the menu bar, and then click **Post to newsgroup**. A window similar to an e-mail client opens.
3. For the subject, type **Super Size**. In the large text box, type **Double the size of a widget**.

4. Click the **Send Now** icon in the upper-left corner of the window.
5. Click **t.p.suggestions**, click **Account** on the menu bar, and then click **Get New Articles in All Groups** to retrieve new articles. Your message appears in the right pane. If you click the message, you see the text of the message in the lower-right pane.

CONFIGURING REMOTE ACCESS TO A SERVER

Sometimes you need remote access to a server so that you can work at the server without being near it. In such a case, the Telnet daemon in Linux and Terminal Services in Windows allow you to execute commands as if you were sitting at the computer. Consider security and processing capacity before you allow remote access. Allowing remote access opens your server to attack more than any other decision. Chapter 10 discusses security in detail. If you let others have remote access to the server, also consider that doing so will increase the processing burden as more users access the server.

Configuring Telnet in Linux

Although you have used the Telnet client to connect to many server programs, you have not used it to connect to a Telnet server. The Telnet server listens at port 23. Its purpose is to create a shell that acts just as if you were logged on locally. However, you cannot connect to a Telnet server with the user name of root. You must first log on as a regular user and then use the su (switch user) utility to become the root user.

To install and enable the Telnet server:

1. Insert Red Hat CD 2 in the drive.
2. In Konqueror, navigate to /RedHat/RPMS and double-click the package that begins with "telnet-server." The Completed System Preparation dialog box opens.
3. Click **Continue** to install the Telnet server.
4. Close the Konqueror window.
5. In a terminal window, type **chkconfig telnet on** and then press **Enter** to enable the Telnet server.
6. Type **service xinetd restart** and then press **Enter** to restart the xinetd daemon so that it will read the configuration files again.

Now you can use a Telnet client from any computer on the same network to log on to the Linux server. Just as you can use a Web browser on any operating system to view pages on a Web server on Linux, so you can use a Telnet client on any operating system to connect to the Linux server. In the following steps, you use a Windows computer to connect to a Linux computer at 192.168.0.100.

To use Telnet to remotely connect to a Linux server:

1. Open a command-prompt window.

   In Windows 2003: Click **Start**, and then click **Command Prompt**.

   In Windows 2000: Click **Start**, point to **Programs**, point to **Accessories**, and then click **Command Prompt**.

2. In the Command Prompt window, type **telnet 192.168.0.100**, which is the IP address of the Linux computer, and then press **Enter**.
3. For a user name, use one besides root that exists on the Linux computer. For example, type **cbranco** and then press **Enter**.
4. For the password, type **password** and then press **Enter**. You are now at a command prompt for the user. Notice that the prompt ends in a dollar sign ($), indicating that you are a regular user.
5. To become the root user, type **su root** and then press **Enter**.
6. For the password, type **password** and then press **Enter**. Notice that the prompt ends in a pound sign (#), indicating that you are a super user, or root.
7. To exit the root account, type **exit** and then press **Enter**. Now you are back at the cbranco account.
8. To exit the cbranco account, type **exit** and then press **Enter**. Now you are back at the command prompt. Type **exit** to close, if necessary.

Telnet and Terminal Services in Microsoft Windows

Connecting remotely to a Windows server is a bit more complicated because Windows depends so heavily on the GUI. However, Windows does include a Telnet server if that is all you need.

Although administrators are accustomed to maintaining servers through a GUI, you can accomplish many tasks by using the command prompt, which is the only interface you have with Telnet. Microsoft has provided much more support for command-line administration in Windows 2003 than was available in Windows NT and Windows 2000. Before Windows, Microsoft networking depended on a single command called `net`. The `net` command was used to start the server, share folders, add and delete users, configure printers, and perform other administration tasks. Some of the useful options, such as `net user`, are not documented in Windows 2000 and Windows 2003, although they still work correctly. The `net user` command has many options; following are the ones most commonly used when adding a user:

```
net user username password /add /fullname:"first last"
/comment:"Appears in description"
```

The `/fullname` and `/comment` are optional. For example, to add a user called mnoia with a password of pass, a full name of Mary Noia, and a description of Accounting Manager, you would type the following command:

```
net user mnoia pass /add /fullname:"Mary Noia"
/comment:"Accounting Manager"
```

Table 9-3 lists other common `net` commands.

Table 9-3 Common `net` commands

Command	Description	Example
`net user`	Lists all users	`net user`
`net user` *`username`*	Displays user information	`net user mnoia`
`net user` *`username`* `/delete`	Deletes a user	`net user mnoia /delete`
`net start`	Lists all services	`net start`
`net start` *`service`*	Starts a service	`net start "FTP Publishing Service"`
`net pause` *`service`*	Pauses a service	`net pause "FTP Publishing Service"`
`net stop` *`service`*	Stops a service	`net stop "FTP Publishing Service"`
`net share`	Lists shared folders and printers	`net share`
`net share` *`name=location`*	Shares a folder	`net share docs=c:\docs`
`net share` *`name`* `/delete`	Deletes a share	`net share docs /delete`
`net use` *`drive: \\computer\share`*	Maps a drive	`net use g: \\web1\docs`
`net` *`command`* `/?`	Gets help for the command	`net use /?`

You can also use a command-line utility to control folder and file permissions. Use the `cacls` command to control Access Control Lists. The basic form of `cacls` is as follows:

```
cacls filename or folder name [options]
```

Some common options are included in Table 9-4.

9

Table 9-4 `cacls` options

Option	Description
`/e`	Changes instead of replaces permission
`/t`	Changes all subfolders
`/g user:perm`	Grants a user specific permissions
	Permissions are:
	f (full control)
	r (read)
	w (write)
	c (change)
	n (none)
`/p user:perm`	As above, except permissions are replaced
`/r user /e`	Revokes permission

You can also use a networking shell called **netsh**. The `netsh` command creates a network shell that allows you to configure and display dozens of network-related items. You can work either within each level of the shell or from the command line to specify all the levels and associated commands. For example, you can add or delete IP addresses to NICs, including gateways and DNS addresses. To add an IP address of 10.1.2.3 and a gateway of 10.1.1.1 to the default NIC, you would type the following commands:

```
netsh interface ip add address "Local Area Connection" 10.1.2.3 255.0.0.0
netsh interface ip add address "Local Area Connection"  gateway=192.168.0.1
```

If you wanted to create a text file with the commands to re-create the IP configuration, you would type the following command:

```
netsh interface ip dump
```

Using the `netsh` diagnostics, you can gather a wealth of information from the server's perspective. You can test connections from the server to a proxy server, DNS servers, and access to services at ports on other computers, among many other things. For example, you can ping the gateway address of each adapter with the following command:

```
netsh diag ping gateway
```

Windows 2003 has added some useful command-line utilities for remote administration. You can create detailed queries of event logs with a script called eventquery.vbs. For example, if you wanted to display any entries in the system log related to errors, you would type the following command:

```
cscript c:\windows\system32\eventquery.vbs /fi "type eq error" /l system
```

You can also manage the network monitor, manage performance, defragment a drive, and even shut down the server remotely. In all, there are nearly 50 new command-line utilities in Windows 2003.

To enable and start the Telnet server:

1. In the Administrative Tools window, click **Computer Management** (double-click it in Windows 2000).
2. In the left pane, expand **Services and Applications**.
3. Click **Services** to display a list of services in the right pane.
4. Scroll down the list of services, right-click **Telnet**, and then click **Properties**. To have the Telnet server start every time you start the server, you would change the startup type to Automatic. If you want the Telnet server to start whenever you order it to do so, you would choose Manual. In this case, change the startup type to **Automatic**, and then click **Apply**.
5. Click **Start** to start the Telnet server.
6. Click **OK** to close the Telnet Properties dialog box.

To connect to a Telnet server on Windows, you can use the steps "To use Telnet to remotely connect to a Linux server," and change the IP address and user information to fit the Windows computer. One of the differences in logging on to a Windows Telnet server instead of a Linux Telnet server is that you can log on as an administrator. There is no "su" capability.

Terminal Services is more complicated. If you need GUI-based access to the server or you are more concerned about security, then Terminal Services is the answer. It provides solutions to two problems related to remote users and administrators.

Some remote users may need access to applications that run only on a specific server. In this Terminal Services mode, you are working with an application server. One reason you may want an application server is that you do not want users to have a proprietary application for security reasons. Another reason could be that because of licensing requirements, you do not want to give all potential users a copy of an application.

Terminal Services also allows an administrator to remotely administer the server. The focus of this section is remote administration.

Windows 2000 and Windows 2003 take slightly different approaches toward installing Terminal Services on the server. In Windows 2003, Terminal Services for administration is already installed, however you have to enable it. In Windows 2003, you have to install Terminal Services only if you want to create an application server. In Windows 2000, when you install Terminal Services, you are asked whether it will be for remote administration or for an application server.

To install Terminal Services in Windows 2000:

1. Open the Control Panel, and then double-click **Add/Remove Programs**.
2. Click **Add/Remove Windows Components**.
3. Scroll and then click the **Terminal Services** check box.

4. Click **Next** to install Terminal Services. The Terminal Services Setup dialog box opens. It requests that you select the mode you want to use. Application server mode would require licensing after 90 days of use.
5. Keep the default of Remote administration mode and click **Next**. This will require access to Windows 2000 files, which are typically on a CD.
6. Click **Finish** to exit the wizard. A dialog box opens stating that the server needs to be restarted.
7. Click **Yes** to restart the server.

To configure Terminal Services in Windows 2003:

1. In the Control Panel, click **System**. The System Properties dialog box opens.
2. Click the **Remote** tab. In the Remote Desktop section, click the **Allow users to connect remotely to this computer** check box.
3. The Remote Sessions message box opens, indicating that all accounts used for remote connections must have passwords. Click **OK**. By default, anyone in the administrators group can access the computer. If you wanted other users to access this computer, you could click the Select Remote Users button to add them.
4. Click **OK** to save the changes.

Terminal Services requires that client software reside on each computer that needs to access Terminal Services on the remote server. Windows 2003 automatically includes the client software. For a Windows 2000 client, however, you have to install the client software manually. If you have a Windows 2000 server and a Windows 2000 client, then you install Terminal Services from floppy disks. If you have a Windows 2003 server and a Windows 2000 client, you have to share the installation folder on the Windows 2003 server and then map a drive to it from the Windows 2000 clients.

To install Windows 2000 client software for Windows 2000 Terminal Services:

1. Find two blank, formatted floppy disks.
2. In the Administrative Tools window, double-click **Terminal Services Client Creator**. The Create Installation Disk(s) dialog box opens.
3. Click **Terminal Services for 32-bit x86 windows**. You will be prompted to insert one disk at a time as Setup copies the installation files. Click **OK**.
4. Click **Cancel** to close the Create Installation Disk(s) dialog box.
5. Take the floppy disks to another Windows 2000 computer, and insert the first floppy disk into the floppy disk drive.
6. At a command prompt, type **a:\setup**, and then press **Enter**. The Terminal Services Client Setup dialog box opens.

7. Click **Continue**. The Name and Organization Information dialog box opens. Type your name and the name of your organization.
8. Click **OK** once, and then click **OK** again to confirm the information. The Licensing agreement dialog box opens.
9. Click **I Agree**. A dialog box opens so you can select the installation location.
10. Click the button in the upper-left corner of the dialog box to start the installation. When asked whether you want all users to have the same configuration, click **Yes**.
11. After installing the files on the first disk, the Setup program asks you for the second disk. Insert it, and then click **OK**.
12. When Setup states that the installation was completed successfully, click **OK**.

Now that you have installed Terminal Services on the Windows 2000 client, you can connect to a Windows server running Terminal Services. When you start the client software, it will ask for the IP address or computer name of the server. You can also adjust the resolution of the connection. Once you connect and log on, your screen appears as if you are working at the server. This means that drive A: is on the remote computer, not yours. It is very important to distinguish between logging off and disconnecting. Once you are connected and logged on, and you close the Terminal Services client window, you disconnect your computer, but your session remains active on the server. This ability can be useful if you want to connect and run a utility that takes a long time, such as defragmenting the drive. If you disconnect, the utility will continue to run. When you connect and log on again, you will see the same screen that last appeared when you disconnected. The effect is similar to locking a workstation. To log off, you must click Start, click Shut Down, and then select Log off before clicking OK. If you press Ctrl+Alt+Del, that would cause you to log off of the client instead of the server.

9

To connect to a Terminal Services Server from Windows 2000:

1. Click **Start**, point to **Programs**, point to **Terminal Services Client**, and then click **Terminal Services Client**. The Terminal Services Client dialog box opens.
2. In the server text box, type **192.168.0.100**.
3. Click **Connect** to connect to the server.
4. Log on as the administrator just as you would as if you were at the server.
5. When you want to log off, click **Start** in the Terminal Services window, click **Shut Down**, click the list arrow, and then click **Log off**. Click **OK**.

To connect to a Windows 2003 Terminal Services server from Windows 2003:

1. Click **Start**, point to **All Programs**, point to **Accessories**, point to **Communications**, and then click **Remote Desktop Connection**.
2. On the Remote Desktop Connection dialog box, type **192.168.0.100**.

3. Click **Connect** to connect to the server.
4. Log on to the server.
5. To log off, click **Start**, and then click **Log Off**.

Understanding Streaming Media Servers

Over the years, the quality of the video and audio over relatively slow connections has increased greatly. Also, users who want to receive high-quality video can now more easily access high-speed DSL and broadband services. Video servers such as those from *www.jumptv.com* offer TV channels from around the world. Internet radio stations are also very popular. Streaming media is useful in organizational environments, too.

You can use streaming media in corporations to improve communication with both employees and customers. For example, you can create a standard library of training materials for new employees that includes video. You can also produce real-time video of a product launch or illustrate the reorganization of the business. In education, online courses that use streaming media can allow students to watch or listen to lectures at any time of the day or night. Educators can also use streaming media to enhance lectures on topics that would be difficult to present in a classroom, such as how to physically configure a network. You can use real-time video in a distributed lecture mode so that as the person is lecturing, students can send questions and comments to him or her.

The communication needs of streaming media differ from those of most of the other software in the Web environment. In the case of FTP, every byte must be transmitted accurately. To achieve this accuracy, FTP uses TCP, which acknowledges every packet and resends packets as needed. With streaming media, the requirements are not so exacting. If a packet is dropped, having it retransmitted would probably delay the stream and cause choppiness. Because of these limitations in TCP, the default transport protocol for streaming media is UDP, which is fast and efficient but does not have the overhead of acknowledging and retransmitting packets. If UDP does not work, clients often try TCP first, and then HTTP. HTTP, which uses TCP, is helpful in cases where security prevents the use of UDP or TCP, or when you want to run your streaming media from a Web server. Although you can use a Web server for streaming media, it is appropriate only when the traffic requirements are low because streaming media files are relatively large and HTTP is less efficient than UDP. In most cases, you should use a streaming media server such as Helix from RealNetworks or Windows Media Services from Microsoft.

Streaming media, unlike the other forms of communication discussed so far in this book, has no standard that everyone follows for each type of data. With SMTP, for example, all e-mail servers know the basic commands so they can interoperate, and e-mail clients can communicate with e-mail servers without knowing who created the SMTP server. This is not the case with streaming media. Streaming media clients from Realnetworks and Microsoft read their own file formats and alternative file formats. Other clients such as Macromedia Flash can read the major file formats. However, imagine being pressured to upgrade your e-mail client frequently to use the most current enhanced SMTP commands. Fortunately, that step is not necessary with e-mail, but it is standard practice with streaming media. Both RealNetworks and Microsoft keep improving their products, but the new versions can make the existing clients incompatible with the latest features. It can also cause support difficulties because of the difficulty entailed in ensuring that you have deployed the correct version of one or more streaming media clients.

To develop an infrastructure for streaming media, you must first decide which file formats to support. The three major formats are Real Media, Windows Media, and QuickTime from Apple. Also important are the MP3 audio format and the MPEG video format.

Another consideration is how you plan to broadcast the streaming media. The simplest but most inefficient technique is **unicast**, in which each packet is sent individually to each client. With unicast, if you have 1,000 connections, you have 1,000 separate streams of data being sent to the clients. In the other method, called **multicast**, you send only one stream of data to an unlimited number of clients. The clients are configured with multicast IP addresses so that only those clients configured correctly receive the stream of data. Although parts of the Internet can use multicast through Mbone, this transmission technique is not common enough to rely on it. Multicast is more appropriate for an organization's intranet. Even then, the organization's routers have to support multicast, which is rare on low-end routers. One consideration when using multicast in an intranet is its similarity to broadcast TV. That is, the stream is sent once and clients have to make sure they are waiting for the transmission. They cannot pause or restart it. With unicast, because each transmission is distinct, you can pause or restart it. Multicast is a good option when many people need to watch a video and they are all available at one time to watch it.

One of today's most popular streaming media servers is Helix Universal Server from RealNetworks. Helix supports all of the file formats mentioned earlier, and more. It requires at least a 500 MHz Intel processor, a 400 MHz Ultra Sparc II processor, or a 375 MHz PowerPC. It supports a variety of operating systems, such as Windows, Solaris, IBM AIX, HP UX, and Linux. In the case of Linux, you must use a kernel version 2.2.13 or later. Although the Helix basic server requires only 256 MB as a minimum, streaming media servers benefit greatly from increased RAM. Storage requirements are more difficult to predict beyond the 18 MB required for the server. The calculation for basic audio is (bit rate of clip in Kbps * length of clip in seconds) ÷ 8 = kilobytes of disk space required to store the audio. Given a one-hour audio file sampled at 8 bits, you would need about 28 MB of disk storage. If you want to have it available for different connection speeds, you have to allow for storage for each rate. Video Storage requirements are even more challenging to calculate because of the different transfer rate possibilities. The 8-second Windows Media sample that comes with the Helix server requires 256 KB of storage. At a transfer rate of 32 Kbps, it would take about 115 MB of storage for one hour of video.

Actually, the Helix server is many servers in one because of the number of protocols that it supports. By default, it configures servers at the ports described in Table 9-5.

Table 9-5 Helix server ports

Protocol	Port	File format
RTSP	554	For RealPlayer: Real Media, MP3, MPEG-1, MPEG-4, QuickTime
HTTP	80	Windows Media, QuickTime, others
PNA	7070	Used by older versions of RealPlayer
MMS	1755	Microsoft's proprietary control protocol for Windows Media Player

Microsoft offers the Windows Media Services (WMS) as part of Windows Components. It has parallels to Internet Information Services, another service that is part of Windows Components. Both servers default to port 80 for HTTP. For that reason, it is better not to have IIS installed on the same server with WMS. You can make the two services work on the same computer by creating a virtual IP address on the NIC and then allowing IIS to use one IP address and WMS to use the other. Another reason not to have IIS and WMS reside on the same server is that WMS is resource-intensive. WMS uses port 80 because some security measures prevent clients from using other ports. By default, HTTP in WMS is disabled. Besides supporting HTTP at port 80, WMS supports MMS at port 1755.

To install WMS:

1. Insert the Windows installation CD. If the installation window opens, click **Exit**.
2. *In Windows 2003:* In the Control Panel, click **Add or Remove Programs**.

   In Windows 2000: In the Control Panel, double-click **Add/Remove Programs**.
3. Click **Add/Remove Windows Components**.
4. Scroll to the last entry, and then select **Windows Media Services**.
5. Click **Next** to install WMS. In Windows 2000, the Terminal Services Setup dialog box opens with the default setting of Remote administration mode. Click **Next** to continue. When the Completing the Windows Components Wizard dialog box opens, click **Finish** to exit the wizard. Click **Yes** to restart the server in Windows 2000.

In Windows 2003, a folder called wmpub contains WMRoot, where the streaming media files are stored. In Windows 2000, the folder called \ASFRoot is used to store the **Advanced Streaming Format (ASF)** files. ASF is the standard file format for WMS. A few sample ASF files are found in the \ASFRoot folder. WMS is typically accessed through a browser. If TechnoWidgets had a WMS server at *wms.technowidgets.com*, for example, you could type *mms://wms.technowidgets.com/sample.asf* from a Windows computer with Windows Media Player installed. When the browser detected the MMS protocol, it would start Windows Media Player and play the sample.

UNDERSTANDING E-COMMERCE SERVERS

E-commerce servers allow an organization to communicate effectively with its customers. An e-commerce server has applications that you can configure. Some of these applications allow the organization to extend them by adding its own applications written in Java or ASP. E-commerce servers can provide services as simple as an online product catalog with a simple shopping cart that allows you to submit a list of products you want to order. An e-commerce Web site can also help you organize and analyze your marketing efforts or offer special promotions over a certain period of time. Such a promotion could be based on individual product prices, volume discounts, shipping discounts, or many other possibilities. You might also want to e-mail sales information to customers. At the same time, e-commerce requires heightened security because credit card information many be transmitted from clients and stored on your computers. Also, you may want customers to be able to manage their own profiles online.

Often e-commerce servers are created using the programming languages mentioned in Chapter 7. However, developing an e-commerce site can be a large and complex undertaking. Purchasing a specialized e-commerce server application or even just critical components such as shopping cart software can improve the quality of your site and allow you to build the site in significantly less time.

Microsoft Commerce Server 2002 is an add-on to IIS that incorporates a number of features required for a typical e-commerce site. This software requires SQL Server 2000 to act as the DBMS holding product, customer, and other information. Commerce Server is integrated into the .NET Framework (described in Chapter 7) to offer increased productivity and greater capabilities for programmers. It supports the latest programming environment, Visual Studio .NET, which makes it easy for programmers to create and modify an e-commerce site. Although Microsoft provides sample solutions you can explore, effective use of this product requires the services of skilled programmers to create and maintain a typical Web site.

Commerce Server supports tens of millions of registered or anonymous users, who can be either customers or trading partners. Users can be tracked with regard to orders so when they return to the site, they can be targeted with specific advertisements or even shown a customized catalog. For example, if you operate an online pet-supply catalog, but the user is interested only in dogs and fish, the product selection and advertisements can reflect the user's preferences. In addition, Commerce Server can support multilingual catalogs and language-specific promotions. You can also program a site for **cross-selling**. Cross-selling involves offering customers products related to other products they have ordered or examined in the past. For example, if a customer is looking for travel books on San Francisco, your site could suggest travel books for California. Another approach built into Commerce Server is the **up-sell**, which involves suggesting a more profitable product related to a customer's interest in a different product.

Commerce Server uses a **pipeline** architecture for order processing and other purposes. A pipeline shows the steps that are needed for a customer to finish a specific business process. For example, the steps needed to process an order include gathering the list of products that the customer wants to order, processing the payment information, selecting the shipping options, and communicating information about the order and shipment of the product with the customer. Naturally, you typically want to customize the steps in the pipeline, so programmers can modify them by adding, deleting, or changing steps.

Authentication on an e-commerce server represents a challenge, because you need to balance flexibility and security. Commerce Server supports standard Secure Sockets Layer connection (discussed in Chapter 10) to a database of users along with Microsoft Passport, which can allow a single user name and password to access multiple sites.

CHAPTER SUMMARY

- You use FTP to transfer files from a server to a client (download) and to transfer files from a client to a server (upload). FTP is commonly employed to download programs, software patches, service packs, music, video, and other binary files. You can configure an FTP server to operate as an anonymous server or you can require a valid logon. Although you can allow uploads to an FTP server, they pose risks because they leave your system vulnerable to hackers. User names and passwords are sent as clear text. FTP uses port 20 for data commands and port 21 for control commands; the actual data transfer takes place over a pair of unprivileged ports.
- You use News servers to set up threaded discussions on a variety of topics. You organize each topic in a newsgroup, such as one interested in Linux security. A News server can be part of Usenet, which contains tens of thousands of topics to which people can contribute. Often, private News servers are used just within an organization. News servers use NNTP and communicate via port 119.
- When configuring remote access to a server via Telnet or Windows Terminal Services, consider that user names and passwords typically are sent using clear text. In Linux, you use ssh (secure shell) to communicate securely. Windows Terminal Services can use Integrated Windows Authentication to securely log on. Both Windows and Linux have command-line Telnet clients for connecting to a Telnet server. To use Terminal Services from a Windows 2000 or earlier client, you must install client software on each computer.
- Streaming media servers allow users to watch videos and listen to audio. Corporations use streaming media to improve communication with their employees and customers. To develop an infrastructure for streaming media, you must first decide which file formats to support. The three major ones are Real Media from RealNetworks, Windows Media from Microsoft, and QuickTime from Apple.

- E-commerce servers allow an organization to communicate more effectively with its customers. Their programs can be as simple as a product catalog that has a simple shopping cart and allows customers to submit a list of desired products. At the other end of the spectrum, a site might enable a company to organize and analyze its marketing efforts over time. Microsoft Commerce Server 2002 is an add-on product for IIS that helps an organization create a sophisticated e-commerce Web presence. Although sample configurations are available, development of a real site takes extensive programming.

Review Questions

1. FTP stands for ______________.
2. Which user name is used with FTP when you do not have a specific user name?
   a. basic
   b. anonymous
   c. an e-mail address
   d. nothing; leave the user name blank
3. What is the command to download multiple files at once?
   a. `getm`
   b. `mget`
   c. `get *`
   d. `gget`
4. FTP servers use which of the following two privileged ports?
   a. 20 and 21
   b. 19 and 21
   c. 20 and 40
   d. 1 and 2
5. Which command do you use in FTP if you do not want be asked whether you want to download each file in a multiple-file download?
   a. `no prompt`
   b. `prompt no`
   c. `no ask`
   d. `ask no`

6. In the Linux FTP server, what is the name of the configuration file?
   a. access.ftp
   b. ftpaccess.conf
   c. ftpaccess
   d. ftp.access
7. In the Linux FTP server, how would you limit the number of failed logins to two?
   a. `logins 2`
   b. `login-limit 2`
   c. `loginfails 2`
   d. `faillogins 2`
8. How do you prevent users from connecting to the FTP server in Linux?
   a. `ftpd stop`
   b. `ftpstop now`
   c. `shutftp`
   d. `ftpshut now`
9. What is the command to limit the number of files downloaded to 50?
   a. `limit-file in 50`
   b. `file-limit out 50`
   c. `file-limit in 50`
   d. `files 50`
10. Approximately how many Usenet newsgroups are there?
    a. 400
    b. 4,000
    c. 40,000
    d. more than 40,000
11. In NNTP, the command to receive a list of valid newsgroups is ________________.
12. NNTP stands for ________________.
13. What is the term used to send a newsgroup message to a News server?
    a. post
    b. send
    c. mail
    d. forward

14. What is the command to enable Telnet?
    a. `Telnet on`
    b. `config Telnet on`
    c. `chkconfig Telnet on`
    d. `configTelnet on`
15. What is the command to list all services on a Windows computer?
    a. `list services`
    b. `net services`
    c. `net start`
    d. `net start services`
16. What is the command to find out whether mnoia is a valid user in Windows?
    a. `net mnoia`
    b. `net user mnoia`
    c. `net mnoia /user`
    d. `net users /user=mnoia`
17. What is the command to change permissions in Windows?
    a. `cacls`
    b. `chgperm`
    c. `permchg`
    d. `You cannot change permissions in Windows.`
18. What is the name of the networking shell?
    a. netshell
    b. nets
    c. net
    d. netsh
19. What is the preferred protocol used by streaming media?
    a. TCP
    b. UDP
    c. HTTP
    d. ICMP
20. Unicast is when each packet is sent individually to each client. True or False?

Hands-on Projects

Project 9-1

Test an FTP server in Windows. Show the importance of using binary mode for transfer of binary files.

To test FTP:

1. Install FTP, if necessary. (See the steps in this chapter for detailed instructions.)
2. *In Windows 2003:* Copy **calc.exe** from \WINDOWS\system32 to \inetpub\ftproot.

   In Windows 2000: Copy **calc.exe** from \WINNT\system32 to \inetpub\ftproot.
3. Rename calc.exe to **newcalc.exe** (right-click **calc.exe**, click **Rename**, type **newcalc.exe**, and then press **Enter**.) You are renaming the file to differentiate it from calc.exe, which is still available from the command-line.
4. Open a command-prompt window. Type **ftp localhost** and then press **Enter** to log on to the FTP server.
5. Type **anonymous** for a user name and press **Enter**, and then type anything for a password and press **Enter**.
6. Type **binary** and then press **Enter** to change the mode to binary. Although the default of ascii would have worked, too, it is always a good idea to change the mode to binary to ensure compatibility with other systems.
7. Type **get newcalc.exe** and then press **Enter** to download the calculator program from the FTP server.
8. Type **bye** and then press **Enter** to end the session with the FTP server.
9. Type **newcalc.exe** and then press **Enter** to start the calculator.

Project 9-2

In this project, you will configure and test FTP in Linux. In the configuration, you will change the number of times that the user can fail to log on correctly to 1. You will also set up messages, readme files, and a banner.

To configure FTP in Linux:

1. Create a text file in var/ftp called **readme** that contains the text **This is the login directory**.
2. Create a directory in /var/ftp called **software**.
3. Create a text file in the software directory called **.message** that contains the text **Welcome to the software directory**.

4. Create a text file in /var/ftp called **welcome.msg** that contains the text **Welcome to our FTP site. The software directory has what you are looking for.**
5. Create a text file in /var called **banner.txt** that contains the text **Just log on with the user name of anonymous and give us your e-mail address for a password.**
6. Open the /etc/ftpaccess file and change the following:
   a. Change loginfails 5 to **loginfails 1**.
   b. At the bottom of the file, add **banner /var/banner.txt**.
7. Save the file and then exit.

To test FTP:

1. In a terminal window, type **ftp localhost** and then press **Enter**. You should see a response with the banner you created. It may take a while for the FTP server to start.
2. For the user name, type **anonymous**; for the password, type **test@pass.com**. If you do not type an e-mail address, you will be disconnected from the FTP server. You should see the welcome message for the logon directory and a reference to the Readme file.
3. Type **cd software** and then press **Enter** to change to the software directory. You should see the message you created for the software directory.
4. Type **ls** and then press **Enter** to view the files in the software directory.
5. Type **bye** and then press **Enter** to close the session. The session should resemble Figure 9-23.

To test the login procedure with a user account:

1. Type **ftp localhost** and then press **Enter**.
2. For the user name, use mnoia or another user besides root.
3. Type an incorrect password and then press **Enter**. What is the response?
4. Type **open localhost** to connect to the FTP server again from the ftp> prompt.
5. Type **ls** and then press **Enter** to see the directories. What directories do you see? You do not see the software directory because you are not in the /var/ftp directory. You are in the user's home directory, such as /home/mnoia.
6. Type **bye** and then press **Enter**.

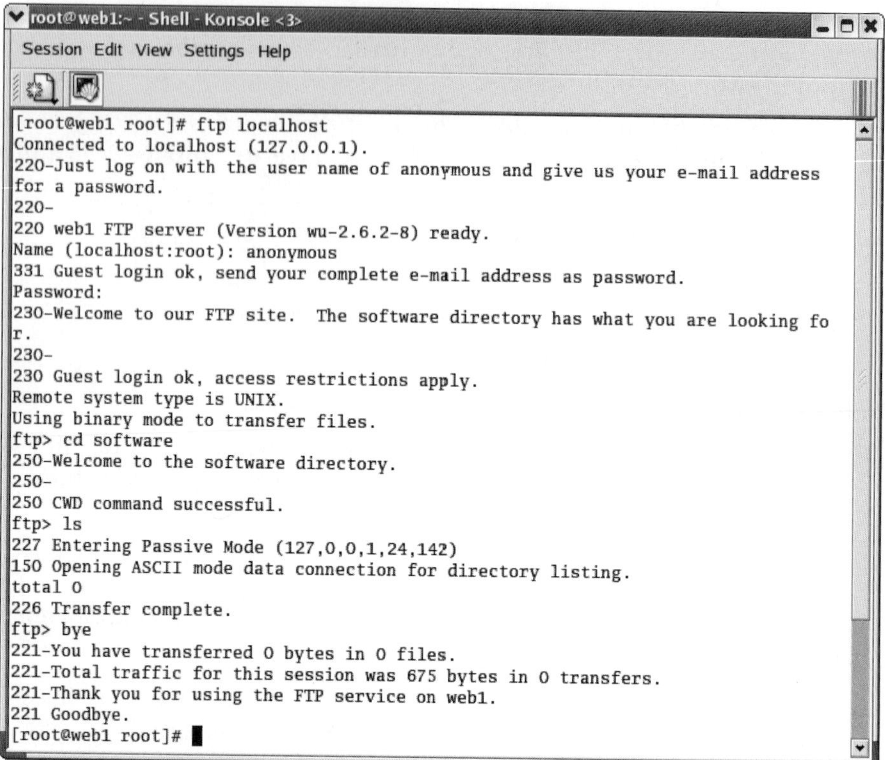

Figure 9-23 FTP session

Project 9-3

In this project, you will configure the News server in Windows to create a newsgroup called web.security. Then you will configure Outlook Express to access the newsgroup and post an article.

To create a newsgroup and test it in Windows:

1. Create a newsgroup called **web.security**.
2. Use **Web Security** as the pretty name with a description of **Security issues of Web servers and DNS servers**.
3. Configure Outlook Express to connect to the News server.
4. Download the newsgroups and subscribe to web.security.
5. Post a message to the web.security newsgroup.
6. Retrieve the message and open it.

Project 9-4

In this project, you will configure the News server in Linux to create a newsgroup called web.security. Then you will configure KNode to access the newsgroup and post an article.

To create a newsgroup and test it in Linux:

1. Make sure that cleanfeed and InterNetworkNews are installed, configured, and started.
2. Create a newsgroup called **web.security** with no moderator.
3. Allow articles to be stored on the server.
4. Test the installation using Telnet.
5. Configure KNode to connect to the News server.
6. Subscribe to the web.security newsgroup.
7. Post an article.
8. Retrieve the article and open it.

Project 9-5

In this project, you will configure and test Telnet in Linux. In Linux, you will shut down FTP and the Web server.

To configure and test Telnet in Linux:

1. Enable Telnet, if necessary. (Refer to the steps in this chapter for detailed instructions.)
2. Restart the xinetd service.
3. From another computer, use Telnet to communicate with the Linux computer using one of the user names created in a previous project.
4. Change to the root user.
5. Shut down the FTP server.
6. Shut down the Web server.
7. Exit the Telnet session.
8. Open a browser and try to connect to the Web server.
9. Use the FTP command line to try to connect to the FTP server.
10. Use Telnet to connect to the server again, and then start the Web server and FTP server from the Telnet prompt.

Project 9-6

In this project, you will configure and test Telnet and Terminal Services in Windows.

To enable and test Telnet in Windows:

1. Install Telnet, if necessary. (Refer to the steps in this chapter for detailed instructions.)
2. From another computer, use Telnet to connect to the Windows server.

3. Type **cd** and then press **Enter** to find your current directory.
4. Type **net start** and then press **Enter** to find which services are running. How many are running?
5. Type **net stop "World Wide Web Publishing Service"** and then press **Enter** to stop the Web server.
6. Use a browser to make sure that the Web server has stopped running.
7. Add a user called **tester** with a password of **pass**.
8. Display all the users on the server.
9. Add an IP address of **192.168.0.200** on the server.
10. Display a list of commands necessary to re-create the existing IP configuration.
11. Ping the DNS servers with **netsh diag ping dns**.

To configure and test Terminal Services in Windows:

1. Install Terminal Services, if necessary. (Refer to the steps in this chapter for detailed instructions.)
2. If you have Windows 2000, install the Terminal Services client software, preferably on another computer.
3. Log on to the server from the client as the administrator.
4. Use Administrative Tools to add a user.
5. In Internet Information Services, stop the Web server.
6. Exit Terminal Services.

Project 9-7

In this project, you will explore the use of the `netsh` command shell. You will learn how to move from context to context and how to display the options that are available. A **context** represents the relative position in the hierarchy of commands in netsh. Just as folders represent positions in a file system and related files exist in a single folder, a context contains related commands that allow you to explore the network settings.

To explore the use of the `netsh` command shell in Windows:

1. Open a command-prompt window.
2. Configure the command-prompt window to display up to 1,000 lines. Click the **c:** icon in the upper-left corner of the command-prompt window, and then click **Properties**. In the Properties dialog box, click the **Layout** tab. Change the height of the screen buffer size to **1000**. Click **OK** twice to exit.
3. At the command prompt, type **netsh** and then press **Enter**.
4. Type **?** and then press **Enter** to list the commands that you can use at this level. You are at the root context. As you see at the bottom of the screen, you can go to the following subcontexts: aaaa, bridge, dhcp, diag, interface, ras, routing, and wins. (Windows 2003 has ipsec and rpc as additional subcontexts.)

5. Type **dump** and then press **Enter**. Describe what happens.
6. Type **diag** and then press **Enter** to move to the diagnostics subcontext.
7. Type **?** and then press **Enter**. Which commands are available in this context?
8. Type **show ?** and then press **Enter** to show the options for the show command.
9. Type **show adapter** and then press **Enter** to show the adapter information.
10. Type **..** and then press **Enter** to move back one level.
11. Type **interface** and then press **Enter** to go to the interface subcontext.
12. Type **show interface** and then press **Enter**. How many interfaces are there?
13. Type **quit** and then press **Enter** to exit the shell.

Project 9-8

You should have already installed Windows Media Server in Windows 2003. In this project, you will enable connections, and then configure and test Windows Media Server.

To enable new connections to the Windows Media Server:

1. In Administrative Tools, click **Windows Media Services**. The Windows Media Services window opens.
2. Expand **WEB1**, and then expand **Publishing Points**.
3. Right-click **<Default> (on-demand)** and then click **Allow New Connections** on the shortcut menu.
4. Close the window.

To test Windows Media Server:

1. In the Address bar of your Web browser, type **mms://localhost/pinball.wmv** and then press **Enter**.
2. The Welcome to Windows Media 9 Series dialog box opens, allowing you to install Windows Media Player. Click **Next**.
3. The Select your Privacy Options dialog box opens. See Figure 9-24. Although you may want to alter the selections if you are accessing streaming media from the Internet, in this project you can just accept the defaults. Click **Next**.
4. The Customize the Installation Options dialog box opens. It lists the files that Media Player understands. Click **Finish** to exit the wizard.
5. In a browser, type **mms://localhost/pinball.wmv** and then press **Enter**. You see a video of a pinball.
6. In Windows Explorer, navigate to \wmpub\WMRoot and click on one of the files with a .wmv extension to see the video.

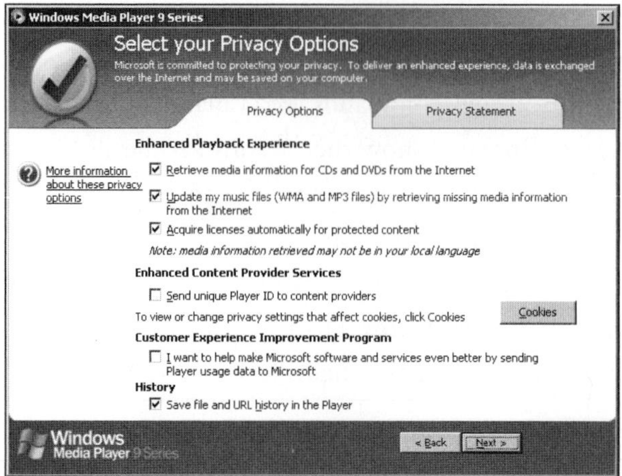

Figure 9-24 Select your Privacy Options dialog box

To configure and test Windows Media Server in Windows 2000:

1. Make sure that you have installed Windows Media Server. What are the names of the sample streaming media files?
2. In a browser, type **mms://localhost/sample.asf** and then press **Enter**. If you do not have audio available, you will get an error. If so, click **Close** to close the error dialog box and allow the media clip to continue without audio.
3. Close the Media Player and the browser.
4. Click **Start**, point to **Programs**, point to **Accessories**, point to **Entertainment**, and then click **Windows Media Player**.
5. In Windows Media Player, click **File** on the menu bar, and then click **Open**.
6. Click **Browse**, navigate to the \ASFRoot folder, and then click **welcome1.asf**.
7. Click **Open**. Then click **OK** to view the clip.

CASE PROJECTS

Case Project 9-1

The purpose of this project is to probe more deeply into FTP clients. What other command options are available for the `ftp` command in Linux? Type `man ftp` to get started. Show some examples. Use Windows Help to explore the details of the `ftp` command. Show some advanced examples of the `ftp` command in Windows. Compare the `ftp` command in Linux and Windows. List the strengths and weaknesses of each. Download an FTP client such as WS-FTP, install it, and test it.

Case Project 9-2

Subscribe to a Microsoft newsgroup. Go to *www.microsoft.com*, search for "newsgroups," and select the link for "All Newsgroups." Pick a newsgroup relevant to this chapter. Configure Outlook Express or KNode to connect to the newsgroup, subscribe to it, and read some messages. Find a newsgroup for Linux, subscribe to it, and read a message. Turn in the URL of the newsgroup, a description of the newsgroup, and a sample message.

Case Project 9-3

Research at least eight other command-line utilities in Windows that would help an administrator to remotely administer a server. Give a description of each utility and at least one example of its use.

Case Project 9-4

Download and install the Helix server from RealNetworks. Write a step-by-step guide to installing and configuring it. Describe any problems you experienced while installing it. Download and install Real Player from RealNetworks. How many of the samples can you get to run? You may also have to download the latest version of Macromedia Flash.

CHAPTER

10

SECURING THE WEB ENVIRONMENT

In this chapter, you will:

- Identify threats and vulnerabilities
- Secure data transmission
- Secure the operating system
- Secure server applications
- Authenticate Web users
- Use a firewall
- Use a proxy server
- Use intrusion detection software

Any time you connect a computer to a network, and especially to the Internet, the computer is open to attack. Although you can minimize the risk, you cannot eliminate it. Minimizing risk can require significant resources, both monetary and human. You also need to balance your need for security with the need to keep your system flexible and user-friendly.

Your Web server is vulnerable to many threats. Attackers might penetrate your system to gather data, change settings, or simply vandalize the server. Attackers do not even need to penetrate your system to do it harm. They can prevent other users from contacting your Web server through a technique known as a denial-of-service (DOS) attack. Because attackers can manipulate TCP/IP to try to harm your system, you should understand how the protocol works. The details will help you recognize common types of attacks and prepare to avoid them.

Both Windows and Linux need to be configured carefully to minimize security problems. In both of these complex operating systems, you must keep software patches up to date because many are released to minimize security vulnerabilities. Web servers that provide only static pages are relatively easy to protect. However, if your Web server provides dynamic pages that interact with a programming language, such as CGI, ASP.NET, or PHP, you must use caution when adding the programming language to the Web server. Programming languages can provide an access point for attackers to enter the Web environment.

To secure data transmission, you can encrypt data in a number of ways, including using Secure Sockets Layer (SSL) and Secure Shell (SSH) technologies. To isolate your Web server environment, you can use a firewall, which blocks unwanted access to ports, and proxy servers, which isolate computers. Intrusion detection software is useful to discover whether and how attackers have penetrated the system. Some intrusion detection software also identifies attempts to penetrate the system.

IDENTIFYING THREATS AND VULNERABILITIES

Although threats to your computer system can come from a variety of sources, this section focuses on threats that come from an Internet connection. First, you should understand the terms that network professionals use to describe a person who attacks a network. Historically, a "hacker" was someone who was very curious about the inner workings of computer systems. Unfortunately, the definition evolved to describe someone who intends to do harm to computer systems. To "hack" now means to penetrate a system. Many authors prefer to use the term "cracker" to denote a hacker with evil intentions. Both hackers and crackers have a high level of knowledge about computer systems. In contrast, some attackers have little or no knowledge of computer systems, such as script kiddies who download applications that can automate attacks on systems. This book uses the general term "attacker" to refer to someone who attempts to access a computer to harm the system or interfere with its data or processes.

Do not assume that no one would want to attack your system. Attackers are often motivated by the challenge of penetrating an organization, no matter what the organization does. Often, they scan IP addresses looking for particular vulnerabilities. Once they find a vulnerability, they penetrate a system without knowing who owns it.

For more information on vulnerabilities and security issues, consult the System Administration, Networking, and Security Institute (SANS) at *www.sans.org* and the Computer Emergency Response Team (CERT) at *www.cert.org*.

Understanding the Major Threats to Your Systems

The most dangerous threat to your Web server is someone penetrating your system to gather data. The data can consist of credit card information for customers, private company data intended only for authorized users, or passwords that attackers need for further penetration. For example, an attacker could gather user names and passwords and use that data to retrieve e-mail messages, find private information that requires authentication, and access the internal network. Someone could gather customer information that could be used by a competitor, such as to analyze pricing information for your products or services.

Attackers do not necessarily have to penetrate your system to gather data; they can also read data as it travels to and from your servers. The data could include sensitive company or client information and user names and passwords that can then be used to access the system more easily.

Another threat involves someone who changes data by **tagging** your Web site. Tagging refers to displaying a message, usually on the home page, that notifies you of the penetration. Tagging can also mean making changes that may cause you economic harm or embarrassment, such as editing your Web pages to discourage potential customers from purchasing products. In addition, an attacker could open your database to add products with embarrassing characteristics, change existing product pricing and descriptions, and delete products. With this level of access, the attacker could potentially add information to the database or operating system to provide a **back door** to your system. A back door represents a hidden access point to allow for significant control of your system.

The most common threat is disruption that prevents your system from functioning normally. These types of disruptions include flooding a computer with data to slow processing and exploiting a flaw in one of your servers, such as the DNS, Web, e-mail, or FTP server, or a weakness in the operating system itself. The flaw could cause the system to malfunction under certain circumstances or to fail completely.

Examining TCP/IP

The vulnerabilities to your system begin with TCP/IP, which was not designed to be secure but rather to allow systems to communicate. When you use TCP/IP in a typical networking environment, you are usually concerned with IP addressing, not with analyzing how TCP/IP works. However, to understand its vulnerabilities and secure your system, you need to understand how TCP/IP allows computers to communicate. Attackers take advantage of ignorance about TCP/IP to access computers connected to the Internet. Chapter 2 provided a brief overview of the structure of TCP/IP. Subsequent chapters explained that applications listen for communication at particular ports, and then accept packets of data. These applications assume that the packets of data are assembled accurately, but an attacker can manipulate the packets to penetrate your system.

When an IP packet enters your computer, the operating system analyzes the packet, which is divided into two parts: the header and data. The data is passed to the Transport layer for analysis. The header contains information about the packet. The following parts of the IP header are related to security:

- *Source address*—The IP address where the packet originated.
- *Destination address*—The end-point IP address.
- *Packet identification, flags, fragment offset*—If the packet needs to be split to send separate sections through a device that cannot accept the size of the original packet, these parts of the packet provide information to reassemble the packet at its destination.
- *Total length*—The length of the packet in bytes.
- *Protocol*—The higher-level protocols to which the data is being sent, including TCP, UDP, and ICMP.

At the level of the IP packet, the operating system handles the communication, making it is easier to detect and drop a malformed packet. The main task at this level is to pass the data to ICMP or a transport protocol such as TCP or UDP.

Like IP, TCP has a packet structure related to the tasks it performs, which primarily involve delivering data to applications. The important header fields are as follows:

- *Source port*—The port number associated with the application at the source IP address.
- *Destination port*—The port number associated with the application at the destination IP address.
- *Sequence number, data offset*—Information used when transmitting data that exceeds the size of the packet. Packets can be sent along different routes, and then arrive out of sequence. The sequence number and data offset information helps to put the packets back together in the correct order.
- *Flags*—The flags define the state of the data exchange. The most important flags are SYN (synchronization), which starts a TCP session; ACK (acknowledgment), which acknowledges the receipt of each packet; and FIN (finish), which ends the session.

You should understand how a TCP connection is created because someone attacking your system might alter what the system expects. Also, when you set up protection, you might need to describe the characteristics of the packets you expect to receive, including the flags. Figure 10-1 shows a standard TCP connection.

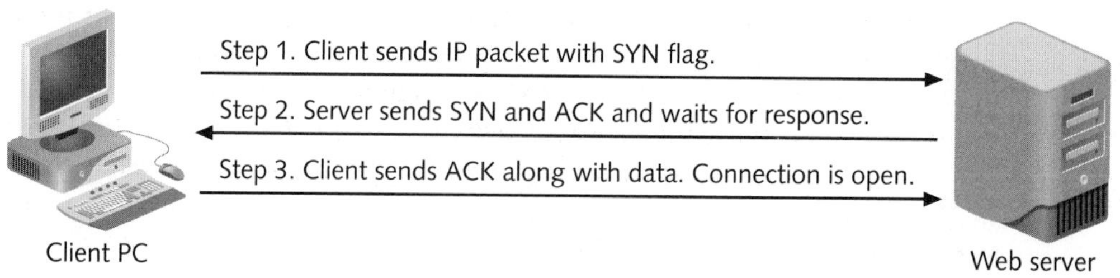

Figure 10-1 Establishing a TCP connection

When the server reads the SYN flag and acknowledges it, the server waits for the client to send an acknowledgment along with the data. If the client continues to send packets with the SYN flag set but never acknowledges it, the server suffers a **SYN flood**, which can consume resources on the server until legitimate traffic is either prevented from accessing the server or response times become very slow.

Attackers can manipulate sequence numbers and data offsets in the header of a data packet to cause a SYN flood and other system malfunctions, even though operating systems continue to improve their response to malformed headers. Later in this chapter, you will learn how to alter your operating system to determine its response to a SYN flood. An inappropriate header can also cause other system problems, especially if it passes through the TCP protocol and is sent to the port of the application protocol, such as HTTP, SMTP, or FTP. At this point, you have to depend on the capabilities of third-party application programmers to make sure the application handles the header appropriately.

As described in Chapter 9, UDP is an unreliable protocol because it does not guarantee the receipt of packets as TCP does. Instead, UDP depends on the application that uses it to provide reliability. UDP is also known as a connectionless protocol because it does not maintain a connection to transmit data, but rather sends each packet separately, which simplifies the structure of the packet. The main parts of each packet are the source port, the destination port, and the data sent to the destination port. Although UDP is most commonly used for DNS, it can also be used to attack systems. Such attacks are difficult to prevent because each UDP packet is sent independently as opposed to the approach TCP uses, which creates a connection to send data.

ICMP is a Network layer protocol that controls communication and reports the status of the communication. For example, ICMP is responsible for responding to a ping request with an echo-reply. If the packet cannot reach the destination, a router responds with a destination-unreachable message. If a computer is sending data more rapidly than the receiving computer can process it, a source-quench control message is returned to the sending computer to slow down communication.

Although it is a simple protocol, ICMP can provide information to an attacker that may prove useful later. By scanning hundreds or thousands of IP addresses, attackers can find those that respond with ICMP messages, and then probe those addresses to see what other services they provide. Attackers also often automate attacks that scan IP addresses to see which ones respond to a ping, and then pursue them in attempts to penetrate the system. When setting security options on servers, an administrator can try to prevent this type of attack by not allowing the server to respond to ICMP messages. Doing so also blocks responses to a ping. For example, if you type `ping www.microsoft.com` at a command prompt, you will not receive an echo-reply from the Microsoft server. That doesn't mean the Microsoft Web servers are down, but merely that Microsoft does not allow you to ping the servers. You can still use a browser to connect to *www.microsoft.com*.

Understanding Vulnerabilities in DNS

DNS seems like a simple system compared to the others in the Web environment, but historically it has been problematic. BIND has been the standard application used to implement DNS. BIND 8 had serious bugs that allowed unauthorized users root access to a server. With root access, someone could cause DNS to stop working or change records to incorrect IP addresses, such as one for a site that would be embarrassing to the organization or a pirate site that could gather credit card information from customers.

BIND 9, a complete revision of the software, has so far proved to be more secure than BIND 8. Because many systems still use BIND 8, however, newer versions of BIND 8 have also been released, primarily to reduce security problems related to remotely accessing the DNS computer and causing a denial of service.

You can find a current list of vulnerabilities of BIND at *www.isc.org/products/BIND/bind-security.html*. For a more detailed list of what has changed in new releases and other related issues, read the announcements at *marc.theaimsgroup.com/?l=bind-announce*.

Understanding Vulnerabilities in the Operating System

Operating systems are so large and complex that they will most likely continue to be vulnerable to attack. In reality, however, most system vulnerabilities are due to inattentive administrators and users running applications that allow attackers to compromise the system. If you are running Windows 2000 with Service Pack 1, or without a service pack, you are responsible for its security vulnerabilities because Microsoft has solved the security problems in Windows 2000 by providing service packs. Likewise, if a patch is available for a new computer virus but you do not install it, you should not blame the manufacturer of the operating system.

One of the most important ways to reduce the vulnerabilities in operating systems is to make sure that you have installed the latest patches. For Microsoft software, go to *www.microsoft.com/downloads*. Search based on the keywords "service pack" and "hotfix." Red Hat describes specific Linux vulnerabilities and ways to eliminate them at *www.redhat.com/support/alerts*.

Operating systems are designed to perform a variety of tasks, but you should use only those features you need to complete your tasks. For example, a useful feature of Windows is mapping a drive on a server. It makes the drive available to the server, although it is not physically connected to the server. However, when that server is connected to the Internet, the mapped drive becomes a vulnerability. Linux also provides utilities such as rlogin that allow remote access and are useful in a trusted environment, but should be avoided when connecting to the Internet. The sections in this chapter on securing the Web environment discuss the specific vulnerabilities and ways to avoid them.

Understanding Vulnerabilities in the Web Server

If your Web server has only static HTML pages with no scripts and allows access only to read pages, you can easily eliminate most vulnerabilities. However, users would find the site dull, and administrators would find it difficult to update pages. Most organizations want to enhance their sites while allowing users to update pages.

When you generate an online form, search a database for information, or restrict parts of your site, you create vulnerabilities. Even security features themselves can pose risks to a Web server. For example, if you require user authentication, but allow the user name and password to be sent as clear text, you have created a vulnerability because an attacker could intercept the clear text. The programming and configuration that makes a Web server useful also creates vulnerability.

Suppose you purchase an e-commerce application for your Web server or hire programmers to create your own e-commerce site. Often, programmers are more skilled in creating software that works correctly than preventing the software from being used incorrectly. Prevention is difficult because there are more ways to cause software to malfunction than there are to make it work correctly. The e-commerce application probably requests information from a user, and programmers can easily test this feature to make sure it requests and accepts data. However, if the programmer does not set the feature to validate the data, the data could cause **buffer overruns**, **cross-site scripting attacks**, and other problems. A buffer overrun, also known as a *buffer overflow*, occurs when a program accepts more data than it anticipated receiving. Although buffer overruns are generally easy for the programmer to test and solve, under certain circumstances they can cause the system to stop or allow an attacker to execute code on the server. A cross-site scripting attack can take place when you display information that someone has entered. If an attacker enters code instead of the requested information, for example, the code could access your database, display system information that could be used in subsequent attacks, or trick an unsuspecting user viewing the message to divulge private information. Microsoft offers a useful article for helping programmers reduce vulnerabilities at *msdn.microsoft.com/msdnmag/issues/02/09/SecurityTips/default.aspx*.

As you learned in Chapter 7, Web Services are program modules that can be accessed remotely. They create significant vulnerabilities when they are used over the Internet because they essentially allow anyone into parts of your programming environment. Programmers who work with Web Services must be very skillful in reducing vulnerabilities. Microsoft has developed the WS-Security Specification to make these services more secure.

Identifying Vulnerabilities in E-mail Servers

In a sense, e-mail servers are vulnerable by design because they are designed to accept data anonymously. Messages themselves can harm the server. For example, imagine a series of 1 GB messages sent to an e-mail server. If the server doesn't have a message size limit, receiving many gigabytes of data could quickly fill up an e-mail server. Although not directly an e-mail vulnerability, being able to transmit malicious code on to an e-mail client can ultimately cause problems for the Web server. Some viruses read an e-mail address book and then send messages to all addresses they find, potentially infecting the recipient computers. Not only is this possibility a problem for the users, but the increased burden on the e-mail servers to deliver these messages can also be severe.

Retrieving your e-mail from the Internet is risky because you send your user name and password to the server in clear text. An attacker can discover private or sensitive information and delete or forward messages without being detected.

The SMTP protocol includes VRFY and EXPN, two commands that can be used to discover valid e-mail names. Because e-mail names are typically the same as user account names, the more e-mail names the attacker can find, the better his or her chance of finding passwords for some accounts.

Some e-mail servers such as sendmail are complex, which does not create a vulnerability but can cause an inexperienced administrator to make mistakes. Older versions of sendmail and other e-mail servers contained more serious vulnerabilities. Attackers could access a connection that identified the version of the servers, providing information that attackers could exploit. For example, some e-mail servers inadvertently let spammers use servers to relay messages.

SECURING DATA TRANSMISSION

Previous chapters emphasized the functionality of the server applications without considering the security of the data being transmitted. Of course, users of your Web site will not want to send sensitive information to your Web site if it might be intercepted and read by someone else. The same can be true with other applications. Users might not want their e-mail user names and passwords sent in clear text and all of their e-mail messages transmitted without encryption. Some applications, such as Telnet, should never be used over the Internet because of their potential security problems.

SSL is the most common method of encrypting data transmissions. Most Web sites that encrypt sensitive information, such as credit card information, use SSL. Another important technology is SSH, which is primarily used to implement a secure version of Telnet and FTP. However, you can also use SSH to create a secure connection with virtually any TCP/IP application.

Using Secure Sockets Layer

Encrypting sensitive data is not useful if you cannot verify the authenticity of the server with which you are communicating. At a minimum, SSL requires a **digital certificate** on the server. A digital certificate is a file issued by a **certification authority (CA)** that identifies a person or organization. To trust the server certificate, a third party, such as VeriSign or Thawte, can act as the CA. The **public key infrastructure (PKI)** defines the system of CAs and certificates.

While the digital certificate verifies who you are communicating with, you also need a way to encrypt your communication session so that only you and the server can see the data. In this case, a **key** processes data so that it becomes unintelligible—a process called *encrypting*. A different key processes the encrypted data to turn it back into the original data, called *decrypting*. Protecting the key that decrypts the data is critically important. Anyone with this key can read the data being transmitted.

PKI relies on **public key cryptography**, which uses two different keys: a **public key** and a **private key**. These keys are bound to the digital certificate issued by the CA. The pair of keys is controlled by a single entity, such as *technowidgets.com*. The public key, which is available to everyone, is used to encrypt data. The private key, which is kept securely on the server, is used to decrypt the data. However, public key cryptography only allows the client computer to send encrypted data to a server; it does not allow the client computer to receive encrypted data and decrypt it. The client computer encrypts a special kind of private key called a session key and sends it to the server. Then the client and the server use the session key to encrypt and decrypt the data. Figure 10-2 shows the series of events that take place to establish a connection using SSL.

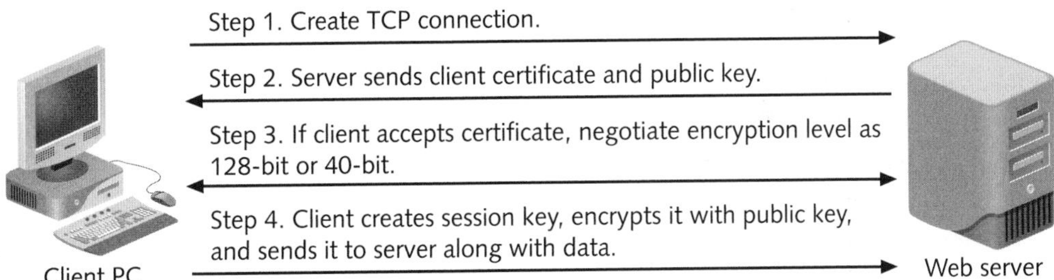

Figure 10-2 Establishing an SSL connection

SSL encrypts TCP packets. As a result, the applications at either end of the connection can use SSL without being altered. If SSL is used with a Web server, the Web pages do not have to be changed—they are encrypted only as they are being sent to a client. 10

Microsoft products such as IIS and Exchange 2000 are SSL-enabled, and Apache is designed to work with SSL. To use SSL with a Web server, you provide a digital certificate from a CA. In the case of SSL on Linux, you can create your own certificate or even use the dummy certificate that was installed with Apache. In Windows, you can use Microsoft Certificate Services to create a CA. In an e-commerce environment you receive a certificate from a third-party CA, but within your organization you can generate your own certificate.

In this section, you learn how to install Certificate Services to become your own CA. In other sections, you learn how to create and install certificates in products such as Exchange and IIS.

To install Certificate Services in Windows:

1. Insert the Windows installation CD in the drive. If the installation window opens, click **Exit**.
2. *In Windows 2003:* In the Control Panel, double-click **Add or Remove Programs**. The Add or Remove Programs window opens. Click **Add/Remove Windows Components**.

   In Windows 2000: In the Control Panel, double-click **Add/Remove Programs**. The Add or Remove Programs window opens. Click **Add/Remove Windows Components**.

3. Select the **Certificate Services** check box. A dialog box opens, warning you that after installing Certificate Services, you cannot rename the computer or change its domain membership. Click **Yes** to accept the warning.
4. Click **Next** to begin the installation.

   In Windows 2000: If you installed Terminal Services, the Terminal Services Setup dialog box opens. In the Terminal Services dialog box, keep the default of Remote administration mode and click **Next**.

   The CA Type dialog box opens, shown in Figure 10-3. (This is called the Certification Authority Type dialog box in Windows 2000.)

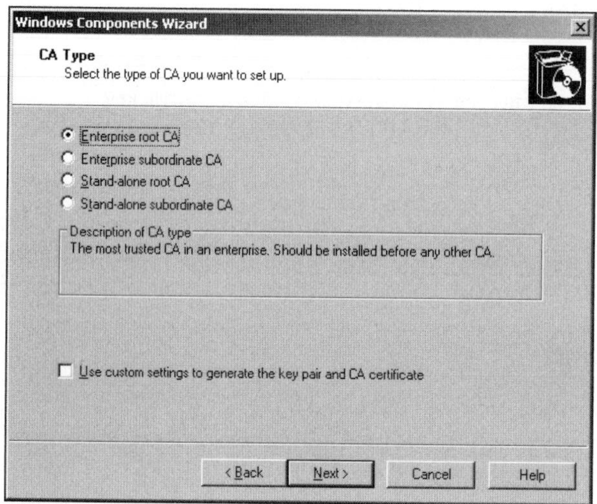

Figure 10-3 CA Type dialog box

You use the Enterprise root CA to integrate the CA with Active Directory. You can use an Enterprise root CA to verify individual users, typically in an intranet, and for smart-card identification. You could choose the Stand-alone root CA option for Internet applications. A stand-alone subordinate CA can issue certificates, but must first obtain a certificate from another CA.

5. Click the **Enterprise root CA** option button, if necessary, and then click **Next**. The CA Identifying Information dialog box opens. See Figure 10-4.
6. Enter a common name, which is often the name of the computer, such as **WEB1**.

   In Windows 2000: This dialog box includes more text boxes than shown in Figure 10-4 to gather information used for generating certificates. Complete these text boxes as accurately as possible.

   In Windows 2003: The Distinguished name suffix is created automatically based on your domain name. When you type the name of your computer, the information in the "Preview of distinguished name" text box includes WEB1.

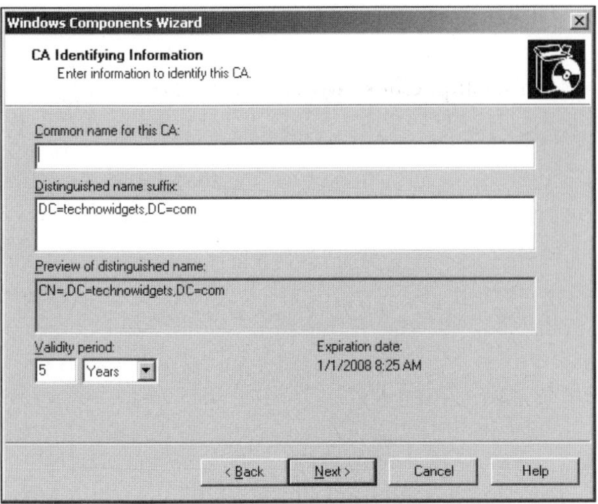

Figure 10-4 CA Identifying Information dialog box

7. Click **Next**. The Certificate Database Settings dialog box opens, as shown in Figure 10-5. (In Windows 2000, this dialog box is called Data Storage Location.) These text boxes specify the locations of the components of the certificate.

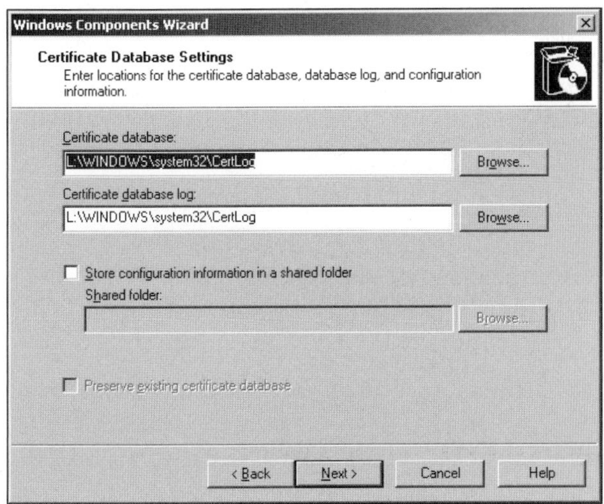

Figure 10-5 Certificate Database Settings dialog box

8. Click **Next**. A dialog box warns you that it needs to stop IIS to complete the installation. Click **Yes** to stop IIS. (Click **OK** in Windows 2000.) If, during installation, a dialog box opens stating that "Active Server Pages (ASPs) must be enabled in Internet Information Services (IIS) in order to allow Certificate Services to provide web enrollment services. . .", click **No**.
9. Click **Finish** to exit the wizard. Then close all open windows.

Using Secure Shell

You use SSH for secure logins. By replacing Telnet with SSH, you can securely log on to Linux or Windows remotely. The SSH server is included in Linux. For Windows servers, SSH is a separate product available for free from *www.openssh.com*. PuTTY, another excellent Telnet and SSH client for Windows, is available for free from *www.chiark.greenend.org.uk/~sgtatham/putty*.

SSH can also encrypt other types of communication based on protocols such as FTP, SMTP, POP3, and IMAP4. This is done through SSH **tunneling** to encrypt traffic from the client to the server. Tunneling allows you to use an unsecure protocol, such as POP3, through a secure connection, such as SSH. One benefit of using SSH with these protocols is that you gain a secure connection without changing any server settings. For example, suppose that you want to download and read your e-mail using POP3, but you do not want anyone to read your password. Your objective is to create an SSH tunnel and then use your e-mail client to receive your e-mail. Although you will learn the specifics of setting up an SSH tunnel in Hands-on Project 10-2, the basic steps are the same no matter what the protocol or operating system. The server application, such as e-mail, does not have to be modified to use SSH.

To tunnel POP3 communication in Windows and Linux:

1. Select a port number above 1023 on your local computer to be used for the tunnel communication. For this example, assume it is port 55555.
2. Configure the SSH client so your local port uses 55555.
3. Configure the SSH client to connect to a host at a specific port. For POP3, assume it is port 110.
4. Use the SSH client to log on remotely to the server.
5. Configure your e-mail client so that the address of the POP3 server is that of your local computer and the port of the POP3 server is 55555. The tunneling feature of the SSH client sends the data from your local computer through the tunnel to POP3 port 110 on the server.

Now you can log on to the e-mail server (securely) and start receiving e-mail.

Securing the Operating System

Recall that one way to make your operating system more secure is to use it only for necessary tasks, such as those related to default file access, user accounts, and services such as printing. You can also enhance security by configuring each computer for a single task such as a Web server or e-mail server, but not both. It is easier to focus on the needs of a single server application, and if one server application becomes compromised, both applications will not be affected.

Avoid running any client programs on a server, including a browser. Although this practice prevents you from easily downloading service packs and patches directly to the server, it also prevents general use of the server to browse the Internet and possibly download or install software that could harm the server. Download service packs and patches to another computer and then transfer them to a CD. Likewise, running an e-mail client on the server is not a problem in itself, but accidentally opening an attachment that contains a virus can harm the server. For this reason, you should not install an e-mail client on a server.

Use the minimum number of user accounts necessary for the server to function. Periodically review these accounts to make sure you understand their purpose. However, if you share administration with others, consult with the other administrators before deleting user accounts that you do not recognize. If these accounts are used by a server program, their removal might cause the program to malfunction. Linux systems often have user accounts that only server programs use.

When making your Web server secure, balance your security needs with ease of use. The most stringent security practice would be to prevent any access to a Web server except by browsers. Users would then have to update pages by sending you e-mail attachments of pages so you could check them out in detail. Unfortunately, this arrangement is inconvenient for all involved. Likewise, although including dynamic Web pages that require programming languages and databases incurs risk, using dynamic pages creates a more appealing Web site than using static pages.

Securing Microsoft Windows

A Windows server connected to the Internet is vulnerable to attack because anyone can access the server. One way to make the server more secure in Windows is to change the name of the administrator account to a name unrelated to administration. Changing the administrator user name and using a challenging password can slow down some types of attacks because attackers generally assume that the administrator name has not been changed.

To further secure a server, examine the services that it runs. The default installation has many services that are not needed by a server connected to the Internet. You can safely disable them, although the server has less functionality when you do so. In the following steps, you disable services not directly related to the Web environment.

To disable a service on Windows:

1. From the Control Panel, open the **Administrative Tools** window. Click **Services**.
2. Double-click the service that you want to disable. The Properties dialog box opens.
3. Use the list box to change the Startup type to **Disabled**. The service is stopped when you either reboot or click Stop.
4. Click **OK** to exit the Properties dialog box for the service.

You can disable the following services from a Windows server:

- Alerter
- Computer browser
- DHCP client
- Distributed file system
- Distributed transaction coordinator
- DNS client
- Messenger
- Print spooler
- Remote Registry service
- RunAs service
- Server
- Task Scheduler
- Workstation

Disabling the DNS client prevents you from resolving DNS names, which makes using a browser difficult. However, as mentioned earlier, you might want to avoid using a browser on a server. Disabling the workstation service prevents you from mapping a drive to another computer to transfer files; it can cause problems if you need to transfer files larger than the capacity of a CD. One solution is to start the service to transfer a large file and then disable it again. The server service allows you to create shares on the server. When connected to a LAN, users can use the shares to directly update those parts of the Web site that they control. Unfortunately, using shares can create security-related problems, such as trying to access shares from the Internet and sending user names and passwords in clear text. As discussed later in this chapter, you can prevent these security problems by using a firewall.

You can also change settings in the Windows **Registry** to enhance security. The Registry is a database of system settings used by both the operating system and applications. You need to be very careful when changing it because if you make a mistake, you could cause the operating system or an application to malfunction.

One Registry setting that you can safely change involves using short filenames. To be compatible with 16-bit programs, long filenames have equivalent versions that are only eight characters long, a format called "8 dot 3." Because it is easier for an attacker to guess an eight-character name than a long name, you should disable the creation of the short filenames.

To disable the generation of short filenames in Windows:

1. Click **Start**, and then click **Run**.
2. Type **regedt32** and then press **Enter** to start the Registry Editor.
3. Click the **plus sign (+)** next to the **HKEY_LOCAL_MACHINE** folder to expand its contents.
4. Use the tree structure of the registry to navigate to SYSTEM\CurrentControlSet\Control\FileSystem.
5. In the right pane, double-click **NtfsDisable8dot3NameCreation**, which is the item that you want to modify. The DWORD Editor dialog box opens, as shown in Figure 10-6. (This is called the Edit DWORD Value dialog box in Windows 2003.) Using a setting of 0 means that the Registry should not disable 8 dot 3 name creation; a setting of 1 means that the Registry should disable short names.
6. In the Value data text box, type **1**, and then click **OK**.
7. Close the Registry Editor window.

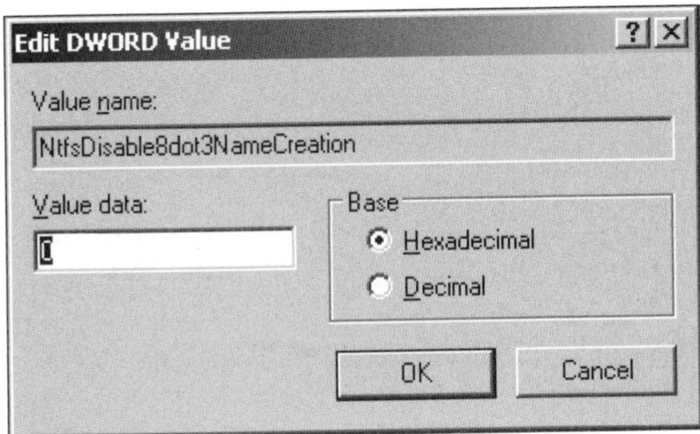

Figure 10-6 Using the Registry Editor to modify a value

Another vulnerability in Windows servers involves user groups. By default, the Everyone group is given significant access to the system drive. You should make the system drive more secure by changing the permissions to the ones described in Table 10-1.

Table 10-1 Permissions to increase Windows security

Folders to secure	Group permissions
c:\	Administrators: Full Control System: Full Control Authenticated users: Read and Execute, List Folder Contents, Read

Table 10-1 Permissions to increase Windows security (continued)

Folders to secure	Group permissions
c:\windows\Repair c:\windows\Security c:\windows\Temp c:\windows\system32\Config c:\windows\system32\Logfiles (In Windows 2000, the default folder is winnt instead of windows)	Administrators: Full Control Creator/owner: Full Control System: Full Control

Securing Linux

As in any operating system, a good way to secure Linux is to run only those services you need. Recall that the services you run provide attackers with the most common entry point into your system. To find out which services are running, you can use the **netstat** command, which has many options. The most useful option for Web servers is **-l**, (the letter ell), which displays the listening server sockets. Figure 10-7 shows a sample of lines from the output of the **netstat** command. Under the Proto heading is the protocol, which is TCP or UDP. Under the Local Address heading, **netstat** displays the IP address and port separated by a colon. If the port is listening on any IP address in the server, an asterisk is used. For example, "*:pop3" means that all IP addresses are listening for POP3 (port 110) packets.

```
Active Internet connections (only servers)
Proto Recv-Q Send-Q Local Address              Foreign Address      State
tcp        0      0 *:pop3                     *:*                  LISTEN
tcp        0      0 *:imap                     *:*                  LISTEN
tcp        0      0 *:http                     *:*                  LISTEN
tcp        0      0 research.technow:domain    *:*                  LISTEN
tcp        0      0 mail.technowidge:domain    *:*                  LISTEN
tcp        0      0 web1.technowidge:domain    *:*                  LISTEN
tcp        0      0 *:ftp                      *:*                  LISTEN
tcp        0      0 *:ssh                      *:*                  LISTEN
tcp        0      0 *:nntp                     *:*                  LISTEN
tcp        0      0 *:smtp                     *:*                  LISTEN
tcp        0      0 *:https                    *:*                  LISTEN
udp        0      0 research.technow:domain    *:*
udp        0      0 mail.technowidge:domain    *:*
udp        0      0 web1.technowidge:domain    *:*
```

Figure 10-7 `netstat -l` command to show services running

As shown in Figure 10-7, many services are running on this computer. To disable a service associated with xinetd, you can use the **chkconfig** command. For example, to disable IMAP, you would type **chkconfig imap off**. To get a complete listing of services controlled by `chkconfig`, you would type `chkconfig –list`. To disable services such as named, you would delete the line you created in /etc/rc.d/rc.local when you installed the service.

If you administer a server that you did not create, other services might be running that you do not know about. Use `netstat` to determine what is running and whether you need each service. Also avoid the printer service (lpd), NFS (Network File System), and any of the "r" services, such as rlogin, rexec, rsh, and rcp. NFS is a good method of sharing files in a trusted environment, but it is dangerous to use on a computer connected to the Internet. The "r" services were once used for remote access, but are now obsolete. SSH has replaced these applications.

Just as with any operating system, you need to check for the latest software patches on a regular basis. For Red Hat Linux, visit *redhat.com/apps/support/errata/index.html*. On this Web page, Red Hat provides links to all of its supported products, not just the latest version.

For more information on Linux security, visit *www.linuxsecurity.com*.

SECURING SERVER APPLICATIONS

When securing server applications, run only one server application on each computer to prevent a breach in one application that might cause problems in another application. As with operating systems, make sure you have the latest software patches for server applications. However, be sure to fully test significant upgrades to any application software. The upgrade may be more secure than the original version, but might introduce incompatibilities or inadvertent configuration problems. Make sure that an upgrade does not cause the same types of problems as an attacker might.

Securing Telnet and FTP

Neither Telnet nor FTP is secure because both send user names and passwords as clear text. However, FTP is useful as an anonymous client for downloading files when security is not an issue. Likewise, using FTP to upload files on an isolated computer does not allow someone to intercept user names and passwords. However, if you use an upload user name that also provides access to other parts of the system, having your user name and password intercepted could compromise the system.

Telnet should never be used over the Internet or any insecure network. With Telnet, you connect to a computer system to execute command-line utilities, which can be dangerous. Instead, you should use SSH, which allows you to perform the same tasks as Telnet, but in a secure environment. Telnet and SSH are similar, so if you know how to use Telnet, SSH will be familiar. Red Hat Linux installs sshd, the SSH server, by default. When you want to remotely connect to another computer running Linux, such as one called *web1.technowidgets.com*, you would type `ssh web1.technowidgets.com`.

When you connect, SSH does not prompt you for a user name, but rather uses the same user name you entered when you logged on to Linux. You can even connect to a remote computer while you are logged on as root. (You cannot log on as root using a Telnet client.) After you type your password in SSH, you can securely execute command-line utilities.

In Windows, you can use PuTTY as an SSH client. With PuTTY, you can use a Windows computer to connect to the secure shell on a Linux computer. To use PuTTY, you download putty.exe from the *www.chiark.greenend.org.uk/~sgtatham/putty* Web site. You can create a \putty folder for putty.exe, and then double-click putty.exe to start the program and open the PuTTY window, as shown in Figure 10-8.

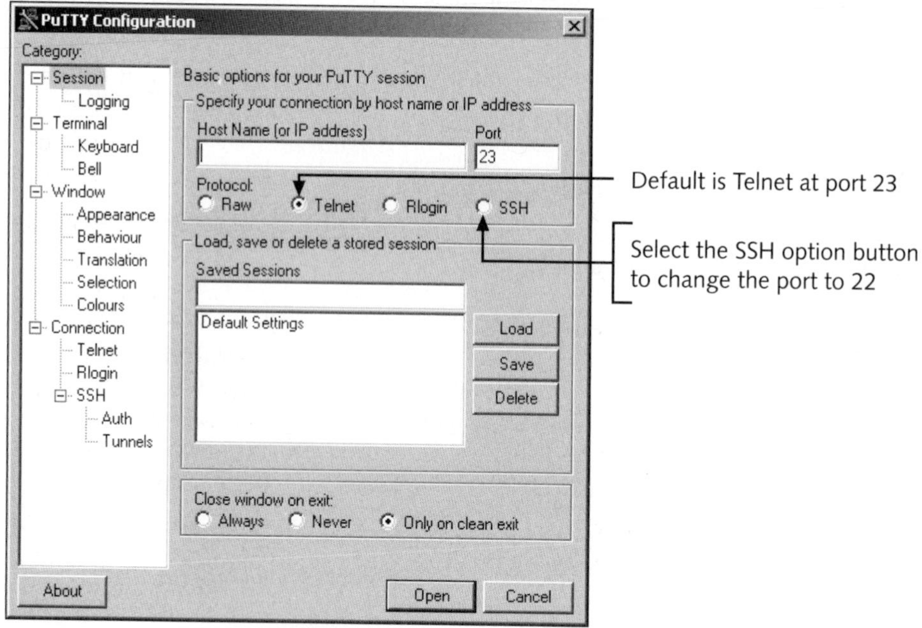

Figure 10-8 PuTTY main window

With PuTTY, you type the IP address or host name and then click the SSH option button. When you click Open, you are prompted for a user name and password.

You can make FTP transfers secure by using SSH on Linux. To do so, use the **`sftp`** command in Linux instead of the `ftp` command to transfer files. Linux then calls a secure FTP server from sshd. The major difference between using FTP and sshd is that your default directory on the Linux computer is your user directory instead of a specific FTP directory. For Windows users, you can download a secure version of FTP called psftp.exe from the same Web page that provides PuTTY, *www.chiark.greenend.org.uk/~sgtatham/putty*.

Securing E-mail Applications

Recall that e-mail servers are the most open systems you have to configure, so an essential part of administering them is minimizing potential problems. Although sendmail is a popular e-mail program, its complexity can cause problems for an inexperienced administrator. An alternative e-mail server is qmail, which was designed to be secure. In fact, in 1997 the qmail creator posted a reward for anyone who could find a security hole in it. So far, no one has found a problem. Another advantage to qmail is that it is easier to configure than sendmail. For more information on qmail, visit *cr.yp.to/qmail.html*.

Although Microsoft Exchange 2000 is reasonably secure for Windows, it is very complex. To better understand the trade-offs involved in using Exchange 2000, refer to Microsoft's 130-page document called "Security Operations for Microsoft Exchange Server 2000," available at *www.microsoft.com/technet/security/prodtech/mailexch/opsguide/default.asp*.

E-mail servers introduce extra security considerations. Attackers can use an e-mail server to do more than simply penetrate your system. For example, they could use e-mail to send a virus or pose as a trusted associate. To help prevent viruses, be sure to purchase quality virus protection software and to keep it updated with the latest enhancements.

By resolving local e-mail addresses to user-friendly names, Exchange 2000 makes it easy for attackers to appear to be trusted associates. For example, if you receive a message from *mnoia@technowidgets.com*, the Outlook client can display Mary Noia as the sender. Although this approach is user-friendly, users cannot verify that the message is truly from Mary. The SMTP protocol that Exchange 2000 uses makes it easy to **spoof** an e-mail address, which presents a fake IP address to gain access or otherwise deceive a person. You may want to set Exchange to show external addresses as Mary Noia [mnoia@technowidgets.com], and then tell users that such an address may not actually be from Mary. To prevent Exchange from resolving a sender's address for external mail, you need to add a value to the Windows Registry. In the Registry, navigate to the following setting: HKEY_LOCAL_MACHINE/SYSTEM/CurrentControlSet/Services/MSExchangeTransport/Parameters/2

You might need to create the Parameters key and the 2 key. At that location, add a value called ResolveP2 and give it a DWORD value of 2. For more details on changing this setting, visit *support.microsoft.com/default.aspx?scid=KB;EN-US;Q288635&*.

Another serious problem with any e-mail server can be denial of service, which occurs when a user receives e-mail until the hard disk fills up. As it is filling up, users would probably notice a significant slowdown in response time. To help prevent denial-of-service problems, you could set a size limit for each user's mailbox.

To set a limit of 100 MB for each Exchange 2000 mailbox:

1. Open the Exchange System Manager.

2. In the left pane, expand **Servers**, **WEB1**, and then **First Storage Group** to display the Mailbox Store.
3. Right-click **Mailbox Store**, and then click **Properties**. In the Mailbox Store Properties dialog box, click the **Limits** tab, shown in Figure 10-9.

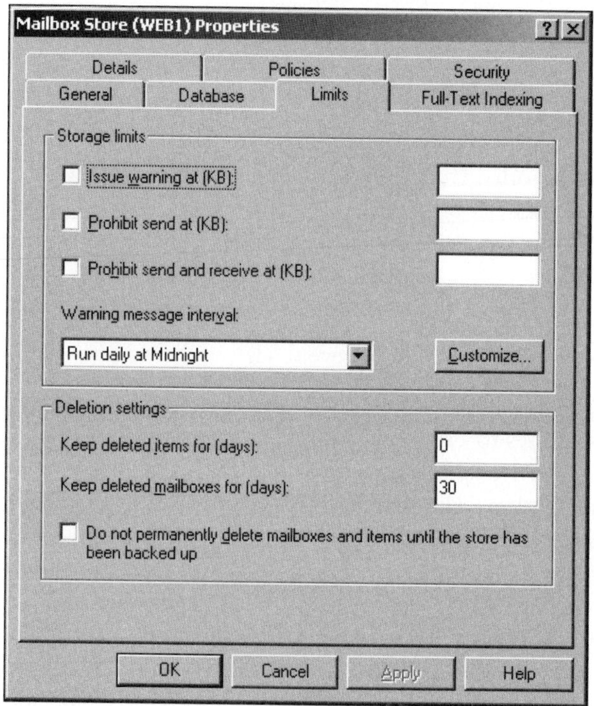

Figure 10-9 Mailbox Store (WEB1) Properties dialog box

4. At a minimum, select the **Prohibit send and receive at (KB)** check box and enter **10000** in the corresponding text box. (Recall that 10,000 KB is the same as 10 MB.) It would also be helpful to users to select the **Issue warning at (KB)** check box and set it to **9000**. To give the user an incentive to clean out his or her mailbox before e-mail messages are blocked, select the **Prohibit send at (KB)** check box, and set it to **9500**.
5. Click **OK** to save the settings and close the dialog box.

Some e-mail systems, such as Exchange 2000, support SSL. To enable SSL on Exchange 2000, you need a digital certificate. If you installed Certificate Services, you can create a certificate as you configure Exchange 2000. An SSL connection is created for each protocol, such as POP3, IMAP4, NNTP, or HTTP. Each of these connections uses a different port. For example, if you configure POP3 to use SSL, the default port is 995. Once you configure SSL for a protocol, you have to configure the client to use SSL and direct it to the appropriate port. Other clients can still use port 110 for normal POP3 communication unless you force users to require SSL.

To enable SSL for POP3 on Exchange 2000:

1. Open the Microsoft Exchange System Manager.
2. Navigate to the **Default POP3 Virtual Server**. See Figure 10-10.

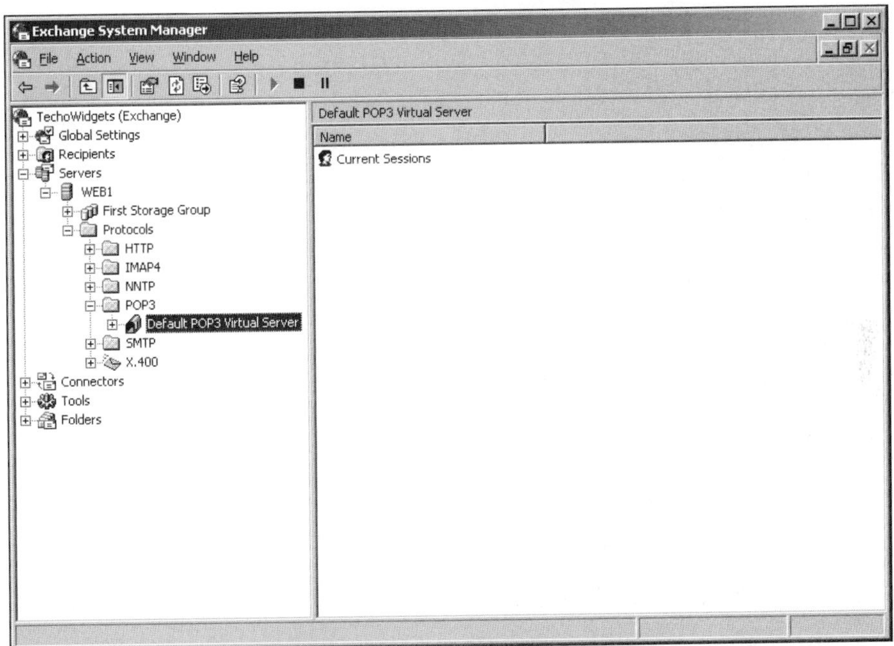

Figure 10-10 Selecting Default POP3 Virtual Server

3. Right-click **Default POP3 Virtual Server**, and then click **Properties**. The Default POP3 Virtual Server Properties dialog box opens.
4. Click the **Access** tab. The dialog box for the access methods opens. See Figure 10-11.
5. Click the **Certificate** button. The Welcome to the Web Server Certificate Wizard opens. This wizard steps you through the process of setting up a certificate for all protocols.
6. Click **Next**. The Server Certificate dialog box opens, as shown in Figure 10-12. (This is called the Current Certificate Assignment dialog box in Windows 2000, which does not have the last two options.) Because you created an Enterprise CA, you should create a new certificate.

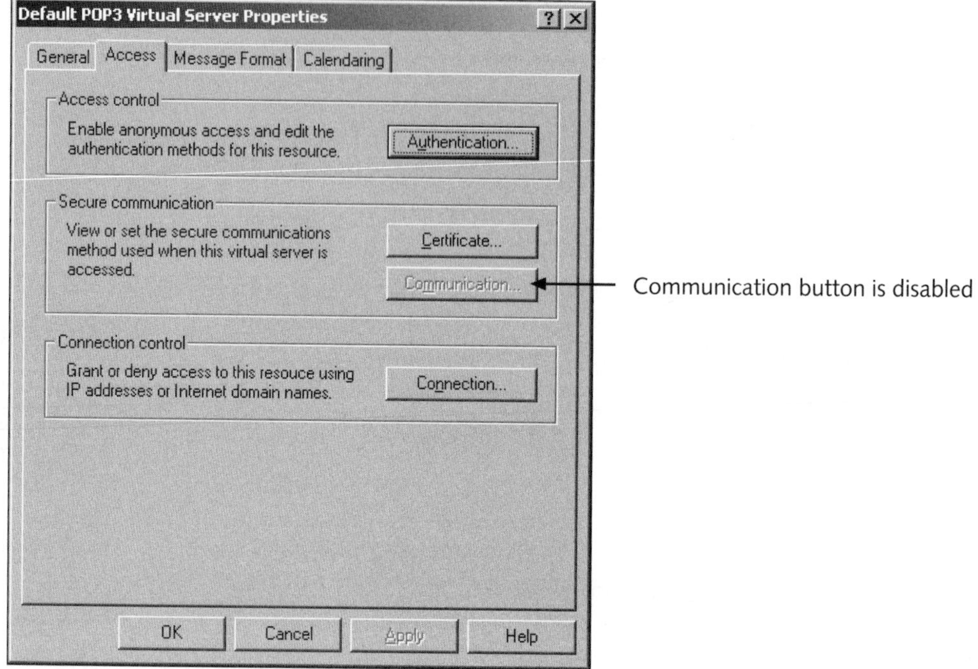

Figure 10-11 Setting access methods for the default POP3 virtual server

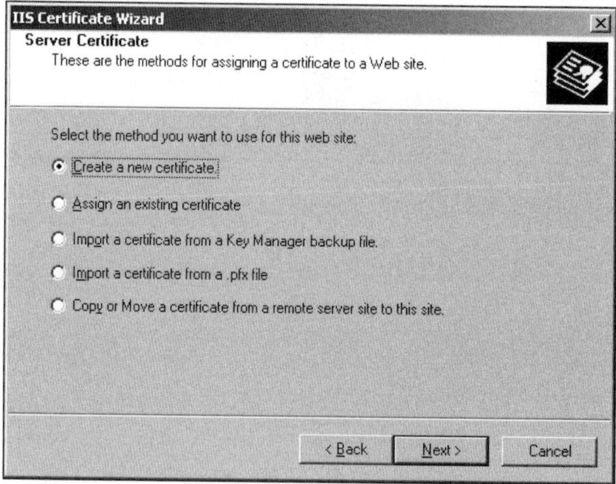

Figure 10-12 Server Certificate dialog box

7. Click **Next**. The Delayed or Immediate Request dialog box opens, shown in Figure 10-13.

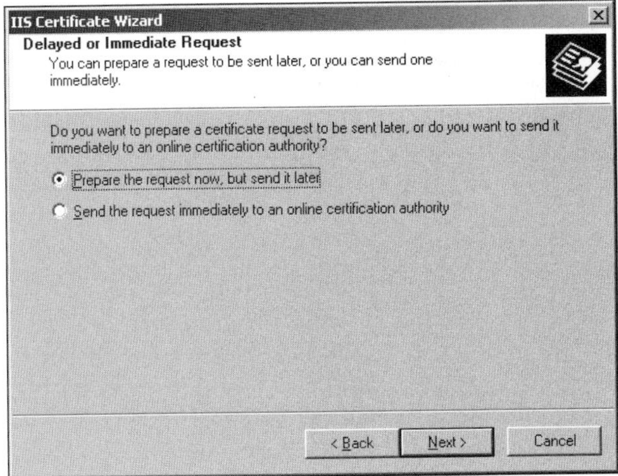

Figure 10-13 Delayed or Immediate Request dialog box

8. Click the **Send the request immediately to an online certification authority** option button, and then click **Next**. The Name and Security Settings dialog box opens, shown in Figure 10-14. You can use this dialog box to create a different name for the certificate and change the bit length of the encryption. The choices for the bit length range from 512 to 16384.

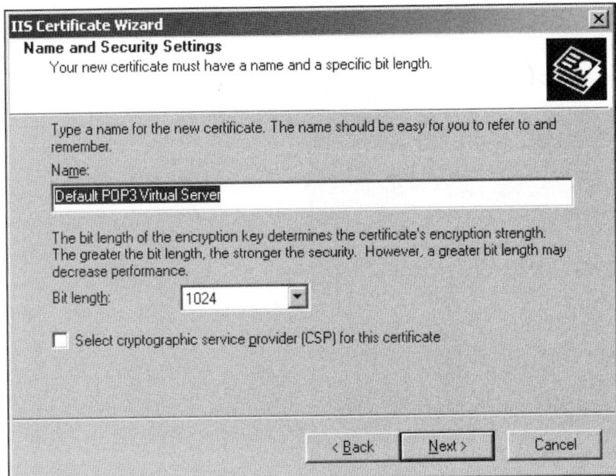

Figure 10-14 Name and Security Settings dialog box

9. Click **Next** to accept the default settings of "Default POP3 Virtual Server" as the name and 512 as the bit length. The Organization Information dialog box opens, shown in Figure 10-15.

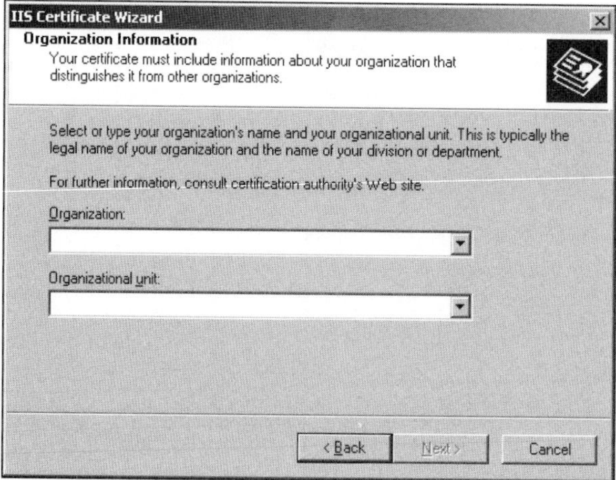

Figure 10-15 Organization Information dialog box

10. In the Organization text box, type **TechnoWidgets** and in the Organizational unit text box, type **Web**. Then click **Next**. The Your Site's Common Name dialog box opens, indicating that you should enter a valid DNS name if you have one.
11. Type **web1.technowidgets.com** for the common name, and then click **Next**. The Geographical Information dialog box opens, shown in Figure 10-16.

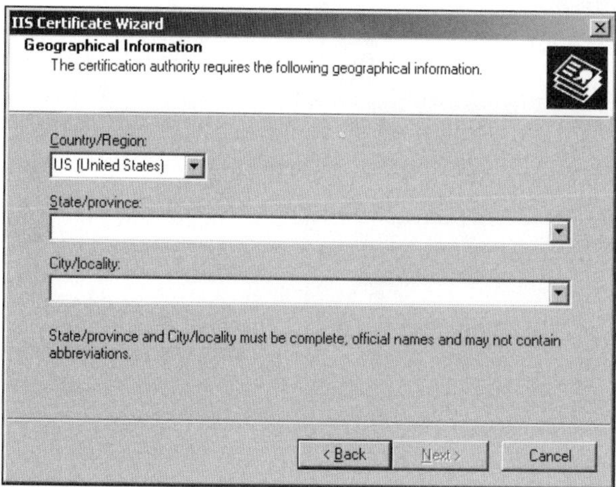

Figure 10-16 Geographical Information dialog box

12. Complete the State/province and City/locality text boxes based on your location, and then click **Next**. The Choose a Certification Authority dialog box opens.

13. Click **Next** to accept the default of your local computer. The Certificate Request Submission dialog box opens with a summary of the information that you entered.

14. Click **Next**, and then click **Finish** to exit the wizard. You return to the Default POP3 Virtual Server Properties dialog box. You are now assigned a certificate, but you still must enable SSL. Compare the Default POP3 Virtual Server dialog box to the one shown in Figure 10-11, in which the Communication button is disabled. Now that you have assigned a certificate, the Communication button is enabled.

15. Click **Communication**. The Security dialog box opens, as shown in Figure 10-17.

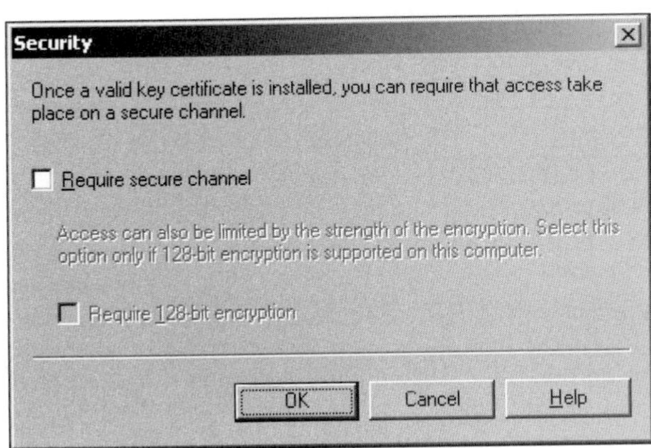

Figure 10-17 Security dialog box

16. Click the **Require secure channel** check box to select it. The option to require 128-bit encryption instead of the standard 40-bit encryption becomes available, but you don't need to select it.

17. Click **OK** to close the Security dialog box. Now you verify the port used for SSL by POP3, if necessary.

18. In the Default POP3 Virtual Server dialog box, click the **General** tab. On this property sheet, you can configure IP addresses, limit the number of connections, and set the connection timeout.

19. Click the **Advanced** button. The Advanced dialog box opens, as shown in Figure 10-18. Notice that the SSL port is 995. If necessary, you could click the Edit button and change the port number.

20. Click **OK** twice to accept the current settings and close the Default POP3 Virtual Server Properties dialog box. Close the Exchange System Manager window.

Now Exchange 2000 can use port 110 for normal POP3 communication and port 995 for those users who require encrypted communication. However, to use SSL for POP3, you still have to configure the client.

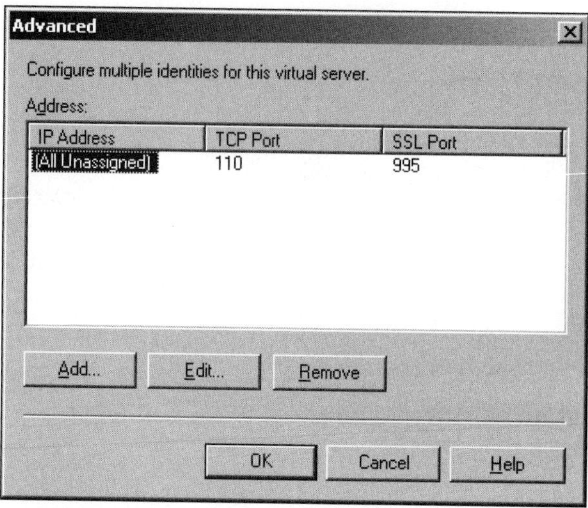

Figure 10-18 Advanced dialog box

To configure Outlook Express to use SSL:

1. Open Outlook Express.
2. Click **Tools** on the menu bar, and then click **Accounts**. The Internet Accounts dialog box opens.
3. Click the **Mail** tab.
4. Click **Properties**. The Properties dialog box for mail opens.
5. Click the **Advanced** tab. This property sheet provides information on server port numbers. See Figure 10-19.
6. In the Incoming mail (POP3) section, click the **This server requires a secure connection (SSL)** check box to select it. Notice that the port automatically changes from 110 to 995.
7. Click **OK** to save the information, and then click **Close** to close the Internet Accounts dialog box.

Securing the Web Server

The best approach to deploying a Web server is to offer the minimum capabilities required. As mentioned earlier, if the site needs only static HTML pages, do not use a programming interface such as ASP or ASP.NET. If certain pages are sensitive, restrict the viewing of the pages through permissions. If programming is allowed, make sure that good coding rules are followed. If you use code developed by a third party, research its security measures and guarantees. Look for product reviews on the Internet and check the company's product information for details on security measures.

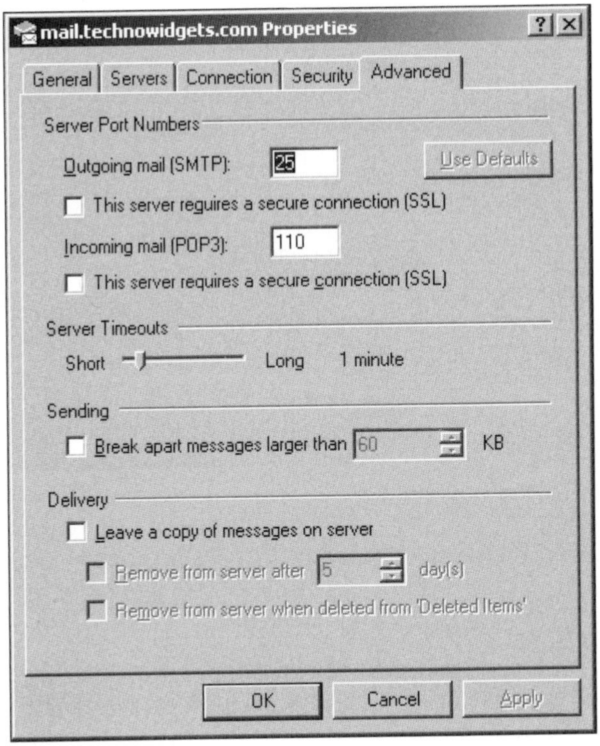

Figure 10-19 Advanced tab of the mail Properties dialog box

Programs running on your Web server present the most potential for problems when maintaining a Web server. The best you can do is to trust the expertise of your programmers. Given that, if an inexperienced user wants to post an interesting CGI script on your server that he found on the Internet, be wary. Even the best of programmers can inadvertently cause serious security problems.

A simple programming issue that can cause serious problems occurs when a database is updated. For example, suppose your server runs an application with a user database. Each user has a user name and a password. Programming texts often show examples where the column name in a table matches the text box name on a form. This nomenclature facilitates documentation, but decreases security because it provides system knowledge to an attacker. Assume that the application has verified your existing user name and password and now prompts you to enter a new password. If the user name is mnoia and the new password is Flores, the SQL statement to update mnoia's password to "Flores" would be:

```
Update users
Set password = 'Flores'
where username = 'mnoia'
```

Although rather subtle, the attacker has to remember that the first and last apostrophes are supplied by the program, so the statement does not have the beginning and ending apostrophe. If the attacker changed the user name on the form as it was sent back to the server, and the column names were the same as the text box names on the form, the attacker could replace "mnoia" with mnoia' or username != ' which would translate as follows:

```
Update users
Set password = 'Flores'
where username = 'mnoia' or username != ''
```

This code would change the passwords for all users to "Flores." Now the attacker would have a much easier time gaining access to the database. One way to mitigate this security risk is to name table columns something difficult to determine, although that would make program development more challenging. An easier approach would be to make sure that just before the password is updated, you execute a SQL statement to confirm that the user name coming from the form is still valid when using the old password.

Commercial Web sites typically need to implement SSL to encrypt sensitive data such as personal information or credit card numbers. Often, a single server is dedicated to SSL traffic. SSL requires extra processing to encrypt Web pages and decrypt information sent by users. By default, SSL for HTTP uses port 443.

Another aspect of Web server security, user authentication, is covered in the "Authenticating Web Users" section later in this chapter.

Securing Apache

As with any application, you must monitor vulnerabilities and patches for Apache. For Apache 2.0, you can find this information at *www.apacheweek.com/features/security-20*. Normally, you download and install a new version of Apache to correct the problems.

Security also means restricting access to certain directories. Chapter 6 introduced the concept of directory control in httpd.conf. For example, you might have a directory with the following configuration:

```
<Directory "/var/www/html/reports">
      order allow, deny
      allow from all
</Directory>
```

These settings allow everyone to see the pages in the reports directory. The settings include three directives:

- *order*—Specifies the order in which the next two items are processed. Specify *order deny, allow* to process the *deny* directive first, then the *allow* directive. Specify *order allow, deny* to process the *allow* directive first. As soon as a directive is true, either the request is allowed or denied. If you specify *order mutual-failure*, both the *allow* and the *deny* directives are processed.
- *allow from*—Describes the hosts that can access the directory. Besides the specific hosts, you can specify all or none.
- *deny from*—Describes the hosts that are prevented from accessing the directory. Besides the specific hosts, you can specify all or none.

Hosts can be described in a number of ways and more than one host can be listed in the *deny from* or *allow from* directive. The host can be an IP address, such as 10.4.6.3, a domain such as *evildoers.org*, or a specific host at a domain such as *branch1.technowidgets.com*. For example, to allow only persons related to *technowidgets.com* to access a directory, you would use the following directives:

```
order allow, deny
allow from technowidgets.com
deny from all
```

To allow access from specific addresses, you could change the directives to the following:

```
order allow, deny
allow from 10.4.5.6 192.168.1.23
deny from all
```

If you wanted to keep anyone from *evildoers.org* from accessing the directory, you would use the following directives:

```
order deny, allow
allow from all
deny from evildoers.org
```


Notice that the *order* directive was changed so that the *deny* directive was processed first.

One drawback to using these directives is that specifying a domain name means the name must be resolved before Apache can determine whether to allow the visitor to the directory. This step takes significant processing power. Also, an attacker can spoof an address to avoid detection.

One common setting in Apache servers focuses on what happens if a default page such as index.html is not found in a directory. By default, if a directory does not have a default page, Apache displays all the files in the directory. This is achieved by the following directive:

```
Options Indexes
```

This option works only if you always remember to include an index.html file in every directory and never leave old files in a directory that may cause problems. For example, you could have a program called findit.jsp that inadvertently causes a security problem. You copy it to another file called newfindit.jsp and modify it until it works. As a good programmer, you maintain an old copy in case you have to start over. After newfindit.jsp works as designed, you might forget to delete findit.jsp. Its presence can continue to cause problems if the old file can be displayed.

Using SSL with Apache on Red Hat Linux involves configuring a virtual server and then restarting the Apache, which you will do in Hands-on Project 10-1. By default, Red Hat Linux installs a dummy certificate. For a real e-commerce site, you would install a valid certificate from a third-party CA. When a browser connects using SSL, it compares the CA to a list of acceptable CAs. If it is not on the list, as is true with a dummy certificate, SSL will warn the user about the certificate.

Securing IIS

For IIS, it is best to start by downloading the latest patches from *www.microsoft.com/technet/security/current.asp*. At this page you can select the version of IIS that you are using and retrieve a list of relevant patches.

Like Apache, IIS allows you to control user access by either denying all hosts by default and specifying who has access, or by allowing everyone by default and denying specific hosts. The details were covered in Chapter 6.

Page requests can be made to a server in many ways. Unfortunately, some such requests can potentially do damage. Because it is difficult to ensure that every program on your server will block problematic requests, Microsoft created a utility called Urlscan. The Urlscan security tool keeps potentially harmful page requests from reaching the server. Depending on the settings, you can restrict the size of the request, limit the type of request, and create a more detailed log of page requests. You can also download a more restrictive version of Urlscan, called Urlscan-SRP. Although installing patches for IIS is always a good idea, Urlscan-SRP would have prevented the ten critical vulnerabilities listed in Microsoft Security Bulletin 02-018, which you can read at *www.microsoft.com/technet/security/bulletin/ms02-018.asp*. These vulnerabilities include buffer overruns that would allow attacker's code to run on the server or cause IIS to fail. Urlscan might also prevent future problems. You can download Urlscan and Urlscan-SRP from *www.microsoft.com/technet/security/tools/urlscan.asp*.

Another tool from Microsoft that can be installed for IIS 5 on Windows 2000 is IIS Lockdown. You can download it from *www.microsoft.com/downloads*. IIS Lockdown has templates for IIS that you can use with Exchange, Commerce Server, SharePoint Portal Server, FrontPage Server Extensions, and other products. This tool can adjust security settings based on the server role. IIS Lockdown is also integrated with Urlscan, so the templates apply configuration options in the Urlscan tool. You can also use the IIS Lockdown tool to remove or disable IIS services such as HTTP, FTP, NNTP, and SMTP.

You can perform other tasks to improve IIS. By default, the \inetpub\ftproot and \inetpub\mailroot folders both have permissions set to Full Control for everyone. They should probably be set to Execute for everyone and Full Control for administrators and system users. Although you used Windows Explorer in Chapter 5 to modify permissions, you can also set permissions from the command prompt. To specify these settings, type the following two lines at the command prompt:

```
xcalcs c:\inetpub\ftproot /e /c /p everyone:x administrators:f system:f /y
xcalcs c:\inetpub\mailroot /e /c /p everyone:x administrators:f system:f /y
```

IIS 5 provides sample files that demonstrate the many capabilities of the Web server. Unfortunately, they were not meant to be accessible from the Internet because some of the samples could be used to compromise the Web server. For this reason, if you are using Windows 2000, you should delete the virtual directories and associated folders in Table 10-2.

Table 10-2 Virtual directories to delete in IIS 5

Virtual directory	Location
IISSamples	\inetpub\iissamples
\IISHelp	\winnt\help\iishelp
\MSADC	\program files\common files\system\msadc

Any server application connected to the Internet can suffer a denial-of-service attack based on a SYN flood. This problem occurs when an attacker initiates a connection by sending the SYN flag. The server waits for the connection to be completed, but the response never comes. As the server waits, the packets it accepts take up memory. Sending thousands of packets with the SYN flag set can force the server to use up so much memory that legitimate traffic cannot get through. The most difficult form of attack to combat is the Distributed DOS, which is launched from multiple computers. However, you can reduce the problems associated with a Distributed DOS attack by modifying the Registry to force the attempted connection to time out sooner and free memory. For the Windows Server 2003 registry, in KEY_LOCAL_MACHINE at System\CurrentControlSet\Services\Tcpip\Parameters\SynAttackProtect, change the default from 0 to 1. For Windows 2000, change the default from 0 to 2.

10

Other registry changes that increase security are described at *support.microsoft.com/default.aspx?scid=kb;EN-US;315669* for Windows 2000 and *support.microsoft.com/default.aspx?scid=kb;en-us;324270* for Windows Server 2003.

Subtle details in script mappings have also been used to attack systems. Consider deleting the mappings that you or your developers do not use. The common ones to delete include .htr, .idc, .stm, .shtm, .shtml, .printer, .htw, .ida, and .idq. The list is shorter in IIS 6.

To delete mappings in IIS 5 and 6:

1. *In Windows 2003:* In Administrative Tools, double-click **Internet Information Services (IIS) Manager**.

   In Windows 2000: In Administrative Tools, double-click **Internet Services Manager**.

2. *In Windows 2003:* Expand WEB1, right-click **Web Sites**, and then click **Properties**.

   In Windows 2000: Right-click **WEB1**, and then click **Properties**. Under Master Properties, click **Edit** to edit the master properties of the Web server. The WWW Service Master Properties dialog box opens.

3. Click the **Home Directory** tab.
4. Click the **Configuration** button to alter the application configuration.
5. Click the mapping, such as **shtm**, and then click **Remove**.
6. A dialog box opens, asking if you want to remove the selected script mapping. Click **Yes**.

7. Repeat Steps 4 through 6 for other mappings as necessary. Click **OK** to close the Application Configuration dialog box.
8. If you installed Exchange or Certificate Services, the Inheritance Overrides dialog box opens. Click **Select All** then click **OK**.
9. Click **OK** to close the Properties dialog box. Close all other open dialog boxes and windows.

To enable SSL on IIS, you need a certificate from a CA. If you have installed Certificate Services, you already have a dummy certificate that you can use. The first task is to associate a certificate with the server. The second task is to enable SSL for the Web server or a directory.

To associate a certificate with IIS:

1. *In Windows 2003:* Open **Internet Information Services** (IIS) Manager.

   In Windows 2000: Open Internet Services Manager.
2. Expand folders as necessary to navigate to Default Web Site. Right-click **Default Web Site**, and then click **Properties**. Notice that the SSL Port text is blank (Windows Server 2003) or it is disabled (Windows 2000).
3. In the Default Web Site Properties dialog box, click the **Directory Security** tab. Under Secure communications, the only button enabled is Server Certificate. This is where you associate the certificate with IIS.
4. Click **Server Certificate**. The Welcome to the Web Server Certificate Wizard dialog box opens.
5. Click **Next**. The Server Certificate dialog box opens. Follow Steps 7-14 in the "To enable SSL for POP3 on Exchange 2000" section. *Note*: Replace references to a POP3 server with the Web server. In the Choose a Certification Authority dialog box, you also need to accept the default port of 443 by clicking **Next**.

To require SSL on the Web site:

1. In the Default Web Site Properties dialog box, click the **Directory Security** tab.
2. In the Secure communications section, click the **Edit** button. The Secure Communications dialog box opens, as shown in Figure 10-20.
3. Click the **Require secure channel (SSL)** check box.
4. Click **OK** twice. In Windows 2000, the Inheritance Overrides dialog box opens. Because you want the whole site to inherit the new value, click **Select All**, and then click **OK**.

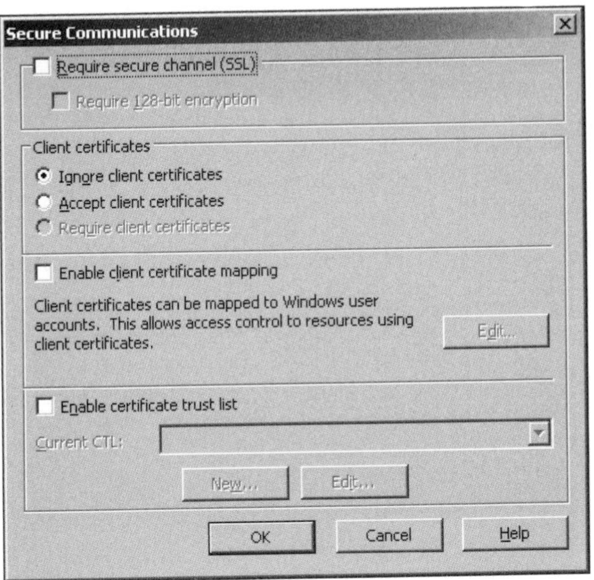

Figure 10-20 Secure Communications dialog box

Authenticating Web Users

You can authenticate users by passing the user name and password in clear text or by using more secure methods. In this section, you will learn about authenticating users based on the capabilities of the operating system (Windows) and the Web server (Apache). Although these methods work as designed, most Web-based authentication takes place with a combination of an SSL connection and a software application that authenticates a user. Use SSL and an application when you need to associate a user name with other information about the user, such as the person's real name, address, phone number, and other personal data. With an application, the user can enter and edit the information. Once the information is entered into a database, other applications can use that information for other purposes, such as mailing a product to a customer.

You can set up authentication on a Web server for the whole Web site or only for selected directories. Each directory can be configured differently, with a different level of authentication, and even different access once the user is authenticated. Both IIS and Apache use HTTP to enable authentication. Basically, HTTP first tries to connect, determines that access is not allowed, and then requests authentication by opening a dialog box that requests the user name and password. This scheme is often used in conjunction with SSL, which uses HTTPS, so the user name and password are encrypted.

Configuring User Authentication in IIS

IIS authenticates Windows users. For low security, you can create an individual user for a directory and then distribute the corresponding user name and password. When someone tries to navigate to the directory, he or she must enter the correct user name and password. A more appropriate use of user authentication is within an intranet. For example, suppose that on a LAN, Mary Noia logs on as mnoia. She decides to use Outlook Web Access to view her e-mail on the Exchange 2000 server. When she navigates to *www.technowidgets.com/exchange*, her user credentials are available to Exchange 2000, and she immediately sees her e-mail without having to log on. Setting up user authentication on an intranet where users log on to the network means that user logons are transparent and users do not have to type their user names and passwords. If a user navigates to a directory and the logged-on user is not authenticated automatically, a dialog box opens and prompts the user for a user name and password.

By default, IIS allows anonymous access. When you installed IIS, a specific guest user was created for anonymous access. If you remove anonymous access or alter NTFS permissions so that the anonymous guest account does not have permission to view a page, IIS uses authenticated access.

There are four types of authenticated access in Windows Server 2003 and three in Windows 2000. The following list describes authentication methods in Windows:

- *Windows integrated authentication*—The most secure method, this type of authentication uses a cryptographic exchange and can authenticate a user without having the password sent to the server. It requires Internet Explorer.
- *Digest authentication for Windows domain servers*—This method sends the password in encrypted form to the server. The advantage of this authentication approach is that it works with proxy servers, as described in a later section. It requires Active Directory and Internet Explorer.
- *Basic authentication*—This method sends the user name and password in clear text. It is compatible with Internet Explorer, Netscape Navigator, and other Web browsers.
- *Passport authentication*—This method is available only on Windows Server 2003. Passport is a centralized form of authentication supported by Microsoft.

Using any of the preceding methods provides any valid user access to the directory or file that you have secured. If you want only specific users or groups to have access, you must modify the NTFS permissions.

To require user authentication on a Windows directory called prod:

1. Create a folder called **\inetpub\wwwroot\prod**.
2. Create a small Web page called **default.htm** in the \inetpub\wwwroot\prod directory.

3. Open **Internet Information Services** (Internet Information Services (IIS) Manager in Windows 2003) and navigate to Default Web Site.
4. Expand **Default Web Site**. In the left pane, the prod directory appears.
5. Right-click **prod**, and then click **Properties**.
6. In the prod Properties dialog box, click the **Directory Security** tab. See Figure 10-21.

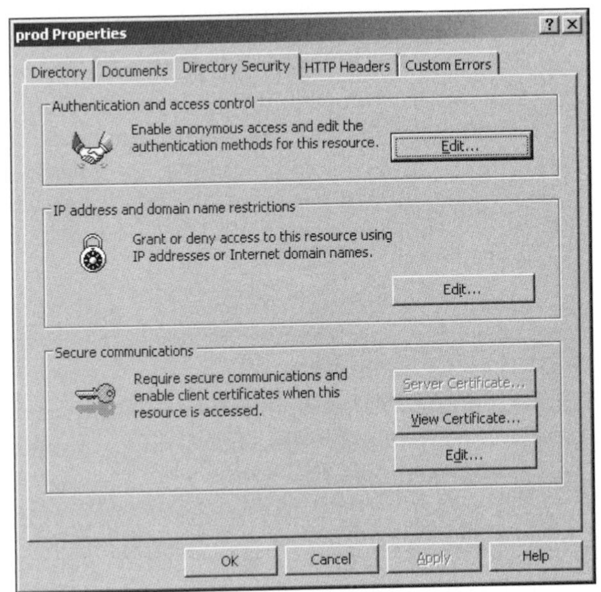

Figure 10-21 Directory Security tab in the prod Properties dialog box

7. *In Windows 2003:* Click the first **Edit** button, which is in the Anonymous access and authentication control frame, then click the **Enable anonymous access** to remove the check mark.

   In Windows 2000: Click the first **Edit** button, which is in the Authentication and access control frame, then click the **Anonymous access** box to remove the check mark.
8. Click **OK** to accept the default authentication access method, and then click **OK** to exit the prod Properties dialog box. Close the IIS window.

If you opened a browser on the server now and tried to display the contents of the prod directory, you would succeed because you are logged on as the administrator. However, if you tried to access the contents of the prod directory from another computer, you would be prompted to enter a valid user name and password.

Configuring User Authentication in Apache

You can use two methods to implement user authentication in Linux. The first method works with a file called .htaccess, which is stored in each directory that requires authentication. The other method stores all user authentication directives in httpd.conf. This section focuses on using the httpd.conf file. You will also configure user authentication via httpd.conf in Hands-on Project 10-8.

The most common way to set up users is to store their account information in a file. You can use a utility called htpasswd to create the user authentication file and insert user names and passwords. You can also create multiple user authentication files. The first time you use the **`htpasswd`** command, you add the **`-c`** directive to create the file, followed by the filename of the user file and the user name that you want to add to the file. Then **`htpasswd`** prompts you to enter the password. After the first use of **`htpasswd`**, you enter the **`htpasswd`** command followed by the name of the user file and the user name. If you want to specify the password along with the command, add **`-b`** followed by the password. For example, to create a user authentication file called users and add three users to it, you could enter the following commands:

```
htpasswd -c users mnoia
htpasswd users fpessoa
htpasswd users lcamoes -b lusiades
```

The .htaccess file defines who is allowed to access a given directory. You need a .htaccess file in each directory that requires security. Using this file provides you with flexibility because it lets you protect specific directories in your hierarchy of directories. However, .htaccess can be difficult to maintain over time, especially when you need to manage many different directories and security needs change over time. With the .htaccess files spread throughout the system, it may be difficult to remember where they are and what they contain. Using the .htaccess file method is turned off by default.

Using httpd.conf to implement user authentication stores all the configuration information in one location so it is easier to maintain. Table 10-3 lists the common httpd.conf user authentication directives and their meaning.

Table 10-3 User authentication directives

Directive	Description
`AuthName`	Specifies descriptive text for user authentication that appears on the user's browser when the request is made to log on. `AuthName` is also known as the realm, and it can be used to remind the user which user name/password to use. Example: `AuthName Internal Product Information`
`AuthType`	Specifies the authentication type, and must be followed by either `Basic` or `Digest`. Use `Basic` to transmit the user name and password in clear text. Use `Digest` to encrypt the user name and password. (Note that few browsers support the `Digest` option.) Example: `AuthType Basic`
`AuthUserFile`	Specifies the complete path to the user authentication file. Example: `AuthUserFile /var/www/users`

Table 10-3 User authentication directives (continued)

Directive	Description

`AuthGroupFile`	Specifies the complete path to the text file that associates users with groups.
	Example: `AuthGroupFile /var/www/usergroups`
	The format of the text file is *<group name>*:*<username>* followed by a space-delimited list of user names associated with the group.
	Example of group files:
	`developers:mnoia fpessoa jdesena`
	`designers:fpessoa cbranco jsampaio lcamoes`

`require`	Defines which users in the user authentication file are allowed access to the directory. There are three options to this directive: `user`, followed by a list of space-delimited user names `group`, followed by a list of space-delimited group names `valid-user`, which allows any user in the user authentication file Examples:
	`require user fpessoa lcamoes`
	`require group developers designers`
	`require valid-user`

10

To put this all together, assume that you have a directory beneath the root of the Web server called devel that only developers should access. In httpd.conf, you would add the following directory configuration:

```
<Location /devel>
AuthName "Developers Only"
AuthType Basic
AuthUserFile /var/www/users
require group developers
</Location>
```

In the following example, any valid user is allowed to see the contents of the newprods directory:

```
<Location /newprods>
AuthName "New Product Information"
AuthType Basic
AuthUserFile /var/www/users
require valid-user
</Location>
```

Using a Firewall

A firewall in a hotel usually involves a concrete-lined stairwell. The ventilation and even the lights are isolated from the rest of the hotel. The concrete prevents fire from entering the stairwell, yet the fireproof doors allow people to enter in case of fire. In a computer network, firewalls implement an access control policy between networks. You want to keep the attackers out, but let legitimate users in. Typically, this means filtering IP packets between two networks. For example, you might want to filter packets between the Internet and the servers in your Web environment. You might also want to filter packets between your internal users and the Internet and between your internal users and your servers in the Web environment. A broader definition of a firewall, therefore, includes any method that isolates two networks. This definition includes proxy servers, as described in the next section. In fact, some products such as Microsoft Internet Security and Acceleration (ISA) Server combine firewall and proxy server functionality.

You filter packets based on three types of IP packets: ICMP, TCP, and UDP. In some firewall products, such as iptables in Linux or the packet-filtering capabilities of Cisco routers, rules are explicitly stated for each packet type. Other firewall products, such as ISA Server from Microsoft, allow you to specify filtering by applications such as e-mail, Web, and FTP. The firewall product then translates these requests internally into specific packet-filtering requirements. Windows Server 2003 comes with a basic firewall product called Internet Connection Firewall, while ISA Server is a product that you purchase.

You have already learned about the port requirements for a variety of servers. You also realize that adding SSL capabilities for applications increases the number of ports that must be accessible on a server. Your objective is to allow all requests to connect to supported applications that exist at particular ports, but to refuse all others. Conversely, from the internal network, you want to allow control over ports that communicate with the Internet. For example, you would want to keep a virus that has infected one of your servers from easily communicating with the Internet. A few years ago, many Windows computers were infected with a virus that directed the computers to attack specific sites such as e-Bay and Yahoo! in a Distributed DOS attack. Filtering ports could help prevent such a virus from doing damage because you could prevent your server from connecting to a Web server at port 80. Naturally, you would still allow browsers from the Internet to connect to your Web server at port 80.

You can filter IP packets in three ways. The most basic approach, **packet filtering**, looks at each packet individually and accepts or rejects the packet based on specified rules. **Circuit-level filtering** controls the complete communication session, as opposed to individual packets. The most sophisticated way to filter packets is through an **application-level filter**. With an application-level filter, the firewall recognizes that the Web or e-mail application, for example, serves as a termination point for traffic between the internal network and the Internet. Instead of simply transferring a packet destined for an internal Web server, an application-level filter opens separate connections between the firewall and the internal server to better control the flow of data.

Packet Filtering Using iptables

The iptables utility is a command-line utility available on Linux to filter packets by creating a script with rules that define your firewall. You typically begin by preventing any packet from entering or leaving your computer, and then determine which packets are acceptable. There are three types of packets to filter: TCP, UDP, and ICMP. You can also set rules depending on the direction of the traffic—that is, input rules for packets destined for the computer, and output rules for packets originating from the computer. For example, suppose you want to filter Web traffic and your IP address connected to the Internet is 38.246.165.200. You analyze five parts of the packet: the type of packet, the destination IP address, the destination port, the source IP address, and the source port. Because the HTTP protocol depends on TCP, you want to accept only TCP packets destined for port 80 at 38.246.165.200. In most cases, the source IP address of the packet does not matter. For Web traffic leaving the computer, you want to make sure that the source IP address is 38.246.165.200 at port 80. Checking packets leaving the computer can help prevent unauthorized programs from communicating with the Internet.

Do not implement a firewall using iptables until you complete Hands-on Project 10-9. If you create the firewall now, you will have problems with some of the other Hands-on Projects.

Now you need to translate your objectives into a script containing a series of iptables commands. First, you must develop a text file that contains the definitions you need to create the firewall. Each line in the script begins with the iptables command followed by one or more options. Table 10-4 defines the iptables options that you need.

Table 10-4 iptables options

Option	Description
`-A`	Appends a rule. Most configurations will begin with this option because you want to add a new rule to the list of existing rules.
`INPUT`	Analyzes packets that are destined for this computer.
`OUTPUT`	Analyzes packets that originate from this computer.
`ACCEPT`, `DROP`, `REJECT`	Defines what to do with the packet. `ACCEPT` allows the packet to be transmitted. `DROP` rejects the packet silently; that is, it does not respond with an ICMP message. `REJECT` rejects the packet and responds with an ICMP message stating that the packet was refused.
`--policy`	Defines an overall characteristic of the iptables configuration. For example: `iptables --policy INPUT DROP` As a default, all packets arriving at this computer will be dropped. Following statements describe specifically which ones will be accepted.
`-s`, `-d`	Defines the source or destination IP address of the packet. The `-s` is followed by the source IP address and the `-d` is followed by the destination IP address.
`-sport`, `-dport`	Defines the source or destination port of the packet. The `-sport` is followed by the source port and the `-dport` is followed by the destination port.
`-p`	Defines the protocol that is being filtered. The `-p` is followed by TCP, UDP, or ICMP.
`-j`	Describes what to do with the packet if the rule is true. It is usually followed by `ACCEPT`.
`--flush`	Deletes any existing rules.

Figure 10-22 shows a simple script to create a firewall that allows only a Web server to operate on the server. If you named the script rc.iptables, you would start the firewall by typing **sh rc.iptables**. Some options have two dashes, as in **--flush**, and **--policy**, whereas other options have a single dash, as in **-d**, **-s**, **-sport**, and **-dport**. Notice that each line specifies only a destination or a source IP address. Because the fourth line specifies a destination address of 38.246.165.200 and a destination port of 80, the source address and source port can be anything. This result makes sense because you want any IP address to access your Web server. The first three lines are standard to any iptables script. The actual filtering starts on line 4. The examples in this section show both INPUT statements to filter packets coming into the server and OUTPUT statements to filter packets leaving the server. Although INPUT statements are essential and the primary purpose of a firewall, you could eliminate the OUTPUT statements with only a slight decrease in effectiveness because there is much less of a chance that unwanted packets would be exiting the server.

```
iptables --flush
iptables --policy INPUT DROP
iptables --policy OUTPUT DROP
iptables -A INPUT  -p tcp -d 38.246.165.200 --dport 80 -j ACCEPT
iptables -A OUTPUT -p tcp -s 38.246.165.200 --sport 80 -j ACCEPT
```

Figure 10-22 Script file for a Web server firewall

The file starts by clearing any previous rules from the iptables rules cache. Then it defaults to dropping packets coming in and leaving from the computer. The last two lines in Figure 10-22 define the two rules to allow packets to be transmitted. They state that if TCP packets destined for IP address 38.246.165.200 arrive at port 80, they should be accepted. TCP packets leaving 38.246.165.200 and coming from port 80 should also be accepted.

Using this firewall, Internet users with a browser could view pages, but you could not type **ping 38.246.165.200** and get a response. The script describes the only traffic that you allow: Because you did not allow ICMP, ping does not work. Also, you could not use ping from the server to test connectivity. To allow ping to work, you would add the following lines to the script:

```
iptables -A INPUT  -p ICMP -d 38.246.165.200 -j ACCEPT
iptables -A OUTPUT -p ICMP -s 38.246.165.200 -j ACCEPT
```

Although no one should use the browser on a server to prevent downloading viruses and other files that could cause problems, you could add such functionality by allowing communication between the browser and Web sites. The browser would then accept packets from any IP address on an unprivileged port. The numbers of unprivileged ports range from 1024 to 65535. The output packets need to go to port 80 but can go to any IP address:

```
iptables -A INPUT  -p tcp -d 38.246.165.200  --sport 1024:65535 -j ACCEPT
iptables -A OUTPUT -p tcp -s 38.246.165.200 --dport 80 -j ACCEPT
```

To allow packets for most other protocols, you would include similar lines in the iptables script. For example, if your e-mail server uses both the SMTP (port 25) and POP3 (port 110) protocols, you would add the following lines to an iptables script file:

```
iptables -A INPUT  -p tcp -d 38.246.165.200 --dport 25 -j ACCEPT
iptables -A OUTPUT -p tcp -s 38.246.165.200 --sport 25 -j ACCEPT
iptables -A INPUT  -p tcp -d 38.246.165.200 --sport 25 -j ACCEPT
iptables -A OUTPUT -p tcp -s 38.246.165.200 --dport 25 -j ACCEPT
iptables -A INPUT  -p tcp -d 38.246.165.200 --dport 110 -j ACCEPT
iptables -A OUTPUT -p tcp -s 38.246.165.200 --sport 110 -j ACCEPT
```

With SMTP, you need to be able to accept SMTP connections from outside your server, which you allow in the first two lines. Your e-mail server also needs to use SMTP to send e-mail to other servers, which you allow in lines 3 and 4. However, with POP3, your server just needs to communicate with users

FTP communicates differently from the other protocols. When the FTP server transmits a file, it uses unprivileged ports, so you have to allow all unprivileged ports for both incoming traffic and outgoing traffic, as seen in lines 5 and 6 in the following code. By allowing all unprivileged ports to be used in communication, you could inadvertently enable attackers to communicate with a database server on your server, because database servers use unprivileged ports. Other applications can also use unprivileged ports. FTP servers are often put on separate servers because they use unprivileged ports and because user names and passwords for FTP are sent in clear text. In fact, because you have to open so many ports for an FTP server, it is often set up outside the firewall. To implement filtering to allow an FTP server to communicate on your server, you would add the following rules. Because FTP requires both ports 20 and 21, you add the first two lines to allow port 21 to be used, and the second two lines to allow port 20 to be used.

Warning: Because of space constraints in the code below, each line of code wraps to a second line. This would be incorrect in the text file that contains these lines. Each new line of code must begin with the "iptables" command.

```
iptables -A INPUT -p tcp --sport 1024:65535
   -d 38.246.165.200 --dport 21 -j ACCEPT
iptables -A OUTPUT -p tcp -s 38.246.165.200 --sport 21
   --dport 1024:65535 -j ACCEPT
iptables -A INPUT -p tcp --sport 1024:65535
   -d 38.246.165.200 --dport 20 -j ACCEPT
iptables -A OUTPUT -p tcp -s 38.246.165.200 --sport 20
   --dport 1024:65535 -j ACCEPT
iptables -A INPUT -p tcp --sport 1024:65535
   -d 38.246.165.200 --dport 1024:65535 -j ACCEPT
iptables -A OUTPUT -p tcp -s 38.246.165.200
   --sport 1024:65535 --dport 1024:65535 -j ACCEPT
```

Other iptables features provide detailed controls by specifying particular NICs in the server for communication and test for specific TCP flags. You can also use iptables to route packets of a particular protocol, such as SMTP or HTTP, to an internal server. In addition, you can use this utility to set up transparent proxying, which allows computers within your organization to have private IP addresses, yet communicate with the Internet without having a browser configuration for a proxy server.

Understanding the Firewall Capabilities of Windows

Both Windows 2000 and Windows Server 2003 can filter incoming TCP and UDP packets through the TCP/IP connection properties. Windows Server 2003 adds the Internet Connection Firewall (ICF), a basic firewall that allows the filtering of TCP and UDP packets and supports logging. ICF permits connections *to* the Internet, but not *from* the Internet. It prevents attackers from penetrating your system through your Internet connection by making sure that any packet coming into your computer is a response to a packet that was sent by your computer. It can work with Internet Connection Sharing, which enables multiple computers on your small network to share an Internet connection. ICF is not available on the Web edition of Windows Server 2003.

To allow Windows to accept connections to the Web server only at port 80:

1. *In Windows 2003:* Click **Start**, point to **Control Panel**, point to **Network Connections**, and then click **Local Area Connection**.

   In Windows 2000: Click **Start**, point to **Settings**, click **Network and Dial-up Connections**, and then double-click **Local Area Connection**. The Local Area Connection Status dialog box opens.
2. Click **Properties**. The Local Area Connection Properties dialog box opens.
3. Highlight **Internet Protocol (TCP/IP)**, and then click **Properties**. The Internet Protocol (TCP/IP) Properties dialog box opens.
4. Click **Advanced**. The Advanced TCP/IP Settings dialog box opens.
5. Click the **Options** tab. Highlight **TCP/IP filtering**, and then click **Properties**. The TCP/IP Filtering dialog box opens, as shown in Figure 10-23.

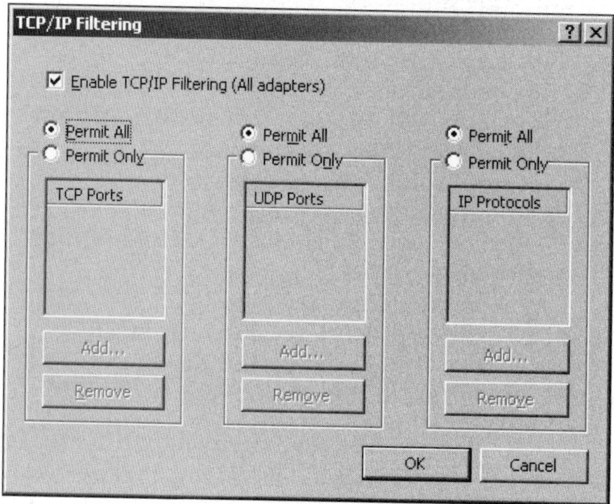

Figure 10-23 TCP/IP Filtering dialog box

6. Above TCP Ports, click the **Permit Only** option button.
7. Below TCP Ports, click **Add**. The Add Filter dialog box opens.
8. Type **80**, and then click **OK**.
9. To save this change you would click OK, but to perform some of the Hands-on Projects, you should not implement filtering. Instead, click **Cancel** until you reach the Local Area Connection Status dialog box, and then click **Close**.

Understanding the Firewall Capabilities of Microsoft Internet Security and Acceleration Server

ISA Server includes firewall capabilities and can be used to cache Web pages. The steps in this section explain how to set up ISA Server to run on the same computer as a Web server, but do not include instructions for installing ISA Server. Although you could install ISA Server with a single NIC, fully testing the configuration requires having two NICs in the computer. One of the NICs represents a connection to the Internet, and the other NIC is connected to the internal network. Review the following steps to compare these setup instructions to the capabilities of iptables in Linux.

To configure packet filtering for ISA Server, you use a GUI called the ISA Management console. When you first install ISA Server, it includes some default filtering. Figure 10-24 shows the default access.

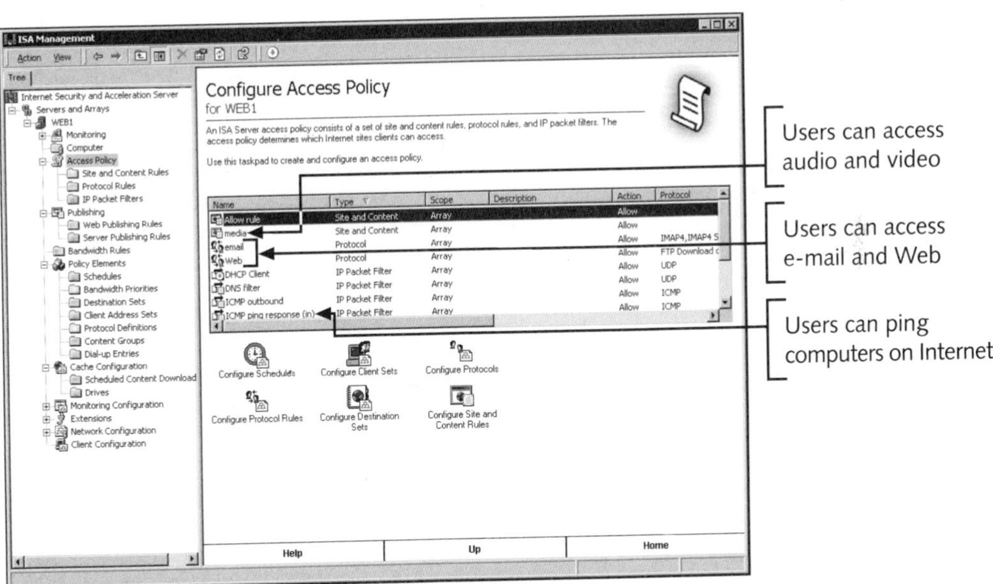

Figure 10-24 Default ISA Server access policy

In the Type column, the Protocol type defines what traffic is allowed to exit the firewall to the Internet. You can see that e-mail and Web access are allowed. The Site and Content type allows you to refine what type of HTTP content is allowed and who can see the content. For example, you could allow HTML documents but block audio and video, except for people in the marketing department. The IP Packet Filter type enables you to exert more detailed control over ports. For example, the DNS filter allows local computers to access a DNS server on the Internet. The ICMP filters allow computers on the Internet to ping your server. You can further control the access policy by restricting the time of day during which people have access.

Although it is best to have only ISA Server running on the firewall, in a small business, you may want to run a Web server on the same computer. To do so, you can create an IP packet filter to allow access to port 80 on the firewall. To perform the following steps, ISA Server must be installed on your Windows server computer.

To allow port 80 on ISA Server in Windows:

1. Click **Start**, point to **All Programs**, (**Programs** in Windows 2000) point to **Microsoft ISA Server**, and then click **ISA Management**.
2. Expand the folders in the left pane until IP Packet Filters appears, and then click **IP Packet Filters**. See Figure 10-25.

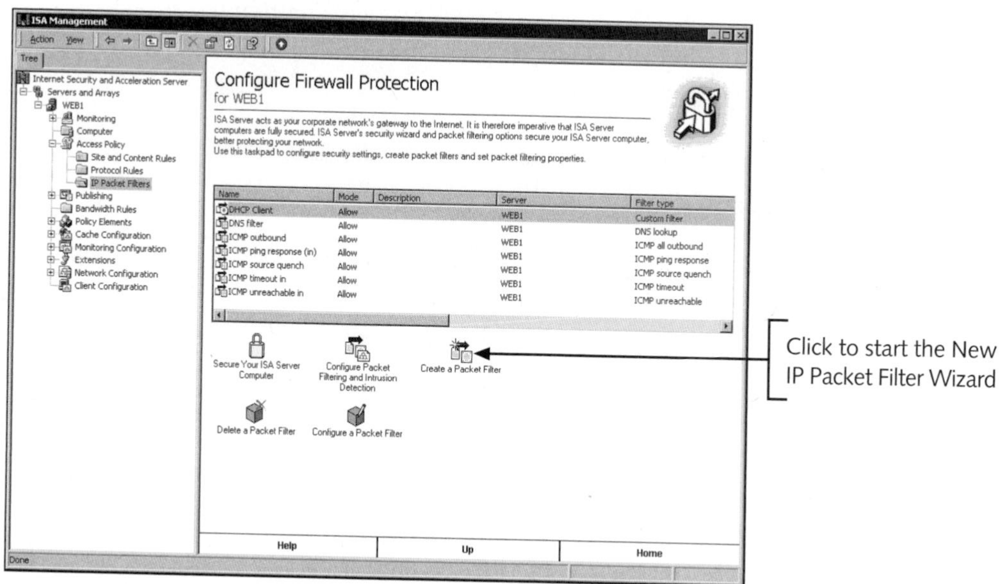

Figure 10-25 Selecting IP packet filters

3. Click the **Create a Packet Filter** icon to start the New IP Packet Filter Wizard. The first dialog box of the wizard opens, requesting the name of the filter you want to create.
4. Type **Web server access**, and then click **Next**. The Filter Mode dialog box opens. Accept the default of "Allow packet transmission."

5. Click **Next**. The Filter Type dialog box opens. Click the list arrow, and then click **HTTP server (port 80)**.
6. Click **Next**. The Local Computer dialog box opens, as shown in Figure 10-26. You can assign the Web server access filter to a specific external IP address if your server has multiple addresses. In an array of firewalls, you could apply this filter to another computer on the perimeter network. Typically, however, you accept the default option to allow access on the default IP addresses for all NICs attached to the external network.

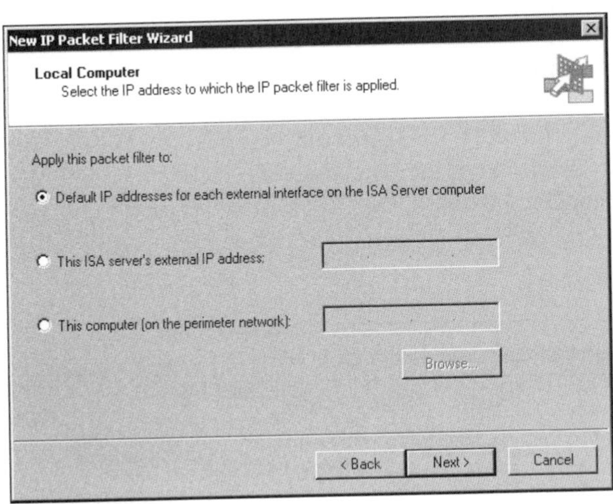

Figure 10-26 Local Computer dialog box

7. Click **Next**. The Remote Computers dialog box opens. You can keep the default of allowing all remote computers to access this port or specify an individual IP address.
8. Click **Next**. The wizard displays a summary of your actions. Click **Finish** to exit the wizard.

Using a Proxy Server

A proxy server delivers content on behalf of a user or a server application. When a proxy server receives requests for files, it acts on behalf of the requester and retrieves the files. Once it has the files, it sends them to the requester.

Proxy servers need to understand the protocol of the application that they proxy. For example, you can use Apache to proxy HTTP and FTP applications, but not streaming media or instant messaging because Apache does not understand those protocols. Some proxy servers, such as ISA Server, can support streaming media, instant messaging, and other protocols.

Proxy servers typically have at least two NICs. One NIC is connected to the Internet, and the other NIC is connected to the internal network. IP routing is disabled between the NICs to isolate them and prevent packets from moving between the internal network and the Internet.

One of two types of proxy servers is the **forward** (or **forwarding**) **proxy server**, which typically isolates internal users from the Internet. Instead of users directly accessing and downloading Web pages, the user's browser contacts the proxy server, which finds the Web page and sends it to the user. As an added benefit, Web pages are usually cached on the proxy server. Thus, if the Web page is already in the cache, the proxy server can send the page to the user more quickly. Caching documents on a proxy server can provide a significant benefit when users have similar requests and your Internet connection cannot directly support all the requests. Figure 10-27 shows an example of a user requesting a Web page that is not in the cache. Figure 10-28 shows an example of a user requesting a Web page that is in the cache. In both cases, the user does not know whether the page came from the Internet or the cache.

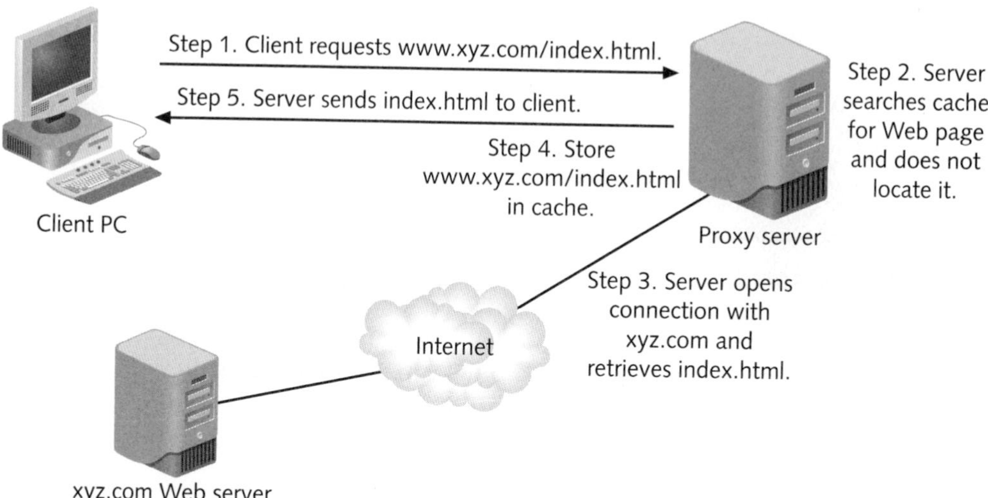

Figure 10-27 Proxy server retrieving a Web page from the Internet

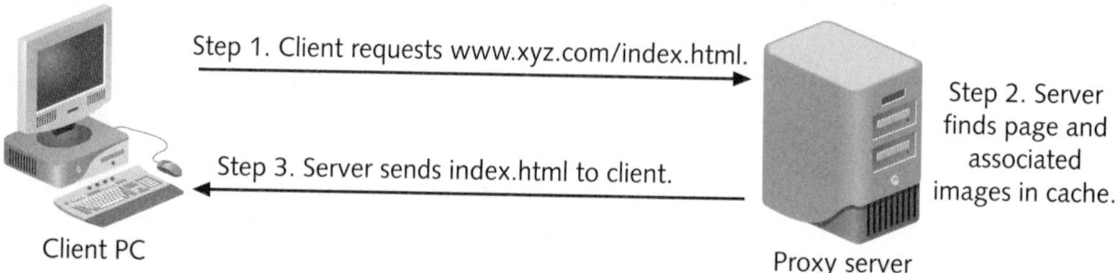

Figure 10-28 Proxy server retrieving a Web page from the cache

The other type of proxy server is a **reverse** (or **reversing**) **proxy server**, which is designed to isolate your Web server environment from the Internet. Instead of DNS pointing to your Web server's IP address, it points to the IP address of your proxy server. When an Internet user requests a Web page, the proxy server retrieves the page from an internal server, and then sends it back to the user. With this scheme, users (and attackers) do not have direct access to your Web environment, which makes it more difficult to penetrate. Figure 10-29 shows how a single IP address can be used to proxy a number of applications. The proxy server decides which server to send the request to based on the port number of the request.

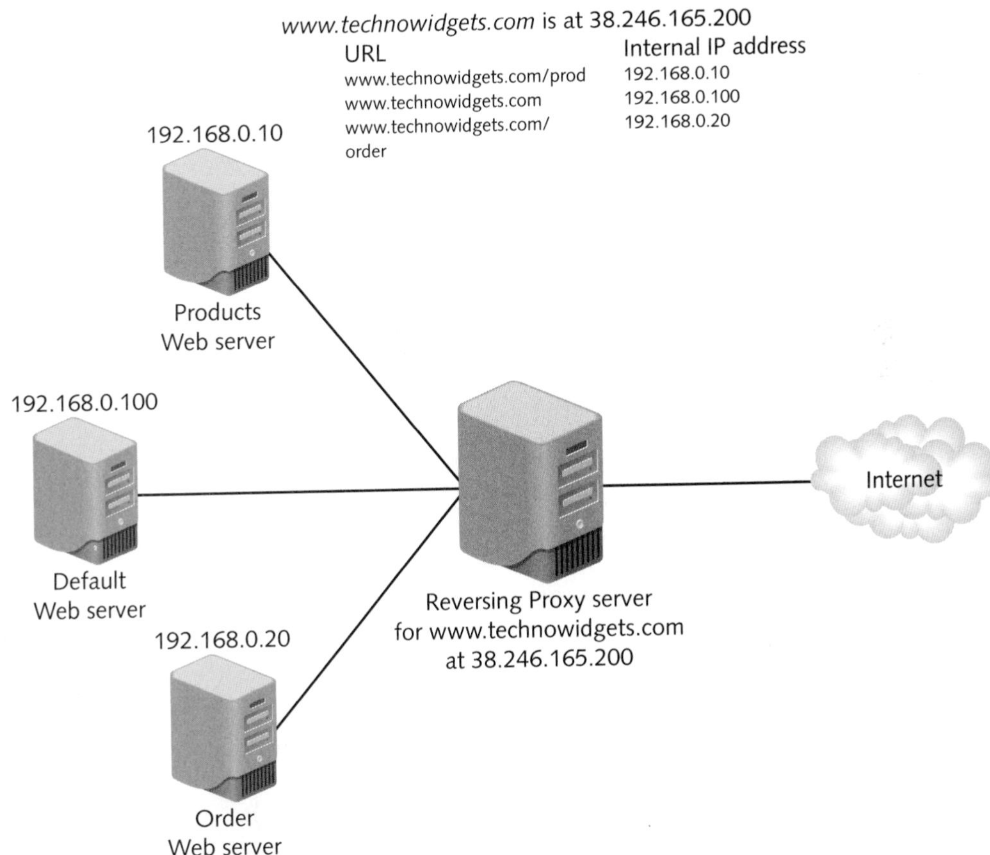

Figure 10-29 Reverse proxy server

Using Apache as a Proxy Server

To set up a forward proxy server, you need two NICs in your server. In the following steps, one NIC is connected to the Internet. The other NIC has an IP address of 192.168.0.100 and is connected to your internal network. The dedicated proxy server is not used as a Web server. You will use port 8080 for it. In Hands-on Project 10-8, you will configure and test this proxy server in a lab environment.

Do not actually implement a proxy server until you perform Hands-on Project 10-8. If you create the proxy server now, you will have problems with some of the other Hands-on Projects.

To configure Apache to become a forward proxy server in Linux:

1. In Linux, open httpd.conf.
2. Press **Ctrl+F** to open the Find dialog box. Type **Listen 80**, and then click **Find**. Change 80 to **8080**.
3. Use the Find dialog box to find **<IfModule mod_proxy.c>** and change the code so that it matches the following code. Most of the changes involve deleting the pound sign (#) at the beginning of the line to turn a comment into an actual configuration line.

```
<IfModule mod_proxy.c>
    ProxyRequests On
    <Proxy *>
        Order deny,allow
        Deny from all
        Allow from 192.168.0.0/24
    </Proxy>
</IfModule>
```

   The only required item is "ProxyRequests On." The statement "Allow from 192.168.0.0/24" allows only those computers connecting from the local network to access the proxy server.

4. Save the file and exit the editor.
5. Type **apachectl restart**, and then press **Enter**.

Because proxy servers use a special protocol, you must configure the browser to use a proxy server. The following steps assume that the computer is on the 192.168.0.0 network and the proxy server is configured as in the preceding steps. Although Linux is commonly used as a proxy server, Internet Explorer, available only on Windows, is by far the most common browser.

To configure Internet Explorer to use a proxy server in Windows:

1. Start Internet Explorer. Click **Tools** on the menu bar, and then click **Internet Options**. The Internet Options dialog box opens.
2. Click the **Connections** tab.
3. Click the **LAN Settings** button. The Local Area Network (LAN) Settings dialog box opens.
4. Click the **Use a proxy server for your LAN** check box to enable the entries for the proxy server.

5. For the address, type **192.168.0.100**. For the port, type **8080**.
6. Click **OK** to close the Local Area Network (LAN) Settings dialog box, and then click **OK** to close the Internet Options dialog box.

To configure Konqueror to use a proxy server in Linux:

1. Open Konqueror.
2. Click **Settings** on the menu bar, and then click **Configure Konqueror**. The Settings window opens.
3. In the left pane, click the **Proxy** icon.
4. Click the **Use Proxy** check box to select it.
5. Click the **Manually specified settings** option button, and then click the **Setup** button to the right of the option button.
6. Click the **HTTP** check box to select it.
7. For the URL, type **http://192.168.0.100**. For the port, accept the default of 8080.
8. Click **OK** twice to close all open dialog boxes and close Konqueror.

When you set up a reverse proxy server, you capture all incoming Web requests and send them to an internal Web server. For example, suppose you have a Web site for *www.technowidgets.com* at 38.246.165.200, which is the IP address of your proxy server, not your Web server. Another NIC on the proxy server is connected to the 192.168.0.0 network. On that network, your Web server is at 192.168.0.50. To create a reverse proxy server, you add the following two lines to your proxy server configuration in httpd.conf:

```
ProxyPass / http://192.168.0.50/
ProxyPassReverse / http://192.168.0.50/
```

You use the `ProxyPass` command when the client must connect to the proxy server to determine where to send the request. However, when the internal Web server responds, it inserts its own host name in the Location header. The `ProxyPassReverse` directive is required to replace the host name of the internal Web server with the host name of the proxy server. If the internal Web server at 192.168.0.50 has a host name of web1, this command would translate a link for *web1/prod/info.htm* into *www.technowidgets.com/prod/info.htm* when it is sent back to the originating client.

You can add to the reverse proxy server to split Web traffic among internal Web servers. For example, if you wanted a request for *www.technowidgets.com/order* to go to a Web server at 192.168.0.20 and a request for *www.technowidgets.com/prod* to go to a Web server at 192.168.0.30, you could add the following lines:

```
ProxyPass /order/ http://192.168.0.20/
ProxyPassReverse /order/ http://192.168.0.20/
ProxyPass /prod/ http://192.168.0.30/
ProxyPassReverse /prod/ http://192.168.0.30/
```

Using ISA Server as a Proxy Server

Although ISA Server has a Web proxy service that functions in a similar manner to using Apache as a proxy server, ISA Server uses a different method to isolate the Internet from your internal network. In Windows 2000 and Server 2003, **Network Address Translation (NAT)** allows you to connect a NIC to your internal network with a private IP address and connect another NIC to the Internet. The private IP addresses are translated into the single Internet IP address as messages are routed to the Internet. When the Internet NIC receives a response to a message, NAT translates the Internet IP address into the individual private IP address, as shown in Figure 10-30. ISA Server makes this process secure through SecureNAT, which translates addresses, and allows you to filter and control traffic to and from the Internet. The advantage of using NAT or SecureNAT is that any version of NAT is based on standards, rather than being designed for a particular computer platform. As a consequence, Macintosh and Linux computers on your network can take advantage of NAT. Another important advantage is that you do not have to configure a browser to use NAT.

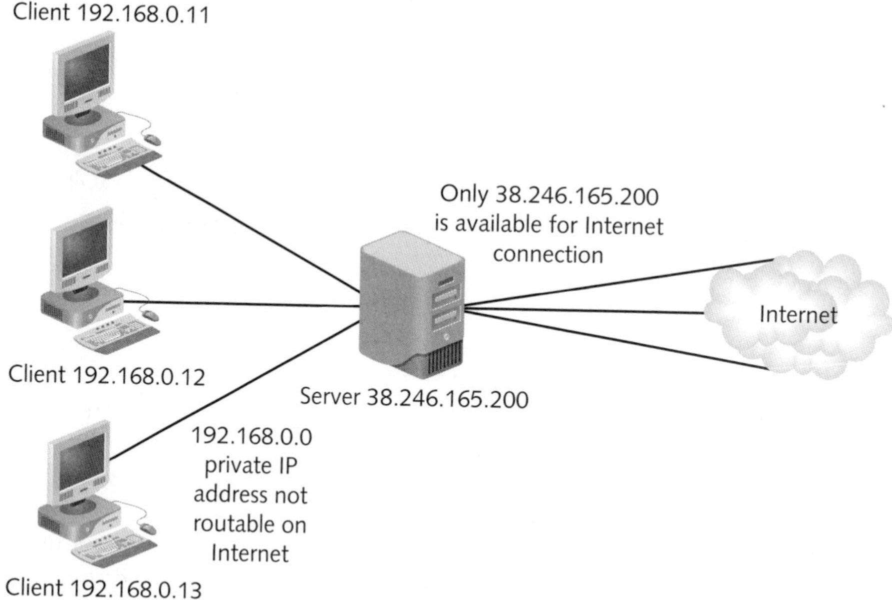

Figure 10-30 Using Network Address Translation

ISA Server includes advanced caching technology to optimize your Internet connection. Besides storing Web pages on disk, it uses available RAM to cache the most frequently requested Web pages. The most common form of caching is forward caching, which caches

Web pages for internal users. ISA Server also supports reverse caching, which caches Web pages requested from a Web server on an internal network by a user on the Internet.

Recall that you can configure ISA Server to use a reverse proxy server for HTTP, FTP, e-mail, and streaming video protocols. In this way, you can isolate all of the servers in your Web server environment from the Internet, thereby increasing the security of the Web server. The one disadvantage of this scheme is that the ISA Server computer becomes the single point of failure. If the ISA Server computer fails or becomes compromised, your users cannot communicate with the Internet, and outsiders cannot communicate with your organization.

To configure a reverse proxy server in ISA Server, you must perform two tasks. The first task is to create a listener, which waits for an Internet user who wants access to your Web server. The second task is to create a Web publishing rule to determine which internal Web server should get the Web request.

To create a default listener on ISA Server in Windows:

1. Open the ISA Management MMC.
2. Right-click the name of your server computer, and then click **Properties**. The Web server Properties dialog box opens.
3. Click the **Incoming Web Requests** tab. You can configure a different listener for each IP address on your Internet interface or you can have one listener for all IP addresses.
4. Click the **Use the same listener configuration for all IP addresses** option button, if necessary. The default configuration appears in the Identification area. See Figure 10-31.
5. Click **OK** to close the Properties dialog box. The ISA Server Warning dialog box opens. Because you made a change that affects the Web proxy service, you should restart the service.
6. Click the **Save the changes and restart the service(s)** option button, and then click **OK**.

To create a Web publishing rule to create a reverse proxy server:

1. In the ISA Management MMC, expand the folders under Publishing in the left pane, and then click **Web Publishing Rules**.
2. Click the **Create a Web Publishing Rule** icon to start the New Web Publishing Rule Wizard.
3. In the first dialog box of the wizard, type an appropriate name, such as **Internal Web**.

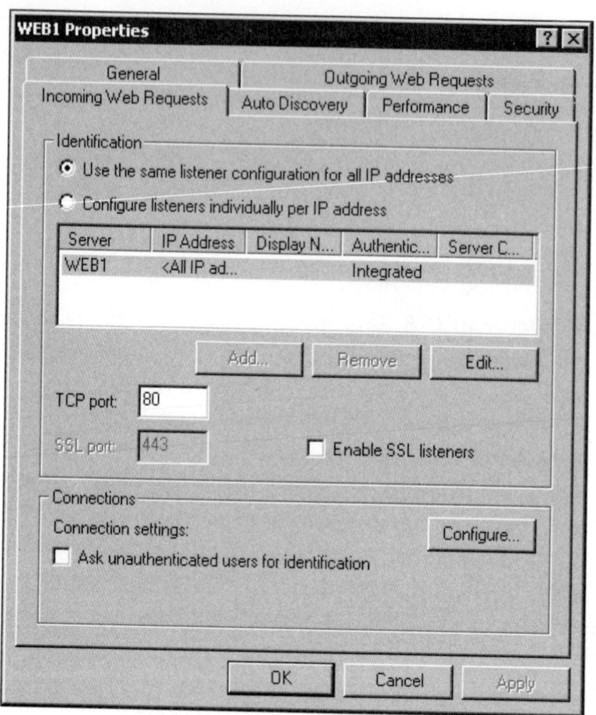

Figure 10-31 Incoming Web Requests tab of the Web server Properties dialog box

4. Click **Next**. The Destination Sets dialog box opens. By default, the settings in this dialog box apply to all destinations, but you can also select individual destination sets. For example, you could direct *www.technowidgets.com/order* to one server, but send *www.technowidgets.com/prod* to another computer. In this way, you could have many Web servers associated with a single domain name.
5. Click **Next**. The Client Type dialog box opens. You use this dialog box either to accept the default of any request from a client or to restrict requests to those received from specific computers or users.
6. Click **Next**. The Rule Action dialog box opens. See Figure 10-32. You use this dialog box to specify how this Web publishing rule should respond to requests by clients. By default, requests are discarded. If you want to redirect Web requests, click the **Redirect the request to this internal Web server** option button. Next, enter the computer name or IP address, such as **192.168.0.115**, in the text box.
7. Click **Next**, and a summary appears. Click **Finish** to exit the wizard.

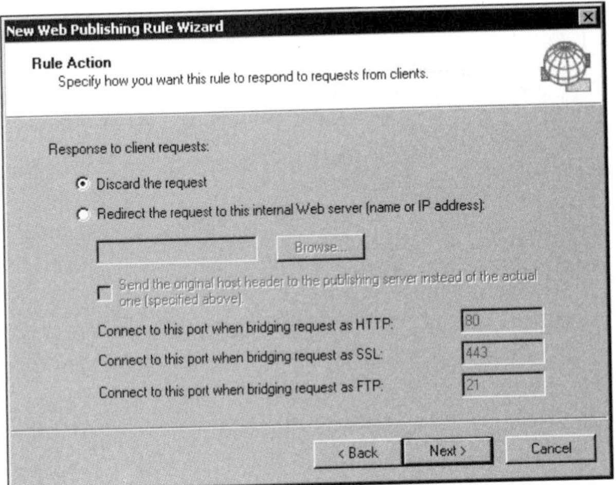

Figure 10-32 Rule Action dialog box

Using Intrusion Detection Software

Because working to secure your systems does not prevent all network and computer intrusions, you also need to find out whether someone has penetrated your system and changed files. In some cases, users or even other administrators might cause problems by accidentally introducing viruses or installing unapproved software. The first line of defense is to use virus protection software from one of the top commercial producers, such as McAfee for Windows computers, and then download updates about once per week. The most common intrusion detection software available for Linux is Tripwire, which is included with Red Hat Linux. A version of Tripwire is also available for Windows computers. ISA Server itself contains several intrusion detection features.

Using Tripwire on Linux

In Tripwire, you can set policies that allow you to monitor any changes to the files on the system. Tripwire can detect file additions, deletions, and changes. By identifying the changes to the files, you can determine which changes are unauthorized and then try to find out the cause of the change.

After installing Tripwire, you configure the policy file to determine which files to monitor. Next, you create a database of monitored files based on the policy file. You then use a utility to compare this database to your existing system. In production systems, you would probably run the utility once daily to check for changes. To protect Tripwire, you password-protect it. Finally, it is a good idea to copy the policy files to a floppy disk for safekeeping in case someone tries to tamper with the ones you actively use.

The most important file that Tripwire installs is the policy file, which contains the details on the files it checks. Fortunately, the policy file was created specifically for Red Hat Linux. If you use a different version of Linux and download the generic version of Tripwire, you would need to determine which files to check and then assign them to a category—tasks that could take hours.

The policy file for Red Hat Linux has more than 1,000 lines and is organized into a series of rules that group files according to function. For example, the 28 default groups for the rules include the following:

- File system and disk administration programs
- Kernel administration programs
- Networking programs
- System administration programs
- Hardware and device-control programs
- System information programs
- Application information programs
- Shell-related programs
- Operating system utilities

To install Tripwire on a Linux computer:

1. Insert Red Hat Linux CD 3 in the CD drive.
2. Double-click the **CD/DVD-ROM** icon on the desktop. Click **Find**.
3. On the CD, navigate to /mnt/cdrom/RedHat/RPMS.
4. Double-click the file that begins with **tripwire**. After a few moments, the Completed System Preparation dialog box opens.
5. Click **Continue** to install Tripwire.
6. Close the Konqueror window.

Next, you must add your e-mail address to the file.

To add your e-mail address to the Tripwire policy file:

1. In a terminal window, type **kedit /etc/tripwire/twpol.txt** and then press **Enter**.
2. Press **Ctrl+F** to open the Find dialog box, and then search for **severity =**. Be sure to insert a space after typing "severity."
3. At the end of the line containing `severity =`, add a comma (,) and then press **Enter**.

4. Type **emailto =** followed by your e-mail address enclosed in double quotation marks. For *mnoia@technowidgets.com*, the first rule would resemble the following:

   ```
   rulename = "Tripwire Binaries",
   severity    = $(SIG_HI),
   emailto  = mnoia@technowidgets.com
   ```

   Press **Enter**. Now if "Tripwire Binaries" is changed, Tripwire sends an e-mail message to mnoia.

5. Search for all the other rules and add your e-mail address to them. Do not change any instances that begin with a pound sign (#), because these are comments. The twenty-fourth instance of adding the e-mail name includes `recourse = false` after `severity =`. Insert a comma at the end of the `recourse = false` line and then add your e-mail name on the next line. You must enter your e-mail name in 25 places, or the next series of steps will not work.

6. Save and exit the file.

   The next task is to make a minor change to the configuration file so that the policy file will work as designed.

7. In the configuration file, allow a specific configuration by editing **/etc/tripwire/twcfg.txt** to change the `LOOSEDIRECTORYCHECKING` setting from "false" to "**true**." 10

Obviously, you do not want the person penetrating the system to be able to modify the configuration. You use a shell script to create a secure site password and a local password. The site password is used for modifying the configuration and policy. The local password is used for generating reports and other features that you can delegate. With the site password, the policy and configuration files are converted to a secure binary form, thereby ensuring that no one has tampered with them.

To create your passwords and secure versions of your configuration and policy in Linux:

1. In a terminal window, type **/etc/tripwire/twinstall.sh** to start the installation script. The script prompts you for a secure password that it uses to digitally sign a number of important Tripwire files.

2. When asked to enter the site keyfile passphrase, type a secure password of at least eight characters, and then press **Enter**. Type the password again to verify it. There is no way to recover this password if you forget it.

   Next, you must enter the local keyfile passphrase. Using a local password lets you delegate some administration tasks.

3. Type a secure password of at least eight characters, and then press **Enter**. Type the local password again to verify it. There is no way to recover this password if you forget it.

4. When asked to enter your site passphrase, type the password that you entered in Step 2. Tripwire generates a secure version of your configuration file, and then asks you to enter your site passphrase again.
5. Type the password that you entered in Step 2. Tripwire generates a secure version of your policy file.

Now that the binary files are ready, you can create the database that Tripwire uses to monitor your system. Type the following command, noting that it contains two dashes:

```
/usr/sbin/tripwire --init
```

Tripwire asks for your local (not site) password. After you enter the password, you might see dozens of errors because some files specified in the default configuration file do not exist on your system. The example policy file that you used was based on a system where every package available on the system was installed. You did not install all the packages, so Tripwire warns you that the files could not be found. Although the missing files will not cause problems on your system, in a production system you should modify your configuration to remove the lines in the policy file that specify the missing files. By removing the lines in the policy file, you will no longer receive reports on the missing files.

To compare the policy reflected in the database against the files that exist in the system, type the following command:

```
/usr/sbin/tripwire --check
```

Tripwire produces a report containing information about any system changes. It displays the report on the screen and puts it in a secure binary file to be used at a later date for comparison. If you run this report based on the example file, you will probably see more than 100 errors because of the packages that you did not install.

The last important task is to move the policy and configuration text files (twcfg.txt and twpol.txt) to a floppy disk for safekeeping. If you leave the files on the computer, a person who penetrated your system could learn which files are being checked.

Using the Intrusion Detection Features of ISA Server

Intrusion detection in ISA Server differs from intrusion detection in Tripwire. ISA Server detects specific methods that attackers can employ to penetrate a system. If it recognizes a specific type of attack, it issues an alert that can be viewed in the event log or in a message on the screen. ISA Server can detect only intrusions that result from attacks that it recognizes. It also focuses on intrusions that could cause the computer to crash, rather than intrusions that could allow someone to gain control of the server. To set up intrusion detection on ISA Server, you use the Intrusion Detection tab of the IP Packet Filters Properties dialog box. Figure 10-33 shows you a list of attacks that ISA Server detects.

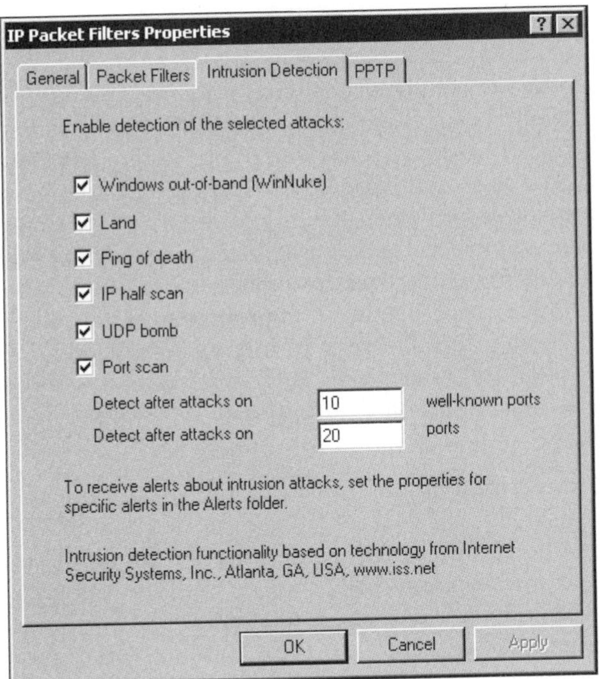

Figure 10-33 Intrusion Detection tab of the IP Packet Filters Properties dialog box

The following list briefly describes the attacks ISA Server detects:

- *Windows out-of-band (WinNuke)*—This is a specific type of denial-of-service attack.
- *Land*—A spoofed packet is sent with the SYN flag set so that the source address is the same as the destination address, which is the address of the server. The server might then try to connect to itself and crash.
- *Ping of death*—The server receives ICMP packets that include large file attachments, which can cause a server to crash.
- *IP half scan*—If a remote computer attempts to connect to a port by sending a packet with the SYN flag set and the port is not available, the RST flag is set on the return packet. When the remote computer does not respond to the RST flag, the result is an IP half scan. In normal situations, the TCP connection is closed with a packet containing a FIN flag.
- *UDP bomb*—This attack uses an UDP packet with an illegal configuration.
- *Port scan*—You determine the threshold for number of ports that are scanned (checked) before an alert is issued.

Chapter Summary

- Every computer connected to the Internet represents a potential target for attack. The most dangerous threat to your system is someone penetrating your system to gather data. However, attackers do not have to actually enter your system to gather information. An alternative method is to read the data as it travels to and from your servers. Another potential threat involves someone changing existing data or simply preventing others from using your system. Attackers use detailed knowledge of TCP/IP to attack systems. DNS has been prone to attack for years because of the weaknesses in BIND, although BIND 9 represents a significant improvement in terms of security. Operating systems, as the most complex part of your environment, are prone to problems that attackers can exploit. To protect them, keep up to date on software patches. E-mail servers are open by design, and preventing certain types of problems such as mail bombs can be difficult.

- Securing data transmission is critical in many instances. The most common method is to use Secure Sockets Layer (SSL), which sends a certificate and a public key to the client. If the client accepts the certificate, they negotiate an encryption level of 128-bit or 40-bit. The client creates a session key and encrypts it with the server's public key. Once the server gets the session key, it is used for the duration of the connection. Microsoft Certificate Services allows you to manage certificates. You can use Secure Shell (SSH) to provide secure logins. It is very popular on Linux systems as a replacement for Telnet. You can also use SSH to tunnel other protocols. Tunneling allows you to send higher-level protocols, such as POP3, across an encrypted channel.

- When you secure an operating system, the best approach is to configure each computer for a single task such as a Web server or an e-mail server, but not both, for two reasons. First, it is easier to focus on the needs of a single server application. Second, if one of the server applications becomes compromised, both applications will be affected if a multiple-task configuration is used. Avoid running any client programs on a server—not even a browser. Always keep the absolute minimum number of user accounts necessary for the server to function. Because attackers can potentially gain entrance to the system through any services that you run on the server, you should keep these services to a minimum on the server.

- You need to be concerned about the security of running any server applications. Telnet and FTP are the least secure programs. Telnet sends your user name and password in clear text, so you should use SSH instead. FTP requires that all unprivileged ports remain open for data transfer, so FTP should either be located outside the firewall or be used behind a sophisticated firewall that opens and closes ports as needed. Because e-mail spoofing is easy to do, users must be wary. SSL is used not only for Web applications, but also for POP3 and SMTP. On Web servers, programmers can inadvertently open security holes that are hard to find and hard to close. CGI scripts can prove very dangerous, because often the languages associated with CGI have full access to the operating system. Other programming languages used on Web servers, such as Active Server Pages, are designed for Web use and keep the programmer somewhat isolated from the operating system.

- You can use any of several approaches to authenticate Web users. You can use the capabilities of the operating system in Windows and special files in Linux. Often, these methods require that the user name and password be sent to the server in clear text. However, Windows integrated authentication uses an encryption method that can authenticate someone without actually sending the password to the server. Microsoft also offers Passport authentication, which allows users to be centrally authenticated for use by servers throughout the Internet.
- Firewalls implement and control access policies between networks. The goal is to keep attackers out, but let legitimate users in. Typically, this means filtering IP packets between the Internet and your network. Filtering is based on three types of IP packets: ICMP, TCP, and UDP. Packet filtering looks at each packet individually and decides, based on stated rules, whether to accept or reject it. Circuit-level filtering focuses on controlling the computer communication session. With an application-level filter, the firewall understands the application, such as Web access or e-mail, and serves as a termination point for traffic between the internal network and the Internet. A Linux utility called iptables is a good firewall. Microsoft's ISA Server acts as a firewall and more.
- A proxy server delivers content on behalf of a user or a server application. It receives requests for files, then acts on behalf of the requester and gets the file. Once it has the file or files, it sends them to the requester. A proxy server needs to understand the application that it proxies. Apache, for example, can proxy Web applications and FTP. ISA server can proxy those and more, such as e-mail. Two types of proxy servers exist. A forward proxy server isolates internal users from the Internet. Instead of users directly accessing and downloading Web pages, the forward proxy server does it for them. A reverse proxy server isolates servers—not users—from the Internet. Internet users want to contact your Web server or e-mail server but instead are sent to your reverse proxy server. The proxy server then contacts the other servers that remain protected in your internal network.
- Intrusion detection software identifies intrusions but does not prevent them. A popular intrusion detection utility in Linux, Tripwire, has a database of files that it monitors. If a file is deleted or changed, you will be able to find out through a report. ISA Server has intrusion detection capabilities, but only for a few specific methods of intrusion.

Review Questions

1. Tagging refers to ________________.
   a. penetrating a site
   b. putting a message on a Web page to show that a penetration occurred
   c. any action by an attacker
   d. infecting a system with a virus

2. A back door represents a hidden access point to allow for significant control of your system. True or False?
3. Which of the following is *not* a part of the IP header?
   a. source address
   b. destination address
   c. destination port
   d. protocol
4. Which of the following is *not* part of the TCP/IP suite?
   a. ICMP
   b. UDP
   c. SMB
   d. IP
5. Which of the following is *not* part of the TCP header?
   a. source address
   b. destination address
   c. destination port
   d. protocol
6. The SYN flag is associated with ______________.
   a. TCP
   b. IP
   c. ICMP
   d. UDP
7. Which protocol is most closely associated with the ping utility?
   a. TCP
   b. IP
   c. ICMP
   d. UDP
8. A buffer overrun is ______________.
   a. anytime someone attacks your system
   b. when a program accepts more data than it had anticipated
   c. a Web server that has too many pages
   d. only caused by a virus
9. PKI stands for ______________.
10. CA stands for ______________.

11. The type of key sent to the user to begin the SSL connection is a ________________.
    a. private key
    b. surrogate key
    c. primary key
    d. public key
12. Which packets does SSL encrypt?
    a. UDP
    b. TCP
    c. ICMP
    d. all of the above
13. Certificates in Windows can be managed by ________________.
    a. Certify Services
    b. Certificate Services
    c. Root Services
    d. Digital Services
14. Tunneling allows you to ________________.
    a. attack a system without being detected
    b. enter through a back door
    c. send an insecure protocol through a secure connection
    d. hide a port
15. Which command do you use to run the Windows Registry Editor?
    a. `regedt32`
    b. `regedit32`
    c. `regedt`
    d. `registryedit32`
16. Which command do you use to turn off Telnet?
    a. `set telnet off`
    b. `telnet off`
    c. `set telnet stop`
    d. `chkconfig telnet off`
17. SSH is used as a replacement for which of the following services?
    a. HTTP
    b. Telnet
    c. FTP
    d. none of the above

18. To present a fake IP address to gain access or otherwise trick a system is called ________________.
19. If you configure SSL for POP3, what is the default port?
    a. 80
    b. 995
    c. 443
    d. 25
20. If you decide to use SSL for POP3, you cannot use unencrypted POP3 using port 110. True or False?

HANDS-ON PROJECTS

Project 10-1

Install and test SSL in Windows and Apache. In Windows, you will first install Certificate Services, if necessary. In Apache, you will use the default dummy certificate.

To install and test SSL in Windows:

1. Install Certificate Services. (See "To install Certificate Services in Windows" earlier in this chapter for instructions.)
2. Associate SSL with the IIS. (See "To associate a certificate with IIS" and "To require SSL on the Web site" earlier in this chapter for instructions.)
3. Create a Web page called **default.htm** with a message such as "Home Page" and store it in \inetpub\wwwroot.
4. In a browser on the server, type **http://localhost** and then press **Enter**. What happens? What is the response from the server?
5. In a browser, type **https://localhost** and then press **Enter**. What happens?

In Chapter 6 you created a virtual directory called in /var/www/research. Your objective is to make the research directory protected by SSL. At the bottom of the httpd.conf file, an entry should appear that looks like the following:

```
<VirtualHost 192.168.0.150>
ServerName research.technowidgets.com
DocumentRoot /var/www/research
</VirtualHost>
```

Although you could add the necessary configuration information for SSL to this entry, it is much easier to modify the sample configuration information in /etc/httpd/conf.d/ ssl.conf, which is included when Apache starts. First, however, you have to disable the existing entry for the virtual host in httpd.conf.

To make the research directory use SSL in Linux:

1. At the bottom of httpd.conf, comment out the preceding lines of code by inserting a pound sign (#) at the beginning of each line. Save the file in the /etc/httpd/conf/httpd.conf folder.
2. Open /etc/httpd/conf.d/ssl.conf for editing.
3. Change <VirtualHost *default*:443> to **<VirtualHost 192.168.0.150:443>**.
4. Change DocumentRoot "/var/www/html" to **DocumentRoot "/var/www/research"**.
5. Change ServerName new.host.name:443 to **ServerName research.technowidgets.com:443**.
6. Save the file, and then exit.
7. Restart Apache.

To test SSL in Apache:

1. Open Konqueror.
2. For the URL, type **https://research.technowidgets.com** and then press **Enter**. Note that the URL begins with "https" and not "http."
3. The Server Authentication dialog box opens, indicating that the authenticity of the certificate could not be verified. This result is to be expected because it is a sample certificate. Click **Continue** to accept it anyway. If this dialog box does not open, you probably forgot to use the HTTPS protocol instead of the HTTP protocol. In this case, the home page of the server opens.
4. Another Server Authentication dialog box opens, asking, "Would you like to accept this certificate forever without being prompted?" Click **Forever**.

   You will see the research site page you created earlier in the chapter.

Project 10-2

For this project, you need both a Windows computer and a Linux computer. You will use SSH to tunnel from Windows to Apache. You can then connect to the Web server on Apache and use SSH to encrypt the session. You will use port 55555 locally for the client side of the tunnel. The first part of the project requires PuTTY.

To tunnel from Windows to Linux Apache:

1. Use a Web browser to visit *www.chiark.greenend.org.uk/~sgtatham/putty* and download PuTTY to any folder. Double-click **putty.exe** to start PuTTY.
2. At the bottom of the left pane, under SSH, click **Tunnels**. Make sure that the Local option button is selected in the bottom of the right pane.
3. For the source port under "Add new forwarded port," type **55555**.
4. For the destination, type the IP address of your Apache server, followed by a colon (:) and **80**. For example, if the IP address is 192.168.0.100, type **192.168.0.100:80**.

5. Click **Add**. The combination of the local port and the destination address appears, as shown in Figure 10-34.

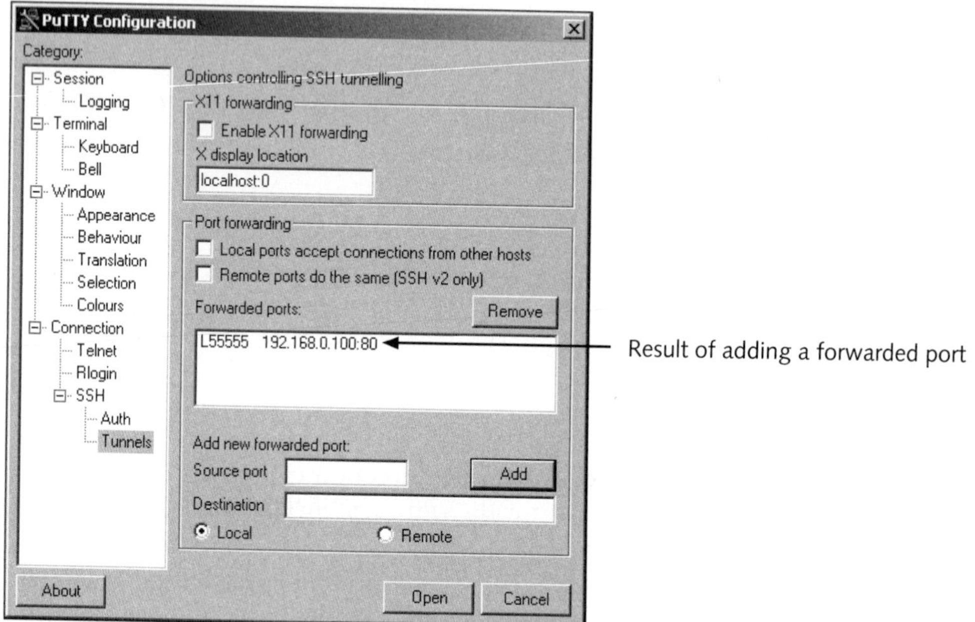

Figure 10-34 PuTTY window after configuring tunnel

6. At the top of the left pane, click **Session**.
7. In the right pane, for host name type the IP address of your Apache server, such as **192.168.0.100**.
8. Click the **SSH** option button.
9. Click **Open** to open a session with the Apache server.
10. The PuTTY Security Alert dialog box opens. Click **Yes** to trust your server.
11. Log on as root.
12. Open your browser. For a URL, type **http://localhost:55555**, and then press Enter. The Apache test page appears.
13. To close the tunnel, open the window for your session, and then type **exit**.

Now you can tunnel from one Linux computer to the Apache server on another server. The following steps assume that the address of the Apache server is 192.168.0.100. If you do not have another Linux computer available, you can use a single computer to tunnel from one port to another. In such a case, on the server use localhost for the IP address. The format for tunneling is -L local_port:remote_host:remote_port.

To tunnel from Linux to Linux Apache:

1. In a terminal window, type **ssh 192.168.0.100 -L 55555:192.168.0.100:80** and then press **Enter**. When asked if you want to continue, type **y**.
2. Type the password for root.
3. Open your browser and type **http://localhost:55555** as the URL. The Apache test page appears.
4. To close the tunnel, open the terminal window for your session, and then type **exit**.

Project 10-3

You can use the Windows Registry to disable the generation of short filenames. This choice makes it more difficult for attackers to guess filenames. You will test the implementation in this project to determine exactly what happens.

To disable the generation of short filenames and test the result in Windows:

1. On the root of drive C:, create a text file called **This is a long file name.txt**.
2. Follow the steps in the chapter to disable the generation of short filenames. See "To disable the generation of short filenames in Windows."
3. Restart the server.
4. On the root of drive C:, create a text file called **Registry changed.txt**.
5. Open a command prompt window, type **dir c:*.txt /X**, and then press **Enter** to display both short and long filenames. What is displayed? Are any items associated with short filenames?

Project 10-4

This project requires both a Windows computer and a Linux computer. You will use an SSH connection to Apache from both Windows and Linux. You will also use secure FTP to transfer files to the Linux server.

To use Windows to upload files securely to Linux:

1. In Windows, at *www.chiark.greenend.org.uk/~sgtatham/putty/download.html*, download **psftp.exe** to any folder. There is no installation program.
2. In Windows, double-click **psftp.exe** to start the secure FTP client. A command-prompt window opens.
3. Type **open**, followed by the IP address of your Linux server. For example, type **open 192.168.0.100**. Then press **Enter**.
4. When psftp displays "Login As:", type **root** and then press **Enter**. If asked whether to trust the host, type **y** and then press **Enter**.
5. When psftp displays "Store key in cache?", type **y** and then press **Enter** so you can connect to the remote host.

6. Type your root password and then press **Enter**. You are at the psftp prompt.
7. Type **pwd** and then press **Enter** to find the remote directory. What is it?
8. Type **binary** and then press **Enter** as you did with the regular FTP client to transfer binary files. What happened? The binary option is not required: psftp.exe transfers both binary and text files without needing special settings.
9. Type **put psftp.exe** and then press **Enter** to upload the file.
10. Type **ls** and then press **Enter** to display files in the remote directory.
11. Type **bye** and then press **Enter** to exit psftp.

If you do not have another Linux computer available, you can use a single computer and localhost for the IP address.

To use Linux to upload named.conf securely to Linux:

1. Open a terminal window, type **sftp 192.168.0.100**, and then press Enter. Type **yes** to trust.
2. Type the password for root.
3. Type **pwd** and then press **Enter** to find the remote directory. What is it?
4. Type **binary** and then press **Enter** as you did with the regular FTP client to transfer binary files. What happened? The binary option is not required: SFTP transfers both binary and text files without needing special settings.
5. Type **lcd /etc** and then press **Enter** to move to a directory that contains the file to transfer.
6. Type **put named.conf** and then press **Enter** to upload the file.
7. Type **ls** and then press **Enter** to display files in the remote directory.
8. Type **bye** and then press **Enter** to exit SFTP.

Project 10-5

In this project, you will secure a directory in both IIS and Apache based on a specific IP address. You will need two computers for this project.

To secure a directory in IIS based on IP address:

1. On the computer that does not have the Web server that you are securing, perform the following task. If the remote computer is a Windows computer, open a command prompt, type **ipconfig**, and then press **Enter** to find your IP address. For Linux, type **ifconfig** and then press **Enter**. Write down the IP address of the computer. This IP address is needed in Step 11.
2. On the Windows computer with IIS, create a folder called **test** in the \inetpub\wwwroot folder.
3. Create a Web page in the test folder called **default.htm** that contains the message **This is a test page**.

4. With the IP address for the remote computer, open Internet Services Manager.
5. Expand the Default Web Site so that you see test in the left pane. This is to the folder you created in Step 2.
6. Right-click **test**, and then click **Properties**.
7. Click the **Directory Security** tab.
8. Under IP address and domain name restrictions, click **Edit**. The IP Address and Domain Name Restrictions dialog box opens.
9. Click the **Denied access** option button to change the default so that no one is allowed to access this directory.
10. Click **Add** to add an exception to the rule.
11. Type the IP address of the remote computer, and then click **OK** until you close the Properties dialog box.
12. From the remote computer, open a browser and type the URL for the server that includes the /test directory. What does it display?
13. On the IIS server, return to the IP Address and Domain Name Restrictions dialog box for the test directory.
14. Select the address that you entered, and then click **Remove**.
15. Click **OK** twice to save the changes and close the Properties dialog box.
16. On the remote computer, close the browser to clear the cache and open it again. Open the browser again and type the URL for the server that includes the /test directory. What is the first line that appears?

To secure a directory in Apache based on IP address:

1. Find the IP address of the remote computer.
2. Create a directory below the root of your Web server (/var/www/html) called **test**.
3. In the directory, create a Web page called **secret.htm** with the message **This is a test page**.
4. Open **httpd.conf** in an editor. On the line following the second occurrence of /Directory, type the following lines. The following code assumes a physical location of /var/www/html/test for the directory and an IP address of 192.168.0.20 for the remote computer.

```
<Directory /var/www/html/test>
      order deny,allow
      deny from all
      allow from 192.168.0.20
</Directory>
```

5. Save and exit the file.
6. Change the file permissions for userfile so Apache can read it. At a terminal prompt type **chmod 744 /etc/userfile** and press **Enter**.

7. Type **apachectl restart** and then press **Enter** to restart your Web server.
8. On the server, open a browser. For the URL, type **http://localhost/test/secret.htm**. What is the first line of the page?
9. On the remote computer, open a browser. For the URL, type **http://192.168.0.100/test/secret.htm**. What is the first line of the page?

Project 10-6

You can use a number of methods to create a more secure IIS, such as changing the permissions on ftproot and mailroot to make them more secure, deleting the vulnerable IIS sample virtual directories, using the Registry to help prevent SYN floods, and deleting some of the more uncommon mappings.

To make IIS more secure:

1. Use xcalcs to secure ftproot and mailroot.
2. *In Windows 2000 only:* Delete the \ISSamples, \IISHelp, and \MSADC virtual directories and the corresponding physical folders.
3. In the Registry, prevent a denial-of-service on IIS based on a SYN flood.
4. Delete the shtm, shtml, and htw mappings in IIS.

Project 10-7

In this project, you will secure IIS and Apache based on user authentication. In both environments, you will create a user called fpessoa with a password of cafebrasileira and secure a directory called campos.

To secure a directory in IIS:

1. In Windows, create a user called **fpessoa** (if you haven't already) with a password of **Azore$3B**. Remember to uncheck the **User must change password at next logon** check box in the New Object – User dialog box.
2. Create a **campos** folder in \inetpub.
3. In the campos folder, create a file called **default.htm** that contains **You made it, Fernando**.
4. In Internet Services Manager, create a virtual directory called **campos** based on the folder you created in Step 2.
5. For the directory security of the campos virtual directory, allow the basic authentication method so you can use a browser other than Internet Explorer.
6. In Windows Explorer, right-click the **campos** folder, and then click **Properties**.
7. Click the **Security** tab, and then click the **Advanced** button.
8. Clear the **Allow inheritable permissions from parent to propagate to this object** check box. The Security dialog box opens. Click **Remove**.

9. Click **Add** to add access to users and groups. The Select User, Computer, or Group dialog box opens.
10. Set the permissions for the fpessoa user, along with the Administrators (Windows 2000) and SYSTEM groups.

    In Windows 2003: Type **fpessoa** in the Enter the object name to select text box and click **OK**. The Permission Entry for campos dialog box opens. Click the **List Folder/Read Data** check box in the **Allow** column, and then click **OK**. You return to the Advanced Security Setting for campos dialog box again. Click **Add**. The Select Users, Computers, or Groups dialog box opens. Type **SYSTEM** in the Enter the object name to select text box and click **OK**. The Multiple Names Found dialog box will open if you installed Exchange 2000. If so, click **OK** to accept the default of **SYSTEM**. The Permission Entry for campos dialog box opens. Click the **Full Control** check box in the **Allow** column, and then click **OK**.

    In Windows 2000: Double-click **fpessoa**, **Administrators**, and **SYSTEM**, and then click OK. You return to the Properties dialog box for the campos folder, which lists Administrators, fpessoa, and SYSTEM in the upper pane. Now you need to select the Administrators and SYSTEM groups and set the permissions. You do not have to set the permissions for fpessoa because the default permissions allow the user to read the contents of the folder. Select **Administrators**, and then click the corresponding check box to allow Administrators Full Control. Select **SYSTEM**, and then click the corresponding check box to allow the system Full Control.
11. Select **Administrators**, and then click the corresponding check box to allow these users Full Control.
12. Select **SYSTEM**, and then click the corresponding check box to allow these users Full Control.
13. Click **OK** to accept the changes.
14. From the remote computer, open a browser. For the URL, type the IP address (be sure to use https) of the Windows server, followed by **/campos**. When prompted for the user name and password, use **fpessoa** to get to the secured page. You do not need to type anything for the domain.

To secure a directory in Apache:

1. Create a directory called **campos** beneath the root of Web server, such as **/var/www/html/campos**.
2. In the campos directory, create a file called **secret.html** and insert the message **You made it, Fernando**.
3. In a terminal window, change to the **/etc** directory. Type **htpasswd -c userfile fpessoa** and then press **Enter**.
4. For the password, type **cafebrasileira**.
5. Open **httpd.conf** in an editor to add the reference to the campos directory.

6. On the line following the second occurrence of /Directory, type the following lines:

```
<Location /campos>
   AuthName "For Fernando Only"
   AuthType Basic
   AuthUserFile /etc/userfile
   require user fpessoa
</Location>
```

7. Restart the Web server.
8. In the browser on the server, type **http://localhost/campos/secret.htm** and then press **Enter**. Notice that the dialog box shows For Fernando Only, just as you typed it for the AuthName.
9. Type the user name of **fpessoa** and the password of **cafebrasileira**. Now you see the Web page with "You made it, Fernando."

Project 10-8

Set up a forward proxy server in Linux. Although you need only a single Linux computer to configure the proxy server, you will need two other computers to test it. Besides the Linux computer for the Apache proxy server, you will need an internal computer that will be configured to use the proxy server to request Web pages. You will also need an external computer, which will serve as the external Web server.

For the proxy server, you will simulate having two NICs by adding a different IP address to the single NIC. This project assumes that all computers share a single network. The internal computer is configured for 192.168.0.20. The Apache proxy server is at 192.168.0.100, and the IP address 10.10.1.100 is added to represent the external network. The IP address for the external computer, which represents a computer on the Internet, needs to be set at 10.10.1.200.

To configure the external computer to use 10.10.1.200 only on a Linux computer:

1. Click the **Red Hat** icon, point to **System Settings**, and then click **Network**.
2. Click **Edit**. The Ethernet Device dialog box opens.
3. Change the IP address to **10.10.1.200**, the subnet mask to **255.0.0.0**, and make the default gateway address blank.
4. Click **OK**, which returns you to the Network Configuration dialog box. Click **Apply** to save the settings, and then click **Close**.
5. Restart the computer.

To configure the external computer to use 10.10.1.200 only on a Windows computer:

1. *In Windows 2003:* In the Control Panel, double-click **Network Connections**, right-click **Local Area Connection**, and then click **Properties**.

   In Windows 2000: On the desktop, right-click **Network Places** and then click **Properties**. Double-click **Local Area Connection**, and then click **Properties**.
2. Select **Internet Protocol (TCP/IP)**, and then click **Properties**.

3. Change the IP address to **10.10.1.200**, the subnet mask to **255.0.0.0**, and make the default gateway blank.
4. Click **OK** twice and close the windows.
5. Restart the computer.

To create a forward proxy server:

1. To add an IP address to the Linux server used as the proxy server, open **/etc/rc.d/rc.local** and change 192.168.0.200 to **10.10.1.100**. Save the file and reboot. In a terminal window, type **ifconfig** and then press **Enter**. You should see the new IP address along with the old ones.
2. Use the steps in the chapter to configure the forward proxy server. (See "To configure Apache to become a forward proxy server in Linux" for details.)
3. On the internal computer, first verify that you cannot reach the external computer by opening the browser and typing the URL of **10.10.1.100**. You cannot reach external computer because the internal computer has an IP address only on the 192.168.0.0 network.
4. On the internal computer, configure the browser to use 192.168.0.100 as the proxy server. Refer to either the steps for "To configure Internet Explorer to use a proxy server in Windows" or "To configure Konqueror to use a proxy server in Linux."
5. On the internal computer, open a browser. For the URL, type **10.10.1.200**. The default page on the external computer opens.

10

Project 10-9

You can use iptables to allow connections to the Web server, secure shell, and FTP. If you did Hands-on Project 10-8, you need to go back into httpd.conf to change "Listen 8080" back to "Listen 80." The following steps assume that the IP address for the server is 192.168.0.100.

To implement iptables in Linux:

1. Create a text file called **firewall**.
2. In the firewall text file, insert the script shown in Figure 10-22. Change the IP address to the IP address of your Linux computer.
3. Add the following information to the file to allow FTP, remembering to replace 192.168.0.100 with your own IP address. Remember that each line must begin with the "iptables" command. Make sure that the commands you type do not wrap as shown below.

```
iptables -A INPUT  -p tcp --sport 1024:65535
   -d 192.168.0.100 --dport 21 -j ACCEPT
iptables -A OUTPUT -p tcp -s 192.168.0.100 --sport 21
   --dport 1024:65535 -j ACCEPT
iptables -A INPUT  -p tcp --sport 1024:65535
   -d 192.168.0.100 --dport 20 -j ACCEPT
```

```
iptables -A OUTPUT -p tcp -s 192.168.0.100 --sport 20
   --dport 1024:65535 -j ACCEPT
iptables -A INPUT  -p tcp --sport 1024:65535
   -d 192.168.0.100 --dport 1024:65535 -j ACCEPT
iptables -A OUTPUT -p tcp -s 192.168.0.100
   --sport 1024:65535 --dport 1024:65535 -j ACCEPT
```

4. Add the ability to connect to secure shell, which is at port 22:

```
iptables -A INPUT  -p tcp -d 192.168.0.100 --dport 22 -j ACCEPT
iptables -A OUTPUT -p tcp -s 192.168.0.100 --sport 22 -j ACCEPT
```

5. From a remote computer, type **ping 192.168.0.100** and then press **Enter**. You should get a response.
6. From the Linux server in the directory where you created the firewall file, type **sh firewall** and then press **Enter**. Now the firewall is running.
7. From a remote computer, type **ping 192.168.0.100** and then press **Enter**. You should *not* get a response. Although ICMP is not available, you should still be able to use the other ports.
8. From a remote computer, open a browser, type **http://192.168.0.100**, and then press **Enter**. You should see the test page.
9. From a remote computer, type **telnet 192.168.0.100** and then press **Enter**. Did you get a response? Why or why not?
10. From a remote Linux computer, type **ssh 192.168.0.100** and then press **Enter**. Did you get a response? Why or why not?
11. From a remote computer, connect using FTP. Did you get a response? Why or why not?

CASE PROJECTS

Case Project 10-1

Design an environment for maximum security. Which software packages will you use? Assume that you have an Apache Web server and Microsoft Exchange 2000. You need to allow users to upload Web pages from the Internet. The e-mail server is very sensitive, so make sure e-mail data is encrypted. Implement as much of the environment as you can.

Case Project 10-2

Research other firewall products. Compare and contrast at least three products. Give details on the features of each, and explain how they could prove useful in a Web environment. The audience for the paper is upper management, so you must explain your needs in basic terms. Select one of the three products as the one your company should purchase.

Case Project 10-3

Visit the Microsoft Web site to download and install all security patches available for IIS. Research the site and implement as many security improvements as possible. Describe each improvement in security that you make. Download and install Urlscan.

Case Project 10-4

Go to the Red Hat and Apache sites to download and install all security patches available for Apache and Linux. If a new version of Apache that improves security, is available, download and install it. Research the sites and implement as many security improvements as possible. Describe each improvement in security that you make.

CHAPTER

11

MONITORING AND ANALYZING THE WEB ENVIRONMENT

In this chapter, you will:

- Monitor operating systems
- Monitor Web servers
- Monitor other Web applications
- Learn about some analysis tools for Web servers

One of the primary tasks of a Web server administrator is to monitor the Web server as it fulfills its tasks. To spot trends over time, you start with a **baseline**, which reflects the status of the system during normal operations and serves as a standard for subsequent comparisons. You need to know which services are running and what types of problems they might experience. In Windows, the Event Viewer logs a variety of information and allows you to see detailed information about the operating system and programs such as Exchange 2000 and DNS. In Linux, syslogd logs information for the operating system and a number of other programs. The log files are typically stored in the /var/log directory.

Besides monitoring the operating system through logs, you can use specialized monitoring tools to analyze performance. In Windows, you can use the Performance Monitor to produce a real-time graph that reflects the performance of the overall system, including details about the hardware. In Linux, a utility called top displays the processes that consume most of the processor's time. You can monitor traffic to and from the Web server and track a variety of information, such as the date and time of the request, the page requested, and technical information related to the request. For both Apache and IIS, you can analyze this information using programs such as WebTrends and 123Loganalyzer, which offer many reports that organize the information in a number of ways. Other server applications in the Web environment such as e-mail, FTP, and DNS have their own logging capabilities to fit the needs of the application and the administrator.

Monitoring Operating Systems

Monitoring operating systems typically involves analyzing **log files**, which contain information recorded by the operating system in response to certain events. For example, you can set criteria to determine when a driver does not load correctly or when the load on the CPU reaches a particular level. Windows provides an integrated GUI for viewing operating system logs, while Linux creates text files that you can open with any text editor.

Primarily, you use logs to detect problems in performance, security, and software that can develop over time. Performance problems can create bottlenecks on your server, and logs help you identify potential problems and resolve current ones. Security logs track information related to issues such as logons, changes to permissions, and access to files. The logs can also indicate which parts of the system started and are running correctly.

When monitoring an operating system, you should first create a baseline near the beginning of the operating system's life cycle when the system is running under a normal load. If you understand the characteristics of the operating system before any changes are made, you can better analyze the effect of changes over time. Save logs at regular intervals so that you can compare them over time and detect server-related trends.

Monitoring Windows

Performance monitoring allows you to compare system performance over time to determine the effects of system changes and increased workload. Figure 11-1 shows the default view of the Performance window, which shows the system monitor in Windows 2003.

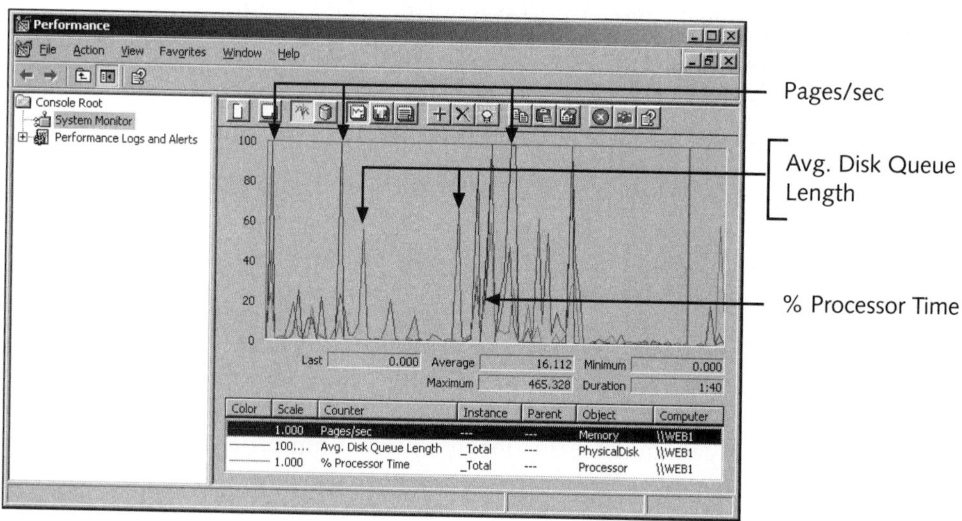

Figure 11-1 Performance window

One line shows the Avg. Disk Queue Length, which gives you a good overall view of disk workload. The disk queue represents data requested to be read from or written to the disk. In general, the longer the queue length, the slower the disk access. Another line shows the % Processor Time, which reflects processor performance. This metric represents how often the processor is used. Measurements should average about 80 percent or lower. The other counter shown in Figure 11-1 is Pages/sec, which tells you how often the operating system does not find data in RAM and must refer to virtual memory on disk. The Pages/sec counter suggests whether you have enough RAM, but can also indicate that you are starting and stopping many applications. The characteristics of the item selected in the bottom panel are displayed under the graph. For example, Figure 11-1 shows that Windows 2003 referenced an average of 16.112 pages/second and a maximum of 465.328 pages/second. Hundreds of counters are available, depending on which programs are installed on the system. If you install all the programs referenced in this book, nearly 100 groups of counters would be available. For example, 14 groups of counters would be for Windows 2003, one group for Active Server Pages, one for FTP, and 19 for Exchange 2000. The FTP Service group contains counters for Bytes Received/sec, Current Connections, and many others. You add counters to the Performance window by using the Add Counters dialog box shown in Figure 11-2.

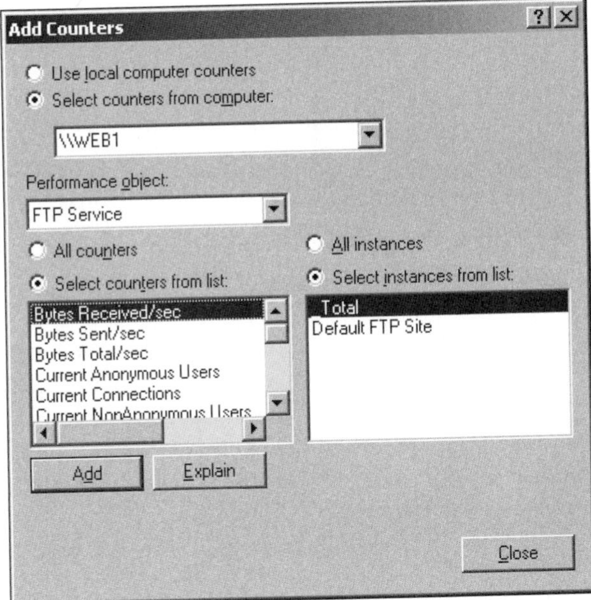

Figure 11-2 Counters for the FTP service

In addition to using the Performance Monitor, you can quickly view system performance using the Windows Task Manager, which you can open by first right-clicking the taskbar and then clicking Task Manager. The Task Manager window includes a number of tabs, including a Performance tab that shows CPU usage and page file usage. See

Figure 11-3. The Processes tab highlights the percentage of CPU time spent on each process and details memory usage of the services and applications that are running. To check the network usage of each NIC, you access the Networking tab; to see which users are connected, you review the Users tab. You can also disconnect users or send a message to a user from the latter tab.

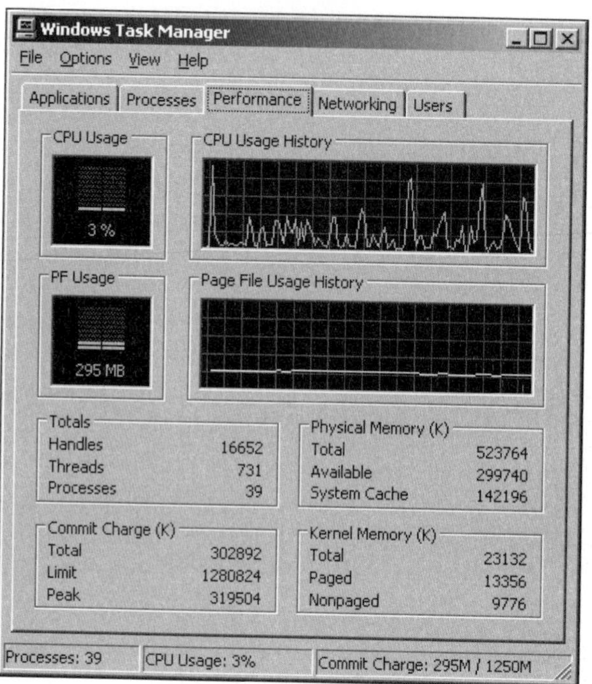

Figure 11-3 Windows Task Manager

Chapters 6 and 10 discussed the services needed to maintain a Web server and identified those that are not needed. The number of services that a Web server uses increases significantly as you add server programs. To track the changes in services, you should document the services with which you begin, and then revise this documentation when you add or delete software. You can use the Services window to provide this information. You can open the Services window in Windows 2003 by clicking Start, pointing to Administrative Tools, and then clicking Services. In Windows 2000, you open the Control Panel, double-click Administrative Tools, and then double-click Services. Figure 11-4 shows the Standard tab of the Services window, where you can set the status and startup type of each service. In Windows 2003, the Extended tab allows you to select a service and get detailed information about what it does.

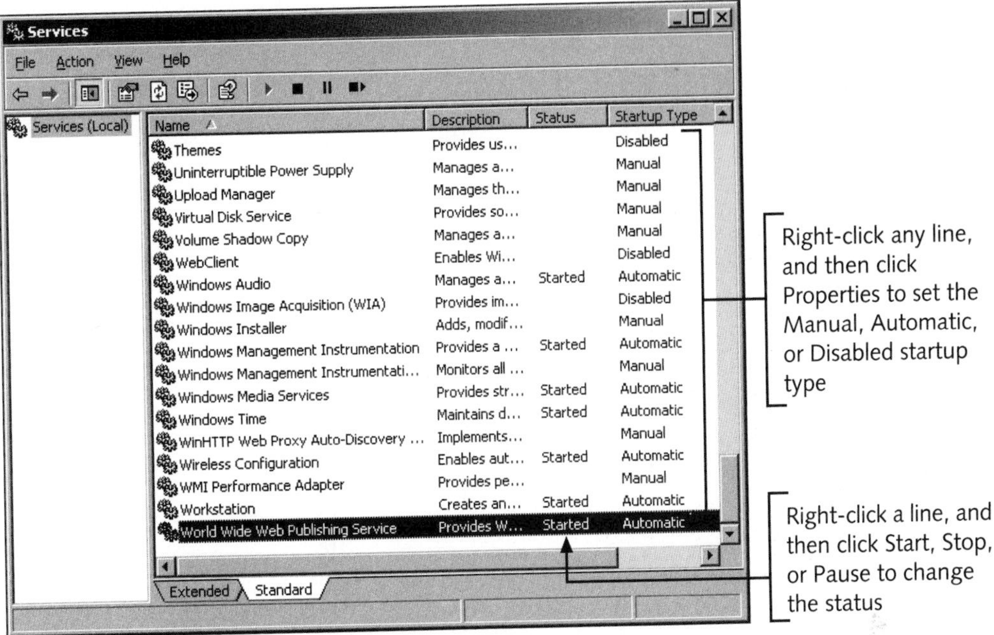

Figure 11-4 Services window in Windows 2003

Services have three statuses: Start, Stop, and Pause. You use the Pause status to prevent others from using the service while allowing the service to continue to run. Not all services support the Pause option.

Some services depend on other services for part of their functionality. With such an arrangement, if one service fails, then one or more other services might also fail. A service can fail for many reasons. For example, a file that the service needs could be changed or deleted, a virus or another type of attack could interrupt the service, or the service could be configured incorrectly. The dependencies can point you to the service that caused the other services to fail. You can monitor these dependencies by viewing the Dependencies tab of the Properties dialog box for any service. Figure 11-5 shows the dependencies for the Windows Management Instrumentation service, which provides an interface for Windows programs to access operating system information.

Notice that this service depends on the Event Log and the Remote Procedure Call (RPC) services. If either service stops, then the Windows Management Instrumentation service will also stop. The Microsoft Exchange Management system component depends on this service as well, so if the Windows Management Instrumentation service stops, Microsoft Exchange Management will also stop. Tracing these dependencies can be useful—for example, if Exchange stops on your Web server, you can see whether Windows Management Instrumentation has stopped before you begin troubleshooting problems with Exchange.

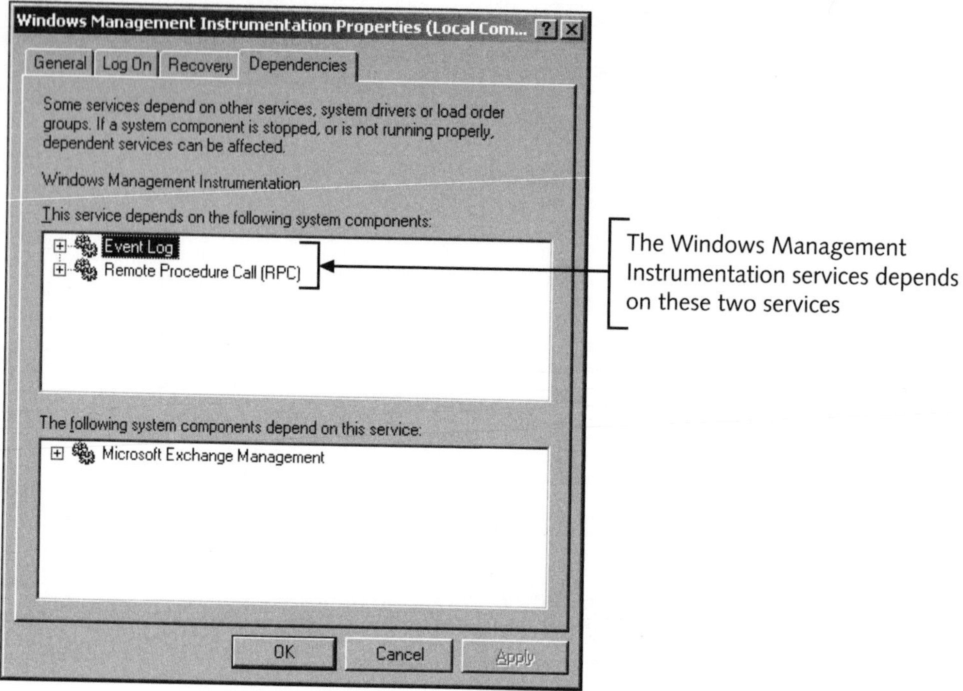

Figure 11-5 Dependencies tab of the Windows Management Instrumentation Properties dialog box

If you want to be notified when a service fails, use the Recovery tab of the Properties dialog box for the particular service. If you want to restart the computer after a failure, you can send a message to computers on the network by using the Restart Computer Options button, as specified in the following steps. However, restarting the computer is an extreme measure. Normally, you restart only the service, which is generally the default option. The Event Viewer shows services that are restarted.

In the following steps, you set Windows to send a message before it restarts a service, which it does only if the service fails three times in a session.

To send a message that a Windows service has failed and the computer is restarting:

1. In Administrative Tools, click **Services**.
2. Scroll down and then double-click **World Wide Web Publishing Service** in the right pane. The World Wide Web Publishing Service Properties dialog box opens.
3. Click the **Recovery** tab.
4. Click the **Subsequent failures** list arrow and then click **Restart the Computer**. (This is called **Reboot the Computer** in Windows 2000.) The Restart Computer Options button is now enabled. See Figure 11-6.

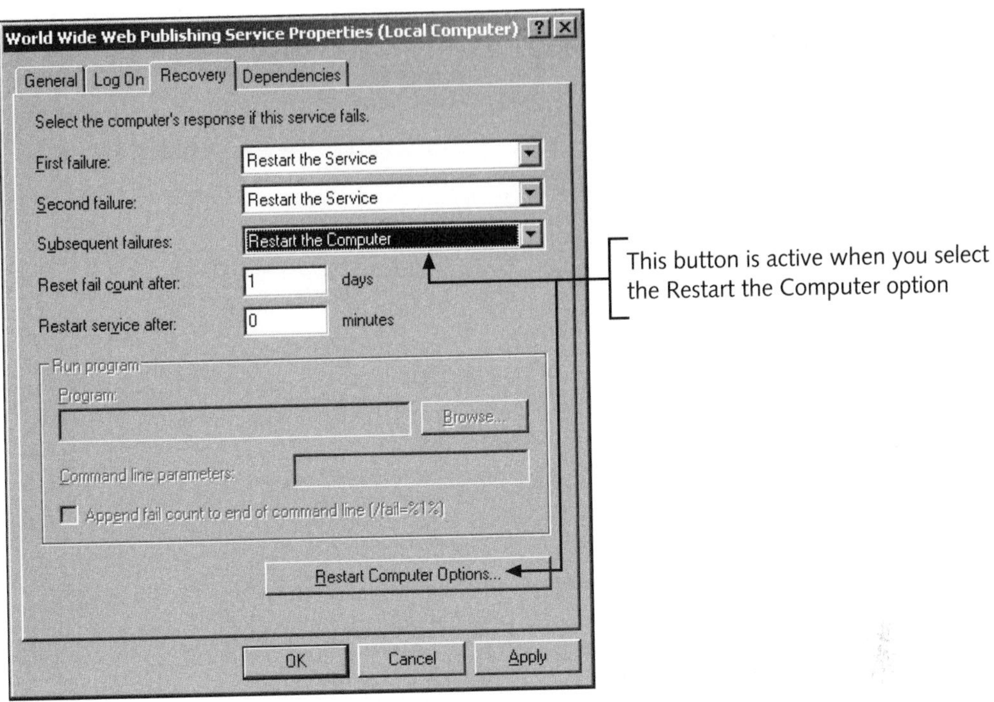

Figure 11-6 Recovery tab of the World Wide Web Publishing Service Properties dialog box

5. Click **Restart Computer Options**. The Restart Computer Options dialog box opens.
6. Accept 1 as the number of minutes to wait before the computer restarts. Click the **Before restart, send this message to computers on the network** check box, and then accept the default message or type **A failed service will force the computer to restart in one minute**.
7. Click **OK** twice to accept the changes and close the window.

Other ways to monitor the server are included in the Computer Management MMC (Microsoft Management Console), which is one of the Administrative tools shown in Figure 11-7. You use the Systems Tools option in the left pane to monitor server performance, alerts, and events such as system startup and shutdown and users connecting to the server and accessing shares.

The Event Viewer shown in the left pane contains six logs that you can monitor. Because the Event Viewer is a common utility, it is also listed in the Administrative Tools window. As shown in Figure 11-8, system events include messages from the operating system. Security events include selected items related to permissions. Any application that wants to track information can use an application event to do so. For example, if you install Exchange 2000, Oracle DBMS, or many other applications, they use application events to record the statuses of various portions of their applications.

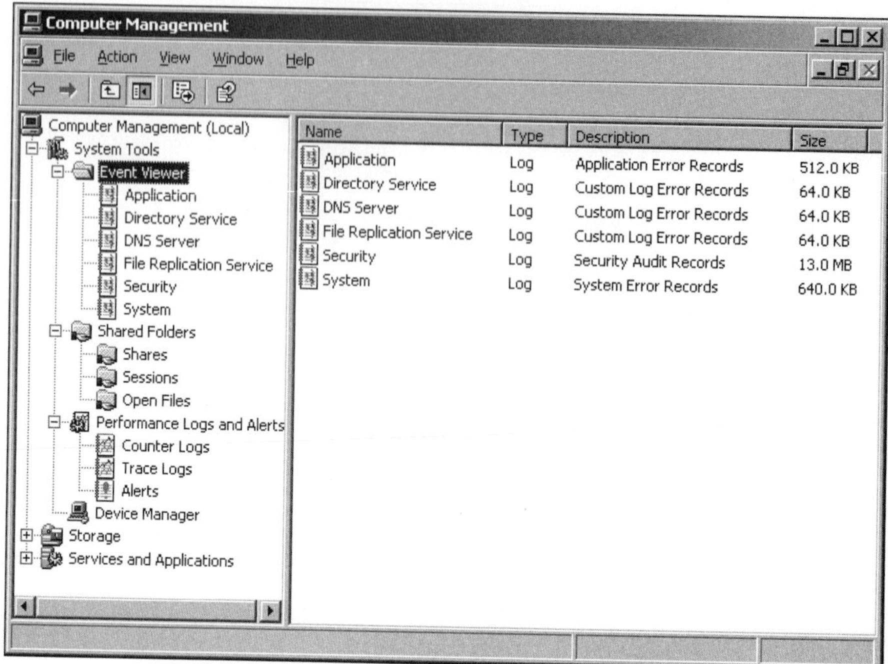

Figure 11-7 Computer Management window

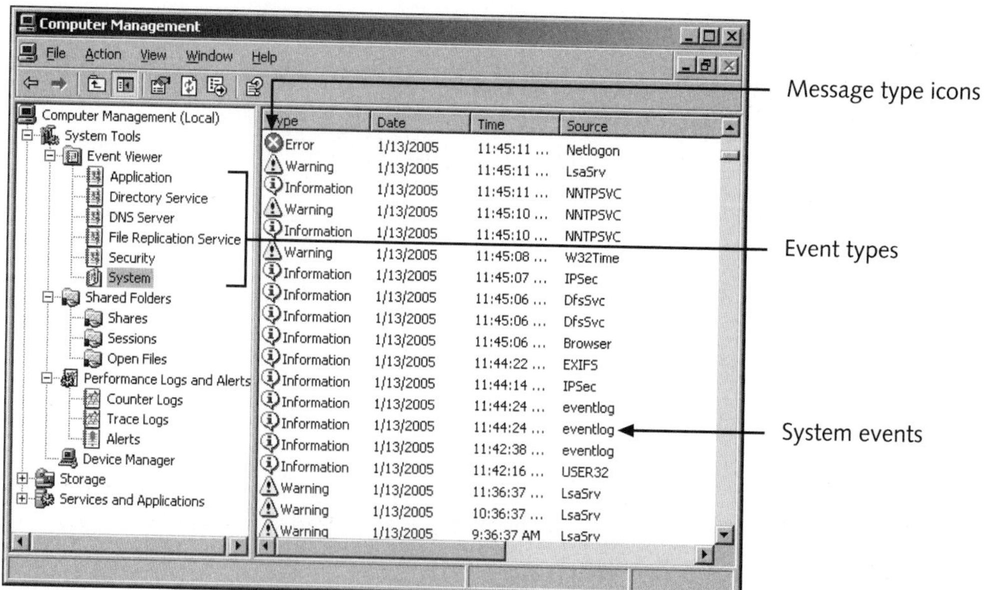

Figure 11-8 Event Viewer

System and application events display three levels of messages: Information, Warning, and Error. Each level has its own icon. The Information messages notify you of important system occurrences such as the Web server, SMTP server, or News server starting. The Warning messages do not necessarily indicate major system problems, but help you to determine whether parts of the system are malfunctioning. For example, Figure 11-9 shows a warning that a virtual root for the News server could not be found, meaning that no newsgroups are available. Error messages are reserved for the most severe problems, such as the server stopping unexpectedly or the Exchange server not starting.

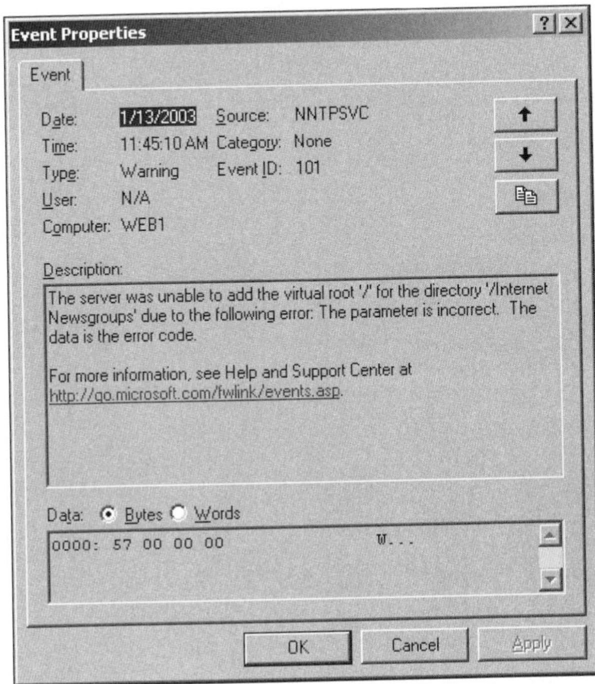

Figure 11-9 Event Properties dialog box for a warning

To observe specific events, you can filter the events that you want to track by using the Filter tab of the System Properties dialog box. Table 11-1 shows the various ways that you can filter events.

Table 11-1 Event filtering

Filter option	Description
Event Type	Track events by message type such as Information, Warning, or Error. Security event types also include Success Audit and Failure Audit.
Event Source	Identify the specific component that caused the message, such as a disk controller or SMTP service.

Table 11-1 Event filtering (continued)

Filter option	Description
Category	Because an event source could be very broad, restrict it according to category, such as Devices, Disk, Network, Printers, Services, Shell, and System Event.
Event ID	Track events by ID, which is a code that describes a specific event. For example, if you receive an error with an event ID of 6008 (unexpected system shutdown), track events by ID to determine whether the system has unexpectedly shut down at other times.
User	Track events by specific users. Although often no user is associated with events, some services such as Exchange and SQL Server use specific users instead of the System account.
Computer	Monitor a specific computer when the MMC is monitoring multiple computers.
From/To	Set either a range or a specific time for the event.

To display all events related to SMTP in Windows:

1. In Administrative Tools, click **Computer Management**.
2. Expand the Event Viewer folder in the left pane, and then click **System** as shown earlier in Figure 11-8.
3. Click **View** on the menu bar, and then click **Filter**. The Filter tab of the System Properties dialog box opens. See Figure 11-10.

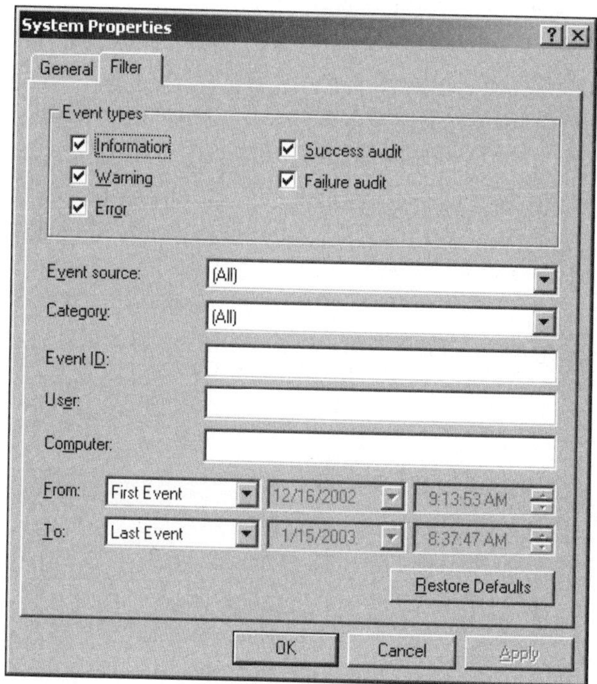

Figure 11-10 Filter tab of the System Properties dialog box

4. Click the **Event source** list arrow, and then click **SMTPSVC**, which is the SMTP service.
5. Click **OK**. The messages related to SMTP are displayed in the right pane of the Computer Management window.

Windows saves event information in logs, which can fill up over time. You can periodically clear the logs or overwrite them as they fill up. Before you clear the logs, be sure to back them up to keep historical records of events. If necessary, you can later retrieve the old logs to review them. In Windows 2003, the default size of the System and Application log files is 16 MB each, and both are overwritten by default when the log files fill. In Windows 2000, the log files are set to a maximum of 512 KB, and events older than seven days in the log files are overwritten. Although these settings are appropriate in most cases, you can modify them if desired by right-clicking a log and then clicking Properties.

To save the Windows System log and clear it:

1. In the Computer Management window, right-click **System**, and then click **Clear all Events** on the shortcut menu. The Event Viewer dialog box opens and asks whether you want to save the System log before clearing it.
2. Click **Yes**. The Save dialog box opens. Navigate to the root of the drive, click the **Create New Folder** button, and then name the new folder **Event Logs**.
3. Double-click the **Event Logs** folder.
4. Type the name of the event log as system followed by the date in yyyymmdd form, as in **system20040721**. Then click **Save** to save the System log file. Close the Computer Management window.

Expand Shared Folders in the left pane of the Computer Management window to monitor shares, sessions, and open files. When you click the Shares folder, a list of shares appears in the right pane, as shown in Figure 11-11. As discussed in Chapter 10, you should use only the minimum number of shares on a Web server. To find out which users are using your shares and how many files they have opened, click the Sessions folder in the left pane of the Computer Management window. You can right-click a user name to disconnect that user. However, if you disconnect the user, any files that the user has open may not close correctly, causing data corruption. The same is true if you select the Open Files folder in the left pane of the Computer Management window and decide to close one or more files.

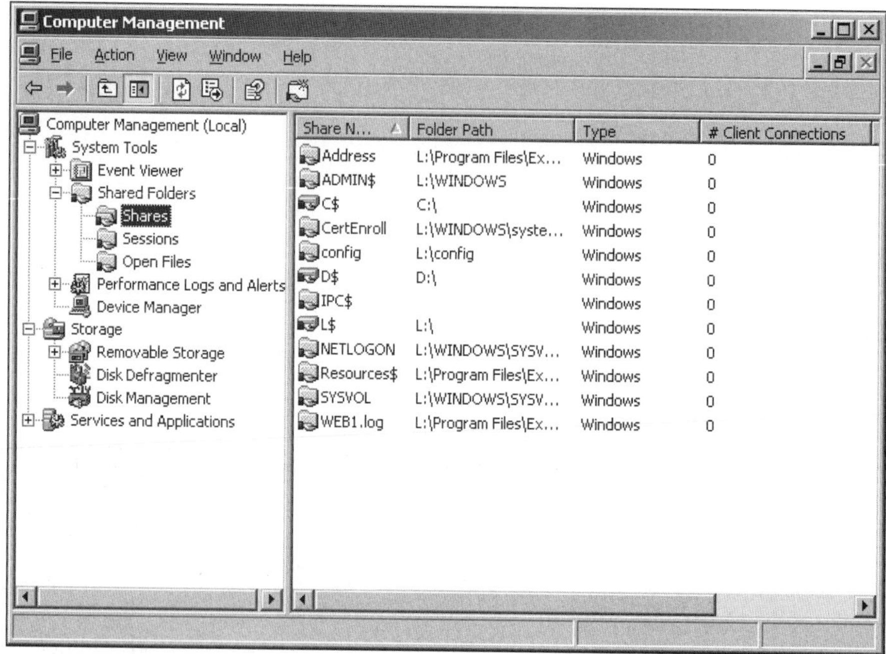

Figure 11-11 Displaying a list of shares

Monitoring Linux

In Linux, logging is controlled by the syslogd daemon, which coordinates operating system messages and some server applications such as e-mail and news. Miscellaneous subsystems use the logging capabilities of syslogd through generic facilities named local0 through local7. **Facilities** represent daemons that use syslogd. Table 11-2 lists the syslogd facilities. Note that Apache uses local7 for logging.

Table 11-2 Common syslogd facilities

Facility	Description
authpriv	User authorization
cron	Messages from the cron system, which is used to execute scheduled commands
daemon	Miscellaneous daemon messages
kern	Kernel (core operating system) messages
local0–local7	For system use; for example, local7 has boot messages and, by default, Apache messages
lpr	Printer messages
mail	E-mail server messages

Table 11-2 Common syslogd facilities (continued)

Facility	Description
news	Network news server messages
syslog	Messages from the syslog system
user	Miscellaneous user-level messages

You control the types of messages for each facility by setting priorities. Eight levels of priorities are possible, as described in Table 11-3. Because some facilities can generate many messages if they are assigned a low priority, be sure to set the priorities at an appropriate level.

Table 11-3 Syslogd priorities

Priority	Description
emerg	Emergency messages indicating that the system is about to stop.
alert	Alert messages, which require immediate action.
crit	Critical messages indicating that a subsystem, such as the News server, has stopped or will not start.
err	General error messages that often report parts of a subsystem are not functioning correctly.
warning	Warning messages that typically reflect portions of applications that are not configured correctly.
notice	Notifications that are not errors but are otherwise important.
info	Messages that provide general information.
debug	Debug messages that often show steps an application completes, which can generate enough information to affect performance. Avoid this priority unless you are working under the supervision of someone who is trying to understand the inner workings of an application.

11

When you installed Linux, a reasonable set of priorities was configured in /etc/syslog.conf. Figure 11-12 lists most of the information in syslog.conf. Note that because Apache uses local7, you can find Apache log files in /var/log/boot.log.

```
*.info;mail.none;authpriv.none;cron.none     /var/log/messages
authpriv.*                                   /var/log/secure
mail.*                                       /var/log/maillog
cron.*                                       /var/log/cron
*.emerg                                      *
uucp,news.crit                               /var/log/spooler
local7.*                                     /var/log/boot.log
```

Figure 11-12 /etc/syslog.conf

In Figure 11-12, the asterisk dot (*.) means all facilities, and the dot asterisk (.*) means all priority levels. Thus, the first line means that all facilities from the level of info and higher will be sent to the /var/log/messages file. The exceptions to that rule are for mail, authpriv, and cron. On the second, third, and fourth lines, all messages for authpriv, mail, and cron are sent to the associated files listed on the right. Any emergency messages are sent to every user logged on to the server.

You can modify syslog.conf depending on your needs. Other symbols besides the asterisk (*) refer to groups of facilities or priorities. The equals sign (=) refers to a specific priority, and the exclamation point (!) excludes the specified priority and any higher level. As an example, assume that instead of sending all mail messages to a single file, you want to split the messages into two files—one for messages from the error level to emergency level and another for the lower priorities except for debug messages. In syslog.conf, you could replace the existing line that logs mail messages with the following commands:

```
mail.err    /var/log/mailerrors
mail.info;mail.!err     /var/log/mailinfo
```

For more information on configuring syslog.conf, see the following man pages:
man syslogd
man syslog.conf

You should regularly check the /var/log directory for log files. Once you read them, you should either archive or delete the files. Log files can grow rapidly on an active system, which can ultimately cause the operating system to stop when they fill the hard disk. The primary file to check is the current messages file. Older messages files are named messages.1, messages.2, and so on. In /var/log, Linux also creates log files for facilities that you have not configured. For example, although you may have not used cron to execute commands on a regular basis, the system has used it and stores logged entries for cron in /var/log.

Not all log files in /var/log are controlled by syslogd. The rpmpkgs file logs the installed applications. The ksyms file maintains detailed system information that system support personnel might need. The lastlog file keeps track of all users and notes when they last logged on. To see that information, type `lastlog` in a terminal window.

Monitoring Web Server Applications and Their Usage

When you monitor Web servers and other server applications, you typically want to monitor two categories of information: one relating to how the Web server functions, and one relating to how people use your system. Information about the Web server indicates whether it is functioning correctly or performing operations incorrectly, such as maintaining a link to a nonexistent page. Information about how people use the Web server includes which pages they access, when they access them, and other related data.

Monitoring IIS

You can use a variety of tools to monitor IIS, including some of the same tools that you use to monitor Windows. The Performance Monitor has specific counters for IIS, and the System event viewer provides information specific to the Web service. That is, the System event viewer indicates whether IIS started and, if it did not start, why it did not start. The IIS logs information about users who access your site, such as the IP address used and the pages viewed. You can turn the IIS logs into informative reports using third-party software such as WebTrends.

The Performance Monitor offers more than 60 counters for IIS and more than 30 counters specifically related to Active Server Pages. Table 11-4 lists some of these counters. The first counter in Table 11-4 helps you monitor your cache. Track this number to make sure it stays high (above 60 percent), because most requests should be supplied by the cache instead of the disk. Also monitor the bandwidth, especially if you are limiting it to reserve bandwidth for another application such as e-mail. Other important counters include one that tracks data that is actually sent and another that tracks the number of users being serviced. The data can be tracked in terms of the number of bytes or the number of files.

Table 11-4 IIS counters

Counter	Description
Cache Hits %	The percentage of requests that are found in the cache without having to search the disk
Total Blocked Async I/O Requests	The number of requests that could not be serviced because of bandwidth throttling
Anonymous Users/sec	The number of anonymous users who are connecting to the Web server, per second
Bytes Total/sec	The total number of bytes sent and bytes received per second
Current Nonanonymous Users	The number of users who, because of security restrictions, log on to the server to get pages
Files Sent/sec	The number of files sent from the Web server per second
Not Found Errors/sec	The number of requests that could not be fulfilled because the page was not found, per second
Total Not Found Errors	The total number of pages not found since the Web server was started
Errors/sec	The number of ASP errors per second
Requests Queued	The number of ASP requests that are waiting to be processed

IIS has extensive logging capabilities to determine not only what users are doing on the system but what the server is doing. To enable or disable logging, you use the Properties dialog box of the Web server. Figure 11-13 shows the Properties dialog box for the default Web server. Notice that the default log format is W3C Extended Log File Format. This format is supported by a number of third-party applications that analyze logs. The default items logged are the date, time, client IP address, method, **URI stem**,

URI query, server port, user name, server IP address, user agent, and protocol status. The URI stem represents the page requested. The optional URI query represents any information being passed to the page for processing.

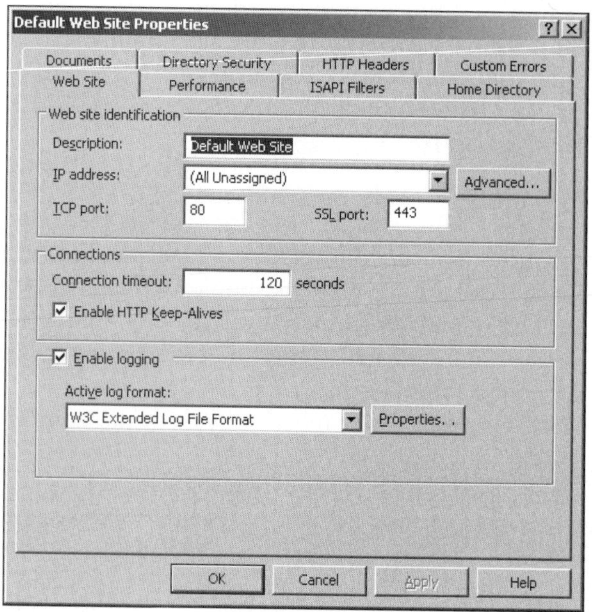

Figure 11-13 Default Web Site Properties dialog box

By default, logging is turned on. Logging is good if you plan to use the information to track users. It can affect performance, however, and can slowly fill a drive. This consideration is especially important if you do not have much free space on your system and your site becomes popular. If you decide that you will not use the logs, you should turn off logging and delete the existing logs. You can always turn on logging at a later date to monitor traffic over a specific amount of time. To turn off logging, you would clear the Enable logging check box in Figure 11-13.

Figure 11-14 shows a sample listing from a log file, with one exception. The actual user agent was Mozilla/4.0+ (compatible;+MSIE+6.0;+Windows+NT+5.0;+.NET+CLR+1.0.3705), which was shortened to Mozilla/4.0+ to improve readability. In this log file, cbranco has logged on to view the default page of /prod. In Windows 2003, the logs are found in the \WINDOWS\system32\LogFiles\W3SVC1 folder. In Windows 2000, the logs are in the \WINNT\system32\LogFiles\W3SVC1 folder. If more virtual Web sites exist, the associated log files would be stored in W3SVC2, and so on.

```
#Software: Microsoft Internet Information Services 6.0
#Version: 1.0
#Date: 2005-09-09 21:27:52
#Fields: date time s-ip cs-method cs-uri-stem cs-uri-query s-port cs-username
   c-ip cs(User-Agent) sc-status
2005-09-09 21:27:52 192.168.0.100 OPTIONS / - 80 - 192.168.0.100 Microsoft-
   WebDAV-MiniRedir/5.1.3590 200
2005-09-09 21:27:52 192.168.0.100 PROPFIND /sysvol - 80 - 192.168.0.100
   Microsoft-WebDAV-MiniRedir/5.1.3590 501
2005-09-09 22:27:10 10.5.3.4 GET /prod - 80 TECHWID\cbranco 10.8.3.88
   Mozilla/4.0+ 301
2005-09-09 22:27:10 10.5.3.4 GET /prod/ - 80 TECHWID\cbranco 10.8.3.88
   Mozilla/4.0+ 403
2005-09-09 22:27:33 10.5.3.4 GET /prod/default.asp - 80 - 10.8.3.88
   Mozilla/4.0+ 401
2005-09-09 22:27:39 10.5.3.4 GET /prod/default.asp id=435 80 - 10.8.3.88
   Mozilla/4.0+ 401
2005-09-09 22:27:39 10.5.3.4 GET /prod - 80 TECHWID\cbranco 10.8.3.88
   Mozilla/4.0+ 301
2005-09-09 22:27:39 10.5.3.4 GET /prod/ - 80 TECHWID\cbranco 10.8.3.88
   Mozilla/4.0+ 403
2005-09-09 22:28:06 10.5.3.4 GET /prod - 80 - 10.8.3.88 Mozilla/4.0+ 401
2005-09-09 22:28:15 10.5.3.4 GET /prod - 80 - 10.8.3.88 Mozilla/4.0+ 401
```

Figure 11-14 Sample IIS log file using the W3C Extended Log File Format

You can alter the information logged by this format. The other items you can log are service name, server name, Win32 status, bytes sent, bytes received, time taken, protocol version, host, cookie, and referrer.

To alter the items logged using the W3C Extended Log File Format:

1. *In Windows 2003:* Open the Internet Information Services (IIS) Manager.

   In Windows 2000: Open Internet Services Manager.
2. Expand the left pane until the Default Web Site appears. Right-click the **Default Web Site**, and then click **Properties** on the shortcut menu. The Properties dialog box for the Web site opens.
3. On the Web Site tab, make sure that the active log format is W3C Extended Log File Format, and then click the **Properties** button. The Logging Properties dialog box opens, as shown in Figure 11-15. (This is called Extended Logging Properties in Windows 2000.) The default dialog box describes the log time period and the location of the log file.

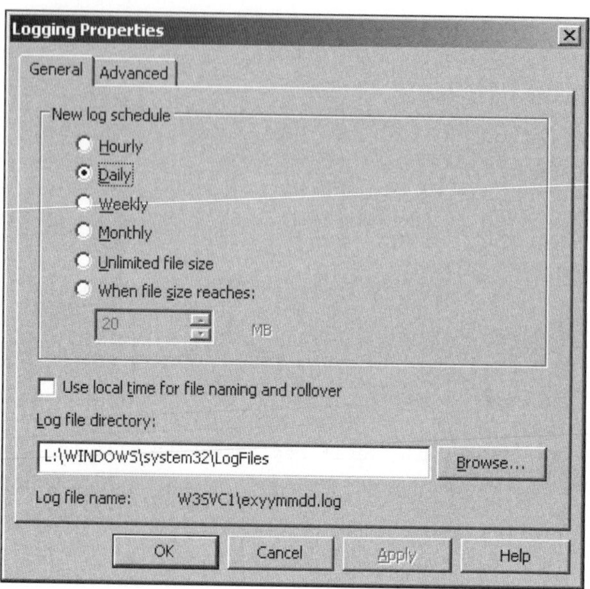

Figure 11-15 Logging Properties dialog box

4. Click the **Advanced** tab (**Extended Properties** tab in Windows 2000) to see which properties you can change. See Figure 11-16. Notice that the items that are logged by default are already enabled.

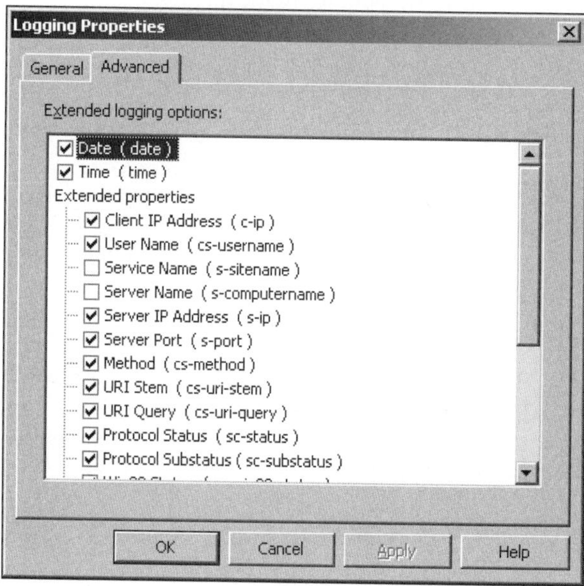

Figure 11-16 Advanced tab of the Logging Properties dialog box

5. Now you could select and deselect properties that you want to log. Often these choices are specified by third-party software. Once you have selected the items you want to log, click **OK** twice to save and exit the property changes. From this point on, the logs will reflect the new settings. Close the IIS window.

You can find more information about the W3C Extended Log File Format at *www.w3.org/TR/WD-logfile.html*.

The Active log format list box in the Properties dialog box for a Web server (shown earlier in Figure 11-13) allows you to change the format of the log file. One of the choices is the NCSA Common Log File Format, an older format that you cannot modify by selecting particular items to log. It stores the remote host name, user name, data time, request type, HTTP status code, and number of bytes sent by the server. Many analysis tools use this format. The following statement is a line from a log in the NCSA Common Log File Format. A user from IP address 10.2.3.5 who accessed a file in the root of the Web server called hello.htm would be logged as follows:

```
10.2.5.3 - - [24/Sep/2002:11:51:44 -0700] "GET /hello.htm HTTP/1.1" 200 294
```

The Microsoft IIS Log Format is similar to the NCSA Common Log File Format except that it logs more information, including the user IP address, user name, request date and time, service, server name, server IP address, time taken, bytes sent, bytes received, service status code (such as 200, which means okay), Windows status code, request type, target of request, and parameters that are passed to a script. Following is an example of the previous request using the Microsoft IIS Log Format:

```
10.2.5.3, -, 9/24/2002, 11:59:10, W3SVC1, WEB1, 10.5.3.4, 200, 308, 294, 200,
0, GET,
/hello.htm, -,
```

Instead of logging the information to a text file, you can log it to a database via ODBC logging. The information stored is the same as that under the Microsoft IIS Log Format. By storing the information in a database, you can more easily extract it and produce reports, although you do increase overhead because more resources are needed to write information to a database.

You can find the SQL Server script needed to create a table called inetlog for ODBC logging at *windows**system32**inetsrv**logtemp.sql* in Windows 2003 or *winnt**system32**inetsrv**logtemp.sql* in Windows 2000.

Monitoring Apache Web Server

The Apache Web server splits its logs between the system logs controlled by syslogd and the transfer log, which stores information about page transfers in and out of the server.

As stated previously, by default, Apache sends all messages to local7 of syslogd, and it stores the results in /var/log/boot.log. Once Apache starts, the following line in the Apache configuration determines the location of the error log:

```
ErrorLog logs/error_log
```

The reference to logs represents the log directory for Apache, which is /var/log/httpd. Apache determines the types of errors logged through the `LogLevel` directive. A few lines below the `ErrorLog` directive, the following statement appears:

```
LogLevel warn
```

This line means that all messages at the warn level and higher will be written to the error_log file. As shown earlier in Table 11-3, the warn level is the first level that logs problems, which is appropriate for a log file. If you used a `LogLevel notice` setting, the log files would fill up with relatively unimportant information. If you used a `LogLevel err` setting, you could miss important configuration problems.

You can create a different error log for each virtual host that you have. Each log uses the same format. For example, in Chapter 7 you created a virtual host called *research.technowidgets.com* by modifying httpd.conf. You could create an error log for *research.technowidgets.com* by adding the following line shown in bold:

```
<VirtualHost 192.168.0.150>
ServerName research.technowidgets.com
DocumentRoot /var/www/research
ErrorLog logs/research-error_log
</VirtualHost>
```

Any errors for the virtual host would then be logged in the research-error_log file. The error log for each virtual host would have a different filename. The type of information in these logs would roughly correspond to the IIS-related information found in System log in Windows. The following is an alternative way of writing that same directive:

```
ErrorLog /var/log/httpd/research-error_log
```

Transfer logs tell you about the use of your Web site. These logs correspond to the IIS logs that you configured in Figures 11-11 to 11-14. By default, the transfer log based on the combined log format is enabled. You enable such logs by removing the comment from one of the lines that begin with `CustomLog` in httpd.conf, such as `CustomLog logs/access_log combined`, as shown in Figure 11-17. If you wanted to use the common log format, you would add a pound sign (#) at the beginning of the `CustomLog logs/access_log combined` line, and then delete the # at the beginning of the `CustomLog logs/access_log common` line. You would restart the Apache Web server to have it recognize the change.

```
LogFormat "%h %l %u %t \"%r\" %>s %b \"%{Referer}i\" \"%{User-Agent}i\"" combined
LogFormat "%h %l %u %t \"%r\" %>s %b" common
LogFormat "%{Referer}i -> %U" referer
LogFormat "%{User-agent}i" agent

#
# The location and format of the access log file (Common Logfile Format).
# If you do not define any access log files within a <VirtualHost>
# container, they will be logged here. Otherwise, if you *do*
# define per-<VirtualHost> access log files, transactions will be
# logged therein and *not* in this file.
#
#CustomLog logs/access_log common
CustomLog logs/access_log combined
#
# If you would like to have agent and referer log files, uncomment the
# following directives.
#
#CustomLog logs/referer_log referer
#CustomLog logs/agent_log agent
```

Figure 11-17 Portion of httpd.conf that defines transfer logs

The format for the transfer log is based on a custom log format. Fortunately, Apache has configured a number of sample formats from which you can choose. First, you have to understand the symbols available in the LogFormat directive, which are listed in Table 11-5.

Table 11-5 LogFormat symbols

Symbol	Description
`%a`	IP address of client.
`%A`	IP address of server.
`%b`	Number of bytes in page sent.
`%{x}e`	Where `x` is an environment variable recognized by the server.
`%f`	The complete file path for the page.
`%h`	Client host name or, if it is not available, the IP address. The host name is enabled by using the `HostNameLookups` directive, which is not enabled by default.
`%{x}i`	Where `x` is a header such as User-Agent, which represents the browser used to request the page.
`%l`	Displays the identity of the client if the directive `IdentityCheck` is on and the client is set up to respond. Not common on the Internet.
`${x}n`	For internal Apache notes based on modules. For example, if a cookie is used by mod_usertrack, the value can be logged by `${cookie}n`.
`%{x}o`	Where `x` is the output header from the server, such as Last-Modified. For example, `%{Last-Modified}o` would list the date that the Web page was last modified.

Table 11-5 LogFormat symbols (continued)

Symbol	Description
`%p`	The TCP port on the server that received the request. It is useful for picking out normal requests to port 80 as opposed to SSL requests to port 443.
`%P`	The process ID that processed the request.
`%r`	The first line of the request, which is typically a GET or POST, such as `GET /test.htm HTTP/1.1`
`%s`	Status of the request. For example, 200 means okay. If the request involves redirection, this represents the status before the redirection.
`%S`	Status of the request. If the request involves redirection, this represents the status after the redirection.
`%t`	The date and time, such as `[25/Sep/2005:10:16:52 -0400]`.
`%{x}t`	Where `x` is the format for time. For example, `%{y/m/d X}t` would produce [02/09/25 10:16].
`%T`	The number of seconds needed to process the request.
`%u`	The user name when you have implemented user authorization.
`%U`	The URL.
`%v`	The server name as provided by the `ServerName` directive. Useful if you have implemented virtual servers.
`%V`	The server name as provided by the `UseCanonicalName` directive. When the server detects a self-referencing URL, it will use the original client's host name if the directive is off, or it will use the value of the ServerName if it is on. In Apache 1.3, it is set to on by default; in Apache 2.0, it is set to off.

Based on the explanations in Table 11-5, you can decipher the formats used by Apache. The first four lines in Figure 11-17 list the formats from httpd.conf.

The reference to access_log is to the file that contains the log information. As new log files are created, the old ones are named access_log.1, access_log.2, and so on. The last part of the directive is the format for the log file. The format is defined by the `LogFormat` directives. Four formats are defined by default in Apache: combined, common, referrer, and agent. You can define your own format and give it a name using `LogFormat`. Then you can define your own `CustomLog`. You can even define multiple logs so that you can keep the combined log but add one with your own definition in a different file.

Figure 11-18 provides an example of requests from the transfer log. The first three lines show what happens when someone requests the default Web page on the Apache Web server. The first line shows that there was a request for the default page with `GET / HTTP/1.1`. You used the `GET` statement in Chapter 6 when you simulated getting a default page using Telnet. In this case, the default page had two images, which are retrieved with separate requests on lines 2 and 3. Line 2 has `GET /icons/apache_pb.gif HTTP/1.1`, and line 3 has `GET /poweredby.png HTTP/1.1`. The more images that you have, the more requests that are generated for each page. In the definition for the combined format in Figure 11-17, the next-to-last item is for the referrer. When there is no referrer, a hyphen (-) acts as the placeholder for that item. The first line (`10.2.5.3 - - [25/Sep/2005:10:16:52 -0400] "GET / HTTP/1.1" 304 - "-" "Mozilla/4.0"`) does not specify a referrer, but the second line (`10.2.5.3 - - [25/Sep/2005:10:16:52 -0400] "GET /icons/apache_pb.gif HTTP/1.1" 304 - "http://10.11.22.33/" "Mozilla/4.0"`) specifies `http://10.11.22.33/` as the referrer, which is the IP address of the server. Thus, although the client requested the Web page, the server requested `/icons/apache_pb.gif` and `/poweredby.png`. The fourth line (`10.2.5.3 - - [25/Sep/2005:10:28:16 -0400] "GET /test.htm HTTP/1.1" 200 31 "-" "Mozilla/4.0"`) includes a simple request for test.htm, which has no images. The last three lines show what happens when the client uses tunneling, as described in Chapter 10. Recall that you used 55555 as the port for the tunnel. The client appears to be 10.11.22.33, which is the first item on the line, but the referrer is http://localhost:55555, which gives the administrator an idea of where the request actually originated.

```
10.2.5.3 - - [25/Sep/2005:10:16:52 -0400] "GET / HTTP/1.1" 304 - "-"
   "Mozilla/4.0"
10.2.5.3 - - [25/Sep/2005:10:16:52 -0400] "GET /icons/apache_pb.gif
   HTTP/1.1" 304 - "http://10.11.22.33/" "Mozilla/4.0"
10.2.5.3 - - [25/Sep/2005:10:16:52 -0400] "GET /poweredby.png HTTP/1.1" 304 -
   "http://10.11.22.33/" "Mozilla/4.0"
10.2.5.3 - - [25/Sep/2005:10:28:16 -0400] "GET /test.htm HTTP/1.1" 200 31 "-"
   "Mozilla/4.0"
10.11.22.33 - - [16/Sep/2005:09:06:43 -0400] "GET / HTTP/1.1" 200 2890 "-"
   "Mozilla/4.0"
10.11.22.33 - - [16/Sep/2005:09:06:43 -0400] "GET /poweredby.png HTTP/1.1" 200
   1154 "http://localhost:55555" "Mozilla/4.0"
10.11.22.33 - - [16/Sep/2005:09:06:43 -
   0400] "GET /icons/apache_pb.gif HTTP/1.1" 200 2326 "http://localhost:55555"
   "Mozilla/4.0"
```

Figure 11-18 Transfer log

Carefully monitor the number of logs you are generating if you turn Apache into a proxy server and have a lot of users who access the Internet. All pages that they request will be logged, which could quickly create very large log files. Nevertheless, the logs remain a good way to keep track of which sites your internal users reference during a day and approximately how much time they spend online. If you use log files, make sure that you have plenty of disk space. Check the log files at regular intervals and archive them if necessary to free space.

Figure 11-19 shows an example of the log file when Apache is used as a proxy server.

```
192.168.0.10 - - [10/Sep/2005:13:26:01 -0400] "GET http://my.yahoo.com/
   HTTP/1.0" 302 74 "-" "Mozilla/4.0 "
192.168.0.10 - - [10/Sep/2005:13:26:02 -0400] "GET http://my.yahoo.com/?myHome
   HTTP/1.0" 200 68924 "-" "Mozilla/4.0 "
192.168.0.10 - - [10/Sep/2005:13:26:02 -0400] "GET
   http://us.i1.yimg.com/us.yimg.com/i/my/qc.js HTTP/1.0" 304 0
   "http://my.yahoo.com/?myHome" "Mozilla/4.0 "
192.168.0.10 - - [10/Sep/2005:13:26:02 -0400] "GET http://us.a1.yimg.com/
   us.yimg.com/a/1-/jscodes/072002/ct_072002.js HTTP/1.0" 304 0 "http://
   my.yahoo.com/?myHome" "Mozilla/4.0 "
192.168.0.10 - - [10/Sep/2005:13:29:15 -0400] "GET
   http://us.news2.yimg.com/us.yimg.com/p/cx/uc/20020910/db/db020910.jpg HTTP/
   1.0" 304 0 "http://my.yahoo.com/?myHome" "Mozilla/4.0 "
192.168.0.10 - - [10/Sep/2005:13:29:15 -0400] "GET
   http://us.news2.yimg.com/us.yimg.com/p/cx/uc/20020910/ga/ga020910.jpg HTTP/
   1.0" 304 0 "http://my.yahoo.com/?myHome" "Mozilla/4.0 "
```

Figure 11-19 Log file when Apache is used as a proxy server

Monitoring Other Web Applications

Virtually all server applications have ways to monitor problems and software functioning. Often, they use the same methods that you have already encountered, such as the Event Viewer in Windows and syslogd in Linux. For example, the BIND 9 DNS server can use a screen to display log files or you can store the logs in a file or have syslogd process and store the logs. Sendmail uses syslogd, while Exchange 2000 uses the Event Viewer and a number of log files.

Monitoring DNS

The BIND 9 DNS server has extensive logging capability and easy-to-use defaults. Often, you need to log DNS information to test a configuration or log specific items such as zone transfers to make sure that they are occurring on a regular basis. In Windows, the Event Viewer includes a category for the DNS server, so there is nothing to configure.

BIND uses a logging statement that you configure in named.conf. You define all the information you need for logging in two parts of this statement. The channel defines where the logging information is sent. The category defines what will be sent to the channel.

If the channel is going to a file, you use the `versions` option to define the number of backup files it will use, and you use the `size` option to set the maximum size of each file. The `print-time` option adds the date and time to the file. For example, you could specify a channel called techno_channel in a file named named.log with up to four backups, so you will have named.log, named.log.0, named.log.1, named.log.2, and named.log.3. Suppose you also want the date and time in the file, and you want to limit the size of each file to 10 MB. You would create the following channel:

```
channel "techno_channel" {
        file "named.log" versions 4 size 10m;
        print-time yes;
};
```

You can use four default channels, which are shown in Figure 11-20. The default_syslog channel states that it will use syslogd for processing and storing the logs. It also states that you could use the reference called daemon in syslog.conf to specify how the messages are handled, just as you learned in a previous section. The **severity** option is similar to the **priority** option in syslogd; it defines the messages used for the channel. In the case of default_syslog, only messages at the info level and higher are sent to the channel. The default_debug channel defines a channel with a filename of named.run. The **severity** option is dynamic, which means that it will display the level of debug information depending on how named.run is started. The default_stderr will send messages with a priority of info and higher to stderr, which is usually the screen. The last channel, called null, defines output as being discarded.

```
channel "default_syslog" {
        syslog daemon;
        severity info;
};
channel "default_debug {
        file "named.run";
        severity dynamic;
};
channel "default_stderr" {
        stderr;
        severity info;
};
channel "null" {
        null;
};
```

Figure 11-20 Default channels in DNS

Once you define the channels, the category information determines what information is sent to the channel. Seventeen categories are defined; the more common ones are listed in Table 11-6.

Table 11-6 Categories in BIND

Category	Description
default	All categories not configured in the logging statement. If no other categories are defined, it means that all logging information is handled by default.
security	Approval and denial of requests.
xfer-in	Zone transfers coming into the server.
xfer-out	Zone transfers leaving the server.
client	Client requests.
resolver	Used with caching servers to log information related to recursive lookups.
queries	Any DNS query.

Because the default category includes all of the other categories, using the default category is a good way to log everything. If you wanted the resolver information sent to the techno_channel, you would write the following complete logging statement in named.conf:

```
logging {
      channel "techno_channel" {
            file "named.log" versions 4 size 10m;
            print-time yes;
      };
      category "resolver" {
            "techno_channel";
      };
};
```

If you do not specify a default category, the following is used:

```
category "default" {
      "default_syslog";
      "default_debug";
};
```

Monitoring E-mail Applications

Monitoring e-mail typically means keeping track of any errors and trying to find possible misuse of the system. You can also use logs to monitor the volume of messages and determine the usage levels of SMTP or HTTP. Although each e-mail application differs in the way that you monitor it, the concepts of what you want to monitor are similar. This section focuses on the e-mail applications installed in Chapter 8.

Monitoring Exchange 2000

Exchange 2000 uses the Application portion of the EventViewer to display general messages about starting and stopping the many components. Because most of these messages are for information only, you should filter the messages to exclude the informational messages created by Exchange 2000. Figure 11-21 shows a sample of the more than 50 messages created when Exchange 2000 starts.

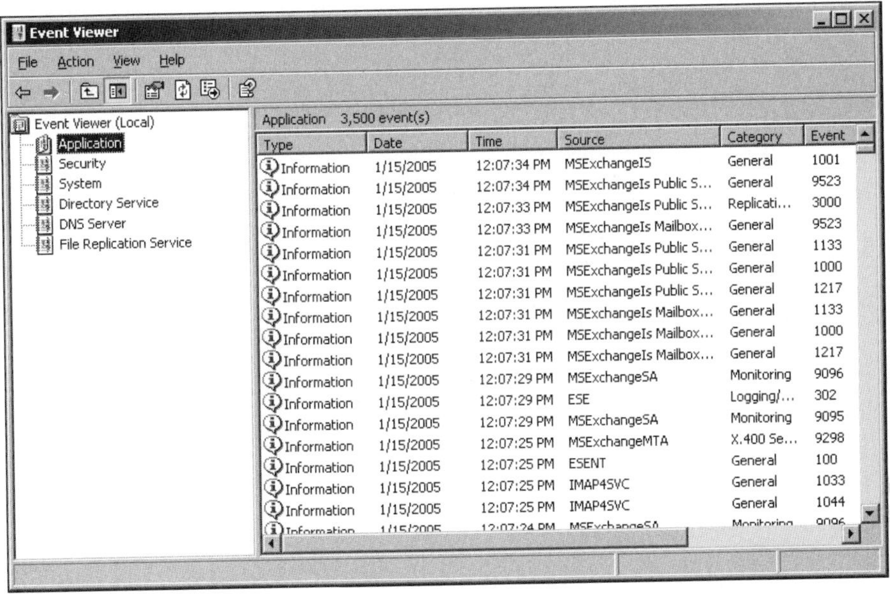

Figure 11-21 Event Viewer showing Exchange 2000 events

You can also log information as Exchange 2000 is being used. You can use four types of logs: audit, protocol, message tracking, and diagnostic. Because they generate large amounts of information that could affect the performance of the server, you should use them only when necessary. The audit log monitors access to mailboxes and analyzes how people use Exchange 2000. It is becoming more widely used in high-security situations, because it allows administrators to determine exactly what someone did at a certain time. Protocol logging allows you to see the commands used by clients and servers for some of the protocols. The message tracking logs give you information about senders and recipients of messages. Diagnostic logging can help you debug detailed problems with the Exchange 2000 services.

Audit logging is complicated and can easily create an extreme load on the server. It requires detailed knowledge of group policies and Windows auditing in general. You can audit everyone who uses the server or just one group or user. You can audit the success or failure of attempts to access mailboxes, public folders, and other Exchange objects. For example, you could audit access to mailboxes to find out how often users check their mail.

Protocol logging can aid you in discovering problems related to SMTP, HTTP, or NNTP, but not POP3 or IMAP4. The purpose of protocol logging is to determine the exact exchange of commands between the client and the server. It should be enabled only while you are trying to solve a specific problem because of the extra burden that it places on the server. Protocol logging is disabled by default. The following steps assume that you have installed Exchange 2000.

To enable protocol logging on SMTP in Windows:

1. Open the Exchange System Manager.
2. In the left pane of the Exchange System Manager window, expand the **Servers** folders until Default SMTP Virtual Server appears. See Figure 11-22.

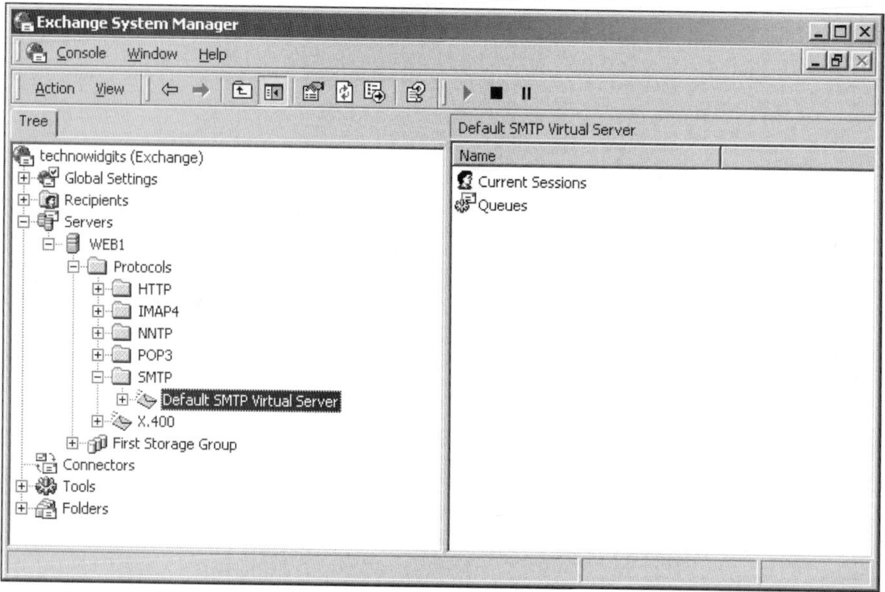

Figure 11-22 Exchange System Manager window

3. Right-click **Default SMTP Virtual Server**, and then click **Properties**. The Default SMTP Virtual Server Properties dialog box opens. See Figure 11-23.
4. On the General tab, click the **Enable logging** check box.
5. Click the **Properties** button to display the Logging Properties dialog box. (This is called the Extended Logging Properties dialog box in Windows 2000.) See Figure 11-24. The text box shows the folder where the log files are stored. Below the text box is the log filename, which is probably SmtpSvc1\exyymmdd.log.

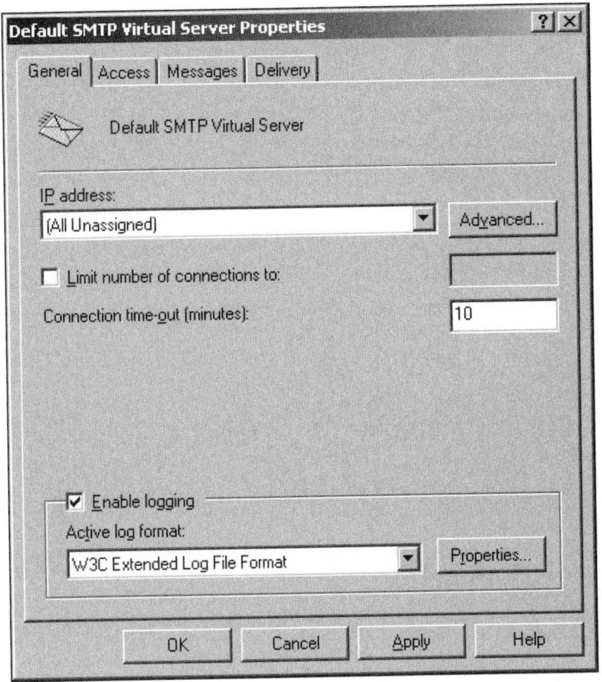

Figure 11-23 Default SMTP Virtual Server Properties dialog box

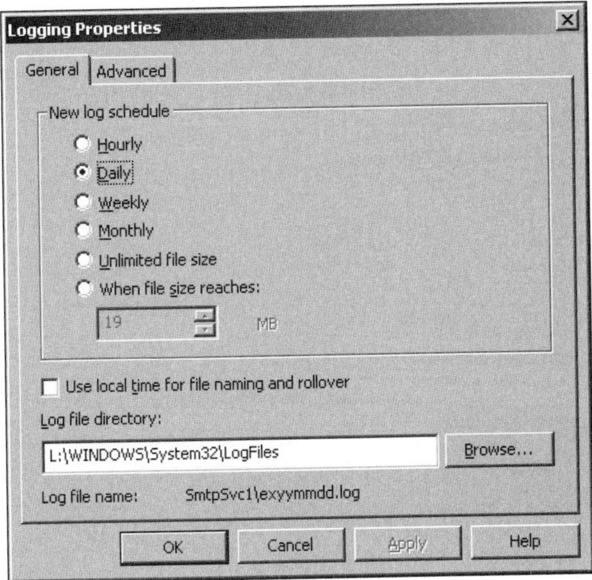

Figure 11-24 Finding the log filename

6. Click **OK** until you return to the Exchange System Manager window, and then close the window.

You can log message information to determine the flow and status of e-mail messages. Once you enable message tracking, you use the Message Tracking Center to search for messages that you want to track. You can search by sender, recipient, or message ID. You can also search over a date range.

To enable message tracking in Exchange 2000:

1. Open Exchange System Manager.
2. In the left pane, expand **Servers**, if necessary.
3. Right-click the name of the server (WEB1 in this example), and then click **Properties**. The WEB1 Properties dialog box opens. See Figure 11-25.

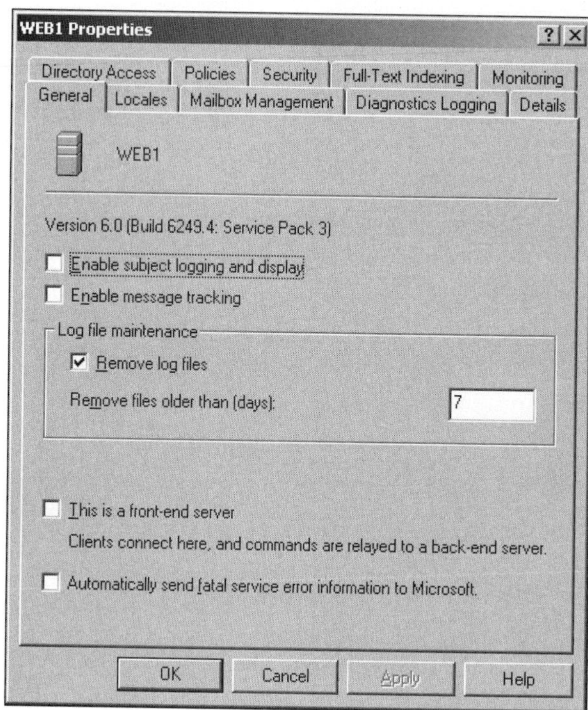

Figure 11-25 WEB1 Properties dialog box

4. On the General tab, click the **Enable message tracking** check box to select it.
5. If you also want to see the subject of the messages, click the **Enable subject logging and display** check box to select it.
6. Click **OK** to save the settings.

To search for messages:

1. In the left pane, expand the **Tools** folder.
2. Click **Message Tracking Center**. The Message Tracking Center information appears in the right pane of the Exchange System Manager window. See Figure 11-26.

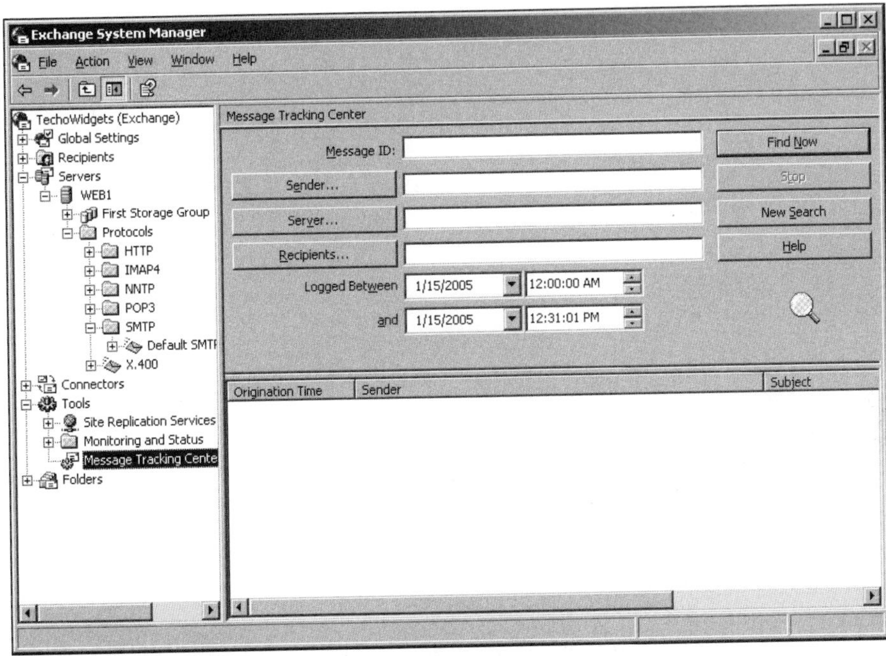

Figure 11-26 Message Tracking Center

3. In the text box next to the Server button, enter the name of the server, such as **Web1.technowidgets.com**, to run a search.
4. You do not have any messages logged yet, so there is nothing to find. However, after Exchange 2000 has been used for a period of time, you could define the sender, recipient, and/or date range and then click the **Find Now** button. In the bottom text box, you would see the date and time the e-mail was sent or received, the sender, and the subject of the e-mail.
5. Close the Exchange System Manager window.

Diagnostic logging is useful to diagnose problems with specific services within Exchange 2000. You configure diagnostic logging by selecting the Diagnostics Logging tab of the WEB1 Properties dialog box shown in Figure 11-25. For each service, you can select from the category to be logged. Once the category is highlighted, you can select the logging level. Figure 11-27 shows an example of the diagnostic categories for the POP3 service. Table 11-7 describes the logging levels.

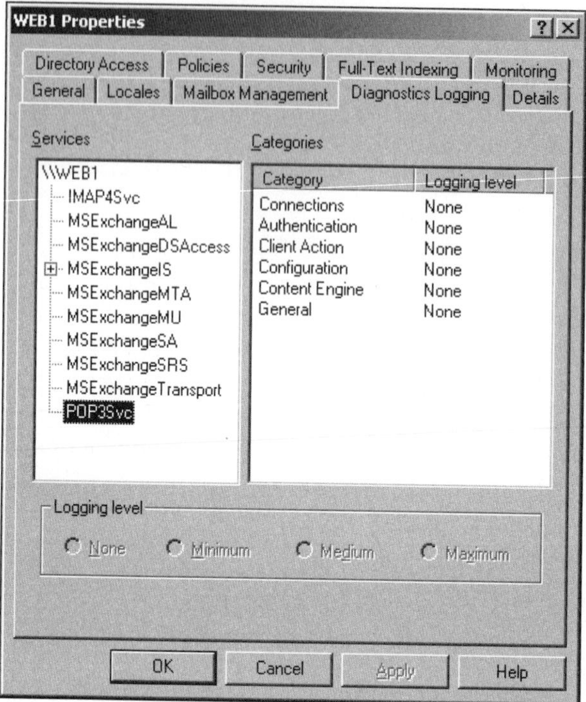

Figure 11-27 Diagnostic categories for the POP3 service

Table 11-7 Logging levels for diagnostic logging

Level	Description
None	Logs only critical errors.
Minimum	One entry for each major task performed by the service. It is usually best to start with this level so you do not generate too much logging information.
Medium	Includes the steps for each task. This choice is best when you have identified the specific service that has the problem.
Maximum	Includes entries for each line of code in the service. This level can cause performance problems in a server.

Monitoring E-mail in Linux

In Linux, syslogd already monitors sendmail and imapd, which includes POP3. In fact, a mail facility is included in syslog.conf, so information is already logged as described in the "Monitoring Linux" section.

Monitoring FTP

Monitor the FTP service to learn which files are being downloaded most often. Although you can monitor FTP user information, FTP is generally implemented with anonymous users, and the logged information on users is probably unreliable. Nevertheless, FTP logs can tip you off to attempted or successful attacks on your server.

As an example, Figure 11-28 shows a few of the dozens of lines logged in a successful attack on a Windows FTP server that ultimately filled the hard drive until Windows failed. Once the administrator noticed that a number of programs were malfunctioning, it was quickly determined that no disk space remained on the server. The administrator started looking at the properties of folders to see which folders were using up the most space, and found that the \InetPub\ftproot folder, instead of having a few megabytes of data, held many gigabytes of data. Upon further investigation, many new folders and files were found to be stored in the \InetPub\ftproot folder and many of them could not be deleted.

To delete the files, the administrator had to use the RM.EXE utility from the Resource Disk. RM.EXE is useful in any situation where files cannot be deleted through conventional methods. To use RM.EXE, you must open a command prompt because it is a command-line utility. It also uses a different syntax for files. For example, to delete everything in the \inetpub\ftproot folder and everything beneath it, you would type `rm -r //C/Inetpub/ftproot/*` and press Enter.

Because a problem was found with the \Inetpub\ftproot folder in this case, the FTP logs were then checked. Instead of a normal listing of files downloaded, the log contained commands with odd characters. A software patch from Microsoft prevented further attacks.

```
#Software: Microsoft Internet Information Services 5.0
#Version: 1.0
#Date: 2005-05-17 00:04:45
#Fields: time c-ip cs-method cs-uri-stem sc-status
00:04:45 172.183.3.168 [44]USER anonymous 331
00:04:48 172.183.3.168 [44]PASS anonymous@on.the.net 230
00:07:46 172.183.3.168 [44]QUIT - 257
09:54:38 217.128.201.34 [48]USER anonymous 331
09:54:38 217.128.201.34 [48]PASS email@notset.com 230
09:56:00 80.14.68.167 [49]USER anonymous 331
09:56:00 80.14.68.167 [49]PASS anonymous@on.the.net 230
09:57:20 80.14.68.167 [49]MKD lab9.files 257
09:58:05 80.14.68.167 [49]MKD .~~.++++;;+%+%+++1++/.+++
( ;;+%+%+[UDF¨]++%+%++;+   550
09:59:25 80.14.68.167 [49]MKD .~~.+++++%+%+++1++/.+++
( +%+%+[+Shrek+_+¨]++%+%+++   550
09:59:58 80.14.68.167 [49]MKD ..+..+T@gGeD+..+..+++_ 257
10:01:41 80.14.68.167 [49]MKD ..+..++bY+ShreK+++...++_++++++ 257
10:02:11 217.128.201.34 [48]QUIT - 200
```

Figure 11-28 Excerpt from FTP log file that recorded an attack

To enable FTP logging in Windows:

1. Open the Internet Information Services window.
2. In the left pane, expand **WEB1**. In Windows 2003, also expand the FTP sites folder.
3. Right-click **Default FTP Site**, and then click **Properties**.
4. Click the **Enable logging** check box to select it, if necessary.
5. Click the **Properties** button to find the location of the log files. The log file directory text box contains the location. In Windows 2003, it is in \WINDOWS\System32\LogFiles; in Windows 2000, it is in \WINNT\System32\LogFiles. Within the LogFiles folder, a folder called MSFTPSVC1 contains individual log files.
6. Click **OK** twice to save the settings, and then close IIS.

By default, Linux logs FTP data, so you do not have to enable this feature. The log files are located in /var/log. The log filenames begin with xferlog and are followed by a number, with the largest number being the oldest file.

Understanding Analysis Tools for Web Servers

Analysis tools extract system data from logs and format the information so that it is easier to read and interpret. For IIS, one of the most popular analysis tools is WebTrends from NetIQ. A free trial of WebTrends is available at *www.webtrends.com*. For Apache, 123LogAnalyzer is popular and easy to configure. A free trial of 123LogAnalyzer is available at *www.123loganalyzer.com*.

WebTrends analyzes log files to help you determine the source of your Web traffic. It also indicates which pages are the most popular, and it tracks this information over time to show how the popularity of a page increases and decreases. For an e-commerce site, you can find out where potential customers stop most often as they store merchandise in a shopping cart and complete the checkout procedure. You can improve your marketing by identifying the products customers looked at and the ones they actually purchased. WebTrends offers nearly 50 different reports in the categories listed in Table 11-8.

Table 11-8 WebTrends reports

Category	Types of reports
General Statistics	These single reports emphasize totals and averages such as total hits, average hits per day, number of page views, average length of visit, and number of unique visitors.
Resources Accessed	The ten reports in this category are related to the number of views for top pages, entry files, exit pages, top directories, and most accessed file types.

Table 11-8 WebTrends reports (continued)

Category	Types of reports
Advertising	There are two basic reports—one on views of advertising and one on users who clicked on an advertisement.
Visitors and Demographics	There are ten reports in this category. In the visitor reports, you can find out how many visitors come back, and how many times they return. If you have user authentication, you can find out which ones visited the site the most. In the demographic reports, you find out where the visitors come from, by country and by state.
Activity Statistics	In this area, you can analyze hits in a variety of ways: by time increment, by day of the week, by hour of the day, by length of visit, by number of views, and by visitors by time increment.
Technical Statistics	You can find out if the site contains any errors, such as a page not found when you click a link. You can also get a report that contains the number of cache hits.
Referrers and Keywords	For sites that get visitors who are referred by other sites, these reports show you which were the most popular originating sites. Also, there are reports on top search engines, phrases, and keywords that get visitors to your site.
Browsers and Platforms	These reports focus on the various types of browsers that access your site and the operating systems used. This information can be useful for your programmers, who need to determine which browsers to code for.

123LogAnalyzer provides many of the same types of reports, but with less detail than may be appropriate for many organizations. In 123LogAnalyzer, the general statistics, activity statistics, browsers, platforms, referrer statistics, and some technical information reports are similar to those that WebTrends offers. A major difference is that WebTrends can compare reports over time, and it has other related products that could help sites analyze their data. WebTrends is available only for IIS, whereas 123LogAnalyzer is available for both IIS and Apache.

Chapter Summary

- Monitoring operating systems typically involves analyzing log files, which serve a number of purposes. In some cases, you can monitor performance criteria through log files. Performance monitoring allows you to analyze performance over time to determine the effects of changes, increased workload, and resource consumption. Security logs track information related to security such as logons, changes to permissions, and access to files.
- When monitoring your system, start with a baseline, which shows you the status of the system at the beginning of its life cycle. Document the services with which you begin, and note changes to them when you add or delete software.

- In Windows, the Event Viewer is the primary utility used to look at operating system information. You can filter events to look at specific ones. Monitoring in Linux centers around syslogd and the logs determined by syslog.conf. Syslogd is used not only for operating system logs, but also for application-specific logs such as e-mail logs.
- You typically monitor information relating to the functioning of the Web server, which indicates whether it is functioning correctly or performing operations incorrectly, such as maintaining a link to a nonexistent page. Information about how people use the Web server includes the pages they are accessing, when they are accessing them, and other related data.
- The Performance Monitor has more than 60 counters for IIS and more than 30 counters for ASP. For IIS, you can enable or disable logging and also select which items will be logged. In Apache, the log information is configured in httpd.conf. The default level for log messages is warn, and the default log definition is called common. You can configure your own log files.
- The BIND 9 DNS server has extensive logging capability. Often, you need to log DNS information to test a configuration or log specific items such as zone transfers to make sure that they occur on a regular basis. In Windows, the Event Viewer automatically generates logs for the DNS server, so there is nothing to configure. Exchange 2000 uses the Application portion of the Event Viewer for general information about starting and stopping the many components. It has four types of logs. The audit log monitors access to mailboxes. Protocol logging allows you to see the commands used by clients and servers for some of the protocols. The message tracking logs give you information about senders and recipients of messages. Diagnostic logging can help you debug detailed problems with the Exchange 2000 services. Monitoring FTP can give you information on which files are downloaded most frequently. Often, you can also use this information to find out if someone is trying to penetrate your system.
- Analysis tools take the data in logs and help you make sense of it in a more easily read format. For IIS, one of the most popular analysis tools is WebTrends from NetIQ. For Apache, 123LogAnalyzer is popular and easy to configure. WebTrends offers nearly 50 different reports related to analyzing hits, page views, visitors, advertising, technical information, and more. 123LogAnalyzer provides many of the same reports, albeit with a bit less detail, but it still may be appropriate for many organizations.

Review Questions

1. ________________ contain information written by the operating system in response to certain criteria and events fitting those criteria.
2. Which of the following would *not* be part of a security log?
   a. logons
   b. changes to permissions
   c. a service not starting
   d. access to files
3. A(n) ________________ shows you the status of the system during normal operations and serves as a standard against which future statuses are compared.
4. In the Windows Performance Monitor, the average disk queue length ________________.
   a. looks at access time only
   b. looks at seek time only
   c. gives you an overall look at disk system workload
   d. looks at track-to-track time
5. There are three levels of messages for the System and Application Event Viewers in Windows. Which of the following is *not* a message level?
   a. information
   b. warning
   c. alert
   d. error
6. If you want to filter an event such as information related to SMTP, which filter would you use?
   a. Event type
   b. Event source
   c. Category
   d. Event ID
7. In the Shared Folder portion of the Computer Management MMC, you can find users who are using your shares in which folder?
   a. Shares
   b. Sessions
   c. Open files
   d. Users

8. In Linux, logging is controlled by ________________.
   a. logsysd
   b. logd
   c. syslogd
   d. sysd
9. Syslogd uses facilities that allow applications such as Apache to implement logging. Which facility does Apache use?
   a. daemon
   b. apache
   c. local7
   d. user
10. Which is the highest priority used by syslogd?
    a. alert
    b. emerg
    c. crit
    d. err
11. In Linux, in which file is information on when users last logged in found?
    a. loglast
    b. lastlog
    c. userlog
    d. loguser
12. In Linux, what is the default directory for log files?
    a. /log
    b. /var
    c. /var/logfiles
    d. /var/log
13. What is the default file format for IIS?
    a. W3C Extended Log File Format
    b. NCSA Common Log File Format
    c. Microsoft IIS Log Format
    d. There is no default.
14. By default, where are Apache log files stored?
    a. /var/log/apache
    b. /var/log/web

c. /var/log/boot
d. /var/log/httpd

15. Transfer logs tell you about ________.
    a. the use of your Web site
    b. Apache errors
    c. FTP information
    d. e-mail transfers
16. Error logs can be set up for each virtual host. True or False?
17. In Apache, which `LogFormat` symbol would you use for the complete path to the page?
    a. `%p`
    b. `%f`
    c. `%a`
    d. `%z`
18. The ________ directory stores the transfer logs for Apache.
19. Which of the following is *not* a type of log in Exchange 2000?
    a. audit
    b. access
    c. protocol
    d. diagnostic
20. WebTrends is a product from Microsoft. True or False?

HANDS-ON PROJECTS

Project 11-1

You monitor the operating system in a variety of ways in Windows. The Event Viewer is an important utility. You should also use the Performance Monitor.

To filter events in Windows:

1. Click **Start**, point to **Administrative Tools**, and then click **Event Viewer**.
2. *In Windows 2003:* Right-click **System**, and then click **Properties**.

   In Windows 2000: Right-click **System Log**, and then click **Properties**.

   The System Properties dialog box opens.

3. Click the **Filter** tab.
4. Deselect all event types except **Warning** and **Error**.
5. Click **OK**. A list of current warnings and errors appears in the right pane.
6. Double-click the first warning or error. What is the description of the warning or error? Next, determine whether there are any other warnings or errors. Although a server in a school computer lab probably has only a few, a server that has been running for a while can have many warnings and errors.
7. Close the window.

To test the Performance Monitor:

1. In Administrative Tools, open the **Performance** window.
2. Right-click anywhere in the blank area of the right pane, and then click **Properties**. The System Monitor Properties dialog box opens. Click the **Data** tab. See Figure 11-29. In Windows 2000, no counters are selected, so skip to step 5.

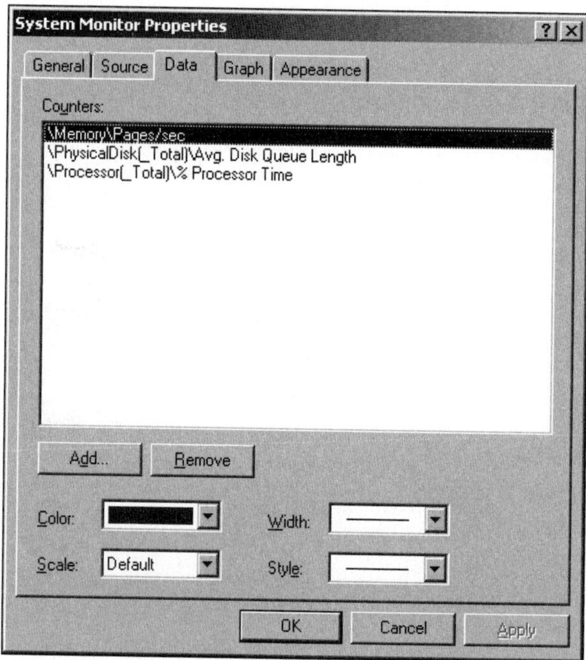

Figure 11-29 Data tab of the System Monitor Properties dialog box

3. The \Memory\Pages/sec should be highlighted. Click **Remove** to remove the \Memory\Pages/sec counter.
4. The \PhysicalDisk(_Total)\Avg. Disk Queue Length counter is now highlighted. Click **Remove** to remove it.

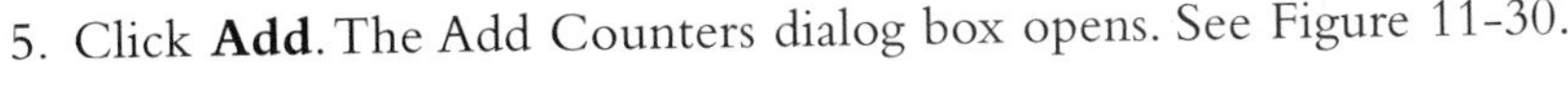

5. Click **Add**. The Add Counters dialog box opens. See Figure 11-30.

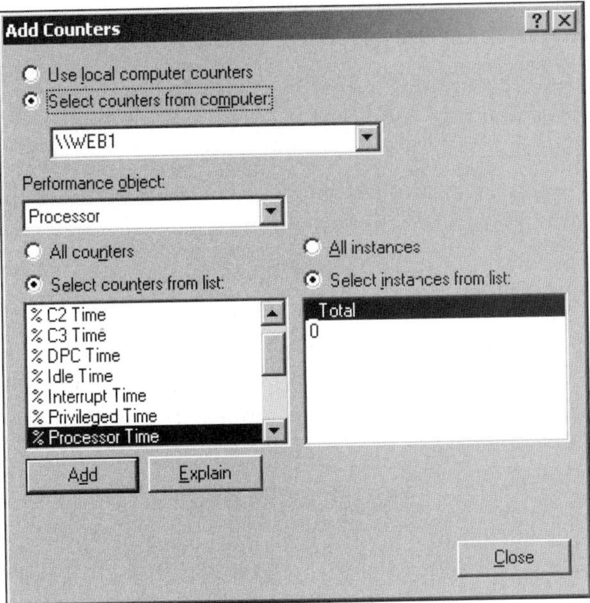

Figure 11-30 Add Counters dialog box

6. In the Performance object list box, select **ICMP**. The list of counters changes to reflect the types of counters available for ICMP.
7. Select the **Messages/sec** counter, and then click **Add**. The graph will now monitor ICMP Messages, which are used by the ping utility.
8. Click **Close** to close the Add Counters dialog box, and then move the System Monitor Properties dialog box so you can see the graph.
9. Open a command-prompt window, ping another computer, and watch the graph. You probably did not see any change in the graph because the scale is set for zero to 100. If you change the scale, you can monitor smaller changes.
10. In the System Monitor Properties dialog box, click the **Graph** tab.
11. Under Vertical scale, change the Maximum from 100 to **2**, and then click **OK** to save the changes.
12. Ping another computer and watch the graph. What changes did you notice? Look along the left scale to approximate the height.
13. Close the command-prompt window and the Performance window.

Project 11-2

In Linux, you can monitor the operating system in a variety of ways. The logs in /var/log are important in Linux. You can use utilities to determine which processes are making the heaviest demands on the processor.

To monitor the performance of Linux:

1. In a terminal window, type **top** and then press **Enter**. The top utility shows you the processes that are using most of the processor's time, with results being updated every five seconds. Which are the top three processes?
2. Open a browser, and then close it. In a terminal window, type **top** again and press **Enter**. Which are the top three processes now?
3. Close the window.
4. In a terminal window, type **vmstat** and then press **Enter**. This command shows you the status of virtual memory. What amounts appear for free, buffer, and cache memory?
5. Type **xload** and then press **Enter**. A window opens to show you the overall load on the server. It shows a small bar every 10 seconds.
6. Open five browser windows, and then close them. How did this activity affect xload?

Project 11-3

The IIS and Apache Web servers allow you to configure log files to display exactly what you want.

In IIS, follow the "To alter the items logged using the W3C Extended Log File Format" steps to create a log with the properties needed to track the following:

- IP address of the client
- Number of bytes sent
- First line of the request (URI stem and query)
- Status of the protocol (request)
- Number of seconds needed to process the request

Open a browser on another computer and view some pages. What effect did this have on the IIS log file?

Project 11-4

Now you will create the same type of log that you did with IIS in Project 11-3.

To create a specially formatted log in Apache:

1. In httpd.conf, find the location of the other instances of LogFormat that Apache created by default.
2. On a line below the last instance of LogFormat, type **LogFormat "%a %b %r %s %T" project**. (These codes are from Table 11-5.)
3. On the next line, you need to create a custom log based on project, and store it along with other logs in a file called project_log. Type **CustomLog logs/ project_log project**.
4. Make sure all proxy configurations are disabled from Chapter 10. If you set up a proxy server in Chapter 10, you need to make sure all proxy configurations are disabled by inserting a pound sign (#) at the beginning of all configuration lines between `<IfModule mod_proxy.c>` and `</IfModule>`.
5. Save httpd.conf and exit.
6. Restart Apache.
7. Open a browser on another computer and view some pages on Apache.
8. Open a terminal window. Type **cat /var/log/httpd/project_log** and then press **Enter** to display the contents of the log.

11

Project 11-5

DNS monitoring can offer insights into how your DNS server is being accessed. In this project, you will create a DNS log in Linux. Use the definition for logging of the techno_channel for reference. The following is the complete example from the chapter. However, one important change has been made for the purpose of this project. The level of category severity has been changed from resolver to queries, which allows you to easily produce entries in the log. In a production environment, this would produce too much output to be used regularly.

To log DNS information:

1. Open a terminal window.
2. Type **kedit /etc/named.conf** and then press **Enter**.
3. On the line above include "/etc/rndc.key"; type the following logging specification:

```
logging {
channel "techno_channel" {
file "named.log" versions 4 size 10m;
print-time yes;
};
```

```
category "queries" {
"techno_channel";
};
};
```

4. Save named.conf and exit.
5. Restart the DNS server by typing **/etc/init.d/named restart** and then press **Enter**.
6. Type **ping www.technowidgets.com** and then press **Enter** to create entries in the log file. You will probably notice that the statement responds more slowly. After a few entries, press **Ctrl+C** to stop the display.
7. Type **cat /var/named/named.log** and then press **Enter** to display the contents of the log.

Project 11-6

In this project, you will set up monitoring for Exchange 2000 by logging SMTP information.

To test logging in Exchange 2000:

1. Make sure that you have completed the "To enable protocol logging on SMTP in Windows" steps in the chapter. Note the location of the log files.
2. Make sure that you have completed "To enable message tracking in Exchange 2000" steps in the chapter.
3. Create an e-mail message. (If you need help, look at Hands-on Projects 8-3 and 8-4.)
4. Follow the "To search for messages" steps in the chapter. What are the results?
5. Display the contents of the SMTP log file. What does it contain?

Project 11-7

This project compares FTP logging in Windows and Linux. It is useful to determine what information is tracked so that you can find out which serves you best. FTP logging is enabled by default in Linux so you just need to generate information for the log by downloading a file.

To create logging information in Linux:

1. Open a terminal window.
2. Copy a file to the root of the FTP server so you can download it. Type **cp /etc/named.conf /var/ftp** and then press **Enter**. (This file is not significant.)
3. Make sure FTP is running by typing **chkconfig wu-ftpd on** and then pressing **Enter**. Then type **service xinetd restart** and press **Enter**. Finally, type **ftprestart** and press **Enter**. If a message appears indicating that two files are missing, you can disregard the message by closing the dialog box.
4. Log on to the FTP server. Type **ftp 192.168.0.100** and then press **Enter**. It may take a minute or so for the FTP server to start and respond.

5. When it responds with "Name (192.168.0.100:root):", type **anonymous** and then press **Enter**.
6. For the password, type **cbranco@technowidgets.com** and then press **Enter**.
7. Type **get named.conf** and then press **Enter** to download the file.
8. Type **bye** and then press **Enter** to exit the FTP client.
9. Type **cat /var/log/xferlog** and then press **Enter** to display the FTP log.

To create logging information in Windows:

1. Follow the "To enable FTP logging in Windows" steps in the chapter. Note the location of the log files.
2. Copy a file to the root of the FTP server so you can download it. In Windows Explorer, copy default.htm from \Inetpub\wwwroot to \Inetpub\ftproot.
3. At a command prompt, type **ftp 192.168.0.100** and then press **Enter**.
4. At the user prompt, type **anonymous** and then press **Enter**.
5. At the password prompt, type **cbranco@technowidgets.com** and then press **Enter**.
6. Type **get default.htm** and then press **Enter** to download the file.
7. Type **bye** and press **Enter** to exit the FTP client.
8. In Windows Explorer, double-click the most recent log file to display the contents.

Compare the log files between Linux and Windows. Which log is more useful and why?

CASE PROJECTS

Case Project 11-1

Download and install WebTrends Analysis Suite for IIS (*www.netiq.com/products/was/trial.asp*). Run the report module. What did you find? Write a one- to two-page paper that describes which parts of the report you think are most useful and why. Which parts of the report do you think are least useful and why?

Case Project 11-2

Download and install 123LogAnalyzer for Apache (*www.123loganalyzer.com/download.htm*). Run the report module. What did you find? Write a one- to two-page paper that describes which parts of the report you think are most useful and why. Which parts of the report do you think are least useful and why?

Case Project 11-3

Research *Microsoft.com* for the best practices related to monitoring one of the following: IIS, SQL Server, Exchange 2000. Create a one- to two-page report with supporting documentation indicating what your company should do. Supporting documentation could be Web pages from the site describing the best practices.

Case Project 11-4

Use the Web to research the best techniques for monitoring Apache. Create a one- to two-page report with supporting documentation indicating what your company should do. Supporting documentation could be Web pages from the site describing the best techniques.

Glossary

access time — The amount of time it takes the drive to retrieve a single piece of data, measured in milliseconds.

Active Directory (AD) — In Windows, AD allows users a single logon for the whole network. It can be used to organize domains.

Active Server Pages.NET (ASP.NET) — The latest generation of programming environment that allows for more productive programming, it is used to create dynamic pages. Based on Active Server Pages (ASP), this Web-based programming language was created by Microsoft for Windows Web servers.

address resolution — The process of converting a computer name to a numeric IP address.

alias — An alternate name, as for a computer or mailbox.

application server — A server that focuses on processing information. For example, a server that contains a DBMS is an application server.

application-level filter — A filter that enables a firewall to recognize that the Web or e-mail application, for example, serves as a termination point for traffic between the internal network and the Internet. Instead of simply transferring a packet destined for an internal Web server, using an application-level filter opens separate connections between the firewall and the internal server to better control the flow of data.

ASP — *See* Active Server Pages.NET.

ASP.NET — *See* Active Server Pages.NET.

authentication — The process of determining a user's true identity.

back door — A hidden access point to allow for significant control of your system.

backbone — A high-speed network that connects other networks.

bandwidth — The theoretical maximum number of bits that can be sent in one second.

baseline — Shows the status of the system during normal operations and serves as a standard against which future statuses are compared.

Berkeley Internet Name Domain (BIND) — The software used for DNS in Linux and other non-Windows servers.

Berkeley Systems Distribution (BSD) — A UNIX standard distributed by Berkeley Systems. Examples of the BSD implementation include FreeBSD and SunOS.

boot loader — The program that starts the operating system.

bottleneck — The component of the server that causes system performance to slow, thereby keeping parts of the system from working optimally.

buffer overrun — When a program accepts more data than it anticipated receiving. Under certain circumstances, buffer overruns can cause the system to stop or allow the attacker to execute code on the server. Also known as a buffer overflow.

bus — The path that data travels between devices.

caching server — A server that is not authoritative for any zone. Instead, it handles queries by asking other servers for information.

CAL — *See* client access license.

canonical name — A host's official name, the first hostname listed for the computer's IP address in the hostname database.

certificate — A software mechanism that guarantees the identity of an organization or user.

certification authority (CA) — An organization that identifies a person or organization. To trust the server certificate, a third party, such as VeriSign or Thawte, can act as the CA.

CGI — *See* Common Gateway Interface.

circuit-level filtering — A type of packet filtering that controls the complete communication session, as opposed to individual packets. Also known as stateful filtering.

CISC — *See* Complex Instruction Set Computer.

client access license (CAL) — A Microsoft license that allows a client computer to connect to a server.

clustering — A technology in which many computers act as one.

Common Gateway Interface (CGI) — A protocol that allows the operating system to interact with the Web server.

Complex Instruction Set Computer (CISC) — A processor architecture that emphasizes the number of different instructions the processor can understand.

contention — A state of data transfer where the more traffic there is, the slower it travels.

cookie — Text that a Web site stores on your disk that can be retrieved by the Web server whenever you visit the site.

cross-selling — A sales technique used on e-commerce sites that involves offering customers products related to other products they have ordered or examined in the past.

cross-site scripting attack — An attack that can take place when you display information that someone has entered. For example, you might display messages that users entered but, instead of a message, the user information could actually contain code that could access your database, display system information that could be used in subsequent attacks, or trick an unsuspecting user viewing the message into divulging private information.

daemon — A term used in Linux to specify a program (more specifically, a process) that runs in the background.

Data Control Language (DCL) — The part of SQL that controls access to the data, often through user names and passwords. Access can be controlled by specific DML statements.

Data Definition Language (DDL) — The part of SQL that creates the tables and other objects in a database.

Data Manipulation Language (DML) — The part of SQL that does the inserting, updating, deleting, and selecting of data. The DML is the most common part of SQL used in programming.

database management system (DBMS) — A system that stores data on a computer in an organized format. It typically uses SQL as the language to define and manipulate the data, and stores data in an organized manner for processing.

DBMS — *See* database management system.

DCL — *See* Data Control Language.

DDL — *See* Data Definition Language.

DDNS — *See* Dynamic Domain Name Service.

demilitarized zone (DMZ) — In a firewall configuration, a protected network containing the Internet servers, such as the e-mail, Web, and FTP servers. These servers are protected from both the Internet and the internal network.

deprecated — A command that is considered obsolete and may be dropped from future versions of the software.

digital certificate — A file issued by a certification authority (CA) that identifies a person or organization.

digital subscriber line (DSL) — Allows you to transfer data at high speeds over conventional telephone lines.

DML — *See* Data Manipulation Language.

DMZ — *See* demilitarized zone.

DNS — *See* domain name service.

DNS round robin — A system configuration where one host is associated with multiple IP addresses. Each IP address is used in succession as requests are made to a Web server.

domain — In Windows, a logical grouping of computers that administrators use to organize common resource needs.

domain account — In Windows, a user account on a server that is valid throughout the domain, which is a logical grouping of computers.

domain local group — A group that has members from the same domain. You can use domain local groups to assign permissions to resources in the same domain.

domain name service (DNS) — A distributed database that translates host names and IP addresses. DNS translates a host name such as *www.microsoft.com* into an IP address. Conversely, it can take an IP address and translate it into a host name.

drive speed — The spindle rotation speed of a disk drive.

DSL — *See* digital subscriber line.

Dynamic Domain Name Service (DDNS) — A service that allows DNS to be automatically updated when the IP address of a workstation changes or a new workstation is added to the network. Only Windows 2000, Windows XP, and Windows 2003 support DDNS.

Dynamic Host Configuration Protocol (DHCP) — A protocol for assigning dynamic IP addresses to devices on a network. DHCP holds a pool of addresses that are given to a computer for a specific amount of time.

dynamic IP address — An address in a LAN environment that can change over time.

dynamic Web page — A page that contains programming statements to customize its output. A number of languages can be used to create dynamic Web pages, including PHP, Perl, ASP, and ASP.NET.

Ethernet — A network technology that connects multiple devices, such as PCs and printers, on a LAN, and passes information from one device to another.

ext3 — The most recent Red Hat Linux file system.

Extensible Markup Language (XML) — A technology that allows developers to create text files that contain tags that define information. Data can then be sent in text form that can be interpreted by otherwise incompatible systems.

external e-mail address — An e-mail address outside of a network.

facility — In Linux, a daemon that uses syslogd.

FAT — *See* File Allocation Table.

fault tolerance — The ability of a system to keep running even when a component fails.

File Allocation Table (FAT) — A file system for Windows that is compatible with all Microsoft operating systems, but offers no security.

file server — A server that focuses on sending and receiving files.

file system — A data structure that provides the input and output mechanisms for an operating system.

File Transfer Protocol (FTP) — A Web service that allows users to upload and download files.

firewall — Software that implements an access control policy between networks. When you want to keep the attackers out, but let legitimate users in, you typically filter IP packets between two networks.

flag — An symbol or characteristic to indicate the state of an item, such as an e-mail message.

foreign key — A column in one table that is related to a primary key in another table.

forward lookup — A zone that contains entries that map names to IP addresses.

forwarding servers — Servers that process requests that DNS servers cannot resolve locally. A forwarding server is not really a separate type of server, but a caching server used in a particular way. Also called a forwarder.

FTP — *See* File Transfer Protocol.

fully qualified domain name (FQDN) — The complete name of the host computer.

global group — A group that has members from the same domain. You can use global groups to assign permissions to resources in any domain, however.

GNOME — A GUI available for Linux, Solaris, and FreeBSD.

GNU General Public License — A license intended to guarantee your freedom to share and change free software, thereby making sure the software is free for all its users.

group — A collection of users with common access needs. You put users in groups and then assign access to groups.

group ID (GID) — A unique number, between 0 an 32767, identifying a set of users in Linux.

group policy — In Active Directory, a policy that enforces network policies.

header — Text sent from the Web server to the browser that contains information about the page. Headers are also used in other TCP/IP protocols to send extra information.

host — An individual computer on a network.

host name — A name that refers to a computer; more specifically, a service running on a computer. For example, *ftp.technowidgets.com*, *www.technowidgets.com*, and *www.productswithpizazz.com* are all host names that could exist on the same computer.

HTML — *See* Hypertext Markup Language.

HTTP — *See* Hypertext Transfer Protocol.

hub — A device used to connect computers. Because hubs are shared devices, as more computers use a hub, traffic can slow.

Hypertext Markup Language (HTML) — The formatting language that browsers use to display text and graphics.

Hypertext Transfer Protocol (HTTP) — A protocol that defines how information is passed between the browser and the Web server.

IDE — *See* Integrated Drive Electronics.

IMAP4 — *See* Internet Mail Access Protocol.

Integrated Drive Electronics (IDE) — The most common hard drive interface available. The controlling electronics are integrated with the hard drive.

Integrated Services Digital Network (ISDN) — A digital dial-up service capable of carrying voice, video, or data communications.

Internet Mail Access Protocol (IMAP4) — A protocol to deliver e-mail messages to e-mail clients. It can have a number of mailboxes and is designed to keep the e-mail on the server.

Internet Mail Service (IMS) — An obsolete add-on that allowed computers to send and receive Internet e-mail by providing the SMTP, POP3, and IMAP4 protocols.

Internet Relay Chat (IRC) — A protocol that allows a chat service to function. A chat service allows two or more users to communicate simultaneously.

Internet service provider (ISP) — The organization that provides you with a connection to the Internet.

intranet — A private network.

IPX/SPX — A set of LAN protocols that was made popular by Novell Netware.

IRC — *See* Internet Relay Chat.

ISAPI filters — Applications that process HTTP requests. For example, Microsoft Exchange installs an ISAPI filter to process Web e-mail.

ISDN — *See* Integrated Services Digital Network.

ISP — *See* Internet service provider.

Itanium — The latest generation of processors from Intel. They are 65-bit processors.

iteration — A programming structure where the same instructions are processed multiple times.

Java Database Connectivity (JDBC) — A technology that enables Java programs to execute SQL statements. Linux uses JDBC in much the same way that Windows uses ODBC. *See also* ODBC.

JavaServer Pages (JSP) — A Web-based scripting language that uses a subset of the Java language. The code is compiled into a Java servlet before it runs for the first time after changes are made to the file.

JSP — *See* JavaServer Pages.

K Desktop Environment (KDE) — A GUI available for Linux, Solaris, and FreeBSD.

KDE — *See* K Desktop Environment.

Kerberos — The default authentication protocol in Windows 2000, Windows 2003, and Windows XP.

kernel — The central, high-security portion of the UNIX/Linux operating system that contains its core elements.

kernel-mode — A mode protected from corruption by another program.

key — A way to encrypt or decrypt data so that it remains private during transfer, but can be read upon receipt.

Konqueror — A program used by the KDE windowing environment for file management and Web browsing.

LAN — *See* local area network.

Lightweight Directory Access Protocol (LDAP) — A protocol used in LAN environments for communications between e-mail clients such as Microsoft Outlook and Exchange.

local account — In Windows, a user account that exists only on a single computer.

local area network (LAN) — A group of connected computers along with the devices and media that connect them.

log files — Files that contain information recorded by the operating system in response to certain events.

LogFormat — A directive that describes the format for data transfer in Apache, stored in httpd.conf. Apache has configured a number of sample formats from which you can choose.

logic — A programming structure where more than one option is possible.

loop — A program construct that performs a sequence of instructions until a particular condition occurs.

loopback — A site that corresponds to an IP address of 127.0.0.1, and is used to test basic TCP/IP connectivity and to facilitate the computer communicating with itself.

Mail Delivery Agent (MDA) — A service responsible for delivering e-mail from the e-mail system to the MUA.

Mail Exchange (MX) — A DNS record used to associate the domain name with the IP address of an e-mail server.

Mail Transfer Agent (MTA) — A service that accepts e-mail from clients and then sends the e-mail to another MTA that stores the e-mail.

Mail User Agent (MUA) — The client software that correctly formats messages and sends them to the MTA.

masquerading — The act of replacing the actual host name of the mail server with the domain name.

Master boot record (MBR) — A sector on the hard disk that contains the boot loader program.

MBR — *See* master boot record.

MDA — *See* Mail Delivery Agent.

mean time between failure (MTBF) — The average time interval that elapses before a hardware component fails and requires service.

MIME — *See* Multipurpose Internet Mail Extensions.

mixed mode — A mode for AD servers that allows Windows NT domain controllers to communicate with Windows 2000 and Windows 2003 domain controllers.

mount — Making the file system recognize a floppy disk, CD, or other device.

MTA — *See* Mail Transfer Agent.

MTBF — *See* mean time between failure.

MUA — *See* Mail User Agent.

multi-boot system — A computer with multiple operating systems. Typically, a menu allows you to choose the desired operating system.

multicast — A technology that allows a single IP packet to go to multiple recipients as opposed to having to send separate IP packets to each individual recipient.

Multipurpose Internet Mail Extensions (MIME) — An e-mail format that converts pictures, sound, and other binary data into text formats.

name resolution — Taking a common name of a network resource—a Web server, for instance—and converting it into a corresponding IP address. The name can be in the form of a DNS host name, such as *www.technowidgets.com*, or, in Windows, a computer name such as Web1.

name resolver — A DNS client. Technically, a name resolver is the client software component that uses the services of one or more name servers.

name server — An application that supports name-to-address and address-to-name translation. Also known as a DNS server.

namespace — A common grouping of related names such as hosts within a LAN.

NAP — *See* network access point.

NAT — *See* network address translation.

native mode — A mode for AD servers that allows only Windows 2000 and Windows 2003 domain controllers to communicate.

NetBEUI — A protocol made popular by Microsoft in the 1980s for small networks.

native mode — A mode for AD servers that allows only Windows 2000 and Windows 2003 domain controllers to communicate.

NetBIOS name — A computer name based on the NetBIOS interface, which was developed in the 1980s to link software with network services and thereby allow computers to communicate with one another.

network access point (NAP) — Each NAP provides a major Internet connection point.

network address translation (NAT) — Allows you to connect one NIC to your internal network with a private IP address and another NIC to the Internet. The private IP addresses are translated into the single Internet IP address as messages are routed to the Internet.

Network News Transfer Protocol (NNTP) — A protocol used in news servers to create threaded discussions in a newsgroup.

newsgroup — A group that shares an interest in information on a specific topic, such as comp.os.linux.security, a newsgroup devoted to Linux security issues, or alt.volkswagen.beetle, a newsgroup for Volkswagen Beetle owners and fans.

NNTP — *See* Network News Transfer Protocol.

normalization — The series of rules for organizing data into tables. Basically, tables are normalized when all the columns not part of the primary key are related solely to the primary key, and not to each other.

NT LanManager (NTLM) — An authentication protocol used by Windows NT, Windows 95, and Windows 98.

NTFS — A high-performance file system for Windows that supports access control and auditing of files and folders.

NTLM — *See* NT LanManager.

Object Linking and Embedding Database (OLE DB) — A database that stores objects that can be embedded in a variety of programs.

ODBC — *See* Open Database Connectivity.

Open Database Connectivity (ODBC) — A technology that acts as an intermediary between the DBMS and the programming language.

Open Source Interconnection (OSI) model — A model that defines the building blocks that divide data communication into discrete parts.

OSI model — *See* Open Source Interconnection model.

Outlook Web Access (OWA) — A Web-based client in Exchange 2000.

packet filtering — A practice where a server examines each packet individually and accepts or rejects the packet based on specified rules.

partition — A logical division of the hard disk.

partition, extended — The part of the drive where more system partitions can be created.

partition, primary — The part of the drive that starts the boot process.

passive mode — A type of data transfer where the FTP server uses port 20 to tell the client which unprivileged port on the server to use for the data transfer, and the client then connects (through its own unprivileged port) to an unprivileged port on the server for the actual data transfer. This type of FTP transfer is the most common method used today.

passwd — A Linux utility to change passwords.

PAT — *See* port address translation.

path — The exact location of a file or folder (Windows) or directory (Linux).

PCI slot — A connector on a computer's motherboard that can accept a variety of hardware adapters.

peering agreement — An agreement by large ISPs to exchange Internet traffic.

Pentium — The most popular 32-bit family of processors from Intel.

Perl — *See* Practical Extraction and Reporting Language.

per seat license — An agreement for using software in a network environments with multiple servers. Each client computer has its own license and can connect to as many servers as you have.

per server license — An agreement for using software in a client/server configuration where all client computers do not need to connect to the server at the same time.

persistent connections — Allows the browser to receive multiple files in one TCP connection.

PHP — *See* PHP Hypertext Protocol.

PHP Hypertext Protocol (PHP) — A Web-based scripting language commonly used with Apache Web servers. Also called PHP Hypertext Preprocessor.

pipeline — An architecture for order processing and other purposes that shows the steps that are needed for a customer to finish a specific business process.

POP3 — *See* Post Office Protocol.

port address translation (PAT) — Translates user ports (program interface) from computers on an internal network to a port on an interface connected to the Internet. This allows multiple users to share a single IP address on the Internet.

Post Office Protocol (POP3) — A protocol used to deliver e-mail to a client. This simple protocol allows for a single inbox.

Practical Extraction and Reporting Language (Perl) — A language that predates the Web and is used to process text.

primary key — In a table, one or more columns whose values uniquely define the contents of the row.

primary server — A server used to store files for a domain. Configuration files refer to the primary server as a master server, for good reason—a primary server is the authority for the current domain, meaning it controls host names and updating the secondary server.

private key — An algorithm kept securely on the server that is used to decrypt data. It is also used to encrypt data if the recipient has the same private key.

program — Software that solves specific problems. For example, a server program is software that runs on a server to solve data transfer problems.

protocol — A set of communication rules.

proxy server — A server that isolates your Web server from the Internet. A proxy server takes requests for pages from the Internet and transfers them to the Web server inside your network.

public key — An algorithm used to encrypt data that can only be decrypted by the corresponding private key.

public key infrastructure (PKI) — A system of public key encryption using digital certificates from Certificate Authorities that verify and authenticate the validity of each party involved in an electronic transaction.

RAID — *See* redundant array of inexpensive/independent disks.

Reduced Instruction Set Computer (RISC) — Processor architecture that focuses on very efficiently processing a few types of instructions.

record — A set of data, usually stored in a database.

redundant array of inexpensive/independent disks (RAID) — Allows multiple drives to operate together as a single drive. A variety of configurations are available.

Registry — A database of system settings used by the Windows operating system and applications.

relaying — The process of sending e-mail to an intermediate MTA before sending the e-mail to its final destination.

reverse lookup — A zone that contains entries that map IP addresses to names.

reverse (or reversing) proxy server — A server designed to isolate your Web server environment from the Internet. Instead of your DNS pointing to your Web server's IP address, it points to the IP address of your proxy server. When an Internet user requests a Web page, the proxy server retrieves the page from an internal server, and then sends it back to the user.

RISC — *See* Reduced Instruction Set Computer.

roaming profile — A profile that lets you access a variety of information about the user, such as desktop settings, Windows Explorer folder options, and Internet Explorer favorites, from other computers on the LAN.

root — The physical location on the Web server where you store your Web pages.

root-level domain — The top of the hierarchy. The root is expressed by a period ("dot"). In common use, the trailing period is usually removed from domain names, but when you configure DNS services, it is important.

root server — A special type of server that identifies the top-level domains on the Internet.

router — A device used to connect one network with another. It can serve many purposes, including connecting an internal network to the Internet.

row — Data stored in a record in a database table.

SCSI — *See* Small Computer System Interface.

secondary server — A server that receives its authority and database from the primary server. The secondary server provides fault tolerance, load distribution, and easier remote name resolution for the primary DNS server.

second-level domain — A level that identifies a particular entity within a top-level domain. The second-level domain name includes the top-level domain.

Secure Shell (SSH) — A protocol that creates a secure connection between two computers. You use it as a replacement for Telnet and to transmit insecure protocols such as POP3.

Secure Sockets Layer (SSL) — A technology that allows for encrypted communication between Web server and browser, thereby increasing the security of a Web site.

sequence — A programming structure where one instruction after another is processed.

service — A program (more specifically, a process) that runs in the background, such as a Web server.

Service Pack — A file issued by Microsoft with improvements and corrections to an operating system after it has been installed.

servlet — A compiled Java program that can be used on a Web server.

shell — In Linux and UNIX, a program that converts commands into instructions the operating system can follow.

signal degradation — A condition that involves the loss of signal strength as a communication signal moves farther from the source.

signed drivers — Drivers certified to work as described.

Simple Mail Transfer Protocol (SMTP) — The protocol used for sending e-mail.

single-boot system — A computer with only one operating system.

Small Computer System Interface (SCSI) — A parallel interface that allows multiple devices to communicate with the local system at the same time. It is commonly used to connect multiple hard drives to a server.

SMP — *See* symmetric multiprocessing.

SMTP — *See* Simple Mail Transfer Protocol.

spammer — Someone who sends unsolicited e-mail, typically to try to sell something.

spoof — To present a fake IP address to gain access or otherwise deceive a person.

SQL — *See* Structured Query Language.

SSH — *See* Secure Shell.

SSL — *See* Secure Sockets Layer.

Start of Authority (SOA) — A type of resource record used by DNS where every domain name has an SOA record in its database that indicates basic properties of the domain and its zone.

stateless — When a protocol is stateless (as is HTTP, for example), each Web page sent to the user is independent of every other Web page that the server sends.

static IP address — An address that is allocated to a computer once and doesn't change.

static Web page — A page that contains only HTML statements and is sent to the browser without any processing. The typical extension for such pages is .htm or .html.

Structured Query Language (SQL) — The language used to interact with a relational DBMS.

subdomain — Second-level domains that are divided into further domain levels, as in the URL *www.arda.jones.name*. In this case, *jones.name* is the second-level domain controlled by the *.name* TLD, and *arda.jones.name* represents the subdomain that a person can register.

switch — A device that allows computers to communicate as if they were directly connected to one another. It produces a virtual connection between the computers.

superuser — A computer user account that allows access to system files and folders.

symmetric multiprocessing (SMP) — A technology that allows a server to divide processes and assign them to the available processors.

synchronization (SYN) flag — Part of the TCP header. The SYN flag is set to signify a request to start a connection.

synchronization (SYN) flood — An attack where many connections are requested, but none is completed, thereby overloading the server.

system account — A special account in Windows that a service can use to have the same privileges as the administrator.

System V — A UNIX standard distributed by AT&T and Sun. Solaris is the most popular example of a System V system.

table — A container of organized data in a database with columns and rows similar to a spreadsheet. Each column describes a specific characteristic of the table.

tagging — Displaying a message, usually on the home page, that notifies you of an attack on your system. Also, making changes that may cause you economic harm or embarrassment, such as editing your Web pages to discourage potential customers from purchasing products.

TCP/IP — *See* Transmission Control Protocol/Internet Protocol.

Telephony API 3.0 — A programming interface that allows efficient multicasting.

terminal adapter (TA) — A device that connects ISDN lines to a LAN; sometimes referred to as an ISDN modem.

threaded discussion — Allows you to post messages in a newsgroup and have others respond.

throughput — The amount of data you can move from one place to another in a given time period.

TLD — *See* top-level domain.

top-level domain (TLD) — Identifies the most general portion of the domain name. It is the "end" portion of the domain name, as in *com*, *edu*, and *org*.

Transmission Control Protocol/Internet Protocol (TCP/IP) — The suite of protocols used in data communication.

tunneling — Allows you to use an insecure protocol, such as POP3, through a secure connection, such as SSH.

UID — *See* user ID.

unicast — A method of communicating each packet of data individually to each client. With unicast, if you have 1,000 connections, you have 1,000 separate streams of data being sent to clients.

Unicode — A set of characters that allows you to use foreign-language character sets in Web pages.

uninterruptible power supply (UPS) — A device with a battery that will supply electricity to computers and other components when an electrical circuit fails.

universal group — A group that can have members from any domain. You can use universal groups to assign permissions to resources in any domain.

unprivileged port — Any port above 1023.

UPS — *See* uninterruptible power supply.

up-selling — A sales technique used on e-commerce sites that involves suggesting a more profitable product related to a customer's interest in a different product.

URI query — In IIS logs, any information being passed to the page for processing.

URI stem — In IIS logs, the page requested.

user ID (UID) — A number assigned to users in Linux. A UID with a value less than 100 is intended for special system users. In Red Hat Linux, when you add a user, the UID starts at 500.

useradd — A Linux utility to add users.

VBScript — A subset of Visual Basic commonly used in writing ASP.

virtual directory — A Web directory that is not physically located beneath the Web root.

virtual host — Adding a second Web site to an existing Web server. The term is most commonly used with Apache.

virtual IP address — An IP address that is added to the IP address for a NIC.

virtual memory — Memory that the processor uses when it does not have enough RAM.

Voice Profile for Internet Mail (VPIM) — A technology that enables you to listen to voicemail through an e-mail client.

WAN — *See* wide area network.

watts — A unit of power that is equal to volts multiplied by amperes (amps).

Web Distributed Authoring and Versioning (WebDAV) — A service that allows the server to share Web-based files.

Web service — One or more programming modules that reside on the Web server and can be accessed from a client computer.

WebDAV — *See* Web Distributed Authoring and Versioning.

wide area network (WAN) — Primarily a public, shared network that connects regions and countries.

Windows Internet Name Service (WINS) — A server that supports computer name resolution for Windows computers that do not support DDNS, such as Windows NT, Windows 95, and Windows 98.

WINS — *See* Windows Internet Name Service.

wire speed — The same speed two computers could achieve if they were physically connected.

XML — *See* Extensible Markup Language.

zone — The set of records contained within a domain. For example, if the domain name for your company is *technowidgets.com*, then you need to create a forward lookup zone for the *technowidgets.com* domain on the primary server. If you had a subdomain that was controlled by another DNS server, it would reside in a separate zone.

Index

A

B

D

E

G

N

O

P

T

X

Y

Z

Microsoft® Windows® Server 2003 Enterprise Edition 180-Day Evaluation

The software included in this kit is intended for evaluation and deployment planning purposes only. If you plan to install the software on your primary machine, it is recommended that you back up your existing data prior to installation.

System requirements

To use Microsoft Windows Server 2003 Enterprise Edition, you need:

- Computer with 550 MHz or higher processor clock speed recommended; 133 MHz minimum required; Intel Pentium/Celeron family, or AMD K6/Athlon/Duron family, or compatible processor (Windows Server 2003 Enterprise Edition supports up to eight CPUs on one server)
- 256 MB of RAM or higher recommended; 128 MB minimum required (maximum 32 GB of RAM)
- 1.25 to 2 GB of available hard-disk space*
- CD-ROM or DVD-ROM drive
- Super VGA (800 × 600) or higher-resolution monitor recommended; VGA or hardware that supports console redirection required
- Keyboard and Microsoft Mouse or compatible pointing device, or hardware that supports console redirection

Additional items or services required to use certain Windows Server 2003 Enterprise Edition features:

- For Internet access:
  - Some Internet functionality may require Internet access, a Microsoft Passport account, and payment of a separate fee to a service provider; local and/or long-distance telephone toll charges may apply
  - High-speed modem or broadband Internet connection
- For networking:
  - Network adapter appropriate for the type of local-area, wide-area, wireless, or home network to which you wish to connect, and access to an appropriate network infrastructure; access to third-party networks may require additional charges

Note: To ensure that your applications and hardware are Windows Server 2003–ready, be sure to visit **www.microsoft.com/windowsserver2003**.

* Actual requirements will vary based on your system configuration and the applications and features you choose to install. Additional available hard-disk space may be required if you are installing over a network. For more information, please see **www.microsoft.com/windowsserver2003**.

Uninstall instructions

This time-limited release of Microsoft Windows Server 2003 Enterprise Edition will expire 180 days after installation. If you decide to discontinue the use of this software, you will need to reinstall your original operating system. You may need to reformat your drive.

0103 Part No. X09-41357